MASTER VISUALLY™

Office XP

Visual

by Shelley O'Hara

From

&

Hungry Minds™

Best-Selling Books • Digital Downloads • e-Books • Answer Networks
e-Newsletters • Branded Web Sites • e-Learning
New York, NY • Cleveland, OH • Indianapolis, IN

Master VISUALLY™ Office XP

Published by
Hungry Minds, Inc.
909 Third Avenue
New York, NY 10022
www.hungryminds.com

Copyright © 2001 Hungry Minds, Inc.

maranGraphics, Inc.
5755 Coopers Avenue
Mississauga, Ontario, Canada
L4Z 1R9

Library of Congress Control Number: 2001092065

ISBN: 0-7645-3599-4

Printed in the United States of America

10 9 8 7 6 5 4 3 2

1V/RT/QZ/QR/IN

Distributed in the United States by Hungry Minds, Inc.

Distributed by CDG Books Canada Inc. for Canada; by Transworld Publishers Limited in the United Kingdom; by IDG Norge Books for Norway; by IDG Sweden Books for Sweden; by IDG Books Australia Publishing Corporation Pty. Ltd. for Australia and New Zealand; by TransQuest Publishers Pte Ltd. for Singapore, Malaysia, Thailand, Indonesia, and Hong Kong; by Gotop Information Inc. for Taiwan; by ICG Muse, Inc. for Japan; by Intersoft for South Africa; by Eyrolles for France; by International Thomson Publishing for Germany, Austria and Switzerland; by Distribuidora Cuspide for Argentina; by LR International for Brazil; by Galileo Libros for Chile; by Ediciones ZETA S.C.R. Ltda. for Peru; by WS Computer Publishing Corporation, Inc., for the Philippines; by Contemporanea de Ediciones for Venezuela; by Express Computer Distributors for the Caribbean and West Indies; by Micronesia Media Distributor, Inc. for Micronesia; by Chips Computadoras S.A. de C.V. for Mexico; by Editorial Norma de Panama S.A. for Panama; by American Bookshops for Finland.

For corporate orders, please call maranGraphics at 800-469-6616 or fax 905-890-9434.

For general information on Hungry Minds' products and services please contact our Customer Care Department within the U.S. at 800-762-2974, outside the U.S. at 317-572-3993 or fax 317-572-4002.

For sales inquiries and reseller information, including discounts, premium and bulk quantity sales, and foreign-language translations, please contact our Customer Care Department at 800-434-3422, fax 317-572-4002, or write to Hungry Minds, Inc., Attn: Customer Care Department, 10475 Crosspoint Boulevard, Indianapolis, IN 46256.

For information on licensing foreign or domestic rights, please contact our Sub-Rights Customer Care Department at 212-844-5000.

For information on using Hungry Minds' products and services in the classroom or for ordering examination copies, please contact our Educational Sales Department at 800-434-2086 or fax 317-572-4005.

For press review copies, author interviews, or other publicity information, please contact our Public Relations department at 317-572-3168 or fax 317-572-4168.

For authorization to photocopy items for corporate, personal, or educational use, please contact Copyright Clearance Center, 222 Rosewood Drive, Danvers, MA 01923, or fax 978-750-4470.

Screen shots displayed in this book are based on pre-released software and are subject to change.

Trademark Acknowledgments

Permissions

 is a trademark of Hungry Minds, Inc.

Hungry Minds™

U.S. Corporate Sales	U.S. Trade Sales
Contact maranGraphics at (800) 469-6616 or	Contact Hungry Minds at (800) 434-3422 or (317) 572-4002.

Praise for Visual books...

"If you have to see it to believe it, this is the book for you!"
–PC World

"I would like to take this time to compliment maranGraphics on creating such great books. I work for a leading manufacturer of office products, and sometimes they tend to NOT give you the meat and potatoes of certain subjects, which causes great confusion. Thank you for making it clear. Keep up the good work."
–Kirk Santoro (Burbank, CA)

"I write to extend my thanks and appreciation for your books. They are clear, easy to follow, and straight to the point. Keep up the good work! I bought several of your books and they are just right! No regrets! I will always buy your books because they are the best."
–Seward Kollie (Dakar, Senegal)

"What fantastic teaching books you have produced! Congratulations to you and your staff."
–Bruno Tonon (Melbourne, Australia)

"Compliments To The Chef!! Your books are extraordinary! Or, simply put, Extra-Ordinary, meaning way above the rest! THANKYOUTHANKYOU THANKYOU! for creating these. They have saved me from serious mistakes, and showed me a right and simple way to do things. I buy them for friends, family, and colleagues."
–Christine J. Manfrin (Castle Rock, CO)

"A master tutorial/reference — from the leaders in visual learning!"
–Infoworld

"Your books are superior! An avid reader since childhood, I've consumed literally tens of thousands of books, a significant quantity in the learning/teaching category. Your series is the most precise, visually appealing and compelling to peruse. Kudos!"
–Margaret Rose Chmilar (Edmonton, Alberta, Canada)

"You're marvelous! I am greatly in your debt."
–Patrick Baird (Lacey, WA)

"Just wanted to say THANK YOU to your company for providing books which make learning fast, easy, and exciting! I learn visually so your books have helped me greatly – from Windows instruction to Web page development. I'm looking forward to using more of your Master Books series in the future as I am now a computer support specialist. Best wishes for continued success."
–Angela J. Barker (Springfield, MO)

"A publishing concept whose time has come!"
–The Globe and Mail

"I have over the last 10-15 years purchased $1000's worth of computer books but find your books the most easily read, best set out and most helpful and easily understood books on software and computers I have ever read. You produce the best computer books money can buy. Please keep up the good work."
–John Gatt (Adamstown Heights, Australia)

"The Greatest. This whole series is the best computer learning tool of any kind I've ever seen."
–Joe Orr (Brooklyn, NY)

maranGraphics is a family-run business
located near Toronto, Canada.

At maranGraphics, we believe in producing great computer books — one book at a time.

maranGraphics has been producing high-technology products for over 25 years, which enables us to offer the computer book community a unique communication process.

Our computer books use an integrated communication process, which is very different from the approach used in other computer books. Each spread is, in essence, a flow chart — the text and screen shots are totally incorporated into the layout of the spread.

Introductory text and helpful tips complete the learning experience.

maranGraphics' approach encourages the left and right sides of the brain to work together — resulting in faster orientation and greater memory retention.

Above all, we are very proud of the handcrafted nature of our books. Our carefully-chosen writers are experts in their fields, and spend countless hours researching and organizing the content for each topic. Our artists rebuild every screen shot to provide the best

clarity possible, making our screen shots the most precise and easiest to read in the industry. We strive for perfection, and believe that the time spent handcrafting each element results in the best computer books money can buy.

Thank you for purchasing this book. We hope you enjoy it!

Sincerely,

Robert Maran
President
maranGraphics
Rob@maran.com
www.maran.com
www.hungryminds.com/visual

CREDITS

Acquisitions, Editorial, and Media Development

Project Editor
Maureen Spears

Acquisitions Editors
Jennifer Dorsey, Martine Edwards

Product Development Supervisor
Lindsay Sandman

Copy Editors
Jill Mazurczyk, Timothy J. Borek

Technical Editor
Lee Musick

Senior Permissions Editor
Carmen Krikorian

Media Development Specialist
Angela Denny

Media Development Coordinator
Marisa Pearman

Editorial Manager
Rev Mengle

Media Development Manager
Laura Carpenter VanWinkle

Editorial Assistant
Amanda Foxworth

Production

Book Design
maranGraphics®

Project Coordinator
Dale White

Layout
LeAndra Johnson
Adam Mancilla
Kristin Pickett
Erin Zeltner

Illustrators
David E. Gregory
Ronda David-Burroughs
Mark Harris
Suzana G. Miokovic
Jill A. Proll
Steven Schaerer

Proofreaders
Laura Albert
Vicki Broyles
Susan Moritz
Marianne Santy

Indexer
TECHBOOKS Production Services

Special Help
Mary Jo Richards
Ryan Steffen

GENERAL AND ADMINISTRATIVE

Hungry Minds, Inc.: John Kilcullen, CEO; Bill Barry, President and COO; John Ball, Executive VP, Operations & Administration; John Harris, Executive VP and CFO

Hungry Minds Technology Publishing Group: Richard Swadley, Senior Vice President and Publisher; Mary Bednarek, Vice President and Publisher; Walter R. Bruce III, Vice President and Publisher; Joseph Wikert, Vice President and Publisher; Mary C. Corder, Editorial Director; Andy Cummings, Publishing Director, General User Group; Barry Pruett, Publishing Director, Visual Group

Hungry Minds Manufacturing: Ivor Parker, Vice President, Manufacturing

Hungry Minds Marketing: John Helmus, Assistant Vice President, Director of Marketing

Hungry Minds Production for Branded Press: Debbie Stailey, Production Director

Hungry Minds Sales: Michael Violano, Vice President, International Sales and Sub Rights

*The publisher would like to give special thanks to Patrick J. McGovern,
without whom this book would not have been possible.*

ABOUT THE AUTHOR

Shelley O'Hara is the author of over 100 books including *Master Word® 2000* for Hungry Minds. She has just completed her first novel and is currently at work on *Look and Learn FrontPage® 2002*.

AUTHOR'S ACKNOWLEDGMENTS

I would like to thank Ted Cains, Rev Mengle, and Maureen Spears for helping me through this project. Also, thank you to Martine Edwards who initially invited me to do this project, to Barry Pruett who finished up the project details, and to Jen Dorsey, who saw me through this project. Finally, I express my appreciation to copy editors Jill Mazurczyk and Tim Borek.

This book is dedicated to my son Michael's class at Immaculate Heart of Mary, Class of 2005. Everyone's name from the current 4th grade class should be in here somewhere. They are an awesome class, and I enjoy each and every one of them, including their current teachers Mrs. Ginny Forbes and Mrs. Julie Monahan.

OFFICE XP

I   USING OFFICE PROGRAMS

1   Getting Started

2   Work with Office Programs and Documents

II   USING WORD

3   Getting Started

4   Edit Word Documents

5   Format Text

6   Format Documents

7   Create Tables

8   Work with Graphics

9   Using Mail Merge

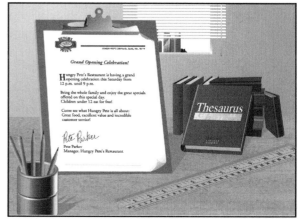

III USING EXCEL

10 Getting Started
11 Edit Workbooks
12 Create Formulas and Functions
13 Format Worksheets
14 Print Worksheets
15 Create Charts
16 Work with Graphics
17 Manage Data in a List

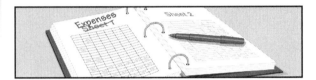

IV USING POWERPOINT

18 Getting Started
19 Create and Edit Slides
20 Add Objects to Slides
21 Format Presentations
22 Fine-tune and Present a Presentation

V USING ACCESS

23 Getting Started
24 Create Tables
25 Change Table Design
26 Create Forms
27 Find and Query Data
28 Create Reports

VI USING OUTLOOK

29 Send and Receive E-mail
30 Organize Messages
31 Manage Information

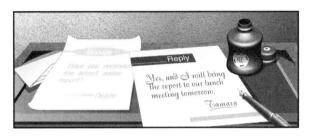

VII USING FRONTPAGE

32 Create a Web Site
33 Enhance a Web Site

VIII SPECIAL OFFICE FEATURES

34 Share Data
35 Customize Office
Appendix A: Install and Troubleshoot Office XP
Appendix B: What's on the CD-ROM

1

1) GETTING STARTED

An Introduction to Microsoft Office XP 4

Start and Exit a Program 6

Work with Windows 8

Using Toolbars 10

Display or Hide a Toolbar 12

Change Toolbar Placement 13

Work with the Task Pane 14

Getting Help 16

2) WORK WITH OFFICE PROGRAMS AND DOCUMENTS

Create a New Document 18

Save and Close a Document 20

Save Documents to Other Locations 22

Save a Document as a Web Page 24

Open a Document 26

Print a Document 28

E-mail a Document 30

Switch among Programs 32

Switch among Documents 33

Find a Document 34

2

3) GETTING STARTED

An Introduction to Word 38
Start Word 40
Parts of the Word XP Screen 41
Type Text 42
Move through a Document 44
Select Text 46

4) EDIT WORD DOCUMENTS

Insert and Delete Text 48
Move or Copy Text 50
Undo Changes 52
Insert a Page Break 53
Find Text 54
Replace Text 56
Using AutoCorrect 58
Check Spelling 60
Check Grammar 62
Using the Thesaurus 64
Count Words 65
Create and Insert an AutoText Entry 66
Insert Date and Time 68
Insert Special Characters 69
Insert Symbols 70

5) FORMAT TEXT

Bold, Italicize, or Underline Text 72

Change the Font Style 73

Change the Font Size 74

Using Special Text Effects 75

Change the Color of Text 76

Highlight Text 77

Align Text 78

Indent Paragraphs 80

Set Tabs 82

Change Line and Paragraph Spacing 84

Add Bullets 86

Create a Numbered List 88

Add Borders or Shading 90

Create a Style 92

Apply a Style 94

Modify a Style 96

Copy Formatting 98

Reveal Formatting 99

Display and Hide Paragraph Marks 100

Change AutoFormat Options 101

6) FORMAT DOCUMENTS

Change the View 102

Zoom In or Out 103

Preview a Document 104

Change Margins 106

Align Text on a Page 108

Change Page Orientation 109

Add Page Numbers 110

Add a Header or Footer 112

Add Footnotes or Endnotes 114

Create Columns 116

Add a Picture Watermark 118

Using Templates 120

TABLE OF CONTENTS

7) CREATE TABLES

Create a Table 122
Type Text in a Table 124
Sort Text 125
Change Column Width 126
Erase Lines 127
Add or Delete a Row or Column 128
Move or Resize a Table 130
Change Table Borders 132
Add Shading or Color to Cells 134
Change Text Position in Cells 135
Using a Table AutoFormat 136

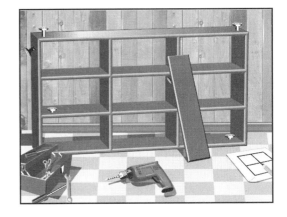

8) WORK WITH GRAPHICS

Add an AutoShape 138
Add a Clip Art Image 140
Add Word Art 142
Insert a Picture 144
Add a Diagram 146
Move or Resize a Graphic 148
Wrap Text around a Graphic 150

9) USING MAIL MERGE

An Introduction to Mail Merge 152
Create a Letter with Mail Merge 154
Print Mailing Labels 164
Print an Envelope 170

3

10) GETTING STARTED

Introduction to Excel 174

Start Excel 176

Parts of the Excel Screen 177

Type Text 178

Type Numbers 179

Fill a Series 180

Enter Dates and Times 182

Using AutoComplete 183

Select a Range of Cells 184

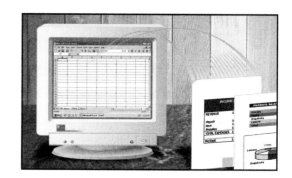

11) EDIT WORKBOOKS

Edit or Delete Data 186

Move or Copy Data 188

Check Spelling 190

Find Data 192

Insert a Row or Column 194

Delete a Row or Column 196

Hide and Unhide Columns 198

Using Cell and Range Names 200

Protect Cells 202

Add and Delete Worksheets 204

Rename a Worksheet 206

Move or Copy a Worksheet 207

12) CREATE FORMULAS AND FUNCTIONS

An Introduction to Formulas and Functions......208

Sum Numbers 210

Enter and Edit Formulas 212

Copy a Formula 214

Enter a Function 216

TABLE OF CONTENTS

13) FORMAT WORKSHEETS

Change Column Width or Row Height 218
Bold, Italic, or Underline 220
Apply a Number Style to Cells 221
Format Numbers 222
Change Font and Font Size 224
Change Font or Fill Color 226
Apply Special Appearance Effects 228
Change Data Alignment 230
Add Borders 232
Copy Formatting 234
Clear Formatting 235
Apply an AutoFormat 236

14) PRINT WORKSHEETS

Preview a Worksheet 238
Print a Worksheet 240
Change Margins 242
Change Page Orientation 244
Change Print Options 245
Insert and View a Page Break 246
Fit a Worksheet to a Page or Pages 248
Repeat Row or Column Headings 249
Add a Header or Footer 250
Create a Custom Header or Footer 252

15) CREATE CHARTS

An Introduction to Charts 254
Create a Chart Using a Wizard 256
Change the Chart Type 260
Format Chart Elements 262

Move or Resize a Chart 264
Delete a Chart 265
Add Data to a Chart 266
Print a Chart 267

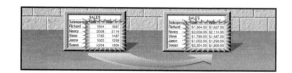

16) WORK WITH GRAPHICS

Add an AutoShape to a Worksheet 268
Add a Text Box 270
Add a Clip Art Image 272
Work with Graphics 274

17) MANAGE DATA IN A LIST

Using a Data List 276
Sort Data in a List 278
Filter Data in a List 280
Add Subtotals to a List 282

4

USING POWERPOINT

18) GETTING STARTED

An Introduction to PowerPoint 286
Create a Blank Presentation 288
Parts of the PowerPoint Screen 289
Using the AutoContent Wizard 290
Using a Design Template 294
Add a Slide 296

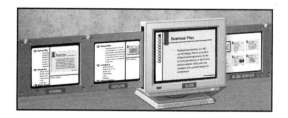

TABLE OF CONTENTS

19) CREATE AND EDIT SLIDES

Select Text 298
Add and Edit Text 300
Move and Copy Text 302
Resize, Add, and Delete Text Boxes 303
Change Views 304
Browse through a Presentation 306
Change the Slide Layout 308

20) ADD OBJECTS TO SLIDES

Add a Table with Text 310
Format a Table 312
Add a Chart 314
Edit and Format a Chart 316
Add an Organization Chart 318
Add a Clip Art Image 320
Add a Picture 322
Add an AutoShape 324
Add WordArt Text Effects 326
Move, Resize, or Delete a Slide Object 328

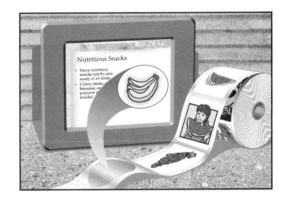

21) FORMAT PRESENTATIONS

Change the Font and Size of Text 330
Change Text Style 332
Change Text Alignment 333
Change Text Color 334
Copy Formatting 335
Format Bulleted and Numbered Lists 336
Animate Slide Objects 338
Use an Animation Scheme 340
Change the Color Scheme 342
Change the Design Template 344
Add or Edit a Header or Footer 346
Use the Slide Master 348

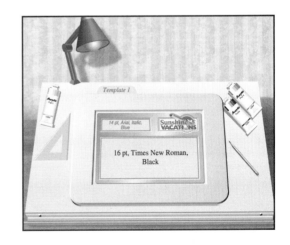

22) FINE-TUNE AND PRESENT A PRESENTATION

Rearrange Slides 350

Delete a Slide 351

Hide a Slide 352

Create a Summary Slide 353

Add Slide Transitions 354

Rehearse a Slide Show 356

Set Up a Slide Show 358

Preview a Slide Show 360

Create Speaker Notes 362

Check Spelling 364

Set Up a Presentation for Printing 366

Print a Presentation 368

5

USING ACCESS

23) GETTING STARTED

An Introduction to Access 372

Parts of a Database 373

Plan a Database 374

Start Access 375

Create a Blank Database 376

Create a Database Using a Wizard 378

Parts of the Database Window 384

Rename or Delete an Object 385

Open and Save a Database 386

TABLE OF CONTENTS

24) CREATE TABLES

Create a Table in Datasheet View 388
Enter Data in Datasheet View 390
Create a Table Using the Wizard 392
Open a Table 396
Understanding Data Types 397
Add or Delete Records 398
Move through Records 400
Select Data 402
Edit Data 404
Zoom into a Cell 406
Change Column Width 407
Hide a Field 408
Freeze a Field 409

25) CHANGE TABLE DESIGN

Change the Table View 410
Rearrange Fields 411
Display Field Properties 412
Add a Field Description 413
Change the Data Type 414
Rename a Field 415
Change the Field Size 416
Select a Data Format 418
Change the Number of Decimal Places 419
Add or Delete a Field 420
Add a Caption 422
Add a Default Value 423
Require an Entry 424
Add a Validation Rule 426
Create a Yes/No Field 428
Create a Lookup Column 430
Use a Lookup Column to Enter Data 432
Create an Index 433
Set the Primary Key 434
Display a Subdatasheet 435
Define Relationships between Tables 436

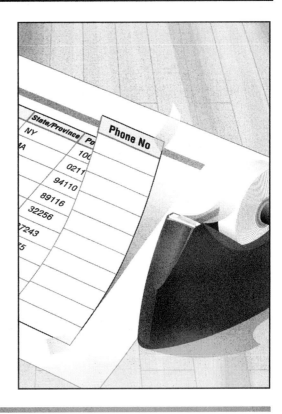

26) CREATE FORMS

Create a Form Using a Wizard 440
Open a Form 444
Move through Records with a Form 446
Edit Data Using a Form 447
Add or Delete a Record 448
Add a Field to a Form 450
AutoFormat a Form 451
Change a Form Control 452
Change the Appearance of Form Controls 454
Change Form Control Colors and Borders 456

27) FIND AND QUERY DATA

Find Data 458
Sort Records 460
Filter Data 462
Filter Data by Form 464
Create a Query Using the Simple Query Wizard 466
Create a Query in Design View 470
Open a Query 474
Change the Query View 475
Set Criteria 476
Examples of Criteria 478
Sort Query Results 479
Perform Calculations 480
Summarize Data 482

28) CREATE REPORTS

Create a Report Using the Report Wizard 484
Open a Report 490
Change the Report View 491
Preview a Report 492
Print Data from a Database 494
Create Mailing Labels 496

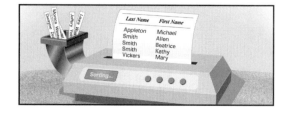

TABLE OF CONTENTS

6

USING OUTLOOK

29) SEND AND RECEIVE E-MAIL

An Introduction to Outlook 502
Start Outlook 503
Using Outlook Today 504
Change the Outlook Window 505
Read Messages 506
Create a New Message 508
Select a Name from the Address Book 510
Attach a File to a Message 512
Open and Save Attachments 514
Reply to or Forward a Message 516

30) ORGANIZE MESSAGES

Open E-mail Folders 518
Print a Message 520
Delete a Message 521
Create a New Mail Folder 522
Move a Message 523
Archive Messages 524
Format a Message 525
Sort and Find Messages 526

31) MANAGE INFORMATION

Keep Notes 528
Create a Task List 530
Manage a Task List 532
Schedule Appointments with Calendar 534
Display the Calendar 536
Manage Contacts 538

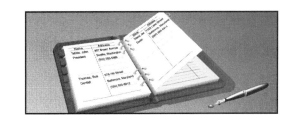

32) CREATE A WEB SITE

Introduction to FrontPage 544
Start FrontPage 545
Create a New Web Site 546
Create a New Page 548
Save a Page 550
Open a Web Page 552
Add or Edit Text on a Page 553
Change Font and Size of Text 554
Using Bold, Italic, or Underline 556
Change Color of Text 557
Change Alignment of Text 558
Indent Text 559
Add Numbers or Bullets 560
Create a Heading 561
Add a Picture 562
Insert a Table 564
Create a Hyperlink 566
Preview and Print a Page 568

33) ENHANCE A WEB SITE

Check Spelling 570
Apply a Theme 572
Add a Hit Counter 574
Work with Web Files and Folders 576
View Web Reports 578
View Hyperlinks 580
Check Site Navigation 582
Publish a Web Site 584

TABLE OF CONTENTS

8

SPECIAL OFFICE FEATURES

34) SHARE DATA

Move or Copy Information between Documents 588
Work with the Clipboard 590
Embed Information 592
Edit Embedded Information 594
Link Information 596
Edit Linked Information 598
Create a File Hyperlink 600
Insert a Web Hyperlink 602

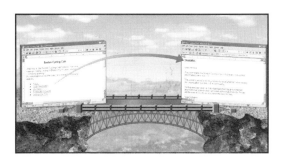

35) CUSTOMIZE OFFICE

Set Toolbar and Menu Options 604
Add or Remove Office XP Features 606
Using Handwriting or Speech Recognition 608
An Introduction to Additional Office XP
      Programs and Features 610

APPENDIX A

Install Office XP 612
Troubleshoot Installation 616

APPENDIX B

What's on the CD-ROM 618
Master Visually Office XP
      on the CD-ROM 620

Master VISUALLY™ Office XP contains straightforward tasks to help you quickly learn the basics of all the Office programs. The book explains how to create a wide variety of documents in Word, Excel, PowerPoint, Access, Outlook, and FrontPage, as well as how to share data within the various Office programs.

This book is designed to help a reader receive quick access to any area of question. You can simply look up a subject within the Table of Contents or Index and go immediately to the task of concern. A *task* is a self-contained unit that walks you through a computer operation step-by-step. That is, with rare exception, all the information you need regarding an area of interest is contained within a task.

Who This Book Is For

This book is for the beginner, who is unfamiliar with the various Office programs. It is also for more computer literate individuals who want to expand their knowledge of the different features that Office XP has to offer.

What You Need To Use This Book

The recommended system configuration to use Microsoft Office XP is Microsoft Windows® 2000 Professional on a computer with a Pentium III processor and 128 megabytes (MB) of RAM. Below are the minimum requirements your computer needs to run each suite of Office XP. Some Office XP features have additional requirements. For questions about your individual requirements, or to learn about additional requirements see www.microsoft.com/office/evaluation/fastfacts.

Minimum Requirements

Computer/Processor: Pentium 133-megahertz (MHz) or higher.

Memory

For all Office XP suites: RAM requirements depend on the operating system used.

- **Windows 98, or Windows 98 Second Edition**
  24MB of RAM plus an additional 8MB of RAM for each Office program (such as Microsoft Word) running simultaneously

- **Windows Me, or Microsoft Windows NT®** 32MB of RAM plus an additional 8MB of RAM for each Office application (such as Microsoft Word) running simultaneously

- **Windows 2000 Professional** 64MB of RAM plus an additional 8MB of RAM for each Office application (such as Microsoft Word) running simultaneously

Hard Disk: Hard disk space requirements will vary depending on configuration; custom installation choices may require more or less

OFFICE XP

pace. Listed below are the minimum hard disk requirements for Office XP suites:

- Office XP Standard
  210MB of available hard disk space
- Office XP Professional and Professional Special Edition
  245MB of available hard disk space

An additional 115MB is required on the hard disk where the perating system is installed. Users without Windows 2000, Windows Me, or Office 2000 Service Release 1 (SR-1) require an xtra 50MB of hard disk space for System Files Update.

The Conventions in This Book

This book uses the following conventions to describe the actions you perform when using the mouse and keyboard. In addition Office XP uses a number of typographic and layout styles to help distinguish different types of information:

- Click means that you press and release the left mouse button. You use a click to select an item on the screen.
- Double-click means that you quickly press and release the left mouse button twice. You use a double-click to open a document or start a program.
- Right-click means that you press and release the right mouse button. You use a right-click to display a shortcut menu, a list of commands specifically related to the selected item.
- Click and Drag means that you position the mouse pointer over an item on the screen and then press and hold down the left mouse button. Still holding down the button, move the mouse to where you want to place the item and then release the button. Dragging and dropping makes it easy to move an item to a new location.
- **Bold** represents information that you type.
- *Italics* indicate the introduction of a new term.
- Numbered steps indicate that you must perform these steps in order to successfully perform the task.
- Bulleted steps give you alternate methods, explain various options, or present what a program will do in responds to the numbered steps.
- Notes are *italicized* statements beneath screen shots that give you additional information to help you complete a task.
- Icons indicate a program button that you must click with the mouse.

 Many tasks in this book are supplemented with a section called Master It. These are tips, hints, and tricks that extend your use of the task beyond what you learned by performing the task itself.

The Organization of Each Chapter

Each task contains an introduction, a set of screen shots, and a set of tips. The introduction tells why you want to perform the task, the advantages and disadvantages of performing the task, a general explanation of task procedures, and references to other related tasks in the book. The screens, located on the bottom half of each page, show a series of steps that you must complete to perform a given task. The tip section gives you an opportunity to further understand the task at hand, to learn about other related tasks in other areas of the book, or to apply more complicated or alternative methods. A chapter may also contain an illustrated group of pages that gives you background information that you need to understand the tasks in a chapter.

The parts of this book are organized in the logical order in which you would learn the Office programs. Beginning chapters contain basic tasks common to all Office programs followed by parts devoted to each individual program. The parts that cover the individual programs go from the simple task of starting and navigating through a program, to more complicated tasks. The final chapters involve more complex tasks that are common to all Office programs.

Part I: *Using Office Programs* introduces you to Office XP. Chapter 1 gives an overview of the various programs and tells you how to navigate within these programs. Chapter 2 contains tasks that show how to use various commands common to all Office programs, such as how to start, close, or save a document.

Part II: *Using Word* discusses how to use the popular word-processing program to create documents. With this part, you learn how to edit and format documents to which you can add tables and graphics. You also learn how to perform a mail merge.

Part III: *Using Excel* shows you how to create a worksheet to which you can add formulas, functions, charts, and graphics. You also learn how to print your worksheet to meet any situation as well as how to manage the data in your worksheet.

Part IV: *Using PowerPoint* shows you how to create a professional presentation. In this part, you learn the basics of creating a simple slide and adding graphics and other objects to that slide to make it more attractive. You also learn how to create an entire presentation complete with notes and handouts, as well as how to time your presentation.

Part V: *Using Access* discusses how to create a database of information, which you can then organize to create tables, forms, and reports. You also learn how to use your data to find the exact information you need to know or present.

Part VI: *Using Outlook* shows you e-mail basics including how to send, receive, and organize your e-mail.

Part VII: *Using FrontPage* illustrates how create a Web page for publication on the Internet.

Part VIII: *Special Features* shows you how to share data between the various Office programs, as well as how to customize these programs. *Appendices* contains supplemental information that shows you how install and troubleshoot Office XP. You also learn how to view the information included on the CD-ROM that comes with this book.

SECTION I

1) GETTING STARTED

An Introduction to Microsoft Office XP 4

Start and Exit a Program 6

Work with Windows 8

Using Toolbars 10

Display or Hide a Toolbar 12

Change Toolbar Placement 13

Work with the Task Pane 14

Getting Help 16

2) WORK WITH OFFICE PROGRAMS AND DOCUMENTS

Create a New Document 18

Save and Close a Document 20

Save Documents to Other Locations 22

Save a Document as a Web Page 24

Open a Document 26

Print a Document 28

E-mail a Document 30

Switch among Programs 32

Switch among Documents 33

Find a Document 34

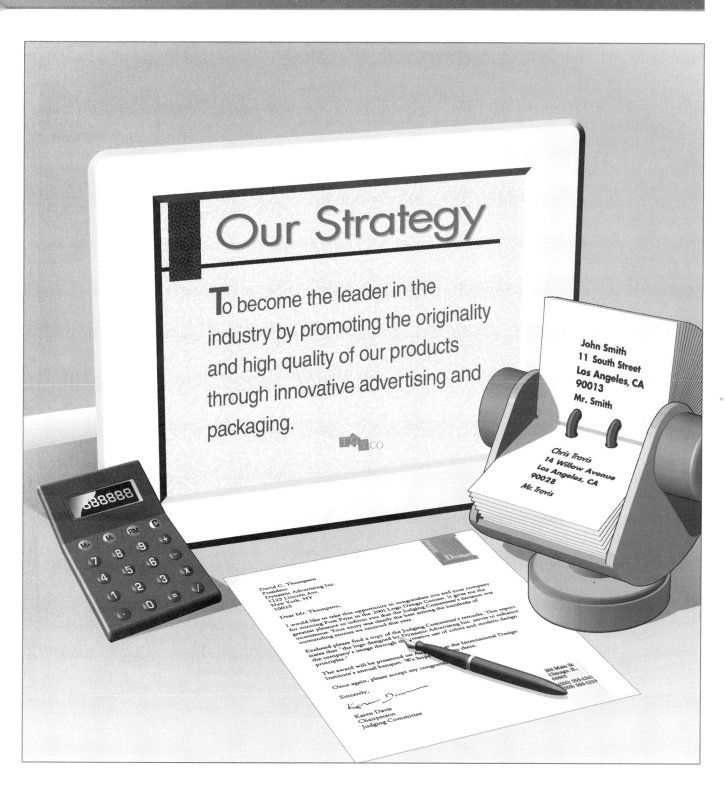

AN INTRODUCTION TO MICROSOFT OFFICE XP

Microsoft Office XP is a collection of programs sold together in one package, called a software suite. Purchasing a software suite is considerably less expensive than buying each program in the suite individually.

Microsoft Office XP is available at computer and electronic superstores. The program comes on a set of CD-ROM disks, so you need a CD-ROM drive to install Office XP.

If you already have a version of Office, but want to upgrade, you can do so. The new version contains a revamped interface, making the programs simpler to use.

Some new computers come with Microsoft Office XP as part of the computer package. In this case, the programs are most likely already installed for you.

All Office XP programs share a common design and work in a similar way. Once you learn one program, you can easily learn the others. Part I, in particular, covers features and aspects common to all Office XP programs.

Create Documents in Word

Word 2002 is a word processing program that lets you create documents such as letters, reports, manuals, and newsletters. Word can help you efficiently work with text in a document. You can edit text, rearrange paragraphs, and check for spelling errors.

In addition, Word has many formatting features to change the appearance of a document. For example, you can apply various fonts, align text, and add page numbers. You can also enhance a document by adding a graphic or creating a table. You can learn more about Word in Part II.

Create Spreadsheets in Excel

Excel is a spreadsheet program you can use to organize, analyze, and attractively present financial data, such as a budget or sales report. Excel allows you to enter and edit data efficiently in a worksheet. You can use formulas and functions to calculate and analyze the data. A *function* is a ready-to-use formula that lets you perform a specialized calculation.

You can enhance the appearance of a worksheet by formatting numbers, changing the color of cells, and adding graphics. Excel can help you create colorful charts based on your worksheet data. Excel also provides tools you can use to manage and analyze a large amount of data in a list. You can learn more about Excel in Part III.

Create Presentations in PowerPoint

PowerPoint is a program that helps you plan, organize, and design professional presentations. You can use your computer screen, the Web, 35mm slides, or overhead transparencies to deliver a presentation.

You can use the features in PowerPoint to edit and organize text in a presentation. PowerPoint also allows you to add objects to the slides including shapes, pictures, charts, and tables. You can further enhance a presentation by changing the color scheme, animating slides, or adding slide transitions. To learn more about PowerPoint, see Part IV.

Create Databases in Access

Access is a database program that allows you to store and manage large collections of information. Many people use a database to store personal information such as addresses, music collections, and recipes. Companies often use a database to store information such as client orders, expenses, inventory, and payroll.

An Access database consists of several components that provide different ways to work with the data. These include tables, forms, queries, and reports. A table is a collection of information about a specific topic, such as a mailing list. Forms provide a quick way to view, type, and change information in a database. Queries help you find specific information in a database. Reports allow you to create and print professionally designed copies of information in a database. You can learn about Access in Part V.

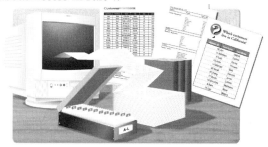

Manage Information in Outlook

Outlook is a program that helps you manage your e-mail messages, appointments, contacts, tasks, and notes, with the primary function being e-mail. You can send, receive, print, save, and handle e-mail messages as well as attach and send files to other recipients.

In addition to e-mail, Outlook includes a Calendar for keeping track of your appointments, Contacts for storing information about the people you communicate with, Tasks for keeping a to-do list, and Notes to create on-screen reminders, similar to paper sticky notes. Learn more about Outlook in Part VI.

Create Web Pages in FrontPage

FrontPage is a program that helps you create, manage, and maintain your own collection of Web pages, called a Web site.

You can use FrontPage to create Web pages that contain text, pictures, tables, and hyperlinks. FrontPage also has many formatting features you can use to enhance your Web site. For example, you can change the color of text, add horizontal lines, or apply a theme to change the overall appearance of a page. When you finish creating the pages for your Web site, you can use FrontPage to publish the site. In addition to FrontPage, other Office XP programs, such as Word, Excel, and PowerPoint, allow you to add hyperlinks to your documents and save your documents as Web pages. You can learn more about creating Web pages in Part VIII.

START AND EXIT A PROGRAM

Office allows you to easily start a program in several ways. You can either start a program using the Start menu or using a shortcut icon.

What happens upon starting a program depends on which program you select.

In Word, Excel, and PowerPoint, a blank document displays so that you can start creating a document, workbook, or presentation.

In Access and FrontPage, you see a blank area and the task pane. You can create a new blank database or Web, or open an existing database or Web.

Although this section illustrates how to start a Word document, you can use the steps to start any Office application. For more information on getting started with Word, Excel, PowerPoint, Access, or FrontPage, see Chapters 3, 10, 18, 23, and 32, respectively.

When you finish working in the program, you must save your documents and then exit the program. Doing so frees up system resources.

START AND EXIT A PROGRAM

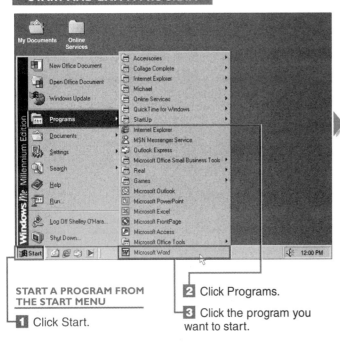

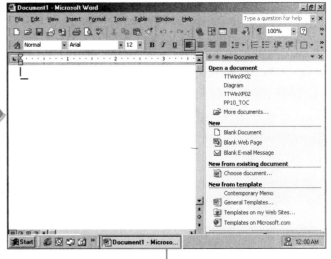

START A PROGRAM FROM THE START MENU

■1 Click Start.

■2 Click Programs.

■3 Click the program you want to start.

■ The program window appears, displaying a blank document.

Note: In Access and FrontPage, you see a blank screen. See Chapter 2 to fill the screen.

■ The Taskbar button displays a button for the program and document.

I do not see my programs listed on the Start menu. Why not?

✔ If the Start menu does not list your programs, you may not yet have installed Office. To install Office, insert the first Office CD-ROM and follow the on-screen instructions.

How do I create a shortcut icon?

✔ The easiest way to create a shortcut icon is to drag the program name from the Start menu to the desktop. Click Start and then click Programs to view a list of Office programs. Click and drag the desired program from the menu to the desktop, and Office automatically creates a shortcut. The program still appears on the Programs list.

How do I delete a shortcut icon?

✔ To delete a shortcut icon, right-click the icon, click Delete, and then confirm the deletion by clicking Yes. Deleting a shortcut does not delete the program.

Why do I want to create a shortcut icon?

✔ If you often use a program, you may want to create a shortcut icon to that program on your desktop. Then you can quickly start the program by clicking the icon.

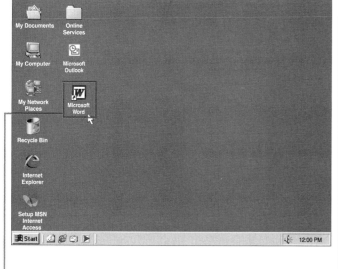

START A PROGRAM FROM A SHORTCUT ICON

■1 Double-click the shortcut icon.

■ The program starts and you see a new blank document on-screen.

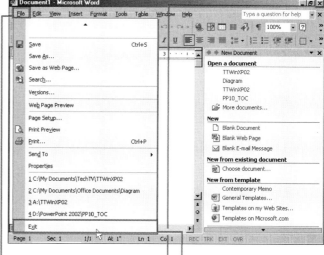

EXIT A PROGRAM

Note: Before you exit a program, save any open documents. See Chapter 2 for more information.

■1 Click File.

■2 Click Exit.

■ You can also click the Close button (☒) for the program window.

WORK WITH WINDOWS

Each program you start or item you open appears in a window on your desktop. Because you can have many windows open on your screen at once, you need to learn how to work with the windows on your desktop. For example, if a window covers important items on your screen, you can move the window to a new location.

You can change the size of a window displayed on your screen by resizing it. You can maximize a window so that it fills the entire screen, or minimize a window so that it shrinks to the size of a button on the taskbar.

You commonly maximize a window to work in a program and to see as much of the program window as

possible. A maximized window does not have borders. Therefore, you cannot move or manually resize a maximized window.

Restoring a window expands it to its original size, a size that does have borders so that you can move or manually resize the window.

WORK WITH WINDOWS

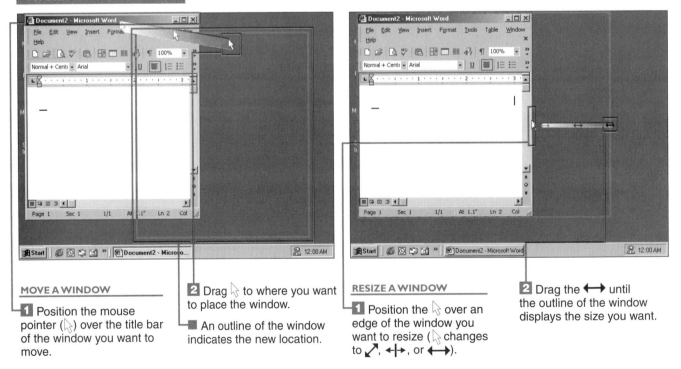

MOVE A WINDOW

1 Position the mouse pointer (⤢) over the title bar of the window you want to move.

2 Drag ⤢ to where you want to place the window.

■ An outline of the window indicates the new location.

RESIZE A WINDOW

1 Position the ⤢ over an edge of the window you want to resize (⤢ changes to ↗, ↔, or ↔).

2 Drag the ↔ until the outline of the window displays the size you want.

Why do the Minimize (▣), Maximize (▢), Restore (▣), or Close (▣) buttons appear more than once in a window?

✔ These buttons appear for the program in which you are working, and for each document within that program window. That is, document windows also have their own set of window controls so that you can move, resize, maximize, and minimize these windows within the program window.

How do I close a window?

✔ Click the Close button ▣ in the top right corner of the window you want to close.

How can I view all the information in a window?

✔ When a window is not large enough to display all the information it contains, scroll bars appear in the window. To move through the information in the window, you can drag the scroll box along a scroll bar or click an arrow button ▲ or ▼ at the end of a scroll bar.

How do I switch to another open window?

✔ You click the button on the taskbar for the window on which you want to work. The window appears in front of all other open windows.

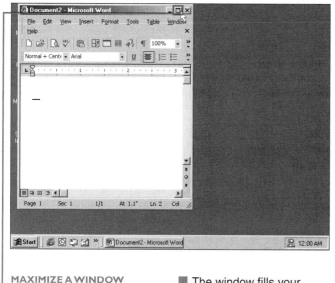

MAXIMIZE A WINDOW

■1 Click the Maximize button (▢) in the window you want to maximize.

■ The window fills your screen and ▢ changes to a Restore button (▣).

■ To return the window to its previous size, click ▣.

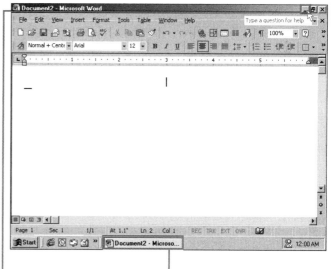

MINIMIZE A WINDOW

■1 Click the Minimize button (▣) in the window you want to minimize.

■ The window reduces to a button on the taskbar.

■ To redisplay the window, click the taskbar button for that window.

USING TOOLBARS

You can use toolbars to select features in a program. Rather than opening a menu and selecting a command, a toolbar button is often faster. A toolbar contains buttons that you can use to select commands and access commonly used features. Office also has an option that allows you to identify what each button does before you select it.

When you first start an Office program, one or more toolbars automatically appear at the top of your screen. Office programs share similar toolbars, which makes the programs easier to learn and use.

Although by default Office displays the Standard and Formatting toolbar on two rows, you can change the toolbars so that they

share one row. You can then move or resize the toolbars when necessary to access the buttons you want. This book assumes the default setting.

If you are not sure what a button does, Office allows you to display the name of a toolbar button with the ScreenTip feature.

USING TOOLBARS

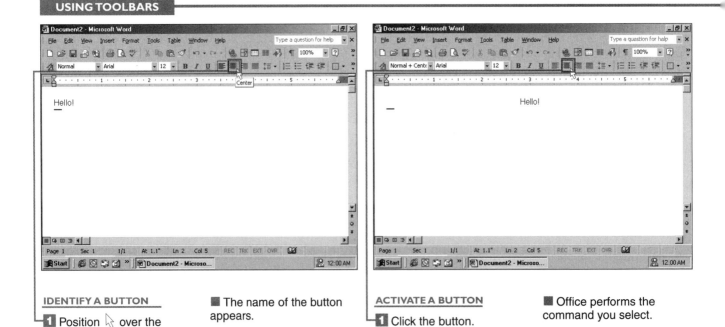

IDENTIFY A BUTTON

■ 1 Position ⬚ over the button.

■ The name of the button appears.

ACTIVATE A BUTTON

■ 1 Click the button.

■ Office performs the command you select.

Why do some buttons look a different shade of gray?

✔ When you click some buttons, you turn on that feature. To indicate that feature is on, Office outlines the button. For example, if you click Bold, the Bold button appears outlined. Toolbar buttons are toggles, which means you can turn off Bold by clicking the button again.

I do not see the name of the button when I use the ScreenTip feature. Why not?

✔ You may have turned off the ScreenTip feature. Click Tools and then Customize. Click the Options tab. Click the Show ScreenTips on toolbars option (☐ changes to ✔) to activate the feature.

What if I see only one row of buttons?

✔ You may find the Office default of combining toolbars into one row confusing. If so, you can display each toolbar in its own row. To do so, click the Tools menu, click Customize, and then click the Options tab. Click the Show Standard and Formatting toolbars on two rows option (☐ changes to ✔).

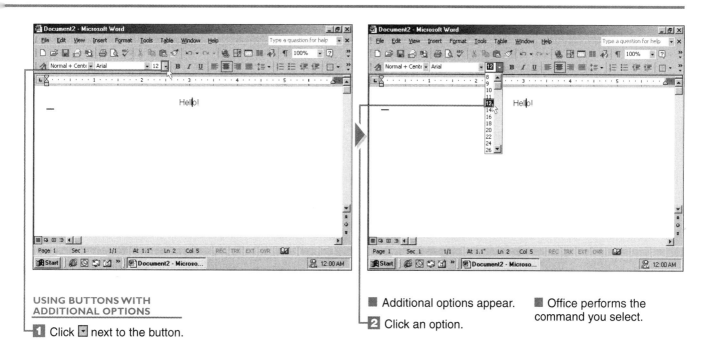

USING BUTTONS WITH ADDITIONAL OPTIONS

1 Click ▾ next to the button.

■ Additional options appear.

2 Click an option.

■ Office performs the command you select.

DISPLAY OR HIDE A TOOLBAR

Each Microsoft Office program offers several toolbars that you can display or hide at any time. Each toolbar contains buttons that help you quickly perform tasks.

When you first start an Office program, one or more toolbars automatically appear on your screen. Most programs display the Standard toolbar, which contains buttons to help you select common commands, such as Save and Print.

In most programs, the Formatting toolbar also automatically appears. The Formatting toolbar contains buttons to help you select formatting commands, such as Bold and Underline.

You can choose which toolbars to display based on the tasks you perform often. For example, if you frequently create and edit tables in Word, you can display the Tables and Borders toolbar.

If you do not use the toolbars, you can turn them off so that they do not take up screen space.

DISPLAY OR HIDE A TOOLBAR

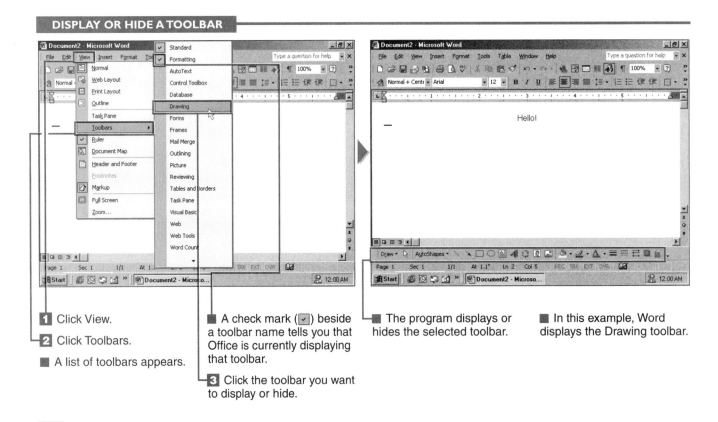

1 Click View.

2 Click Toolbars.

■ A list of toolbars appears.

■ A check mark (☑) beside a toolbar name tells you that Office is currently displaying that toolbar.

3 Click the toolbar you want to display or hide.

■ The program displays or hides the selected toolbar.

■ In this example, Word displays the Drawing toolbar.

CHANGE TOOLBAR PLACEMENT

You can move a toolbar to the top, bottom, right, or left edge of your screen to meet your work needs. When you place a toolbar next to the edge of the window, you are "docking" it.

You can also make the toolbar a floating palette, placing it anywhere on-screen. With this type of placement, you can change the size of the toolbar.

How do I move a floating toolbar back to the top of the screen?

✔ To return a floating toolbar to the top or other edge of the screen, click and drag the title bar to the top until it is "docked" against that edge of the window.

Can I change the size of the toolbar?

✔ Yes. To resize a floating toolbar, position the over an edge of the toolbar. Click and drag the edge of the toolbar until it reaches the size you want.

CHANGE TOOLBAR PLACEMENT

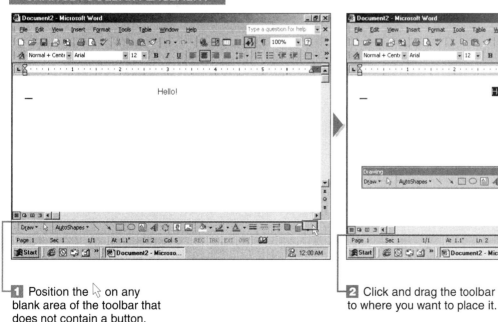

1 Position the on any blank area of the toolbar that does not contain a button.

2 Click and drag the toolbar to where you want to place it.

■ The toolbar appears in the new location.

WORK WITH THE TASK PANE

A new feature with Microsoft Office XP, the task pane appears by default along the right edge of the program window. This pane displays various options that relate to the current task, providing fast access to commonly performed commands. For example, if you select Blank Document under New, Office creates a new blank document.

You can select which features Office displays in the task pane, and you can move back and forward between task pane options you display. You can also close or resize the task pane as needed.

The options in the task pane work similar to Web links. That is, you click the option to select that feature. When you point to the option, Office underlines it and the

mouse pointer changes to the shape of a hand with a pointing finger.

For some task pane options, you perform other actions rather than selecting a link. For example, when you search for text, you type the text to find in the text box in the task pane. The task pane may also include drop-down lists from which you can select options.

WORK WITH THE TASK PANE

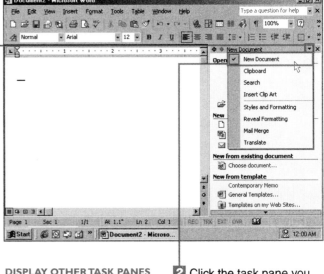

USING TASK PANE OPTIONS

1 Start an Office XP program.

Note: See Chapter 2 to start a program.

■ The New Document task pane appears.

Note: If the task pane does not appear, click View and then click Task Pane.

2 Click an option on the task pane.

■ Office executes your command.

DISPLAY OTHER TASK PANES

1 Click ▾ next to the task pane title bar.

■ A list of other task panes appears.

2 Click the task pane you want to display.

■ Office places a ✓ next to your selection and displays the new task pane.

If I close the task pane, how can I redisplay it?

✔ Click View and click the Task Pane command. Office redisplays the task pane.

How can I move back and forth among different task panes?

✔ You can click the Forward (⬛) and Back (⬛) task pane buttons to scroll among different task panes. Note that these buttons only appear if you display other task panes using the drop-down list.

Do the task panes in all Office applications have the same options?

✔ Yes and no. The task panes share some common options including the New document task pane, the Clipboard, and Search. But the other available task panes vary from application to application. For example, Word includes task panes for working with styles and mail merge. Because these options do not pertain to Excel, Excel does not include them.

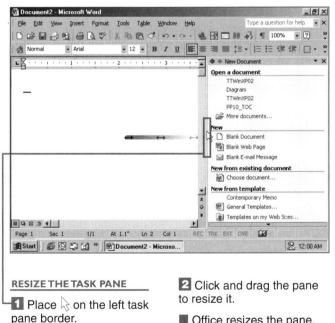

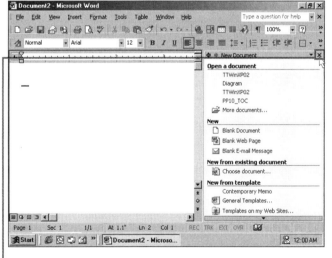

RESIZE THE TASK PANE

1 Place ⬚ on the left task pane border.

■ ⬚ changes to ↔.

2 Click and drag the pane to resize it.

■ Office resizes the pane.

CLOSE THE TASK PANE

1 Click ⊠.

■ Office closes the task pane.

GETTING HELP

You can get help on tasks, commands, and features in Office programs using one of several help options.

New with Office XP is the Type a question button in the menu bar. With this option, you can quickly and easily type a question and see a list of related help topics.

You can also display the Help window by clicking the Help button in the toolbar or selecting the Help command from the Help menu. The Help window provides several ways to get help, including using the Answer Wizard, which is the same as Type a question button, browsing through a table of contents of help topics, or looking for a particular topic in the index, as covered in the following questions.

In previous versions of Office, an Office Assistant appeared. This icon prompted you for help on certain tasks and was available for typing a question. Although the Office Assistant no longer appears by default in Office XP, you can assess the assistant via the Help menu.

GETTING HELP

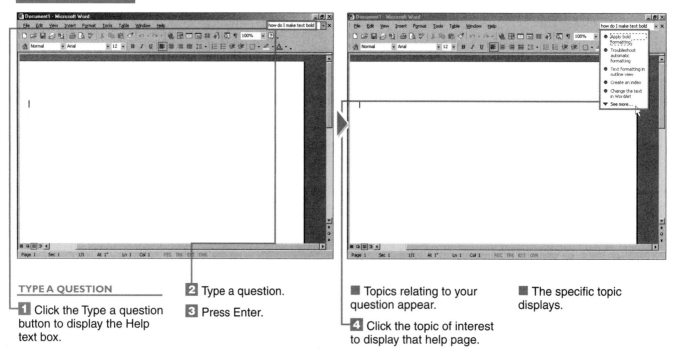

TYPE A QUESTION

1 Click the Type a question button to display the Help text box.

2 Type a question.

3 Press Enter.

■ Topics relating to your question appear.

4 Click the topic of interest to display that help page.

■ The specific topic displays.

How do I use the index?
✔ In the help window, click the Index tab. Then type the keyword you want to look up and click Search. In the bottom part of the dialog box, you see a list of matching help topics. Click the help topic of interest.

What is the purpose of the toolbar buttons in the Help window?
✔ You can use the toolbar buttons in the Help window to navigate back and forward among previous topics. You can also print a topic and change the view of the Help window. Click the Options button (🖻) to display other Help commands.

What other Help commands are available?
✔ You can click the Help menu to display a list of other help topics including accessing help from the Web, getting information about the current program version, and displaying the Office Assistant.

What is the Office Assistant?
✔ In previous versions of Office, the Office Assistant was an on-screen icon that appeared by default when you started an Office application. This has been replaced with the Type a question text box in the menu bar.

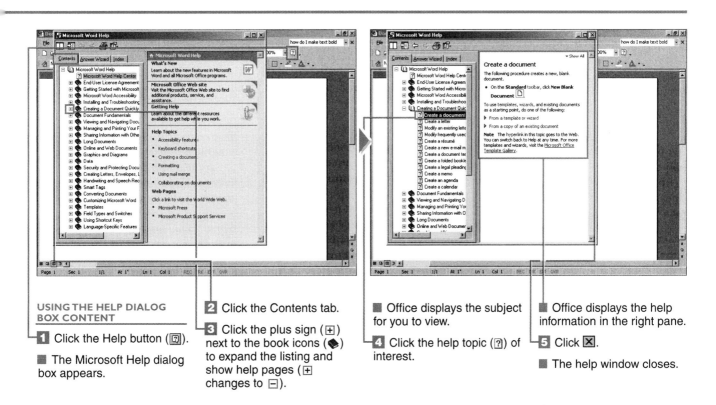

USING THE HELP DIALOG BOX CONTENT

1 Click the Help button (🗗).

■ The Microsoft Help dialog box appears.

2 Click the Contents tab.

3 Click the plus sign (⊞) next to the book icons (📖) to expand the listing and show help pages (⊞ changes to ⊟).

■ Office displays the subject for you to view.

4 Click the help topic (🗐) of interest.

■ Office displays the help information in the right pane.

5 Click ✖.

■ The help window closes.

CREATE A NEW DOCUMENT

Office allows you to create a new document in one of three ways: using the default template, an Office template, or the task pane. Each document is like a separate piece of paper. Creating a new document is similar to placing a new piece of paper on your screen.

When you start most programs, Office displays a blank document based on the default template. You simply type text to create a document. The default template defines the page margins, default font, and other settings appropriate for that program's typical document. A *template* is a pre-designed document, which may include text, formatting, and even content.

You can also create documents based on other templates by selecting from several common document types.

The task pane also includes options for creating new documents. These options vary from program to program. To learn more about the task pane, see Chapter 1.

CREATE A NEW DOCUMENT

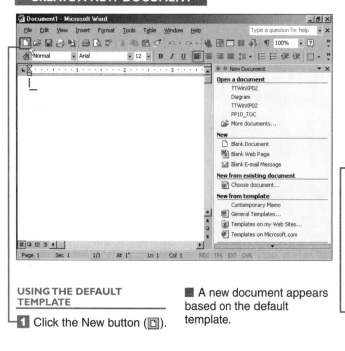

USING THE DEFAULT TEMPLATE

1 Click the New button ( ).

■ A new document appears based on the default template.

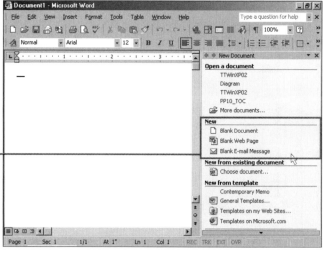

USING THE TASK PANE

1 Click the type of document you want to create under the New section in the task pane.

■ Office creates a new blank document based on that option.

Do I have to close a document before I can create a new one?

✔ No. You can have several documents open at the same time, although closing a document when you finish working on it frees up system resources.

Can I use a wizard to create a document?

✔ Yes. Some programs include *wizards*. Like templates, wizards include pre-designed formatting and text. Unlike templates, wizards lead you step-by-step through the process of creating the document. Wizards are covered where appropriate in each of the main program parts of this book. For example, you can find out how to use the PowerPoint presentation wizard in Part IV.

Can I create my own templates?

✔ Yes. First, create the document with all the text and formatting you want to include. Click File and then Save As. Type a template name and then click the Save as type ⯆ and click Template as the file type. Note that the name of the actual template file type varies depending on the program. When you save the document as a template, you make this template available in that particular program.

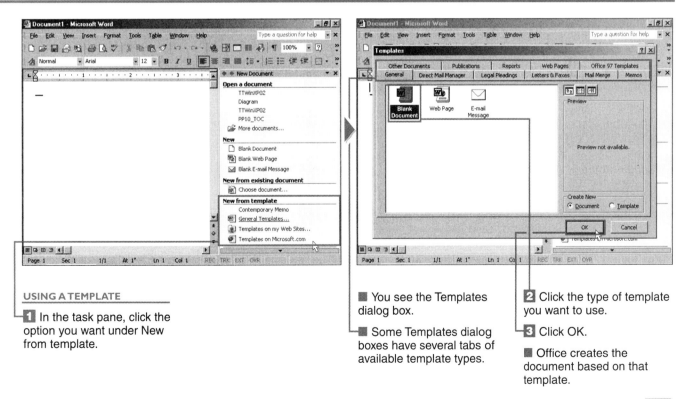

USING A TEMPLATE

◥1 In the task pane, click the option you want under New from template.

◼ You see the Templates dialog box.

◼ Some Templates dialog boxes have several tabs of available template types.

◥2 Click the type of template you want to use.

◥3 Click OK.

◼ Office creates the document based on that template.

SAVE AND CLOSE A DOCUMENT

You can save your document to store it for future use. To avoid losing your work, remember to regularly save changes you make to a document.

The first time you save a document, you assign it a name and a location. After that, you can simply use the Save button to save the document as you work.

For file names, you can type up to 255 characters, including spaces. The program automatically assigns a file extension, which indicates the type of file.

Although Office saves your document in a default document folder, you have several options for selecting a different location. See the section "Save Documents to

Other Locations" for more information concerning the Place bar, which gives you access to commonly used folders.

When you finish working with your document, you can close and remove it from your screen. You can continue working with other documents until you exit the program.

SAVE AND CLOSE A DOCUMENT

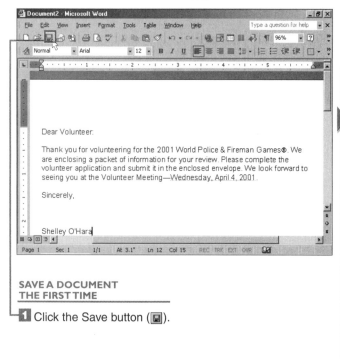

SAVE A DOCUMENT THE FIRST TIME

1 Click the Save button ( ).

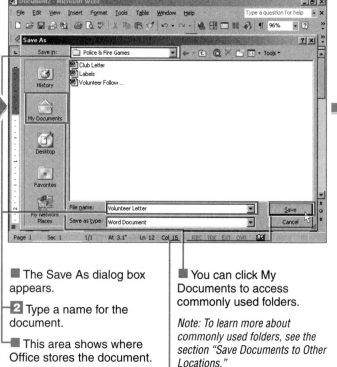

■ The Save As dialog box appears.

2 Type a name for the document.

■ This area shows where Office stores the document.

■ You can click My Documents to access commonly used folders.

Note: To learn more about commonly used folders, see the section "Save Documents to Other Locations."

3 Click Save.

How do I share my document with someone that does not have Office XP?

✔ Office lets you save most documents in other formats. For example, you can save a Word document as plain or rich text, or as other program types and versions. Click the Save as ▼ in the Save As dialog box, click the format, and then click Save. Office may prompt you to install the appropriate filter. To do so, insert the Office CD-ROM and follow the on-screen instructions.

How can I save a previously saved copy of the document with a different name?

✔ Click File and then Save As. Type the new name and then click Save.

How do I change the default folder location?

✔ This varies from program to program. In Excel, click Tools, Options, and then the General tab. Type the default file location in the Default file location box. In Word, click Tools, Options, and then the File Locations tab. Select the type of file, click the Modify button, and then click the default folder. For instructions on other programs, see the Office online help.

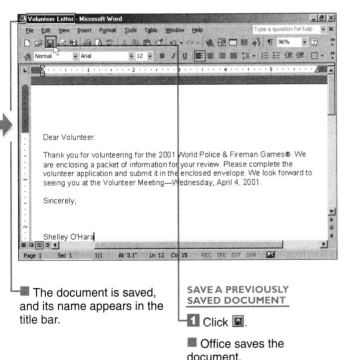

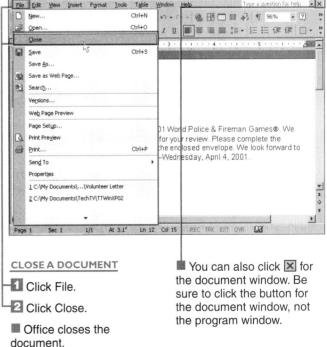

■ The document is saved, and its name appears in the title bar.

SAVE A PREVIOUSLY SAVED DOCUMENT

1 Click 🖫.

■ Office saves the document.

CLOSE A DOCUMENT

1 Click File.

2 Click Close.

■ Office closes the document.

■ You can also click ☒ for the document window. Be sure to click the button for the document window, not the program window.

SAVE DOCUMENTS TO OTHER LOCATIONS

To keep your documents organized, you can set up folders and save similar documents together. Doing so helps you quickly find a document again when you want to work on it. You can use the Office program to create folders for your documents.

When you save a document, you can select the drive and folder where you want to save the document. You can use the Save in drop-down list to select another drive. You can also select another folder from the folders listed in the dialog box.

The Places bar in the Save As dialog box also lets you quickly access commonly used folders. The History folder lets you locate recently used folders. The My Documents folder, which is the default folder, provides a convenient place to save documents on which you are currently working. The Desktop folder lets you quickly save your document on the Windows desktop. The Favorites folder provides a place to save a document you frequently access.

SAVE DOCUMENTS TO OTHER LOCATIONS

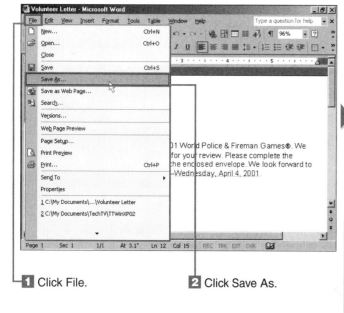

1 Click File.

2 Click Save As.

■ The Save As dialog box appears.

3 Type a name for the document.

■ To save a document to another folder, you can double-click the folder you want to use in the folder list.

What if I do not see the folder I want listed?

✔ If the Save As dialog box does not list the folder you want, you may need to navigate through the folder structure to find the folder. Click the Up One Level button (⬆) to display a higher level of folders.

What is My Network Places folder?

✔ If you are connected to a network, you can click the My Network Places button in the Places bar to access folders on the network.

How do I create a new folder?

✔ You can create a new folder from the Save As dialog box. To do so, click the Create New Folder button (📁). Type a folder name and click OK. Office creates and opens the folder so that you can save the document to this new location.

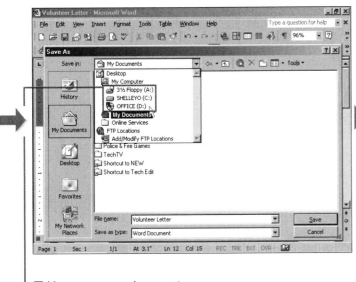

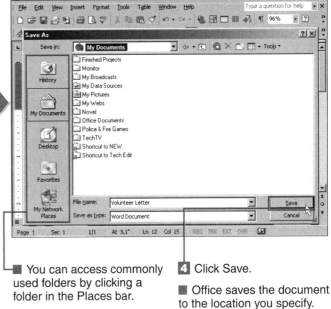

■ You can save a document to another drive by clicking the Save in ▾ and clicking a drive from the drives and folders listed.

■ You can access commonly used folders by clicking a folder in the Places bar.

4 Click Save.

■ Office saves the document to the location you specify.

SAVE A DOCUMENT AS A WEB PAGE

You can save a Word document, Excel workbook, or PowerPoint presentation as a Web page. This lets you place information on the Internet or on your company's intranet.

When saving information as a Web page, you can specify a file name and title for the page. The file name is the name you use to store the page on your computer. The title is the text that appears at the top of the Web browser window when a reader views your page.

After you save information as a Web page, you can transfer, or *publish*, the page to a computer that stores Web pages, called a Web server. Publishing the page on a Web server makes it available for other people to view. For more information on Web publishing, see Part VIII.

To learn more about creating Web pages in FrontPage, Office's Web design program, see Part VII.

SAVE A DOCUMENT AS A WEB PAGE

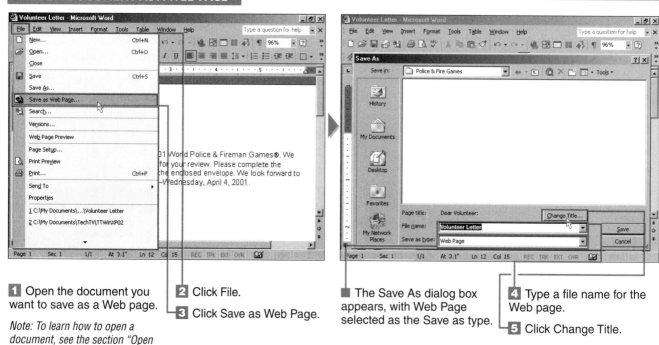

1 Open the document you want to save as a Web page.

Note: To learn how to open a document, see the section "Open a Document."

2 Click File.

3 Click Save as Web Page.

■ The Save As dialog box appears, with Web Page selected as the Save as type.

4 Type a file name for the Web page.

5 Click Change Title.

Can I see how a page looks on the Internet?

✔ Before publishing a page, you can preview the page in a Web browser to make sure it appears the way you want. Click File, Web Page Preview.

Can I save an Access report as a Web page?

✔ Yes. Display the report you want to save as a Web page. Click File, Export. Click the Save as type area, click HTML Documents, and click Save. Then click OK in the HTML Output Options dialog box.

Can I save an individual Excel worksheet as a Web page?

✔ When you save an Excel file as a Web page, you can opt to save the entire workbook or just the current worksheet. To save a worksheet as a Web page, in Excel click File and then Save As. The Save As dialog box appears. Click the Selection: Sheet option (O changes to ●). To save the entire workbook as a Web page, click the Entire Workbook option (O changes to ●).

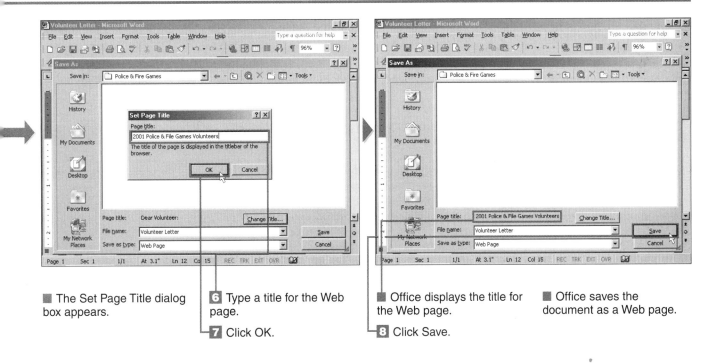

■ The Set Page Title dialog box appears.

6 Type a title for the Web page.

7 Click OK.

■ Office displays the title for the Web page.

8 Click Save.

■ Office saves the document as a Web page.

OPEN A DOCUMENT

You can open a saved document and display it on your screen to review and make changes to it. To open a document, you need to know its location — the drive and folder where Office stores your document.

Using the Open dialog box, you can access a particular drive and folder in one of three ways. You can use

the Places bar to quickly display the contents of commonly used folders. See the section "Save Documents to Other Locations" for more information. You can also use the Look in drop-down list to display other drives and folders on your system. Alternatively, you can double-click any of the files listed in the Open dialog box to view a folder's content.

You can open documents in other file formats if you have the proper file converter installed. You simply select the file, and the program converts automatically. If the document does not convert, and a file converter is available, but not installed, Office prompts you to insert one of your Office CD-ROM disks. Follow the on-screen instructions and try opening the file again.

OPEN A DOCUMENT

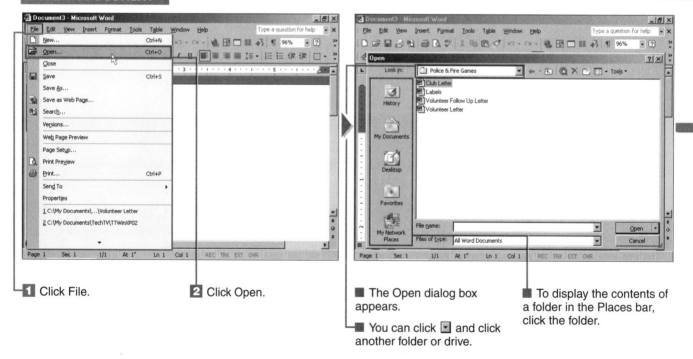

1 Click File.

2 Click Open.

■ The Open dialog box appears.

■ You can click ▦ and click another folder or drive.

■ To display the contents of a folder in the Places bar, click the folder.

How can I quickly open a document with which I recently worked?

✔ Most Office programs remember the names of the last documents with which you worked. To quickly open one of these documents, click File and then the name of the document you want to open from the bottom of the menu. Alternately, you can click the recently opened files listed in the new task pane. Click the file you want to open under the Open a document area.

Can I sort the icons displayed in the Open dialog box alphabetically by name?

✔ Yes. Sorting icons can help you find the document you want to open more easily. Click the ⊡ beside the Views button (🖽) in the Open dialog box and then click Arrange Icons. You can then click an option to sort the icons by file name, file type, file size, or by the date the files were last modified.

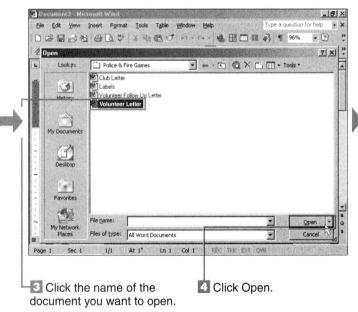

3 Click the name of the document you want to open.

4 Click Open.

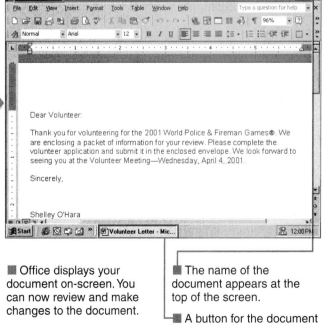

■ Office displays your document on-screen. You can now review and make changes to the document.

■ The name of the document appears at the top of the screen.

■ A button for the document appears on the taskbar.

PRINT A DOCUMENT

You can produce a paper, or hard copy of any open document. Before you print your document, make sure the printer is on and contains an adequate supply of paper. Check your specific printer manual for questions on operating your printer.

If you have more than one printer, the Office program allows you to

select the printer you want to use. This is useful if you want to use different printers to print different types of information. For example, you may want to use a black-and-white printer to print a draft of your document and a color printer to print the final version.

You can print multiple copies of your document, for example, when you are printing a brochure or

handouts for a presentation. You can also specify the part of your document you want to print. You can print the entire document, a range of pages, or just the selected text.

Although the options in the Print dialog box vary among different applications, you can use the steps in this section for printing any document in Office.

PRINT A DOCUMENT

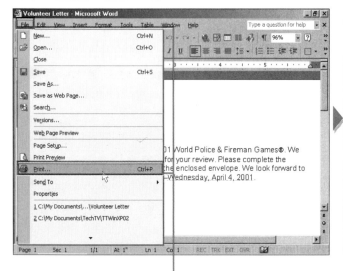

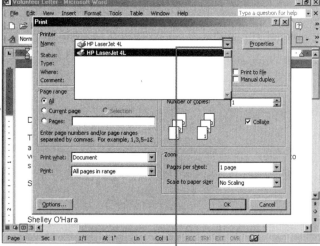

1 Click anywhere in the document or page you want to print.

■ You can print only some of the text in the document by selecting the text you want to print.

Note: See Chapter 4 to learn how to select text.

2 Click File.

3 Click Print.

■ The Print dialog box appears.

■ You can click 🔽 and click a different printer.

How do I quickly print an entire document?

✔ Click the Print button (). This sends your document to the default Windows printer, and quickly prints an entire document.

How can I preview my document before I print it?

✔ To preview a document, click File and then Print Preview. Doing so gives you an idea of how the document appears on the printed page. You can then make any changes before you print.

How do I stop a print job?

✔ You can cancel a job in the print queue. If the document is short, you may not have time to stop it. If it is a long document or if you are printing several documents, you can display the queue and stop the print job.

Double-click the printer icon in the taskbar; Office displays this icon as you print a document. You see the print queue. Click the print job you want to cancel, click Document, and then Cancel Printing. Click ☒ to close the print queue window.

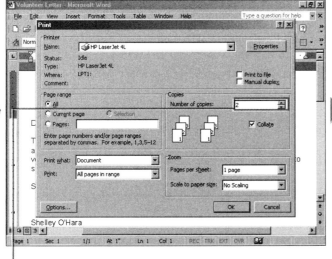

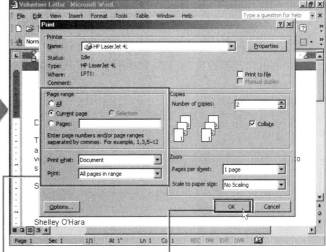

■ To print more than one copy of the document, you can double-click this area and then type the number of copies you want to print.

4 Click the print options you want to use.

Note: These options vary from program to program.

■ If you are not sure what an option does, you can right-click the option and select What's This to display a ScreenTip explanation.

5 Click OK.

■ Office prints your document.

E-MAIL A DOCUMENT

Y ou can e-mail the document on your screen to other people on the Internet or your corporate intranet. The contents of the document appear in the body of the e-mail message.

Before you e-mail a document, you must set up Microsoft Outlook. To learn more about Outlook, see Part VI.

You can send a document to more than one person. You must know the exact address of the recipient(s) and enter the address of each person you want to receive the document in the To area.

Entering an address in the Cc, or carbon copy, area allows you to send a copy of the document to a person who is not directly involved

but may find the document of interest.

When you e-mail a document, the program may suggest a subject for the e-mail message based on the name of the document. You can enter a different subject, which helps the recipient quickly identify the contents of the message.

E-MAIL A DOCUMENT

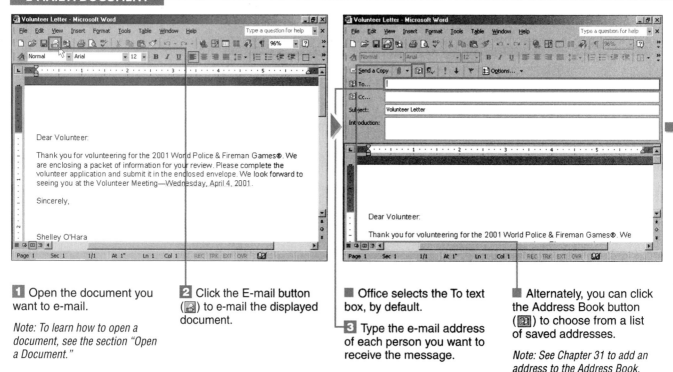

■ Open the document you want to e-mail.

Note: To learn how to open a document, see the section "Open a Document."

2 Click the E-mail button (🗐) to e-mail the displayed document.

■ Office selects the To text box, by default.

3 Type the e-mail address of each person you want to receive the message.

■ Alternately, you can click the Address Book button (📖) to choose from a list of saved addresses.

Note: See Chapter 31 to add an address to the Address Book.

How do I change the subject of the message?

✔ If a subject already exists, you can click and drag the ▷ over the existing subject and then type a new subject.

Can I send my documents as attachments?

✔ Yes, you can also send documents as attachments to regular e-mail messages. To do so, simply attach the file to the message. See Chapter 30 for more information on attaching files.

A toolbar appears when I create an e-mail message. What are these toolbar buttons for?

✔ You can use these buttons to set the priority of the message as well as attach a file or add a signature or set options for the e-mail. See Part VI for more information on Outlook e-mail buttons.

How do I send the message to several people?

✔ To type more than one address, separate each address with a semicolon (;).

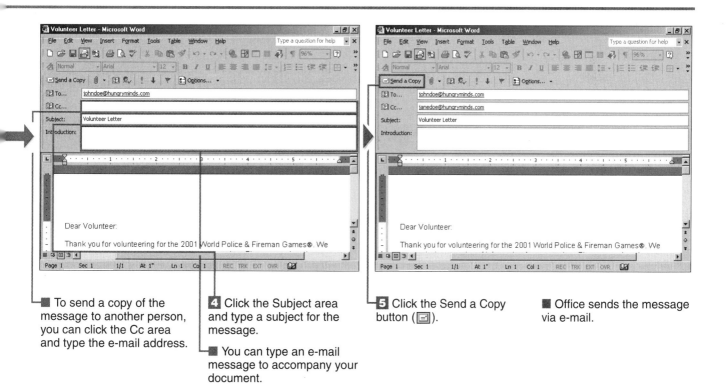

■ To send a copy of the message to another person, you can click the Cc area and type the e-mail address.

4 Click the Subject area and type a subject for the message.

■ You can type an e-mail message to accompany your document.

5 Click the Send a Copy button (🖃).

■ Office sends the message via e-mail.

SWITCH AMONG PROGRAMS

With Windows, you can have more than one program running at a time. Each program or document you have running has its own taskbar button. You can easily switch among different programs.

For example, you might want to view data in Excel while composing a document in Word. You might want to

copy a chart from Excel to a Word document. Switching programs enables you to *multitask* — work with several types of programs and information at once.

Note that switching among programs is not the same as switching among documents within a program. Please see "Switch among Documents" for more information.

Can I use the keyboard to switch programs?

✔ Yes. You can press Alt+Tab to cycle through all the open programs. When the one you want is selected, release the Alt+Tab keys.

Can I close programs from the taskbar button?

✔ Yes. Right-click the button and then click Close. If you have not saved your document, you are prompted to do so. Then Office closes the document and the program.

SWITCH AMONG PROGRAMS

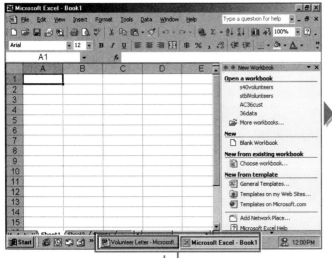

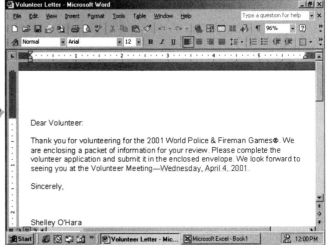

1 Start an Office program.

2 Start a second Office program.

Note: To learn how to start a program, see Chapter 1.

■ Windows displays a taskbar button for each program. Windows indicates the current program with an outlined button.

3 Click the button of the program to which you want to switch.

■ Windows displays the program.

SWITCH AMONG DOCUMENTS

Most Office programs let you have many documents open at once. You can switch among all of your open documents.

The ability to have multiple documents open and to switch among them is useful. For example, you may want to view an outline in one Word document as you write a chapter in another Word document.

You can display the names of all your open documents in a list and then select the document to which you want to switch.

You can also use the taskbar to switch among documents. The taskbar displays a button for each document you have open. To switch to the document you want to display on your screen, click the button for that document on the taskbar.

What other Window commands are available?

✔ Depending on the program, you may see different Window commands. For example, in Excel, you can freeze the panes of the worksheet. In Word, you can split the document screen into two sections and scroll independently.

SWITCH AMONG DOCUMENTS

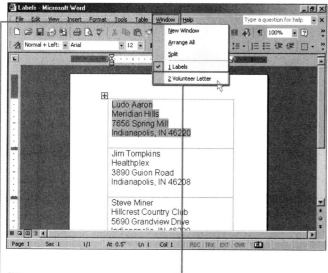

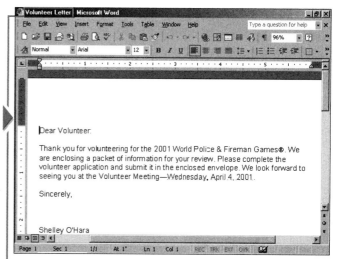

1 Open a number of documents in one program.

Note: To learn how to open documents, see the section "Open a Document."

2 Click Window.

3 Click the name of the document to which you want to switch.

■ The program adds a ☑ next to the document name.

■ The document appears. The name of the current document appears in the title bar.

FIND A DOCUMENT

If you cannot remember the name or location of a document you want to open, you can have the particular Office program search for the document using search criteria you specify.

The basic search looks for a particular text phrase in the locations you specify. You can also select a file type to limit the search.

It is best to limit the search. Otherwise, the search may take a long time, or you may get too many matches. First, think of a unique word or phrase in the document. If you search for a common word, again, you may get so many matches that the search results are not useful.

Second, limit the search to a particular drive or folder if possible. Doing so saves time because the program does not have to search the entire hard drive(s).

Third, select the type of file. For example, if you know the document is a Word document, limit the search to that document type.

FIND A DOCUMENT

1 In the task pane, click ⊡ and click Search.

Note: If the task pane is not displayed, click Views and then click Task Pane.

■ The Search task pane appears.

2 Type the text to find.

3 Click ⊡ and click the locations to search.

4 Click ⊡ and click the file types to include in the search from this list.

Can I use the search feature without accessing it in the task pane?

✔ You can search for a document in the Open dialog box. Click Tools and then click Search. In the Search dialog box, type the text to find. Click ☑ and click the drive or file to search. Click ☑ and click a file type. Click Search to start the search.

Can I search using Windows?

✔ Yes. Windows also includes a command for searching for files or folders. Click Start, click Search in Windows ME, or Find in Windows 95 or 98, and then click Files or Folders. Complete the dialog box that appears.

What does the Advanced link in the Search task pane do?

✔ The Advanced link searches for other file properties such as size, template, and number of words. To use the link, select a property and a condition and type a value to match. Next, click the Advanced link and complete the criteria for the search. You see a list of documents that match your selected criteria.

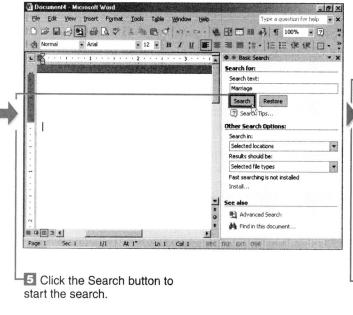

5 Click the Search button to start the search.

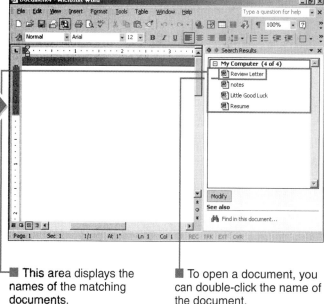

■ This area displays the names of the matching documents.

■ To open a document, you can double-click the name of the document.

SECTION II

3) GETTING STARTED

An Introduction to Word 38
Start Word 40
Parts of the Word XP Screen 41
Type Text 42
Move through a Document 44
Select Text 46

4) EDIT WORD DOCUMENTS

Insert and Delete Text 48
Move or Copy Text 50
Undo Changes 52
Insert a Page Break 53
Find Text 54
Replace Text 56
Using AutoCorrect 58
Check Spelling 60
Check Grammar 62
Using the Thesaurus 64
Count Words 65
Create and Insert an AutoText Entry 66
Insert Date and Time 68
Insert Special Characters 69
Insert Symbols 70

5) FORMAT TEXT

Bold, Italicize, or Underline Text 72
Change the Font Style 73
Change the Font Size 74
Using Special Text Effects 75
Change the Color of Text 76
Highlight Text 77
Align Text 78
Indent Paragraphs 80
Set Tabs 82
Change Line and Paragraph Spacing 84

USING WORD

Add Bullets 86

Create a Numbered List 88

Add Borders or Shading 90

Create a Style 92

Apply a Style 94

Modify a Style 96

Copy Formatting 98

Reveal Formatting 99

Display and Hide Paragraph Marks 100

Change AutoFormat Options 101

6) FORMAT DOCUMENTS

Change the View 102

Zoom In or Out 103

Preview a Document 104

Change Margins 106

Align Text on a Page 108

Change Page Orientation 109

Add Page Numbers 110

Add a Header or Footer 112

Add Footnotes or Endnotes 114

Create Columns 116

Add a Picture Watermark 118

Using Templates 120

7) CREATE TABLES

Create a Table 122

Type Text in a Table 124

Sort Text 125

Change Column Width 126

Erase Lines 127

Add or Delete a Row or Column 128

Move or Resize a Table 130

Change Table Borders 132

Add Shading or Color to Cells 134

Change Text Position in Cells 135

Using a Table AutoFormat 136

8) WORK WITH GRAPHICS

Add an AutoShape 138

Add a Clip Art Image 140

Add Word Art 142

Insert a Picture 144

Add a Diagram 146

Move or Resize a Graphic 148

Wrap Text around a Graphic 150

9) USING MAIL MERGE

An Introduction to Mail Merge 152

Create a Letter with Mail Merge 154

Print Mailing Labels 164

Print an Envelope 170

AN INTRODUCTION TO WORD

Word allows you to efficiently produce documents for business or personal use, such as newsletters, reports, letters, and essays. Word offers many features that make it easy for you to create professional-looking documents.

For more information on Word, you can visit the following Web site: www.microsoft.com/word.

Enter and Edit Text

Word includes many features, such as templates and wizards, to help you create documents. You save time by setting up common types of documents, such as letters, memos, and reports. The AutoText feature stores text you frequently type, such as an address, so you do not have to repeatedly type the same text.

You can also easily make changes to the text, editing the words and organization of a document until it makes the best sense. You can add or delete text as well as check for spelling and grammar mistakes.

To learn more about entering text, see Chapter 3. For more information on the AutoText feature, see Chapter 4. You can learn more about templates and wizards in Chapter 5.

Format Text

Word allows you to enhance the appearance of text by using text and paragraph formatting options. Formatting options include changing font sizes, styles, and colors to help make important text stand out. Paragraph formatting options include changing the amount of space between lines of text or aligning text in different ways. Formatting text can help you organize the information in a document so that it is easy for your reader to review and understand it. For example, headings help identify key sections. Bulleted lists identify main points.

To speed formatting, you can apply one of Word's existing styles, or create your own style to help you apply the same formatting to many areas of a document. You can learn how to format text and use styles in Chapter 5.

Format Documents

In addition to formatting the text, you can also make some changes to the overall appearance of the document. For example, you can add page numbers, or display text in newspaper-style columns.

Features such as footnotes or endnotes allow you to provide additional information about text in a document.

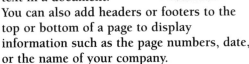

You can also add headers or footers to the top or bottom of a page to display information such as the page numbers, date, or the name of your company.

You can change the margins for a document, center text on a page, or specify whether you want to print a document in the portrait or landscape orientation. To learn more about formatting your document, see Chapter 6.

View and Print Documents

You can display your document in one of several views, each appropriate for the task at hand. For writing, you may find the Normal view helpful because this view focuses on the text rather than the formatting of the document. When you work with special features such as columns, you may want to use Print Layout view, which shows the effects of page formatting. If you are creating an outline, you can change to Outline view.

Before printing a hard copy, Word allows you to preview a document to see how it looks on the page. You can use Word to create print envelopes and mailing labels as well as documents.

To learn more about page views, see Chapter 6. To learn more about printing a document, see Chapter 7.

Send and Publish Documents

Besides printing documents, you can also send them via e-mail to others. You can also use Word to create a Web document and publish this document as part of a Web site. For more about sending and publishing Word documents, see Chapter 2.

Insert Tables

Tables help you organize and neatly display information in a document. Word lets you insert a table on the screen similar to drawing a table with a pen and paper. You can enhance the appearance of a table by changing the cell borders, adding shading to cells, and aligning the position of text in cells. For more on creating and formatting tables, see Chapter 8.

Insert Graphics

Word comes with many types of graphics you can use to enhance the appearance of a document. Graphics such as text effects, AutoShapes, and professionally designed clip art can help make a document more interesting or help draw attention to important information.

After adding a graphic to a document, you can further enhance the document by wrapping text around the graphic. To learn more about using graphics in a Word document, see Chapter 9.

Mail Merge

Word's Mail Merge feature allows you to quickly produce personalized letters and mailing labels for each person on a mailing list. This is useful if you want to send the same document, such as an announcement, change of address notification, or advertisement to many people. To learn how to do a mail merge, see Chapter 10.

START WORD

Word is a word processing program that you can use to create letters, memos, reports, manuscripts, brochures, newsletters, and flyers. You can create basically any type of document, which can include text, pictures, tables, or other elements.

When you start Word, a blank document appears on your screen. You can type text into this new document. The flashing vertical line, also called the *insertion point,* indicates the current position of the cursor — where Word inserts text when you type. The small horizontal line indicates the end of the document. Although you cannot click past this line, the line continues to move as long as you type text. You use the I-beam cursor to place the insertion point within existing text. You can learn more about typing and moving within the document in the sections "Type Text" and "Move Through a Document."

After you start Word, the taskbar displays a button for the Word program. Before you save and name a document, Word gives your document a default name, which appears on the taskbar button.

START WORD

1 Click Start.

2 Click Programs.

3 Click Microsoft Word.

■ The Microsoft Word window appears, displaying a blank document.

■ The insertion point indicates where Word places text when you type.

■ The taskbar button displays a button for the program and document.

PARTS OF THE WORD XP SCREEN

T he Word screen displays several items
to help you perform tasks efficiently.

Title Bar

Displays the name of
the document and the
program name.

Standard Toolbar

Contains buttons to help you
select common commands, such
as Save and Print.

Menu Bar

Lists the menu names.

Ruler

Enables you to set paragraph
formatting options such as tabs
and indents.

Document Area

The blank area where you
type.

View Buttons

Enable you to switch to a
different view of the document.

Formatting Toolbar

Contains buttons to help you
select formatting commands,
such as Styles, Font, and Font
Size.

Scroll Bars

Allow you to move through
the document.

Task Pane

Displays pertinent commands
for the current task. For
example, if you are creating a
new document, the pane
includes options for opening a
saved document or creating a
new document.

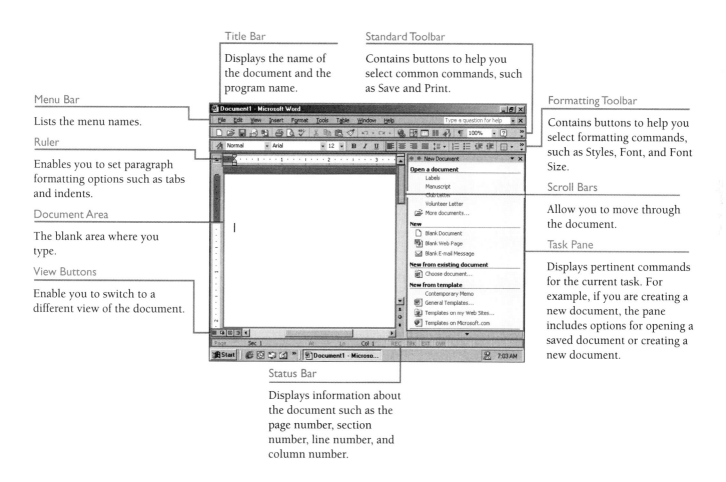

Status Bar

Displays information about
the document such as the
page number, section
number, line number, and
column number.

TYPE TEXT

You can type text into your document quickly and easily and let Word help you with its built-in features. Simply press the keys on the keyboard, and as you type, the characters appear on-screen, and the insertion point moves to the right.

Word has a word wrap feature, which automatically moves your text to the next line when it reaches the end of a line. You press Enter only when you want to start a new line or paragraph. You should not press Enter at the end of each line. Pressing Enter creates *hard breaks,* which make it difficult to add or delete text because the breaks do not adjust automatically at the end of each line.

As you type, Word automatically checks your document for spelling and grammar errors, underlining any errors that it finds. Word also corrects hundreds of common typing, spelling, and grammar errors for you. For example, Word automatically replaces "istead" with "instead" as you type. For more about the AutoCorrect feature, see Chapter 4.

Word's AutoText feature helps you quickly enter common words and phrases in your document. For example, you can quickly enter salutations, such as "To Whom It May Concern:". You can also quickly enter the days of the week, months of the year, or your name, which Word creates as an AutoText entry automatically). For more information on the AutoText feature, see Chapter 4.

TYPE TEXT

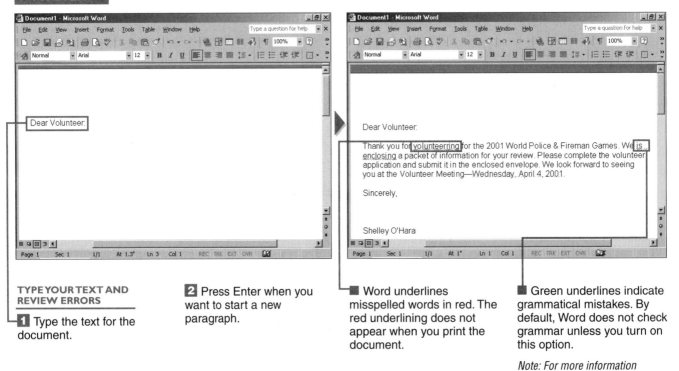

TYPE YOUR TEXT AND REVIEW ERRORS

1 Type the text for the document.

2 Press Enter when you want to start a new paragraph.

■ Word underlines misspelled words in red. The red underlining does not appear when you print the document.

■ Green underlines indicate grammatical mistakes. By default, Word does not check grammar unless you turn on this option.

Note: For more information concerning Grammar and Spelling checks, see Chapter 5.

Can I enter text anywhere in my document?

✔ Word's Click and Type feature lets you quickly type text in any part of your document. In the Print Layout or Web Layout view, double-click the location where you want to place your text and then type the text you want to add.

Word capitalizes everything that I type. What did I do wrong?

✔ If you press the Caps Lock key, Word enters all text in uppercase letters. You can press the Caps Lock key again to turn off this feature. If you accidentally type text and want to change the case, click Format, and then Change Case.

How can I quickly insert the current date and time into my document?

✔ Click where you want the date and time to appear in your document. Click Insert, and then click Date and Time. Select the format you want to use for the date and time and then click OK.

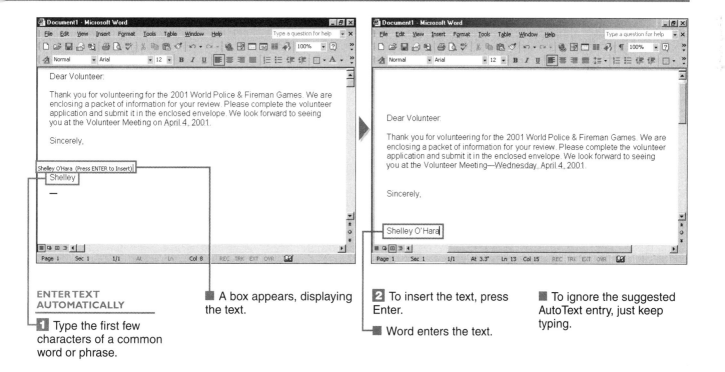

ENTER TEXT AUTOMATICALLY

1 Type the first few characters of a common word or phrase.

■ A box appears, displaying the text.

2 To insert the text, press Enter.

■ Word enters the text.

■ To ignore the suggested AutoText entry, just keep typing.

MOVE THROUGH A DOCUMENT

Word allows you to move quickly through a document, saving you time when you type and edit. When you want to edit or select text, you need to place your insertion point at the spot in the document you want to change. You can use either the mouse or the keyboard to move to the insertion point.

In longer documents, you can also display the other pages of a document. You can move through the document screen by screen or page by page. Word also provides shortcuts for moving quickly to the top of the document and the end of the document.

You can also use scroll bars to scroll up and down or left and right. The location of the scroll box on the scroll bar indicates which area of the document you are viewing. When you drag a scroll box, Word displays a yellow box containing the page number.

MOVE THROUGH A DOCUMENT

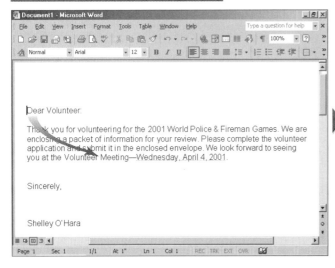

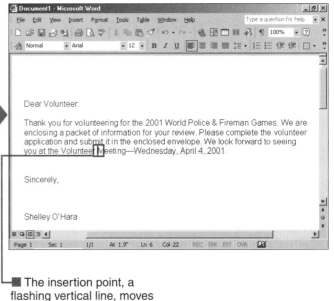

MOVE THE INSERTION POINT

1 Move the I-beam cursor (I) to the spot where you want to move.

2 Click the mouse.

■ The insertion point, a flashing vertical line, moves to the new location.

How do I use the keyboard to move through a worksheet?

✔ You can use any of the following keys and key combinations to move through a document:

Press	To move
Left Arrow	Left one character
Right Arrow	Right one character
Up Arrow	Up one line
Down Arrow	Down one line
Home	To the beginning of the line
End	To the end of the line
Ctrl + Home	To the top of the document
Ctrl + End	To the end of the document

I have a mouse with a special wheel. How do I use this to scroll?

✔ You can purchase a mouse that has a small wheel between the left and right mouse buttons. Moving this wheel lets you quickly scroll through a document.

How can I quickly move to another page?

✔ If you know the page number, you can use the Go To command. Click Edit, and then Go To. In the Find and Replace dialog box, click the Go To tab and click Page in the Go to what box. Type the page number in the Enter page number box and click Go To.

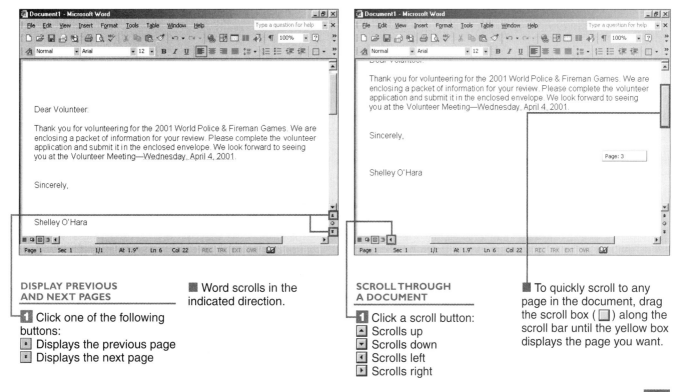

DISPLAY PREVIOUS AND NEXT PAGES

■1 Click one of the following buttons:

⬆ Displays the previous page

⬇ Displays the next page

■ Word scrolls in the indicated direction.

SCROLL THROUGH A DOCUMENT

■1 Click a scroll button:

⬆ Scrolls up

⬇ Scrolls down

◀ Scrolls left

▶ Scrolls right

■ To quickly scroll to any page in the document, drag the scroll box (☐) along the scroll bar until the yellow box displays the page you want.

SELECT TEXT

The most common task you perform when creating a document is selecting the text with which you want to work. You may select text when you want to perform common editing tasks such as copying or moving a text block, or when you want to implement a format change such as increasing the font size or making the text bold.

You can select as much text as you want, including a single character, a word, a line, an entire paragraph, or even the whole document.

When you select text, it appears reverse video — usually white text on a black background — on your screen so that you can tell which text you selected. Once selected,

you can then perform any action you want on the selected text.

You can select text using one of several methods: the mouse, the keyboard, or the selection bar. The selection bar is the white area along the left edge of the screen.

USING THE MOUSE

1 Click at the start of the text you want to select.

2 Drag across the text to select it.

■ Word selects the text.

Are there shortcuts for selecting text?

✔ Word includes several shortcuts for selecting text:

- To select a word, double-click the word.
- To select a sentence, press the Ctrl key and click within the sentence you want to select.
- To select a paragraph, triple-click within the paragraph.

How do I deselect text?

✔ To deselect text, click outside the selected area.

How do I select all the text in my document?

✔ The easiest way to select all of the text in the document is to use the keyboard shortcut. Press the Ctrl key and then press the A key. You can also click Edit, and then click Select All.

I accidentally deleted text. What happened?

✔ If you select text, and you type anything, even a single character, Word replaces the text with the typing. If this happens, simply click Edit and then Undo to undo the deletion.

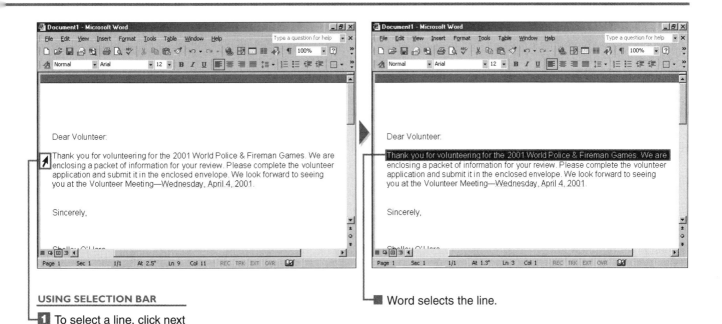

USING SELECTION BAR

1 To select a line, click next to the line in the selection area.

■ Word selects the line.

INSERT AND DELETE TEXT

Y ou can insert and delete text in your document. The capability to add and remove text in a document makes Word an efficient editing tool because instead of retyping when you want to make changes, you can simply add or delete text, and Word adjusts the existing text.

When you add new text to your document, the existing text moves to make room for the text you add. You can also add a blank line to your document. Adding a blank line between paragraphs can help make your document easier to read.

You can remove text or a blank line you no longer need from your

document. You can also select any amount of text you want to remove from your document, such as a few characters, a sentence, or an entire paragraph. When you remove text from your document, the remaining text moves to fill any empty spaces.

INSERT TEXT

■1 Click where you want to insert the new text.

■ You can press the Up, Down, Right, or Left arrow keys to move the insertion point in any direction.

■2 Type the text you want to insert.

■ You can insert a blank line by pressing Enter.

■ The text you type appears where the insertion point flashes on the screen. Word adjusts existing text to make room.

Can I recover text I accidentally deleted?

✔ You can click the Undo button () to recover your text. For more information on the Undo feature, see the section "Undo Changes."

Why does the existing text in my document disappear when I insert new text?

✔ When you turn on the Overtype feature, Word replaces existing text with the text you insert. When Overtype is on, OVR appears in the status bar. To turn off the Overtype feature, press Insert.

Can I delete characters as I type?

✔ Yes. If you make a mistake, you can press Backspace to delete characters to the left of the insertion point. You can also delete characters to the right of the insertion point by pressing Delete.

Can I quickly change the text I inserted to uppercase letters?

✔ Word offers five case styles you can use to change the appearance of text in your document: Sentence case, lowercase, UPPERCASE, Title Case, and tOGGLE cASE. Select the text you want to change. Click Format, Change Case, and then click the case you want to use (○ changes to ◉).

DELETE TEXT

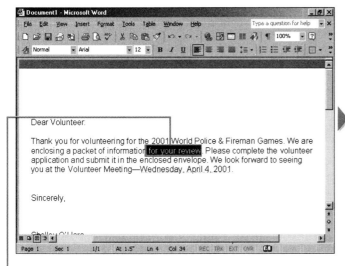

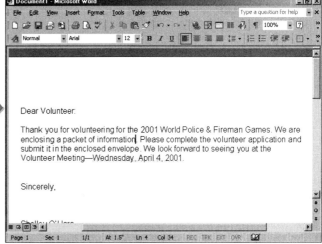

1 Select the text you want to delete.

2 Press Delete to remove the text.

■ Word deletes the selected text and adjusts the existing text accordingly.

MOVE OR COPY TEXT

You can reorganize your document by moving text from one location to another. Moving text can help you find the most effective structure for your document. For example, you may want to reorder the paragraphs in a document so that they flow better.

When you move text, the text disappears from its original location in your document and moves to the new location.

In addition to moving text, you can also copy text to a different location in your document. This is helpful when you want to use the same information, such as an address, in several locations in your document. When you copy text, the text appears in both the original and new location.

When you move or copy text to a new location in your document, Word shifts the existing text to

make room for the text you move or copy.

For both tasks, Word uses the metaphor of cutting, copying, and pasting. You use the Cut and Paste buttons to move text, and Copy and Paste buttons to copy text.

MOVE TEXT

1 Select the text you want to move.

Note: To select text, see Chapter 3.

2 Click the Cut button ( ).

3 Click where you want to place the cut text.

4 Click the Paste button ( ).

■ Word moves the text to the new location.

Is there another method to cut or copy text?

✔ Yes. You can also drag and drop text. To move text, select the text, place over the text, and then drag the text to the new location. To copy, follow the same procedure, but hold down Ctrl as you drag.

While working with selected text, I often drag and drop the text by accident. Is there a way to turn off this feature?

✔ Yes. Click Tools and then click Options. Click the Edit tab, deselect the Drag-and-drop text editing option (☑ changes to ☐), and then click OK.

Why does the Clipboard toolbar appear when I move or copy text using the toolbar buttons?

✔ The Clipboard toolbar may appear when you cut or copy two pieces of text in a row, copy the same text twice, or place copied text in a new location and then immediately copy other text. This toolbar lets you select what you copy. For more information on working with the Clipboard and moving and copying text to other programs, see Chapter 34.

COPY TEXT

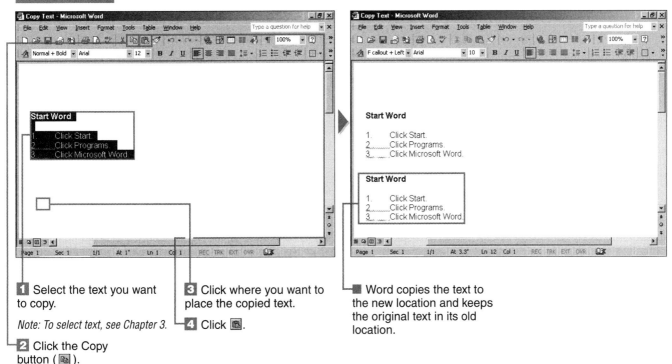

1 Select the text you want to copy.

Note: To select text, see Chapter 3.

2 Click the Copy button (📋).

3 Click where you want to place the copied text.

4 Click 📋.

■ Word copies the text to the new location and keeps the original text in its old location.

UNDO CHANGES

Word remembers the last changes you made to your document. If you change your mind, you can cancel them by using the Undo feature.

The Undo feature can cancel your last editing and formatting changes. For example, you can cancel editing changes such as deleting a

paragraph or typing a sentence. You can also cancel formatting changes such as underlining a word or increasing the size of text.

You can use the Undo feature to cancel one or many changes at once. Word stores a list of changes you make to your document. When you select the change you want to

cancel from the list, Word cancels the change and all the changes you have made since that change.

You can also "undo" the undo. That is, you can cancel the undo changes by using the Redo button.

UNDO CHANGES

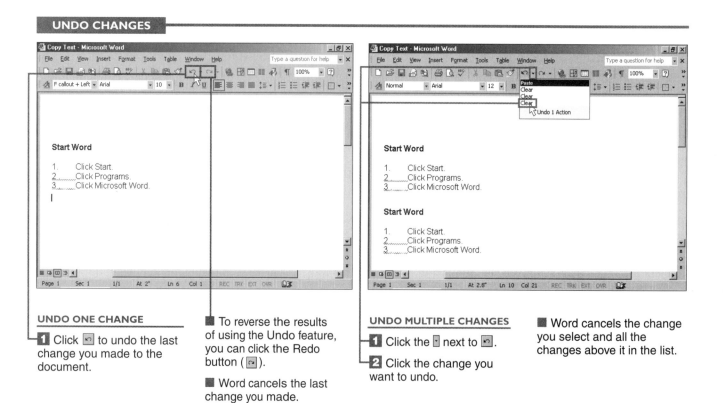

UNDO ONE CHANGE

1 Click ![undo icon] to undo the last change you made to the document.

■ To reverse the results of using the Undo feature, you can click the Redo button (![redo icon]).

■ Word cancels the last change you made.

UNDO MULTIPLE CHANGES

1 Click the ■ next to ![undo icon].

2 Click the change you want to undo.

■ Word cancels the change you select and all the changes above it in the list.

INSERT A PAGE BREAK

If you want to start a new page at a specific place in your document, you can insert a page break. Word automatically determines the length of the pages by the paper size and margin settings you set, and inserts a page break when you enter text past the bottom of a page.

When you insert a break in Normal view, Word places a dotted line where the page break occurs, but does not show the text broken into pages. In Print Layout view, you see the actual pages. To learn about the various views in Word, see Chapter 6.

What are the Section break types options in the Break dialog box?

✔ Word allows you to break your document into sections instead of pages. When you break your document into different sections, you can apply formatting to different parts of your document. See Chapter 6 for more information on sections and section breaks.

How do I remove a page break?

✔ To remove the page break, you can click it in Normal view and press Delete.

INSERT A PAGE BREAK

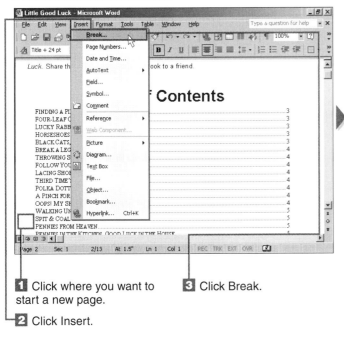

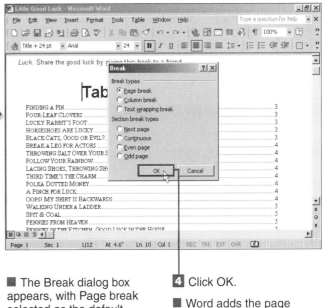

1 Click where you want to start a new page.

2 Click Insert.

3 Click Break.

■ The Break dialog box appears, with Page break selected as the default option.

4 Click OK.

■ Word adds the page break to the document.

FIND TEXT

If your document is short, finding a particular word, phrase or passage by skimming the text is easy. If the document is longer, however, skimming to find the section of interest is tedious. Instead of skimming your document, you can use the Find feature to locate text.

By default, when you search for text in your document, Word finds the text even if it is part of a larger word. For example, if you search for "place" Word also finds "places," "placement," and "commonplace."

The word or phrase you want to find may appear in several locations in your document. After you start the search, Word finds and highlights the first instance of the word or phrase. You can

continue the search to find the next instance of the word or phrase, or cancel the search at any time.

The More button allows you to narrow your search by matching case, finding whole words, or using wildcards.

To learn how to replace the words you find, see the section "Replace Text."

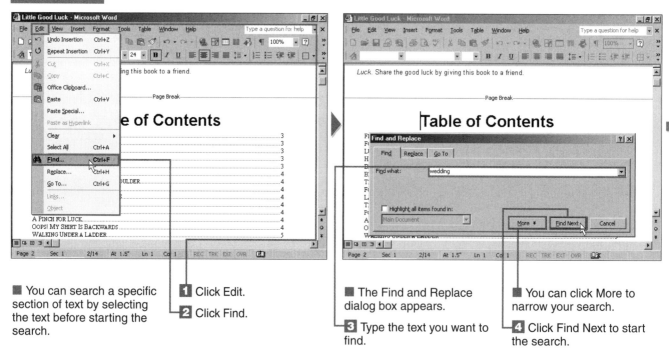

■ You can search a specific section of text by selecting the text before starting the search.

1 Click Edit.

2 Click Find.

■ The Find and Replace dialog box appears.

3 Type the text you want to find.

■ You can click More to narrow your search.

4 Click Find Next to start the search.

How do I move the Find and Replace dialog box so I can view my document?

✔ Position ⌖ over the title bar of the Find and Replace dialog box, and then drag the dialog box to a new location.

What does the Use wildcards option do?

✔ You can click wildcards (☐ changes to ✔), a More button option, to insert wildcard characters in your search. The ? wildcard represents any single character. For example, "h?t" finds "hit" and "hut." The * wildcard can represent many characters. For example, "h*t" finds "heat" and "haunt."

What does the Match case option do?

✔ You can click Match case (☐ change to ✔), a More button option, to find words that exactly match uppercase and lowercase letters. With this option, for example, "Letter" does not find "letter" or "LETTER."

What does the Find whole word option do?

✔ You can click Find whole words only (☐ change to ✔), a More button option, to search for words that are not part of a larger word. With this option, for example, "work" does not find "homework" or "coworker."

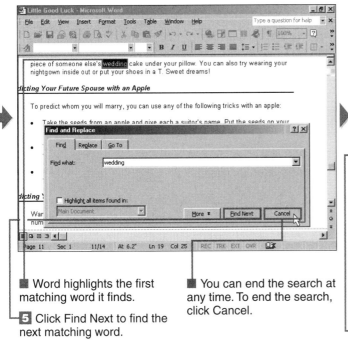

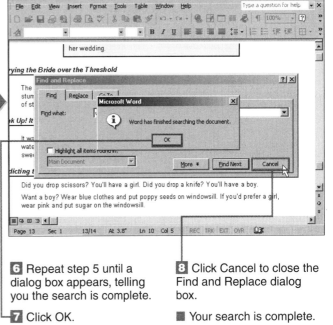

■ Word highlights the first matching word it finds.

5 Click Find Next to find the next matching word.

■ You can end the search at any time. To end the search, click Cancel.

6 Repeat step 5 until a dialog box appears, telling you the search is complete.

7 Click OK.

8 Click Cancel to close the Find and Replace dialog box.

■ Your search is complete.

REPLACE TEXT

The Replace feature can locate and replace every occurrence of a word or phrase in your entire document or only part of it.

This is useful if you need to replace a name throughout a document. For example, if you have a letter to ABC Inc. and you want to send the same letter to XYZ Corp., Word can replace ABC Inc. with XYZ Corp. throughout the document.

The Replace feature is also useful if you repeatedly misspell a name in your document. For example, you can quickly change all occurrences of McDonald to Macdonald.

Word locates and highlights each occurrence of the word or phrase in your document. You can replace the found word or phrase, or ignore the match. If you are sure of the replacements, you can also replace

all the occurrences of the word or phrase in your document at once.

The More button allows you to narrow your search by finding specific formatting. To learn more about the matching case, finding whole words only, and wildcard options of this button, see the section "Find Text."

REPLACE TEXT

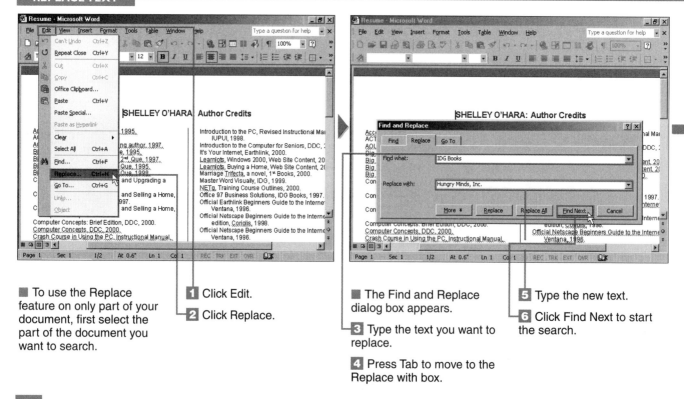

■ To use the Replace feature on only part of your document, first select the part of the document you want to search.

1 Click Edit.

2 Click Replace.

■ The Find and Replace dialog box appears.

3 Type the text you want to replace.

4 Press Tab to move to the Replace with box.

5 Type the new text.

6 Click Find Next to start the search.

Can I use the Replace feature to change the formatting of text in my document?

✔ Yes. In the Find and Replace dialog box, remove any text from the Find what and Replace with areas, and click More. Click the Find what area, click Format, and select a format property. If a dialog box appears, select the property you want to replace and click OK. Click the Replace with area and repeat the process to specify your new formatting.

How do I stop the formatting search?

✔ Click the Find what area and click No Formatting. Then click the Replace with area and click No Formatting again.

When I clicked Replace all, Word made changes I did not want. What do I do?

✔ You can always click 🔄 to reverse your replacements. To prevent undesirable replacements, try clicking Replace a few times to see whether the change is what you want. For example, if you replace *man* with *person*, you can end up with *personager* instead of *manager.* It is a good idea to use the More button options with Replace all to narrow your search.

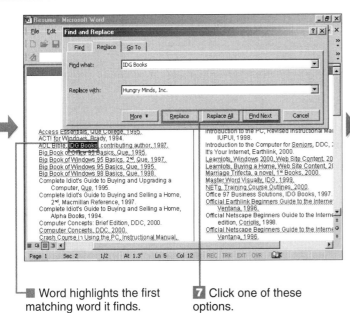

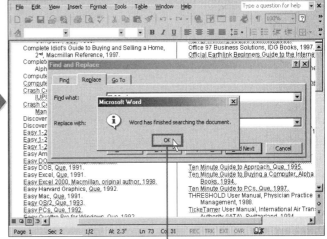

■ Word highlights the first matching word it finds.

7 Click one of these options.

Replace	Replaces the word.
Replace All	Replaces all.
Find Next	Ignores the word and continues the search.

8 Continue confirming or ignoring replacements.

■ You can click Cancel to end the search.

■ A dialog box appears when the search is complete.

9 Click OK to close the dialog box.

■ Your search is complete.

USING AUTOCORRECT

Word automatically corrects hundreds of typing, spelling, and grammar errors as you type. The AutoCorrect feature uses its list of common errors and Word's dictionary to correct errors in your document. You can add your own words and phrases to the AutoCorrect dictionary.

The AutoCorrect feature replaces common errors such as "aboutthe,"

"includ," and "may of been" with the correct word or phrase.

The feature capitalizes the first letter of new sentences and the names of days. It also inserts symbols into your document when you type certain characters. For example, when you type (r), the ® symbol automatically appears in your document. This is useful when you want to quickly insert

symbols into your document that do not appear on your keyboard.

You can review a list of AutoCorrect entries and add new entries. For example, suppose that you consistently misspell or mistype cabinet. You can add an AutoCorrect entry for the incorrect spelling with its correct spelling so that Word automatically corrects it.

USING AUTOCORRECT

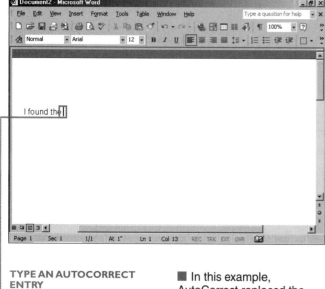

TYPE AN AUTOCORRECT ENTRY

1 Type an incorrect spelling of a word.

■ Word automatically replaces the incorrect word with the correct one.

■ In this example, AutoCorrect replaced the misspelled word teh with the, but you can use the AutoCorrect feature with any misspelled word.

ADD AN AUTOCORRECT ENTRY

1 Click Tools.

2 Click AutoCorrect Options.

58

What other types of errors does the AutoCorrect feature correct?

✔ When you type two consecutive uppercase letters, the AutoCorrect feature converts the second letter to lowercase. The feature also corrects accidental usage of the Caps Lock key. If you no longer want the feature to automatically correct some types of errors, display the AutoCorrect dialog box and click each option you do not want to use.

Can I delete an AutoCorrect entry?

✔ Yes. In the AutoCorrect dialog box, select the entry you want to delete and then click Delete.

The AutoCorrect feature did not replace a spelling error in my document. Why?

✔ The AutoCorrect feature automatically replaces a spelling error when there is only one suggestion to correct the error. To have the AutoCorrect feature always correct a spelling error, right-click the misspelled word. Click AutoCorrect and then click the word you want to always replace the misspelled word.

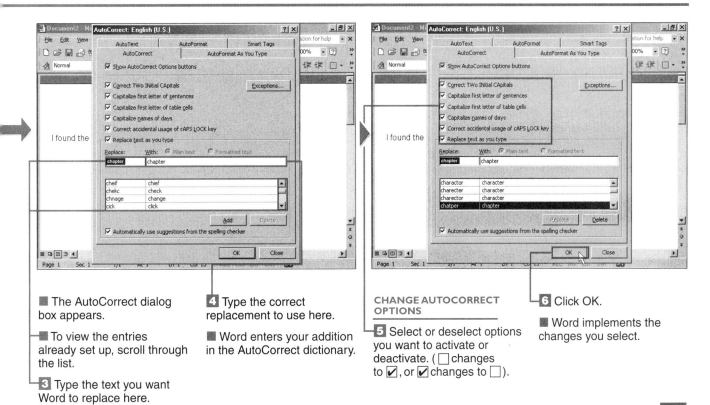

■ The AutoCorrect dialog box appears.

■ To view the entries already set up, scroll through the list.

3 Type the text you want Word to replace here.

4 Type the correct replacement to use here.

■ Word enters your addition in the AutoCorrect dictionary.

CHANGE AUTOCORRECT OPTIONS

5 Select or deselect options you want to activate or deactivate. (☐ changes to ✔, or ✔ changes to ☐).

6 Click OK.

■ Word implements the changes you select.

59

CHECK SPELLING

Word checks your document for spelling as you type. You can correct the errors Word finds to make sure your document is professional and accurate. A misspelled word can mar an otherwise perfect document, creating an impression of sloppy work or carelessness.

Word's spell check feature works by comparing every word in your document to words in its

dictionary. If Word does not find the word in the dictionary, it flags it. Word underlines spelling errors in red. These underlines appear only on the screen and not in your printed document. A flagged word does not necessarily indicate a misspelling; the word is just not in Office's dictionary.

You can correct spelling errors one at a time as you create your document. You can also find and

correct all spelling errors at once when you finish creating your document. No matter how you decide to use the Spelling feature, Word offers suggestions for correcting your errors.

Word automatically corrects common spelling errors, such as "adn" and "recieve," as you type. For information on the AutoCorrect feature, see "Using AutoCorrect."

CHECK SPELLING

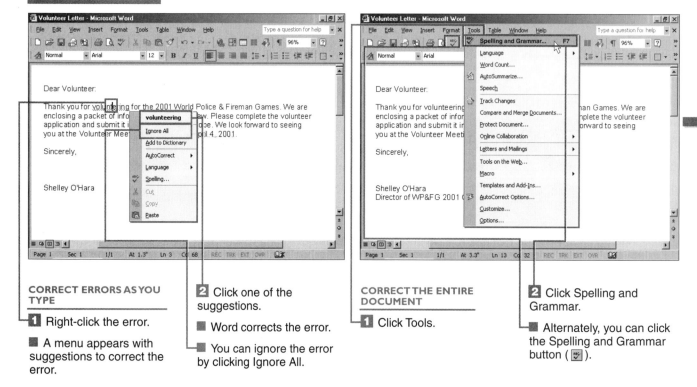

CORRECT ERRORS AS YOU TYPE

1 Right-click the error.

■ A menu appears with suggestions to correct the error.

2 Click one of the suggestions.

■ Word corrects the error.

■ You can ignore the error by clicking Ignore All.

CORRECT THE ENTIRE DOCUMENT

1 Click Tools.

2 Click Spelling and Grammar.

■ Alternately, you can click the Spelling and Grammar button ( ).

Does a spell check ensure the document does not have any mistakes?

✔ No. You still must proofread your document. Word only recognizes spelling errors, not whether you use the word correctly. For example, to, two, and too all have different meanings and uses. If spelled correctly, Word does not flag them, even if you use them incorrectly.

Can I prevent Word from underlining spelling errors?

✔ If the underlining Word uses to indicate spelling errors distracts you, you can hide it. Click Tools and then click Options. Click the Spelling & Grammar tab and then click the Hide spelling errors in this document option.

How can I stop Word from flagging words that are spelled correctly?

✔ Word flags any words that do not exist in its dictionary as misspelled. You can add a word to the dictionary so that Word recognizes it during future spell checks. Right-click the word you want to add to the dictionary and then select Add.

If you want to have Word automatically correct the word, click AutoCorrect in the Spelling and Grammar dialog box.

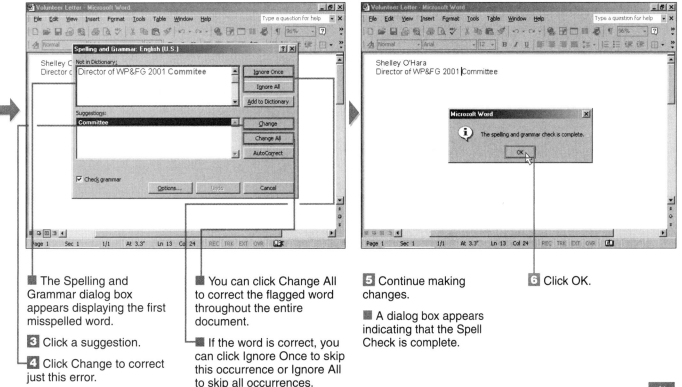

■ The Spelling and Grammar dialog box appears displaying the first misspelled word.

3 Click a suggestion.

4 Click Change to correct just this error.

■ You can click Change All to correct the flagged word throughout the entire document.

■ If the word is correct, you can click Ignore Once to skip this occurrence or Ignore All to skip all occurrences.

5 Continue making changes.

■ A dialog box appears indicating that the Spell Check is complete.

6 Click OK.

CHECK GRAMMAR

You can have Word check your document for grammatical errors. By default, Word does not check grammar, but you can turn on this feature to let Word flag any grammatical errors it finds. To learn more about the spell check feature, see the section "Check Spelling."

The grammar check feature finds errors such as capitalization problems, punctuation mistakes, misused words, and common mistakes such as passive voice or misuse of a pronoun.

For some mistakes, Word makes suggested corrections. You can use one of these suggestions. In addition, you can ignore the flagged error, edit the sentence, or view an explanation of the error.

Word uses a certain writing style with set rules by default. You can change to a different writing style and select which settings Word checks for you.

Keep in mind that you still need to proofread your work because the grammar checker is not perfect and it may not find all the mistakes in a document.

CHECK GRAMMAR

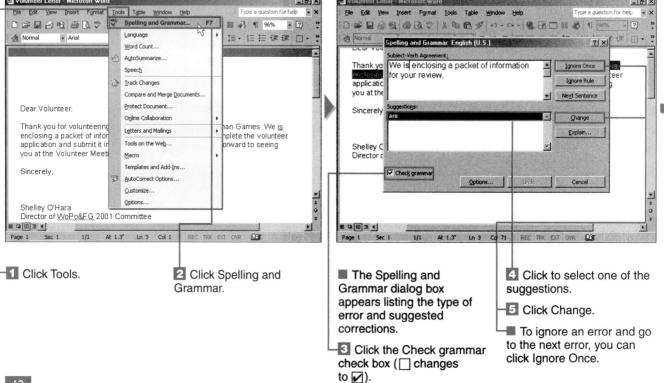

■ Click Tools.

2 Click Spelling and Grammar.

■ The Spelling and Grammar dialog box appears listing the type of error and suggested corrections.

3 Click the Check grammar check box (☐ changes to ☑).

4 Click to select one of the suggestions.

5 Click Change.

■ To ignore an error and go to the next error, you can click Ignore Once.

Can I have Word always check grammar?

✔ Yes. If you click Check grammar (☐ changes to ☑), Word automatically checks grammar during spell checks. You can also click Tools and then click Options. Click the Spelling & Grammar tab and click the Check grammar with spelling option (☐ changes to ☑). To check grammar as you type, click the Check grammar as you type check option (☐ changes to ☑). Word underlines Grammar errors in green.

How can I view the rules Word uses to check for grammar mistakes?

✔ Click Tools and then Options. Click the Spelling & Grammar tab. Click ▼ in the Writing style box and click a writing style from a list. You can also view the settings for the selected writing style by clicking the Settings button.

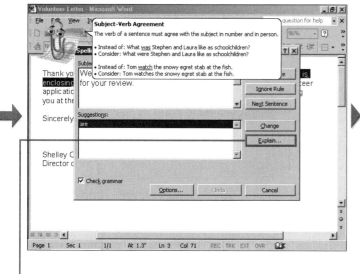

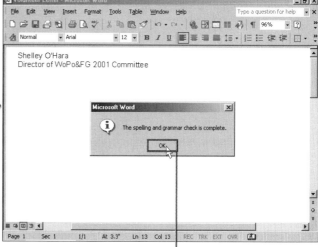

■ To see an explanation of the error, click Explain.

6 Continue making changes.

■ Word completes the spell and grammar check.

7 Click OK to close the dialog box.

USING THE THESAURUS

You can use a thesaurus to replace a word in your document with one that is more suitable, a synonym that shares the same meaning. Using the thesaurus included with Word is faster and more convenient than searching through a printed thesaurus.

If the word you want to replace has more than one meaning, you can select the correct meaning and

Word displays the synonyms for the meaning.

If you do not see a word that fits your situation, you can use the Look Up button in the Thesaurus dialog box to view synonyms for any of the listed words.

If the Thesaurus does not offer a suitable replacement for the word, you do not have to make a replacement. You can simply cancel out of the Thesaurus.

What if Word cannot find the word I select?
✔ If Word cannot find your selection in the Thesaurus, it displays the closest match. You can select from these words or you can type another word for Word to check.

USING THE THESAURUS

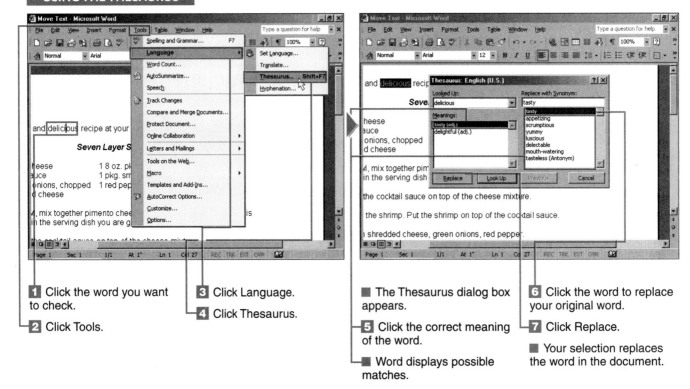

1 Click the word you want to check.

2 Click Tools.

3 Click Language.

4 Click Thesaurus.

■ The Thesaurus dialog box appears.

5 Click the correct meaning of the word.

■ Word displays possible matches.

6 Click the word to replace your original word.

7 Click Replace.

■ Your selection replaces the word in the document.

COUNT WORDS

You can quickly determine the number of words in your document as well as other document statistics such as the number of pages, characters, paragraphs, and lines.

Counting words in a document is useful if your document must contain a specific number of words. For example, most newspapers and magazines specify that you submit a certain number of words before they are accepted.

You can count the words in your entire document or just a specific section of selected text. When you count the words in an entire document, you can opt to include the words in any footnotes and endnotes in the document by selecting the Include footnotes and endnotes option.

What do I use the Show Toolbar box in the Word Count dialog box for?

✔ You can click Show Toolbar to display a toolbar with the total word count. The toolbar also contains a Recount button. Click this button to recount the words. To close the toolbar, click ☒.

COUNT WORDS

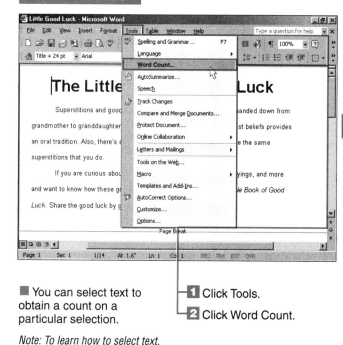

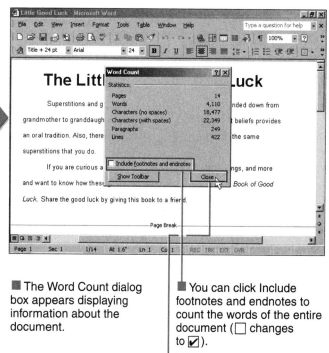

■ You can select text to obtain a count on a particular selection.

Note: To learn how to select text, see Chapter 3.

1 Click Tools.

2 Click Word Count.

■ The Word Count dialog box appears displaying information about the document.

■ You can click Include footnotes and endnotes to count the words of the entire document (☐ changes to ☑).

3 Click Close to close the Word Count dialog box.

CREATE AND INSERT AN AUTOTEXT ENTRY

You can use the AutoText feature to store text you use frequently. This lets you avoid typing the same text over and over again.

Word includes several built-in AutoText entries to use in your document. For example, the Closing category stores entries such as "Best wishes," and "Thank you,". The Mailing Instructions category stores entries such as "CONFIDENTIAL" and "VIA FACSIMILE." The Salutation category stores entries such as "Dear Sir or Madam:" and "To Whom It May Concern:".

In addition to these predefined AutoText entries, you can create your own, For example, you can create AutoText entries, complete with their own text formatting, such as a mailing address, legal disclaimer, or closing remark. Word stores most AutoText entries you create in the Normal category.

You can insert a built-in or created AutoText entry into your document quickly and easily.

CREATE AN AUTOTEXT ENTRY

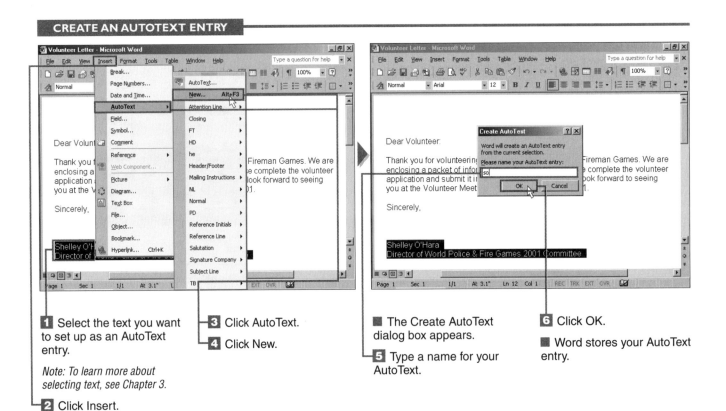

1 Select the text you want to set up as an AutoText entry.

Note: To learn more about selecting text, see Chapter 3.

2 Click Insert.

3 Click AutoText.

4 Click New.

■ The Create AutoText dialog box appears.

5 Type a name for your AutoText.

6 Click OK.

■ Word stores your AutoText entry.

How can I quickly insert an AutoText entry into my document?

✔ When you type the name of an AutoText entry in your document, a box appears on your screen displaying the AutoText entry. To insert the AutoText entry, press Enter. To ignore the AutoText entry, continue typing.

Can I delete an AutoText entry?

✔ To delete an entry, click Insert, click AutoText, and then click AutoText. Click the AutoText entry you want to delete and then click Delete.

How can I access the AutoText feature more quickly?

✔ You can display the AutoText toolbar on your screen. The toolbar allows you to quickly access AutoText entries using a drop-down list and also allows you to create new entries. To display the AutoText toolbar, click View, click Toolbars, and then click AutoText.

You can also start to type the AutoText entry you want and when the suggested entry displays in the small popup window, press F3 or Enter to insert the suggested text entry.

INSERT AN AUTOTEXT ENTRY

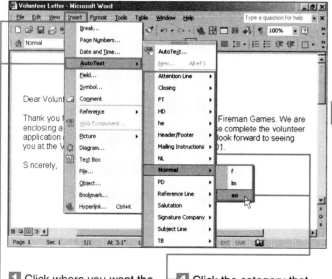

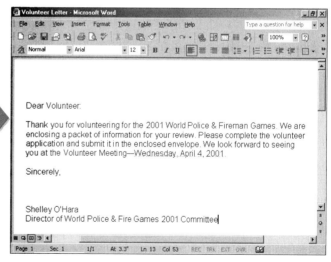

1 Click where you want the AutoText entry to appear.

2 Click Insert.

3 Click AutoText.

4 Click the category that stores the text you want to use.

5 Click the AutoText entry you want to insert.

■ The text appears in the document.

INSERT DATE AND TIME

Word provides a quick method to insert the date and time, which you can include in documents such as letters, or invoices that require a time stamp.

You can select from several date formats including, for example, 2/13/2001, Tuesday, February 13, 2001, and others. You can also select from several time formats including standard time or military time. Some formats include both the date and time.

By default, Word inserts the date and time simply as text, which you can modify and delete like other text.

What if I want to update the date and time every time I open my document?

✔ You can insert the date and time as a special code that Word updates by clicking the Update automatically option (☐ changes to ☑). You might use this option, for example, in a template that you use repeatedly to ensure that Word inserts the current date rather than a set date. When you click this option, the date appears as regular text, but is really a field code, inserted in brackets. You can easily update the code by selecting it and pressing F9.

INSERT DATE AND TIME

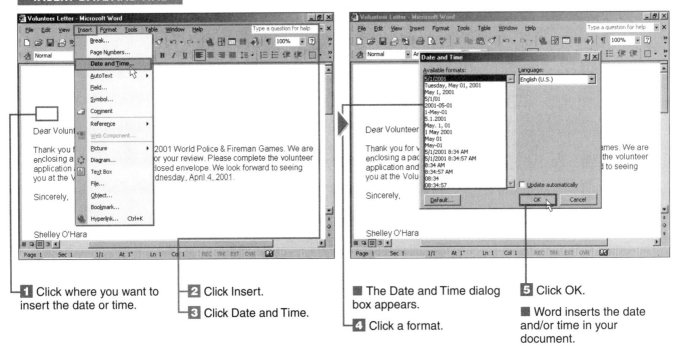

1 Click where you want to insert the date or time.

2 Click Insert.

3 Click Date and Time.

■ The Date and Time dialog box appears.

4 Click a format.

5 Click OK.

■ Word inserts the date and/or time in your document.

INSERT SPECIAL CHARACTERS

In some documents, you may want to insert special typographical characters such as an em dash, an ellipsis, or other special characters.

You can select from a list of common typographical characters and insert them quickly into a document. You can also insert them using the listed shortcut key. To learn

how to insert characters or symbols with shortcut keys, see the section "Insert a Symbol."

Word's AutoCorrect feature can also help you quickly insert some symbols into your document as you type. For more information on the AutoCorrect feature, see "Using AutoCorrect."

What do I use the hyphenation characters for?

✔ If you use hyphenation in a document, you can also insert symbols that help control where hyphenation occurs. You can insert a nonbreaking hyphen to prevent hyphenating a word or an optional hyphen to allow hyphenation. For more information on hyphenation, consult online help.

INSERT SPECIAL CHARACTERS

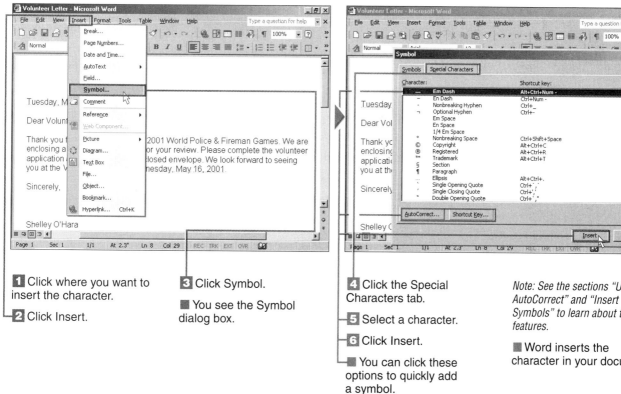

1 Click where you want to insert the character.

2 Click Insert.

3 Click Symbol.

■ You see the Symbol dialog box.

4 Click the Special Characters tab.

5 Select a character.

6 Click Insert.

■ You can click these options to quickly add a symbol.

Note: See the sections "Using AutoCorrect" and "Insert Symbols" to learn about these features.

■ Word inserts the character in your document.

INSERT SYMBOLS

Y ou can insert symbols into your document that do not appear on a standard keyboard. Symbols you can insert into your document include uppercase and lowercase accented letters, arrows, fractions, and special symbols such as hearts, check marks, and others.

You can choose a symbol from one of the sets of symbols, which Word calls fonts. Two popular fonts that

Word offers are Symbol and Wingdings. The Symbol font contains symbols for mathematical equations. The Wingdings font contains bullet, arrow, and other symbols.

You can insert as many symbols as you want while the Symbol dialog box is open.

Word's AutoCorrect feature can also help you quickly insert some

symbols into your document as you type. For more information on the AutoCorrect feature, see "Using AutoCorrect."

You can also insert special characters, such as em dashes and hyphens. For more information, see the section "Insert Special Characters."

INSERT SYMBOLS

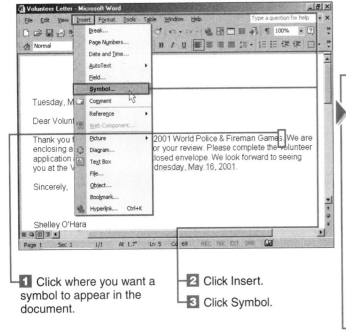

1 Click where you want a symbol to appear in the document.

2 Click Insert.

3 Click Symbol.

■ The Symbol dialog box appears, displaying the symbols in the current font.

4 Click ▼ in the Font box to view a list of fonts.

5 Click the font you want to use.

■ You see the available characters in that font.

Can I use a shortcut key to quickly insert a symbol?

✔ Yes. Word displays the shortcut keys at the bottom of the Symbol dialog box. To insert a symbol, click where you want the symbol to appear in your document and then press the appropriate shortcut key for the symbol.

Why does the Symbol dialog box display a Subset area for some fonts?

✔ Word often divides fonts with many different symbols into subcategories, or subsets, to make the symbols easier to find. You can click the Subset ⯆ to display the subsets for the current font, and click the subset you want to display.

How can I create my own shortcut key for a symbol?

✔ In the Symbol dialog box, select the symbol and then click Shortcut Key. Click in the Press new shortcut key area and then press the keys you want to use, such as Alt + P. You must use a key combination that is not already assigned. Click Assign and then click Close.

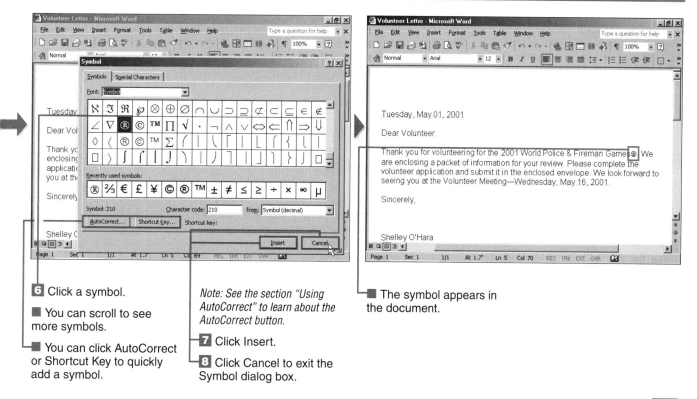

6 Click a symbol.

■ You can scroll to see more symbols.

■ You can click AutoCorrect or Shortcut Key to quickly add a symbol.

Note: See the section "Using AutoCorrect" to learn about the AutoCorrect button.

7 Click Insert.

8 Click Cancel to exit the Symbol dialog box.

■ The symbol appears in the document.

BOLD, ITALICIZE, OR UNDERLINE TEXT

You can use the Bold, Italic, and Underline features to change the style of text in your document. You use these features more than other formatting options to help you emphasize information and enhance the appearance of your document.

You can use one feature at a time or any combination of the three features to change the style of text.

The Bold feature makes text appear darker and thicker than other text. You can bold headings and titles to make them stand out from the rest of the text in your document.

The Italic feature tilts text to the right. You may want to italicize quotations and references in your document.

The Underline feature adds a line underneath text, which is useful for emphasizing important text, such as key words in your document. Keep in mind that it may confuse Web visitors if you use underlining in a Word document that you include on a Web site because Web building programs use this formatting for hyperlinks. To learn more about building a Web site, see Part VII.

BOLD, ITALICIZE, OR UNDERLINE TEXT

1 Select the text you want to change.

Note: To learn how to select text, see Chapter 3.

2 Click one of the following buttons:

B Bold
I Italic
<u>U</u> Underline

■ The text you selected appears in the new style.

■ The button for that text style appears outlined.

■ You can remove the text style by selecting the same text and clicking the appropriate button again.

CHANGE THE FONT STYLE

You can enhance the appearance of your document by changing the design, or font, of the text.

You can quickly change the font using the Font drop-down list. Word lists the available fonts from which you can choose with the most recently applied fonts appearing at the top of the list.

This allows you to quickly select fonts you use often.

The other fonts in the list appear in alphabetical order. Because fonts appear in the list as they appear in your document, you can preview a font before you select it.

The fonts you have available depend on your printer and your

particular computer setup. These fonts have been added either by you or by other application programs.

You can install additional fonts to your computer to use in all your programs, including Word. You can obtain fonts from computer stores and on the Internet. Consult your Windows manual to add fonts to your computer.

CHANGE THE FONT STYLE

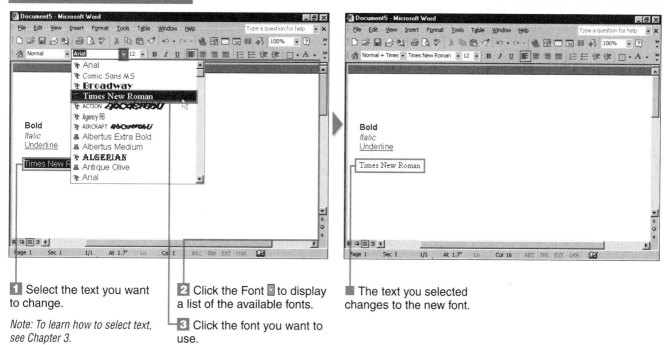

1 Select the text you want to change.

Note: To learn how to select text, see Chapter 3.

2 Click the Font ☷ to display a list of the available fonts.

3 Click the font you want to use.

■ The text you selected changes to the new font.

CHANGE THE FONT SIZE

Y ou can increase or decrease the size of text to fit the needs of your document. Generally, you use larger text to draw attention to specific sections, or to make your text easier to read. By contrast, smaller text allows you to fit more information on a page making it ideal for margin notes, end notes, or footnotes. Word

measures the size of text in points with 72 points in an inch.

By default, Word applies the Times New Roman font and a text size of 12 points. You can change just the font size of specific text or the default setting itself. Word automatically adjusts the line spacing for text you change.

You can either change your font size using the Font Size drop-down list, which offers a range of sizes, or using the Font dialog box. For more on the Font dialog box and instructions on changing the default font, see the section "Using Special Text Effects."

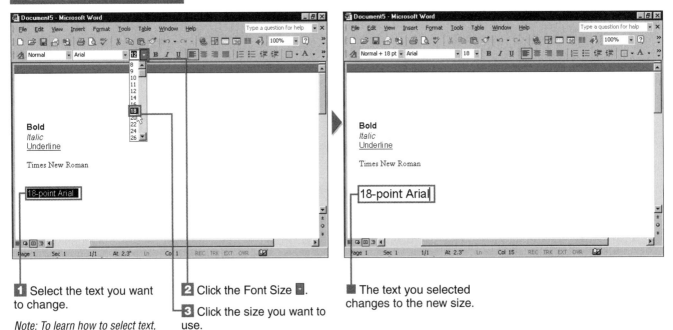

1 Select the text you want to change.

Note: To learn how to select text, see Chapter 3.

2 Click the Font Size ▪.

3 Click the size you want to use.

■ The text you selected changes to the new size.

USING SPECIAL TEXT EFFECTS

You can use the various special effects options in the Font dialog box to enhance the appearance of your document. You can apply Strikethrough to indicate text that you want to delete without actually deleting it. The Superscript and Subscript options place text above or below the line of text making them ideal for footnote numbers, and mathematical and chemical formulas. You can use the Shadow, Emboss, Engrave, or Outline

options to give text a three-dimensional or outline look. The Small caps and All caps options allow you to change text to different sizes of uppercase letters.

In addition, you can apply several effects — including the commonly used bold, underline, and italic styles — all at once. To learn how to quickly apply the format font, see the sections "Bold, Italicize, or Underline Text," "Change the Font Style," and "Change the Font Size."

How do I change the default font setting for new documents?

✔ In the Font dialog box, click the font options you want to apply, and then click the Default button. In the dialog box that appears, click Yes. The new default only applies to new, not already existing documents.

USING SPECIAL TEXT EFFECTS

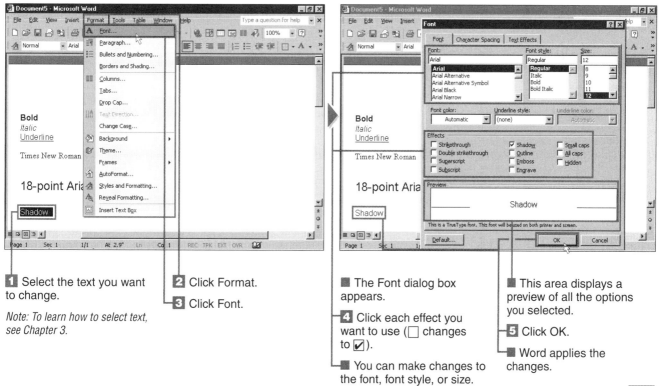

1 Select the text you want to change.

Note: To learn how to select text, see Chapter 3.

2 Click Format.

3 Click Font.

■ The Font dialog box appears.

4 Click each effect you want to use (□ changes to ✔).

■ You can make changes to the font, font style, or size.

■ This area displays a preview of all the options you selected.

5 Click OK.

■ Word applies the changes.

CHANGE THE COLOR OF TEXT

You can select from a wide variety of text colors and apply them to your document. You generally change the color of text to draw attention to headings or important information, or to enhance the overall appearance of your document.

Because colored text appears in shades of gray when you have a black and white printer, consider applying it only when you have a colored printer or if you plan to display your text on-screen or on a Web site.

You can quickly apply color using the Font Color button or apply color as well as other font properties using Font dialog box. To quickly change other font properties, see the sections "Bold, Italicize, or Underline Text," "Change the Font Style," and "Change the Font Size." See the section "Using Special Text Effects" for more on the Font dialog box.

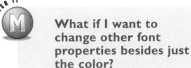

What if I want to change other font properties besides just the color?

✔ Click Format and then click Font. Click ⏷ in the Color box and click a color. You can then change other font properties and click OK to apply your changes.

CHANGE THE COLOR OF TEXT

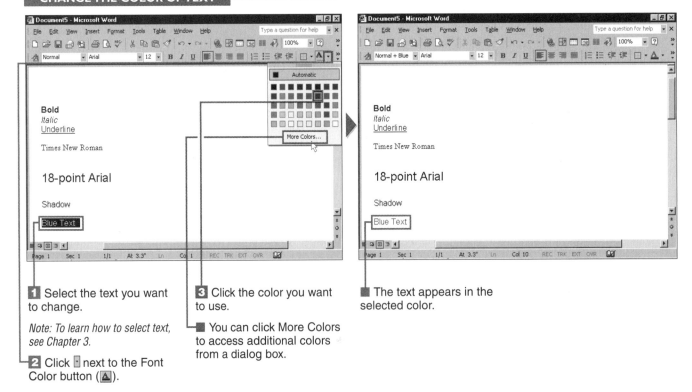

1 Select the text you want to change.

Note: To learn how to select text, see Chapter 3.

2 Click ⏷ next to the Font Color button (△).

3 Click the color you want to use.

■ You can click More Colors to access additional colors from a dialog box.

■ The text appears in the selected color.

HIGHLIGHT TEXT

Y ou can use the highlight feature in your document to mark text you want to review later, or that you want your reader to notice. Word offers several colors you can use to highlight text.

When you highlight text, Word changes the background color of the text making it stand out from the rest of the text in your document.

When you print a document that contains colored or highlighted text using a black-and-white printer, the highlighted text appears in shades of gray. For best printing results, consider applying the highlight option only when you have a color printer. For black-and-white printers, consider using a light highlight color, such as yellow, so you can clearly read your text.

How do I remove highlighting from my text?

✔ To remove highlighting, select the highlighted text. Click the Highlight button (🖉) and then click None. Word removes the highlighting.

Can I activate the Highlight button without selecting text?

✔ Yes. Without selecting text, click 🖉, and click and drag the mouse pointer ⬚ over any text you want to highlight. When you finish, click 🖉 again or press Esc.

HIGHLIGHT TEXT

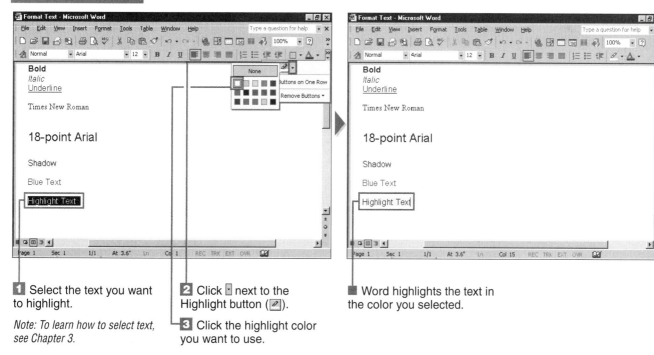

1 Select the text you want to highlight.

Note: To learn how to select text, see Chapter 3.

2 Click ⬚ next to the Highlight button (🖉).

3 Click the highlight color you want to use.

■ Word highlights the text in the color you selected.

ALIGN TEXT

Y ou can use the alignment buttons on the Formatting toolbar to change the alignment of text in your document. By default, Word aligns text along the left margin.

In addition to left alignment, Word allows you to center text between the left and right margins as well as align text along the right margin. You use the center-align option to

make headings and titles in your document stand out and look professional. You can apply the right-align option to make a return address appear at the top of a letter you are creating.

You can also justify text, which aligns your document along both the left and right margins making your text fit neatly on a line. You apply this option to text that

appears in columns, such as newspaper columns.

You can also use Word's Click and Type feature to align text you enter in a document. Available only in the Print Layout and Web Layout views, the Click and Type feature lets you left align, center align, or right align new text quickly.

ALIGN TEXT

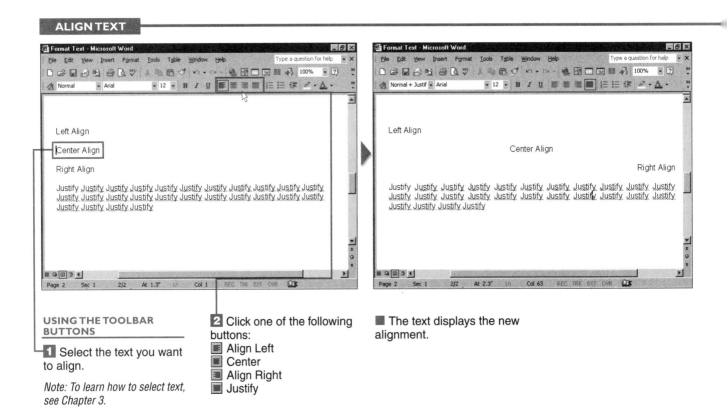

USING THE TOOLBAR BUTTONS

1 Select the text you want to align.

Note: To learn how to select text, see Chapter 3.

2 Click one of the following buttons:
▪ Align Left
▪ Center
▪ Align Right
▪ Justify

▪ The text displays the new alignment.

Word did not justify the last line of my paragraph. Why not?
✔ By default, Word does not justify the last line of a paragraph. To do so, click the end of the line and then press the Shift + Enter keys.

Can I apply different alignments within a single line of text?
✔ Yes. For example, you can left align your name and right align the date on the same line. Move the ▷ across the page until it changes to the first alignment you want. Double-click and type. Move ▷ again until the second alignment appears within the line and double-click and type.

Can I use the menus to change alignment?
✔ Yes. You can also click Format and then click Paragraph. In the Indents and Spacing tab of the Paragraph dialog box, click the alignment you want from the Alignment drop-down list and then click OK.

How do I undo an alignment?
✔ To undo an alignment, click the Undo button (⬅), or select another alignment. Alignment buttons are not toggles. You cannot click the same button to turn "off" an alignment. You must select another alignment button.

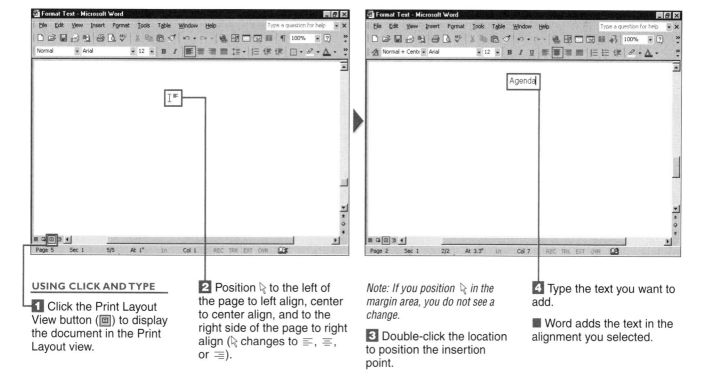

USING CLICK AND TYPE

1 Click the Print Layout View button (▣) to display the document in the Print Layout view.

2 Position ▷ to the left of the page to left align, center to center align, and to the right side of the page to right align (▷ changes to ≡, ≡, or ≡).

Note: If you position ▷ in the margin area, you do not see a change.

3 Double-click the location to position the insertion point.

4 Type the text you want to add.

■ Word adds the text in the alignment you selected.

INDENT PARAGRAPHS

You can use the Indent feature to make paragraphs in your document stand out.

Word allows you to indent the left edge of a paragraph several ways. You can indent the first line of a paragraph. This saves you from having to press Tab at the beginning of new paragraphs.

You can also indent all but the first line of a paragraph to create a

hanging indent. You may want to use hanging indents when creating a resume, glossary, or bibliography. Hanging indents are also useful for numbered lists.

You can indent all the lines in a paragraph. This is useful when you want to set quotations apart from the rest of the text in your document.

You can also indent the right edge of all the lines in a paragraph,

which helps when you want to emphasize a block of information in your document.

To apply a simple left indent, you use the toolbar buttons. You apply other indents using the Paragraph dialog box.

INDENT PARAGRAPHS

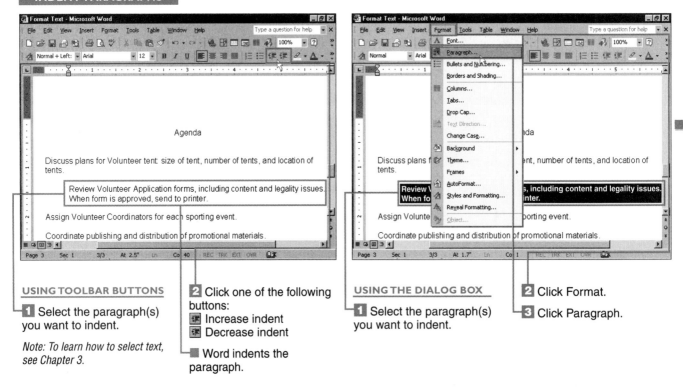

USING TOOLBAR BUTTONS

■1 Select the paragraph(s) you want to indent.

Note: To learn how to select text, see Chapter 3.

■2 Click one of the following buttons:
　Increase indent
　Decrease indent

■ Word indents the paragraph.

USING THE DIALOG BOX

■1 Select the paragraph(s) you want to indent.

■2 Click Format.

■3 Click Paragraph.

Can I set the indents using the Ruler?
✔ Yes. If the Ruler is not displayed, click View and then Ruler. Then drag the appropriate indent marker:

- Drag ▽ to set a first line indent.
- Drag ▤ to set a left indent.
- Drag ▣ to set a hanging indent.

Can I set indents for more than one paragraph?
✔ Yes. To set indents for several paragraphs, select the paragraphs you want to format and set the indent. If you want to set the indent for just one paragraph, you can just click within that paragraph and set the indent.

What other options can I set using the Paragraph dialog box?
✔ You can set the alignment using the Alignment drop-down list. You can also set line and paragraph spacing. See the section "Change Line and Paragraph Spacing."

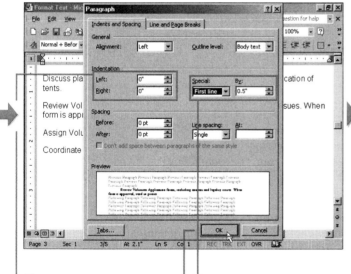

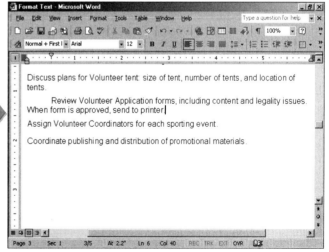

■ You see the Indents and Spacing tab of the Paragraph dialog box.

4 Type a value in the left and right indent fields.

■ To set a first-line or hanging indent, you can click ▾ in the Special box and click the indent type. Type the amount to indent in the By box.

5 Click OK.

■ The paragraph is indented.

SET TABS

Y ou can use tabs to line up columns of information at specific positions in your document. Word automatically places a tab every 0.5 inch across a page. You can either use the default by pressing the Tab key, or set your own tabs.

You should use tabs instead of spaces to line up information. If you use spaces, the information may not line up properly when you print your document.

Word offers several types of tabs from which to choose. The tab you add depends on how you want to line up your information. When you choose the Left Tab, Word lines up the left side of your text with the tab. The Center Tab lines up the center of your text with the tab. When you choose the Right Tab, Word lines up the right side of your text with the tab. You can use the Decimal Tab to line up the decimal points in numbers. Finally, the new Bar Tab inserts a vertical line at the tab stop.

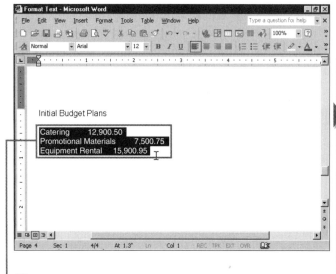

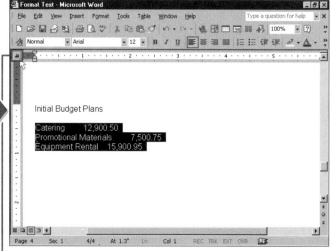

1 Select the text you want to contain the new tab settings.

Note: If the ruler is not displayed, click View and then Ruler.

Note: To learn how to select text, see Chapter 3.

2 Click the tab marker until the type of tab you want to add appears.

- Left Tab
- Center Tab
- Right Tab
- Decimal Tab
- Bar Tab

How can I move a tab?

✔ To move a tab, select the paragraph(s) containing the tab. The tab setting for the selected paragraph(s) appears on the ruler. Drag the tab to a new location on the ruler.

What is another method to align columns of information?

✔ For detailed columns, creating a table is a better way to align data. You have a great deal more flexibility in formatting and setting up a table. See Chapter 7 for more information on tables.

Is there a dialog box available to set tabs?

✔ Yes. You can also use the Tabs dialog box. This method enables you to set a tab at a certain inch-mark, select a tab type, and also use leader characters, such as a row of dots, before a tab. Leader characters make information such as a table of contents easier to read. Select the text for which you want to set tabs. Click Format and then click Tabs. Type the tab stop position, click the tab alignment, select the type of leader, and click OK.

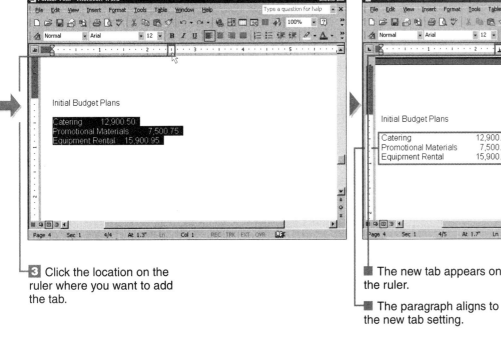

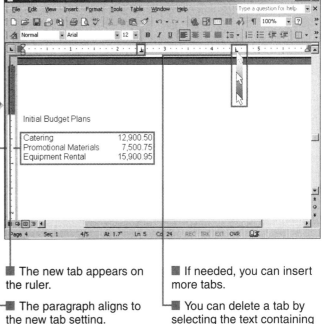

■3 Click the location on the ruler where you want to add the tab.

■ The new tab appears on the ruler.

■ The paragraph aligns to the new tab setting.

■ If needed, you can insert more tabs.

■ You can delete a tab by selecting the text containing the tab and dragging the tab downward off the ruler.

CHANGE LINE AND PARAGRAPH SPACING

Y ou can change the amount of space between the lines of text and the space between paragraphs in your document. *Line spacing* is the distance between two lines of text, while *paragraph spacing* is the distance between two paragraphs.

You can choose a line spacing option such as Single, 1.5 lines, or Double. By default, each new document uses single line spacing. Word uses the text size to

determine line spacing size, which it measures in points. For example, if you select single line spacing for text using a 10-point font size, the line spacing is approximately 10 points.

You can also add space above or below a paragraph. Using paragraph spacing is better than pressing Enter because you have more control over the exact amount of space between paragraphs.

For paragraph spacing, you can select the amount of points to add. Keep in mind that there are 72 points to an inch. You can set spacing before a paragraph, or after a paragraph, or both. For example, you might want to add space just after document headings so that your headings are not too close to the body text.

CHANGE LINE AND PARAGRAPH SPACING

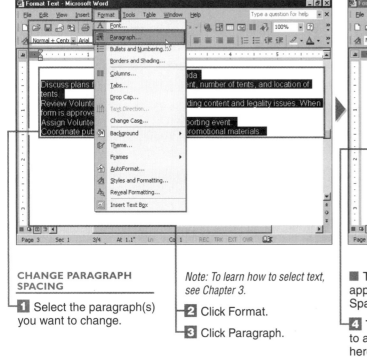

CHANGE PARAGRAPH SPACING

■1 Select the paragraph(s) you want to change.

Note: To learn how to select text, see Chapter 3.

■2 Click Format.

■3 Click Paragraph.

■ The Paragraph dialog box appears with the Indents and Spacing tab selected.

■4 Type the amount of space to add before the paragraph here.

■5 Type the amount of space to add after the paragraph here.

Can I use the keyboard to change line spacing?

✔ Yes. Select the text you want to change. Press Ctrl + 1 to apply single line spacing, Ctrl + 5 to apply 1.5 line spacing, and Ctrl + 2 to apply double line spacing.

How can I quickly change just the line spacing?

✔ On the formatting toolbar, click the Line Spacing ▾ next to the Line Spacing button. Then click the line spacing increment you want to use.

How do you use the At least, Exactly, and Multiple spacing options?

✔ You use the At least option to specify the minimum point size you want to use for line spacing. You use the Exactly option to ensure all lines are evenly spaced. You use the Multiple option to specify a line spacing that is a multiple of single line spacing. All three options require you to type a point value in the At area.

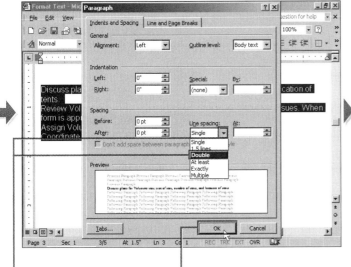

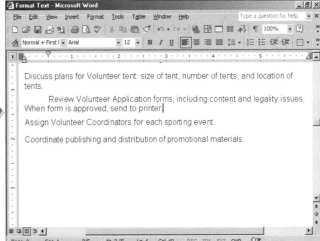

CHANGE LINE SPACING

6 Click ▾ in the Line spacing box.

7 Click a Line spacing option.

■ If you click the At least, Exactly, or Multiple spacing option, you can change the number of points you want to use for spacing in the At box.

8 Click OK.

■ Word changes the spacing.

■ In this example, the paragraphs are double-spaced.

ADD BULLETS

Y ou can begin each item in a list with a bullet. Bullets can help make the list easier to read. You use bullets for items in no particular order, such as items in a shopping list, agenda, and key points in a document.

You can format a document with bullets in one of two ways. You can quickly insert bullets in the default

style with the Bullet button on the formatting toolbar. The default bullet is a round button, but this button applies the last bullet style you used.

If you want another style other than the default, you can select a bullet style that suits your document using the Bullets and Numbering dialog box. For

example, you may want to use round or square bullets in a formal business letter, while you may use arrow or check mark bullets in more informal documents.

When you add bullets, Word automatically formats the paragraph(s) as hanging indents.

ADD BULLETS

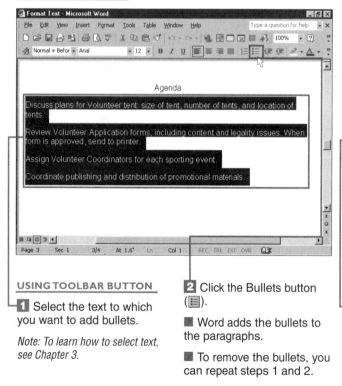

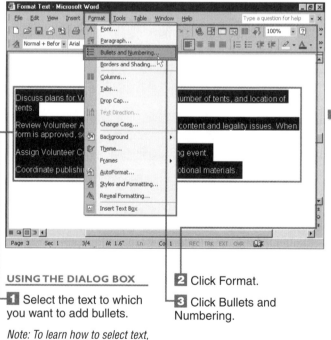

USING TOOLBAR BUTTON

1 Select the text to which you want to add bullets.

Note: To learn how to select text, see Chapter 3.

2 Click the Bullets button (▤).

■ Word adds the bullets to the paragraphs.

■ To remove the bullets, you can repeat steps 1 and 2.

USING THE DIALOG BOX

1 Select the text to which you want to add bullets.

Note: To learn how to select text, see Chapter 3.

2 Click Format.

3 Click Bullets and Numbering.

How can I create a bulleted list as I type?

✔ Type * followed by a space. Then type the first item in the list. Press Enter, and Word automatically starts the next item with a bullet. To end the bullets, press Enter twice or press Backspace to delete the bullet and indent. You must click the Automatic bulleted lists option (○ changes to ●) in the AutoCorrect dialog box for this feature to work. See the section "Change AutoFormat Options" to learn more about this feature.

Can I insert other bullet symbols?

✔ Yes. Click the Bulleted tab in the Bullets and Numbering dialog box, and click a bullet style. Click Customize and click the desired bullet character. You can also select the indent amount for the bullet and text. You can also click Character or Picture to choose from a wide variety of other symbols or images. To replace the old style with your selection, click OK.

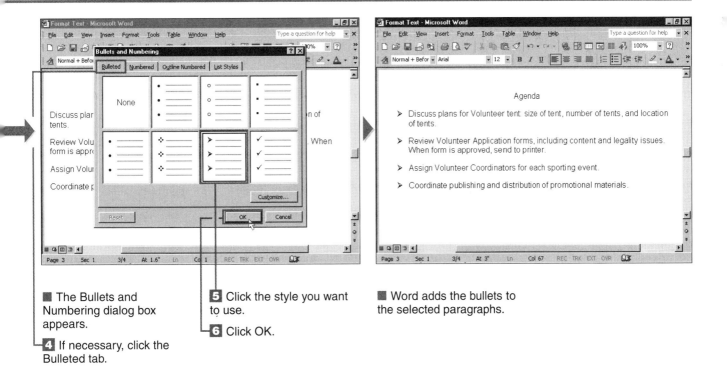

■ The Bullets and Numbering dialog box appears.

4 If necessary, click the Bulleted tab.

5 Click the style you want to use.

6 Click OK.

■ Word adds the bullets to the selected paragraphs.

CREATE A NUMBERED LIST

You can begin each item in a list with a number to make your document easier to read. You use numbers for items in a specific order such as directions or steps.

The Number list feature has several advantages over typing the list manually. You avoid typing and incorrectly numbering your text by simply clicking a button. Also, when you add or delete an item to a numbered list, Word automatically renumbers the entire list for you.

You have two methods for inserting a numbered list. You can use the toolbar button to quickly select the default numbering style, or use the Bullets and Numbering dialog box to select from a set of styles. Word offers a variety of number styles to suit your document, including numbers, letters, and Roman numerals.

When you create a numbered list, Word automatically formats the paragraph(s) as hanging indents.

CREATE A NUMBERED LIST

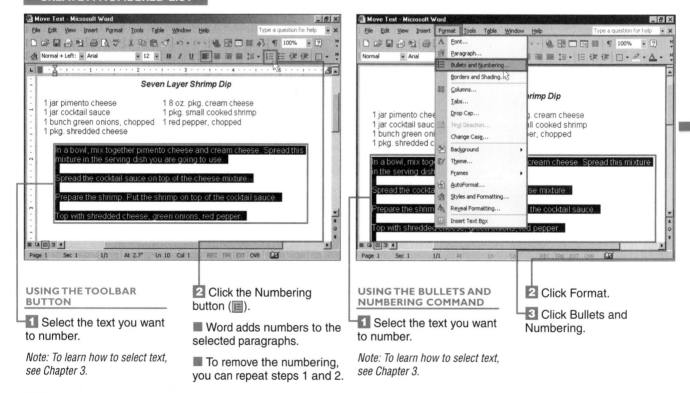

USING THE TOOLBAR BUTTON

■1 Select the text you want to number.

Note: To learn how to select text, see Chapter 3.

■2 Click the Numbering button (☰).

■ Word adds numbers to the selected paragraphs.

■ To remove the numbering, you can repeat steps 1 and 2.

USING THE BULLETS AND NUMBERING COMMAND

■1 Select the text you want to number.

Note: To learn how to select text, see Chapter 3.

■2 Click Format.

■3 Click Bullets and Numbering.

How can I create a numbered list as I type?

✔ To create a numbered list as you type, type 1., insert a space and then type the first item in the list. Press Enter and Word automatically starts the next item with the next number. To end the numbered list, press Enter twice or press Backspace. You click the Automatic numbered lists option (○ changes to ◉) in the AutoCorrect dialog box for this feature to work. See the section "Change AutoFormat Options" to learn more about this feature.

Can I change the number Word uses to start my list?

✔ Yes. On the Numbered tab, click Customize. In the Start at area, enter the number you want to use to start the list and then click OK.

What other options do I have for lists?

✔ You can also create outlines and custom lists. For more information on these features, consult Word's online help.

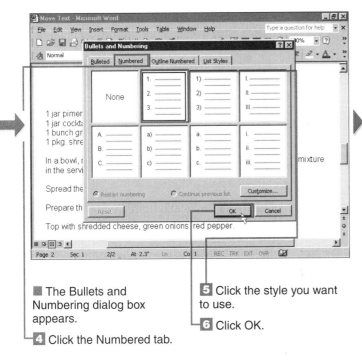

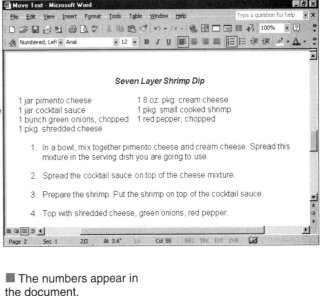

■ The Bullets and Numbering dialog box appears.

4 Click the Numbered tab.

5 Click the style you want to use.

6 Click OK.

■ The numbers appear in the document.

ADD BORDERS OR SHADING

You can add borders and shading to the text of your document to set off a particular section of text, or to make a heading stand out. You add a border or shading to text in the Borders and Shading dialog box, which gives you precise control over the various options.

For borders, Word has several preset options, including a box,

shadow, 3D, and a custom option. You can also select the line style, color, and width of the border.

You can use the Custom border option to add a border above, below, on the right, on the left, or a combination, to a text block. You can also use this option when you want to vary the line style for each border you add.

Word allows you to add shading using the Shading tab. Here, you can select a color or pattern for your shaded text.

To quickly add a border without entering the Borders and Shading dialog box, you can also use the Border button to display a palette of common border choices.

ADD BORDERS

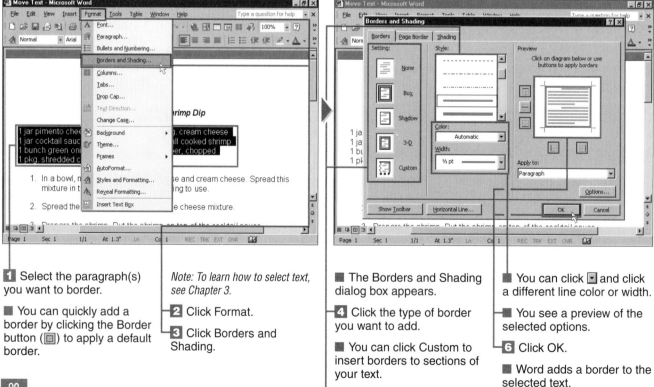

■1 Select the paragraph(s) you want to border.

■ You can quickly add a border by clicking the Border button (▣) to apply a default border.

Note: To learn how to select text, see Chapter 3.

■2 Click Format.

■3 Click Borders and Shading.

■ The Borders and Shading dialog box appears.

■4 Click the type of border you want to add.

■ You can click Custom to insert borders to sections of your text.

■5 Click a line style.

■ You can click ▼ and click a different line color or width.

■ You see a preview of the selected options.

■6 Click OK.

■ Word adds a border to the selected text.

Can I add a page border?

✓ Yes. To do so, click the Page Border tab where you find options similar to paragraph borders. Click one of the predefined settings. Then select the line style, color, and width. Unlike text borders, you can add art to page borders by clicking the Art ▪ and selecting an image.

Can I combine colors and patterns for shading?

✓ Yes. Click the Shading tab. Click the color you want to use. Then click the Style ▪ and click a pattern. You can also select a color for the pattern by clicking the Color ▪ and clicking a color in the Patterns section.

How do I add a custom border?

✓ To add custom borders, click Custom. Then make your choices for line style, color, and width. In the Preview area click the side of the text block where you want to add a border. You can change border styles for each side of the text block. When you click OK, Word adds the border(s) per your specification.

ADD SHADING

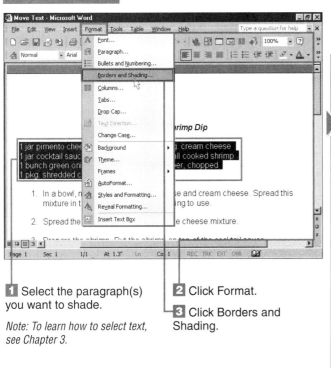

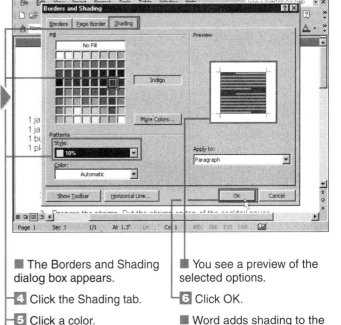

1 Select the paragraph(s) you want to shade.

Note: To learn how to select text, see Chapter 3.

2 Click Format.

3 Click Borders and Shading.

■ The Borders and Shading dialog box appears.

4 Click the Shading tab.

5 Click a color.

■ You can click ▪ and click a pattern for your shading.

■ You see a preview of the selected options.

6 Click OK.

■ Word adds shading to the text.

CREATE A STYLE

You can create and save a style that allows you to apply multiple formatting changes to text in one step.

Word allows you to create two types of styles — paragraph and character. A paragraph style includes formatting that changes the appearance of entire paragraphs, such as text alignment, tab settings, and line spacing.

A character style includes formatting that changes the appearance of individual characters, such as bold, underline, and text color as well as the font and size of characters.

You can store your style in a template so that you can apply the modified style to text in new documents you create. If you do not store the style, you can apply

the style to text only in the current document. For information on applying one of Word's built-in styles or a style that you have created, see the section "Apply a Style."

CREATE A STYLE

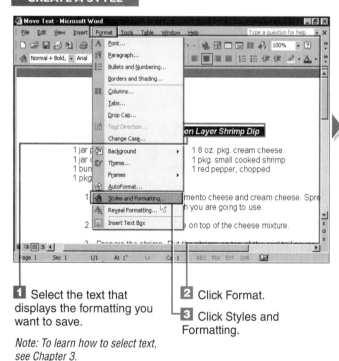

1 Select the text that displays the formatting you want to save.

Note: To learn how to select text, see Chapter 3.

2 Click Format.

3 Click Styles and Formatting.

■ The Styles and Formatting options appear in the task pane.

4 Click New Style.

How can I quickly create a paragraph style for the current document?

✔ Select the paragraph that displays the formatting you want to save. On the Formatting toolbar, click the Style area. Type a name for the new style and then press Enter.

Can I assign a keyboard shortcut to a newly created style?

✔ Yes. In the New Style dialog box, click the name of the style to which you want to assign a keyboard shortcut. Click Format and then click Shortcut Key. Click the Press new shortcut key area and then press the keys you want to use for the keyboard shortcut. Click Assign and then click Close.

Can I have Word automatically update my paragraph style?

✔ Yes. In the New Style dialog box, click the name of the style you want Word to update automatically. Click the Automatically update option (☐ changes to ☑). When you change the formatting of an already formatted paragraph, Word automatically updates the style and all the paragraphs formatted with the style.

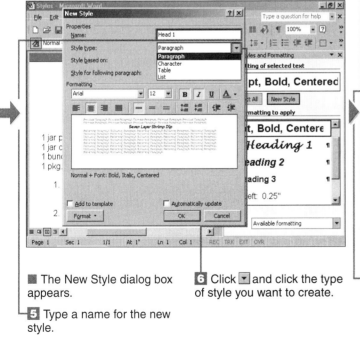

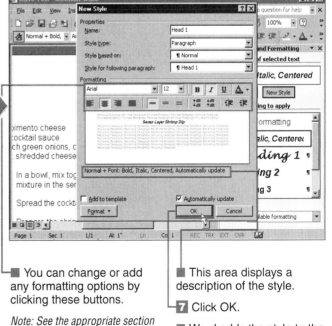

■ The New Style dialog box appears.

5 Type a name for the new style.

6 Click ▾ and click the type of style you want to create.

■ You can change or add any formatting options by clicking these buttons.

Note: See the appropriate section in this chapter for more on a specific option.

■ This area displays a description of the style.

7 Click OK.

■ Word adds the style to the document.

APPLY A STYLE

You can quickly format the text in your document by applying a style to it. Styles can save you time when you want to apply the same formatting to many different areas in a document. Styles also help you keep the appearance of text in a document consistent.

For example, if you manually format all your document headings, you may accidentally use different formatting for each heading, which may confuse your reader. Applying a style ensures that all the document headings contain the same formatting.

Word includes several styles you can apply to text in your document. You can also create a style and apply it. To create a style, see the section "Create a Style."

You have two methods for applying a style. You can quickly access the Style drop-down list, where Word displays a list of the most common and recently used styles. Alternately, you can display the Style and Formatting task pane, where you can both change and apply a style.

APPLY A STYLE

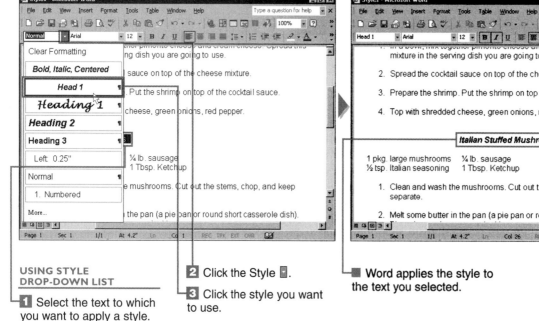

USING STYLE DROP-DOWN LIST

1 Select the text to which you want to apply a style.

Note: To learn how to select text, see Chapter 3.

2 Click the Style ▪.

3 Click the style you want to use.

■ Word applies the style to the text you selected.

How do I close the task pane?

✔ You can close the task pane by clicking its Close button (☒). For more on task panes, see Chapter 1.

How can I change which styles Word lists in the task pane?

✔ Click the ▾ in the Show area located in the task pane, and select which option you want to display. You can opt to display Available formatting, Formatting in use, Available styles, All styles, or Custom.

Can I apply additional formatting to text with a style?

✔ Yes. You can make any formatting changes you want. However, Word does not save this new formatting unless you click the Automatically update option box (☐ changes to ☑) in the New Style dialog box. See the section "Create a Style" for more on this option. If you have not selected this option, you need to update the style. See "Modify a Style."

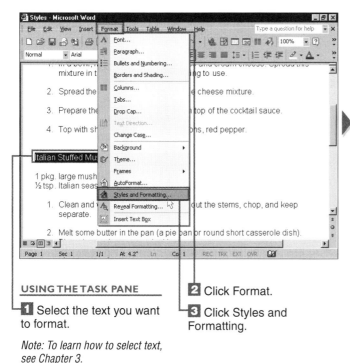

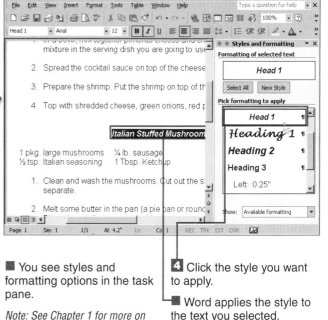

USING THE TASK PANE

1 Select the text you want to format.

Note: To learn how to select text, see Chapter 3.

2 Click Format.

3 Click Styles and Formatting.

■ You see styles and formatting options in the task pane.

Note: See Chapter 1 for more on using the task pane.

4 Click the style you want to apply.

■ Word applies the style to the text you selected.

MODIFY A STYLE

You can change a created style and when you do so, Word automatically changes all the text formatted using the style. This helps you quickly update the appearance of the document. Modifying the style allows you to experiment with several formats until the document appears the way you want.

Modifying a style also ensures consistency in a document's formatting. Rather than worry about changing all the headings in a document, you can apply a heading style to the text. When you need to modify that style, you modify it only once; Word updates all paragraphs formatted with that style, saving you time and ensuring accuracy.

You can modify a style in one of two ways. You can select new formatting options in the Modify Style dialog box. Alternately, you can modify text formatted with the style you want to change, and then update the style with the Update to Match Selection option.

MODIFY A STYLE

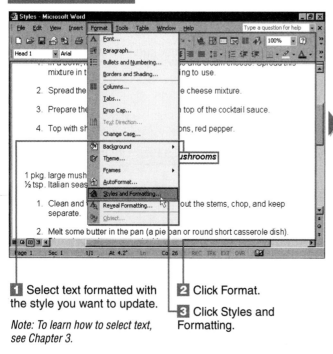

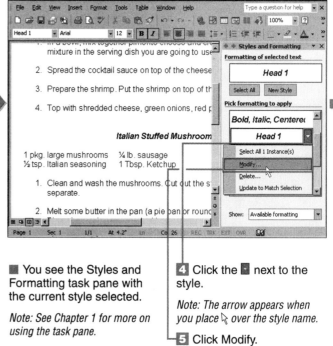

1 Select text formatted with the style you want to update.

Note: To learn how to select text, see Chapter 3.

2 Click Format.

3 Click Styles and Formatting.

■ You see the Styles and Formatting task pane with the current style selected.

Note: See Chapter 1 for more on using the task pane.

4 Click the ⬛ next to the style.

Note: The arrow appears when you place ⬚ over the style name.

5 Click Modify.

What types of formatting changes can I make to a style?

✔ Using the buttons in the Formatting area of the Modify Style dialog box, you can change the font type, size, style, and color. You can also change alignment, paragraph and line spacing, and indents. Alternately, you can click the Format button to set tabs, add borders or frames, assign a shortcut key, or add numbering.

How do I delete a style?

✔ From the Styles and Formatting task pane, click ▾ next to the style and then click Delete. Word changes text using the deleted style to the default Normal style.

How do I use the Update to Match Selection option to modify a style?

✔ Make formatting changes to any of the text you want to modify and then select the text. From the Styles and Formatting task pane, click ▾ next to the style and then click Update to Match Selection.

Can I select all text that has a certain style applied to it?

✔ Yes. To do so, click ▾ next to the style in the Styles and Formatting task pane and then click the Select All command. Word selects all text formatted with this style in your document.

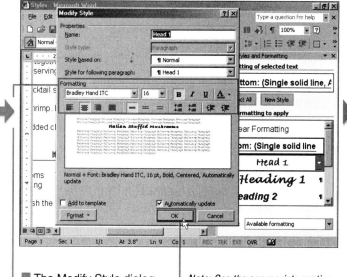

■ The Modify Style dialog box appears.

6 Make any changes to the formatting.

Note: See the appropriate section in this chapter for more on a specfic option.

7 Click OK.

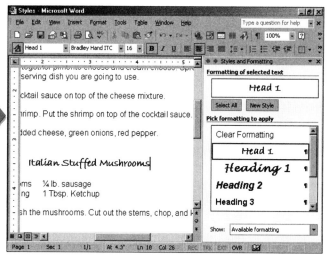

■ All the text that uses the modified style displays your changes.

COPY FORMATTING

I f you need to use the same formatting only once or twice, and do not want to go to the trouble of creating a style, you can make one area of text in your document look exactly like another by copying the formatting. For more on creating and applying styles, see the sections "Create a Style" and "Apply a Style."

If you copy the formatting of text that contains more than one type of the same formatting, such as multiple fonts, Word copies only the first type of formatting. For example, if you select a paragraph that contains the Times New Roman font followed by the Arial font, Word copies only the Times New Roman font.

MASTER IT

Can I copy formatting to several areas in my document at once?

✔ Yes. To do so, perform the steps in this section, except double-click the Format Painter button (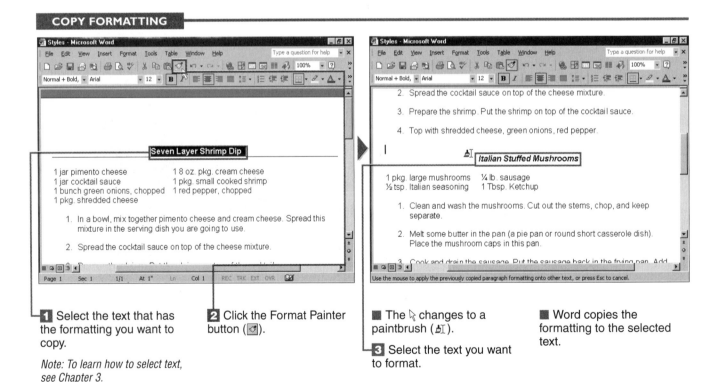). When you finish selecting all the text to which you want to copy formatting, press Esc to stop copying the formatting.

COPY FORMATTING

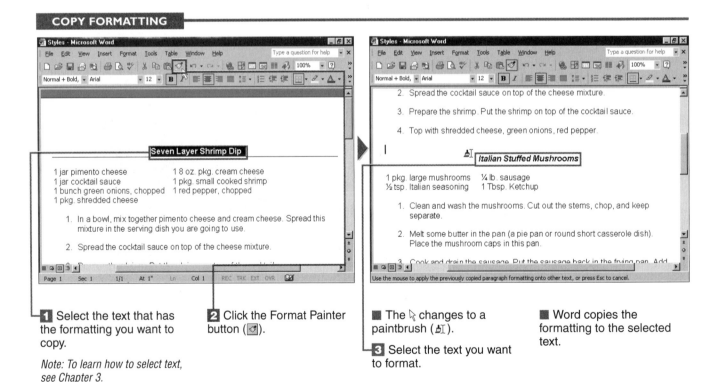

1 Select the text that has the formatting you want to copy.

Note: To learn how to select text, see Chapter 3.

2 Click the Format Painter button (🖌).

■ The ▷ changes to a paintbrush (🖌I).

3 Select the text you want to format.

■ Word copies the formatting to the selected text.

REVEAL FORMATTING

If your document contains several formatting changes, or if you are working in a document created by another person, you may want to display the formatting for a particular section of text. This enables you to determine the existing formatting so you can accurately update it.

When you select this feature, Word displays the Reveal Formatting task pane, showing sample text formatted like the selected text. The task pane includes options for comparing, distinguishing, and showing formatting marks. The task pane also lists formatting for the selected text including the font and language, paragraph alignment, indentation, tabs, and any section formatting. For more information on section formatting, see your Word documentation.

How do I compare formatting?

✔ Select the first text that you want to compare. Then select the second text selection. Next, in the Reveal Formatting task pane, check the Compare to another selection. The task pane lists samples of both selections and notes any formatting differences. You might do this to ensure consistent formatting between similar document sections, such as document headings.

REVEAL FORMATTING

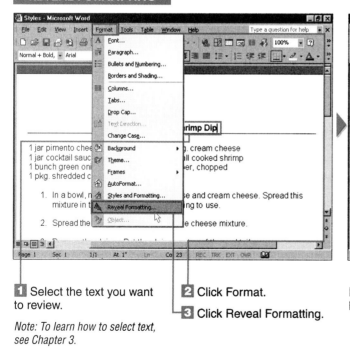

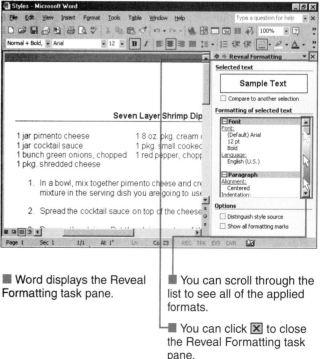

■1 Select the text you want to review.

Note: To learn how to select text, see Chapter 3.

■2 Click Format.

■3 Click Reveal Formatting.

■ Word displays the Reveal Formatting task pane.

■ You can scroll through the list to see all of the applied formats.

■ You can click ☒ to close the Reveal Formatting task pane.

DISPLAY AND HIDE PARAGRAPH MARKS

You can display paragraph and other formatting marks in your document. Formatting marks can help you edit your document and check for errors such as extra spaces between words.

Word displays several formatting marks. For example, the paragraph mark (¶) symbol indicates where you pressed Enter to start a new

paragraph in the document. A small arrow (→) indicates where you pressed Tab to indent text. The space mark (□) symbol shows where you pressed the Spacebar to leave a blank space.

When you display formatting marks, Word also displays hidden text in your document. Word underlines text with a dotted line

(.....) to indicate hidden text. Formatting marks appear only on your screen; Word does not print them in your document.

When you finish reviewing your document with formatting marks, you can once again hide them.

DISPLAY AND HIDE PARAGRAPH MARKS

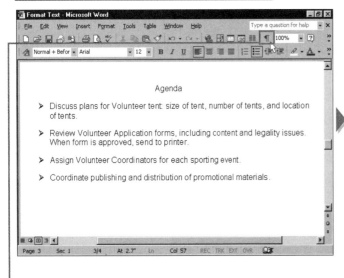

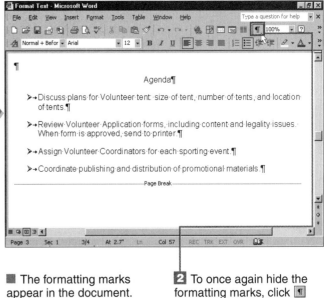

1 Click the Show/Hide Paragraph button (¶) to display formatting marks in a document.

■ The formatting marks appear in the document.

2 To once again hide the formatting marks, click ¶ again.

CHANGE AUTOFORMAT OPTIONS

You can change the default formatting Word automatically makes to your text as you type. You can review all the automatic changes Word makes and deactivate some or all of the options.

By default, if you type two hyphens, Word replaces them with an em dash (—). Word also replaces certain fractions with the fractional character; for example, Word replaces 1/2 with ½. As another example, Word replaces ordinals (1st) with

superscript (1st). Word also applies some styles and formatting. For example, if you type an asterisk (*), press Tab, type text, and press Enter, Word formats the paragraph as a bulleted list item.

You can review and change these and many other options in the AutoFormat As You Type and AutoFormat tabs of the AutoCorrect dialog box. For more information on AutoCorrect tab in this dialog box, see Chapter 4.

How do I determine what an option does?

✔ If you do not know what an option does, right-click the option and select What's This to display a pop-up explanation of the option.

CHANGE AUTOFORMAT OPTIONS

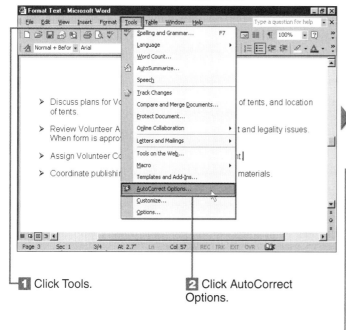

1 Click Tools.

2 Click AutoCorrect Options.

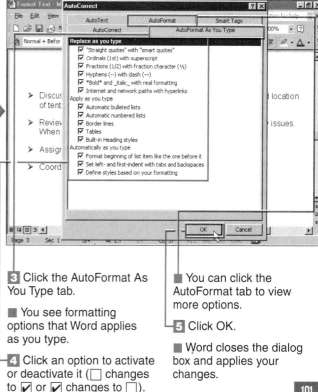

3 Click the AutoFormat As You Type tab.

■ You see formatting options that Word applies as you type.

4 Click an option to activate or deactivate it (☐ changes to ☑ or ☑ changes to ☐).

■ You can click the AutoFormat tab to view more options.

5 Click OK.

■ Word closes the dialog box and applies your changes.

CHANGE THE VIEW

Word offers several ways to display your document. You can choose the view that best suits your needs.

The Normal view simplifies your document so that you can quickly enter, edit, and format text. Word does not display top or bottom margins, headers, footers, or page numbers in this view. You use this view most often when composing a document.

The Print Layout view displays your document as it appears on a printed page and includes top and bottom margins, headers, footers, and page numbers. This view is most appropriate when making formatting changes to the entire document, as illustrated in this chapter.

Word offers two additional views: Outline view and Web Layout view, which displays your document as it appears in a Web browser. For more information on the Outline view, see your Word documentation or consult Microsoft's online help. For more information on Web publishing, see Part VIII.

CHANGE THE VIEW

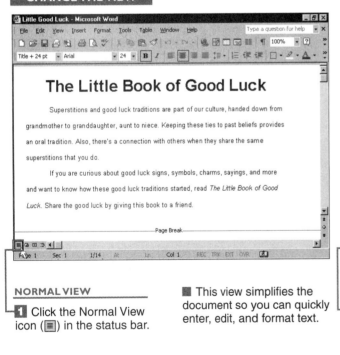

NORMAL VIEW

1 Click the Normal View icon (▤) in the status bar.

■ This view simplifies the document so you can quickly enter, edit, and format text.

PRINT LAYOUT VIEW

1 Click the Print Layout View icon in the status bar (▣).

■ This view displays the document as it appears on a printed page.

ZOOM IN OR OUT

Word lets you enlarge or reduce the display of text on your screen. You can increase the zoom setting to view an area of your document in more detail or decrease the zoom setting to view more of your document at once.

Word offers specially designed zoom settings. The Page Width setting fits your document neatly across the width of your screen. The Text Width setting ensures all text is visible across the width of your screen. The Whole Page and Two Pages settings display one or two full pages on your screen. The view in which you display your document determines which zoom settings Word makes available to you. If the available zoom settings do not suit your needs, Word

allows you to enter a specific zoom setting.

When you save your document, Word saves the zoom setting with it. The next time you open your document, it appears in the zoom setting you selected.

Changing the zoom setting does not affect the size of your document when it is printed.

ZOOM IN OR OUT

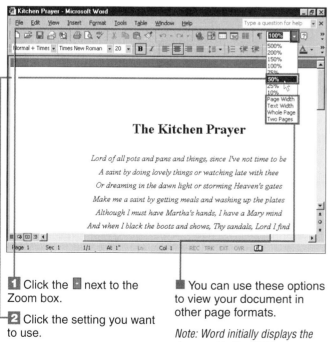

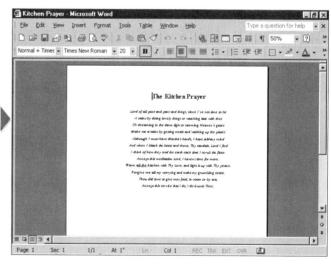

1 Click the ▪ next to the Zoom box.

2 Click the setting you want to use.

■ Alternately, you can type a setting into the Zoom box.

■ You can use these options to view your document in other page formats.

Note: Word initially displays the document in the 100% zoom setting.

■ The document appears in the new zoom setting.

PREVIEW A DOCUMENT

Y ou can use the Print Preview feature to see how your document looks when you print it.

The Print Preview feature allows you to view the layout of information on a page in your document. If your document contains more than one page, you can use the scroll bar to view the other pages.

You can magnify an area of a page in your document. This allows you to view the area in more detail.

You can have Word display several pages in the Print Preview window at once, which allows you to view the overall style of a long document.

Depending on the setup of your computer, Word can display 12, 24, or more pages in the Print Preview window.

When you finish using the Print Preview feature, you can close the Print Preview window to return to your document.

Although you cannot edit your document in Print Preview, you can visually adjust the margins of your document without doing so manually in the Page Setup dialog box. To learn more about margins, see the section "Change Margins."

PREVIEW A DOCUMENT

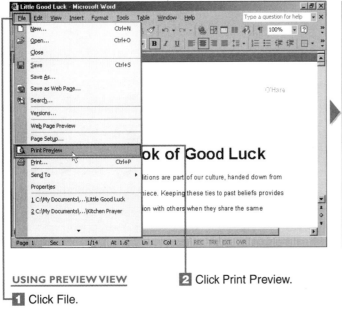

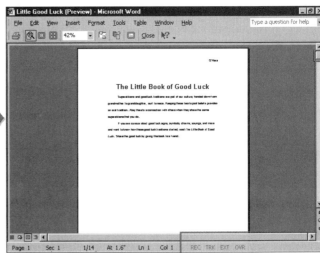

USING PREVIEW VIEW

1 Click File.

2 Click Print Preview.

■ The Print Preview window appears, displaying a page from the document.

■ You can use the scroll bar (▨) to view other pages.

Is there a quicker way to access the Print Preview dialog box?

✔ Yes. You can click the Print Preview button (🔍), located on the Standard toolbar, to quickly preview the document.

How do I change the margins in Print Preview?

✔ To change the margins in print preview, display the Ruler by clicking the Ruler button. Then click the ⤢ over the margin you want to change. Drag the margin to a new location.

Can I shrink the text in my document to fit on fewer pages?

✔ If the last page in your document contains only a few lines of text, Word can shrink the text in your document to fit on one less page. In the Print Preview window, click the Shrink to Fit button (🔲) to shrink the text.

Can I print directly from the Print Preview window?

✔ Yes. To print your document directly from the Print Preview window, click the Print button.

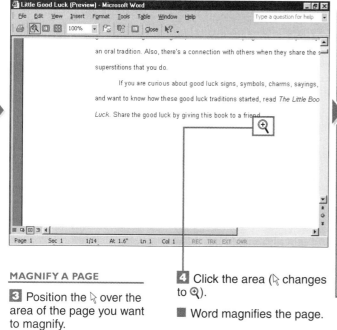

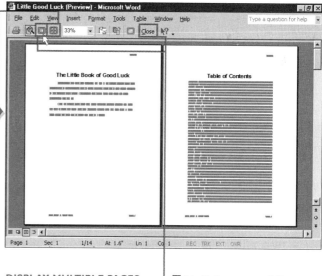

MAGNIFY A PAGE

3 Position the ⤢ over the area of the page you want to magnify.

4 Click the area (⤢ changes to 🔍).

■ Word magnifies the page.

DISPLAY MULTIPLE PAGES

5 Click the Multiple Pages button (▦).

6 Drag across the page indicators to select the number of pages to display.

■ Multiple pages of the document appear.

■ To display one page again click the One Page button (▢).

7 Click the Close button to exit Print Preview.

CHANGE MARGINS

You can change the margins to suit your needs. A margin is the amount of space between the text in your document and the edge of your paper.

Every page has a margin at the top, bottom, left, and right edges of a page. By default, Word automatically sets the top and bottom margins to 1 inch, and the left and right margins to 1.25 inches.

Increasing the size of margins increases the white space on your page. This can help make your document easier to read. Reducing the size of margins lets you fit more information on a page.

Note that most printers cannot print right to the edge of a page and require that you use a margin of at least 0.25 inch on all sides. You can check the manual that came with your printer for more

information about its exact settings.

A change to the margins affects all the pages of your document. To change the margins for only specific pages in your document, you must divide your document into sections.

CHANGE MARGINS

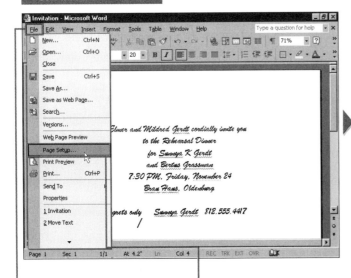

1 In the document you want to change, click File.

2 Click Page Setup.

■ You see the Page Setup dialog box, with the Margins tab selected.

3 Press Tab to move to the margin you want to change.

■ Word selects the current value.

4 Type the new value.

■ Alternately, you can click the spin arrows (▲, ▼) to change the value.

Can I change the left and right margins for only part of my document?

✔ Yes. Select the text on the pages you want to change and follow the steps in this section. In the Page Setup dialog box, click ▼ in the Apply to box, click Selected text, and click OK. Word sets up sections in the document and applies the margin settings to just the selected text.

What other method can I use to change my margins?

✔ You can visually drag the margin marker in Print Preview to change the page margins. See the section "Preview a Document" for more information.

Can I change the units Word uses to measure a page?

✔ Yes. Select the Tools menu and then click Options. Click the General tab and in the Measurement units area, click ▼ and then click the units you want.

I cannot see the margin changes on-screen. Why not?

✔ In Normal view, you cannot see the margin changes. You must either change to Print Layout view, or preview the document, to see the margins. See the section "Preview a Document" for more information.

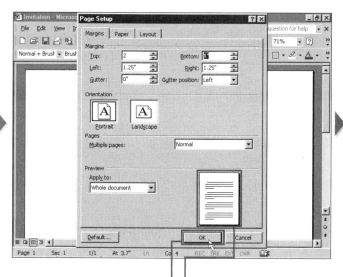

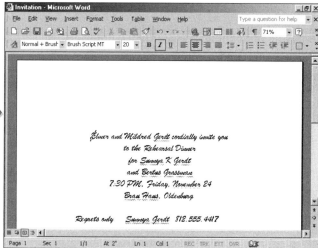

■ You can repeat steps 3 and 4 for each margin you want to change.

■ You see a preview of your changes here.

5 Click OK.

■ Word changes the margins of your document.

ALIGN TEXT ON A PAGE

Y ou can vertically align text on each page of your document to fit your needs. You can opt to align the page to the top, center, or bottom of the page, or to justify the page text.

By default, Word vertically aligns documents to the top. When you select center, Word aligns the text between the top and bottom margins of the page. When you select bottom alignment, your text aligns to the bottom of your document. The justified option

spaces your text evenly on the page. You might apply these alignments as special effects to make the text appear at the bottom or spread out between the two margins.

You can apply center aligning to create title pages and short memos. For information on margins, see "Change Margins."

Remember that you cannot see alignment changes in Normal View. You must switch to Print Layout

What if I want to remove the vertical alignment of my document?

✔ To later remove the alignment, perform steps 1 through 6 in this section. Then click Top and OK to apply the change.

view or Print Preview to see any changes. See the sections "Change the View" and "Preview a Document" for more information.

ALIGN TEXT ON A PAGE

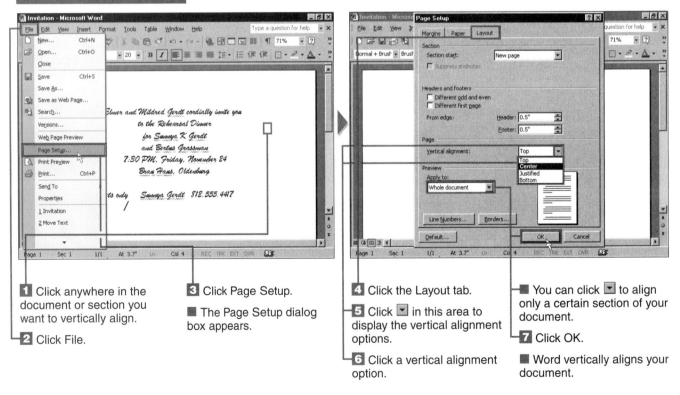

1 Click anywhere in the document or section you want to vertically align.

2 Click File.

3 Click Page Setup.

■ The Page Setup dialog box appears.

4 Click the Layout tab.

5 Click ▼ in this area to display the vertical alignment options.

6 Click a vertical alignment option.

■ You can click ▼ to align only a certain section of your document.

7 Click OK.

■ Word vertically aligns your document.

CHANGE PAGE ORIENTATION

You can change the orientation of pages in your document to fit your page content. Orientation refers to the way that Word prints information on a page.

Portrait is the standard page orientation, and you use it to print most documents, such as letters, memos, reports, and brochures. The portrait orientation prints information across the short side of a page. Landscape orientation prints

information across the long side of a page. Certificates and tables are often printed using the landscape orientation.

You can change the page orientation for only specific pages in your document. For example, in a report, you can print a page displaying a table in the landscape orientation and print the rest of the pages in the report in the portrait orientation.

How do I apply a different orientation for only part of a document?

✔ To change the orientation for part of a document, select the text you want to change and follow steps 1 through 5 in this section. Click ▾ in the Apply to box and select the Selected text option.

CHANGE PAGE ORIENTATION

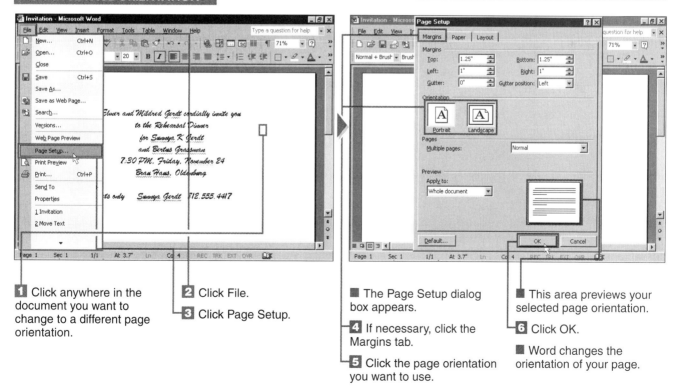

■ Click anywhere in the document you want to change to a different page orientation.

② Click File.

③ Click Page Setup.

■ The Page Setup dialog box appears.

④ If necessary, click the Margins tab.

⑤ Click the page orientation you want to use.

■ This area previews your selected page orientation.

⑥ Click OK.

■ Word changes the orientation of your page.

ADD PAGE NUMBERS

Y ou can have Word number the pages in your document. Numbering pages can help make a long document easier to organize and can help your reader keep pages in order.

Word can display page numbers at the top or bottom of the pages in your document. When you add page numbers, Word sets up headers or footers for the

document. When you add, remove, or rearrange text in your document, Word automatically adjusts the page numbers for you. You can also hide the page number on the first page of your document, which is useful when your first page is a title page.

You can choose to align your page numbers to the left, right, or center. You can also use the inside or

outside alignment if you plan to bind your document.

You can preview the position and alignment settings you choose for the page numbers. Page numbers display on your screen only in the Print Layout view or Print Preview. See the sections "Change the View" and "Preview a Document" for more information.

ADD PAGE NUMBERS

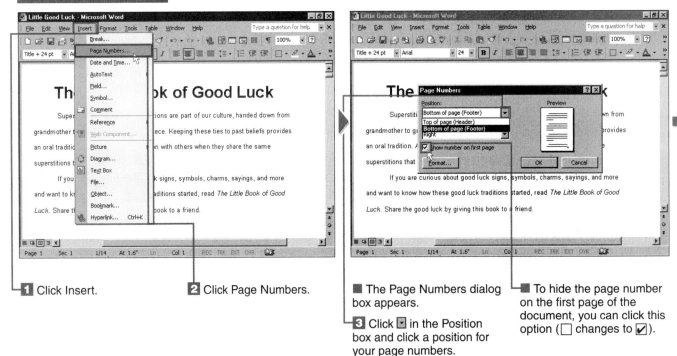

1 Click Insert.

2 Click Page Numbers.

■ The Page Numbers dialog box appears.

3 Click ▼ in the Position box and click a position for your page numbers.

■ To hide the page number on the first page of the document, you can click this option (☐ changes to ☑).

Can I specify a format for my page numbers, such as letters or Roman numerals?

✔ Yes. In the Page Numbers dialog box, click the Format button. Click the Number format area and click the format you want to use for the page numbers. Then click OK.

What are headers and footers?

✔ *Headers* and *footers* appear at the top (header) and bottom (footer) of your document. When you add page numbers, Word creates a header or footer, depending on the position you select. You can also include other document information in a header or footer. See the section "Add a Header or Footer" for more information.

How do I remove page numbers from my document?

✔ To remove page numbers, you must delete the page number from the document's header or footer. To display headers and footers, select the View menu and then click Header and Footer. Select the page number in the header or footer and then press the Delete key. For more information on headers and footers, see the section "Add a Header or Footer."

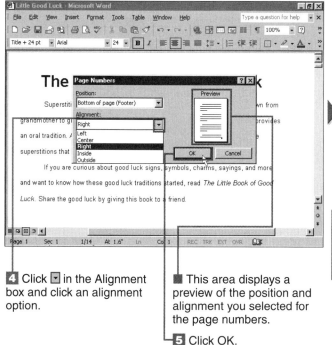

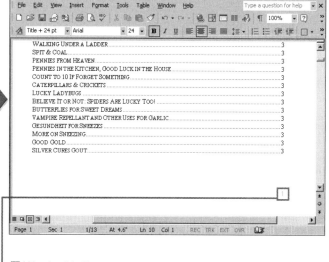

■4 Click ▾ in the Alignment box and click an alignment option.

■ This area displays a preview of the position and alignment you selected for the page numbers.

■5 Click OK.

■ Word adds the page numbers to your document. You may have to scroll to the bottom or top of the page to view the page numbers.

ADD A HEADER OR FOOTER

You can add a header and footer to every page in your document to give your document a more professional look. A *header* appears at the top, while a *footer* appears at the bottom, of each page.

A header or footer can contain information such as a company name, author's name, or chapter title. You can edit and format this text as you would any other text in

your document. See Chapter 5 for more information on formatting text.

You can use the Header and Footer toolbar buttons to insert special information. You can, for example, insert the page number and the total number of document pages into a header or footer. If you add, remove, or rearrange text, Word automatically adjusts the page numbers for you.

You can also quickly insert the date and time into a header or footer, which Word updates automatically every time you open or print your document.

Word displays the headers and footers in a document only in the Print Layout view and Print Preview. See the sections "Change the View" and "Preview a Document" for more information.

ADD A HEADER OR FOOTER

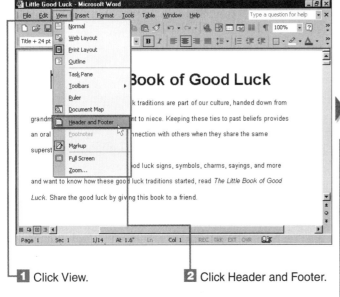

1 Click View.

2 Click Header and Footer.

■ Word displays the Header and Footer toolbar, and dims the text in the document.

3 To create a header, type the header text.

Note: For more on formatting text, see Chapter 5.

4 Click the Switch Between Header and Footer button (📑) to display the Footer area.

How do I delete a header or footer?

✔ Click the View menu and then click Header and Footer. Select all the information in the Header or Footer area and then press Delete.

What other information can I quickly insert into a header or footer?

✔ On the Header and Footer toolbar, you can click Insert AutoText, and then select information, such as the document's author, you want to insert. You can also click one of the other buttons on the toolbar: ⊞ inserts Page Numbers, ⊠ inserts Total Number of Pages, ⊞ inserts the Date, and ◷ inserts the Time.

What formatting options do a header and footer automatically include?

✔ A header and footer include some predefined tabs such as a center tab and a right-aligned tab. This formatting sets up three areas for information: one at the left margin, one centered on the page, and one at the right margin. You can press Tab to move and type text in the center or right edge of the header or footer.

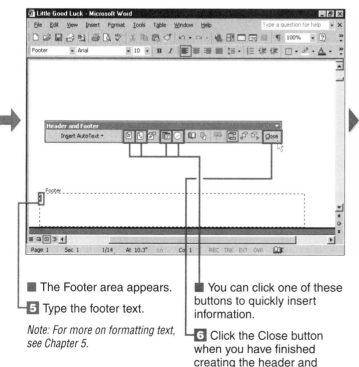

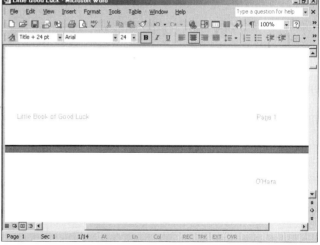

■ The Footer area appears.

5 Type the footer text.

Note: For more on formatting text, see Chapter 5.

■ You can click one of these buttons to quickly insert information.

6 Click the Close button when you have finished creating the header and footer.

■ Word inserts the header and footer information per your specifications.

■ You may have to scroll through the document to view the bottom or top of the page. Here you can see the footer from one page and the header on the next page.

ADD FOOTNOTES OR ENDNOTES

You can add a footnote or endnote to your document to provide additional information about specific text. Footnotes and endnotes can contain information such as an explanation, comment, or reference for the text. *Footnotes* appear at the bottom of a page. *Endnotes* appear at the end of a document. Word displays the footnote or endnote area of your document in the Print Layout view.

Word numbers the footnotes or endnotes you add, beginning with the number 1 or Roman numeral i. You can enter any amount of text for a footnote or endnote.

After you insert your footnote or endnote, you can see it in any view. When you hold the mouse pointer over the number, Word displays the footnote or endnote text.

If you add or remove footnotes or endnotes, Word automatically adjusts the numbers of the footnotes or endnotes in your document. Word also ensures that the text you type for a footnote always begins on the same page as the footnote number.

ADD FOOTNOTES OR ENDNOTES

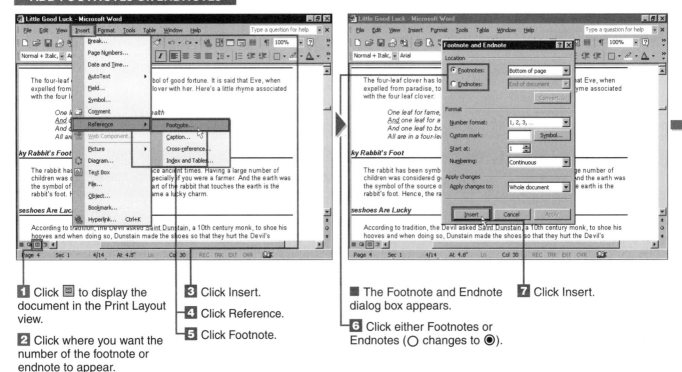

1 Click 🔲 to display the document in the Print Layout view.

2 Click where you want the number of the footnote or endnote to appear.

3 Click Insert.

4 Click Reference.

5 Click Footnote.

■ The Footnote and Endnote dialog box appears.

6 Click either Footnotes or Endnotes (○ changes to ●).

7 Click Insert.

How do I edit an existing footnote or endnote?

✔ You can edit a footnote or endnote as you would edit any text in your document. To quickly display the footnote or endnote area, double-click the footnote or endnote number in your document.

Can I have Word print endnotes on a separate page?

✔ To print endnotes on a separate page, insert a page break directly above the endnote area. To insert a page break, click Insert and then click Break. Click Page break (○ changes to ●), and then click OK.

Can I change the formatting of footnotes or endnotes?

✔ Yes. In the Footnote and Endnote dialog box, select the options you want to change. You can select a number format, a custom mark, the starting number, and type of numbering. Continuous is the default, but you can also restart numbering in each section.

Can I delete a footnote or endnote?

✔ You can delete a footnote or endnote you no longer need. Select the footnote or endnote number in your document and then press Delete.

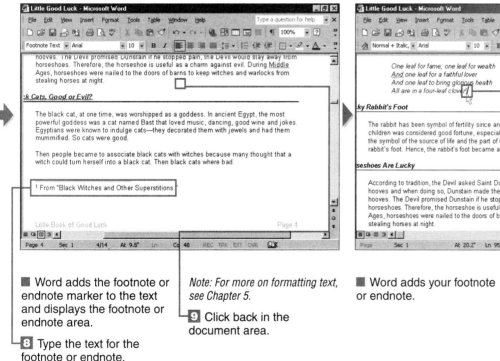

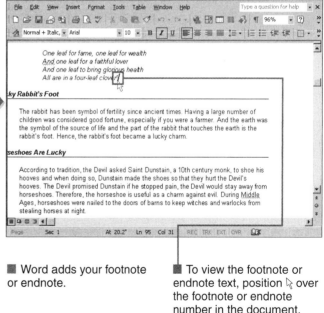

■ Word adds the footnote or endnote marker to the text and displays the footnote or endnote area.

8 Type the text for the footnote or endnote.

Note: For more on formatting text, see Chapter 5.

9 Click back in the document area.

■ Word adds your footnote or endnote.

■ To view the footnote or endnote text, position ℞ over the footnote or endnote number in the document.

CREATE COLUMNS

You can display text in columns like those you find in a newspaper. This document format is useful for creating documents such as newsletters and brochures and can make your document easier to read.

You can create one, two, or three columns of equal size. You can also create two columns and have one column wider than the other. Using one wide column can add an interesting visual effect to your document.

Regardless of the number of columns you create, Word fills one column with text before starting a new column. You can control where Word places text by inserting column breaks. You can also have Word display a vertical line between the columns.

In the Print Layout view, Word displays columns side-by-side. The Normal view displays text in a single column. See the section "Change the View" for more information. The columns appear when you print your document, whether you display them on your screen or not.

CREATE COLUMNS

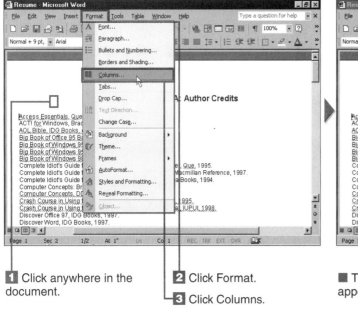

1 Click anywhere in the document.

2 Click Format.

3 Click Columns.

■ The Columns dialog box appears.

4 Click the column format you want to use.

Can I create columns for just part of the document?

✔ Yes. To create columns for part of your document, select the text you want to format as columns. Then follow the steps below.

How do I move text from one column to the top of the next column?

✔ You must insert a column break. Click where you want to insert the break. Click Insert and then click Break. Click the Column break option (○ changes to ◉) and then click OK.

How can I quickly create columns?

✔ To create columns of equal size, click the Columns button (▦) on the Standard toolbar. Then drag ↘ over the number of columns you want to create.

How do I change the width of the columns?

✔ While creating the columns, deselect the Equal column width option (❑ changes to ☑). Then type the width and spacing for each column. For already created columns, drag the column indicators which appear in the Print Layout view. Click and drag ↘ until the column edge is in the new position.

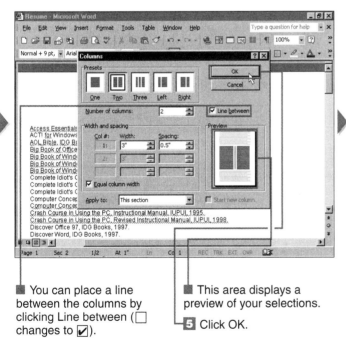

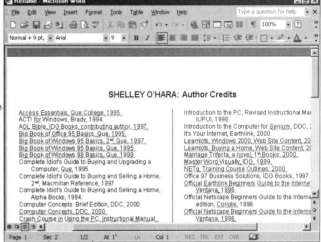

■ You can place a line between the columns by clicking Line between (❑ changes to ☑).

■ This area displays a preview of your selections.

5 Click OK.

■ The text in the document appears in columns.

■ To remove columns, you can repeat steps 1 through 3, click One in the Presets area, and click OK.

ADD A PICTURE WATERMARK

You can make your page more visually interesting by adding a watermark. A *watermark* is an image or text that prints faintly in the background on all the pages of the document.

You can use any type of picture file as a watermark whether it be your own picture, or a sample picture available in Word. For example, you might include a company logo.

When you add a watermark, Word requires that you select a picture, and, by default, opens the My Pictures folder. You can select the pictures from this folder or change to another folder to select the picture file to insert.

You can also choose to add a text watermark. For example, you might include a club or family name as a background in your document. In

this case, you type the text you want to include and then specify the font, size, color, and layout for the text.

Although the watermark does not appear in Normal view, you can select Print Layout view and Print Preview to see your watermark. See the sections "Change the View" and "Preview a Document" for more information.

ADD A PICTURE WATERMARK

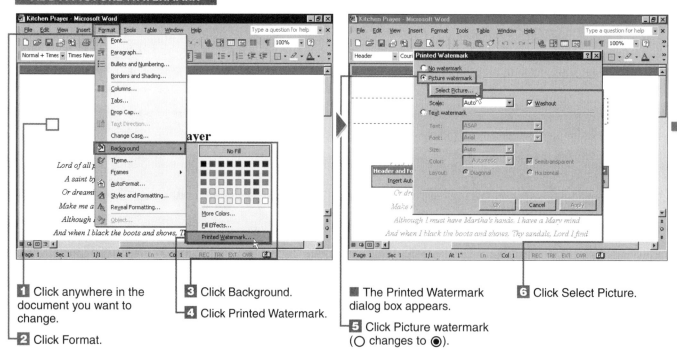

1 Click anywhere in the document you want to change.

2 Click Format.

3 Click Background.

4 Click Printed Watermark.

■ The Printed Watermark dialog box appears.

5 Click Picture watermark (○ changes to ◉).

6 Click Select Picture.

How do I remove a watermark?

✔ To remove a watermark, click No watermark in the Printed Watermark dialog box. Word removes your watermark with all its content.

How do I add watermark text?

✔ Follow steps 1 through 4 in this section and click the Text watermark option (○ changes to ◉). Type the text you want to use in the Text box. You can then select the font, size, and color for your text. You can also select either diagonal or horizontal for the layout of the watermark. When you click OK, Word adds the text watermark to your document.

How do I scale the picture?

✔ You can change the size of the picture by clicking ▣ in the Scale box. Auto, the default, leaves the picture at the current size. You can select a percentage with larger numbers to create bigger images.

What are the other background options?

✔ You can also add a background color or fill, although you use these options more for Web pages, not printed documents. For more information on creating Web pages, see Part VIII of this book.

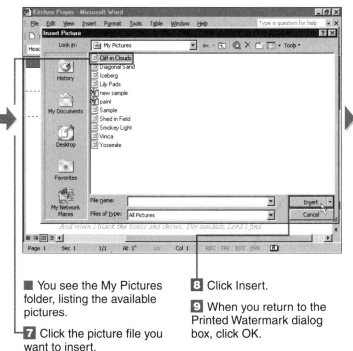

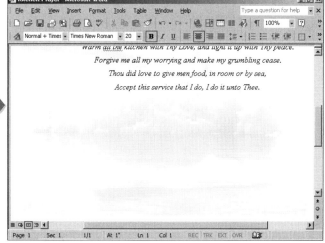

■ You see the My Pictures folder, listing the available pictures.

7 Click the picture file you want to insert.

8 Click Insert.

9 When you return to the Printed Watermark dialog box, click OK.

■ Word adds the picture watermark to your document.

USING TEMPLATES

Rather than making a lot of individual formatting options, you may want to start with a document that includes some formatting (and even text) already set up for you. To do so, you can use templates to save time when creating common types of documents, such as letters, faxes, memos, and reports. Templates provide the layout and formatting so you can concentrate on the content of your document.

When you select a template, a document immediately appears on your screen with areas for you to fill in your personalized information. For example, the Contemporary Memo template provides areas for the name of the person to whom you are sending the memo, the date, and the subject of the memo. You can replace the sample text in a template with the text you want to use.

Other templates provide other layouts and appropriate text for the document type. For example, letter templates provide address areas. Fax templates provide areas to type recipient information such as name, company, phone, and fax numbers as well as your name, company, and phone numbers.

USING TEMPLATES

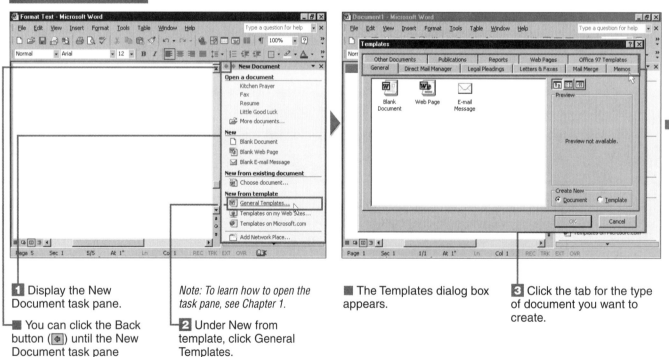

■1 Display the New Document task pane.

■ You can click the Back button (⬅) until the New Document task pane displays.

Note: To learn how to open the task pane, see Chapter 1.

■2 Under New from template, click General Templates.

■ The Templates dialog box appears.

■3 Click the tab for the type of document you want to create.

A Microsoft Office dialog box appears when I click a template. Why?

✔ When you select an uninstalled template or wizard, Word asks you to insert a particular CD-ROM into your CD-ROM drive. Insert the CD-ROM and then click OK to install the template or wizard.

Can I create my own templates?

✔ Yes. Open the document you want to use as the basis for the template. Click File and then Save As. Type a name for the template and then click the Save as type ▼, click Document Template and then click Save. Office lists the template on the General tab in the Templates dialog box.

What are the Wizard templates in the Template dialog box?

✔ In addition to templates, you can select a wizard to guide you step by step through the process of creating a document. Click a wizard in the Template dialog box and then follow the on-screen instructions. The steps vary depending on the wizard you select. After the wizard creates the document, you can modify the text to add your content.

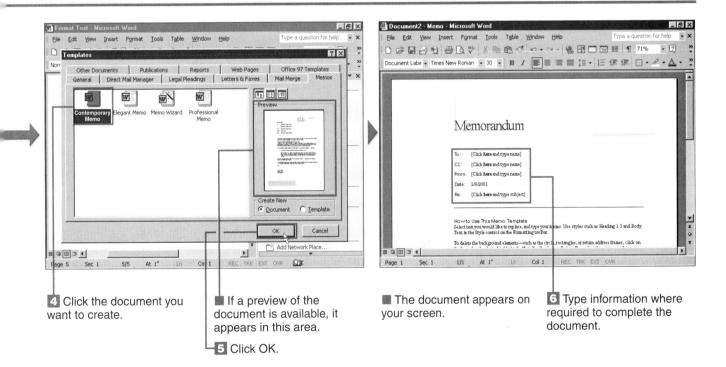

■4 Click the document you want to create.

■ If a preview of the document is available, it appears in this area.

■5 Click OK.

■ The document appears on your screen.

■6 Type information where required to complete the document.

CREATE A TABLE

You can create a table to neatly display information, such as columns of numbers, in your document. Word lets you draw a table as you would draw it with a pencil and paper, or create a table using the default style.

A *table* consists of rows, columns, and cells, where a *row* is a horizontal line of cells, a *column* is a vertical line of cells, and a *cell* is the area where a row and column intersect. You enter text into individual cells. For more on entering text, see the section "Type Text in a Table."

Drawing a table gives you a great deal of flexibility because you can select the style for each line in the table. And you can draw each column and row to the size you want.

When you create a table with the default style, you can select the number of rows and columns to include. The default table style makes the columns all the same size, but you can format the table to fit your needs.

CREATE A TABLE

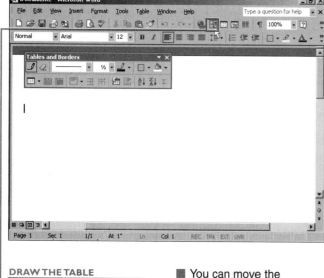

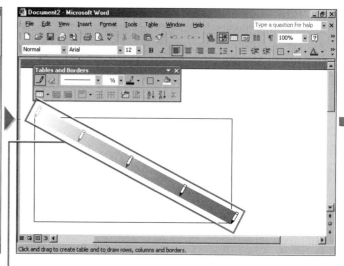

DRAW THE TABLE

1 Click the Tables and Borders button (▦).

■ The Tables and Borders toolbar appears.

■ You can move the toolbar out of the way by clicking ▹ over the title bar and dragging it to a new location.

2 Position the ▹ where you want the top left corner of the table to appear (▹ changes to ✐).

3 Drag ✐ until the outline of the table is the size you want.

How do I create a default table?

✔ Click the Insert Table button (▤) on the Standard toolbar. Then drag ⬚ over the number of rows and columns you want the table to contain.

Do I have to make the columns even?

✔ No. You can draw the lines anywhere within the table to create the column and row sizes you need. You can also keep one combined row at the top for a table title.

Can I change the line styles in my table?

✔ Yes. You can apply a different style or thickness. To change the line style, click the Line Style ▣ and click a style. To change the thickness of the line, click the Line Weight ▣ and click a thickness. By default, the thickness is measured in points. The higher the number, the thicker Word makes the line. The drop-down list shows examples of each line thickness.

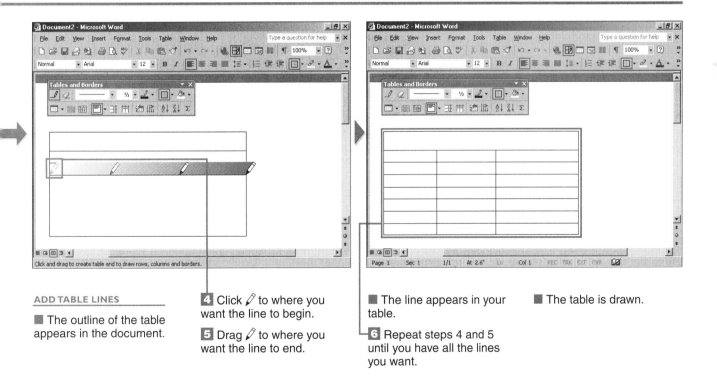

ADD TABLE LINES

■ The outline of the table appears in the document.

4 Click ✎ to where you want the line to begin.

5 Drag ✎ to where you want the line to end.

■ The line appears in your table.

6 Repeat steps 4 and 5 until you have all the lines you want.

■ The table is drawn.

TYPE TEXT IN A TABLE

You can enter data quickly and easily into a created table. Like typing in a document, Word wraps text to the next line within a cell and adjusts the row height. You can insert a paragraph break within the cell to create two paragraphs within the cell. To learn how to draw or insert a default table, see the section "Create a Table."

You can edit and format text in a table as you would edit and format any text in your document. To learn more about formatting text, see Chapter 5.

Can I add blank lines within the cells of my table?
✔ You can press Enter if you want to end the paragraph and/or insert a blank line, or paragraph break, within the cell.

How do I quickly move from cell to cell?
✔ To advance to the next cell, press Tab.

How do I quickly add more rows to my table?
✔ To add another row to a table, press Tab in the last row and column of the table. Word automatically adds a new row.

TYPE TEXT IN A TABLE

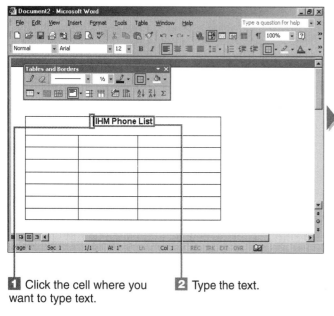

1 Click the cell where you want to type text.

2 Type the text.

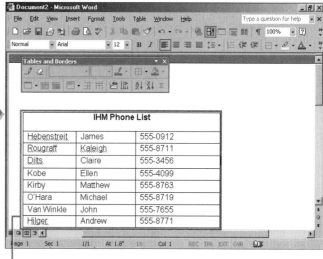

3 Repeat steps 1 and 2 until you type all the text.

■ You can make any formatting changes to the entries.

Note: To learn more about how to format text, see Chapter 5.

■ The table is complete.

SORT TEXT

Y ou can alphabetize the entries in a table, selecting any of the columns to use as the sort column. The Tables and Borders toolbar conveniently provides two buttons for sorting: Sort Ascending and Sort Descending. The buttons sort text as well as numeric

entries. Although these commands appear in the Table menu, you can use them to sort any text in a document. That is, you can sort any paragraphs in a document, even if the text does not appear in table form.

How can I undo a sort?

✔ If you sort a table and do not like the results, you can click the Undo button (🖾). If you frequently sort a table and want have the option of returning it to its original order, consider adding a column to number your rows. You can then use this column to sort and return the table to its original order. To learn how to enter text or numbers, see the section "Type Text in a Table."

SORT TEXT

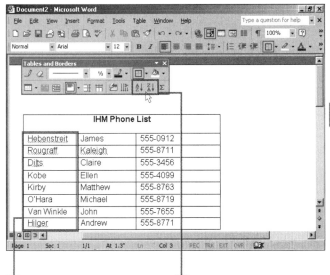

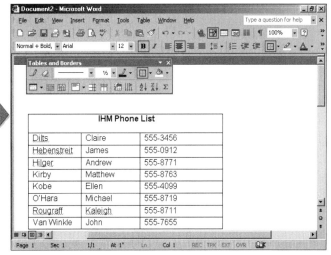

1 Click in the column you want to sort.

2 Click the Sort Ascending (🔼) or Sort Descending (🔽) button.

■ Word sorts the table alphabetically in ascending or descending order.

CHANGE COLUMN WIDTH

After you create a table, you can change the width of its columns. You may do so to make more room for the entries. Or if the entries are short, you can make the column narrower to reduce the amount of white space, or to fit your table onto one page.

You cannot change the width or height of a single cell. When you make changes to the column width, all the cells in the column are affected.

When you change the width of a column, Word displays a dotted line on your screen to indicate the new width.

Can I change the row height also?

✔ Yes. Word automatically adjusts the size of the row, depending on the size of the font. For information on changing the font size, see Chapter 5. You can also adjust the row height in the same way as you adjust the column width: by dragging the row border. Most often, you do not need to adjust the row height because the default size is usually just right.

CHANGE COLUMN WIDTH

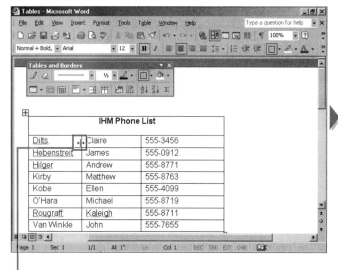

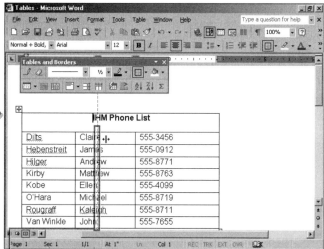

1 Position I over the right edge of the column you want to change (I changes to ↔).

2 Drag the column edge to a new position.

■ A dashed line shows the new position.

ERASE LINES

You can easily erase the interior and exterior lines of a table when you no longer need them. For example, you can erase the interior lines between two or more small cells to create one large cell to display a title at the top of your table. You can also create a title cell when you create the table by not drawing the columns in this row. You might erase the exterior lines of a table as a special effect when you structure the layout of a page. When you erase the lines that make up the outside of your table, remember that the table does not have a solid border when you print it. For more on printing a document, see Chapter 2.

Word highlights the lines that you select to erase. If you erase a line between two cells that contain text, the text appears in the new, larger cell. If you have two cells with different text formats, you must change the format of all the text in the new, larger cell. For information on formatting text, see Chapter 5.

ERASE LINES

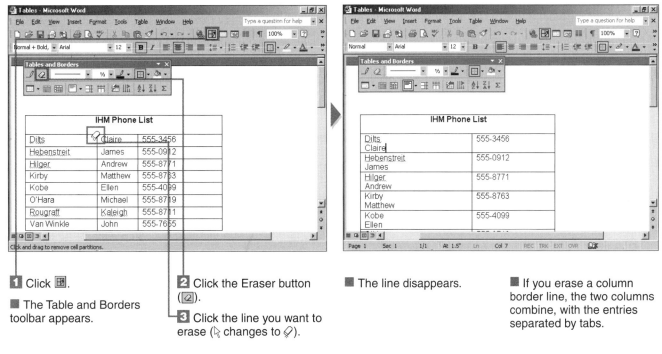

1 Click .

■ The Table and Borders toolbar appears.

2 Click the Eraser button (🖉).

3 Click the line you want to erase (🔖 changes to 🖉).

■ The line disappears.

■ If you erase a column border line, the two columns combine, with the entries separated by tabs.

ADD OR DELETE A ROW OR COLUMN

If you want to insert additional information into an existing table, you can add a row or column. To learn how to create a table, see the section "Create a Table."

When you add a new row or column, start by selecting where

you want to place that row or column. You can place the new row above or below the existing row. You can insert the new column to the left or right of the current column. You can access these four commands through the menu, or through buttons on the Tables and Border toolbar.

You can delete a row or column you no longer need. When you delete a row or column from your table, you also delete all the information in the cell. If you accidentally delete a row or column, you can use the Undo feature to restore the lost information.

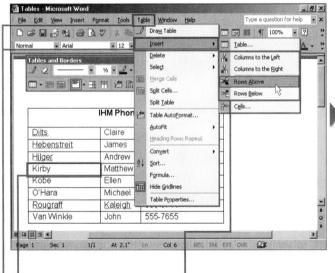

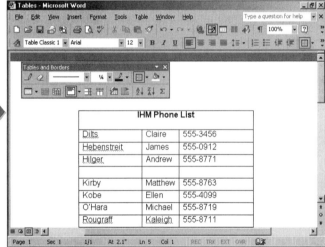

1 Click within the row or column where you want to insert the new row.

2 Click Table.

3 Click Insert.

4 Click Rows Above, Rows Below, Columns to the Left, or Columns to the Right.

■ To add a new row to the end of the table, you can click in the last cell of the table and press Enter.

■ If you add a row, Word adds it either above or below the insertion point. If you add a column, Word adds it either to the left or to the right of the insertion point.

Is there a button I can use to add cells?

✔ Yes. You can also use the Insert Table button (▢) in the Tables and Borders toolbar to add cells. Click ▾ next to this button and then select the command you want: Column to the Left 🖳, Column to the Right 🖳, Rows Above 🖳, or Rows Below 🖳.

How do I delete text?

✔ Select the text by dragging I across it and then press Delete. Word deletes the text, but the table cell remains.

Can I add several rows or columns at once?

✔ Yes. To do so, select the number of columns or rows you want to add in your existing table. Then insert the columns or rows. The number of rows or columns you select determines the number of rows or columns Word inserts into your table.

How can I delete an entire table?

✔ If you select a table and press Delete, Word deletes the text, but the table structure remains. To delete the entire table, click within the table. Then click Table, Delete, and then Table.

DELETE A ROW OR COLUMN

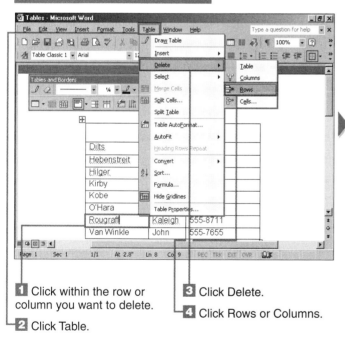

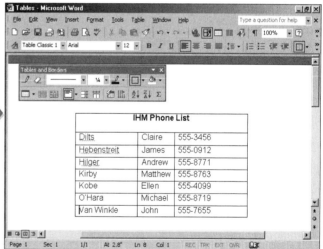

1 Click within the row or column you want to delete.

2 Click Table.

3 Click Delete.

4 Click Rows or Columns.

■ Word removes the row or column and all of its contents from the table.

MOVE OR RESIZE A TABLE

Word allows you to move or resize your table giving greater flexibility in document layout. You generally move or resize a table to accommodate data deletions or additions. For more on creating a table, see the section "Create a Table."

You can move a table from one location in your document to another. When you position the mouse pointer over a table, the move table handle appears at the top left corner of the table allowing you to move the table to a new location.

You can change the size of a table to suit your document. Resizing a table does not change the size of the entries in the table. When you position the mouse pointer over a

table, the table resize handle appears at the bottom right corner of the table.

Please note that Word can only display the move and table resize handles in the Print Layout view. See Chapter 6 to learn more about using the various views in Word.

MOVE A TABLE

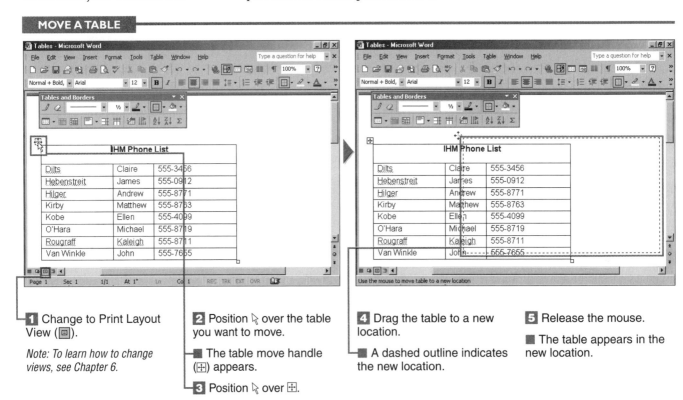

1 Change to Print Layout View (▣).

Note: To learn how to change views, see Chapter 6.

2 Position ▷ over the table you want to move.

■ The table move handle (⊞) appears.

3 Position ▷ over ⊞.

4 Drag the table to a new location.

■ A dashed outline indicates the new location.

5 Release the mouse.

■ The table appears in the new location.

Can I change the alignment of my table?

✔ Yes. Word allows you to align a table to the left, center, or right of a page. To select the table you want to align differently, position ▷ over the table until the table move handle appears. Then click the handle. To change the alignment of the table, click the Left align (▤), Center (▤), or Right align (▤) button on the Formatting toolbar.

I see a double vertical line with two arrows. What does this mean?

✔ If you see two vertical lines with arrows, you have positioned the pointer on the border of a column. You can use this pointer to resize the column width. See "Change Column Width" in this chapter.

How do I undo a change?

✔ If you move or resize a table by accident, you can undo the change by clicking ▷.

RESIZE A TABLE

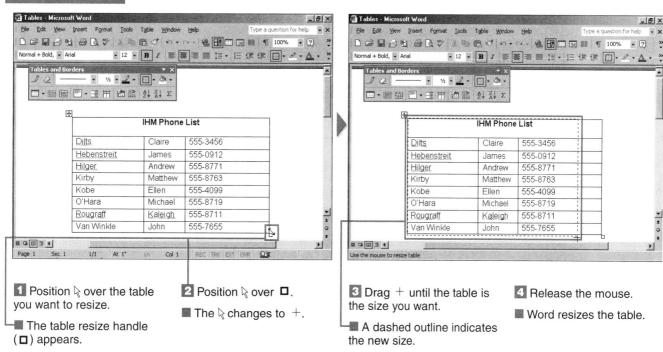

1 Position ▷ over the table you want to resize.

■ The table resize handle (□) appears.

2 Position ▷ over □.

■ The ▷ changes to +.

3 Drag + until the table is the size you want.

■ A dashed outline indicates the new size.

4 Release the mouse.

■ Word resizes the table.

CHANGE TABLE BORDERS

You can enhance the appearance of your table by changing the borders. By default, Word uses a solid, thin, black line for the borders of your table and cells.

You can change the border for a cell, a range of cells, or your entire table. Changing the border for specific cells in your table can help

you separate data or emphasize important information.

Word offers several line styles from which you can choose. You can also select a line thickness and color for the border. Word uses the line style, thickness, and color you select for the border for all the new tables you create until you exit the program.

After you select the various border options, you must specify to which sides of the table you want to apply the border. For example, you can apply an outside, an inside, a right, or a left border. Changing only some of the borders for the cells you select can give your table an interesting visual effect.

CHANGE TABLE BORDERS

CHANGE THE LINE STYLE

1 Click 🔳.

■ The Tables and Borders toolbar appears.

2 Click the ▪ next to the Line Style button.

3 Click the line style you want to use.

CHANGE THE LINE WEIGHT

4 Click the ▪ next to the Line Weight button.

5 Click the line thickness you want to use.

Does Word have an AutoFormat option for tables?

✔ Yes. You can automatically apply pre-designed formatting, such as borders and shading, to your table with the Table AutoFormat feature. For more information on the Table AutoFormat feature, see "Using a Table AutoFormat."

Can I remove a border from my table?

✔ Yes. You generally remove a border when you use a table to organize the placement of information in your document and do not want the border to appear when you print your table. Click No Border from the Line Style drop-down list and then click the border you want to remove.

I removed a border from my table, but a faint border still displays on my screen. How do I remove the faint border?

✔ Word displays faint borders, called gridlines, for each table you create. To remove all the gridlines from a table, click Table and then click Hide Gridlines. To once again display the gridlines, click Table then click Show Gridlines.

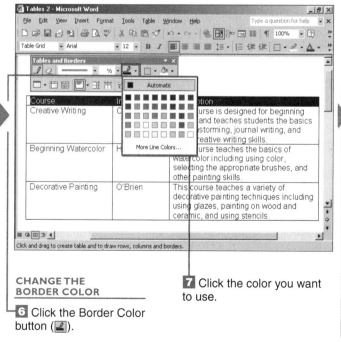

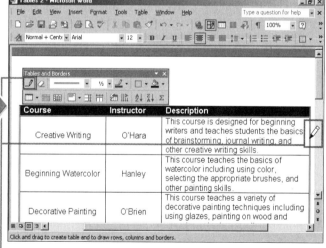

CHANGE THE BORDER COLOR

6 Click the Border Color button (▨).

7 Click the color you want to use.

APPLY FORMATTING

8 Click the Draw Table button (▨) (ℜ changes to ✎).

9 Drag the ✎ over the border you want to change.

10 Follow steps 2 through 9 for any other borders you want to change.

■ The border(s) is formatted with the options you selected.

133

ADD SHADING OR COLOR TO CELLS

You can draw attention to an area of your table by adding shading or color to cells, which changes the background of the cells.

Word offers several shades of gray you can add to the cells in your table. The available shades of gray range from light gray to black. Word also offers several colors you

can use, including blue, yellow, and violet.

If you use a black-and-white printer, any color you add to cells appears as a shade of gray when you print your table. If you have a color printer or if you display the document rather than print it, the colors appear as selected.

Make sure the shading or color you want to add to cells works well with the color of your text. For example, readers may find black text on a violet background difficult to read.

If you no longer want cells in your table to display shading or color, you can easily remove the shading or color from the cells.

ADD SHADING OR COLOR TO CELLS

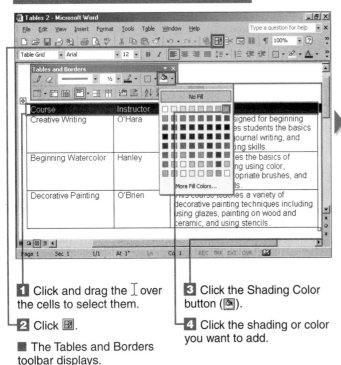

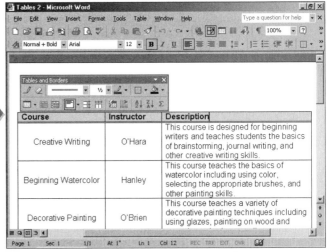

1 Click and drag the I over the cells to select them.

2 Click 🔳.

■ The Tables and Borders toolbar displays.

3 Click the Shading Color button (🔲).

4 Click the shading or color you want to add.

■ The cells display the shading or color.

■ To remove shading or color from cells, you can repeat steps 1 through 3, and then click No Fill.

CHANGE TEXT POSITION IN CELLS

You can enhance the appearance of your table by changing the position of text in cells. Changing the position of text can help you lay out the text in your table to suit your needs, or make long lists of information easier to read. For example, you can align chapter titles in a table of contents at the top left of cells and

align the page numbers at the top right of the adjacent cells.

By default, Word aligns text at the top left of a cell. However, Word provides nine options that combine the left, right, center, top, and bottom alignment positions. For example, you can center headings and titles horizontally and

vertically in cells to make the text stand out.

When you change the position of text that fills an entire cell, you may need to increase the column width or row height to see the change. To change the column width or row height, see the section "Change the Column Width."

CHANGE TEXT POSITION IN CELLS

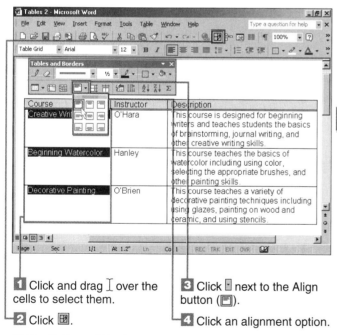

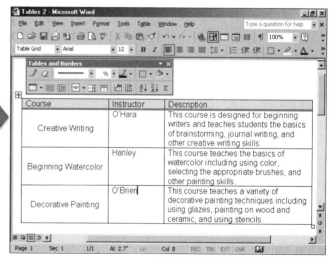

1 Click and drag I over the cells to select them.

2 Click 🔲.

■ The Table and Borders toolbar displays.

3 Click ⬚ next to the Align button (🔲).

4 Click an alignment option.

■ The text displays the new alignment.

USING A TABLE AUTOFORMAT

Word offers many ready-to-use designs, which you can apply to give your table a new appearance or to help make the information in your table easier to read. The AutoFormat allows you to apply several table properties at once, saving you time and effort.

Some of the types of table designs include Simple, Classic, Colorful, and 3-D effects. The Simple designs use only basic formatting. The

Classic designs use simple borders and conservative colors. The Colorful designs use color combinations that make your table stand out. The 3-D effects designs give your table the appearance of depth.

A table design includes formatting options such as borders, fonts, shading, and color. You can specify which formatting options you want Word to apply to your table. You can also have Word apply special

formatting, such as italics, to the heading rows in your table. You can opt to apply special formatting to the last row, first column, and last column.

You can preview a table design to determine if the design suits your table or document. When you apply an AutoFormat, Word replaces any previous formatting changes with the new options.

USING A TABLE AUTOFORMAT

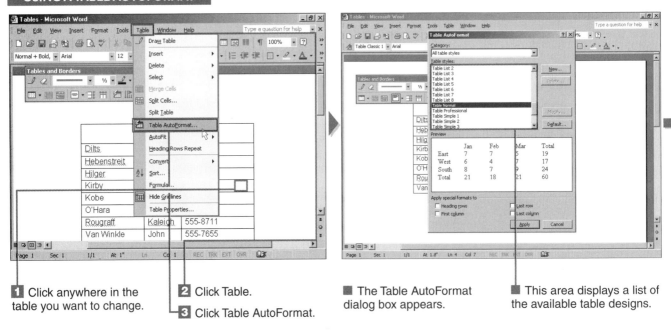

1 Click anywhere in the table you want to change.

2 Click Table.

3 Click Table AutoFormat.

■ The Table AutoFormat dialog box appears.

■ This area displays a list of the available table designs.

What is the purpose of the AutoFit command?

✔ The AutoFit command in the Table menu changes the size of your table based on the amount of text in the table. This ensures that the text fits neatly in your table. You can have the table resize to fit the contents, the window, or a fixed column width. You can also opt to distribute the rows and/or columns evenly so that they are all the same size.

Is there another way to display the Table AutoFormat dialog box?

✔ Yes. Click ⊞ on the Standard toolbar. When the Tables and Borders toolbar appears, click the Table AutoFormat button (🖼).

Can I apply a table design to only part of my table?

✔ No. Word applies the design to the entire table. To change only part of your table, you must select the cells you want to change and then format those cells. To change table borders, see "Change Table Borders." To add shading or color to cells, see "Add Shading or Color to Cells."

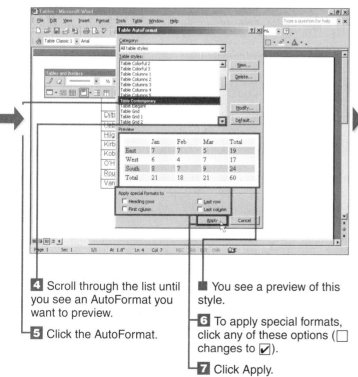

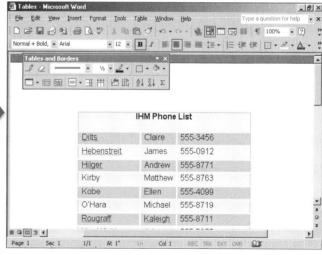

4 Scroll through the list until you see an AutoFormat you want to preview.

5 Click the AutoFormat.

■ You see a preview of this style.

6 To apply special formats, click any of these options (☐ changes to ☑).

7 Click Apply.

■ Word displays the table with the new design replacing any previously made formatting changes.

■ To remove the formatting, you can perform steps 1 through 4, click Table Normal 1, and click Apply.

ADD AN AUTOSHAPE

Word provides many ready-made shapes, called AutoShapes, that you can add to enhance the appearance of your document or draw attention to important information.

You can display AutoShapes only in the Print Layout and Web Layout views where Word offers several categories of AutoShapes, including Lines, Basic Shapes, Block Arrows,

Callouts, and Stars and Banners. To learn more about the Print Layout or Web Layout views, see Chapter 6.

Each category contains individual AutoShapes, which, upon selection, Word creates with its *Canvas*, or drawing program and places within a bounding box. You can later move and resize the AutoShape to better suit your needs. You can also delete an AutoShape you no longer need.

For information on moving, resizing, or deleting a graphic, see the section "Move or Resize a Graphic."

As you draw, your object covers the background text in the document. You can change the placement of the text and graphics. See the section "Wrap Text Around a Graphic" for more information.

ADD AN AUTOSHAPE

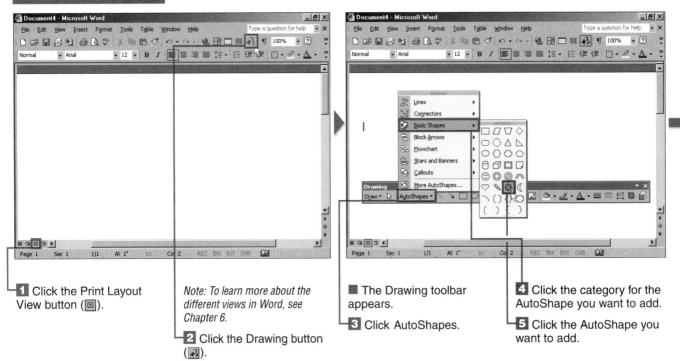

1 Click the Print Layout View button (▣).

Note: To learn more about the different views in Word, see Chapter 6.

2 Click the Drawing button (▧).

■ The Drawing toolbar appears.

3 Click AutoShapes.

4 Click the category for the AutoShape you want to add.

5 Click the AutoShape you want to add.

How can I quickly draw a shape?
✔ You can use the buttons on the Drawing toolbar. Click the Line button (□) to draw a line, the Arrow button (□) to draw an arrow, the Rectangle button (□) to draw a rectangle, and the Oval button (□) to draw an oval. Click where you want to place the shape and drag ⊞ until it is the size you want.

How do I draw a square or circle?
✔ On the Drawing toolbar, click □ to draw a square, or ○ to draw a circle. Then hold down Shift as you draw the shape.

Can I add text to an AutoShape?
✔ Yes. Right-click the AutoShape you want to change. Click Add Text and then type the text you want the AutoShape to display. When you finish typing, click outside the AutoShape.

Can I draw my own shape?
✔ Yes. On the Drawing toolbar, click AutoShapes ▾, select the Lines category, and then click the Freeform tool (□). When you finish drawing your shape, double-click to stop drawing.

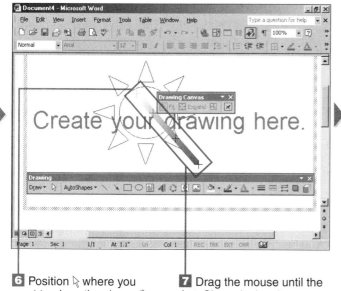

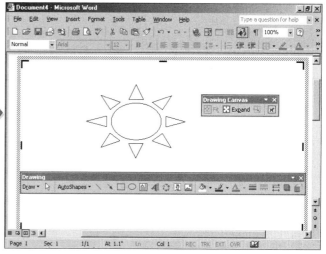

6 Position ▷ where you want to place the shape (▷ changes to +).

7 Drag the mouse until the AutoShape is the size you want.

■ The AutoShape appears in the document.

ADD A CLIP ART IMAGE

Word includes professionally designed clip art images you can add to your document. You can add clip art images to make your document more interesting and entertaining.

The first time you select this command, Office prompts you to search for and categorize the images. Follow the on-screen prompts.

Rather than browse through images, the XP version of Word lets you type a keyword and then search for matching images.

Unlike other types of graphics, such as AutoShapes and text effects, Word can display most clip art images in the Normal and Outline views as well as the Print Layout and Web Layout views. For more information on the views, see Chapter 6.

After you add a clip art image, you can move and resize the clip art image to suit your document. You can also delete a clip art image you no longer need. For information on moving, resizing, or deleting a graphic, see the section "Move or Resize a Graphic."

ADD A CLIP ART IMAGE

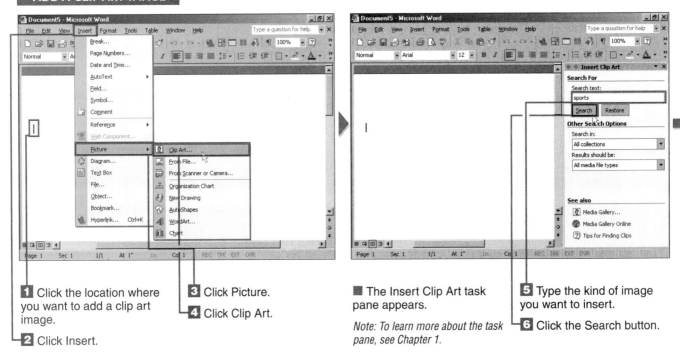

1 Click the location where you want to add a clip art image.

2 Click Insert.

3 Click Picture.

4 Click Clip Art.

■ The Insert Clip Art task pane appears.

Note: To learn more about the task pane, see Chapter 1.

5 Type the kind of image you want to insert.

6 Click the Search button.

How can I limit my search?

✔ You can limit the search to a particular folder or drive. To do so, click the Search in 🔽, which is under Other Search Options in the Insert Clip Art task pane, and click the drives and/or folders you want to search (☐ changes to ☑).

To limit the search to a particular media file type, click the Results should be 🔽, and click the type of file.

Can I edit a clip art image?

✔ Yes. To do so, click the image. You see the Picture toolbar. You can use the buttons on this toolbar to change the brightness of the image, crop the image, rotate the image, and make several other changes.

Where can I find more clip art images?

✔ If you are connected to the Internet, you can visit Media Gallery Online, a Web site, to find additional clip art images. In the Insert Clip Art task pane, click the Clips Online button and then follow the instructions on your screen.

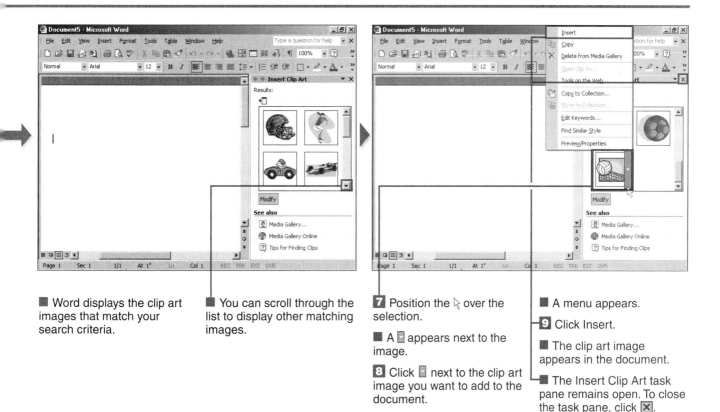

■ Word displays the clip art images that match your search criteria.

■ You can scroll through the list to display other matching images.

7 Position the 🔧 over the selection.

■ A ▫ appears next to the image.

8 Click ▫ next to the clip art image you want to add to the document.

■ A menu appears.

9 Click Insert.

■ The clip art image appears in the document.

■ The Insert Clip Art task pane remains open. To close the task pane, click 🗙.

ADD WORD ART

You can use the WordArt feature to add text effects to your document. You can add text effects that shadow, stretch, or make text appear three-dimensional. Text effects are useful for adding interesting headings to documents such as newsletters, flyers, or brochures.

Word can display text effects only in the Print Layout and Web Layout views. For more information on these views, see Chapter 6.

After you select the type of text effect you want to use, Word requires that you type the text for a text effect. Because Word's spelling check feature does not check WordArt for errors, you may consider checking your text before inserting it.

After you add a text effect, you can move and resize the text effect to suit your document. You can also delete a text effect you no longer need. For information, see the section "Move or Resize a Graphic."

When you select a text effect, Word automatically displays the WordArt toolbar. You can use the buttons on the toolbar to perform tasks such as changing the shape of a text effect or increasing and decreasing the space between characters.

ADD WORD ART

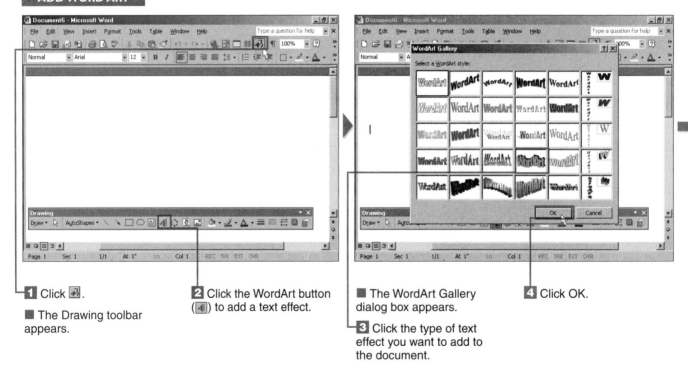

1 Click 🔄.

■ The Drawing toolbar appears.

2 Click the WordArt button (🔳) to add a text effect.

■ The WordArt Gallery dialog box appears.

3 Click the type of text effect you want to add to the document.

4 Click OK.

Can I add a text effect to existing text in my document?

✔ Yes. To do so, select the text you want the text effect to display and perform steps 1 through 4 in this section. Then perform step 6 to display the text effect in your document.

Can I edit the text in a text effect?

✔ Yes. To display the Edit WordArt Text dialog box so that you can change a text effect, double-click the text effect. Or select the text effect and then click the Edit Text button on the WordArt toolbar.

Can I change how the text effect looks?

✔ Yes. You can display the WordArt Gallery to select another style. You can double-click the word effect to display the text and select another font, font style, or font size. You can also use other buttons on the WordArt toolbar to change the shape or alignment of the text.

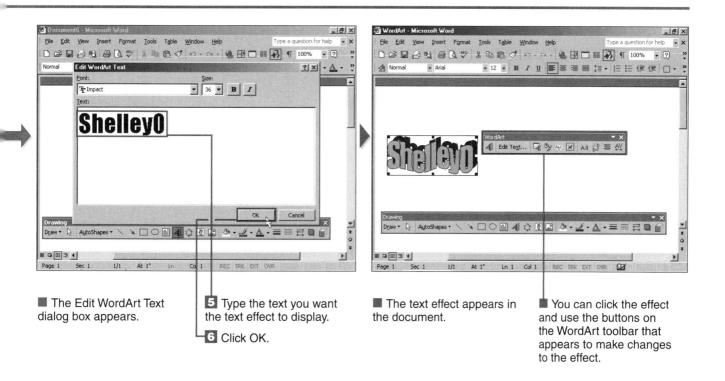

■ The Edit WordArt Text dialog box appears.

5 Type the text you want the text effect to display.

6 Click OK.

■ The text effect appears in the document.

■ You can click the effect and use the buttons on the WordArt toolbar that appears to make changes to the effect.

INSERT A PICTURE

Word allows you to insert pictures that you store on your computer. You can, for example, insert a digital photograph or a scanned image as well as most types of graphic files.

You use either the From File command or the From Scanner or Camera command to insert pictures. When you select From File, Word displays the pictures in

the My Pictures file by default. You can switch to another drive or folder to find the picture you want to insert. You can also preview your files before you select the picture you want to insert.

When you select From Scanner or Camera, the program that runs these options helps you find and select the appropriate image. If you have both a scanner and a camera

installed, Office may ask which you want to use before letting the appropriate program step you through the rest of the process.

After you insert a picture, you can move and resize the image to suit your document. You can also delete a picture you no longer need. For information on moving, resizing, or deleting a graphic, see the section "Move or Resize a Graphic."

INSERT A PICTURE

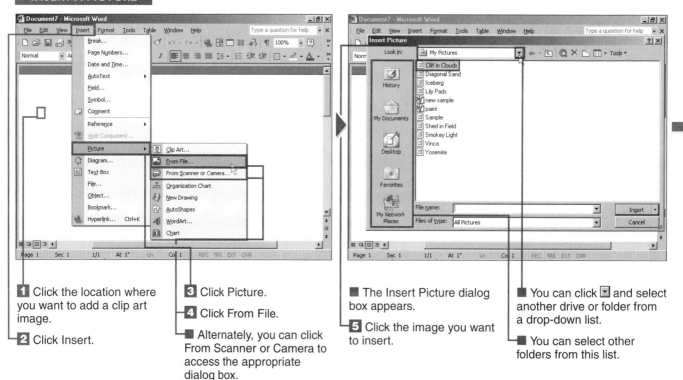

1 Click the location where you want to add a clip art image.

2 Click Insert.

3 Click Picture.

4 Click From File.

■ Alternately, you can click From Scanner or Camera to access the appropriate dialog box.

■ The Insert Picture dialog box appears.

5 Click the image you want to insert.

■ You can click ▼ and select another drive or folder from a drop-down list.

■ You can select other folders from this list.

How can I view other file types?

✔ By default, Word shows all picture file types in the Insert Picture dialog box. To limit the list to a particular file type, click the Files ▾ and click Files of type.

What happens if I choose to insert a picture from a camera?

✔ When you select the From Camera command, the camera software opens and displays a dialog box. From this dialog box, you can select the image to insert. For cameras, Word transfers the stored pictures from the camera and imports them into the document.

How do I insert a scanned image?

✔ When you select the From Scanner, the TWAIN driver — the driver that controls and recognizes your scanner — starts the appropriate scanner software. You can operate the scanner using the software to scan the image. After you scan the image, Word adds it to your document.

■ You can preview an image by clicking ▾ next to the Views button (▥) and selecting Preview.

6 Click Insert.

■ Word inserts the image into your document.

ADD A DIAGRAM

Word allows you to insert simple diagrams into your document. You might, for example, include an organizational chart of your company. As another example, you can include flow charts of common tasks or procedures.

You can select from several pre-designed diagrams. You can then add or replace the sample text with text for your particular diagram contents.

When you insert a diagram, a diagram-specific toolbar appears on-screen. You can use the buttons in this toolbar to select different formatting options. For example, with an organization chart, you can select different layouts, or add other boxes for subordinates or assistants. For more information on organizational charts commonly included in presentations, see Chapter 21.

Word can display a diagram only in the Print Layout and Web Layout views. For more information on these views, see Chapter 6.

After you add a diagram, you can move and resize it to suit your document. You can also delete a diagram you no longer need. For information on moving, resizing, or deleting a graphic, see the section "Move or Resize a Graphic."

ADD A DIAGRAM

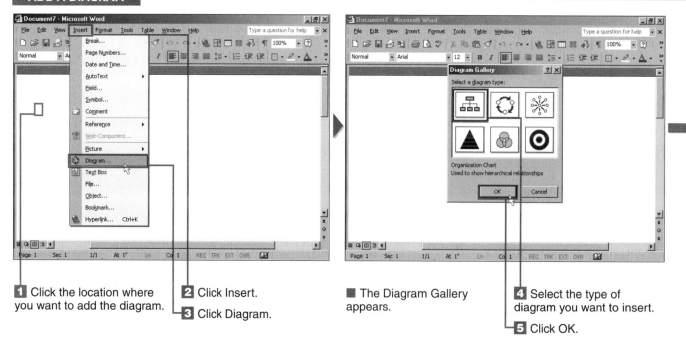

1 Click the location where you want to add the diagram.

2 Click Insert.

3 Click Diagram.

■ The Diagram Gallery appears.

4 Select the type of diagram you want to insert.

5 Click OK.

How can I view a description of the various diagrams?

✔ When you click a diagram in the Diagram Gallery, Word displays the name of the diagram and a short description in the Diagram Gallery dialog box. You can use this information to determine whether you want to insert a particular diagram.

What other types of charts can I insert?

✔ You can also insert charts such as graphs or pie charts, which you commonly use in PowerPoint presentations. See Chapter 21 for more information on creating charts.

How do I edit text in a diagram?

✔ To edit text you have included as part of the diagram, click within the diagram and within the particular text you want to change. You should see the flashing insertion point. You can then edit or make any formatting changes to the text.

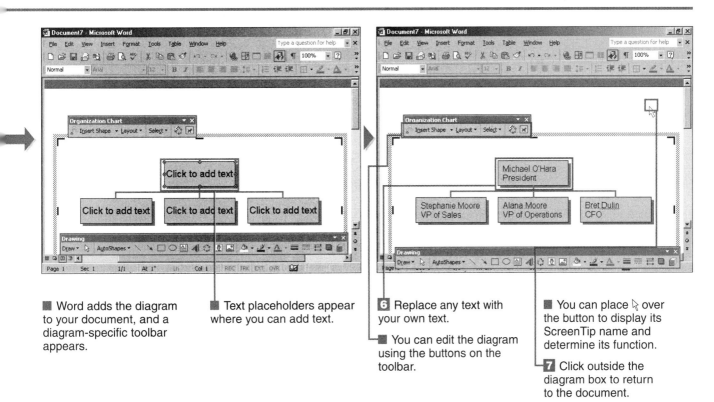

■ Word adds the diagram to your document, and a diagram-specific toolbar appears.

■ Text placeholders appear where you can add text.

6 Replace any text with your own text.

■ You can edit the diagram using the buttons on the toolbar.

■ You can place ⍾ over the button to display its ScreenTip name and determine its function.

7 Click outside the diagram box to return to the document.

■ The diagram is complete.

MOVE OR RESIZE A GRAPHIC

You can move or copy a graphic from one location in your document to another. When you move a graphic, the graphic disappears from its original location in your document. When you copy a graphic, the graphic appears in both the original and new locations.

You can change the size of a graphic to suit your document. The resizing handles that appear when you select a graphic allow you to change the height and width of the graphic. You use the top and bottom handles to change the height of the graphic, the side handles to change the width of the

graphic, and the corner handles to change the height and width of the graphic at the same time.

To make any of these changes, you select the graphic first. Note that when the graphic is selected, not only do the selection handles appear, but the Picture toolbar is also displayed automatically.

MOVE A GRAPHIC

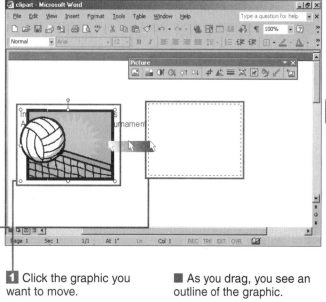

1 Click the graphic you want to move.

2 Drag the graphic to a new location.

■ As you drag, you see an outline of the graphic.

■ The graphic appears in the new location.

■ To copy a graphic, hold down the Ctrl key as you perform step 2.

What can I do if I have trouble moving a clip art image?

✔ Word treats inline images as characters. However, you can change your clip art image from an inline image to a floating image by clicking the image you want to change. Click Format and then Picture. Click the Layout tab and then an option other than In line with text in the Wrapping style area. For information on the Wrapping style options, see the section "Wrap Text Around a Graphic."

How do I align images in my document?

✔ You can align graphics by their left, right, top, or bottom edges. To display the Drawing toolbar, click the Drawing button ( ) on the Standard toolbar. Then press Shift as you click each graphic you want to align. On the Drawing toolbar, click Draw. Click Align or Distribute and then click the alignment you want to use.

How can I delete a graphic?

✔ Click the graphic and press the Delete key. Doing so removes the graphic and any elements within that graphic, including the text.

RESIZE A GRAPHIC

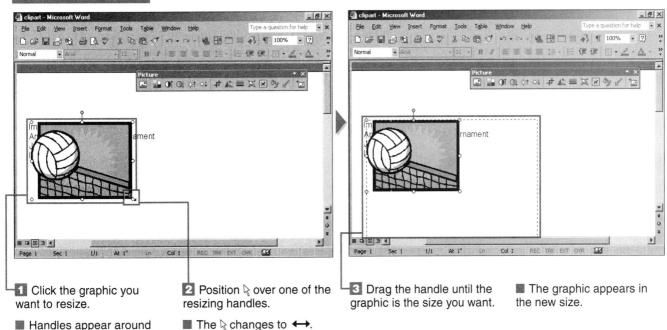

1 Click the graphic you want to resize.

■ Handles appear around the graphic.

2 Position ⌖ over one of the resizing handles.

■ The ⌖ changes to ↔.

3 Drag the handle until the graphic is the size you want.

■ The graphic appears in the new size.

WRAP TEXT AROUND A GRAPHIC

After you add a graphic to your document, you can wrap text around the graphic to enhance the appearance of the document.

Word offers several ways you can wrap text around a graphic. You can have Word wrap text to form a square around a graphic or fit

tightly around the edges of a graphic. Word also lets you place a graphic behind or in front of text. You can also choose the In line with text option to have Word position the graphic within the text of the document. Note that Word does not allow you to select the In line with text option with certain graphics, such as AutoShapes.

You can choose how you want to align a graphic with the text in your document. This lets you specify around which side(s) of the graphic you want the text to wrap. Word can align the graphic to the left, center, or right of the text. If you do not want Word to change the alignment of a graphic, you can choose the Other option.

WRAP TEXT AROUND A GRAPHIC

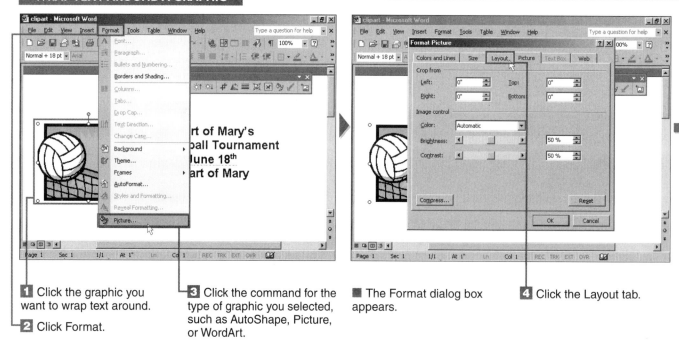

■1 Click the graphic you want to wrap text around.

■2 Click Format.

■3 Click the command for the type of graphic you selected, such as AutoShape, Picture, or WordArt.

■ The Format dialog box appears.

■4 Click the Layout tab.

Can I change the amount of space between text and a graphic?

✔ For some wrapping styles, you can specify the amount of space you want to display between text and the edge of a graphic. Click the graphic you want to change. Display the Format dialog box and then click the Layout tab. Click the Advanced button and choose the Text Wrapping tab. In the Distance from text area, enter the amount of space you want to display in each of the appropriate boxes.

Does Word offer additional wrapping styles?

✔ You can wrap text around a graphic using the Through or Top and bottom wrapping styles. To display the additional wrapping styles, click the Advanced button in the Format dialog box and then click the Text Wrapping tab. Select the option you want and then click OK.

How can I further format the graphic?

✔ The Format dialog box includes several other tabs with options for adding a border, setting a specific size, or formatting the picture. These options vary depending on the type of graphic with which you are working.

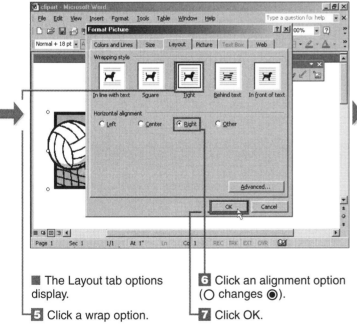

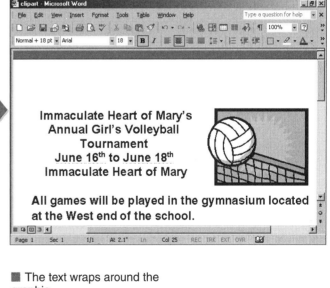

■ The Layout tab options display.

■ **5** Click a wrap option.

6 Click an alignment option (○ changes ◉).

7 Click OK.

■ The text wraps around the graphic.

AN INTRODUCTION TO MAIL MERGE

You can use the Mail Merge feature to quickly produce a personalized letter for each individual on your mailing list. Useful for when you often send the same document, such as a letter, an announcement, notification, or advertisement, to many people, a mail merge saves you from having to type information such as the name and address for a person on each letter.

You can also use the Mail Merge feature to print a mailing label for each person on your mailing list so that you do not have to type individual labels. You can then use these labels on envelopes or other mailing packages.

Whether you use the Mail Merge feature to produce personalized letters or print mailing labels, the Mail Merge Wizard guides you through the steps of performing a mail merge.

Create a Main Document

The first step in performing a mail merge is to create a main document. A *main document* is a letter you want to send to each person on your mailing list. Basically, you start with this main document so that Word makes the connection between this document and its type (form letters, labels, for example), and the data source.

Keep in mind that letters and mailing labels are not the only uses for a merge document. You can also mail merge other document types. For example, you can do a mail merge to create name badges for a convention or to create cards for your Rolodex. When you use the main document to create award certificates, you can print them on special paper that you specifically purchase for these purposes.

Even though this is the first step, you most often just select the document type, create or retrieve the data source, and then compose the letter. To learn how to create a main document, see the section "Create a Main Document."

Create and Save the Data Source

After you create a main document, you must create a data source. A *data source* contains the information that changes in each

letter, such as the name and address of each person on your mailing list. A data source consists of *fields*, which are specific categories of information. Each field has a name, such as Last Name or City. When you complete all the fields for a specific person, you create a record, which contains all the information for one person on your mailing list.

Make sure you plan ahead and determine the information you want your data source to include. Word contains some predefined fields. You can select from a set of pre-designed fields in an address list, or you can customize the address list, adding and deleting fields.

You need to create a data source only once. After your initial work, you can use the data source for future mail merges where you require the same list of names and addresses. To use a previously created data source, you must open the data source after creating the main document. You can also use data from another program. For information about sharing data among programs, see Chapter 34.

Complete the Main Document

After you set up the main document — basically just select the type of document — and type the appropriate data in the data source, you can complete the main document. To complete the main document, you type the text of the letter you want to send. You also insert special instructions into the main document. These instructions, called *mail merge field codes*, tell Word where to place the personalized information from the data source. For example, when you insert the mail merge field code for Last Name in the document, Word pulls the specific information from each record and inserts the last name in the document. Word aids you in this step by providing some pre-designed blocks of information including an address block and a greeting line.

In addition to the mail merge codes, you can type the text of the document, using any of the editing and formatting features of Word. For example, you can make text bold, change the font, use different page margins, and so on. Also, just because you include a mail merge code in the data source does not mean that you have to use it in the main document. You may use some merge fields from the data source more than once, and you may not use other merge fields at all.

Merge the Main Document and Data Source

After you complete the main document, you can combine, or *merge*, the main document and the data source to create a personalized letter for each person on your mailing list. Word replaces the mail merge codes in the main document with the personalized information from the data source.

CREATE A LETTER WITH MAIL MERGE

Y ou can use the Mail Merge feature to quickly produce a personalized letter for each individual on your mailing list.

To do so, you must start by creating a *main document*, which contains the text that remains the same in each letter you send to the people on your mailing list. You can create your main document from a new or existing document.

You can type your text for the document as you go, or you can simply set up the window for the main document, create the data source, and then go back and complete the main document. The latter method is more common because you can then insert the mail merge codes and type the text as needed.

Although Word offers different types of main documents including

form letters, mailing labels, catalogs, or envelopes, this section shows how to create a form letter. For information on mailing labels, see "Print Mailing Labels" later in this chapter. Envelopes are similar to mailing labels; again, you can get a general idea of the process from "Print an Envelope."

CREATE A LETTER WITH MAIL MERGE

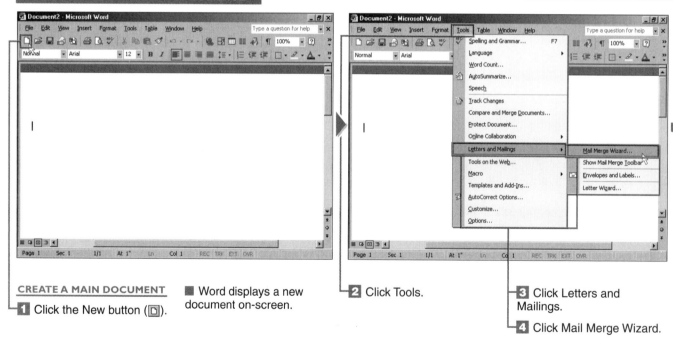

CREATE A MAIN DOCUMENT

◼ **1** Click the New button (◻).

◼ Word displays a new document on-screen.

◼ **2** Click Tools.

◼ **3** Click Letters and Mailings.

◼ **4** Click Mail Merge Wizard.

Can I have Word automatically insert the current date and time into a main document?

✔ Yes. Once you insert a date or time, Word automatically updates the information each time you open or print the document. Click where you want the date and time to appear. Click Insert, select Date and Time and then click the format you want to use. Click the Update automatically option (☐ changes to ☑) and then click OK.

How do I use the main document with a different data source?

✔ You can use the same main document with a different data source to create letters using the data in that data source. To do so, open the main document. Word automatically displays the Mail Merge task pane, listing the current associated data source. You can select a different list by clicking the Select a different list link, and then clicking the list you want to use.

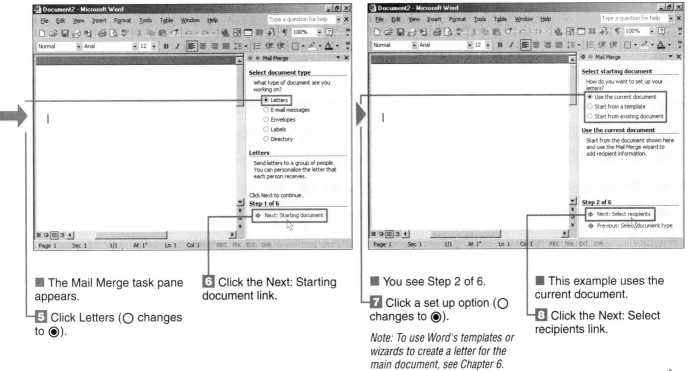

■ The Mail Merge task pane appears.

5 Click Letters (○ changes to ◉).

6 Click the Next: Starting document link.

■ You see Step 2 of 6.

7 Click a set up option (○ changes to ◉).

Note: To use Word's templates or wizards to create a letter for the main document, see Chapter 6.

■ This example uses the current document.

8 Click the Next: Select recipients link.

CONTINUED ▶

CREATE A LETTER WITH MAIL MERGE
(CONTINUED)

The next step in performing a Mail Merge is to create a *data source*, which contains the personalized information that changes in each letter, such as the name and address of each person on your mailing list.

A data source contains fields and records. A *field* is a specific category of information in a data source. For example, a field can contain the first names of all the people on your mailing list. A *record* is a collection of information about one person in a data source. For example, a record can contain the name, address, telephone number, and account information for one person. Make sure you take time to plan and properly set up the data source to determine the fields you need.

Word provides an address list with common field names for form letters. A *field name* is a name, such as Last Name or City, assigned to each field. If you do not want to include a particular field, simply skip that field in the Enter Address Information dialog box. You can also delete the field by customizing the address information.

CREATE A LETTER WITH MAIL MERGE (CONTINUED)

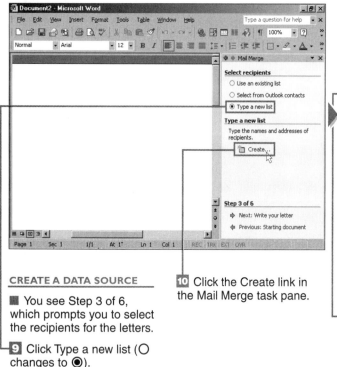

CREATE A DATA SOURCE

■ You see Step 3 of 6, which prompts you to select the recipients for the letters.

9 Click Type a new list (○ changes to ⦿).

10 Click the Create link in the Mail Merge task pane.

■ The New Address List dialog box appears.

11 Type the information for each field, pressing Tab to move from field to field.

Note: If a field is not appropriate, you can skip it. You do not have to complete each field, especially fields you do not plan to use in your letter.

How can I change which fields Word includes?

✔ You can customize fields by clicking Customize in the New Address List dialog box, which displays the Customize Address List dialog box.

To delete a field, select the field, click the Delete button, and then confirm the deletion by clicking Yes. To rename a field, click the field, click the Rename button, type a new name, and press Enter. To add a field, click the Add button, type a field name, and click OK. When you finish customizing, click OK.

Can I use other sources of data?

✔ Yes. You can use contacts from Outlook or from another database, such as Access. For more information on sharing data among programs, see Chapter 34.

How do I use an existing list?

✔ To use an existing list, click the Use an existing list option from the Step 3 of 6 Mail Merge task pane in the wizard. You see the Select Data Source dialog box. Select the data source file you want to use and then click Open.

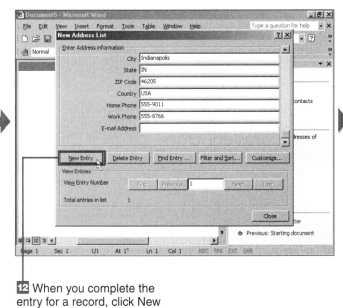

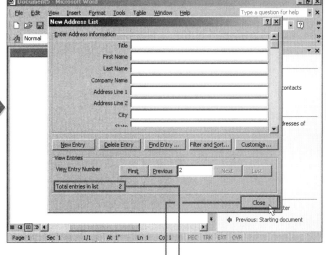

12 When you complete the entry for a record, click New Entry.

■ Word adds the record to the data source, and displays a new blank record.

13 Continue adding records until you add all the records you want to include in the address list.

■ You can see the number of entries in your list.

14 Click Close.

CONTINUED

CREATE A LETTER WITH MAIL MERGE
(CONTINUED)

After you add the records, you must save all your information as a file. By default, Word saves the data source as an Office Address List in the My Data Sources folder. With the wizard, you simply type the file name you want to use.

After you save the data source, you see the Mail Merge Recipients data list, where you can view the recipients. You can also select which recipients to include, sort recipients, search for a particular recipient, and make other selections.

The first row of the recipient list displays your chosen field names. Each of the following rows in the table contains the information for one person. Text that does not fit on one line in the table appears on one line when you print the letters.

You can use any data source you create in future mail merges. Before using a data source again, make sure the information is up-to-date. You can always open, edit, and save a data source as you would any document.

CREATE A LETTER WITH MAIL MERGE (CONTINUED)

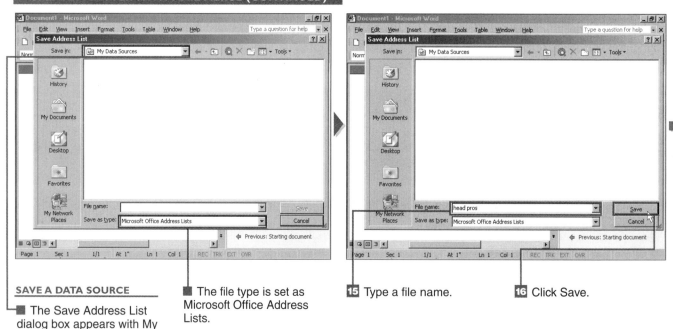

SAVE A DATA SOURCE

■ The Save Address List dialog box appears with My Data Sources folder.

■ The file type is set as Microsoft Office Address Lists.

15 Type a file name.

16 Click Save.

How can I redisplay the Mail Merge Recipient dialog box?

✔ Use the Previous links in the Mail Merge pane to return to the step for selecting the list. Then click the Edit recipient list link.

How do I browse through my entered the information?

✔ You can scroll through the list using the horizontal scroll arrows to see additional fields. If you have several records, the list also includes vertical scroll arrows. Use these to scroll through the list.

How do I edit a record?

✔ Select the record you want to change and then click Edit. You see the Enter Address Information dialog box. Make any changes and click Close.

Can I add a record to the recipient list?

✔ You cannot add a record directly to this list. You can add a record by clicking Edit and then clicking New Entry. Type the information and click Close.

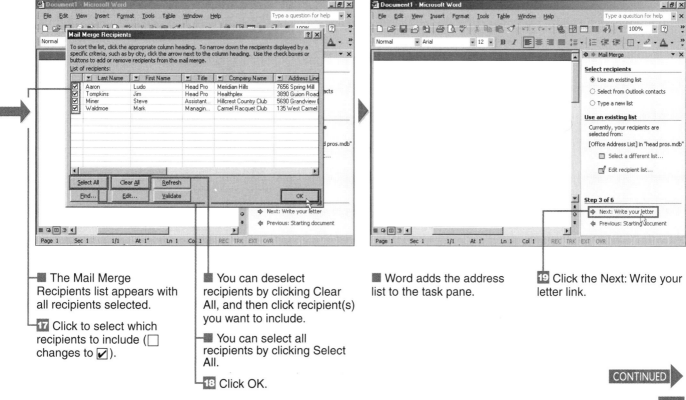

■ The Mail Merge Recipients list appears with all recipients selected.

17 Click to select which recipients to include (☐ changes to ☑).

■ You can deselect recipients by clicking Clear All, and then click recipient(s) you want to include.

■ You can select all recipients by clicking Select All.

18 Click OK.

■ Word adds the address list to the task pane.

19 Click the Next: Write your letter link.

CONTINUED

CREATE A LETTER WITH MAIL MERGE
(CONTINUED)

To complete the main document, you type the text you want to include in the letter. You must insert special instructions into the document to tell Word where to place the personalized information from the address list.

The instructions you insert into the main document are called merge fields. A *merge field* is a specific category of information in a data

source, such as First Name, City, or State. The available merge fields match the fields in the address list you completed for each person.

Word aids you in inserting this key information by allowing you to use links to insert common information such as an address block and a greeting.

You can also insert as many merge fields as you need in any other

location. The location of a merge field in the main document indicates where the corresponding information from the data source appears when you print the letters. In the main document, a merge field begins and ends with brackets.

After you complete the main document, you can merge the main document and the data source to create your letters.

CREATE A LETTER WITH MAIL MERGE (CONTINUED)

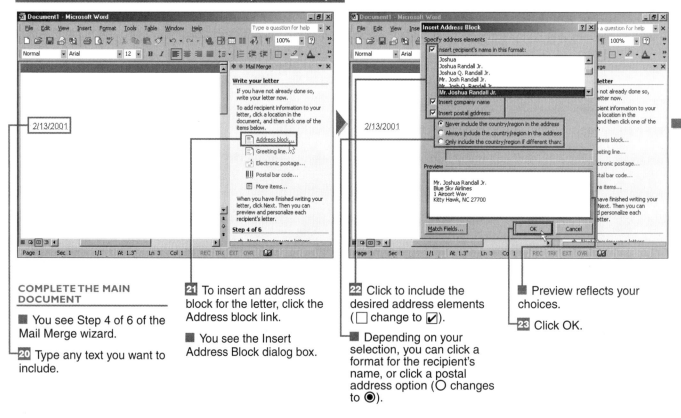

COMPLETE THE MAIN DOCUMENT

■ You see Step 4 of 6 of the Mail Merge wizard.

20 Type any text you want to include.

21 To insert an address block for the letter, click the Address block link.

■ You see the Insert Address Block dialog box.

22 Click to include the desired address elements (□ change to ☑).

■ Depending on your selection, you can click a format for the recipient's name, or click a postal address option (○ changes to ◉).

■ Preview reflects your choices.

23 Click OK.

How do I insert a single merge field?

✔ The links enable you to insert blocks of information in common formats. You may also want to include a merge field in the body of the letter. To do so, click the More items link. You see the Insert Merge Field dialog box. Click the field you want to insert and then click Insert. When you finish inserting fields, click Close.

Can I manually add a merge field by typing the name of the merge field in brackets?

✔ No. You must use the Insert Merge Field dialog box to insert the merge field into the letter.

How do I delete a merge field I have added by mistake?

✔ To delete a merge field, click the field to select it, and press the Delete key.

Can I format a merge field?

✔ You can format a merge field as you would format text in any document. When you merge the main document with the data source, the personalized information in each letter displays the formatting you apply to the merge field.

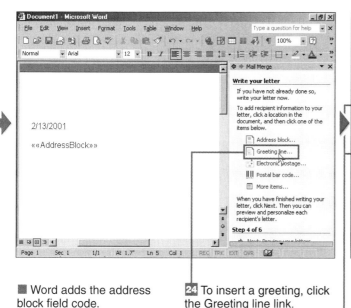

■ Word adds the address block field code.

24 To insert a greeting, click the Greeting line link.

■ The Greeting Line dialog box displays.

25 Click ▼ and select a greeting, name format, and a punctuation symbol.

■ The preview displays how the greeting line will appear.

26 Click OK.

27 Type the rest of the letter.

28 When the letter is complete, save it.

Note: See Chapter 3 for information on saving a Word document.

CONTINUED

CREATE A LETTER WITH MAIL MERGE
(CONTINUED)

After you complete the main document, you can preview how your letters will look when you merge the main document and the data source. Previewing lets you temporarily replace the merge fields in the main document with the information for a person on your mailing list.

You can preview the merged letters to make sure they look the way you want. This can help you find and correct any errors before you waste time and money printing the letters for every person on your mailing list.

After you preview the letters to ensure there are no errors, you can combine the main document and the data source to create a personalized letter for each person on your mailing list.

To conserve hard drive space, do not save the merged document. You can easily re-create the merged document at any time by merging the main document and the data source again.

You can print the personalized letters in the merged document as you would print any Word document. For more information on printing a document, see Chapter 2.

CREATE A LETTER WITH MAIL MERGE (CONTINUED)

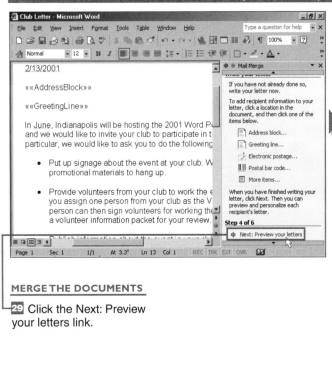

MERGE THE DOCUMENTS

29 Click the Next: Preview your letters link.

■ The main document displays the information for the first record from the data source.

■ To preview the information for other records, you can click the Next or Previous buttons (>> or <<).

30 When you finish previewing the information, click the Next: Complete the merge link.

When previewing merged documents, how can I quickly display the information for a record of interest?

✔ You can scroll through the recipient list using the scroll buttons in the Mail Merge task pane. If you have many recipients, you can search for an individual recipient by clicking the Find a recipient link. Type an entry to find, select to look in all fields or a particular field by clicking the appropriate option, and then click Find Next. Click Cancel to close the Find Entry dialog box.

Can I go back in the merge process to change something?

✔ Yes. You can use the Previous link in the Mail Merge task pane to go back a step. You can go back and make any changes to any of the previous steps.

Do I have to include all the recipients?

✔ No. You can exclude a particular recipient by clicking the Exclude Recipient link when previewing letters. You can also select to print a letter for just the current record or for a range of records when you merge to the printer.

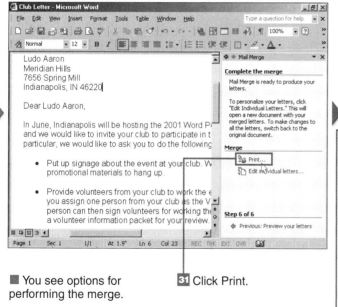

■ You see options for performing the merge.

31 Click Print.

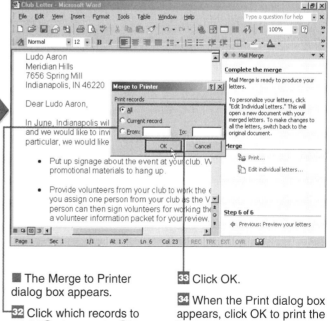

■ The Merge to Printer dialog box appears.

32 Click which records to print (○ changes to ◉).

33 Click OK.

34 When the Print dialog box appears, click OK to print the letters.

■ Word prints the letters.

PRINT MAILING LABELS

You can use the Mail Merge feature to print a label for every person on your mailing list. You can use labels for addressing envelopes and packages, labeling file folders, and creating name tags.

You merge the information from an existing data source to print labels. A data source contains the

personalized information that changes on each label, such as the name and address of each person on your mailing list. Make sure to update the information in the data source. Most often you use the data source that you used to create the letters, but you can create a new data source. To create a data source, see steps 9 through 16 of "Create a Letter with Mail Merge."

Word can print on many popular label products and label types. You can check your label packaging to determine which label product and type of label you are using.

Before you begin, make sure you consult your printer's manual to determine if the printer can print labels and which label products your printer supports.

PRINT MAILING LABELS

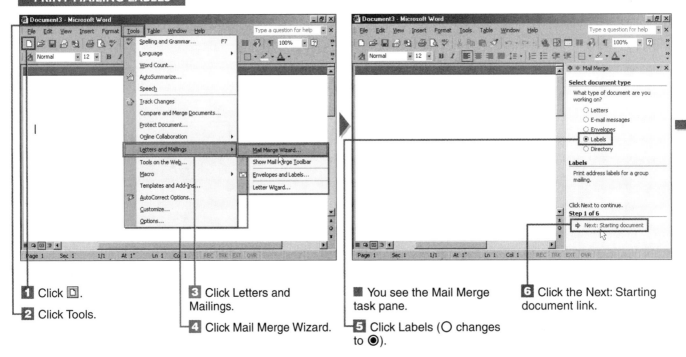

1 Click ⬜.

2 Click Tools.

3 Click Letters and Mailings.

4 Click Mail Merge Wizard.

■ You see the Mail Merge task pane.

5 Click Labels (○ changes to ◉).

6 Click the Next: Starting document link.

Should I specify the kind of printer I am using?

✔ You should specify the kind of printer you are using so that Word can display the appropriate label products and label types. In the Label Options dialog box, click either the Dot matrix or Laser and ink jet options (○ changes to ◉).

Can I create my own labels without using the Mail Merge feature?

✔ Yes. To do so, use the Envelopes and Labels command. Click Tools, Letters and Mailings, and then Envelopes and Labels. Click the Label tab. You can then select the type of label, type the label address, and print the labels.

Can I specify where I want Word to look for labels in my printer?

✔ If you are using a laser or ink jet printer, you can specify where you want Word to look for the labels. This is useful if you want to feed the labels into your printer manually or if your printer has more than one tray. In the Label Options dialog box, click the Tray area to specify where you want Word to look for the labels.

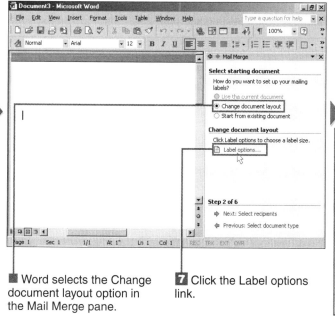

■ Word selects the Change document layout option in the Mail Merge pane.

7 Click the Label options link.

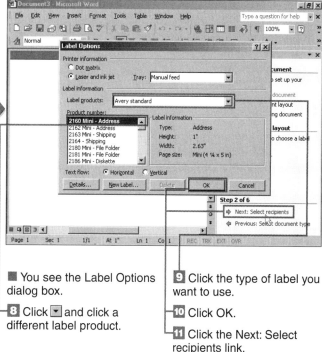

■ You see the Label Options dialog box.

8 Click ▼ and click a different label product.

9 Click the type of label you want to use.

10 Click OK.

11 Click the Next: Select recipients link.

CONTINUED ▶

PRINT MAILING LABELS (CONTINUED)

Most often you use an existing data source when you are creating mailing labels. You can also create a new one. For information on setting up a data source, see steps in the subsection "Create a Data Source" in the section "Create a Letter with Mail Merge."

When you select a data source, you see all of the persons in that address list. By default, Word selects all persons in the list. You can select or deselect which persons you want to include. The list conveniently provides buttons for selecting and clearing selections.

After you select the data source, you next set up the mailing label format. Word helps you set up a mailing label by providing a link for an Address block. This address block contains a predefined address and includes the common format of name, address, city, state, and zip code.

PRINT MAILING LABELS (CONTINUED)

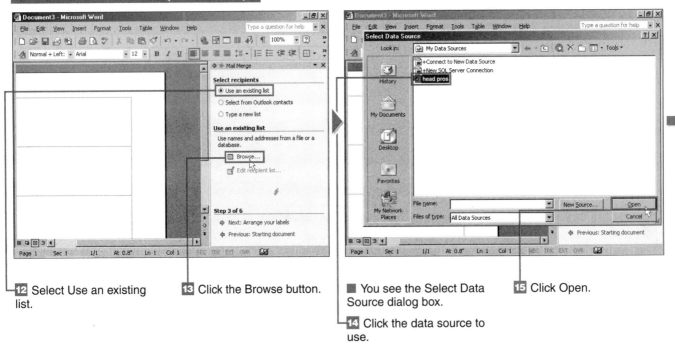

12 Select Use an existing list.

13 Click the Browse button.

■ You see the Select Data Source dialog box.

14 Click the data source to use.

15 Click Open.

Can I edit information in the list?

✔ Yes. To do so, click the Edit recipient list link in the Mail Merge task pane. You can then edit any of the existing records to update the information. Select the record to update and click Edit.

Can I add entries to the Address list?

✔ Yes. To do so, click the Edit recipient list link in the Mail Merge task pane. Then click Edit. The Address Information dialog box appears. Click New Entry and type the information for the new recipient.

Can I search for a particular record?

✔ Yes. In the Mail Merge Recipient dialog box, click Find. Then type what text to find and which fields you want to search. You can look in all fields or select a specific field. Click Find Next until you find the record you want. Click Cancel to close the Find Entry dialog box.

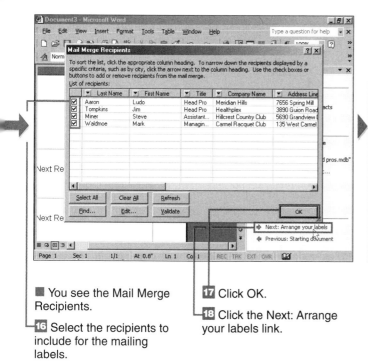

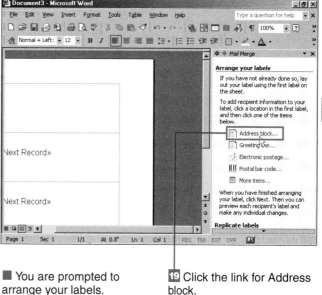

■ You see the Mail Merge Recipients.

16 Select the recipients to include for the mailing labels.

17 Click OK.

18 Click the Next: Arrange your labels link.

■ You are prompted to arrange your labels.

19 Click the link for Address block.

CONTINUED ▶

PRINT MAILING LABELS (CONTINUED)

You can select a format for the name in the address block. You can also select which items to include in the address. For example, you can select whether to include the company name or the country and region.

When you set up the Address block, you do so for one label. You can then copy your setup for all the labels in the document.

Note that your document may look different than the labels that appear in this section. The number of columns and size of the labels depend on your selections when you set up the label options.

When you complete the merge and print, you can select which records to print. By default, Word prints all records, but you can select the current record or a range of records.

Before you merge, save the label document. Doing so allows you to use this document for other address lists. Due to its large size, you do not need to save the label document after you merge. You can always merge the main document with the data source at any time.

PRINT MAILING LABELS (CONTINUED)

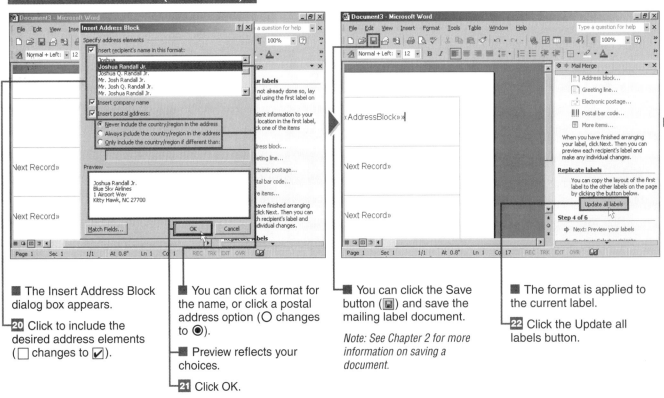

■ The Insert Address Block dialog box appears.

20 Click to include the desired address elements (□ changes to ☑).

■ You can click a format for the name, or click a postal address option (○ changes to ⊙).

■ Preview reflects your choices.

21 Click OK.

■ You can click the Save button (🖫) and save the mailing label document.

Note: See Chapter 2 for more information on saving a document.

■ The format is applied to the current label.

22 Click the Update all labels button.

Why do the labels say Next Record?

✔ The Next Record code is a specific code to tell Word to pull information from the next record for that label. You do not need to worry about including this field code; Word includes it automatically.

How do I print the labels?

✔ Insert the sheets of labels into the printer. Check your printer documentation for proper label insertion. To print, click the Print link in the Mail Merge task pane and then in the Merge to Printer dialog box, select which records to print, and click OK. In the Print dialog box, click OK to print the labels.

What if the preview is not what I want?

✔ If the preview of the labels does not look correct, you can back up through the steps and make any appropriate changes. To do so, click the Previous step link and then make the change. As another alternative, you can click the Edit individual labels link after completing the merge. You can then directly check and edit the merged labels.

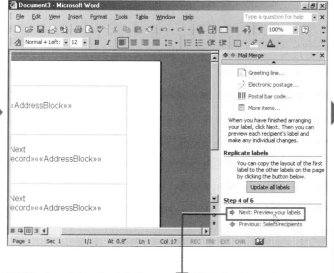

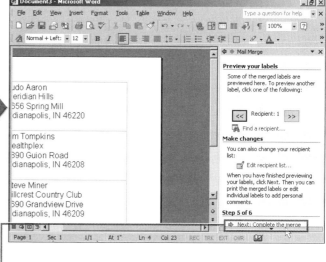

■ Word updates the labels to include the address block information.

23 Click the Next: Preview your labels link.

■ You see a preview of the current labels.

24 Click the Next: Complete the merge link.

■ You can now either edit the individual labels or print by clicking the appropriate link.

Note: For more on printing a document, see Chapter 2.

PRINT AN ENVELOPE

Y ou can use Word to print an address on an envelope. Printing an address directly on an envelope saves you from creating and attaching a label, or using a typewriter to address the envelope.

Before you begin, make sure your printer allows you to print envelopes. You can consult the

manual that came with your printer to determine your printer's capabilities.

Word scans your document to find a delivery address for the envelope. You can use the address Word finds or enter another address.

You can specify a return address for the envelope, or, if you do not want a return address, you can omit it.

You generally omit the return address if your company uses custom envelopes that already display a return address. When you specify a return address, Word allows you to save it, and uses it as the return address every time you print an envelope. This saves you from having to type the same return address repeatedly.

PRINT AN ENVELOPE

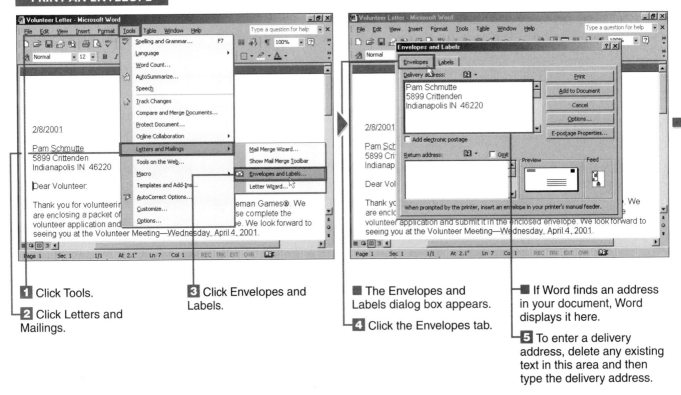

1 Click Tools.

2 Click Letters and Mailings.

3 Click Envelopes and Labels.

■ The Envelopes and Labels dialog box appears.

4 Click the Envelopes tab.

■ If Word finds an address in your document, Word displays it here.

5 To enter a delivery address, delete any existing text in this area and then type the delivery address.

How do I specify the size of the envelope I want to print?

✔ In the Envelopes and Labels dialog box, click Options. Click the Envelope size area and then click the envelope size you want to use. You can select from the most common envelope sizes. After you select the size, click OK.

Can I add E-postage?

✔ Yes, if you have the software installed to print and manage E-postage. In the Envelopes and Labels dialog box, click E-postage Properties. Complete the on-screen dialog boxes to add the E-postage to your envelope.

How do I change the font for my delivery or return address?

✔ In the Envelopes and Labels dialog box, click Options. Then click the Font button for the address you want to change. In the dialog box that appears, select the font options you want to apply and then click OK. Be sure you do not make changes that make the text too big to fit on the envelope.

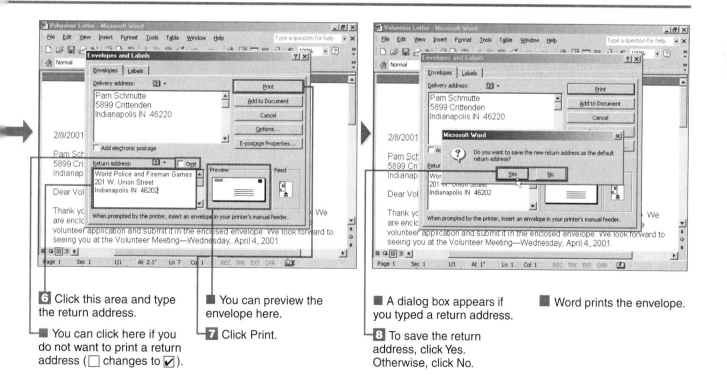

⬛ Click this area and type the return address.

⬛ You can click here if you do not want to print a return address (☐ changes to ☑).

⬛ You can preview the envelope here.

7 Click Print.

⬛ A dialog box appears if you typed a return address.

8 To save the return address, click Yes. Otherwise, click No.

⬛ Word prints the envelope.

10) GETTING STARTED

Introduction to Excel 174

Start Excel 176

Parts of the Excel Screen 177

Type Text 178

Type Numbers 179

Fill a Series 180

Enter Dates and Times 182

Using AutoComplete 183

Select a Range of Cells 184

11) EDIT WORKBOOKS

Edit or Delete Data 186

Move or Copy Data 188

Check Spelling 190

Find Data 192

Insert a Row or Column 194

Delete a Row or Column 196

Hide and Unhide Columns 198

Using Cell and Range Names 200

Protect Cells 202

Add and Delete Worksheets 204

Rename a Worksheet 206

Move or Copy a Worksheet 207

12) CREATE FORMULAS AND FUNCTIONS

An Introduction to Formulas
and Functions 208

Sum Numbers 210

Enter and Edit Formulas 212

Copy a Formula 214

Enter a Function 216

SECTION III

13) FORMAT WORKSHEETS

Change Column Width or Row Height 218
Bold, Italic, or Underline 220
Apply a Number Style to Cells 221
Format Numbers 222
Change Font and Font Size 224
Change Font or Fill Color 226
Apply Special Appearance Effects 228
Change Data Alignment 230
Add Borders 232
Copy Formatting 234
Clear Formatting 235
Apply an AutoFormat 236

14) PRINT WORKSHEETS

Preview a Worksheet 238
Print a Worksheet 240
Change Margins 242
Change Page Orientation 244
Change Print Options 245
Insert and View a Page Break 246
Fit a Worksheet to a Page or Pages 248
Repeat Row or Column Headings 249
Add a Header or Footer 250
Create a Custom Header or Footer 252

15) CREATE CHARTS

An Introduction to Charts 254
Create a Chart Using a Wizard 256
Change the Chart Type 260
Format Chart Elements 262
Move or Resize a Chart 264
Delete a Chart 265
Add Data to a Chart 266
Print a Chart 267

16) WORK WITH GRAPHICS

Add an AutoShape to a Worksheet 268
Add a Text Box 270
Add a Clip Art Image 272
Work with Graphics 274

17) MANAGE DATA IN A LIST

Using a Data List 276
Sort Data in a List 278
Filter Data in a List 280
Add Subtotals to a List 282

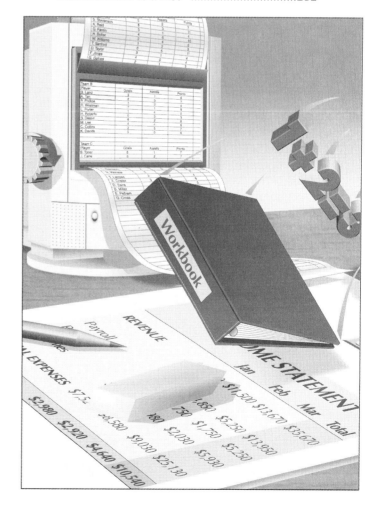

INTRODUCTION TO EXCEL

Excel is a spreadsheet program that you use to work with and manipulate numerical data. With Excel, you can perform calculations, analyze data, and present information. Excel can help you manage your business and personal finances.

A *workbook*, the name for an Excel file, contains a collection of *worksheets* that store and keep related data together. The worksheet itself is a grid of columns and rows, and you type data into a cell — the intersection of a column and row.

For more information on Excel, you can visit the following Web site: www.microsoft.com/excel.

Type and Edit Data

Excel has many automated features that let you efficiently type and edit data in a worksheet, saving you time and effort. For example, Excel automatically fills a series of numbers or text for you. Likewise, with the AutoComplete feature, Excel finishes data or text as you begin to type. For example, when you begin to type a day of the week, Excel can complete your entry automatically. After you enter data in a worksheet, you can add new data, delete data, or move data to a new location as well as check the text in a worksheet for spelling errors. Excel remembers the last changes you made to a worksheet, so you can undo changes you regret. For more information regarding typing and editing data in Excel, see the sections in this chapter and Chapter 11.

Formulas and Functions

Formulas and functions help you perform calculations and analyze data in a worksheet. In Excel, a *formula* is a simple equation that contains mathematical operations and references cells within your worksheet or in another worksheet. For example, you might build a multiplication

formula to calculate the sales tax on a sales amount. *Functions* are ready-to-use, built-in formulas that let you perform specialized calculations on your data. The most common function is AutoSum, which you can use to sum a range of numbers.

After you create a formula, or insert a function, you can copy them to other cells in a worksheet. Excel automatically changes the cell references in the new formulas or functions for you. If you change a number you use in a formula or function, Excel automatically recalculates and displays the new result. See Chapter 12 for more on formulas and functions.

Formatting Worksheets

Excel includes many formatting features that can help you change the appearance of a worksheet. For example, you can change the width of columns and the height of rows to better fit the data in a worksheet or add borders or color to cells.

Excel's formatting features can also help you add emphasis to important data in a worksheet. For example, you can use bold, italic, and underline styles to call attention to key data. You can also make data in a worksheet easier to read by changing the font and size, or by changing the appearance of numbers using formats such as currency or percent. See Chapter 13 for more on formatting worksheets.

Printing

Excel has several features to help you preview and print a worksheet to your specifications. You can add a header or footer to print additional information, such as your name or the date, at the top or bottom of each page. You can also specify how you want your data to print on a page, adjust the margins for the worksheet, or change the size of the printed data so it fits on a specific number of pages. See Chapter 14 for more on printing in Excel.

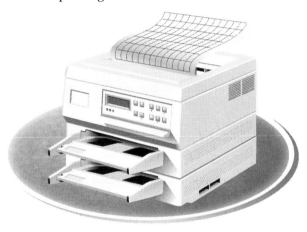

Charts

Excel helps you create colorful charts to help better illustrate the data in a worksheet. For example, a chart may show sales over time so that your audience can visually see the trend of the sales pattern. You can choose from many chart types, such as Bar, Line, Area, and Pie charts. If you change the data in the worksheet, Excel automatically updates the chart to display the changes. You can then move and resize a chart on a worksheet to suit your needs.

Graphics

Excel includes many graphics, such as text boxes, text effects, and AutoShapes, which you can use to illustrate and call attention to information in worksheets and charts. AutoShapes include simple shapes, such as ovals and rectangles, and more complex shapes, such as stars and arrows. You might use a graphic, such as an arrow, to point out an important part of the worksheet.

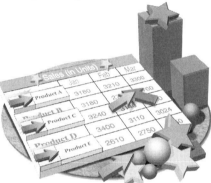

Managing Data in a List

Excel provides powerful tools that allow you to manage and analyze a large collection of data, such as a mailing or product list. After you organize data into a list, you can sort the data in different orders or filter the data to display only the data that meets certain criteria. You can also add subtotals to the list to help summarize the data.

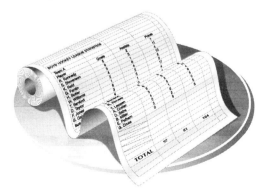

START EXCEL

Excel is a spreadsheet program that helps you organize, analyze, and attractively present data, most often numerical data. You can use Excel to present data such as sales projections, budgets, profit and loss statements, and expenses.

When you start Excel, a blank worksheet appears on your screen. A *worksheet* is a grid of rows and columns, and the intersection of a row and column is a *cell*. Cells store the data, such as text and numbers, which you enter into a worksheet.

After you enter your data, you can change the appearance of the worksheet, perform calculations on the data, and produce a paper copy of the worksheet.

When you first start Excel, you may see the task pane. You can use this task pane to perform common tasks. For more information on working with the task pane, see Chapter 2.

START EXCEL

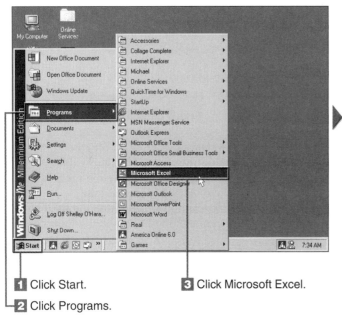

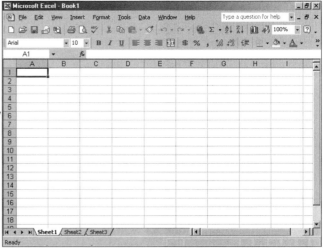

1 Click Start.

2 Click Programs.

3 Click Microsoft Excel.

■ The Microsoft Excel window appears, displaying a blank worksheet.

PARTS OF THE EXCEL SCREEN

The Excel screen displays several items to help you perform tasks efficiently.

Although most of these items appear by default, you can turn some of them, such as the toolbars, on and off. You can also customize certain screen elements so that they appear differently.

Your screen may look different depending on your monitor settings and how you set up your system.

Title Bar

Displays the name of the program and the workbook. If you open a new, unsaved workbook, you see Book 1.

Standard Toolbar

Contains buttons to help you select common commands, such as Save and Print.

Menu Bar

Provides access to lists of commands available in Excel.

Formatting Toolbar

Contains buttons to help you select formatting commands, such as Font Size and Underline.

Name Box

Displays the cell reference for the active cell.

Active Cell

The cell into which you are currently typing data. It displays a thick border.

Cell

The area where a row and column intersect.

Formula Bar

Displays the contents of an active cell.

Row

A horizontal line of cells, which Excel identifies with numbers.

Column

A vertical line of cells, which Excel identifies with alpha characters.

Scroll Bars

Allow you to move through the worksheet.

Status Bar

Displays information about the task you are performing.

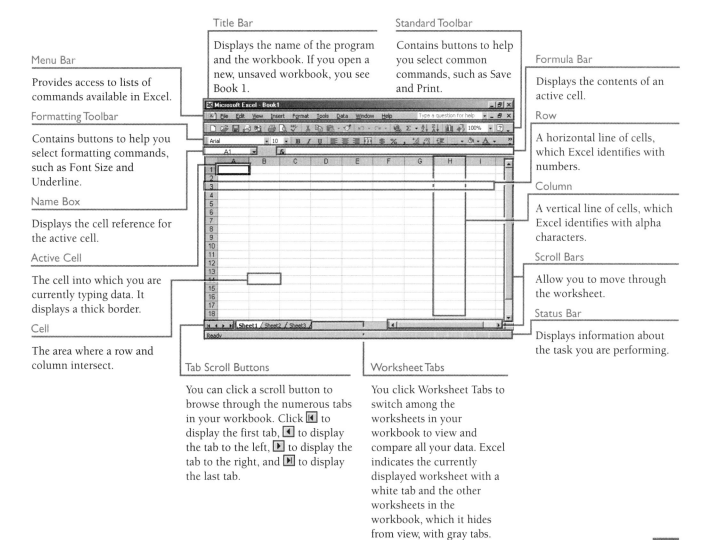

Tab Scroll Buttons

You can click a scroll button to browse through the numerous tabs in your workbook. Click ◄ to display the first tab, ◄ to display the tab to the left, ► to display the tab to the right, and ► to display the last tab.

Worksheet Tabs

You click Worksheet Tabs to switch among the worksheets in your workbook to view and compare all your data. Excel indicates the currently displayed worksheet with a white tab and the other worksheets in the workbook, which it hides from view, with gray tabs.

TYPE TEXT

You can type text into your worksheet quickly and easily. By default, Excel automatically left aligns text, which appears in the active cell and in the formula bar at the top of your worksheet. If you make a typing mistake, you simply press Backspace to remove the incorrect data and then retype the correct data.

Due to the size of a cell, Excel may not display all of the text

you type. If the cell next to the active cell does not contain data, the data spills over into that cell, although the entry is really contained only in the current active cell. If the cell next to the active cell contains data, Excel truncates the entry. To view all the text in a truncated cell, you can change the width of a column, as covered in Chapter 14.

How do I save my work?

✔ To save a workbook, click File, and then Save As. All worksheets in the workbook are saved. See Chapter 2 for more on saving documents.

TYPE TEXT

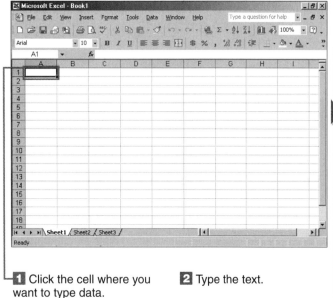

1 Click the cell where you want to type data.

2 Type the text.

■ The data you type appears in the active cell and the formula bar.

■ You can click the X (☒) to cancel the entry or the checkmark (☑) to enter the entry.

3 Press Enter to accept the data and move down one cell.

■ To enter the data and move one cell in any direction, press the up, down, right, or left arrow keys.

TYPE NUMBERS

You can type numbers into your worksheet quickly and easily. By default, Excel automatically right aligns numbers in cells in the active cell, and they appear in the formula bar at the top of your worksheet.

Excel displays large numbers either in scientific notation or as a series of ### signs. To see the whole number, you can widen the column. See

Chapter 14 for more information.

To enter numerical data, you can use the keys on the top row of the keyboard, or the numeric keypad, usually at the far right of the keyboard.

How does Excel differentiate between numbers like ZIP codes and actual values?

✔ Excel cannot tell the difference between numbers that function more as text, such as phone numbers, ZIP codes, and social security numbers, and actual values. To make a numeric entry as text, type an apostrophe (') before the number.

How do I enter numbers using the numeric keypad?

✔ To activate the numeric keypad, press the Num Lock key. A NUM in the status bar indicates that the keypad is active.

TYPE NUMBERS

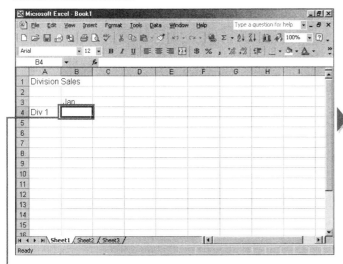

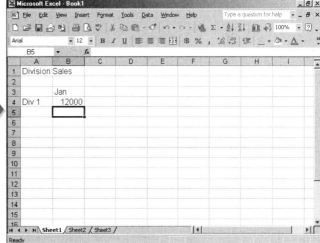

1 Click the cell where you want to type data.

2 Type the number.

■ For a negative number, type a minus sign (-) before the entry or type the entry in parentheses.

3 Press Enter.

■ Excel enters the number and moves the active cell down one row.

FILL A SERIES

Excel can save you time by completing a text or number series for you. A *series* is a sequence of data that changes, such as a range of consecutive numbers. You can complete a series in a row or column.

Excel completes a text series based on the text in the first cell. Excel

can complete a text series such as the days of the week or the months of the year, which you can use to create column labels. If Excel cannot determine the text series you want to complete, it copies the text in the first cell to the cells you select.

Excel completes a number series based on the numbers in the first

two cells. These numbers tell Excel what increment to use for the series. For example, you can create a series of even numbers by typing 2 in the first cell and 4 in the second cell.

FILL A SERIES

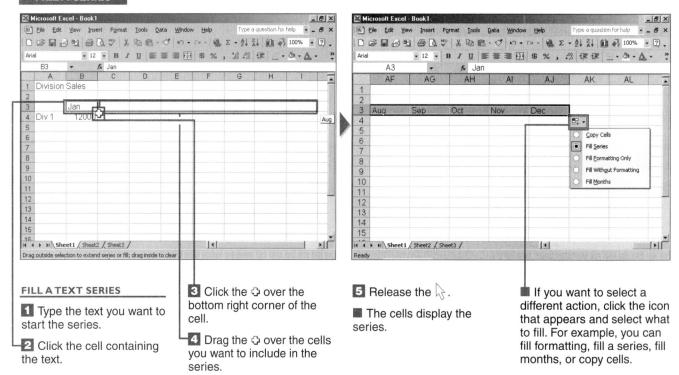

FILL A TEXT SERIES

1 Type the text you want to start the series.

2 Click the cell containing the text.

3 Click the ✛ over the bottom right corner of the cell.

4 Drag the ✛ over the cells you want to include in the series.

5 Release the ⬚.

■ The cells display the series.

■ If you want to select a different action, click the icon that appears and select what to fill. For example, you can fill formatting, fill a series, fill months, or copy cells.

How can I complete a series for the days of the week without including Saturday and Sunday?

✔ Click the cell containing the day of the week you want to start the series. Press the right mouse button as you drag the ⌖ over the cells you want to include in the series. Then select Fill Weekdays from the menu that appears.

When I try to fill a series, Excel fills it with the same entries. Why?

✔ If Excel cannot figure out the text series to fill, it simply copies the entry. Also, if you select only one numeric entry, Excel copies that entry. You have to select the first two entries so Excel knows the pattern to use in the series.

Can I create my own custom series?

✔ Yes. Select the cells containing the data you want to include in the series. Click Tools and then click Options. Click the Custom Lists tab and click Import. Then click OK.

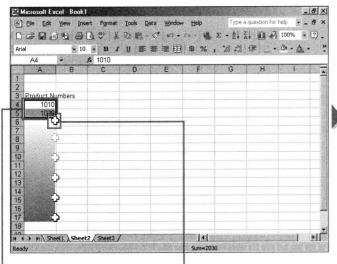

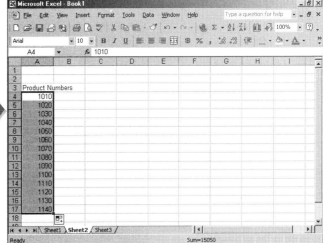

FILL A NUMBER SERIES

1 Type the first two numbers you want to start the series.

2 Select the cells containing the numbers you entered.

3 Position the ⌖ over the bottom right corner of the selected cells.

4 Drag the ⌖ over the cells you want to include in the series.

5 Release the ⌖.

■ The cells display the series.

ENTER DATES AND TIMES

As you create a worksheet, you may want to enter dates and times. As an example, you can use dates in invoices and other billing worksheets. You can use times for speed testing or time-stamping the completion of a task.

Excel uses the format for the date and time that matches how you entered the date and time. To format numeric entries differently, see Chapter 14.

Although the date and time look like regular dates and times, they are actually numeric entries. Excel stores dates as a serial number so that you can use the dates in calculations. For example, you can subtract one date from another to figure the days past due for an account. Likewise, because Excel stores times as a fractional value of 24 hours, you can use times in calculations.

How do I quickly enter today's date?
✔ Press Ctrl+ semicolon (;).

What formats can I use to type a date?
✔ You can type the following formats: 3/17, 3/17/01, 17-Mar, 17-Mar-01, Mar-01, or Mar-17.

What formats can I use to type a time?
✔ You can type 1:30, 1:30 PM, or 13:30.

ENTER DATES AND TIMES

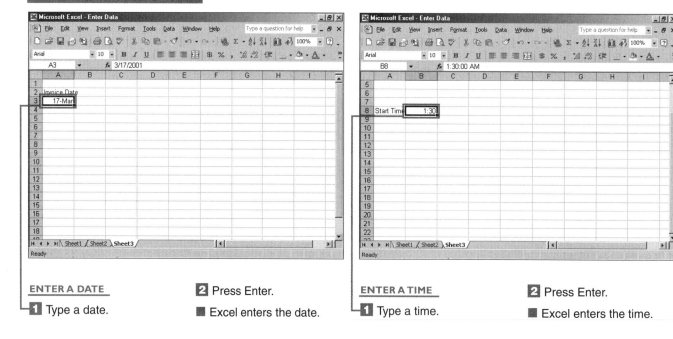

ENTER A DATE

1 Type a date.

2 Press Enter.

■ Excel enters the date.

ENTER A TIME

1 Type a time.

2 Press Enter.

■ Excel enters the time.

USING AUTOCOMPLETE

Excel compares the text you type to text in other cells in the column. If the first few letters you type match the text in another cell in the column, Excel can complete the text for you. This feature, called AutoComplete, can save you time when you

need to type the same text into many cells in a column.

Note that AutoComplete works only on text entries. It does not work on numeric, date, or time entries.

What if I do not want to use the AutoComplete entry?

✔ You do not have to enter the AutoComplete entry. To enter different text, you can continue typing.

Sometimes I type an entry and Excel changes it. Why does this happen?

✔ A related feature to AutoComplete is AutoCorrect, which automatically corrects common spelling errors. You can view the various changes this feature makes by opening the Tools menu and selecting AutoCorrect. For more information on spell checking, see Chapter 11.

USING AUTOCOMPLETE

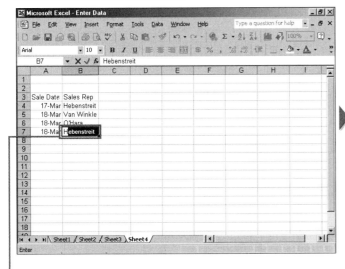

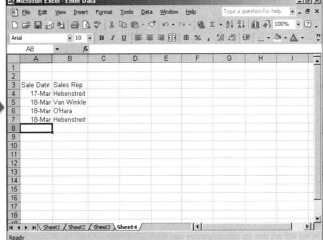

1 Start typing the entry.

■ Excel displays the matching entry.

2 To enter the text Excel provides, press Enter.

■ Excel adds the entry to that cell.

SELECT A RANGE OF CELLS

Before performing many tasks in Excel, you must select the cells with which you want to work. For example, if you want to change the appearance of entries by making them bold or changing the font, you must select the cells containing data you want to change. Likewise, if you want to copy a group of cells or move cells to another location, you start by selecting the cells you want to move.

Selected cells appear in reverse video on your screen. This makes the selected cells stand out from the rest of the cells in your worksheet.

Excel calls a group of cells a *range* and indicates them with a range reference. The range reference consists of the upper leftmost cell, followed by a colon, and then the lower rightmost cell. For example, the range A1:C4 contains A1, A2, A3, A4, B1, B2, B3, B4, C1, C2, C3, and C4.

Excel also lets you quickly select all the cells in a row or column.

SELECT A RANGE OF CELLS

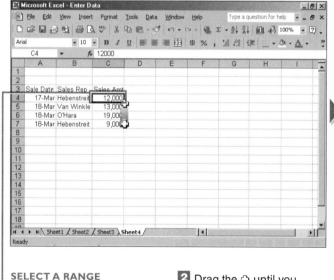

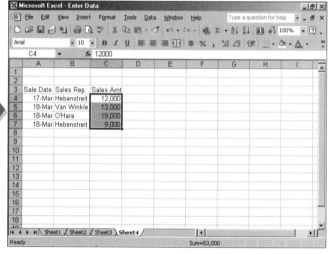

SELECT A RANGE

1 Click the ✛ over the first cell you want to select.

2 Drag the ✛ until you select all the cells you want.

■ The cells in that range are selected.

How do I select all the cells in my worksheet?

✔ To select all the cells in your worksheet, click the blank area to the left of the heading for column A and above the heading for row 1. You can also press Ctrl+A to select all the cells in your worksheet.

How can I select rows or columns that are not beside each other?

✔ To select rows or columns that are not beside each other in your worksheet, press the Ctrl key as you click the numbers of the rows or letters of the columns you want to select.

Can I quickly select a large group of cells?

✔ Yes. Click the first cell in the group you want to select and then scroll to the end of the group. Press the Shift key as you click the last cell in the group. Excel selects all the cells between the first and last cell you select.

How do I deselect a cell?

✔ After you finish working with selected cells, you can click any cell in the worksheet to deselect the cells.

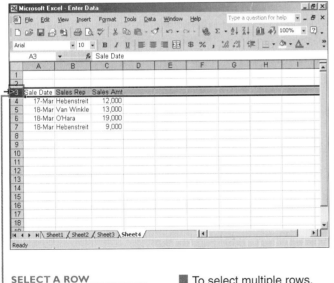

SELECT A ROW

1 Click the number of the row you want to select.

■ To select multiple rows, click the number of the first row and drag the ➜ until your select all the rows you want.

■ Excel selects the row.

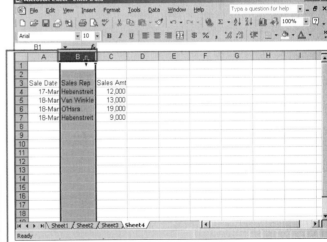

SELECT A COLUMN

1 Click the letter of the column you want to select.

■ To select multiple columns, click the letter of the first column and drag the ↓ until you select all the columns you want.

■ Excel selects the column.

EDIT OR DELETE DATA

Excel allows you to edit, correct mistakes, and update your data in your worksheet. The flashing insertion point in the cell indicates where Excel removes or adds data. You can move the insertion point to another location in the cell.

When you remove data using the Backspace key, Excel removes the characters to the left of the insertion point. When you remove data using the Delete key, Excel removes characters to the right of the insertion point. When you add data, Excel inserts the characters you type at the location of the insertion point.

You can delete data you no longer need from a single cell or a group of cells in your worksheet. This editing technique differs from deleting characters within a cell in that you delete the entire contents of the selected cell(s).

EDIT DATA

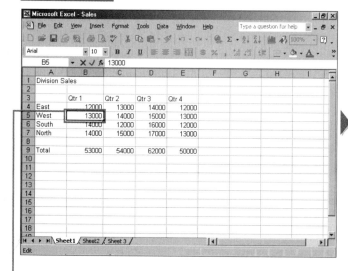

1 Double-click the cell you want to edit.

■ A flashing insertion point appears in the cell.

2 Press the left or right arrow key to move the insertion point.

3 Press Backspace to remove characters to the left of the insertion point, or press Delete to remove characters to the right of the insertion point.

4 Type the new data.

5 Press Enter.

■ Excel updates the entry.

I want to edit or enter data in a large worksheet. Can I display my worksheet headings?

✔ Yes. You can freeze the row and/or column headings so that they remain on-screen. Select a cell below and to the right of where you want to freeze. Click Window and then click Freeze Panes. To undo the freeze, click Window, Unfreeze Panes. Any rows above and any columns to the left of the active cell remain on-screen when you scroll through the worksheet.

What if I want to replace data in the cell?

✔ Click the cell containing the data you want to replace. Type the new data and press Enter.

Can I edit data using the formula bar?

✔ Yes. Click the cell containing the data you want to edit. The data in the cell appears in the formula bar. Click in the formula bar and then perform steps 2 through 5 to edit the data.

Can I undo a change?

✔ Yes. Click the Undo button or click Edit, and then Undo. If you change your mind before typing the change, press Esc to exit the cell without making the changes.

DELETE DATA

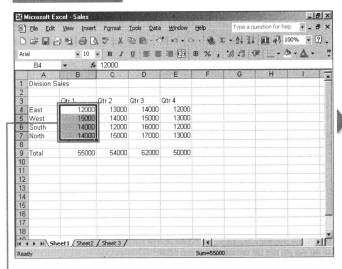

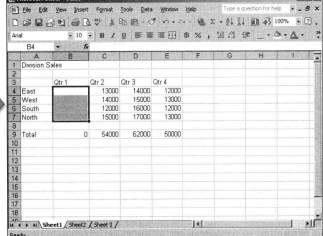

1 Select the cell(s) containing the data you want to delete.

Note: To learn how to select cells, see Chapter 10.

2 Press Delete.

■ The data in the cell(s) you selected disappears.

■ Excel updates any formulas that reference the deleted cells.

MOVE OR COPY DATA

Y ou can reorganize your worksheet by moving data from one location to another. Moving data can help you find the most effective structure for a worksheet. When you move data, the data disappears from its original location in your worksheet.

You can place a copy of data in a different location in your worksheet. This saves you time

because you do not have to retype the data. When you copy data, the data appears in both the original and new location.

To move or copy data, you first cut or copy the selected cells and then paste them. To do so, you use the Cut, Copy, and Paste buttons on the Standard toolbar. When you select a cell to which you want to move or copy your data, the new

cell becomes the top left cell of the new block of data.

If the cells you move or copy contain a formula, Excel may change the cell references in the formula so that the formula still uses the correct cells. For more information on formulas, see Chapter 12.

MOVE DATA

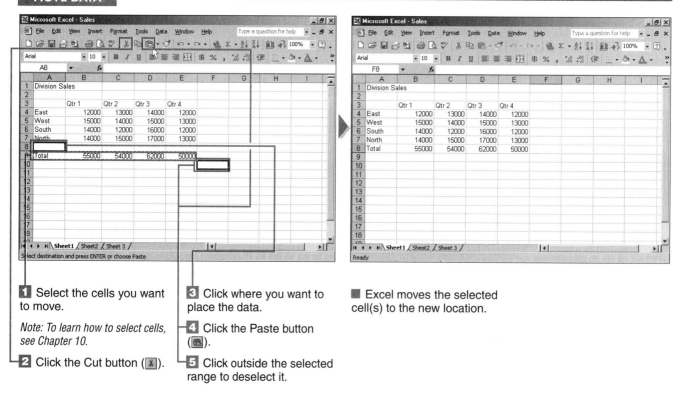

1 Select the cells you want to move.

Note: To learn how to select cells, see Chapter 10.

2 Click the Cut button (✂).

3 Click where you want to place the data.

4 Click the Paste button (📋).

5 Click outside the selected range to deselect it.

■ Excel moves the selected cell(s) to the new location.

Why does Excel ask if I want to replace the contents of the destination cells?

✔ This message appears when you try to paste data to a location that already contains data. To replace the existing data with the selected data, click OK. To cancel the paste, click Cancel.

How can I move or copy data to a different worksheet?

✔ Perform steps 1 and 2 in this section. Click the tab of the worksheet where you want to place the data and then perform steps 3 and 4.

Why does the Clipboard toolbar appear when I move or copy data using the toolbar buttons?

✔ The Clipboard toolbar may appear when you cut or copy two pieces of data in a row, copy the same data twice, or place copied data in a new location and then immediately copy other data.

New with this version of Excel, you also see a Clipboard Smart Tag (📋▾) when you cut or copy. You can click the ▾ next to this button to select what you paste. To learn more about the Office Clipboard, see Chapter 34.

COPY DATA

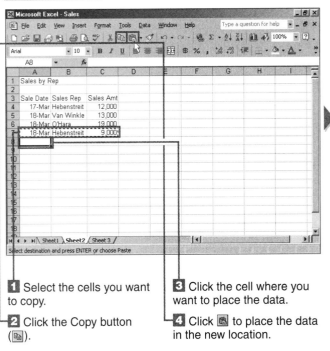

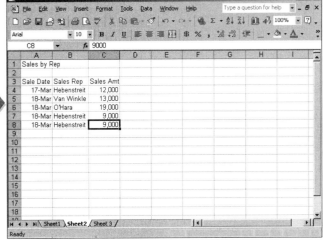

1 Select the cells you want to copy.

2 Click the Copy button (📋).

3 Click the cell where you want to place the data.

4 Click 📋 to place the data in the new location.

■ Excel copies the selected cell(s).

CHECK SPELLING

Y ou can quickly find and correct spelling errors in your worksheet.

Excel allows you to check the spelling of words in an entire worksheet or only specific cells. When you check the spelling of an entire worksheet, Excel also automatically checks any charts in the worksheet for spelling errors. To check the spelling of only specific cells, you must select the cells before you begin.

Excel checks every word in your worksheet and considers every word not in its dictionary as misspelled. For example, Excel may flag company names or certain terminology, which you know are not misspelled, but which do not exist in the dictionary.

When Excel flags a word, it selects that cell in the worksheet and lists the flagged word in the dialog box. Excel provides a list of suggestions for correcting any spelling errors.

You can replace with a suggestion, or you can ignore the error and continue checking your worksheet.

Excel automatically corrects common spelling errors as you type. For example, Excel automatically replaces "frmo" with "from" and "omre" with "more."

CHECK SPELLING

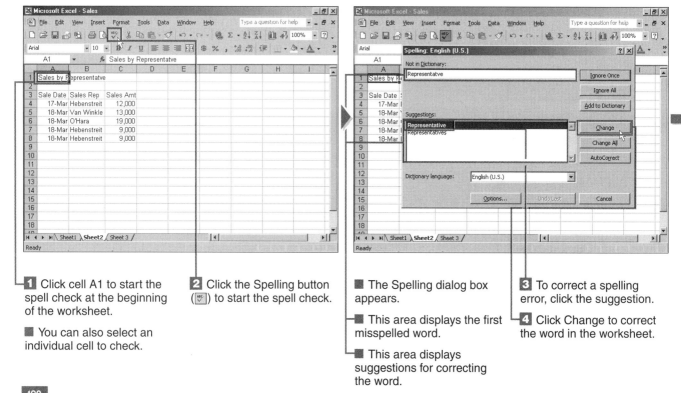

1 Click cell A1 to start the spell check at the beginning of the worksheet.

■ You can also select an individual cell to check.

2 Click the Spelling button (✓) to start the spell check.

■ The Spelling dialog box appears.

■ This area displays the first misspelled word.

■ This area displays suggestions for correcting the word.

3 To correct a spelling error, click the suggestion.

4 Click Change to correct the word in the worksheet.

Can I add a word to Excel's dictionary?

✔ Because Excel's dictionary does not contain many names and technical terms, your technical or company document may contain "misspellings." You can add a word to the dictionary so that Excel recognizes it during future spell checks. When Excel displays the word in the Spelling dialog box, click the Add button to add the word to the dictionary.

Can I have Excel automatically correct a spelling error I often make?

✔ Yes. When Excel displays the misspelled word in the Spelling dialog box, select the correct spelling of the word. Then click the AutoCorrect button. The next time you make the same error, Excel automatically corrects the error.

How can I check the spelling of several worksheets at once?

✔ Press the Ctrl key as you click the tab of each worksheet you want to check. Then perform steps 1 through 6 in this section. To later ungroup the worksheets, hold down the Ctrl key as you click each worksheet tab again.

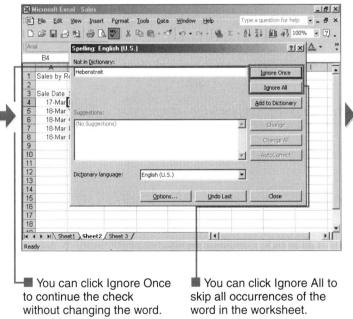

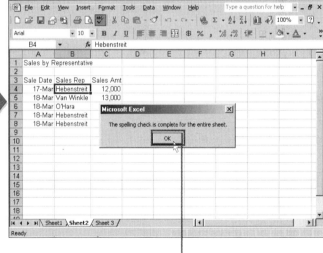

■ You can click Ignore Once to continue the check without changing the word.

■ You can click Ignore All to skip all occurrences of the word in the worksheet.

5 Continue to correct or ignore misspelled words.

■ A dialog box appears, telling you the spell check is complete.

6 Click OK to close the dialog box.

FIND DATA

You can use the Find feature to quickly locate a word, phrase, or number in your worksheet.

You can have Excel search your entire worksheet or only specific cells. To have Excel search only specific cells, you must select the cells before starting the search.

By default, Excel finds the data you specify even if it is part of a larger word or number. For example, searching for the number 105 locates cells that contain the numbers 105, 2105, and 1056.

After you start the search, Excel finds and selects the cell containing the first instance of the word or number, which may appear in

several locations in your worksheet. You can continue the search to find the next instance of the word or number or end the search at any time.

If Excel cannot find the word or number for which you are searching, a dialog box appears directing you to check the data you specified.

FIND DATA

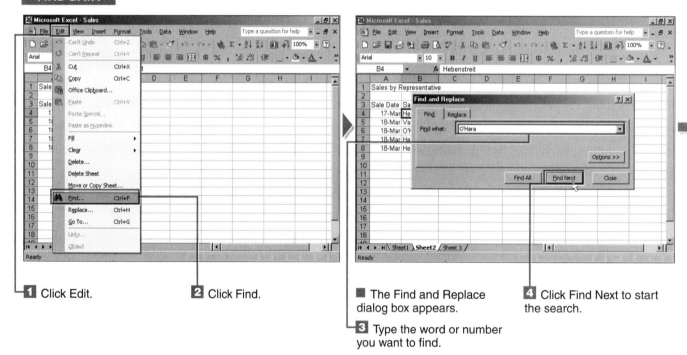

1 Click Edit.

2 Click Find.

■ The Find and Replace dialog box appears.

3 Type the word or number you want to find.

4 Click Find Next to start the search.

Can I have Excel find a word only when it is capitalized?

✔ You can have Excel find words with exactly matching uppercase and lowercase letters. In the Find dialog box, click Options and then click the Match case option (☐ changes to ☑).

Can I search for the exact contents of a cell?

✔ You can find cells that contain only an exact match for the data you specify. In the Find dialog box, first click Options. Then click the Find entire cells only option (☐ changes to ☑).

Can I search for an entry and replace it with another entry?

✔ Yes. Click Edit, then Replace. In the Replace tab of the Find and Replace dialog box, type both the entry to find and your replacement text or number. Click Find Next to start the search. To replace the word or number with the new data, click Replace. To replace all occurrences of the word or number in your worksheet with the new data, click Replace All. To ignore the word or number and continue with the search, click Find Next.

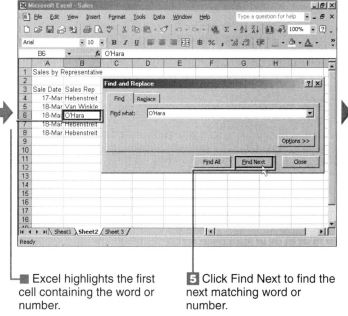

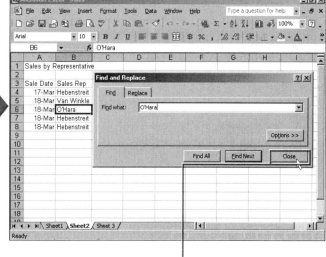

■ Excel highlights the first cell containing the word or number.

5 Click Find Next to find the next matching word or number.

Note: You do not see a message if the entire worksheet is searched; the dialog box remains open and continues to cycle through the worksheet if you click Find Next.

6 To close the Find dialog box at any time, click Close.

INSERT A ROW OR COLUMN

When you want to insert additional data into your worksheet, you can add a row or column.

When you insert a row, the selected row and the rows that follow shift downward. When you insert a column, the selected column and the columns that follow shift to the

right. Excel automatically adjusts the row numbers and column letters in your worksheet for you.

The row you insert is the same height as the row above it. The column you insert is the same width as the column to its left.

When you insert a row or column, Excel automatically updates any

formulas affected by the insertion. For information on formulas, see Chapter 12.

After Excel inserts the new row or column, you can type data into this row or column. See Chapter 10 for information on entering data.

INSERT A ROW

1 To select a row, click the row number.

2 Click Insert.

3 Click Rows.

■ The new row appears and all the rows that follow shift downward.

■ You can click the Format Painter button (🗹) to format your row.

How do I insert several rows or columns at once?

✔ Excel inserts as many rows or columns as you select. For example, to insert three columns, select three columns to the right of where you want the new columns to appear. Click ⬇ over the letter of the first column you want to select, then drag to highlight the three columns. Click Insert, and then Columns. Excel inserts three columns into your worksheet.

Can I insert a group of cells instead of an entire row or column?

✔ Yes. Select the cells where you want the new cells to appear. Click Insert and then click Cells. Then click an option to specify whether you want to shift the existing cells down or to the right (○ changes to ●).

Can I select the formatting for the new row or column?

✔ Yes. When you insert a row or column, a Format Painter Smart Tag (◁) appears next to the new row or column. Click the ⬇ and click to apply the formatting, or no formatting, to the appropriate column or row.

INSERT A COLUMN

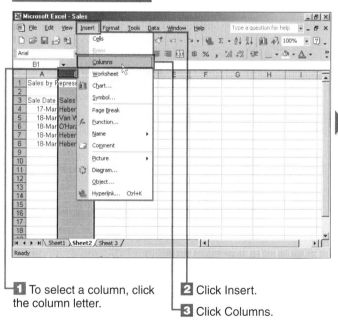

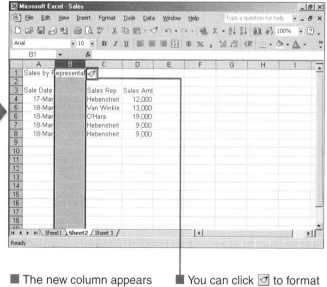

1 To select a column, click the column letter.

2 Click Insert.

3 Click Columns.

■ The new column appears and all the columns that follow shift to the right.

■ You can click ◁ to format your column.

DELETE A ROW OR COLUMN

You can delete a row or column from your worksheet to remove data you no longer need. When you delete a row or column, Excel deletes all the data in the row or column.

To delete a row or column, you must first select the row or column you want to delete. The numbers along the left side of your worksheet identify each row. The letters along the top of your worksheet identify each column.

When you delete a row, the remaining rows in your worksheet shift upward. When you delete a column, the remaining columns shift to the left. Excel automatically adjusts the row numbers and column letters in your worksheet for you.

If you do not want to delete a row or column, you can use the Undo command to immediately return the row or column to your worksheet. See "Edit or Delete Data" for information on using Undo.

DELETE A ROW

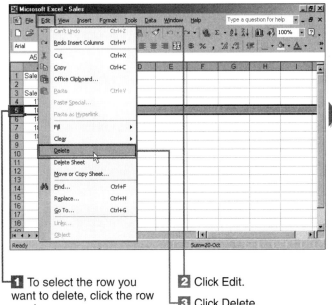

1 To select the row you want to delete, click the row number.

2 Click Edit.

3 Click Delete.

■ The row disappears and all the rows that follow shift upward.

How do I delete several rows or columns at once?

✔ Click the row number or column letter of the first row or column you want to delete. To select columns not adjacent to each other, press the Ctrl key as you click the row numbers or column letters of the other rows or columns you want to delete. To select columns that are contiguous, press the Shift key and click on the last column or row. Click Edit menu and then click Delete.

Can I delete a group of cells instead of an entire row or column?

✔ Yes. Select the cells you want to delete. Click Edit and then click Delete. Then click an option to specify how you want to shift the remaining cells (○ changes to ●).

Why does #REF! appear in a cell after I delete a row or column?

✔ If #REF! appears in a cell in your worksheet, you may have deleted data that Excel needs to calculate a formula. Before you delete a cell, make sure that it does not contain data that Excel uses in a formula. For information on formulas, see Chapter 12.

DELETE A COLUMN

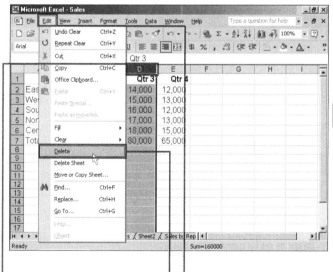

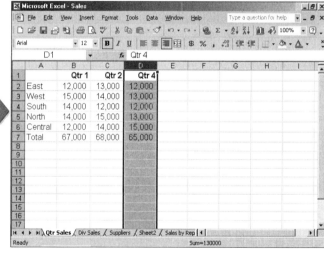

1 To select the column you want to delete, click the column letter.

2 Click Edit.

3 Click Delete.

■ The column disappears and all the columns that follow shift to the left.

HIDE AND UNHIDE COLUMNS

I f you do not want other people to view confidential data in your worksheet, or if you want to reduce the amount of displayed data on your screen, you can hide the columns containing the data. Hiding data helps you work with specific data and can make your worksheet easier to read.

Hiding columns does not affect the data in a worksheet but may affect

macros. Formulas and functions in the worksheet continue to work when you hide them. You can also use the data from cells in hidden columns when entering formulas and functions in your worksheet.

Hidden columns do not appear in the worksheet, as shown by the letter numbering of the columns, or when you print your worksheet. This allows you to produce a

printed copy of your worksheet without including confidential data.

You can redisplay hidden columns at any time to view the data in the columns.

HIDE COLUMNS

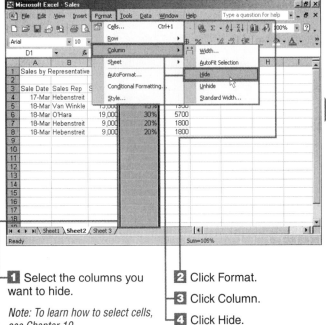

1 Select the columns you want to hide.

Note: To learn how to select cells, see Chapter 10.

2 Click Format.

3 Click Column.

4 Click Hide.

■ Excel hides the columns you selected.

Can I hide rows in a worksheet?

✔ Yes. Select the rows you want to hide. From the Format menu, select Row and then click Hide. To redisplay the rows, select the rows directly above and below the hidden rows. From the Format menu, select Row and then click Unhide.

If I hide column A, how do I redisplay the column?

✔ Choose the Edit menu and then select Go To. In the Reference area, type A1 and then press the Enter key. From the Format menu, select Column and then click Unhide.

Can I hide an entire worksheet in my workbook?

✔ Yes. From the Format menu, select Sheet and then click Hide. To redisplay the worksheet, select the Format menu, click Sheet, and then click Unhide. Click the name of the worksheet you want to redisplay and then click OK.

Does hiding data protect the worksheet?

✔ No. Keep in mind that someone could unhide the columns. If you want to protect the worksheet, you can assign a password which prevents others from changing your data and unhiding data. See the section "Protect Cells" for more information.

UNHIDE COLUMNS

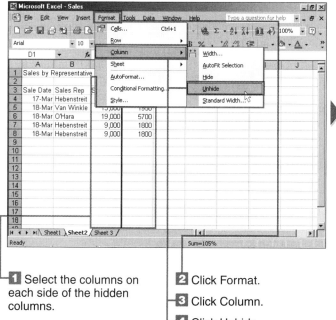

1 Select the columns on each side of the hidden columns.

Note: To learn how to select cells, see Chapter 10.

2 Click Format.

3 Click Column.

4 Click Unhide.

■ Excel displays the hidden columns.

USING CELL AND RANGE NAMES

You can assign a name to a cell or range of cells. Assigning a name to a section of data makes it easier to find the data, or to use that cell or range in a formula.

You can use up to 255 characters for a cell name. The name must begin with a letter or an underscore character (_). You can use any other character, including letters, numbers, and punctuation marks, in the name, but you cannot include spaces. You also cannot use a cell reference as a name. For example, you cannot name a cell D4.

After you assign a name, you can go to that cell or range using the Reference box.

You can also type the name in a formula. Doing so makes a formula much easier to understand. For example, you can create a formula such as =Income-Expenses, rather than =C4-D4 to track which section of data you use in a calculation.

USING CELL AND RANGE NAMES

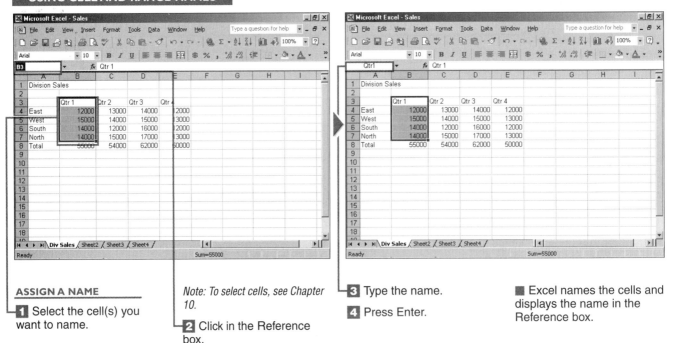

ASSIGN A NAME

1 Select the cell(s) you want to name.

Note: To select cells, see Chapter 10.

2 Click in the Reference box.

3 Type the name.

4 Press Enter.

■ Excel names the cells and displays the name in the Reference box.

Can I insert a cell name in a formula using menus?

✔ Yes. When you want to insert the name in a formula, click Insert, click Name and then click Paste from the submenu. You can then select the name you want from the dialog box and click OK.

How do I delete an assigned name?

✔ Click Insert and then click Name. From the submenu, click Define. Click the name to delete and then click Delete. Click OK.

Is there a quick way to assign names using my column and row labels?

✔ Yes. If you want to use the row and column headings as names, you can do so by clicking Insert, Name, and then Create. Click what to use as the names: top row, left column, bottom row, right column (☐ changes to ☑). You can click more than one option. Click OK to assign the name.

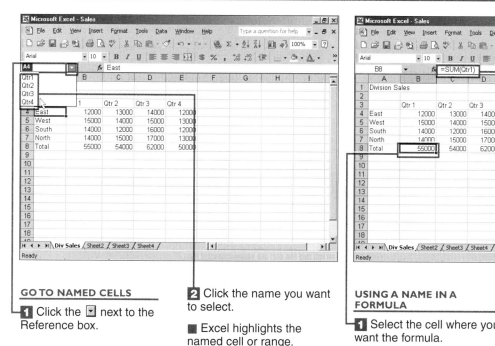

GO TO NAMED CELLS

■1 Click the ▼ next to the Reference box.

■2 Click the name you want to select.

■ Excel highlights the named cell or range.

USING A NAME IN A FORMULA

■1 Select the cell where you want the formula.

Note: To select cells, see Chapter 10.

■2 Type a formula with the named cell(s).

Note: To learn more about creating formulas, see Chapter 12.

■3 Press Enter to enter the formula.

PROTECT CELLS

You can protect cells in a worksheet to prevent others from changing them or accidentally changing them yourself. This can help you when you have complicated formulas and key data that you do not want others to change on a shared worksheet.

By default, Excel locks and protects all cells, but does not activate this feature until you turn on worksheet protection. To activate the feature,

you must unlock the cells to which you want others to have access and then turn on the protection feature to lock all other cells.

When you protect a worksheet, you can also specify what a user can and cannot do. You can allow them to or prevent them from selecting locked or unlocked cells, formatting cells, inserting or deleting columns and rows, and making other changes.

If a user tries to edit or make unauthorized changes to the worksheet, an error message appears.

To further protect your worksheet, you can also assign a password. When you do so, no one can unprotect the cells without typing the password.

PROTECT CELLS

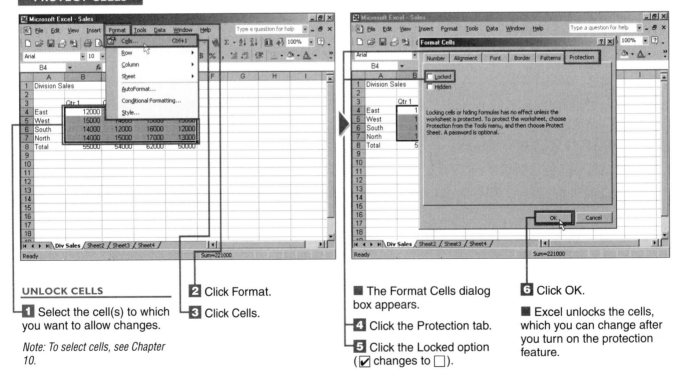

UNLOCK CELLS

■1 Select the cell(s) to which you want to allow changes.

Note: To select cells, see Chapter 10.

■2 Click Format.

■3 Click Cells.

■ The Format Cells dialog box appears.

■4 Click the Protection tab.

■5 Click the Locked option (☑ changes to ☐).

■6 Click OK.

■ Excel unlocks the cells, which you can change after you turn on the protection feature.

How do I turn off the protection feature?

✔ Click Tools, Protection, and then Unprotect Sheet. If you assigned a password, type the password and click OK.

Can I protect the structure of the entire workbook?

✔ Yes. You can protect the structure of the workbook from being changed and assign a password. To use these protection features, click Tools, Protection, Protect Workbook.

I protected my worksheet, but now I cannot make changes to any cells. What is wrong?

✔ By default, Excel locks all cells. Therefore, if you turned on protection, you or any other user cannot make changes to any of the cells. You must unlock the cells before you protect the worksheet. If you forgot to do so, turn off worksheet protection, unlock the cells, and then turn on worksheet protection.

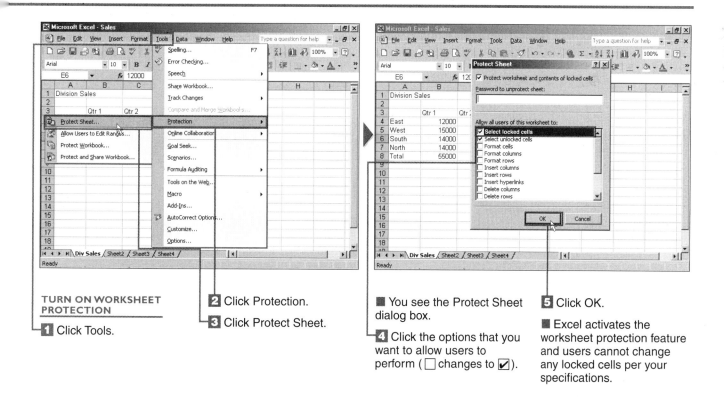

TURN ON WORKSHEET PROTECTION

1 Click Tools.

2 Click Protection.

3 Click Protect Sheet.

■ You see the Protect Sheet dialog box.

4 Click the options that you want to allow users to perform (☐ changes to ☑).

5 Click OK.

■ Excel activates the worksheet protection feature and users cannot change any locked cells per your specifications.

ADD AND DELETE WORKSHEETS

The worksheet you display on your screen is one of several worksheets in your workbook. You can insert a new worksheet to add related information to your workbook.

By default, workbooks contain three worksheets, but you can insert as many new worksheets as you need. Inserting a new worksheet can help you better

organize the information in your workbook. For example, you can store information for each division of a large company on a separate worksheet in one workbook.

To learn how to move among worksheets as well as the Parts of an Excel screen, see Chapter 10. To change the default name on the Worksheet tab, see the section "Rename a Worksheet."

When you no longer need a worksheet, you can delete the worksheet from your workbook. After you delete a worksheet, Excel permanently deletes the worksheet and all its data from your workbook. Be sure that you really want to delete the worksheet because you cannot restore your data after you delete it.

ADD A WORKSHEET

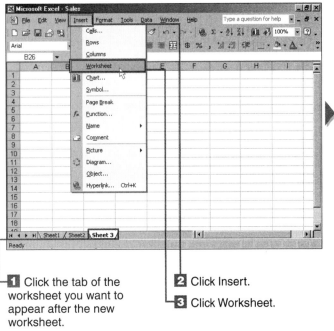

1 Click the tab of the worksheet you want to appear after the new worksheet.

2 Click Insert.

3 Click Worksheet.

■ Excel adds the new worksheet and displays a tab for it.

Can I change the order of the sheets?

✔ Yes. You can change the order of the worksheets with the workbook. To do so, see "Move or Copy a Worksheet."

I deleted a worksheet by mistake. Is there any way to get my data back?

✔ No. When you delete a worksheet, you also permanently delete the data. Be careful when deleting worksheets because you cannot undo this task.

Can I apply a color code to the worksheets?

✔ Yes. You might use color-coding to identify similar worksheets within a workbook. To apply a color code to a tab, right-click the worksheet tab and click Tab Color. Click the color you want to use from the palette of colors and then click OK. Excel applies the color.

To remove the color, follow the same steps, but click No Color from the palette of colors.

DELETE A WORKSHEET

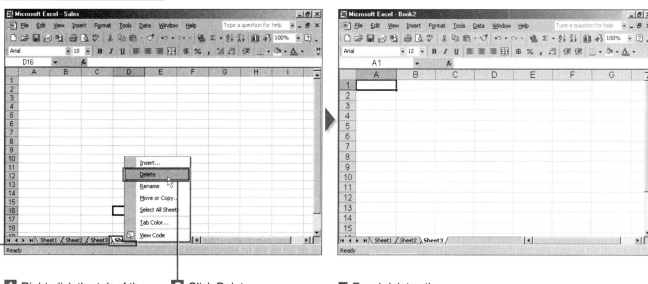

1 Right-click the tab of the worksheet you want to delete.

2 Click Delete.

■ Excel deletes the worksheet tab and all the data on your worksheet.

RENAME A WORKSHEET

You can give each worksheet in your workbook a descriptive name. Excel automatically provides a name, such as Sheet1, for each worksheet in a workbook. You can rename a worksheet to better describe its contents. This helps you and other users more easily identify and find worksheets of interest.

Excel allows you to use up to 31 characters, including spaces, to name a worksheet. You cannot use the following characters in a worksheet name: \ / : ? * [ ]. Each worksheet in

a workbook must have a unique name. Generally, short worksheet names are better than long worksheet names because they allow you to display more worksheet tabs on your screen at once.

After you rename a worksheet, you cannot use the Undo feature to return the worksheet to its original name. You can, however, rename the worksheet again, using the original name.

When I type a name for a worksheet, I receive an error message. Why?

✔ If you type the same name as an existing worksheet, Excel displays an error message. Click OK and type a new name.

RENAME A WORKSHEET

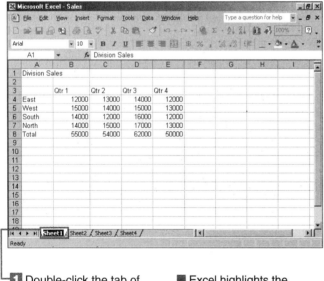

1 Double-click the tab of the worksheet you want to rename.

■ Excel highlights the current name.

2 Type a new name.

3 Press Enter.

■ Excel renames the worksheet.

MOVE OR COPY A WORKSHEET

You can move a worksheet to a new location, allowing you to reorganize the data in a workbook. For example, you can arrange your workbook so that frequently used worksheets are beside each other. Likewise, you can copy a worksheet when you plan to make major changes and you want to have a copy of the worksheet without the changes.

You move and copy worksheets using the Move and Copy dialog box. The only difference between the two operations is that you must select the Create a copy option to copy instead of move a worksheet.

Moving worksheets may cause calculations or charts based on the transferred data to recalculate incorrectly. If this happens, you can

edit the formulas so that they refer to the moved sheet. See Chapter 12 for more information on formulas.

After you move a worksheet, you cannot use the Undo feature to return the worksheet to its original location in the workbook. You can, however, use the same procedure to move the worksheet back to its original location.

MOVE OR COPY A WORKSHEET

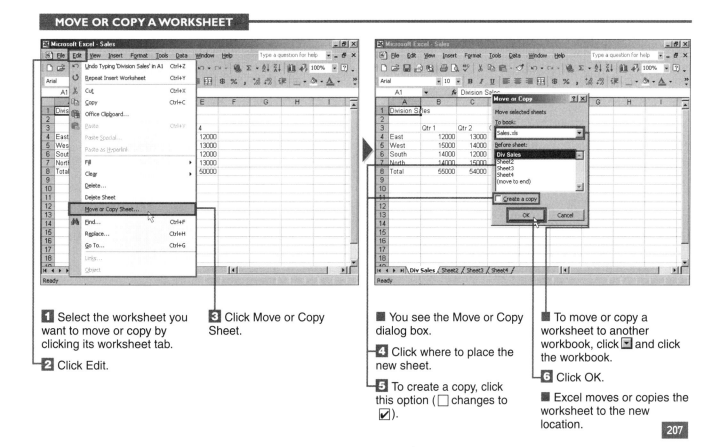

1 Select the worksheet you want to move or copy by clicking its worksheet tab.

2 Click Edit.

3 Click Move or Copy Sheet.

■ You see the Move or Copy dialog box.

4 Click where to place the new sheet.

5 To create a copy, click this option (□ changes to ✓).

■ To move or copy a worksheet to another workbook, click ▾ and click the workbook.

6 Click OK.

■ Excel moves or copies the worksheet to the new location.

AN INTRODUCTION TO FORMULAS AND FUNCTIONS

Formulas

Excel allows you to use formulas to calculate and analyze data in your worksheet. A formula always begins with an equal sign (=), and includes cell references, and some type of mathematical operator. For example, the formula = C4 + C5 takes the value in C4 and adds it to C5.

In a formula, it is better to use cell references rather than typing the value directly because this utilizes Excel's ability to recalculate a formula when you change the value in any cell(s) references. If you change the value in C4 in the preceding example, the results automatically update. If you type a value, you must manually edit the formula.

You can use arithmetic operators in formulas to perform mathematical calculations. Arithmetic operators include the addition (+), subtraction (-), multiplication (*), division (/), percent (%), and exponent (^) symbols.

You can use comparison operators, which return values of TRUE or FALSE, in formulas to compare two values. Comparison operators include the greater than (>), less than (<), equal to (=), greater than or equal to (>=), less than or equal to (<=), and not equal to (<>) symbols.

Excel performs calculations in a specific order. Excel calculates percentages first and then exponents, followed by multiplication and division. Excel then calculates addition and subtraction, followed by comparison operators.

You can use parentheses ( ) to change the order in which Excel performs calculations. Excel calculates the data inside the parentheses first. For example, in the formula = 10 * (1 + 2), Excel performs the addition before the multiplication.

Pizza Parlor		
ORDERS		
	A	B
1	Pizza	600
2	Spaghetti	200
3	Garlic Bread	400
4	TOTAL	1200

=B1+B2+B3

Functions

Excel offers over 200 functions to help you analyze data, including financial, math and trigonometry, date and time, and statistical functions. A function is a ready-to-use formula that you can use to perform a calculation on the data in your worksheet. Excel's functions allow you to perform calculations without having to type long, complex formulas.

A function always begins with an equal sign (=). Excel encloses the data it uses to calculate a function in parentheses ( ).

Each cell or number Excel uses in a function is called an argument. Each function requires some arguments; you must include them. Some functions include optional arguments. When you create a formula, Excel helps you by prompting which arguments to enter.

Examples of Formulas and Functions

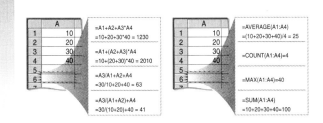

Errors in Formulas

An error message appears when Excel cannot properly calculate a formula. Errors in formulas are often the result of typing mistakes. You can correct an error by editing the data in the cell containing the error.

indicates the column is too narrow to display the result of the calculation.

#DIV/0! indicates the formula divides a number by zero (0). Excel considers a blank cell to contain a value of zero.

#NAME? indicates the formula contains a function name or cell reference Excel does not recognize.

#REF! indicates the formula refers to a cell that is not valid. For example, a cell used in the formula may have been deleted.

#VALUE! indicates the formula contains a cell reference for a cell that Excel cannot use in a calculation. For example, the formula may refer to a cell containing text.

#N/A indicates the formula refers to a value that is not available.

#NULL! indicates the formula refers to an intersection of cells that do not intersect. This may occur when there is a space between two cell references instead of a comma (,) or colon (:).

A circular reference occurs when a formula refers to the cell containing the formula. Excel cannot calculate a formula that contains a circular reference and displays a warning message on your screen when it finds this type of error.

When an error message appears in a cell, you see an Error button. Click the down arrow and select from available commands to get help, ignore the error, or show the formula auditing toolbar. Excel includes auditing tools to check the formulas and functions in a worksheet.

SUM NUMBERS

The most common calculation in a worksheet is to sum a group of numbers. You can quickly calculate the sum of a list of numbers in your worksheet using AutoSum.

You can use the AutoSum feature to quickly add numbers in rows or columns. When you use AutoSum, you can select a cell below or to the right of the cells containing the

numbers you want to add. The AutoSum feature automatically inserts the SUM function in the cell you select.

Excel outlines the cells it uses in the AutoSum calculation with a dotted line. The program guesses which cells you are likely to want to sum by looking at the entries above or to the left of the current cell. If Excel outlines the wrong

cells, you can select the cells you want to use in the calculation.

You can use the AutoCalculate feature to display the sum of numbers without entering a formula in your worksheet. When you select two or more cells, AutoCalculate displays the sum of the selected cells in the bottom right corner of your screen.

SUM NUMBERS

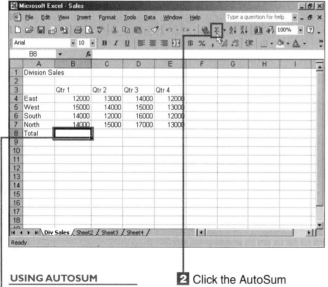

USING AUTOSUM

1 Click the cell below or to the right of the cells containing the numbers you want to add.

2 Click the AutoSum button (Σ).

■ Excel outlines the cells it will use in the calculation with a dotted line.

■ If Excel does not outline the correct cells, you can select the cells containing the numbers you want to add.

Note: To learn how to select a cell, see Chapter 10.

Can I have AutoSum perform other calculations?

✔ Yes. Select the cells you want to calculate and then click ▥ next to the AutoSum button (**Σ**). Select the function you want to include.

How can I check my formulas?

✔ Excel includes several auditing tools for checking formulas. Click Tools and then click Formula Auditing. You can then use the commands in this menu to trace formulas. Tracing formulas show you which cells are referenced or dependent on other cells. You can also trace errors.

Can I select other calculations for AutoCalculate?

✔ Yes. Select the cells and then right-click the area in the bottom right corner of your screen that displays AutoCalculate results. From the menu that appears, select the calculation you want to perform. Average calculates the average value of a list of numbers. Count calculates the number of items in a list, including text. Count Nums calculates the number of values in a list. Max finds the largest value in a list. Min finds the smallest value in a list.

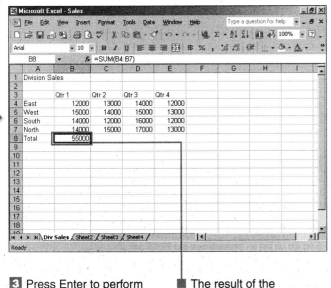

3 Press Enter to perform the calculation.

■ The result of the calculation appears.

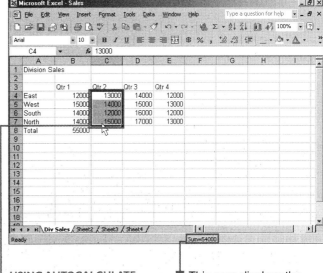

USING AUTOCALCULATE

1 Select the cells you want to include in the calculation.

■ This area displays the sum of the cells you selected.

ENTER AND EDIT FORMULAS

You can enter a formula into any cell in your worksheet. A formula helps you calculate and analyze data in your worksheet. A formula always begins with an equal sign (=).

When entering formulas, use cell references instead of actual data whenever possible. For example, type the formula = **A1 + A2** instead of = **10 + 30**. When you use cell references and you change the value in one of the cells referenced in the formula, Excel automatically redoes the calculations for you. For example, if you base your sales commissions on a value of 10% and then change the value to 12%, all the commissions in your worksheet automatically change.

A cell displays the result of a formula, while the formula bar displays the formula itself.

You should always be careful to enter the correct cell references and mathematical symbols in a formula. Errors in formulas are often the result of typing mistakes. You can edit a formula to correct an error or change the formula. When you edit a formula, Excel outlines each cell you use in the formula with a different color.

ENTER AND EDIT FORMULAS

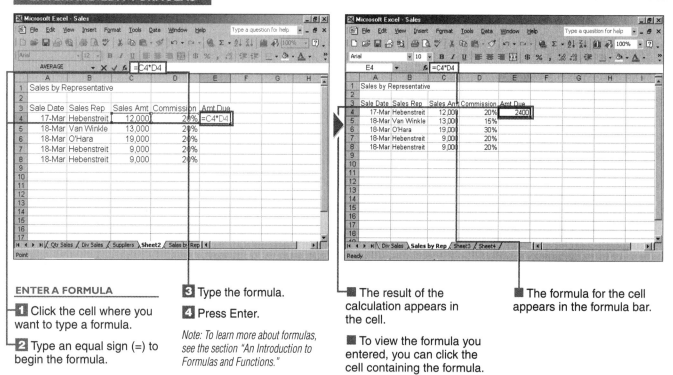

ENTER A FORMULA

1 Click the cell where you want to type a formula.

2 Type an equal sign (=) to begin the formula.

3 Type the formula.

4 Press Enter.

Note: To learn more about formulas, see the section "An Introduction to Formulas and Functions."

■ The result of the calculation appears in the cell.

■ To view the formula you entered, you can click the cell containing the formula.

■ The formula for the cell appears in the formula bar.

Can I reference a cell in another worksheet?

✔ Yes. To do so, type the worksheet name, followed by an exclamation mark and the cell reference (**Sheet1!A1**, as an example).

You can also simply go to that worksheet and click the cell to include as you are building the formula.

Can I reference a cell in another workbook?

✔ Yes. To do so, type the workbook name in square brackets and then type the worksheet name, followed by an exclamation mark and the cell reference (for example, **[Budget.xls]Sheet1!A1**).

How can I view the relationship of cells and formulas?

✔ You can use Excel's auditing tools. To trace precedents (cells that are included in a formula), select the cell that contains the formula and then click Tools, Formula Auditing, Trace Precedents.

To trace dependents (see which formulas reference a particular cell), select the cell that contains the value. Then click Tools, Formula Auditing, Trace Dependents.

Excel draws tracer lines to indicate the relationship between the cell(s) and formula(s). To remove these arrows, click Tools, Formula Auditing, Remove All Arrows.

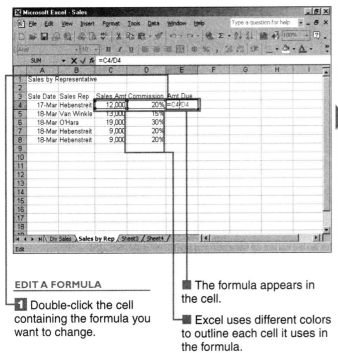

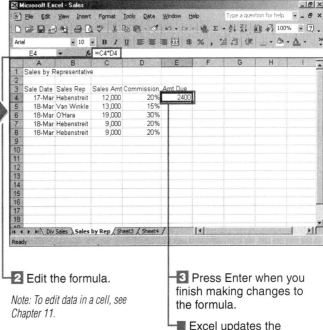

EDIT A FORMULA

■1 Double-click the cell containing the formula you want to change.

■ The formula appears in the cell.

■ Excel uses different colors to outline each cell it uses in the formula.

■2 Edit the formula.

Note: To edit data in a cell, see Chapter 11.

■3 Press Enter when you finish making changes to the formula.

■ Excel updates the formula, and displays the new results.

COPY A FORMULA

I f you want to use the same formula several times in your worksheet, you can save time by copying the formula.

Excel automatically adjusts any cell references so you avoid manually re-creating each formula.

There are two types of cell references you can use in a formula — relative and absolute.

A *relative* reference changes when you copy a formula. If you copy a

formula to other cells, Excel automatically changes the cell references in the new formulas. For example, when you copy the formula =A1+A2 from cell A3 to cell B3, the formula changes to =B1+B2.

If you do not want Excel to change a cell reference when you copy a formula, you can use an *absolute* reference, which always refers to the same cell. You make a cell reference absolute by typing a

dollar sign ($) before both the column letter and row number. If you copy the formula to other cells, Excel does not change the reference in the new formulas. For example, when you copy the formula =$A$7*B2 from cell B4 to cell C4, the formula changes to =$A$7*C2.

COPY A FORMULA

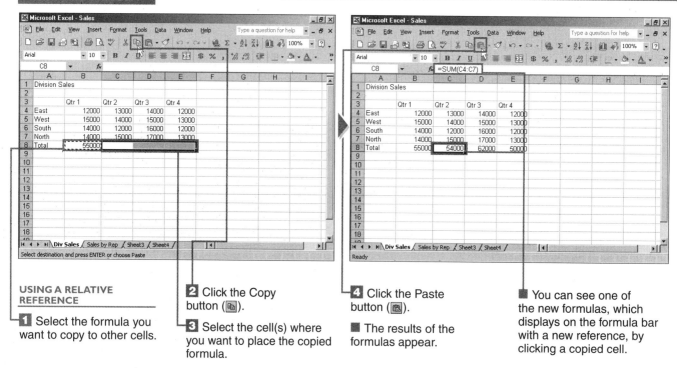

USING A RELATIVE REFERENCE

1 Select the formula you want to copy to other cells.

2 Click the Copy button (▣).

3 Select the cell(s) where you want to place the copied formula.

4 Click the Paste button (▣).

■ The results of the formulas appear.

■ You can see one of the new formulas, which displays on the formula bar with a new reference, by clicking a copied cell.

What is another method for copying formulas?

✔ You can also drag a formula to copy it. Select the cell, hold down Ctrl, and drag it to its new location. You can also fill the formula, which is the same as copying. To fill a formula, select it and then drag the fill handle. See Chapter 10 for more information on filling a series.

Excel automatically copied a formula. How did this happen?

✔ Excel can pick up a pattern of worksheet entries and may automatically copy a formula from the cell above it. If this is what you want, you can simply continue entering the row entries and let Excel complete the formula cells. If not, you can type a new entry in the cell.

Is there another way to create an absolute reference?

✔ Yes. In a formula, select the cell reference you want to make absolute. Press F4 until dollar signs ($) appear in the appropriate places.

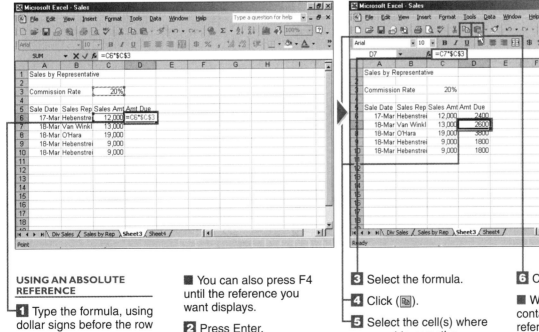

USING AN ABSOLUTE REFERENCE

1 Type the formula, using dollar signs before the row and/or column you want to make absolute.

■ You can also press F4 until the reference you want displays.

2 Press Enter.

3 Select the formula.

4 Click (📋).

5 Select the cell(s) where you want to copy the formula.

6 Click (📋).

■ When you copy a formula containing an absolute reference, the absolute reference does not change.

ENTER A FUNCTION

A function is a ready-to-use formula that you can use to perform a calculation in your worksheet.

Excel offers over 200 functions from which to choose, grouping the functions into categories according to their use. If you do not know which category contains the function you want to use, you can choose the All category to display a list of all the functions.

You can specify the cells containing the numbers you want to use in a function. Each cell or number in a function is called an argument. A function may require one or more arguments.

The arguments in a function are enclosed in parentheses and separated by commas (,) or a colon (:). When commas (,) separate arguments, Excel uses each argument to perform the

calculation. For example, =SUM(A1,A2,A3) is the same as the formula =A1+A2+A3. When a colon (:) separates arguments, Excel uses the specified arguments and all arguments between them to perform the calculation. For example, =SUM(B1:B3) is the same as the formula =B1+B2+B3.

ENTER A FUNCTION

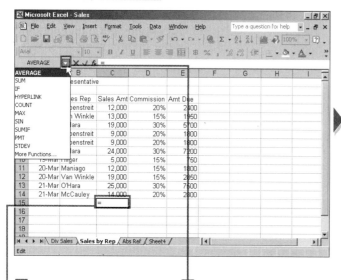

■1 Click the cell where you want to enter a function.

■2 Type the = sign.

■ Excel displays a list of functions in the Reference box. The last function entered is displayed.

■3 Click ▼ next to the Reference box and select the function you want to insert.

Note: If the function is not listed, click More Functions.

■ Excel displays the Function Arguments dialog box which prompts you for the appropriate arguments for the function and gives you a description.

■ Excel may guess which cell or range you want to use in the function and enter it for you.

What is another method for entering a function?

✔ You can also click Insert and then Function. You see the Insert Function dialog box. Select the function and then click OK. Complete the arguments for the function and then click OK.

This method also enables you to search for a particular function. You can type what you want to do and then click Go. Or you can limit the list to a particular category of function by displaying the Or select a category drop-down list and select the category you want.

How can I quickly enter the numbers I want to use for a function?

✔ When entering numbers for a function in the Formula Argument dialog box, you can select a group of cells by dragging over them in the worksheet rather than selecting each cell individually.

Can I type a function without using the command?

✔ If you know the name of the function you want to use, you can enter the function directly into a cell. You must start the function with an equal sign (=), enclose the arguments in parentheses ( ), and separate the arguments with commas (,) or a colon (:).

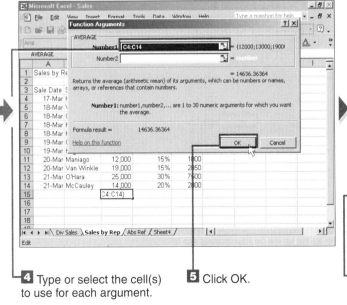

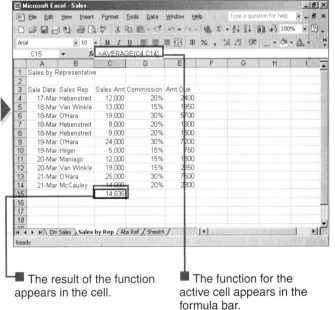

4 Type or select the cell(s) to use for each argument.

Note: The arguments you must complete depend on the function you are inserting.

5 Click OK.

■ The result of the function appears in the cell.

■ The function for the active cell appears in the formula bar.

CHANGE COLUMN WIDTH OR ROW HEIGHT

You can improve the appearance of your worksheet and display hidden data by changing column width and row height.

Cells with text too long for the cell spill into the cell to the right. If the cell to the right contains data, Excel truncates the entry. Numeric

entries display as #### in the cell. You can change the column width to display all the text in a cell. As you change the column width, Excel displays a small box containing the average number of characters that fit in the cell. You can opt to have Excel automatically adjust the column width to fit the longest item in the column.

You can change the height of rows to add space between the rows of data in your worksheet. As you change the row height, Excel displays a small box containing the size of the row in points, with one inch containing 72 points. As with column height, you can have Excel automatically adjust the row height to fit the tallest item in the row.

CHANGE COLUMN WIDTH

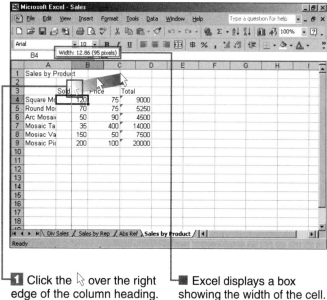
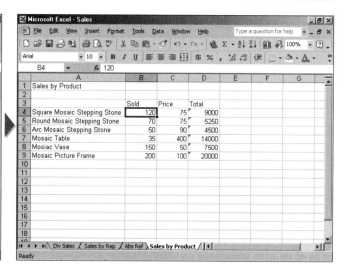

1 Click the ⬚ over the right edge of the column heading.

2 Drag the column edge until the dotted line displays the column width you want.

■ Excel displays a box showing the width of the cell.

■ The column displays the new width.

Can I change the width of several columns or the height of several rows at once?

✔ Yes. Click and drag the ⌖ over the headings of the columns or the headings of the rows you want to change. Then drag the right edge of any column heading or the bottom edge of any row heading.

How do I specify an exact row height?

✔ Click the heading of the row you want to change. Click Format, click Row, and then click Height. Then type the height you want to use and click OK.

How do I set Excel to automatically adjust all of the column widths in the worksheet?

✔ Select the entire worksheet by clicking the worksheet selector button above the row number and to the left of the column letters. Then double-click the column divider between columns A and B. Excel adjusts all of the worksheet columns to fit the contents of each column.

How do I specify an exact column width?

✔ Click the heading of the column you want to change. Click Format, click Column, and then click Width. Type the width you want to use and click OK.

CHANGE ROW HEIGHT

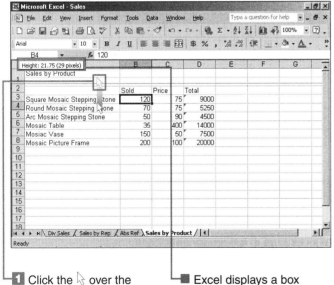

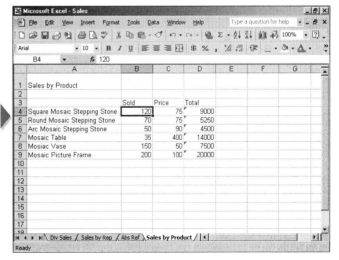

1 Click the ⌖ over the bottom edge of the row heading.

2 Drag the row edge until the dotted line displays the row height you want.

■ Excel displays a box showing the width of the cell.

■ The row displays the new height.

BOLD, ITALIC, OR UNDERLINE

You can use the Bold, Italic, and Underline features to emphasize and enhance the style of data in your worksheet. You can apply one or all of these features quickly using the appropriate buttons on the formatting toolbar.

The Bold feature makes the selected data appear darker and thicker than other data in your worksheet. You can use the Bold feature to emphasize row and column headings or other important information.

The Italic feature tilts the selected data to the right. You may want to italicize notes or explanations you add to your worksheet.

The Underline feature adds a line underneath the selected data. You can underline data to emphasize specific data in your worksheet, such as subtotals and totals.

You can also use the Format Cells dialog box to apply these styles as well as other text effects. For more information, see the section "Apply Special Appearance Effects" for more information. In addition to changing the font style using bold, italic, or underline, you can also select a different font or font size. See "Change Font and Font Size."

BOLD, ITALIC, OR UNDERLINE

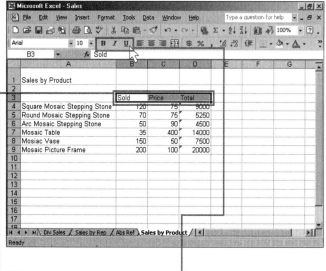

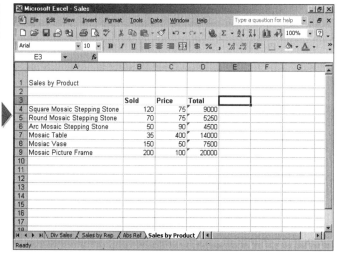

1 Select the cells containing the data you want to change.

Note: To select cells, see Chapter 10.

2 Click one of the following buttons:

- **B** Bold
- *I* Italic
- <u>U</u> Underline

■ The data displays the style you selected.

■ You can remove a style by repeating steps 1 and 2.

APPLY A NUMBER STYLE TO CELLS

You can quickly change the appearance of numbers in your worksheet to make it easier for other people to understand what the values in your worksheet represent. Excel gives you five numbering style options: Currency, Percent, Comma, Increase Decimal, and Decrease Decimal. When you change the format of numbers, you do not change the value of the numbers.

You use Currency format, which adds a dollar sign ($) and two decimal places to a number, when you want to display a number as a monetary value.

The Percent format changes a decimal number, such as 0.05, into a percentage, such as 5%.

The Comma format makes a long number easier to read by adding

commas and two decimal places to the number.

You can increase or decrease the number of decimal places a number displays. If you want to select other number formats, change the look of these styles, or customize each style, see the section "Format Numbers" which covers using the dialog box method to apply a style.

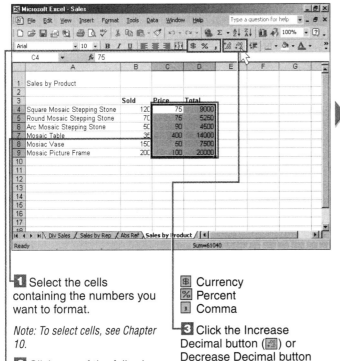

1 Select the cells containing the numbers you want to format.

Note: To select cells, see Chapter 10.

2 Click one of the following buttons:

$ Currency
% Percent
, Comma

3 Click the Increase Decimal button (🔲) or Decrease Decimal button (🔲) to change the number of decimal places.

■ Excel displays the numbers in the selected format and may adjust the column width as necessary.

FORMAT NUMBERS

Y ou can display the numbers in your worksheet in many different ways to fit your situation. For example, you can display the number 11500 as $11,500.00 to express total sales or display the number .075 as 7.5% to express the percent of completion on a project.

When you change the format of a number, the value of the number does not change.

Excel offers several number format categories including Currency, Date, Time, Percentage, and Scientific. The category you choose determines the available options. For example, the Currency category allows you to select options such as the number of decimal places and how you want negative numbers to appear.

The Format Cells dialog box displays a sample of the formatting

options you select. This allows you to see how numbers in your worksheet appear in the new format.

When you format a column of numbers, the number signs (#) may appear in each cell of the column indicating that the new format is too wide for the column. To change the column width, see the section "Change Column Width or Row Height."

FORMAT NUMBERS

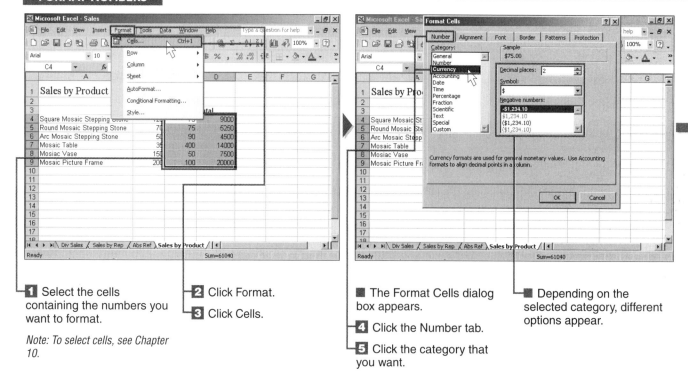

1 Select the cells containing the numbers you want to format.

Note: To select cells, see Chapter 10.

2 Click Format.

3 Click Cells.

■ The Format Cells dialog box appears.

4 Click the Number tab.

5 Click the category that you want.

■ Depending on the selected category, different options appear.

What is a faster method for changing the number format?

✔ You can select from three common number formats — currency, percent, and comma — by using these buttons on the Formatting toolbar. See the section "Apply a Number Style to Cells." Use this method when you do not need to view the complete list of styles and when you do not need to make changes to the formatting options for any of the styles.

How do I remove a number format I added to my data?

✔ Select the cells containing the data from which you want to remove a number format. In the Format Cells dialog box, click the General category. Then click OK to remove the number format from the data.

Can I create a custom number format?

✔ Yes. You can base your custom number format on an existing number format. In the Format Cells dialog box, click the category for the type of number format you want to create and click any options you want to use. Then click the Custom category. The Type area displays a code for your custom number format. You can modify the code to further customize the number format.

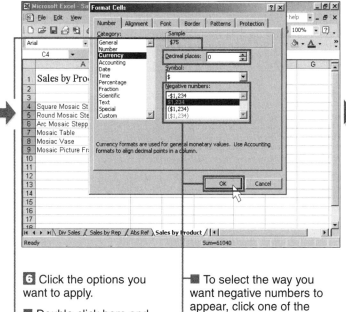

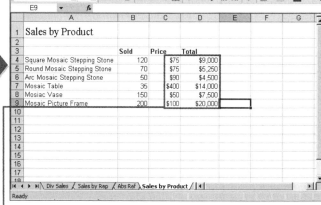

6 Click the options you want to apply.

■ Double-click here and type the number of decimal places you want the numbers to display.

■ To select the way you want negative numbers to appear, click one of the available styles.

7 Click OK.

■ Excel displays the selected number formatting.

CHANGE FONT AND FONT SIZE

You can enhance the appearance of your worksheet by changing the design, or font, of data. By default, Excel uses the Arial font, but you can apply another font to draw attention to headings or emphasize important data in your worksheet. You can also change the default font. See the section "Apply Special Appearance Effects" to learn more.

Excel fonts display in the list as they appear in your worksheet so you preview a font before you select it.

Most fonts in the list display either the TT or a printer icon. The TT symbol indicates the font is a TrueType font, which means the font prints exactly as it appears on your screen. The printer symbol, indicating a printer font, may print differently than it appears on your screen.

In addition to changing the font, you can also increase or decrease the size of data in your worksheet. By default, Excel uses a data size of 10 points, with 72 points making an inch. Larger data is easier to read, but smaller data allows you to fit more information on your screen and on a printed worksheet.

CHANGE FONT

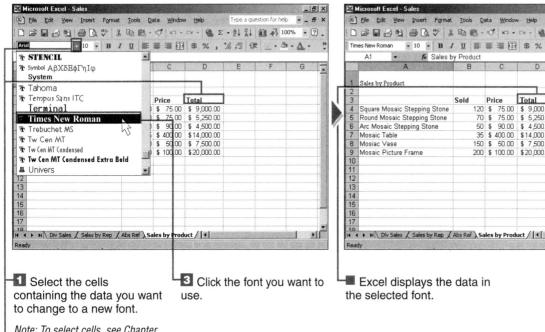

■1 Select the cells containing the data you want to change to a new font.

Note: To select cells, see Chapter 10.

■2 Click the ■ next to the Font box.

■3 Click the font you want to use.

■ Excel displays the data in the selected font.

How do I change the font or size of only some of the data in a cell?

✔ Double-click the cell containing the data you want to change. Drag the ⌖ over the data you want to change. Then select the font or font size using the drop-down lists.

Can I shrink data so it fits neatly in a cell?

✔ Yes. Select the cell containing the data you want to shrink. Click Format and then click Cells. Click the Alignment tab, click the Shrink to fit option (☐ changes to ✔) and then click OK.

Can I decrease the size of data Excel displays on my screen without affecting the data's appearance on a printed worksheet?

✔ You can use the Zoom feature to decrease the size of data on your screen without affecting the appearance of the data when you print your worksheet. Click the ▾ next to the Zoom box (100% ▾) and click a zoom percentage. The smaller the number, the smaller the data appears on-screen.

CHANGE FONT SIZE

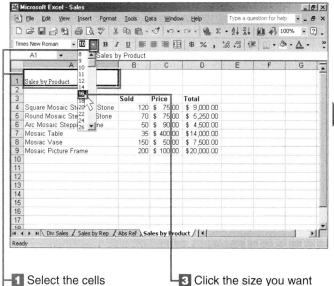

1 Select the cells containing the data you want to change to a new size.

Note: To select cells, see Chapter 10.

2 Click the ▾ next to the Font Size box.

3 Click the size you want to use.

■ Excel displays the data in the selected size.

CHANGE FONT OR FILL COLOR

Y ou can add a variety of colors to your worksheet to enhance its appearance by changing the font or fill color.

You can change the color of data in a cell to draw attention to titles or other important data in your worksheet. You can also change the background, or fill color, of cells. You may change the background

color of cells when you want to distinguish between different areas in your worksheet. For example, in a worksheet that contains monthly sales figures, you can use a different background color for each month.

When adding color to your worksheet, make sure you choose background cell colors and data

colors that work well together. For example, red data on a blue background is difficult to read.

To learn how to apply multiple formatting features, including color, to your worksheet, see the section "Apply an AutoFormat."

CHANGE FONT

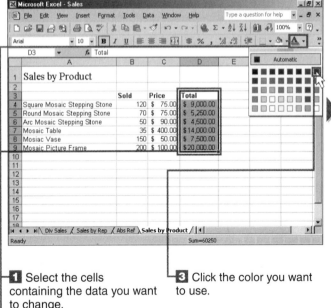

1 Select the cells containing the data you want to change.

Note: To select cells, see Chapter 10.

2 Click the ☉ next to the Font Color button (**A**).

3 Click the color you want to use.

■ The data changes to the new color.

■ To remove a color from data, you can perform steps 1 through 3, except click Automatic in step 3.

What effects can I apply to change the background of cells when I have a black-and-white printer?

✔ You can add a pattern to the background of cells. Select the cells you want to display a pattern. Click Format, click Cells and then click the Patterns tab. Click the Pattern ▼ and click the pattern you want to use. You can also click a color. Click OK to apply the pattern.

Can I have negative numbers automatically appear in red?

✔ Yes. Select the cells to which you want to apply this change. Click Format, click Cells, and then click the Number tab. In the Category area, click Number or Currency. In the Negative numbers area, click the appropriate option and then click OK.

How can I quickly change the color of data in my worksheet?

✔ The Font Color button (▲) on the Formatting toolbar displays the last selected data color. To quickly apply this color, click the cells containing the data you want to change and then click ▲.

CHANGE FILL COLOR

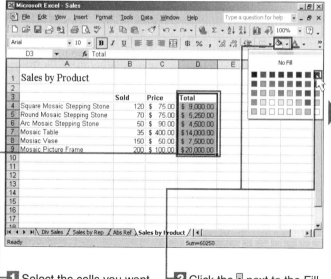

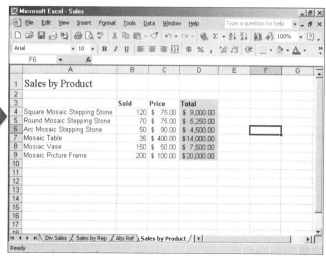

1 Select the cells you want to change to a different color.

Note: To select cells, see Chapter 10.

2 Click the ▼ next to the Fill Color button (▨).

3 Click the cell color you want to use.

■ The cells change to the new color.

■ To remove a color from cells, you can perform steps 1 through 3, except click No Fill in step 3.

APPLY SPECIAL APPEARANCE EFFECTS

Excel includes three effects you can apply to data. The Strikethrough effect, which displays a line through the middle of the data, is useful when you are editing a worksheet and want to suggest deleting that data. Useful for mathematical and chemistry equations, the Superscript and Subscript effects decrease the size of the data and move it either slightly above or slightly below the line of regular-sized data.

In addition, Excel offers several underline styles you can use to help you draw attention to important data, such as totals.

You use the Format Cells dialog box to add these special effects as well as change the design, style, and size of data in your worksheet, which is useful when you want to quickly enhance the appearance of your worksheet by changing several formatting options at once. The

dialog box also lets you make formatting changes that are not available with the Formatting toolbar. See the sections "Change Font and Font Size" and "Bold, Italic, or Underline" for more information on using the Formatting toolbar.

APPLY SPECIAL APPEARANCE EFFECTS

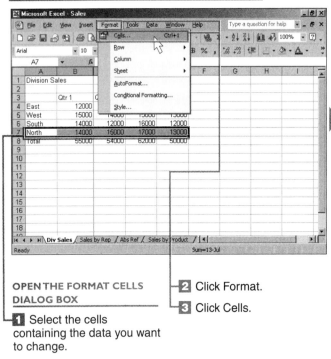

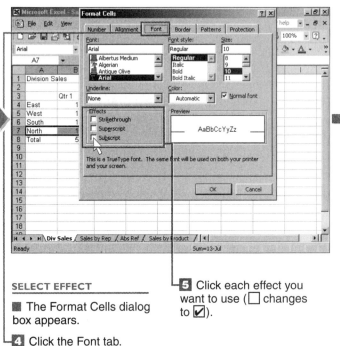

OPEN THE FORMAT CELLS DIALOG BOX

1 Select the cells containing the data you want to change.

Note: To select cells, see Chapter 10.

2 Click Format.

3 Click Cells.

SELECT EFFECT

■ The Format Cells dialog box appears.

4 Click the Font tab.

5 Click each effect you want to use (□ changes to ☑).

What determines which fonts are available in Excel?

✔ The available fonts depend on the fonts installed on your computer and printer. Excel includes several fonts, but other programs on your computer and the built-in fonts on your printer may provide additional fonts.

How do I change the color of data in the cells I selected?

✔ In the Format Cells dialog box, click the Color ☑ to display a list, and then click the color you want to use.

Can I change the default font setting Excel uses for all my new workbooks?

✔ Yes. Click the Tools menu, click Options and then click the General tab. In the Standard font area, click the font and size you want Excel to use for the default font setting. You must exit and restart Excel to apply the change.

What are the options for underlining data?

✔ You can select single, double, single accounting, or double accounting. The accounting underline styles add a little bit of space between the data and underline.

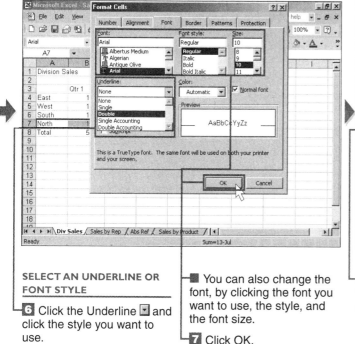

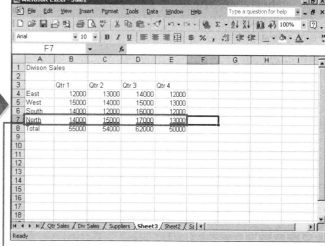

SELECT AN UNDERLINE OR FONT STYLE

6 Click the Underline ☑ and click the style you want to use.

■ You can also change the font, by clicking the font you want to use, the style, and the font size.

7 Click OK.

■ Excel makes the changes to the appearance of the selected cells.

CHANGE DATA ALIGNMENT

You can change the way Excel aligns data within cells in your worksheet. Doing so can enhance the appearance of the data, making column headings align with numeric entries.

The default for text entries, the left align option lines up data with the left edge of a cell. The default for numeric entries, the right align

option lines up data with the right edge of a cell. The center option aligns data between the left and right edges of a cell.

You can also center a title across a worksheet. When you use this alignment option, Excel merges the selected cells into one cell and then centers the entry within the cell.

In addition to changing the alignment, you can apply indenting to move data away from the left edge of a cell. When you indent data, make sure the cell width can accommodate all the data without hiding part of it. To change the column width, see the section "Change Column Width or Row Height."

CHANGE DATA ALIGNMENT

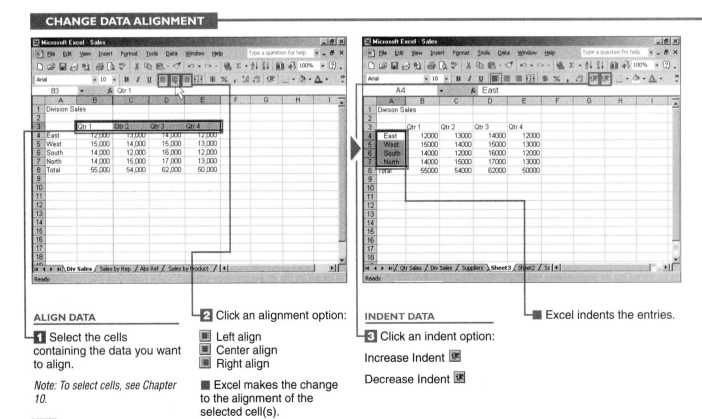

ALIGN DATA

1 Select the cells containing the data you want to align.

Note: To select cells, see Chapter 10.

2 Click an alignment option:

▤ Left align
▤ Center align
▤ Right align

■ Excel makes the change to the alignment of the selected cell(s).

INDENT DATA

3 Click an indent option:

Increase Indent ▦

Decrease Indent ▦

■ Excel indents the entries.

How do I align data vertically in cells?

✔ Select the cells containing the data you want to align vertically. Click Format menu, click Cells and then click the Alignment tab. Click the Vertical ⬛ and click the alignment option you want to use. Then click OK.

How can I rotate data in cells?

✔ Select the cells containing the data you want to rotate. Click Format, click Cells and then click the Alignment tab. In the Orientation area, double-click the box beside Degrees and type the number of degrees you want to rotate the data. Alternately, you can click the clock-like indicator in that area. Then click OK.

Can I display long lines of text in a cell?

✔ Yes. You can display long lines of text in a cell by wrapping the text. Select the cell containing the text you want to wrap. Click Format, click Cells and then click the Alignment tab. Click the Wrap text option and then click OK. This changes the height of the entire row.

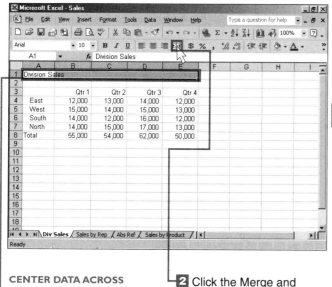

CENTER DATA ACROSS COLUMNS

1 Select the cells you want to center the data across.

Note: The first cell should contain the data you want to center.

2 Click the Merge and Center button (🔳).

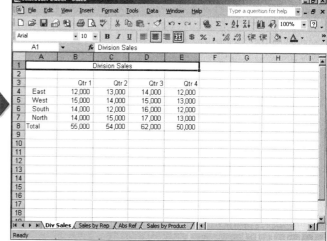

■ Excel centers the data across the cells you selected.

ADD BORDERS

You can add borders to enhance the appearance of your worksheet and divide your worksheet into sections. Adding borders can help make important data in your worksheet stand out. For example, in a financial worksheet, you may want to add borders to the cells containing subtotals and totals.

Excel offers three preset borders: none, an outline around the selected data, and inside borders within the selected data. You can also create a custom border to suit your needs. You have several line styles including broken, bold, and double lines. Although the default border color is black, you can select a color that better suits your worksheet.

You can specify which types of borders you want to add to the selected cells. For example, you can add a top, bottom, left, or right border to cells. You can also add diagonal borders to cells when you want to indicate that data in the cells is no longer valid.

You can preview the borders before you add them to your worksheet to determine if you like the change before applying it.

ADD BORDERS

1 Select the cells you want to display borders.

Note: To select cells, see Chapter 10.

2 Click Format.

3 Click Cells.

■ The Format Cells dialog box appears.

4 Click the Border tab.

■ To use a preset border, you can click a Preset option and then skip to step 9.

5 Click the line style you want to use for a border.

6 Click ☑ and click a color from this list.

How can I quickly add borders to my worksheet?

✔ Select the cells you want to display borders. Click the ▣ beside the Borders button (▣) on the Formatting toolbar. A selection of common border types appears. Click the type of border you want to use. You can also use Excel's AutoFormat feature to quickly add borders and color to your worksheet. For information on the AutoFormat feature, see "Apply an AutoFormat."

How do I remove borders I have added to my worksheet?

✔ Perform steps 1 through 4 in this section, and then click the None button. Excel removes the borders.

Can I print the gridlines displayed on my screen instead of adding borders?

✔ Yes. Click File and then click Page Setup. Click the Sheet tab and click the Gridlines option. Then click OK. Excel prints the worksheet gridlines when you print the worksheet.

Can I turn off the gridlines on my screen so I can more clearly see the borders I have added?

✔ Yes. Click Tools and then click Options. Click the View tab and deselect the Gridlines box (☐ changes to ☑). Then click OK.

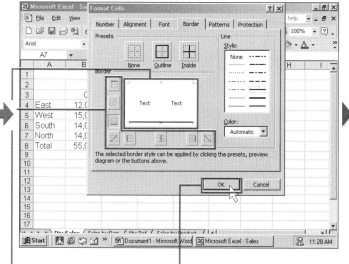

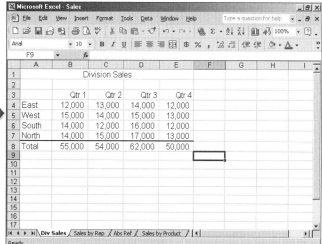

7 Click the button displaying the location of border you want to add.

■ This area displays a preview.

8 Repeat steps 5 through 7 for each border you want to add to the selected text.

9 Click OK.

■ The cells display the border you selected.

COPY FORMATTING

After you format one cell to suit your needs, you can use the Format Painter feature to copy the formatting to other cells in your worksheet.

You can copy formatting to make all the headings in your worksheet look the same, giving your worksheet a consistent appearance. You can also copy number formatting, such as currency, date,

or percentage, and data formatting, such as font, size, or alignment. Excel also allows you to copy cell formatting, such as cell color or borders.

The only formatting that Excel does not copy is the row height or column width of the cells. To learn how to change the height or width of a cell, see the section "Change Column Width or Row Height."

MASTER IT

Can I copy formatting to several areas in my worksheet at once?

✔ Yes. To do so, perform the steps in this section, except double-click the Format Painter button (▨) in step 2. When you finish selecting all the cells you want to display the formatting, press Esc. Excel stops copying the formatting.

COPY FORMATTING

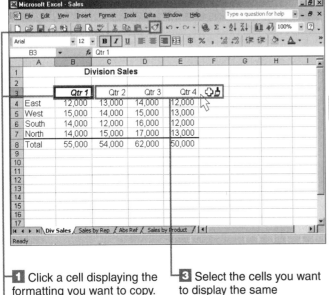

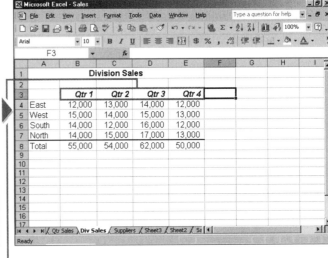

1 Click a cell displaying the formatting you want to copy.

2 Click the Format Painter button (▨).

■ The ▨ changes to ▨▨.

3 Select the cells you want to display the same formatting.

Note: To select cells, see Chapter 10.

■ The cells display the formatting.

CLEAR FORMATTING

You can remove all the formatting from cells in your worksheet. When you clear formatting from cells, the data in the cells appears as you originally entered it. For example, if you clear the formatting from cells containing dates, the dates change to numbers.

You can clear many different types of formatting from cells, including currency, percentage, alignment, font, and color. Clearing formatting does not reverse any changes you made to the row height or column width.

You may need to clear formatting after you remove data from a cell. If you do not clear the formatting, Excel applies the formatting to any new data you enter in the cell. To learn how to type data into a cell, see Chapter 10. To delete data from a cell, see Chapter 11.

If two or more words or numbers in a cell display different formatting, Excel clears the formatting from only the first word or number.

CLEAR FORMATTING

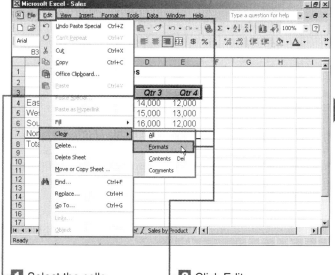

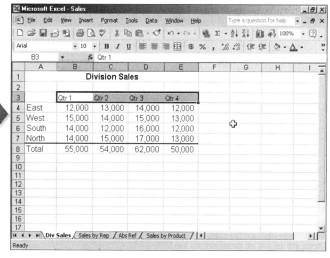

1 Select the cells containing the formatting you want to remove.

Note: To select cells, see Chapter 10.

2 Click Edit.

3 Click Clear.

4 Click Formats.

■ Excel clears the formatting from the cells you selected.

APPLY AN AUTOFORMAT

You can give your worksheet a new appearance by applying AutoFormats, which are a series of ready-to-use designs Excel offers for your use and convenience. An AutoFormat provides the formatting so you can concentrate on the content of your worksheet.

Some of the types of AutoFormats include Accounting, Colorful, and 3-D Effects. The Accounting AutoFormats format numbers as currency. The Colorful AutoFormats emphasize data by changing the color of the cells you selected. The 3-D Effects AutoFormats give the selected cells the appearance of depth.

Excel shows a preview of each available AutoFormat, which allows you to determine which AutoFormat suits the content, purpose, and intended audience of your worksheet.

You can specify which formatting options you want Excel to apply to the selected cells. For example, you may not want to use the font or border options of a particular AutoFormat.

When you apply an AutoFormat to your worksheet, Excel analyzes the selected cells and finds the row or column labels and totals. Excel then applies the appropriate formatting to these special cells.

APPLY AN AUTOFORMAT

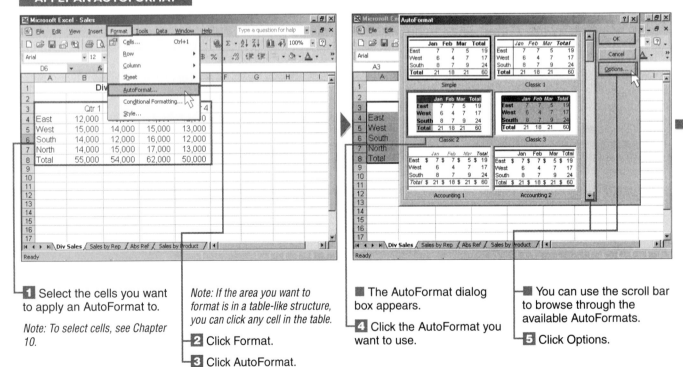

1 Select the cells you want to apply an AutoFormat to.

Note: To select cells, see Chapter 10.

Note: If the area you want to format is in a table-like structure, you can click any cell in the table.

2 Click Format.

3 Click AutoFormat.

■ The AutoFormat dialog box appears.

4 Click the AutoFormat you want to use.

■ You can use the scroll bar to browse through the available AutoFormats.

5 Click Options.

Why do I get an error message when I select one cell to apply AutoFormat?

✔ Excel does not apply an AutoFormat to a single cell. If you select only one cell, Excel cannot determine which cells in your worksheet you want to format and asks you to select a range of cells.

What is the Width/Height option used for?

✔ The Width/Height option changes the selected cell dimensions based on the amount of data in the cells and neatly displays data. If you later remove an AutoFormat using the steps in this section, the columns and rows do not return to their original size.

When I enter data to the right or below the cells where I applied an AutoFormat, Excel automatically formats the new data. How can I stop this?

✔ To turn off the automatic formatting, click Tools and then click Options. Click the Edit tab and deselect the Extend list formats and formulas option (☑ changes to ☐). Click OK to apply the option.

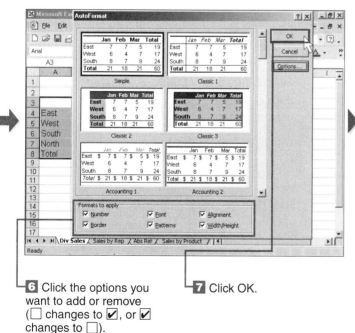

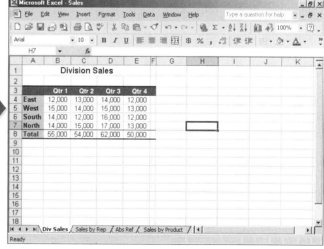

6 Click the options you want to add or remove (☐ changes to ☑, or ☑ changes to ☐).

7 Click OK.

■ The cells display the AutoFormat you selected.

■ To remove an AutoFormat, you can follow steps 1 through 3, click None in step 4, and then click OK.

PREVIEW A WORKSHEET

Y ou can use the Print Preview feature to see how your worksheet looks before you print it. Using the Print Preview feature can help you confirm any applied changes to options, thus saving you time and paper.

The Print Preview window indicates which page you are viewing and the total number of

pages in your worksheet. If your worksheet contains more than one page, you can easily view the other pages. You can also magnify an area of a page in your worksheet to view it in more detail.

If you have a black-and-white printer, the pages in the Print Preview window display in black and white. If you have a color

printer and have changed the color of your date, you see the entries in color when you preview.

When you finish with the Print Preview feature, you can close the Print Preview window to return to your worksheet. You can also print your worksheet following the steps in the section "Print a Worksheet."

PREVIEW A WORKSHEET

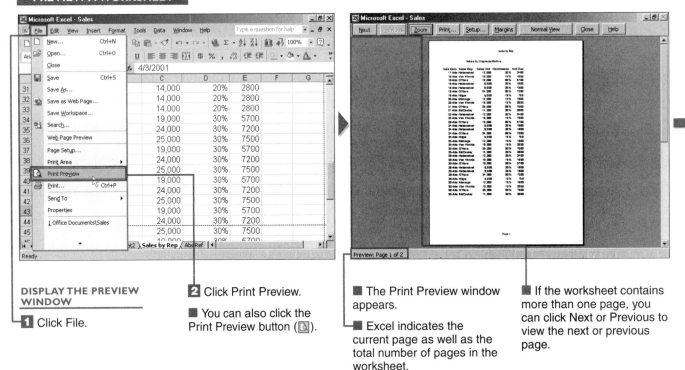

DISPLAY THE PREVIEW WINDOW

■1 Click File.

■2 Click Print Preview.

■ You can also click the Print Preview button (🔍).

■ The Print Preview window appears.

■ Excel indicates the current page as well as the total number of pages in the worksheet.

■ If the worksheet contains more than one page, you can click Next or Previous to view the next or previous page.

Excel does not display gridlines in the Print Preview window. Why not?

✔ By default, Excel does not print gridlines. To print gridlines, click Setup in the Print Preview window. Click the Sheet tab and then click the Gridlines option (☐ changes to ☑). Click OK and Excel displays your gridlines.

Can I change the margins in the Print Preview window?

✔ Yes. You can click the Margins button to change the margins in the Print Preview window. Then click and drag the margin you want to change to a new location.

How do I print my worksheet directly from the Print Preview window?

✔ Click Print. Excel returns to your worksheet and opens the Print dialog box. For information on printing, see the section "Print a Worksheet."

Why does the Print Preview window display only a chart from my worksheet?

✔ If you click a chart in your worksheet before you click the Print Preview command, the Print Preview window displays only the chart. To preview the worksheet, click outside the chart and then preview again.

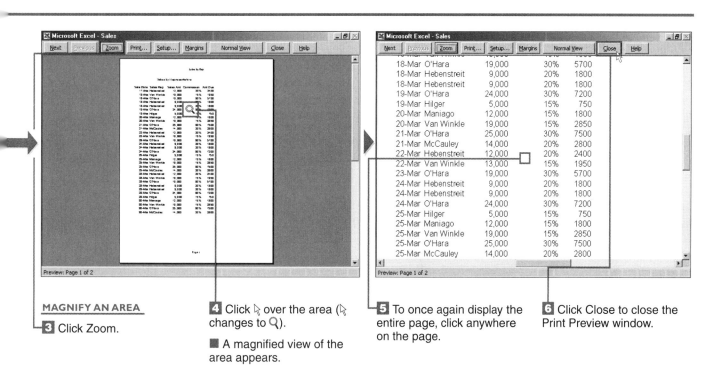

18-Mar	O'Hara	19,000	30%	5700
18-Mar	Hebenstreit	9,000	20%	1800
18-Mar	Hebenstreit	9,000	20%	1800
19-Mar	O'Hara	24,000	30%	7200
19-Mar	Hilger	5,000	15%	750
20-Mar	Maniago	12,000	15%	1800
20-Mar	Van Winkle	19,000	15%	2850
21-Mar	O'Hara	25,000	30%	7500
21-Mar	McCauley	14,000	20%	2800
22-Mar	Hebenstreit	12,000	20%	2400
22-Mar	Van Winkle	13,000	15%	1950
23-Mar	O'Hara	19,000	30%	5700
24-Mar	Hebenstreit	9,000	20%	1800
24-Mar	Hebenstreit	9,000	20%	1800
24-Mar	O'Hara	24,000	30%	7200
25-Mar	Hilger	5,000	15%	750
25-Mar	Maniago	12,000	15%	1800
25-Mar	Van Winkle	19,000	15%	2850
25-Mar	O'Hara	25,000	30%	7500
25-Mar	McCauley	14,000	20%	2800

MAGNIFY AN AREA

3 Click Zoom.

4 Click ⬚ over the area (⬚ changes to Q).

■ A magnified view of the area appears.

5 To once again display the entire page, click anywhere on the page.

6 Click Close to close the Print Preview window.

PRINT A WORKSHEET

You can produce a paper copy of a worksheet you display on your screen. This is useful when you want to present the worksheet to a colleague or refer to the worksheet when you do not have access to your computer.

If you have more than one printer installed on your computer, you can choose to which printer you want to send your worksheet. Before printing, make sure you turn on the printer and that it contains an adequate supply of paper and toner or ink.

Excel allows you to specify the part of your workbook you want to print. You can print a selection of cells, an entire worksheet, or all the worksheets in the workbook. To print a selection of cells, you must select the cells before you follow the steps in this section.

If the part of the workbook you want to print contains several pages, you can specify which pages you want to print.

PRINT A WORKSHEET

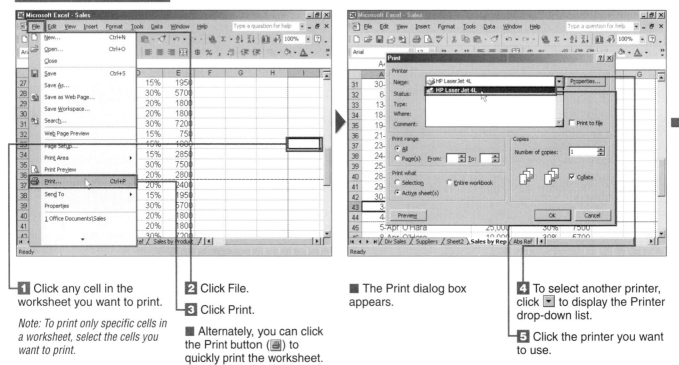

1 Click any cell in the worksheet you want to print.

Note: To print only specific cells in a worksheet, select the cells you want to print.

2 Click File.

3 Click Print.

■ Alternately, you can click the Print button (🖨) to quickly print the worksheet.

■ The Print dialog box appears.

4 To select another printer, click ▼ to display the Printer drop-down list.

5 Click the printer you want to use.

Can I print multiple copies of a worksheet?

✔ You can print multiple copies of a worksheet, workbook, or selection of cells. In the Print dialog box, double-click the Number of copies area and then type the number of copies you want to print.

Can I print more than one worksheet in my workbook?

✔ Yes. Press the Ctrl key as you click the tab for each worksheet you want to print. Then perform steps 2 through 7 in this section, except click Active sheet(s) in step 6 (○ changes to ◉).

How can I quickly print an area of my worksheet that I frequently print?

✔ Select the area you frequently print. Click File, click Print Area, and then click Set Print Area. When you click 🖨 Excel prints the data only in the print area you set. To later clear the print area, click File, click Print Area, and then click Clear Print Area.

How do I print only a selected number of cells?

✔ Select the cells you want to print. Follow steps 2 and 3 in this section. Click the Selection option in the Print dialog box and then click OK.

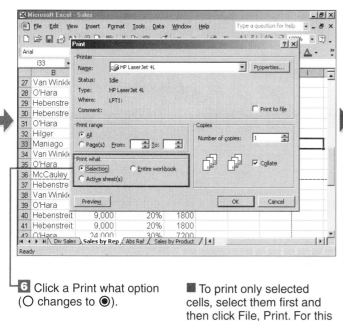

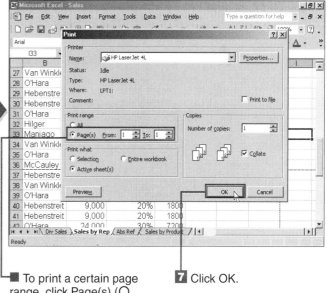

6 Click a Print what option (○ changes to ◉).

■ To print only selected cells, select them first and then click File, Print. For this option, click Selection.

■ To print a certain page range, click Page(s) (○ changes to ◉) and type the range of pages you want to print.

7 Click OK.

■ Excel prints the worksheet.

CHANGE MARGINS

Y ou can change the margins to suit the layout of your Excel worksheet, to fit more or less data on a page, or to accommodate specialty paper. For example, if you print on company letterhead, you may need to increase the size of the top margin. If you print on three-hole punched paper, you may want to increase the size of the left margin.

A *margin* is the amount of space between data and the top, bottom, left, or right edge of your paper. Excel automatically sets the top and bottom margins to 1 inch and the left and right margins to 0.75 inch.

Most printers cannot print right to the edge of a page and require that you set all margins to at least 0.25 inch. Consult your printer manual

for more information on your printing capabilities.

To avoid wasting paper, consider previewing your document to ensure your margins are correct before you print. For more on the preview feature, see the section "Preview a Worksheet." For more on printing your worksheet, see the section "Print a Worksheet."

CHANGE MARGINS

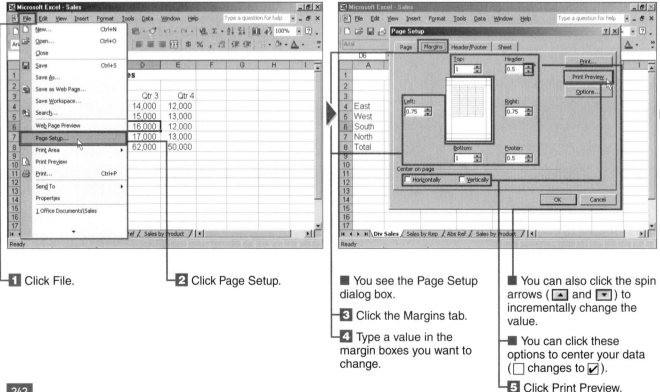

■ **1** Click File.

■ **2** Click Page Setup.

■ You see the Page Setup dialog box.

3 Click the Margins tab.

4 Type a value in the margin boxes you want to change.

■ You can also click the spin arrows (▲ and ▼) to incrementally change the value.

■ You can click these options to center your data (☐ changes to ☑).

5 Click Print Preview.

Can I access and change settings for my printer?

✔ Yes. To view the available options for your particular printer, click Options. You see the Properties dialog box for your particular printer. You can use this dialog box to select default options, such as the page orientation, for your printer. Make your changes and click OK to apply them.

Can I change the margins in the Print Preview view?

✔ Yes. Click Print Preview. If the margins do not display, click Margins. Click the margin you want to change and drag the margin to a new location.

What other margin settings can I change?

✔ You can also change the margins for the header and footer. The default margin setting is .5 inch. See "Add a Header or Footer" for information on adding headers and footers to your worksheet.

What do the Center on page options do?

✔ Rather than change the margins, you might center the page to place it between the top and bottom or left and right margins. To do so, click the appropriate option (☐ changes to ☑).

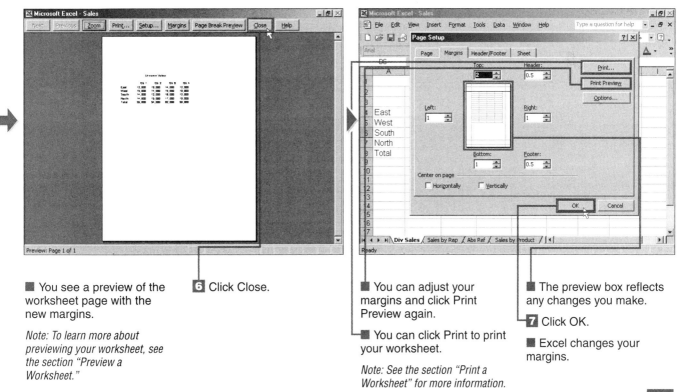

■ You see a preview of the worksheet page with the new margins.

Note: To learn more about previewing your worksheet, see the section "Preview a Worksheet."

6 Click Close.

■ You can adjust your margins and click Print Preview again.

■ You can click Print to print your worksheet.

Note: See the section "Print a Worksheet" for more information.

■ The preview box reflects any changes you make.

7 Click OK.

■ Excel changes your margins.

CHANGE PAGE ORIENTATION

You can change the page orientation and thus the direction that a worksheet prints on a page.

Excel allows you to print worksheets using the portrait or landscape orientation. By default, Excel prints worksheets across the short side of a page, in the portrait orientation. This orientation is useful for printing worksheets that have more rows than columns. When you have a worksheet with

more columns than rows, you can print the worksheet in the landscape orientation, which rotates the worksheet so the data prints across the long side of a page.

Changing the page orientation only affects the current worksheet, and not your other worksheets or workbooks. Also, it does not change the way the current worksheet appears on-screen.

To make sure that your orientation change does not affect the elements in your worksheet, you can use Print Preview to see how the worksheet appears when printed. For more information on Print Preview, see "Preview a Worksheet."

After you change your page orientation, you can print your worksheet. See the section "Print a Worksheet" for more information.

CHANGE PAGE ORIENTATION

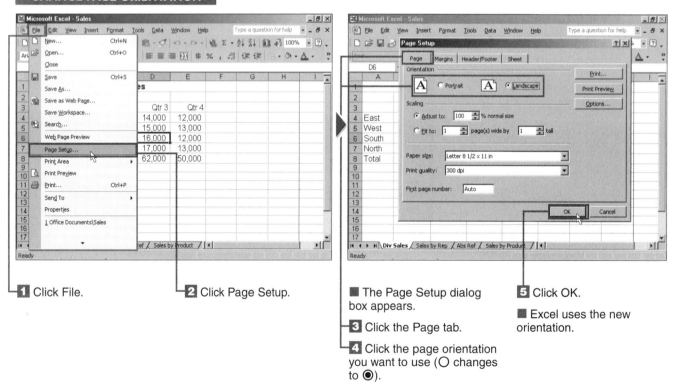

■ Click File.

2 Click Page Setup.

■ The Page Setup dialog box appears.

3 Click the Page tab.

4 Click the page orientation you want to use (○ changes to ◉).

5 Click OK.

■ Excel uses the new orientation.

CHANGE PRINT OPTIONS

You can use the print options Excel offers to change the way your worksheet appears on a printed page. Changing the print options for your worksheet allows you to create a printout that suits your needs.

You can select the Gridlines option to have Excel print lines around each cell in a worksheet. This can help make the data in a large worksheet easier to read.

The Black and white option prints a colored worksheet in black and white, which is useful when you have a color printer but want to print a black-and-white draft of a worksheet.

The Draft quality option helps reduce printing time because it quickly prints a rough draft of a worksheet without gridlines and most graphics.

When you click the Row and column headings option, Excel

prints the row numbers and column headings in your worksheet.

Changing the print options only changes the way your worksheet appears on a printed page and not the appearance of your worksheet on the screen.

After you select the options you want, you can print your worksheet. See the section "Print a Worksheet" for more information.

CHANGE PRINT OPTIONS

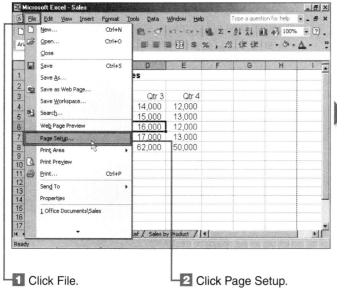

1 Click File.

2 Click Page Setup.

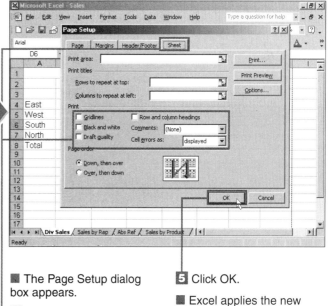

■ The Page Setup dialog box appears.

3 Click the Sheet tab.

4 Click each print option you want to apply (☐ changes to ☑).

5 Click OK.

■ Excel applies the new settings when you print the worksheet.

Note: To print a worksheet, see the section "Print a Worksheet."

INSERT AND VIEW A PAGE BREAK

You can insert a page break when you want to start a new page at a specific place in your worksheet. A *page break* defines where one page ends and another begins.

By default, Excel automatically starts a new page by inserting a page break for you when you fill a page with data. However, you may need to insert your own page break

to ensure that related data appears on the same page when you print your worksheet.

Inserting a horizontal page break above a row prints the rows below the break on a new page. Inserting a vertical page break to the left of a column prints the columns to the right of the break on a new page.

Before you print your worksheet, you can preview all the page breaks

in the worksheet. In this view, page breaks inserted by Excel appear as dotted blue lines. Page breaks you insert appear as solid blue lines. You can adjust the page breaks, as needed, in this view.

The page break lines are not printed when you print the worksheet.

INSERT A PAGE BREAK

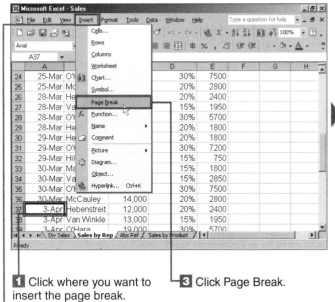

1 Click where you want to insert the page break.

2 Click Insert.

3 Click Page Break.

■ A dotted line appears on the screen. This line defines where one page ends and another begins.

How do I remove a page break?

✔ Select a cell that is directly below or directly to the right of the page break you want to remove. Click Insert and then click Remove Page Break.

Can I remove all the page breaks I inserted in my worksheet at once?

✔ Yes. Click the blank area to the left of column A and above row 1 to select the entire worksheet. Click Insert and then click Reset All Page Breaks.

Can I insert horizontal and vertical page breaks at the same time?

✔ Yes. Click the cell directly below and to the right of where you want the horizontal and vertical page breaks to appear. Click Insert and then click Page Break. Excel divides the worksheet into quadrants with the selected cell as the top right corner in the bottom right quadrant. You might use this type of page break to divide a worksheet into pages both horizontally and vertically.

VIEW A PAGE BREAK

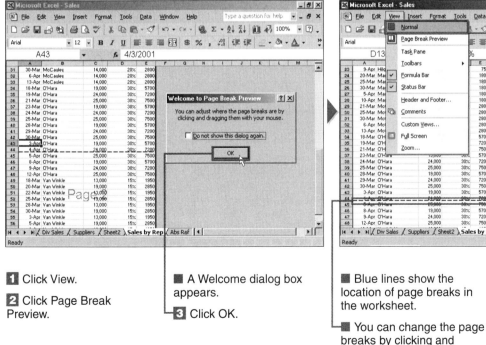

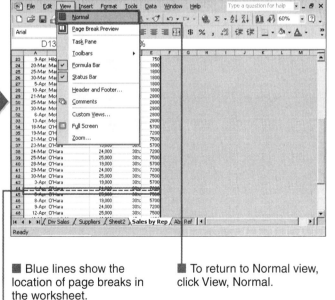

1 Click View.

2 Click Page Break Preview.

■ A Welcome dialog box appears.

3 Click OK.

■ Blue lines show the location of page breaks in the worksheet.

■ You can change the page breaks by clicking and dragging the blue indicator line.

■ To return to Normal view, click View, Normal.

247

FIT A WORKSHEET TO A PAGE OR PAGES

xcel allows you to reduce the size of printed data so that you can print your worksheet on a specific number of pages. This is useful when the last page of your worksheet contains a small amount of data that you want to fit on the previous page.

To change the size of printed data, you must specify how many pages you want the data to print across

and down so that Excel can resize your data.

When you change the size of printed data, Excel ignores any inserted page breaks in your worksheet. For information on page breaks, see "Insert and View a Page Break."

Changing the size of printed data does not affect the way your worksheet appears on-screen.

However, if you try to fit your worksheet on too few pages, the data may become too small to read. You may need to adjust the number you enter before Excel fits your data correctly. Consider viewing your document with the Print Preview feature before printing, as illustrated in the section "Preview a Worksheet." To print your worksheet, see the section "Print a Worksheet."

FIT A WORKSHEET TO A PAGE OR PAGES

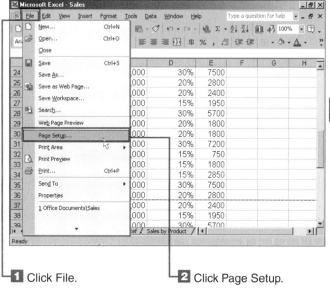

1 Click File.

2 Click Page Setup.

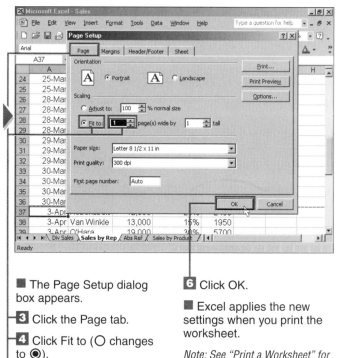

■ The Page Setup dialog box appears.

3 Click the Page tab.

4 Click Fit to (○ changes to ◉).

5 Type the width and height of your data in pages.

6 Click OK.

■ Excel applies the new settings when you print the worksheet.

Note: See "Print a Worksheet" for more on printing.

REPEAT ROW OR COLUMN HEADINGS

If your worksheet prints on more than one page, you can print the same row or column labels on every page.

Repeating row or column labels can help make the data in a long worksheet easier to understand. For example, repeating column labels in a worksheet containing product information can help you avoid confusing data in the

"Quantity Sold" column with data in the "Quantity in Stock" column.

You need to select only one cell in each row or column of labels you want to print on every page. If the Page Setup dialog box covers the labels you want to repeat, you can move the dialog box to a new location.

Repeating labels on printed pages does not affect the way your

worksheet appears on the screen. You can use the Print Preview feature to preview how the repeated labels look when you print your worksheet. See the section "Preview a Worksheet" for more information.

Once you specify which row or column headings to repeat, you can print your worksheet. See the section "Print a Worksheet" to learn more.

REPEAT ROW OR COLUMN HEADINGS

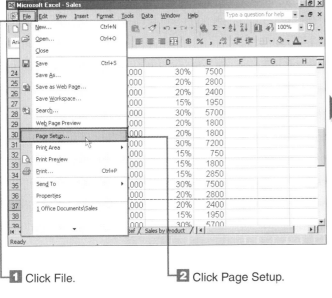

1 Click File.

2 Click Page Setup.

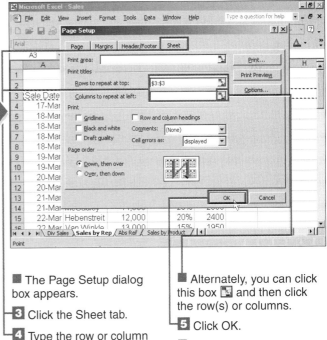

■ The Page Setup dialog box appears.

3 Click the Sheet tab.

4 Type the row or column reference(s) you want to repeat.

■ Alternately, you can click this box 🔲 and then click the row(s) or columns.

5 Click OK.

■ When you print the worksheet, Excel includes the specified rows and columns.

ADD A HEADER OR FOOTER

You can add a header or footer to display additional information on each page of your worksheet. A header or footer can contain information such as your name, the page number, and the current date.

By default, a header appears 0.5 inch from the top of a printed page, and a footer appears 0.5 inch from the bottom of a printed page. A

worksheet can contain only one header and one footer.

Excel provides many headers and footers elements from which you can choose. If your worksheet contains budget or financial information, you may want to choose a header that contains the word "Confidential." If you frequently update the data in your worksheet, you may want to choose

a footer that includes the current date every time the worksheet is printed.

To see how a header or footer appears before you print your worksheet, you can use the Print Preview feature. See the section "Preview a Worksheet" for more information on this option.

ADD A HEADER OR FOOTER

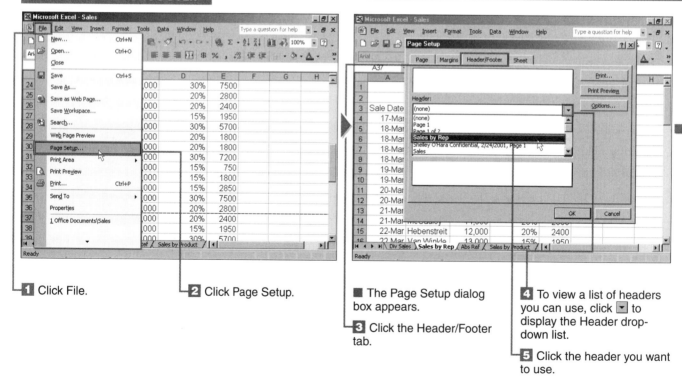

1 Click File.

2 Click Page Setup.

■ The Page Setup dialog box appears.

3 Click the Header/Footer tab.

4 To view a list of headers you can use, click ▼ to display the Header drop-down list.

5 Click the header you want to use.

How do I remove a header or footer?

✔ Click View and then click Header and Footer. The Page Setup box appears. To remove a header, click the Header area ⏷ and then click (none). To remove a footer, click the Footer area ⏷ and then click (none).

Can I modify the text in the header or footer?

✔ No. You can only select another of the available header or footer options. If you want to change the text, create a custom header or footer, as covered in "Create a Custom Header or Footer."

How do I change where the header and footer prints on the page?

✔ You can change the header or footer margins to print them further or closer from the edge of the page. See "Change Margins" for information on changing margins, including header and footer margins.

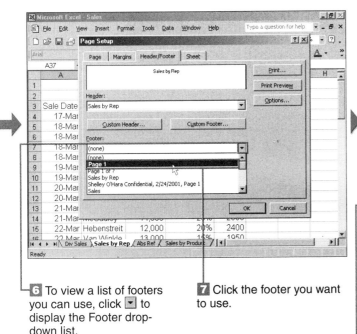

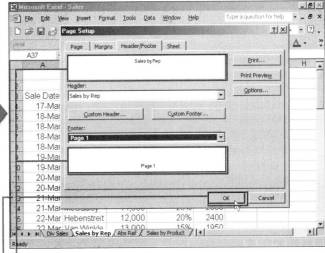

■6 To view a list of footers you can use, click ⏷ to display the Footer drop-down list.

■7 Click the footer you want to use.

■ These areas display a preview of the header and footer.

■8 Click OK to add the header or footer to the worksheet.

■ Excel prints the headers and footers when you print the worksheet.

Note: See the section "Print a Worksheet" for more information.

CREATE A CUSTOM HEADER OR FOOTER

Excel includes several predefined headers and footers. If none suits your needs, you can create a custom header or footer. Custom headers and footers include three sections in which you can enter text: a left section, a center section, and a right section. You can enter text in any of the sections as needed.

The Header and Footer dialog boxes also include buttons for formatting text, or inserting workbook and worksheet information such as the number of pages, the name of the workbook, or the current date.

Custom footers use the default margins: a header appears 0.5 inch from the top of a printed page, and a footer appears 0.5 inch from the bottom of a printed page. A worksheet can contain only one header and one footer. However, you can include both a header and footer on the same page.

To see how a custom header or footer appears before you print your worksheet, you can use the Print Preview feature. See the section "Preview a Worksheet" for more information on this option.

CREATE A CUSTOM HEADER OR FOOTER

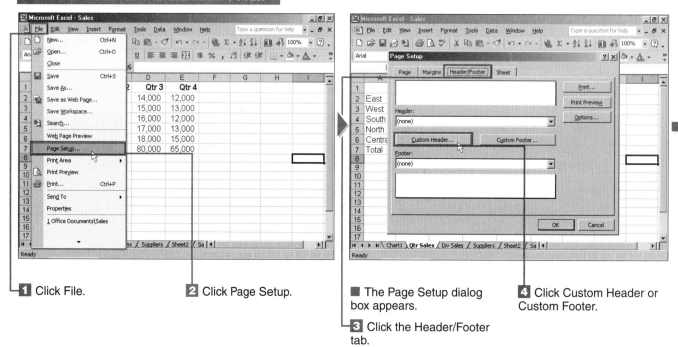

1 Click File.

2 Click Page Setup.

■ The Page Setup dialog box appears.

3 Click the Header/Footer tab.

4 Click Custom Header or Custom Footer.

My custom header runs into the data in my worksheet. What can I do?

✔ You can increase the top or bottom margin to allow more space for a header or footer. Click File and click Page Setup. Then click the Margins tab. Double-click the Top or Bottom area and type a larger number. Then click OK. See "Change Margins" for more information on changing margins.

Can I format the text of the header or footer?

✔ Yes. To do so, click the Font button (▲). You see the Font dialog box. Select the font, font style, and font size and then click OK.

Can I insert the page number?

✔ Yes. You can insert the page number by clicking the Page Number button (▣). If you want to insert the total number of pages, click the Total Pages button (▣).

What other elements can I include in the header or footer from the dialog box buttons?

✔ You can also include the date, time, workbook name, or worksheet name by clicking the appropriate buttons in the dialog box.

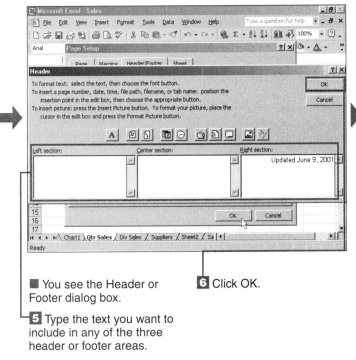

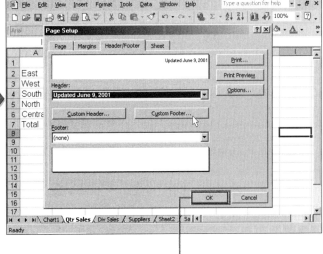

■ You see the Header or Footer dialog box.

5 Type the text you want to include in any of the three header or footer areas.

6 Click OK.

■ Previews of the header and footer appear in the Page Setup dialog box.

7 Click OK.

■ Excel prints the headers and footers when you print the worksheet.

Note: See the section "Print a Worksheet" for more information.

AN INTRODUCTION TO CHARTS

One of the main components of Excel is its ability to take the numerical data in your worksheet and create a chart.

Charts help visually show the data in meaningful ways that you may not see clearly when viewing the pure numbers. For example,

charting data as a line chart can help you spot trends, while charting data as a pie chart helps you see which product is a best-seller.

Types of Charts

Excel provides many types of charts to choose from, and one of the main decisions when creating a chart is selecting a chart that best conveys the message you want. The following table describes the most common chart types.

Excel Chart Types

Type of Chart	Example	Description
Column		Compares values from different categories.
Bar		Similar to a column chart, only the bars are horizontal.
Line		Shows changes in values over time. Good for showing trends.
Pie		Shows the relationship of each value to the overall total.
Area		Shows both trends as well as the contribution of each value to the whole.

Excel also includes some specialized chart types that include those you use in scientific studies to show various data points (XY, bubble, and radar), variations of other chart types (doughnut, surface, cylinder, cone, and pyramid), and a chart for showing stock values.

Parts of a Chart

A chart is made of different elements, each of which contributes to the overall meaning and appearance of the chart. You can customize each element as indicated, using the various tasks in this chapter. To understand how to create a chart to fit your situation, take some time to familiarize yourself with the different parts of a chart.

Chart Title

You can use chart titles to label the various parts of your chart including the name of the chart, and the x and y axis.

Plot Area

The area on which Excel draws your chart. You can change the background color as well as the lines that Excel displays to represent your data.

Data Marker

The individual value represented by one number from the worksheet and charted as one element in the chart. A collection of data markers makes up a data series.

Data Series

A data series is a collection of one set of data values. For example, a data series may include sales for one particular year in your company.

Legend

The legend contains the key to the values in the chart. You can choose whether to display the legend as well as select its placement.

Category Names

The names that appear along the x-, or category axis. Excel pulls these categories from the worksheet.

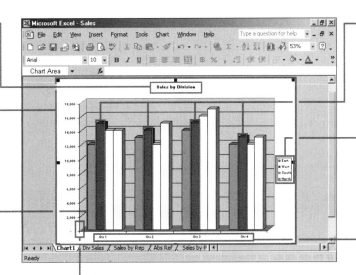

Axes

Excel plots most charts using an x-axis and a y-axis—also called the horizontal and vertical axis. Excel also has chart types that include a third axis, called the z-axis. You can choose how Excel formats and labels the various axes. If you are charting two points, two axes are enough. When you need to plot three points or variables–for example, temperature, pressure, and volume–then select a chart type with three axes.

CREATE A CHART USING A WIZARD

Y ou can create a chart to graphically display your worksheet data and make it easier to understand.

To create the chart, you must first organize the data for your chart into rows and columns, which you can make consecutive or non-consecutive. If you include the column or row labels in your selection, Excel uses them as titles in the chart. To learn how to enter data for your chart, see Chapter 10.

When creating a chart to plot several data values — for example,

all of the divisions of a company for the four quarters of the year — you do not select the totals. Doing so would chart these values, which is not appropriate for the purpose of the chart. On the other hand if you want to create a pie chart and wanted to compare totals of each division, then you would include totals.

After you select your data, you can use the Chart Wizard to help you create the chart. The wizard allows you to determine the type of chart you want to create, such as a

Column, Pie, or Area chart, as well as specify whether you want to plot your worksheet data by rows or columns.

You can add titles to a chart to identify the chart's subject. By default, Excel designates the X-axis title as the categories you include in your data, and the Y-axis title as the unit of measure you use in the chart. If you create a 3-D chart, Excel may allow you to add a title to the Z-axis.

CREATE A CHART USING A WIZARD

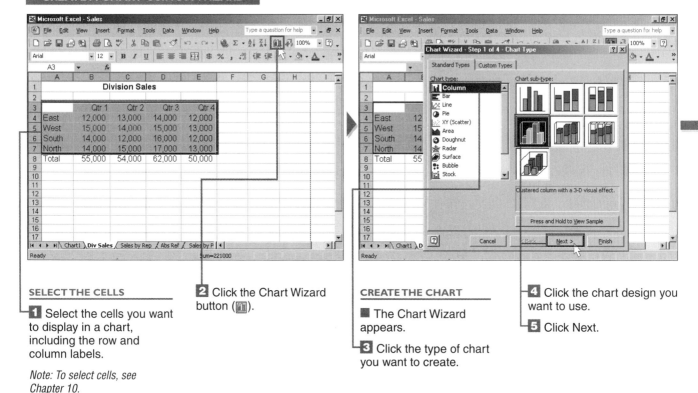

SELECT THE CELLS

■1 Select the cells you want to display in a chart, including the row and column labels.

Note: To select cells, see Chapter 10.

■2 Click the Chart Wizard button (📊).

CREATE THE CHART

■ The Chart Wizard appears.

■3 Click the type of chart you want to create.

■4 Click the chart design you want to use.

■5 Click Next.

How can I preview my chart type selection in the Chart Wizard?

✔ After you select a chart type and design for your chart, you can click the Press and Hold to View Sample button to see what the chart looks like in your worksheet.

Can I change the chart type after I create a chart?

✔ You can change the chart type at any time after creating a chart. To change the chart type, see "Change the Chart Type."

Can I change the chart titles after I create a chart?

✔ Yes. In the completed chart, click the title you want to change. Type the new title and then press Enter.

Is there a keyboard shortcut to quickly create a chart?

✔ Yes. You can quickly create a chart that displays Excel's default chart settings. Select the cells containing the data you want to display in the chart and then press F11. The chart appears on its own sheet in your workbook.

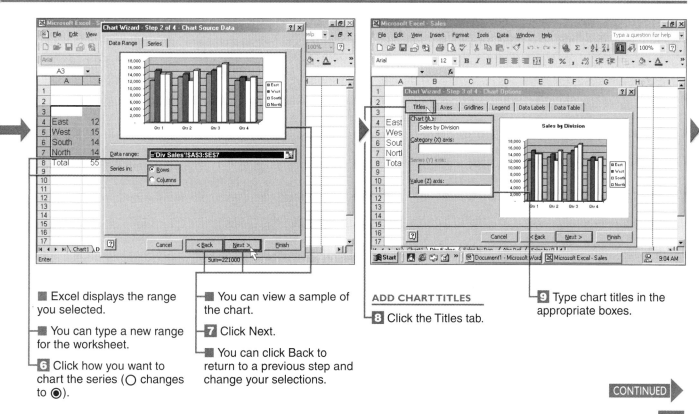

■ Excel displays the range you selected.

■ You can type a new range for the worksheet.

6 Click how you want to chart the series (○ changes to ◉).

■ You can view a sample of the chart.

7 Click Next.

■ You can click Back to return to a previous step and change your selections.

ADD CHART TITLES

8 Click the Titles tab.

9 Type chart titles in the appropriate boxes.

CONTINUED

CREATE A CHART USING A WIZARD
(CONTINUED)

After you create your chart and add titles, Excel allows you to create a legend for your chart. A *legend* is a key that identifies each data series in your chart. *Data series* are related data representing one row or column from your worksheet. When you display more than one data series in a chart, Excel uses different colors, patterns, or symbols to help you identify each data series.

Excel gives you several options for displaying the legend. You can locate the legend at the bottom, top, right, left, or top-right corner of the chart. You can also opt to display your chart on the same worksheet as the data, or on its own sheet — called a chart sheet.

After you select your chart options, Excel displays the chart on your screen. Excel also displays the Chart toolbar, which automatically appears on your screen when you select the chart.

The handles that appear around a chart allow you to resize the chart. For information on resizing a chart, see "Move or Resize a Chart."

CREATE A CHART USING A WIZARD (CONTINUED)

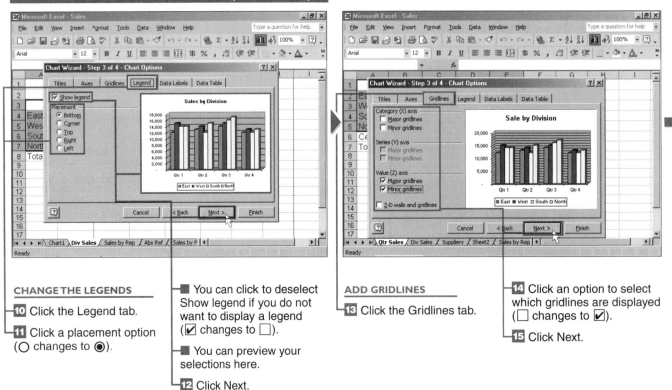

CHANGE THE LEGENDS

-10 Click the Legend tab.

-11 Click a placement option (○ changes to ◉).

■ You can click to deselect Show legend if you do not want to display a legend (☑ changes to ☐).

■ You can preview your selections here.

-12 Click Next.

ADD GRIDLINES

-13 Click the Gridlines tab.

-14 Click an option to select which gridlines are displayed (☐ changes to ☑).

-15 Click Next.

What happens if I change data used in a chart?

✔ If you change data used in a chart in the underlying worksheet, Excel automatically updates the chart.

How can I format a chart?

✔ You can format each area of a chart individually. For more information, see the section "Format Chart Elements."

How can I hide the legend for my chart?

✔ Click a blank area of the chart. On the Chart toolbar, click the Legend button (▤) to hide or display the legend.

Can I add a data table that includes the data I used for my chart within the chart?

✔ Yes. Click a blank area of the chart. On the Chart toolbar, click the Data Table button to add or remove a data table at any time.

Can I move the Chart toolbar?

✔ Yes. Position the ▷ over the title bar of the Chart toolbar and then drag the toolbar to a new location on your screen.

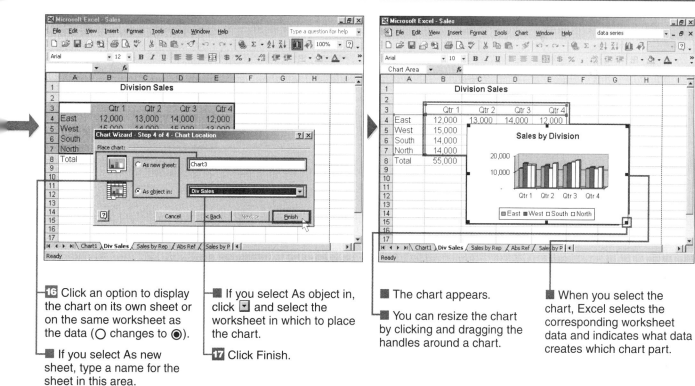

■16 Click an option to display the chart on its own sheet or on the same worksheet as the data (○ changes to ●).

■ If you select As new sheet, type a name for the sheet in this area.

■ If you select As object in, click ▣ and select the worksheet in which to place the chart.

■17 Click Finish.

■ The chart appears.

■ You can resize the chart by clicking and dragging the handles around a chart.

■ When you select the chart, Excel selects the corresponding worksheet data and indicates what data creates which chart part.

CHANGE THE CHART TYPE

You can change the chart type to present your data more effectively. Excel provides 14 standard chart types and approximately 70 designs including Column, Bar, Line, Area, and Pie charts, which are the most popular chart types. In most cases, the individual elements in the chart, such as the columns, bars, lines, areas, or pie sections, represent a data series. *Data series* are related data representing one row or column from your worksheet.

Because each chart type presents data in a specific way, your chart

type depends on your data and on your preference for presenting it.

A *column chart* shows changes to data over time, or compares individual items. You might compare sales of different divisions and quarters, for example.

A *bar chart* compares individual items.

A *line chart* shows changes to data at regular intervals. You might, for example, plot the yearly sales of a company to notice any sales trends.

An *area chart* shows the amount of change in data over time.

A *pie chart* shows the relationship of parts to a whole. You might, for example, plot the total sales of each product to see how much each product contributes to the overall sales total. A pie chart can show only one data series at a time.

To learn how to create a chart, see the section "Create a Chart Using a Wizard."

CHANGE THE CHART TYPE

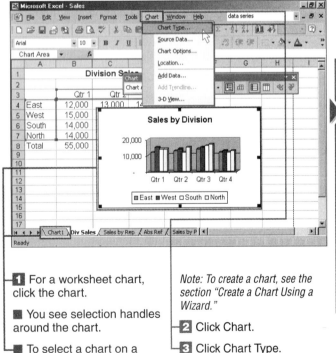

1 For a worksheet chart, click the chart.

■ You see selection handles around the chart.

■ To select a chart on a separate worksheet, click the tab containing the chart.

Note: To create a chart, see the section "Create a Chart Using a Wizard."

2 Click Chart.

3 Click Chart Type.

■ The Chart Type dialog box appears.

4 Click the chart type you want to use.

5 Click the chart design you want to use.

What is the difference between the Pie and Doughnut chart types?

✔ While pie and doughnut charts are both useful for showing the relationship of parts to a whole, they differ in the amount of information they can display. A pie chart can display only one data series, but a doughnut chart can display multiple data series with each ring of a doughnut chart representing a data series.

How can I quickly change the chart type?

✔ Click a blank area in the chart you want to change. On the Chart toolbar, click the ▪ beside the Chart Type button (▥ ▾) and then select the chart type you want to use. If the Chart toolbar is not displayed, click View, Toolbars, Chart.

What chart types are available on the Custom Types tab in the Chart Type dialog box?

✔ The Custom Types tab contains custom chart types that are based on standard chart types but include additional formatting. For example, you can use the Columns with Depth custom chart type to create a two-dimensional chart with three-dimensional columns.

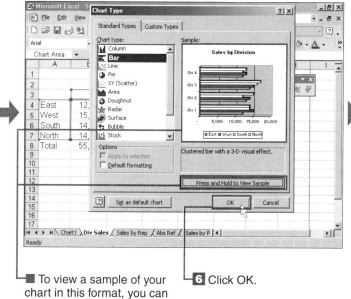

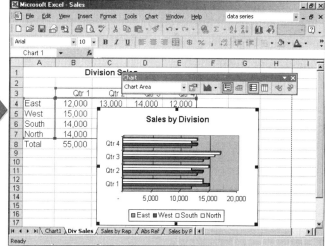

■ To view a sample of your chart in this format, you can click and hold your ⏸ on the Press and Hold to View Sample button.

6 Click OK.

■ Excel updates the chart to the new chart type.

FORMAT CHART ELEMENTS

You can format each individual element that makes up a chart. You can do so to enhance the appearance of each element so that the chart displays your data in the most effective manner possible.

Depending on the item you select, the options vary and only the most common are described here. For chart titles, you can format the font, font style, and font size, alignment, border, and pattern.

For data series, you can format the color and pattern. For some chart types — bar and column, for example — you can also select a different shape for the series, including pyramid, cone, or cylinder. For the chart axes, you can include lines and define their style, color, and weight. For the legend, you can change the font and placement as well as add a pattern and border.

FORMAT CHART ELEMENTS

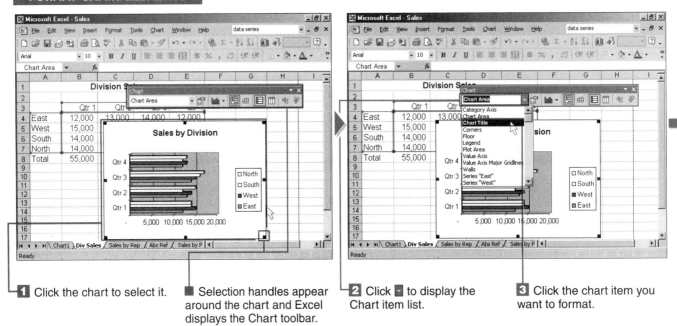

1 Click the chart to select it.

■ Selection handles appear around the chart and Excel displays the Chart toolbar.

2 Click ⊡ to display the Chart item list.

3 Click the chart item you want to format.

What if I make a change that I do not like?

✔ If you make a formatting change that you do not like, you can undo the change. To do so, click the Undo button (⟲).

I do not see the Chart toolbar. How can I display it?

✔ When you select the chart, the Chart toolbar should be displayed. If it is not, be sure the chart is selected. If the chart is selected, you may have closed the toolbar. To redisplay the toolbar, click View, Toolbars, Chart.

What is another method to make a change to a chart element?

✔ As an alternative to selecting the item to format from the Chart toolbar, you can also double-click the item you want to change. The appropriate dialog box for the selected item appears. Make your changes and click OK.

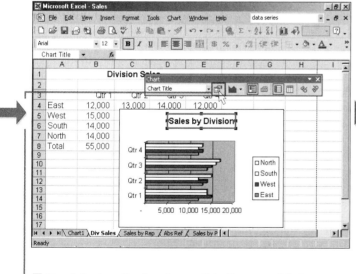

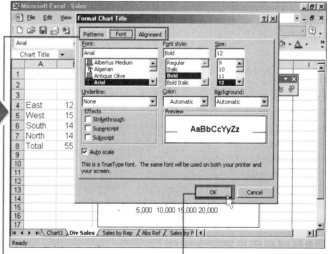

■ Excel displays the item in the Chart toolbar.

Note: The name of the button varies depending on the selected item.

4 Click the Format button (🖼).

■ You see the dialog box with formatting options for that item. The tabs and options vary depending on what you select.

5 Make any changes using the various tabs.

6 Click OK.

■ Excel updates the chart with your new selections.

MOVE OR RESIZE A CHART

You can move a chart to another location in your worksheet or change the size of a chart. You might move a chart if it covers your data. You can change the chart size if the chart information is too small to read.

For both moving and resizing, you use the handles that appear around the chart when you select it. Top and bottom handles allow you to change chart height while side handles allow you to change the chart width. Corner handles allow you to change both dimensions at the same time.

Can I move the slices in a pie chart?

✔ Yes. Click the pie chart and then click the slice you want to pull out. Selection handles appear around the slice. Click a slice and then drag it away from the chart.

Can I move a chart to its own chart sheet?

✔ Yes. Click a blank area in the chart. Open the Chart menu and then select the Location command. Click the As new sheet option button. Type a name for the chart sheet and then click OK.

MOVE OR RESIZE A CHART

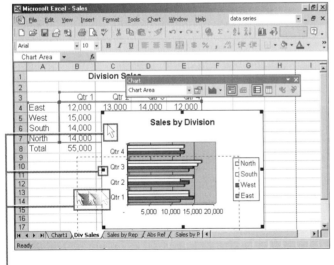

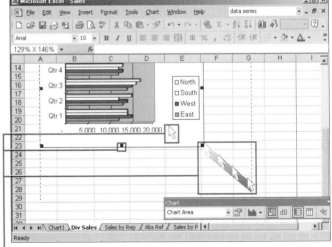

MOVE A CHART

1 Click over a blank area in the chart.

■ Selection handles appear.

2 Click and drag the chart to a new location.

■ To copy a chart, you can press the Ctrl key as you drag.

3 Release the mouse.

■ The chart appears in the new location.

RESIZE A CHART

1 Click a blank area in the chart.

■ Selection handles appear.

2 Click and drag a handle.

■ To resize the chart without changing the height-to-width ratio, press the Shift key as you drag a corner handle.

3 Release the mouse.

■ The chart resizes.

DELETE A CHART

You can delete a chart you no longer need from your worksheet. You may need to delete a chart when you alter the data on your worksheet or when the chart information is outdated.

When you delete a chart in Excel, your data remains intact, but your chart disappears. You can retrieve a chart if you immediately use the Undo feature. See Chapter 4 for more on using Undo. If you save your workbook after you delete a chart, your deletion is permanent and you must re-create the chart if you did not intend to delete it. For more information on creating a chart, see the section "Create a Chart Using a Wizard."

How do I delete a chart that is on a chart sheet?

✔ You must delete the chart sheet. Right-click the tab for the chart sheet you want to delete. Click Delete on the menu that appears. Then click OK in the confirmation dialog box that appears.

DELETE A CHART

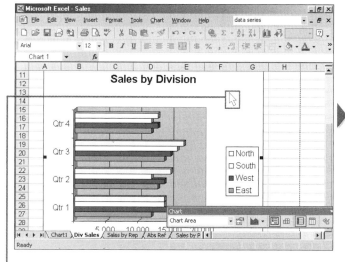

DELETE A CHART

1 Click a blank area in the chart to select it.

2 Press Delete.

■ Excel deletes the chart.

265

ADD DATA TO A CHART

After you create a chart, you can add a new data series to the chart and avoid creating a new chart. A *data series* is a group of related data representing one row or column from your worksheet. The ability to add a new data series to a chart is useful when the chart needs to be updated over time. For example, a chart containing monthly sales figures needs to be updated with a new data series each month. Excel

automatically updates the legend when you add a new data series to a chart. To learn more about creating a chart, see the section "Create a Chart Using a Wizard."

You can add a new data series to any chart type with the exception of a pie chart. This is because a pie chart displays only one data series. For more on changing the chart type, see the section "Change the Chart Type."

Just as you can add data, you can also delete data within a chart. Perhaps you added a data series that is not pertinent. In that case, you can delete it.

If you add or delete data and change your mind, you can Undo the change using the Undo button.

ADD DATA TO A CHART

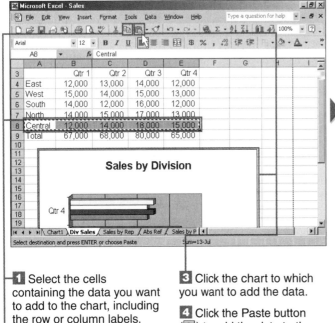

■1 Select the cells containing the data you want to add to the chart, including the row or column labels.

■2 Click the Copy button (📋) to copy the data.

■3 Click the chart to which you want to add the data.

■4 Click the Paste button (📋) to add the data to the chart.

■ The data appears in the chart.

■ To delete a data series in a chart, you can click the data series you want to delete and then press Delete.

266

PRINT A CHART

You can print a chart with the worksheet data or on its own page so that you have a hardcopy of your data for a presentation or meeting.

Printing a chart with the worksheet data is useful if you want the data and the chart to appear on the same page. When you print a chart on its own worksheet, the chart expands to fill the page. The printed chart may look different from the chart on your screen. For example, you may find that the chart's legend is smaller.

If you are using a black-and-white printer to print the chart, the colors in the chart appear as shades of gray. If you have a color printer, the chart prints in the colors you have selected.

Can I preview a chart before I print it?

✔ Yes. You preview a chart the same way you preview a worksheet. This allows you to see how the chart looks before you print it. Click the Print Preview button (🔍).

Can I send the document directly to the printer?

✔ Yes. To do so, click the Print button (🖨) in the Standard toolbar. When you click this button, the document is sent to the default printer. Use the File, Print command when you want to change print options such as the number of copies or the printer that is used.

PRINT A CHART

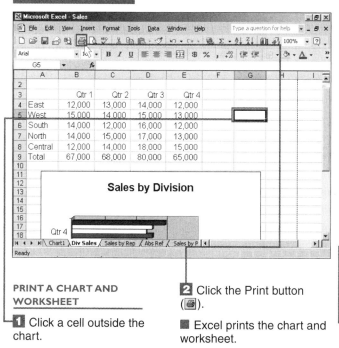

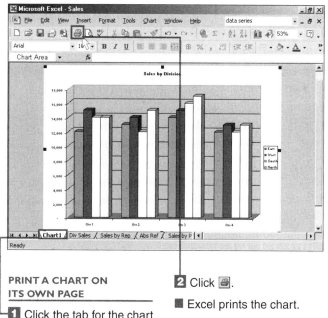

PRINT A CHART AND WORKSHEET

1 Click a cell outside the chart.

2 Click the Print button (🖨).

■ Excel prints the chart and worksheet.

PRINT A CHART ON ITS OWN PAGE

1 Click the tab for the chart sheet.

2 Click 🖨.

■ Excel prints the chart.

ADD AN AUTOSHAPE TO A WORKSHEET

Excel provides many ready-made shapes, called AutoShapes, that you can add to your worksheet or chart.

Adding an AutoShape is a fast and easy way to enhance the appearance of your worksheet. You can also add AutoShapes to help illustrate information or draw attention to important data.

Excel offers several categories of AutoShapes from which you can choose. You can select a category to find the AutoShape you want to add. For example, the Lines category contains lines and arrows. The Basic Shapes category contains rectangles, ovals, crosses, and hearts. The Stars and Banners category contains ribbons and stars with 8, 16, or 32 points.

When you add an AutoShape to your worksheet, Excel lets you specify the location for the AutoShape and the size you want the AutoShape to display. You can later move and resize the Auto-Shape to suit your worksheet. You can also delete an AutoShape you no longer need. For information on moving, resizing, or deleting a graphic, see the section "Work with Graphics."

ADD AN AUTOSHAPE TO A WORKSHEET

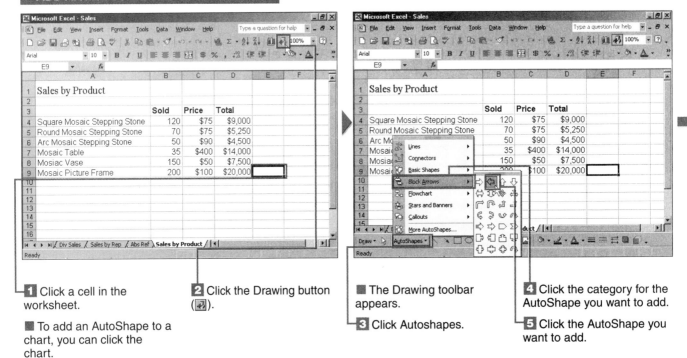

1 Click a cell in the worksheet.

■ To add an AutoShape to a chart, you can click the chart.

2 Click the Drawing button (🗏).

■ The Drawing toolbar appears.

3 Click Autoshapes.

4 Click the category for the AutoShape you want to add.

5 Click the AutoShape you want to add.

Can I control how an AutoShape appears in my Worksheet?

✔ When drawing an AutoShape, you can hold down Alt to have an AutoShape fit perfectly within cell borders. You can hold down Ctrl to draw an AutoShape from the center outward. You can hold down Shift to maintain the height-to-width ratio of an AutoShape.

Can I add text to an AutoShape?

✔ Yes. Click the AutoShape and then type the text you want to add. You cannot add text to some AutoShapes.

How can I change the appearance of an AutoShape?

✔ You can use the buttons on the Drawing toolbar to change the appearance of an AutoShape. Click the AutoShape you want to change. To change the color of an AutoShape, click next to the Fill Color button and then select a color. To add a shadow, click the Shadow button and then select a shadow. To add a 3-D effect, click the 3-D button and then select a 3-D effect.

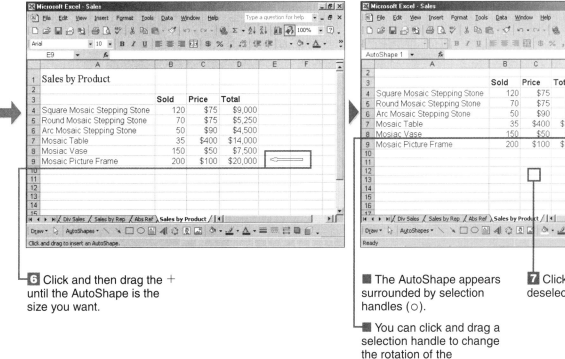

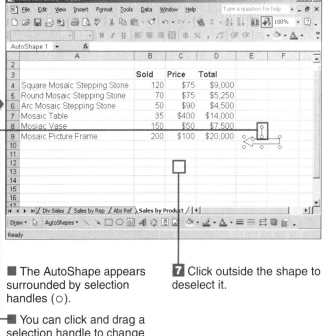

6 Click and then drag the + until the AutoShape is the size you want.

■ The AutoShape appears surrounded by selection handles (○).

■ You can click and drag a selection handle to change the rotation of the AutoShape.

7 Click outside the shape to deselect it.

ADD A TEXT BOX

You can add a text box to your worksheet or chart to display additional information.

Text boxes are useful for displaying your comments. You can also use text boxes to label, identify, or describe specific items in your worksheet or chart. The text you type in a text box wraps to fit the width of the text box.

After you add a text box, you can move and resize the text box to suit your worksheet. You can also delete a text box you no longer need. For information on moving, resizing, or deleting a graphic, see the section "Work with Graphics."

In addition to text boxes, Excel offers AutoShapes that are specifically designed to display

text, such as the AutoShapes in the Stars and Banners or Callout categories. These AutoShapes let you neatly display additional text in your worksheet. For more information on AutoShapes, see "Add an AutoShape to a Worksheet."

ADD A TEXT BOX

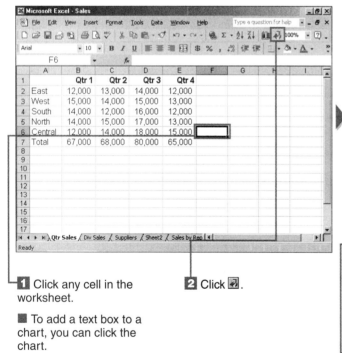

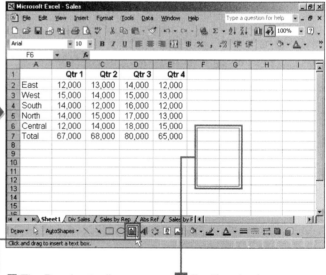

1 Click any cell in the worksheet.

■ To add a text box to a chart, you can click the chart.

2 Click ■.

■ The Drawing toolbar appears.

■ You can hide the Drawing toolbar by clicking ■ again.

3 Click the Text Box button (■).

4 Position + where you want to begin drawing the text box.

5 Drag + until the text box is the size you want.

Can I add a hidden note to a cell?

✔ Yes. You can attach a note to a cell rather than a text box so that it does not appear in the worksheet. Select the cell to which you want to add the note. Click Insert and then click Comment. A red diagonal, or comment indicator, appears in the corner of the cell, and Excel adds a comment box with your name. Type the comment and click outside the comment box. You can display the box by placing the mouse pointer on the comment indicator.

How can I change the border of a text box?

✔ Select the text box and then use the buttons on the Drawing toolbar to change the border. To change the color of the border, click ▪ next to the Line Color button (✎) and select a color. To give the text box a dashed border, click the Dash Style button (▤) and select a dash style.

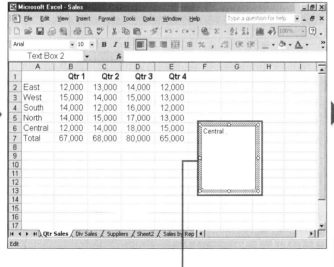

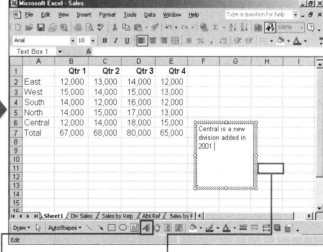

■ The text box appears.

6 Type the text you want to appear in the text box.

■ Word adds the text box to your worksheet.

■ You can select and format the text in the text box.

■ You can also insert WordArt text using the Insert WordArt button (◀).

Note: To learn more about selecting and formatting text, see Chapters 3 and 5. For more on WordArt, see Chapter 8.

7 Click outside the text box to deselect it.

ADD A CLIP ART IMAGE

Excel includes professionally designed clip art images you can add to your document. You can add clip art images to make your document more interesting and entertaining. You might, for example, use a clip art image as your logo or to add interest to a report.

The first time you select this command, Excel prompts you to

search for and categorize the images. Follow the on-screen prompts.

Rather than browse through images, you type a keyword and then search for matching images. You can find clip art images of flowers, animals, buildings, and many other types of objects. You can also, in addition to the images provided with Office, purchase clip art images or find them online.

After you add a clip art image, you can move and resize the clip art image to suit your document. You can also delete a clip art image you no longer need. For information on moving, resizing, or deleting a graphic, see the section "Work with Graphics."

ADD A CLIP ART IMAGE

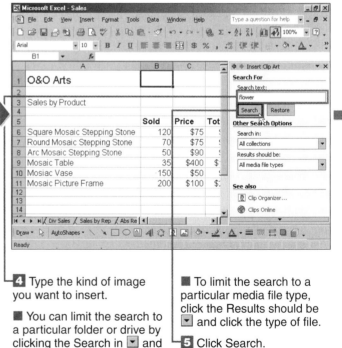

1 Click the location where you want to add a clip art image.

2 Click .

■ The Drawing toolbar displays.

3 Click the Insert Clip Art button (■).

■ The Insert Clip Art task pane appears.

4 Type the kind of image you want to insert.

■ You can limit the search to a particular folder or drive by clicking the Search in ■ and checking what you want to search.

■ To limit the search to a particular media file type, click the Results should be ■ and click the type of file.

5 Click Search.

Can I browse through the clip art images?

✔ Yes. To do so, click the link for Clip Organizer. You see the Microsoft Clip Organizer with a collection list of folders on the left side of the window. Open the folder you want to explore by clicking the plus sign next to the folder. To see the images within a particular folder, click that folder. You can insert an image from this window by clicking ☑ next to the image, selecting Copy, clicking the document where you want to place the image, and selecting Paste.

Where can I find more clip art images?

✔ If you are connected to the Internet, you can visit Microsoft's Design Gallery Live Web site to find additional clip art images. In the Insert ClipArt task pane, click Clips Online and then follow the instructions on your screen.

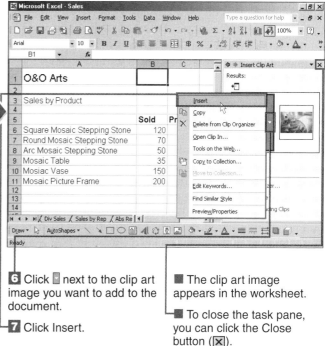

■ Excel displays the clip art images that match your search criteria.

6 Click ☑ next to the clip art image you want to add to the document.

7 Click Insert.

■ The clip art image appears in the worksheet.

■ To close the task pane, you can click the Close button (☒).

WORK WITH GRAPHICS

You can move, resize, or delete a graphic you added to your worksheet or chart to suit your needs.

You can move a graphic to another location in your worksheet. If you add a graphic to a chart, you cannot move the graphic outside the chart area.

When you select a graphic, handles appear around the graphic. The handles allow you to change the size of the graphic. The handles at the top and bottom of a graphic allow you to change the height of the graphic. The handles at the sides of a graphic allow you to change the width of the graphic.

The handles at the corners of a graphic allow you to change the height and width of the graphic at the same time.

You can also delete a graphic you no longer need from your worksheet.

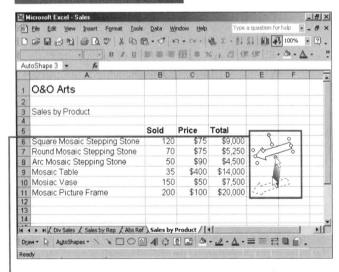

MOVE A GRAPHIC

1 Position the ⌖ over an edge of the graphic you want to move.

2 Drag the graphic to a new location.

■ The graphic appears in the new location.

Note: You cannot move a graphic on a chart outside the chart area.

■ To copy a graphic, press Ctrl as you perform step 2.

RESIZE A GRAPHIC

1 Click the graphic you want to resize.

■ Handles (○) appear around the graphic.

2 Click ⌖ over one of the border handles.

3 Drag the handle until the graphic is the size you want.

■ Excel resizes the graphic.

How can I maintain the height-to-width ratio of a graphic I am resizing?

✔ To maintain the height-to-width ratio, press the Shift key as you drag one of the corner handles.

How do I rotate a graphic?

✔ Click the graphic you want to rotate. If the Drawing toolbar is not displayed, click the Drawing button 📐 on the Standard toolbar. Then click the green Rotate handle. Drag to rotate the graphic. Note that you cannot rotate some graphics.

Can I change several graphics at the same time?

✔ Yes. Click the first graphic you want to change. Press Shift as you click the other graphics. You can now move, resize or delete all the graphics at the same time.

Can I cancel a change I made to a graphic?

✔ Excel remembers your last changes. Click the Undo button (🔄) on the Standard toolbar to immediately cancel a change you make to a graphic.

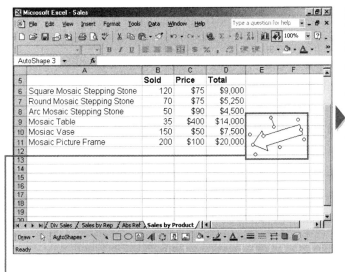

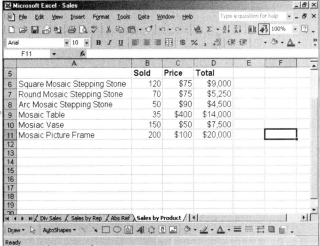

DELETE A GRAPHIC

1 Click the graphic.

2 Press Delete.

■ Excel deletes the graphic.

USING A DATA LIST

Excel provides powerful tools for organizing and analyzing a large collection of data in a list.

Common lists include mailing lists, price lists, sales lists, phone directories, product lists, library book catalogs, and music collections.

The first row in a list contains column labels, which describe the data in each column.

Each row in a list contains one record. A record is a group of related data, such as the name and address of one person on a mailing list.

You can create and store a list of data in a worksheet. You can enter data in a list by typing the data directly in the worksheet. You can also use a data form to type data in a list. A data form allows you to focus on one record at a time.

You should create only one list in a worksheet. If you use the worksheet for other data or calculations, consider leaving at least one blank column and row between the list and the other data to prevent unwanted data from appearing in the data form.

USING A DATA LIST

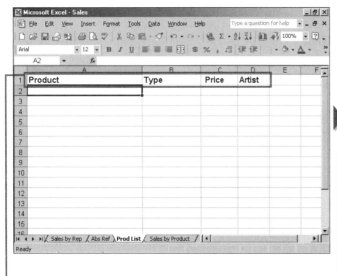
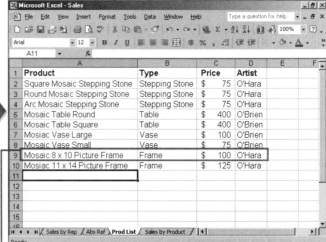

CREATE A DATA LIST

1 Type the column labels that describe the data you plan to type into each column.

■ Format the column labels, for example, make them bold, to ensure that Excel recognizes the text as column labels.

Note: See Chapter 13 for more information on formatting data.

2 Type the information for each record.

Note: Do not leave any blank rows within the list. Doing so could cause problems when sorting and filtering.

3 Save the workbook.

Note: For information on saving, see Chapter 2.

How do I delete a record using a data form?

✔ You can click Delete to delete the currently displayed record. Excel permanently deletes the record and cannot restore it.

How do I search for a specific record using a data form?

✔ Click Criteria. Click the area beside the label of the column you want to use to find the record. Then type the data you want to find. Click Find Prev or Find Next to display the previous or next matching record.

Can I edit a record in a data form?

✔ Yes. Display the record you want to edit. You can use the record navigation buttons to move from record to record until the one you want displays. Then click the area containing the data you want to change and then edit the data as you would edit any data. If you regret changes you make to a record, you can click Restore to undo the changes. You must click Restore before you move to another record.

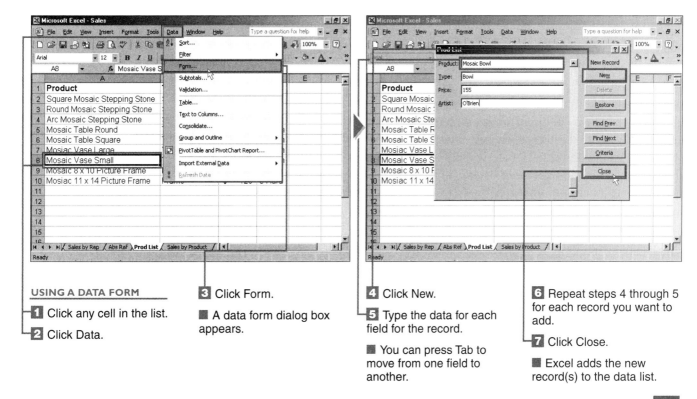

USING A DATA FORM

█1 Click any cell in the list.

█2 Click Data.

█3 Click Form.

■ A data form dialog box appears.

█4 Click New.

█5 Type the data for each field for the record.

■ You can press Tab to move from one field to another.

█6 Repeat steps 4 through 5 for each record you want to add.

█7 Click Close.

■ Excel adds the new record(s) to the data list.

SORT DATA IN A LIST

Y ou can organize a list by changing the order of the records.

You can select the column you want to use to sort the data in a list. For example, you can sort a mailing list by the name, company name, state, or zip code column. You can also sort data by more than one column. For example, if you are sorting by

the last name column and a last name appears more than once, you can sort by a second column, such as the first name column.

You can sort the data in a list by up to three columns. You can sort the data in a list by letter, number, or date. An ascending sort arranges data from lowest to highest. For example, 0 to 9, A to Z, or Jan-99

to Dec-99. A descending sort arranges data from highest to lowest. For example, 9 to 0, Z to A, or Dec-99 to Jan-99.

You should save your workbook before sorting data in case you do not like the results of the sort. To save a workbook, see Chapter 2.

SORT DATA IN A LIST

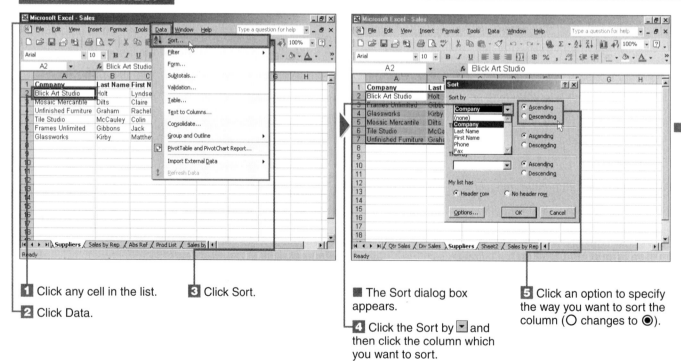

■ 1 Click any cell in the list.

■ 2 Click Data.

■ 3 Click Sort.

■ The Sort dialog box appears.

■ 4 Click the Sort by ▼ and then click the column which you want to sort.

■ 5 Click an option to specify the way you want to sort the column (○ changes to ◉).

How can I quickly sort a list?

✔ Click any cell in the column by which you want to sort. To sort from 0 to 9 or A to Z, click the Sort Ascending button (📊) on the Standard toolbar. To sort from 9 to 0 or Z to A, click the Sort Descending button (📊) on the Standard toolbar.

How do I sort a column of weekdays or months according to their calendar order?

✔ By default, Excel sorts weekdays and months alphabetically. To sort weekdays or months according to their calendar order, select Options in the Sort dialog box. Click the First key sort order drop-down list and then select the sort order you want to use.

Can I perform a case sensitive sort?

✔ Yes. A case sensitive sort sorts data by capitalization. For example, a case sensitive ascending sort would place "ann" before "Ann." Click Options in the Sort dialog box and then check the Case sensitive checkbox (☐ changes to ☑).

How do I undo a sort?

✔ To immediately reverse the results of a sort, click the Undo button (🔄) on the Standard toolbar.

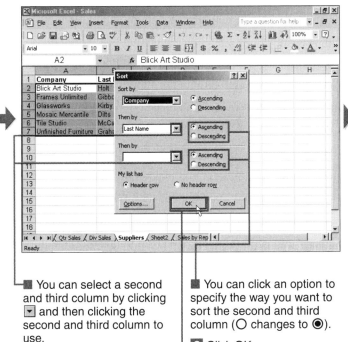

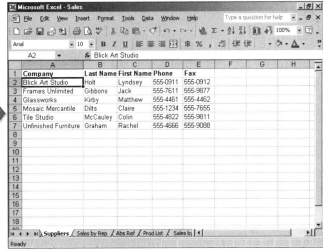

■ You can select a second and third column by clicking ▼ and then clicking the second and third column to use.

■ You can click an option to specify the way you want to sort the second and third column (O changes to ⊙).

6 Click OK.

■ The list appears in the new order.

FILTER DATA IN A LIST

Y ou can filter a list to display only the records containing the data you want to review.

The AutoFilter feature allows you to analyze data by placing related records together and hiding the records you do not want to see.

You can select the column containing the data you want to use

to filter the list. You can also specify the data you want Excel to compare to each record in the list as well as how Excel should compare the data to each record. Telling Excel how to compare the data allows you to display records containing data within a specific range. For example, in a list containing customer names and purchase amounts, you can display

only customers whose purchases were greater than $1,000.00.

After you filter a list, Excel displays the row numbers of the records that match the condition you specified in a different color. Excel also hides the non-matching records. Excel does not delete them; they are simply not displayed in the filtered list.

FILTER DATA IN A LIST

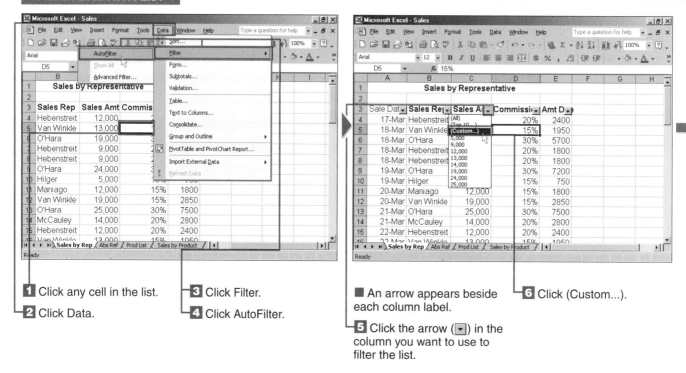

1 Click any cell in the list.

2 Click Data.

3 Click Filter.

4 Click AutoFilter.

■ An arrow appears beside each column label.

5 Click the arrow (▼) in the column you want to use to filter the list.

6 Click (Custom...).

How can I quickly filter data in a list?

✔ Click the ▾ in the column and list and then select the data you want to use to filter the list. The list displays only the records containing the data you selected.

How do I display the top 10 records in a list?

✔ Click the ▾ in the column you want to use to filter the list and then click (Top 10...). In the Top 10 AutoFilter dialog box, click the Items area. To display the top 10 records, click Items. To display the top 10% of the records, click Percent.

How do I redisplay all the data?

✔ To redisplay all the data, click the ▾ next to the filtered column and click (All).

Can I filter with more than one criteria?

✔ Yes. Perform steps 1 through 9 in this section to specify the first condition. In the areas below the first condition, repeat steps 7 through 9 to specify the second condition. Click either the And or the Or option, if you want both or either conditions to be met (○ changes to ●).

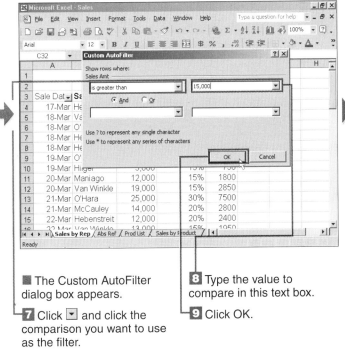

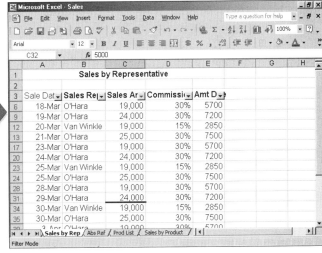

■ The Custom AutoFilter dialog box appears.

7 Click ▾ and click the comparison you want to use as the filter.

8 Type the value to compare in this text box.

9 Click OK.

■ The list displays only the records matching the data you specify.

■ Excel temporarily hides the other records.

■ You can turn off the AutoFilter feature and redisplay the entire list by performing steps 2 through 4.

ADD SUBTOTALS TO A LIST

You can quickly summarize data by adding subtotals to a list.

You can use subtotals to help you analyze the data in a list and quickly create summary reports for the data. For example, in a list containing employee names and sales figures, you can use subtotals to find the total sales made by each

employee and the grand total of all the sales.

Before you add subtotals to a list, sort the column you want to use to group the records.

You can use the Subtotals feature to perform several types of calculations, such as calculating the sum of values, counting the number of

values, calculating the average value, or finding the maximum or minimum value.

After adding subtotals to a list, you can display just the grand total, the subtotals and the grand total, or all the data. By default, Excel displays subtotals below each group of data in a column.

ADD SUBTOTALS TO A LIST

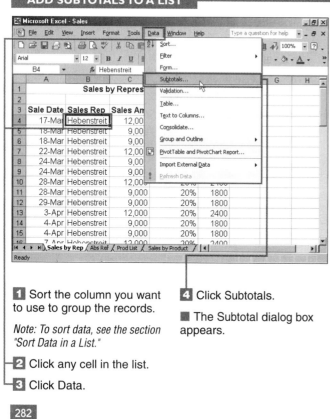

1 Sort the column you want to use to group the records.

Note: To sort data, see the section "Sort Data in a List."

2 Click any cell in the list.

3 Click Data.

4 Click Subtotals.

■ The Subtotal dialog box appears.

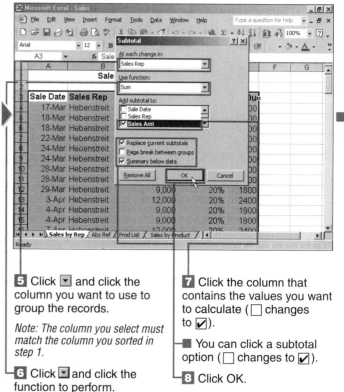

5 Click ▾ and click the column you want to use to group the records.

Note: The column you select must match the column you sorted in step 1.

6 Click ▾ and click the function to perform.

7 Click the column that contains the values you want to calculate (☐ changes to ☑).

■ You can click a subtotal option (☐ changes to ☑).

8 Click OK.

Can I create a chart based on the subtotals in my list?

✔ Yes. Click to display only the subtotals and grand total. Select the cells containing the subtotals and row labels you want to display in the chart. Then create the chart. See Chapter 15 to create a chart. If you later hide or display data in the list, Excel automatically hides or displays the data in the chart.

How do I remove subtotals from my list?

✔ Perform steps 2 through 4 in this section and then click the Remove All button.

How do I display subtotals above each group of data in a column?

✔ Perform steps 2 through 4 in this section and then uncheck the Summary below data option.

Can I hide the data I use in a subtotal?

✔ Yes. Minus signs appear to the left of your subtotaled list. Click a minus sign (⊟) to hide the data you use in a subtotal. Click the plus sign (⊞) to redisplay the data.

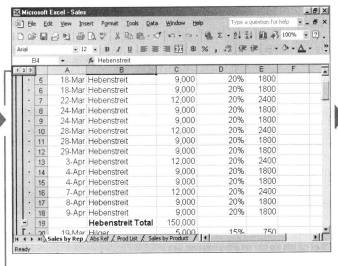

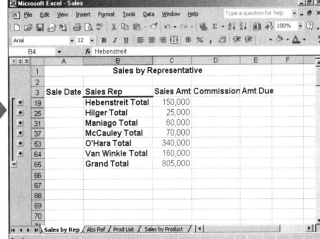

■ The list displays the subtotals and/or a grand total. You can scroll through the list to see the other totals.

9 Click an option to hide or display data.

■ You can click **1** to display only grand total.

■ You can click **2** to display only subtotals and grand total.

■ You can click **3** to display all data.

■ You see the totals you selected.

■ This example shows the subtotals and grand totals.

SECTION IV

18) GETTING STARTED

An Introduction to PowerPoint 286

Create a Blank Presentation 288

Parts of the PowerPoint Screen 289

Using the AutoContent Wizard 290

Using a Design Template 294

Add a Slide 296

19) CREATE AND EDIT SLIDES

Select Text 298

Add and Edit Text 300

Move and Copy Text 302

Resize, Add, and Delete Text Boxes 303

Change Views 304

Browse through a Presentation 306

Change the Slide Layout 308

20) ADD OBJECTS TO SLIDES

Add a Table with Text 310

Format a Table 312

Add a Chart 314

Edit and Format a Chart 316

Add an Organization Chart 318

Add a Clip Art Image 320

Add a Picture 322

Add an AutoShape 324

Add WordArt Text Effects 326

Move, Resize, or Delete a Slide Object 328

21) FORMAT PRESENTATIONS

Change the Font and Size of Text 330
Change Text Style 332
Change Text Alignment 333
Change Text Color 334
Copy Formatting 335
Format Bulleted and Numbered Lists 336
Animate Slide Objects 338
Use an Animation Scheme 340
Change the Color Scheme 342
Change the Design Template 344
Add or Edit a Header or Footer 346
Use the Slide Master 348

22) FINE-TUNE AND PRESENT A PRESENTATION

Rearrange Slides 350
Delete a Slide 351
Hide a Slide 352
Create a Summary Slide 353
Add Slide Transitions 354
Rehearse a Slide Show 356
Set Up a Slide Show 358
Preview a Slide Show 360
Create Speaker Notes 362
Check Spelling 364
Set Up a Presentation for Printing 366
Print a Presentation 368

AN INTRODUCTION TO POWERPOINT

PowerPoint helps you plan, organize, design, and deliver professional presentations. Using PowerPoint, you can use a computer screen, the Web, 35mm slides, or overhead transparencies to deliver a presentation. PowerPoint also allows you to create handouts for the audience and speaker notes to help you when delivering the presentation.

For more information on PowerPoint, you can visit the following Web site: www.microsoft.com/powerpoint.

Create Presentations

PowerPoint offers several ways to create a presentation. By default, when you start the program, PowerPoint creates a blank presentation. You can start from scratch, adding the slides and formatting that suit your particular presentation needs. Or you can use the AutoContent Wizard, which guides you step-by-step through the process of creating a presentation. The AutoContent Wizard lets you select from several common presentation types and includes formatting, slides, and sample text. You can replace the sample content with your own. You can also use a design template.

Creating and Editing Slides

A presentation is made up of slides, and as you build a presentation, you add the slides, selecting from various layouts. Each layout has a placeholder for text or other objects. You can add the text and objects to create the slides. You can also edit the content as needed.

When you create or edit a presentation, you can choose among several different views: Normal view for working on the slide content, Outline view for developing the content in outline format and viewing the overall organization, Slide Sorter view for rearranging, deleting, and adding slides, and Slide Show for previewing a slide.

Add Objects to Slides

Most slides contain other items besides text, and PowerPoint enables you to add several different types of objects to a slide. For example, you may want to display a table of information. You can also add a chart, which is useful for displaying trends, showing the relationship of numeric data, and illustrating other main points. Office includes a separate charting program that you access from PowerPoint to create and add charts to a slide. You can also use Office's built-in diagramming program to add diagrams such as organization charts or flow charts.

In addition to tables and charts, you can also add graphic elements to a slide, including AutoShapes, pictures, clip art images, and WordArt, which creates special text effects. You can use these elements to enhance the slide or to make a particular point. For example, you may include pictures of your products, or, in a company meeting, include pictures of your company's leaders.

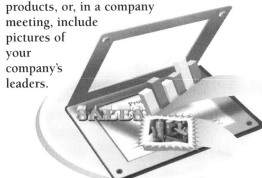

Enhance a Presentation

You can make a slide stand out and grab your audience's attention in several ways. You can emphasize text on a slide using common text styles including bold, italic, underline, or shadow. You can change the font, font size, or color of text. You also can use one of PowerPoint's many ready-to-use designs to give all the slides a consistent format. You can still make changes to individual slides, but a design automatically makes key formatting changes. As another alternative, you can select from several color schemes to enhance a presentation.

You can use special effects such as a slide object or a sound on your slide. Animation can help emphasize important points and keep the audience's attention throughout the presentation.

Fine-tune and Make a Presentation

After you finish the individual slides, you need to step back and consider the overall presentation. You may want to fine-tune your presentation by checking its organizational flow and rearranging slides so that you present your ideas in a logical order. You can also check the spelling, create a summary slide, and add transitions.

You can create and refer to speaker notes to keep focused as you give the presentation. You can also create handouts so that your audience has something to take with them or to refer to during the presentation.

You may also have special considerations for setting up the presentation, depending on whether you are printing the presentation, giving the presentation as a slideshow, or broadcasting the presentation over the Web.

CREATE A BLANK PRESENTATION

PowerPoint is a program that helps you plan, organize, and design professional presentations.

Each time you start PowerPoint, you see a blank presentation, with one slide. You can start building the presentation from scratch,

adding slides as you need them. You create a blank presentation when you know what style, content, and formatting options you want, or when none of the design templates match your needs.

If you do not want to start from scratch, you can create a new

presentation using the AutoContent Wizard or a design template. These options are available in the New Presentation task pane. See the sections "Using the AutoContent Wizard" and "Using a Design Template" for more information.

CREATE A BLANK PRESENTATION

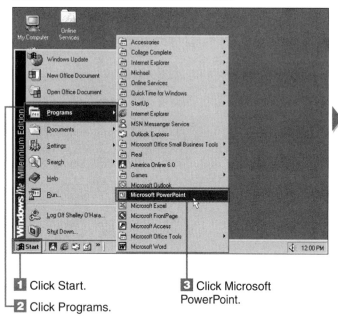

1 Click Start.

2 Click Programs.

3 Click Microsoft PowerPoint.

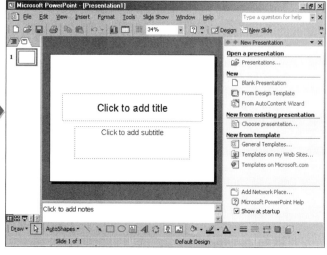

■ The Microsoft PowerPoint window appears.

■ PowerPoint creates a blank presentation.

Note: To close the PowerPoint program, see Chapter 2.

PARTS OF THE POWERPOINT SCREEN

The PowerPoint screen displays several items to help you perform tasks efficiently.

Menu Bar

Provides access to lists of commands available in PowerPoint.

Formatting Toolbar

Contains buttons to help you select formatting commands, such as Font Size and Underline.

Outline Tab/Slides Tab

Lets you switch between outline or slide view.

Slide Pane

Displays the current slide.

View Buttons

Allow you to quickly change the way the presentation displays on the screen.

Title Bar

Displays the name of the program and the presentation. If you have not saved the presentation, you see a default name.

Standard Toolbar

Contains buttons to help you select common commands, such as Save and Open.

Task Pane

Displays options for creating a new presentation.

Notes Pane

Displays the speaker notes for the current slide.

Drawing Toolbar

Contains buttons to help you add objects to the presentation.

Status Bar

Provides information about the slide displayed on the screen and the current presentation.

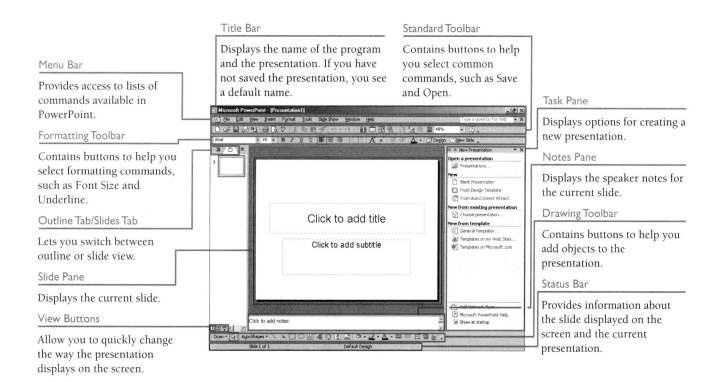

USING THE AUTOCONTENT WIZARD

You can use the AutoContent Wizard to quickly create a presentation. The wizard asks you a series of questions and then sets up a presentation based on your answers. The AutoContent Wizard provides a design and sample text for the slides in the presentation.

The wizard offers several categories of presentations, including General, Corporate, Projects, Sales/Marketing, and Carnegie

Coach. The Carnegie Coach category contains presentations provided by Dale Carnegie Training, which include tips on how to improve your presentations. If you are not sure which category is best for your needs, you can list all of the available presentations.

After you select a category, you can then choose the presentation that most closely matches the goal or message of your planned

presentation. The content and format options that the wizard uses depend on this choice.

You can decide what media to use to display your presentation. You can choose to output your presentation as an on-screen presentation, Web presentation, black-and-white overhead transparencies, color overheads, or 35mm slides.

USING THE AUTOCONTENT WIZARD

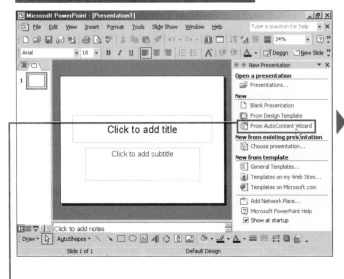

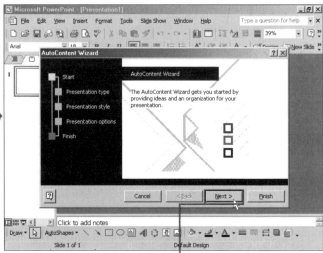

■1 Click the From AutoContent Wizard link in the task pane.

Note: When you start PowerPoint, the task pane displays. If it does not display, click File, New.

■ You see a description of the AutoContent Wizard as well as an outline of the steps you need to complete.

■2 Click Next.

When I select a presentation, PowerPoint says it is not available. What is the problem?

✔ When you install Office, you can select what to install. Your installation may not have included all of the presentations. PowerPoint prompts you to insert an Office CD-ROM to install the appropriate presentation.

How can I restart the wizard or go back to previous wizard dialog boxes?

✔ You can cancel the wizard at any time by clicking Cancel. You can also go back a step and change one of your previous selections by clicking Back.

Can I use a template or start from scratch to create a presentation?

✔ Yes. You can use a design template, which includes the formatting for the slide presentation, but not the content. You use templates when you have content, but want some help with formatting. You can also create a blank presentation and start from scratch, when you know what style, content, and formatting options you want, or when none of the design templates match your needs. See the sections "Create a Blank Presentation" and "Using a Design Template" for more information.

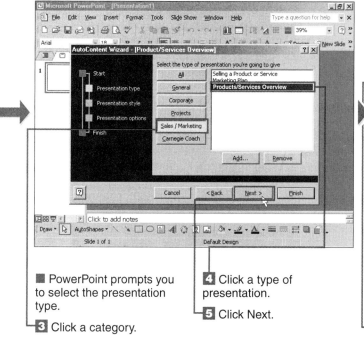

■ PowerPoint prompts you to select the presentation type.

3 Click a category.

4 Click a type of presentation.

5 Click Next.

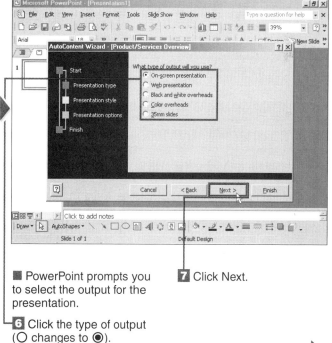

■ PowerPoint prompts you to select the output for the presentation.

6 Click the type of output (○ changes to ◉).

7 Click Next.

CONTINUED ▶

USING THE AUTOCONTENT WIZARD (CONTINUED)

The AutoContent Wizard allows you to specify a title for your presentation. The title appears on the first slide in the presentation.

You can choose to display footer text on each slide. Footer text is useful when you want the audience to keep certain information in mind during your presentation, such as

your name or the name of your company.

You can also choose to include the date and slide number on each slide. If you include the date, PowerPoint automatically updates the date each time you open the presentation.

After you answer the questions to build your presentation,

PowerPoint creates it in the Normal view. The Normal view displays the sample text in the presentation and the current slide. The sample text and the appearance of the slides depend on the information you supply the AutoContent Wizard. You can replace the sample text PowerPoint provides with your own information. To edit text, see Chapter 19.

USING THE AUTOCONTENT WIZARD (CONTINUED)

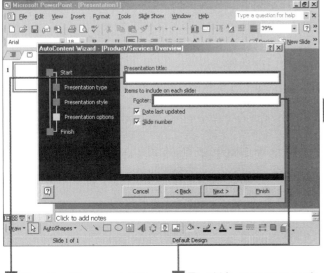

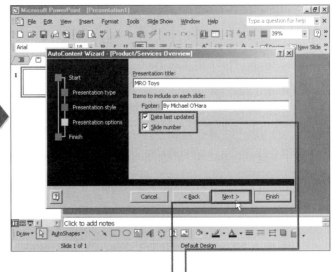

■8 Type the title you want to appear on the first slide in the presentation.

■9 To add footer text to each slide in the presentation, click this area and then type the text.

■ PowerPoint automatically adds the date and slide number to each slide in the presentation.

■ If you do not want to add the date or slide number, you can deselect the option you do not want to include (☑ changes to ☐).

■10 Click Next.

Do I have to include all the slides in the AutoContent presentation?

✔ No. The wizard includes a particular set of slides with content and layouts for particular messages. You can complete the slides you want, rearrange them, and delete any you do not want. See Chapter 19 for creating and editing slides. See Chapter 22 for rearranging and deleting slides.

Keep in mind that the set of slides PowerPoint displays depends on the presentation type. Also, each slide has a text placeholder. You can use these content samples as guides on what to typically include in the selected presentation type.

Do I have to answer all the questions in the AutoContent Wizard?

✔ No. You can click Finish at any time to create a presentation based on the answers you have provided so far. The AutoContent Wizard uses default settings for the questions you do not answer.

Can I change the footer text on my slides later?

✔ Yes. Click View then click Header and Footer. For more information, see Chapter 21.

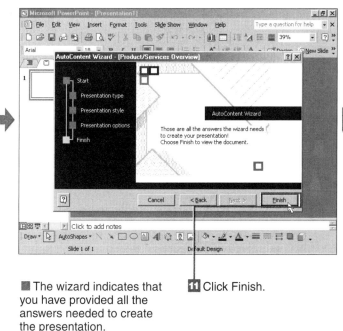

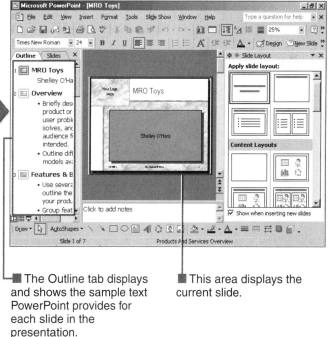

■ The wizard indicates that you have provided all the answers needed to create the presentation.

11 Click Finish.

■ The Outline tab displays and shows the sample text PowerPoint provides for each slide in the presentation.

■ This area displays the current slide.

USING A DESIGN TEMPLATE

You can use a design template to help create a professional-looking presentation. Design templates are useful when you know what information you want to include in your presentation, but you want to choose a design for the slides.

When you create a presentation using a design template,

PowerPoint creates only the first slide and displays it in Normal view. You can add additional slides to your presentation as you need them, and PowerPoint applies the same design template to each addition.

PowerPoint provides several design templates from which you can choose. Each design template

conveys a specific mood and includes fonts, text colors, and a background that work well together. You can preview a design template to determine if it is appropriate for your presentation. For additional design templates, you can visit the following Web site: http://templategallery.microsoft.com/templategallery/.

USING A DESIGN TEMPLATE

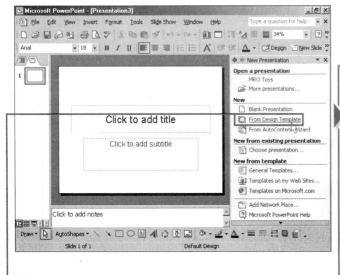

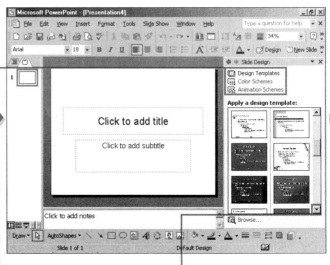

1 Click From Design Template in the New Presentation task pane.

Note: When you start PowerPoint, the task pane displays. If it does not display, click File, New.

■ The Slide Design task pane displays, listing the design template used in this presentation first as well as other available templates listed next.

2 Scroll through the list of available presentations until you see one that you want to use.

Can I create a new presentation while working in PowerPoint?

✔ Yes. Click the appropriate option in the task pane. You can select to create a new blank presentation, a presentation from a design template, or a presentation using the AutoContent Wizard. If the task pane is not displayed, click File and then click New.

Can I apply the template to just one slide?

✔ Yes. To do so, click ▼ next to the template you want to apply and then select Apply to Selected Slides.

Can I change a design template later?

✔ You can change the design template for a presentation at any time. Click the Design button (🗹 Design) in the Formatting toolbar. Use the options in the Slide Design task pane to make your selections. For more information on changing templates, see Chapter 21.

Can I view larger versions of the sample slides in the design templates?

✔ Yes. To do so, click ▼ next to the design template you want to see and then select Show Large Previews.

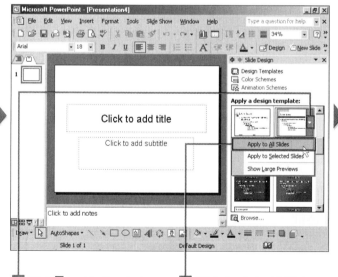

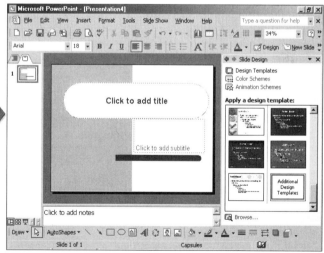

3 Click ▼ next to the design template you want to use.

Note: The ▼ appears when your ▷ is over the template.

4 Click Apply to All Slides.

■ PowerPoint adds the design template to the presentation.

■ To add additional slides to the presentation, see the section "Add a Slide."

ADD A SLIDE

You can insert a new slide into your presentation to add a new topic you want to discuss. PowerPoint inserts the new slide after the current slide on your screen.

By default, PowerPoint adds a bulleted list slide, but you can select another layout for the new

slide in the Apply slide layout task pane. Using a slide layout saves you from having to arrange and position items on a slide.

PowerPoint provides several slide layouts, each with certain areas for different types of content to suit the purpose of the slide.

If you select a slide layout that does not suit your needs, you can change the layout later. After PowerPoint adds a new slide to your presentation, you can add the items you want to appear on the slide. To change the slide layout, or to add text or edit existing text, see Chapter 19.

ADD A SLIDE

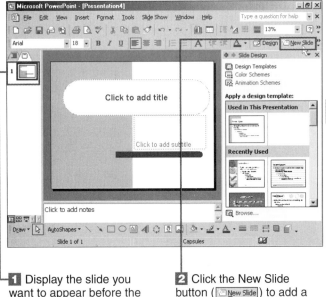

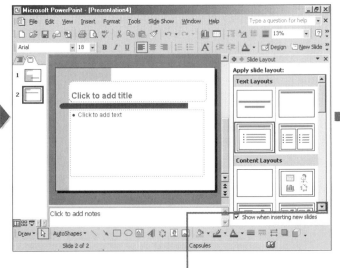

1 Display the slide you want to appear before the new slide.

Note: You can use the slide navigation buttons in the scroll bar to display the slide.

2 Click the New Slide button (New Slide) to add a new slide.

■ PowerPoint adds a bulleted list slide and displays the Slide Layout task pane.

Note: If you have used a design template, the slide uses the settings from this design template.

3 Scroll through the layouts until you see the layout you want.

What slide layouts are available?

✔ You can select from many different types of layouts including text layouts, object layouts, and text and object layouts. For example, one layout may include a table placeholder and a placeholder for a chart. You might use this to list a table of information and then a chart that relates to the table. You can get a good idea of what the layout includes from the sample in the Apply slide layout task pane.

Can I insert a duplicate slide?

✔ Yes. Select the slide you want to duplicate and then click Insert and then Duplicate Slide.

What is the purpose of the little icons in the sample layouts?

✔ Each icon represents a placeholder for an object you can insert in the slide. For example, the title placeholder looks like a dark bar, and chart placeholders look like mini-charts.

How do I add content to the slide?

✔ Chapter 19 covers how to add text to a slide or edit existing text. Chapter 20 covers how to add objects to a slide.

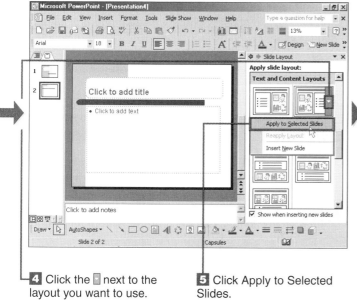

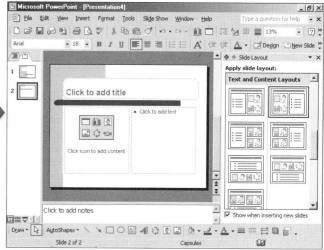

4 Click the ▾ next to the layout you want to use.

5 Click Apply to Selected Slides.

■ PowerPoint applies the new slide layout to the new slide.

SELECT TEXT

Before changing text in a presentation, you often need to select the text with which you intend to work. For example, you must select the text you want to move, delete, or change to a new font. PowerPoint allows you to select a single word, a bullet point, any amount of text, or an entire slide, and highlights your selected text on your screen.

The Slides view allows you to select and work with text efficiently on all the slides in your presentation or just the current slide. When you want to work with and select large portions of your presentation at once, consider using Outline view. See the section "Change Views" for more information on the various views in PowerPoint.

After you finish working with selected text, deselect the text. If you begin typing within selected text, PowerPoint replaces the selected text with the text you type.

PowerPoint contains text on a slide in a text placeholder or text box. Often you may need to select the text box. For example, if you want to move text around on the slide, you select the text box.

SELECT TEXT

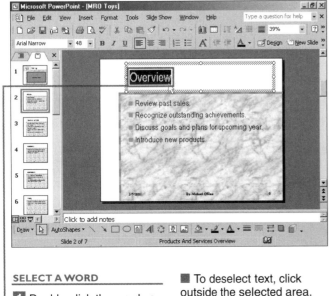

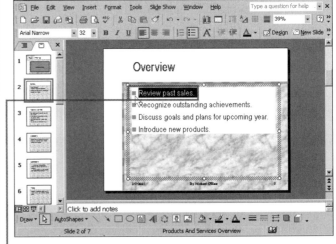

SELECT A WORD

1 Double-click the word you want to select.

■ The word is selected.

■ To deselect text, click outside the selected area.

SELECT A BULLET POINT

1 Click the bullet beside the point you want to select.

■ That bullet point is selected.

Can I select text using the keyboard?

✔ Yes. To select characters, press the Shift key as you press the left arrow or right arrow key. To select words, press the Shift+Ctrl keys as you press left arrow or right arrow key.

How do I select all the text in my presentation?

✔ Click the text in the Outline pane and then press Ctrl+A. You can also click Edit and then click Select All.

How do I select all the text on the current slide?

✔ Click a blank area on the slide in the Slide pane and then press Ctrl+A. PowerPoint displays a thick border around all the selected text rather than highlighting it.

Can I select text in other views?

✔ You can select text in Outline view as you would select text in the Normal view. You cannot select text in the Slide Sorter view. For more information on the views, see the section "Change Views."

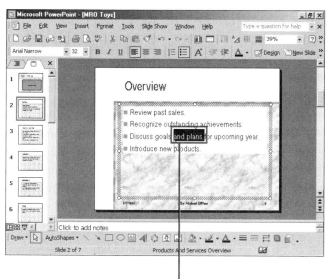

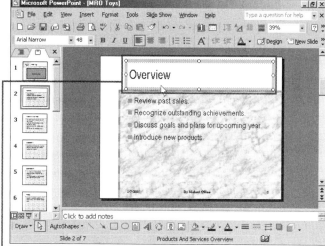

SELECT ANY AMOUNT OF TEXT

1 Position the ▷ over the first word you want to select.

2 Drag the ▷ over the text you want to select.

■ The text is selected.

SELECT A TEXT BOX

1 Click the text box you want to select.

■ Selection handles appear around the text box, indicating it is selected.

ADD AND EDIT TEXT

You can change the text on a PowerPoint slide very easily. You might need to do this for a variety of reasons:

• When you create a new slide, PowerPoint includes text placeholders for the different text items on that particular slide. These placeholders vary depending on the particular layout. You can replace the placeholders with your text.

See Chapter 18 for information on adding slides and selecting a layout.

• In a like manner, the AutoContent Wizard supplies sample text. You can replace the placeholders or sample text with your text.

• If you have already placed text in your presentation, PowerPoint also lets you edit the text. This is useful when you need to

correct a mistake, update the information on a slide, or remove text you no longer need from your presentation. PowerPoint allows you to delete a character, a word, a bullet point, or an entire slide. You can also add text to the existing text if you need to provide more content on a slide.

ADD AND EDIT TEXT

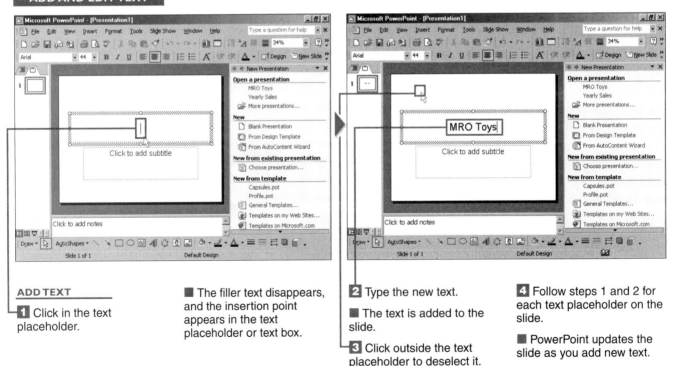

ADD TEXT

1 Click in the text placeholder.

■ The filler text disappears, and the insertion point appears in the text placeholder or text box.

2 Type the new text.

■ The text is added to the slide.

3 Click outside the text placeholder to deselect it.

4 Follow steps 1 and 2 for each text placeholder on the slide.

■ PowerPoint updates the slide as you add new text.

Why do some words in my presentation display a red underline?

✔ If PowerPoint does not recognize a word in your presentation, it considers the word misspelled and underlines the word with a red line. To spell check your presentation and remove the red underlines, see Chapter 22.

Can I edit text in other views?

✔ You can edit text in Outline view the same way you edit text in Slides view. You cannot edit text in the Slide Sorter view. For more information on the views, see the section "Change Views."

Can I add a new slide to my presentation?

✔ Yes. To add a new slide to your presentation, click the New Slide button (New Slide). See Chapter 18 for more information on adding slides.

Can I insert a new bullet on my slide?

✔ Yes. If you forgot to include an idea when you created your presentation, you can add a new point to a slide. To add an item to a bulleted list, press Enter after the last item and then type the new item.

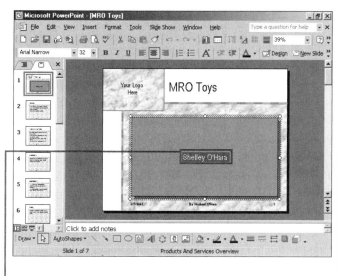

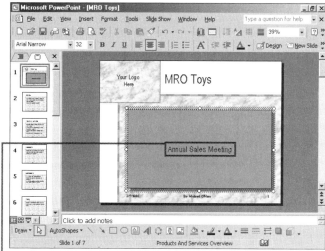

REPLACE EXISTING TEXT

1 Select the text you want to replace with new text.

Note: For help on selecting text, see the section "Select Text."

2 Type the new text.

■ The text you type replaces the selected text.

DELETE TEXT

1 Select the text you want to delete.

2 Press Delete to remove the text.

■ To delete one character at a time, click to the right of the first character you want to delete. Then press Backspace or Delete once for each character you want to delete.

MOVE AND COPY TEXT

You can move text in your presentation to reorganize your ideas. You can also copy text from one location in your presentation to another.

When you move text, the text disappears from its original location in your presentation. Most commonly you move an entire text box, with all of the text in that area. You can also move a word, phrase, or point. For information on moving a slide, see Chapter 22.

Before you can move text, you must select the text or text box you want to move. A solid line or dotted insertion point indicates the location of your text as you are moving it. When you move a text box, you see an outline of the text box as you drag it to its new location.

Copying text saves you time because you do not have to retype the text. When you copy text, the text appears in both the original and new locations.

MOVE AND COPY TEXT

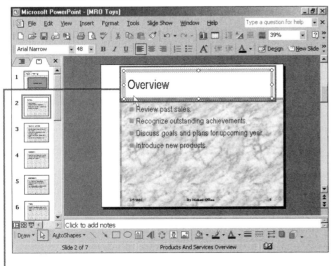

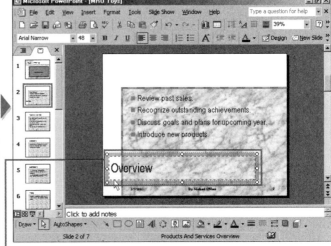

1 Select the text or text box you want to move or copy.

2 To move or copy partial text, position the ↳ anywhere over the selected text; to move or copy an entire text box, place the ↳ on any border of the text box.

3 Drag the ↳ where you want to place the text.

Note: To copy text, press the Ctrl key as you perform step 3.

■ The text is moved or copied.

RESIZE, ADD, AND DELETE TEXT BOXES

When you create a new slide, the layout determines which text boxes PowerPoint includes on a slide as well as the size of the text box. If needed, you can adjust the size of the text box. For example, if you need to make the text box larger, you can do so to allow for more text. If a text box is too big, you can make it smaller to make room for other items you want to include such as a chart or table.

You can also draw new text boxes on-screen so that you can add text to any spot on the slide, regardless of the original text placeholders.

For example, you may want more areas of text than the sample layouts include.

If you do not need a particular text box, you can delete it from the slide layout. PowerPoint deletes the text box and all text inside it.

RESIZE, ADD, AND DELETE TEXT BOXES

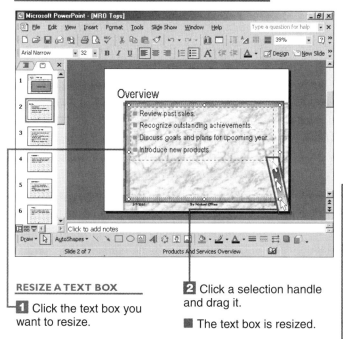

RESIZE A TEXT BOX

1 Click the text box you want to resize.

2 Click a selection handle and drag it.

■ The text box is resized.

ADD A TEXT BOX

1 Click the Text Box button (▣).

2 Click and drag to draw the text box.

3 Type text in the text box.

DELETE A TEXT BOX

1 Click the text box.

2 Press Delete.

■ PowerPoint deletes the text box.

CHANGE VIEWS

PowerPoint offers several ways to display your presentation on-screen. You can choose the view that best suits your needs. If you make changes to a slide in one view, the other views also display the changes.

The Normal view displays all the text in your presentation, the current slide, and the speaker notes for the current slide. Normal view has two tabs: Outline and Slides.

Using the Slides tab, you can work with all the parts of your presentation in a single screen.

The Outline tab in Normal view displays all the text in your presentation, a miniature version of the current slide, and the speaker notes for the current slide. This view is useful for developing the content and organization of your presentation. You can also hide the slide content and display just the titles in this view.

The Slide Sorter view displays a miniature version of each slide to provide an overview of your entire presentation. This view is useful for adding, deleting, and reorganizing slides. To learn how to change the slide order, see Chapter 22.

CHANGE VIEWS

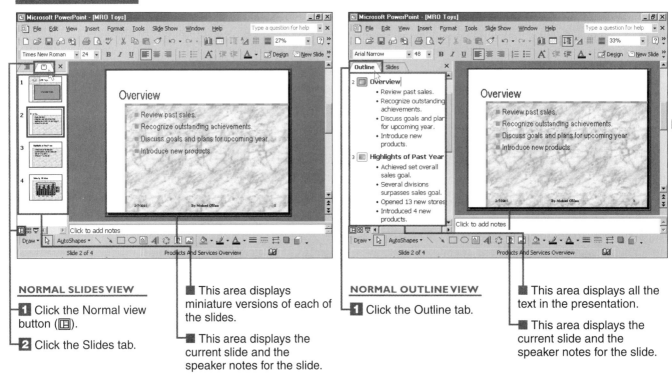

NORMAL SLIDES VIEW

■1 Click the Normal view button (▣).

■2 Click the Slides tab.

■ This area displays miniature versions of each of the slides.

■ This area displays the current slide and the speaker notes for the slide.

NORMAL OUTLINE VIEW

■1 Click the Outline tab.

■ This area displays all the text in the presentation.

■ This area displays the current slide and the speaker notes for the slide.

Does PowerPoint offer any other views?

✔ PowerPoint also offers the Notes Page view. The Notes Page view displays the current slide and the speaker notes for the current slide. To display your presentation in the Notes Page view, select View, and then click Notes Page.

What do I use the Slide Show button for?

✔ The Slide Show button (⬚) allows you to view a slide show of your presentation on your screen. For information on viewing a slide show, see Chapter 22.

Can I change the size of an area of the screen in the Normal view?

✔ In the Normal view, PowerPoint divides its screen into panes. You can change the size of the panes to display more of the pane. Position the ⬚ over the vertical or horizontal bar that separates the panes and then drag the bar to a new location.

Can I magnify part of my presentation?

✔ Yes. Magnifying part of a presentation can make text on the screen easier to read and work with. Click the area you want to magnify. Click the ⬚ next to the Zoom button and click a zoom percentage.

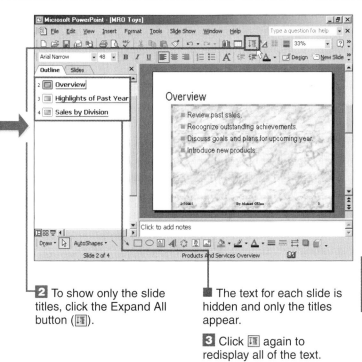

2 To show only the slide titles, click the Expand All button (⬚).

■ The text for each slide is hidden and only the titles appear.

3 Click ⬚ again to redisplay all of the text.

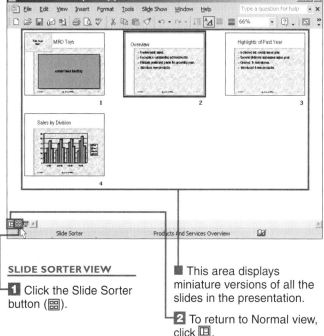

SLIDE SORTER VIEW

1 Click the Slide Sorter button (⬚).

■ This area displays miniature versions of all the slides in the presentation.

2 To return to Normal view, click ⬚.

BROWSE THROUGH A PRESENTATION

Your computer screen cannot display your entire presentation at once. You must browse through the presentation to view the text or slides that PowerPoint does not display on your screen. In the Slides and Outline view, you can use the scroll bar to scroll up or down through all the text in your presentation.

When you are browsing from slide to slide, the status bar displays the number of the current slide and the total number of slides in the presentation.

To quickly browse through your presentation, you can drag the scroll box along the scroll bar. When you drag the scroll box, PowerPoint displays a yellow box containing the number and the title of the slide that will appear on your screen.

You can also display the previous or next slide in your presentation.

And finally, in Outline view, you can browse through the contents of the outlined slides using the scroll bar in that pane.

BROWSE THROUGH A PRESENTATION

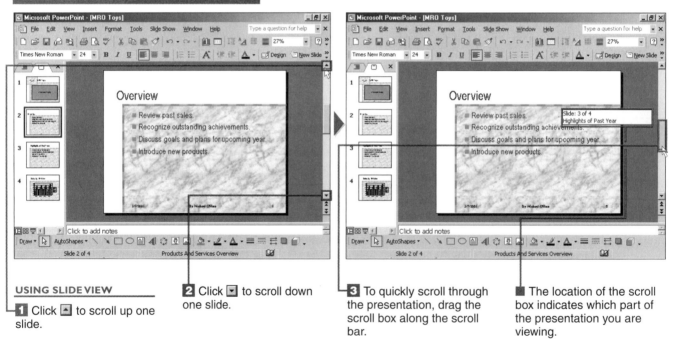

USING SLIDE VIEW

1 Click ▲ to scroll up one slide.

2 Click ▼ to scroll down one slide.

3 To quickly scroll through the presentation, drag the scroll box along the scroll bar.

■ The location of the scroll box indicates which part of the presentation you are viewing.

How can I browse through the speaker notes in my presentation?

✔ In the Normal Slides view, you can click the ▲ or ▼ in the Notes pane, located at the bottom of the window, to display the speaker notes for the current slide. You can also change the size of the panes by dragging the border of the panes.

How do I use a wheeled mouse to browse through my presentation?

✔ Moving the wheel between the left and right mouse buttons lets you quickly browse through your presentation. The Microsoft IntelliMouse is a popular wheeled mouse.

How can I use my keyboard to browse through my presentation?

✔ In Outline view, you can press the up or down arrow keys to browse through your presentation one line at a time. In Slides view, you can press the Page Up or Page Down key to browse through your presentation one slide at a time. You can also press the Home key to move to the first, or the End key to move to the last, slide in your presentation.

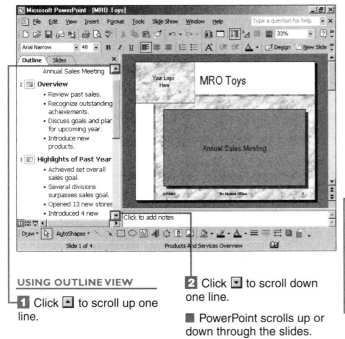

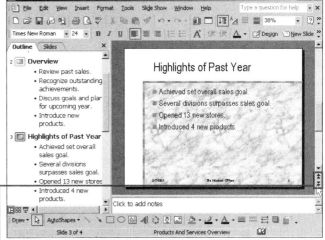

USING OUTLINE VIEW

1 Click ▲ to scroll up one line.

2 Click ▼ to scroll down one line.

■ PowerPoint scrolls up or down through the slides.

DISPLAY PREVIOUS OR NEXT SLIDE

1 Click the appropriate button.

■ To display the previous slide, click ▲.

■ To display the next slide, click ▼.

CHANGE THE SLIDE LAYOUT

You can change the layout of a slide in your presentation to accommodate text and objects you want to add.

PowerPoint offers several slide layouts from which you can choose. Most slide layouts display a different arrangement of placeholders, which allow you to

easily add objects to a slide. PowerPoint has slide layouts available that allow you to add objects such as a bulleted list, table, chart, clip art image, or media clip. If you want to design your own slide layout, you can use the blank layout. To learn how to create a blank presentation, see Chapter 18.

PowerPoint displays the Slide Layout task pane with miniature versions of each slide layout.

After you apply a layout to a slide, you can add the appropriate object to a placeholder on the slide. Any text a placeholder contains disappears when you type your text or add an object.

CHANGE THE SLIDE LAYOUT

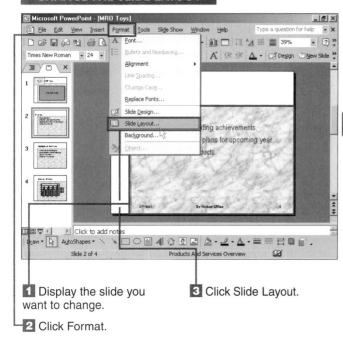

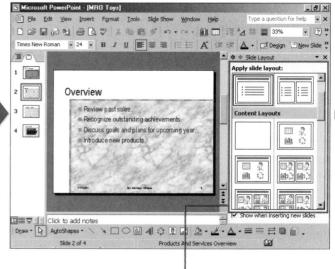

1 Display the slide you want to change.

2 Click Format.

3 Click Slide Layout.

■ The Slide Layout task pane appears.

■ This area displays the available layouts.

■ You can use the scroll bar to browse through the layouts.

Can I change the size of a placeholder on a slide?

✔ Yes. Click the placeholder you want to change. You can drag the handles, which appear around the placeholder, to resize the placeholder.

What types of objects can I add to a slide?

✔ Each slide layout includes different placeholders for different items. You can add charts, organizational diagrams, pictures, movie clips, tables, bulleted lists, and more. If the slide contains only text, see the section "Add and Edit Text." See Chapter 20 to learn how to create the object for any other kind of placeholder.

Can I change the slide layout at any time?

✔ You should not change the slide layout after you add an object to a slide. The object remains on the slide even after PowerPoint adds the placeholders for the new slide layout. This can cause the slide to become cluttered with overlapping objects and placeholders.

I rearranged the placeholders on a slide, but I do not like the result. How can I change back to the last slide layout I applied?

✔ Display the slide you want to change. Click the ▪ next to the slide layout and click Reapply Layout.

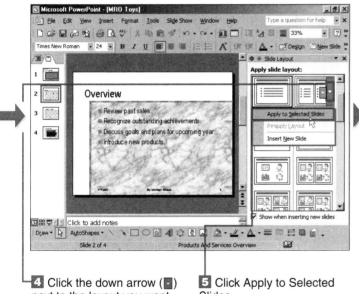

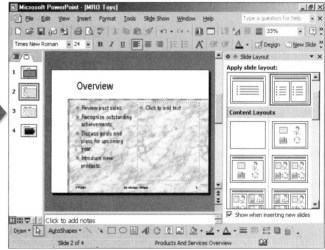

4 Click the down arrow (▪) next to the layout you want to apply to the slide.

5 Click Apply to Selected Slides.

■ The slide appears in the new layout.

6 Replace any new slide objects.

■ The slide is completed.

ADD A TABLE WITH TEXT

You can create a table to neatly display information on a slide. Tables can help you organize lists of information, such as a table of contents or a price list.

Before you add a table to a slide, you should change the layout of the slide to create space for the table. That is, select a slide layout that contains a placeholder for a table.

For information on adding new slides, see Chapter 18. For information on changing the slide layout, see Chapter 19.

A table is made up of rows, columns, and cells. A *row* is a horizontal line of cells. A *column* is a vertical line of cells. A *cell* is the area where a row and column intersect.

You can enter any amount of text in a cell. When the text you enter reaches the end of the cell, PowerPoint should automatically wrap the text to the next line in the cell. The height of the cell increases to accommodate the text you type.

You can edit and format text in a table as you would edit and format any text in your presentation.

ADD A TABLE WITH TEXT

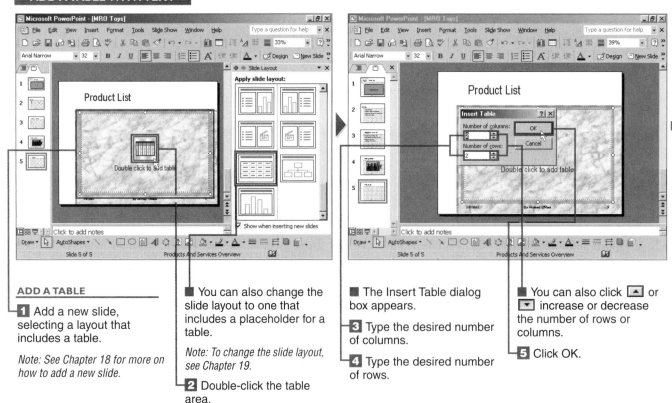

ADD A TABLE

1 Add a new slide, selecting a layout that includes a table.

Note: See Chapter 18 for more on how to add a new slide.

■ You can also change the slide layout to one that includes a placeholder for a table.

Note: To change the slide layout, see Chapter 19.

2 Double-click the table area.

■ The Insert Table dialog box appears.

3 Type the desired number of columns.

4 Type the desired number of rows.

■ You can also click ▲ or ▼ increase or decrease the number of rows or columns.

5 Click OK.

Can I add a table without changing the layout of the slide?

✔ Yes. Click the Insert Table button (▭) on the Standard toolbar. Then drag the mouse pointer over the number of rows and columns you want the table to contain.

How do I delete the contents of cells in a table?

✔ To select the contents of the cells, drag the mouse pointer over the cells. Then press Delete to delete the contents of the cells you selected.

Can I format the text?

✔ Yes. You can use any of the formatting buttons on the Formatting toolbar to make changes to the text. For example, you might want to make the table column headings bold. Or you can change the alignment of the entries within a cell using any of the alignment buttons. For more information on formatting, see Chapter 21.

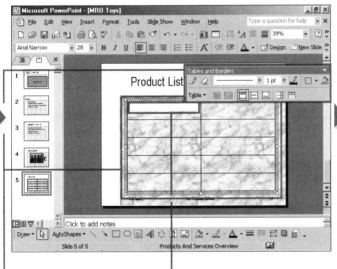

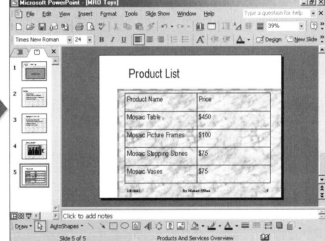

■ The table and the Tables and Borders toolbar appear.

■ You can click and drag the table handles to move or resize the table.

■ You can click the buttons on the toolbar to change the table's appearance.

ENTER TEXT IN A TABLE

6 Click the cell where you want the text to appear.

7 Type the text.

8 Repeat steps 6 and 7 until you type all the text.

■ The content of the table is completed.

FORMAT A TABLE

After you add a table to a slide, you can change the width of columns and the height of rows. This can help improve the layout of your table. If you want to insert additional information into your table, you can also add a row or column to the table.

When you change the width of a column or the height of a row, PowerPoint displays a dashed line on your screen to indicate the new width or height.

You cannot change the width or height of a single cell. When you make changes to the column width or row height, all the cells in the column or row are affected.

When you add a row, the new row appears above the selected row.

When you add a column, the new column appears to the left of the selected column. After you add a row or column, the table may no longer fit on the slide. You may need to move or resize the table to make the table fit on the slide. For information on moving or resizing an object, see "Move, Resize, or Delete a Slide Object."

FORMAT A TABLE

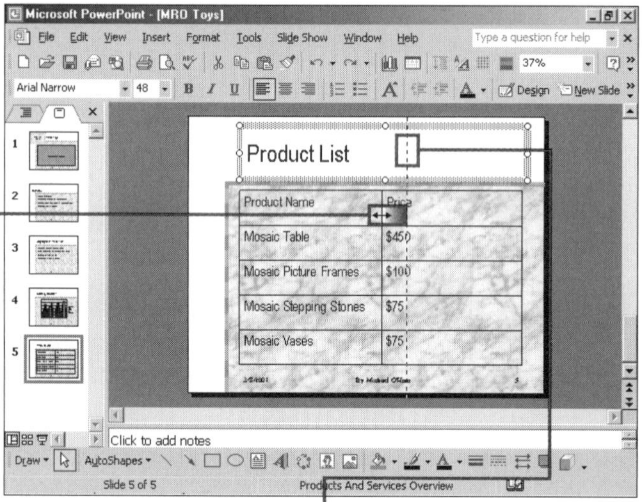

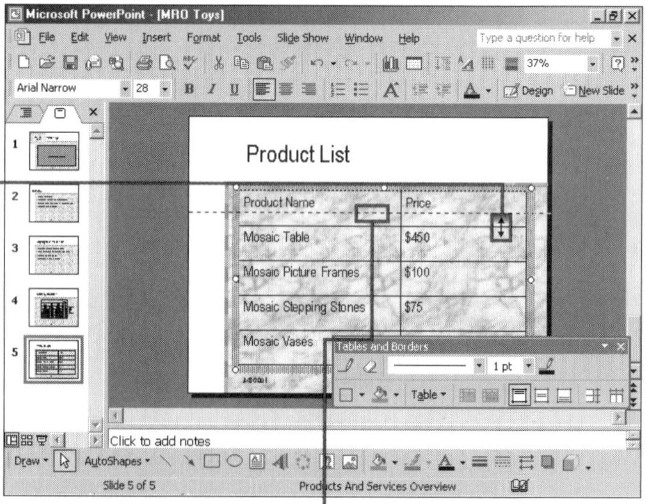

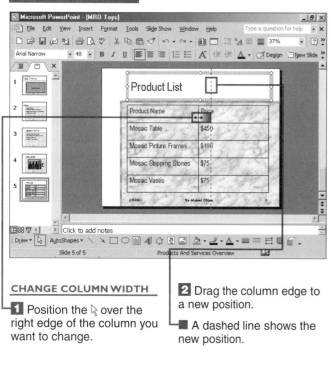

CHANGE COLUMN WIDTH

1 Position the ↖ over the right edge of the column you want to change.

2 Drag the column edge to a new position.

■ A dashed line shows the new position.

CHANGE ROW HEIGHT

1 Position the ↖ over the bottom edge of the row you want to change.

2 Drag the row edge to a new position.

■ A dashed line shows the new position.

What other formatting changes can I make?

✔ You can use the buttons on the Tables and Borders toolbar to change the appearance of the table. You can select different border styles, add a fill color to selected cells, change the vertical alignment of entries in a cell, and more. If you are unsure of what a button does, put the mouse pointer over the button. The ScreenTip or button name should appear.

How do I delete a row or column?

✔ To select the row or column you no longer need, drag the mouse over all the cells in the row or column. Click the Cut button (✂) on the Standard toolbar to delete the row or column.

Can I delete an entire table from a slide?

✔ Yes. You can delete a table as you would delete any object on a slide. For more information, see "Move, Resize, or Delete a Slide Object."

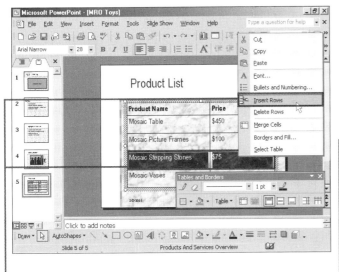

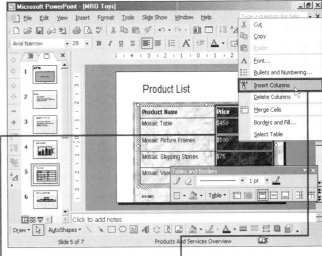

ADD A ROW

1 Click and drag the ↳ over all the cells in the row.

2 Right-click anywhere in the row.

3 Click Insert Rows.

■ PowerPoint adds the new row above the selected row and all the rows that follow shift downward.

■ To add a row to the bottom of a table, click the bottom right cell and then press Tab.

ADD A COLUMN

1 Click and drag the ↳ over all the cells in the column.

2 Right-click anywhere in the column.

3 Click Insert Columns.

■ PowerPoint adds the new column to the left of the selected one.

ADD A CHART

You can add a chart to a slide to show trends and compare data. Adding a chart is useful when a slide in your presentation contains numerical data. A chart is more appealing visually and often easier to understand than a list of numbers.

The Microsoft Graph program allows you to add a chart to a slide in your presentation. This program

is automatically installed on your computer during the standard Office installation.

When you add a chart to a slide, the menus and toolbars from Microsoft Graph appear on your screen. Microsoft Graph also displays a datasheet for the chart. A datasheet is similar to an Excel worksheet, with rows, columns, and cells, except that you cannot

use formulas in a Microsoft Graph datasheet.

The sample data in the datasheet gives you the basic structure of a chart; you replace this data with the contents of the chart you want to create. As you enter data in the datasheet, the chart on the slide automatically changes to display the new data.

ADD A CHART

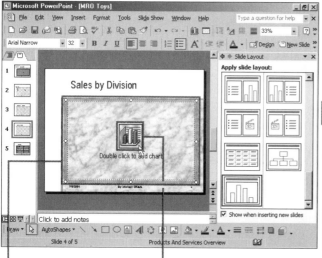

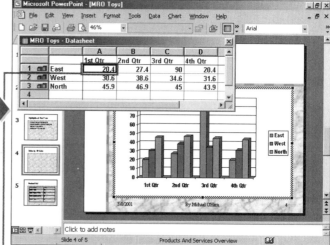

■1 Add a new slide, selecting a layout that includes a chart object.

Note: To add a new slide, see Chapter 18.

■ You can also change the slide layout to one that includes a placeholder for a chart.

Note: To change the slide layout, see Chapter 19.

■2 Double-click the chart area.

■ A datasheet appears, displaying sample data to show you where to enter your information.

■3 Click a cell.

■4 Type your data.

■5 Press Enter.

■ To remove data from a cell and leave the cell empty, click the cell and then press Delete.

■6 Repeat steps 3 through 5 until you finish typing all of your data.

How can I add a chart without changing the slide layout?

✔ You can click the Insert Chart button (📊) on the Standard toolbar and then perform steps 4 through 7 below to add a chart to any slide.

Can I move, resize, or delete a chart I added?

✔ You can move, resize, or delete a chart as you would any object on a slide. For more information, see "Move, Resize, or Delete a Slide Object."

Can I add a chart from Excel?

✔ Yes. In Excel, click a blank area of the chart and then select the Copy button (📋) on the Standard toolbar. In PowerPoint, display the slide you want to add the chart to and then click the Paste button (📋) on the Standard toolbar. When you use this method to add a chart, you cannot use Microsoft Graph to change the data displayed in the chart.

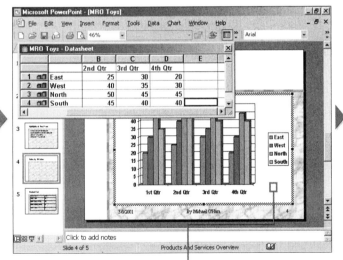

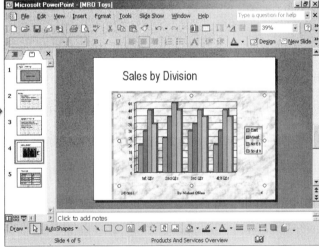

■ As you enter data, PowerPoint updates the chart on the slide.

7 Click a blank area on the slide to hide the datasheet.

■ The datasheet disappears and you can clearly view the chart on the slide.

EDIT AND FORMAT A CHART

You can change a chart you added to a slide. You can edit the data in the datasheet at any time to update the data plotted in the chart. You can also change the chart type, or make other changes to the chart element. For example, you can hide or display a chart legend, or hide or display the gridlines for the chart axes.

To make changes to a chart, the chart must be active. An active chart is surrounded by a thick border and selection handles.

Microsoft Graph allows you to change the chart type to suit your data. You can choose from several available chart types. The area, column, and line charts are useful

for showing changes to values over time. A pie chart is ideal for showing percentages.

You can plot data by row or column. Changing the way data is plotted determines what information appears on the X-axis.

EDIT AND FORMAT A CHART

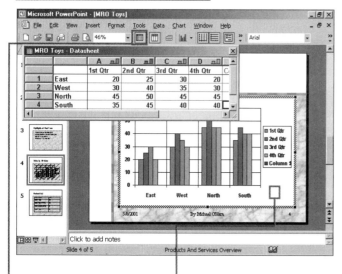

EDIT A CHART

1 Double-click the chart area to activate the chart.

■ If the datasheet does not display, click the View Datasheet button (▥).

2 Make any editing changes to the data.

3 Click back on the slide to hide the datasheet.

■ PowerPoint updates the data.

CHANGE CHART TYPE

1 Double-click the chart area to activate the chart.

Note: If you do not see the toolbar buttons mentioned in this section, click the ⊡ at the end of the toolbar.

2 Click the ⊡ next to the Chart Type button (▥ ▾).

3 Click the type of chart you want to use.

Why does a dialog box appear instead of the datasheet when I double-click a chart?

✔ The chart is already active. When you double-click an active chart, a Format dialog box appears. You can use this dialog box to format the selected chart item. For example, if you double-click the legend on a selected chart, you see options for formatting the legend. Click Cancel to close the dialog box.

Does the datasheet appear in my on-screen presentation?

✔ The datasheet does not appear in your on-screen presentation or when you print your presentation. To make the data in the datasheet part of your on-screen and printed presentation, click the Data Table button (▦).

Where can I find more chart types?

✔ To display more chart types, click the Chart menu and then choose Chart Type instead of using the Chart Type button in the toolbar. Click the chart type and then select the design you want to use.

How do I add a title to a chart?

✔ From the Chart menu, select Chart Options and then choose the Titles tab. Click the Chart title area and type a title for the chart. You can also add a title for each axis in your chart.

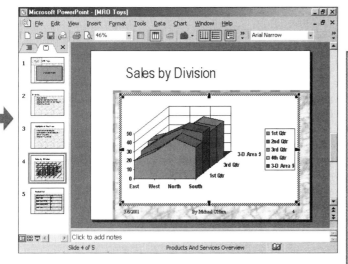

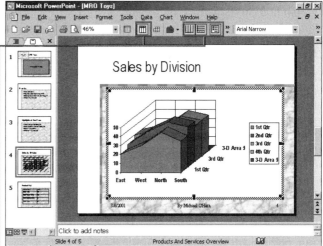

■ PowerPoint updates the chart to the new chart type.

CHANGE OTHER CHART OPTIONS

1 Click the appropriate option button:

By Column button (▦) changes how the chart plots.

Legend button (▤) hides the legend.

Category Axis Gridlines (▦) or Value Axis Gridlines (▤) buttons hide or display gridlines.

2 PowerPoint updates your chart accordingly.

ADD AN ORGANIZATION CHART

Another type of object that you can insert on a slide is an organizational chart. You might include, for example, the organization chart for your company or for a particular division.

Like other slide objects, you start by selecting a slide layout that includes the organization chart. You can also change the slide layout to

one that contains an organization chart object. For information on adding slides, see Chapter 18. For information on changing slide layouts, see Chapter 19.

When you are creating an organization chart, the Organization Chart toolbar appears on-screen. You can use the buttons in this toolbar to select different formatting options. For example,

you can select different layouts for the chart boxes. You can also add other boxes for subordinates or assistants.

After you add a diagram, you can move and resize it to best fit your slide. You can also delete a diagram you no longer need. For information on moving, resizing, or deleting a graphic, see "Move, Resize, or Delete a Slide Object."

ADD AN ORGANIZATION CHART

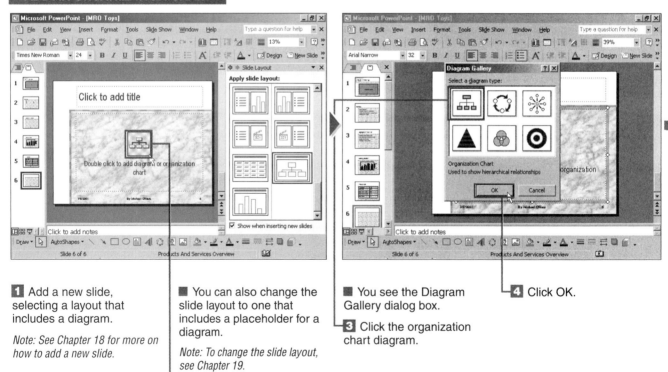

1 Add a new slide, selecting a layout that includes a diagram.

Note: See Chapter 18 for more on how to add a new slide.

■ You can also change the slide layout to one that includes a placeholder for a diagram.

Note: To change the slide layout, see Chapter 19.

2 Double-click the organization chart area.

■ You see the Diagram Gallery dialog box.

3 Click the organization chart diagram.

4 Click OK.

What changes can I make to the diagram?

✔ When you select a diagram, PowerPoint automatically displays the appropriate toolbar for that diagram type. You can use the buttons on the toolbar to make formatting changes.

If you are not sure what a button does, move the mouse pointer over the button to display its ScreenTip name.

What other types of diagrams can I insert?

✔ You can also insert flow charts and other diagrams by selecting the appropriate diagram type from the Diagram Gallery dialog box.

How do I edit text in a diagram?

✔ To edit text you have included as part of the diagram, click within the diagram and within the particular text you want to change. You should see the flashing insertion point. You can then edit or make any formatting changes to the text.

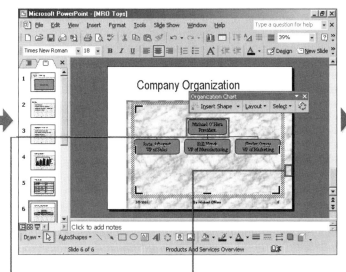

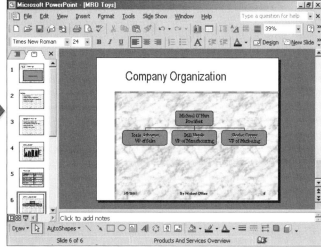

■ Text placeholders appear where you can add text.

6 Click outside the diagram.

■ PowerPoint adds the object to the slide.

5 Click in each text box and replace the filler text with your own text.

ADD A CLIP ART IMAGE

You can add a clip art image to a slide to make your presentation more interesting and entertaining. A clip art image can illustrate a concept and help the audience understand the information in your presentation.

Before you add a clip art image to a slide, you should change the layout of the slide to create space for the clip art image.

The Microsoft Clip Organizer contains a wide variety of images. You can scroll through the list to find a clip art image of interest. Or you can search for an image by typing a keyword or phrase to match.

The Picture toolbar automatically appears on your screen when you add a clip art image to a slide. You can use the buttons on the Picture toolbar to make changes to the clip art image. You can move or resize a clip art image you add to a slide. You can also delete a clip art image you no longer need. For information on moving, resizing, or deleting an object, see "Move, Resize, or Delete a Slide Object."

ADD A CLIP ART IMAGE

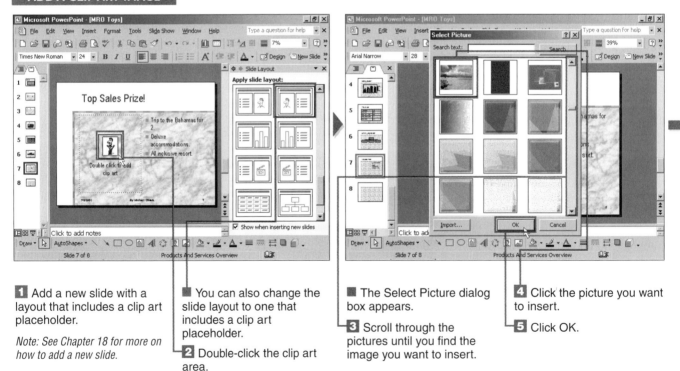

■1 Add a new slide with a layout that includes a clip art placeholder.

Note: See Chapter 18 for more on how to add a new slide.

■ You can also change the slide layout to one that includes a clip art placeholder.

■2 Double-click the clip art area.

Note: To change the slide layout, see Chapter 19.

■ The Select Picture dialog box appears.

■3 Scroll through the pictures until you find the image you want to insert.

■4 Click the picture you want to insert.

■5 Click OK.

Can I have the same clip art image appear on each slide in my presentation?

✔ Yes. You can add a clip art image to the Slide Master to have the image appear on each slide in your presentation. For information on the Slide Master, see Chapter 21.

How can I quickly find a clip art image of interest?

✔ You can search for clip art images by typing a word or phrase describing the clip art image you want to find into the Search text field of the Select Picture dialog box and then clicking the Search button.

Can I add a clip art image without changing the layout of my slide?

✔ Yes. Click the Insert Clip Art button ([🖼]) on the Drawing toolbar and perform steps 4 to 6 in this section.

Where can I find more clip art images?

✔ If you are connected to the Internet, you can visit Microsoft's Design Gallery Live Web site to find additional clip art images. To access this link, click Insert, Picture, Clip Art to display the Insert Clip Art pane. Then click the Clips Online link.

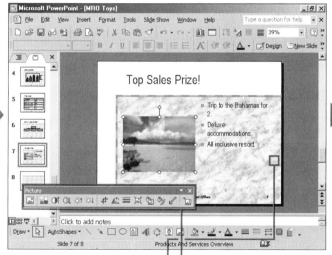

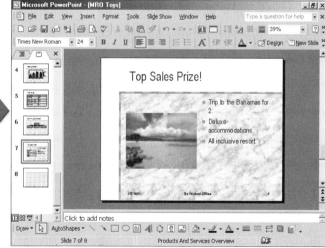

■ The clip art image and Picture toolbar appear.

■ You can click and drag the selection handles around the image to move or resize it.

■ You can click the buttons on the Picture toolbar to change the clip art image.

6 Click anywhere on the slide.

■ PowerPoint adds the clip art image.

ADD A PICTURE

You can add a picture stored on your computer to a slide in your presentation. Adding a picture is useful if you want to display your company logo or a picture of your products on a slide, for example.

PowerPoint allows you to use several popular graphics file formats, including Enhanced Metafile (.emf), Graphics Interchange Format (.gif), JPEG

(.jpg), Portable Network Graphics (.png), Windows Bitmap (.bmp), and Windows Metafile (.wmf).

By default, PowerPoint opens the My Pictures folder, but you can change to any other folder or drive on your computer. You can use the Places Bar to quickly locate the picture in a folder you frequently use.

The Picture toolbar automatically appears on your screen when you

add a picture to a slide. You can use the buttons on the Picture toolbar to change the appearance of the picture.

You can move and resize a picture to suit your slide. You can also delete a picture you no longer need. For information on moving, resizing or deleting an object, see "Move, Resize, or Delete a Slide Object."

ADD A PICTURE

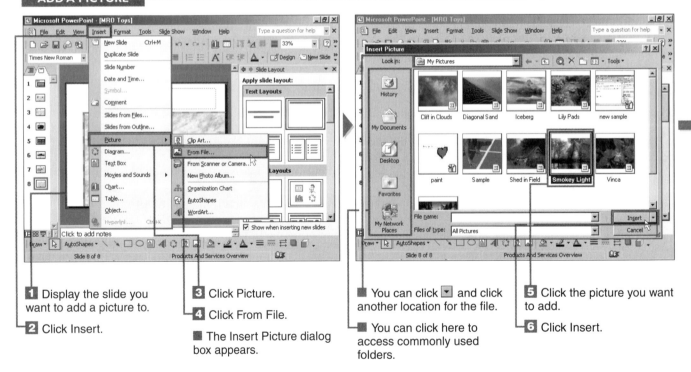

1 Display the slide you want to add a picture to.

2 Click Insert.

3 Click Picture.

4 Click From File.

■ The Insert Picture dialog box appears.

■ You can click ▼ and click another location for the file.

■ You can click here to access commonly used folders.

5 Click the picture you want to add.

6 Click Insert.

The picture I added covers text on my slide. How can I move the picture behind the text?

✔ You can change the order of objects on the slide. Click the picture. On the Drawing toolbar, click the Draw button. Select Order and then choose Send to Back.

Can I have the same picture appear on each slide in my presentation?

✔ You can add a picture to the Slide Master to have the picture appear on each slide in your presentation. For information on the Slide Master, see Chapter 21.

How can the buttons on the Picture toolbar help me change the appearance of a picture?

✔ You can use the More Contrast button (⬚) or Less Contrast button (⬚) to change the contrast of a picture. You can use the More Brightness button (⬚) or Less Brightness button (⬚) to change the brightness of a picture. The Crop button (⬚) allows you to trim the edges of a picture.

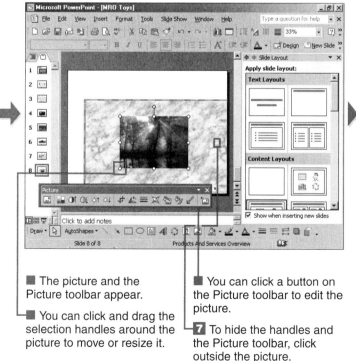

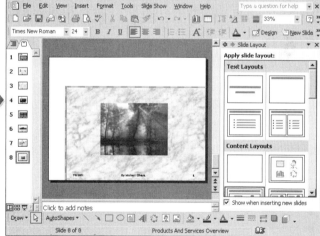

■ The picture and the Picture toolbar appear.

■ You can click and drag the selection handles around the picture to move or resize it.

■ You can click a button on the Picture toolbar to edit the picture.

7 To hide the handles and the Picture toolbar, click outside the picture.

■ PowerPoint adds the picture to the slide.

ADD AN AUTOSHAPE

Y ou can add simple shapes, called AutoShapes, to the slides in your presentation. Adding AutoShapes can help emphasize important information on your slides.

PowerPoint offers several categories of AutoShapes from which you can choose. For example, in the Basic Shapes category, you can find rectangles, ovals, and triangles. In the Block Arrows category, you can find bent and curved arrows. The Stars and Banners category includes stars and ribbons. The Callouts category contains AutoShapes you can use to add captions. You can use entries from the Action buttons to help your audience navigate through a presentation, especially in presentations broadcast or if you present via a kiosk.

When you add an AutoShape to a slide, PowerPoint lets you specify the location for the AutoShape and the size you want the AutoShape to display. You can later move and resize an AutoShape to suit your slide. You can also delete an AutoShape you no longer need. For information on moving, resizing, or deleting an object, see "Move, Resize, or Delete a Slide Object."

ADD AN AUTOSHAPE

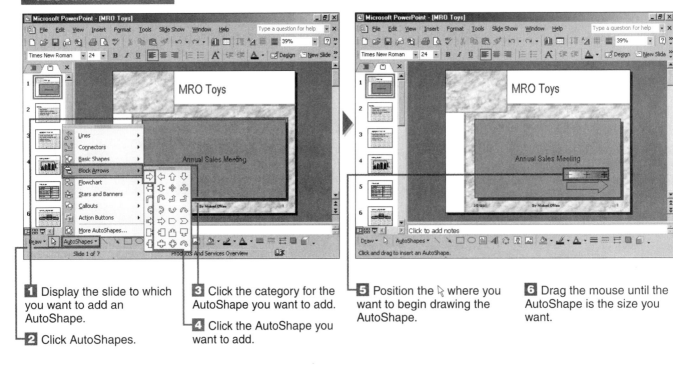

1 Display the slide to which you want to add an AutoShape.

2 Click AutoShapes.

3 Click the category for the AutoShape you want to add.

4 Click the AutoShape you want to add.

5 Position the ⩊ where you want to begin drawing the AutoShape.

6 Drag the mouse until the AutoShape is the size you want.

How can I change the appearance of an AutoShape?

✔ You can use the buttons on the Drawing toolbar. Click the AutoShape you want to change. To change the inside color, click the ▾ beside the Fill Color button (🖎) and then select a color. To change the line color, click the ▾ beside the Line Color button (🖋) and then click a color. To add a shadow, click the Shadow button (▣) and then click a shadow. To add a 3-D effect, click the 3-D button (🖼) and then click a 3-D effect.

Can I add a texture to an AutoShape?

✔ Yes. PowerPoint offers several textures, such as marble and canvas, which you can use to enhance an AutoShape. Click the AutoShape you want to change. Click the ▾ beside 🖎 and then click Fill Effects. Click the Texture tab and click the texture you want to use. Then click OK.

Can I add text to an AutoShape?

✔ Yes. Click the AutoShape and then type the text you want to add. You cannot add text to some AutoShapes.

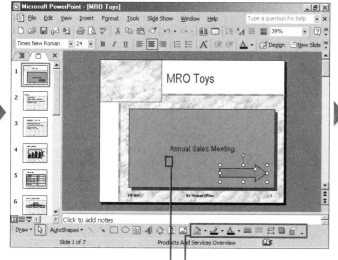

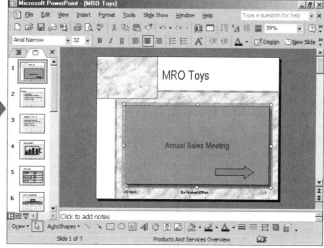

■ The AutoShape appears on the slide. Selection handles appear around the AutoShape letting you resize or move the shape.

7 Make any changes to the AutoShape.

8 Click outside the AutoShape.

■ PowerPoint adds the AutoShape to the slide.

ADD WORDART TEXT EFFECTS

You can use the WordArt feature to add text effects to your slides. A text effect can help enhance the appearance of a title or draw attention to an important point in your presentation.

If changing the font, size, and color of text does not allow you to achieve the look you want, you can add a text effect that skews,

rotates, shadows, or stretches the text. You can also make text appear three-dimensional.

When typing the text for a text effect, be careful not to make any spelling errors. PowerPoint's spell check feature does not check the spelling of text effects.

When you add a text effect, PowerPoint automatically displays

the WordArt toolbar. You can use the buttons on the toolbar to change the appearance of the text effect. You can also move and resize a text effect to suit your slide or delete a text effect you no longer need. For information on moving, resizing, or deleting an object, see "Move, Resize, or Delete a Slide Object."

ADD WORDART TEXT EFFECTS

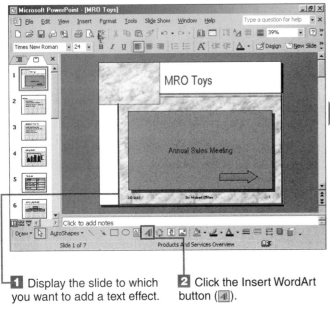

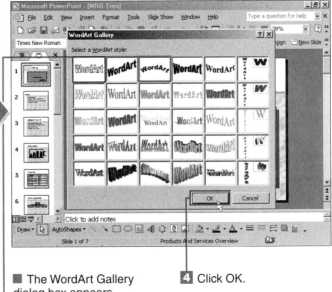

1 Display the slide to which you want to add a text effect.

2 Click the Insert WordArt button (📶).

■ The WordArt Gallery dialog box appears.

3 Click the type of text effect you want to add to the slide.

4 Click OK.

Can I change the shape of the WordArt?

✔ Yes. Click the WordArt object. The WordArt toolbar displays. Click the WordArt Gallery button (☐) and select the new style for the WordArt object.

How do I edit WordArt text?

✔ Double-click the text effect you want to edit. The Edit WordArt Text dialog box appears. You can use this dialog box to edit the text effect or change the font and size of the text effect. You can also bold and italicize the text effect.

How can I change the color of a text effect?

✔ Click the text effect you want to change and then use the buttons on the Drawing toolbar. To change the inside color, click the ☐ beside ☐ and then select the color you want to use. To change the line color, click the ☐ beside ☐ and then select the color you want to use.

What is the green handle used for?

✔ You can use the green handle to drag the AutoShape and change its rotation. Simply click this handle and drag until the shape is rotated to the degree you want.

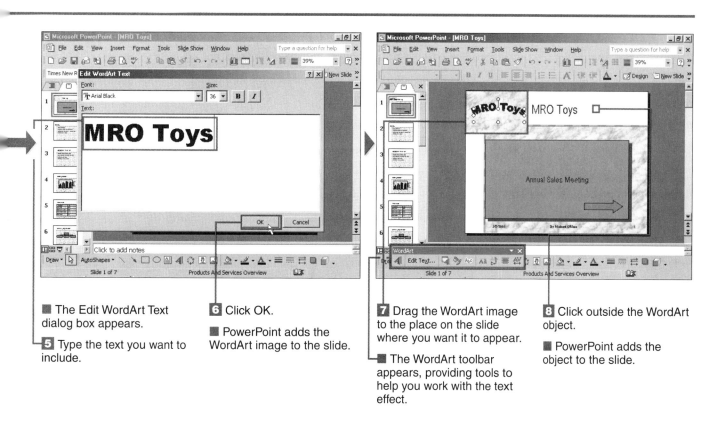

■ The Edit WordArt Text dialog box appears.

5 Type the text you want to include.

6 Click OK.

■ PowerPoint adds the WordArt image to the slide.

7 Drag the WordArt image to the place on the slide where you want it to appear.

■ The WordArt toolbar appears, providing tools to help you work with the text effect.

8 Click outside the WordArt object.

■ PowerPoint adds the object to the slide.

MOVE, RESIZE, OR DELETE A SLIDE OBJECT

Y ou can move, resize, or delete an object on a slide. An object can include an AutoShape, chart, clip art image, picture, table, text box, or WordArt text. PowerPoint allows you to move an object to another location on a slide. This is useful if an object covers other items on a slide. You can also copy an object from one location to another. This allows you to use the same object in more than one location on a slide.

When you select an object, selection handles appear around the object. These handles allow you to resize the object. The handles at the top and bottom of an object allow you to change the height of the object. The handles at the sides of an object allow you to change the width of the object. The handles at the corners of an object allow you to change the height and width of the object at the same time.

You can also delete an object you no longer need from a slide.

MOVE, RESIZE, OR DELETE A SLIDE OBJECT

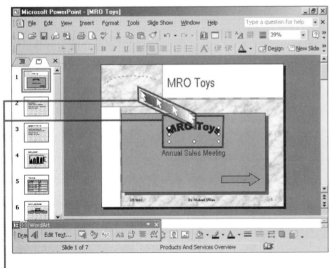

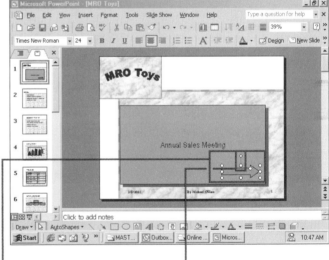

MOVE AN OBJECT

1 Click the object you want to move.

2 Place the ⌖ on the object border and drag the object to a new location.

■ The object appears in the new location.

Note: To copy an object, press the Ctrl key as you perform step 2.

RESIZE AN OBJECT

1 Click the object you want to resize.

■ Selection handles appear around the object.

2 Position the ⌖ over one of the handles.

Can I move or copy an object from one slide in my presentation to another?

✔ Yes. Select the object you want to move or copy. On the Standard toolbar, click 🔳 to move the object or 🔳 to copy the object. Display the slide you want to move or copy the object to and then click 🔳 on the Standard toolbar.

How can I move an object to exactly where I want it?

✔ If you are having difficulty moving an object using the mouse, you can nudge the object using the keyboard. Select the object you want to move. Press the Ctrl key and press the left, right, up, or down arrow to move the object.

How can I cancel a change I made to an object?

✔ PowerPoint remembers the last changes you made. You can click the Undo button (🔳) on the Standard toolbar to immediately cancel a change you regret.

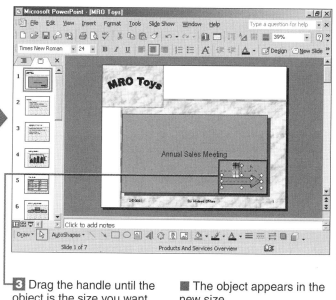

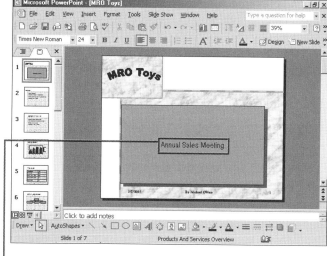

3 Drag the handle until the object is the size you want.

■ The object appears in the new size.

DELETE AN OBJECT

1 Click the object you want to delete.

2 Press Delete.

■ PowerPoint deletes the object.

Note: You may need to press Delete again to remove the placeholder for the object from the slide.

CHANGE THE FONT AND SIZE OF TEXT

Y ou can enhance the appearance of a slide by changing the design, or *font*, of text. PowerPoint also allows you to increase or decrease the size of text in your presentation. Larger text is easier to read, but smaller text enables you to fit more information on a slide.

PowerPoint provides a list of fonts from which to choose. Fonts you

used most recently appear at the top of the list, allowing you to quickly select fonts you use often. The fonts appear in the list as they appear in your presentation. This lets you preview a font before you select it.

You should consider your audience when choosing a font. For example, you may want to use an informal font, such as Comic Sans MS, for a

presentation you are delivering to your co-workers. A conservative font, such as Times New Roman, may be more appropriate for a presentation you are delivering to clients.

You should not use more than three different fonts in your presentation. Using too many fonts can make your presentation difficult to follow.

CHANGE THE FONT AND SIZE OF TEXT

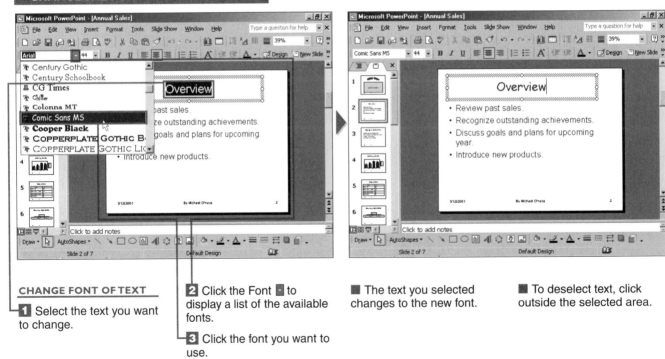

CHANGE FONT OF TEXT

■1 Select the text you want to change.

■2 Click the Font ▾ to display a list of the available fonts.

■3 Click the font you want to use.

■ The text you selected changes to the new font.

■ To deselect text, click outside the selected area.

I plan to deliver my presentation on a computer screen. Which font should I use?

✔ Use a font that is easy to read on a computer screen, such as Arial, Tahoma, Times New Roman, or Verdana.

Can I replace a font throughout my presentation?

✔ You can replace a font on all the slides in your presentation with another font. From the Format menu, click Replace Fonts. Click the Replace area and then select the font you want to replace. Click ▼ in the With box and click the font you want to use. Click Replace and PowerPoint makes the change. When the change has been made, click Close.

Is there another way to change the size of text?

✔ You can use the Increase Font Size button (A) or Decrease Font Size button (A) on the Formatting toolbar to change the size of text. Select the text you want to change, and then click the appropriate button until the text is the size you want. Each click increments the font to the next larger size within that font.

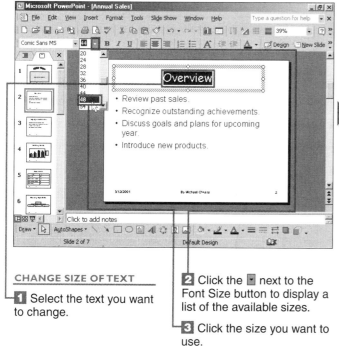

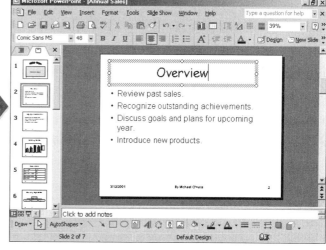

CHANGE SIZE OF TEXT

1 Select the text you want to change.

2 Click the ▼ next to the Font Size button to display a list of the available sizes.

3 Click the size you want to use.

■ The selected text changes to the new size.

■ To deselect text, click outside the selected area.

CHANGE TEXT STYLE

Y ou can use the Bold, Italic, Underline, and Shadow features to change the style of text on slides in your presentation. Changing the style of text allows you to emphasize important information and enhance the appearance of slides.

You can use one feature at a time or any combination of the four features to change the style of text.

The Bold feature makes text appear darker and thicker than other text. You can bold headings and titles to make them stand out from the rest of the text on your slides.

The Italic feature tilts text to the right. You may want to italicize quotations on your slides.

The Underline feature adds a line underneath text. This is useful for emphasizing important words or phrases on your slides.

The Shadow feature adds a three-dimensional effect to text and is useful for creating eye-catching slide titles.

Avoid overusing the Bold, Italic, Underline, and Shadow features, as this can make the text on your slides difficult to read and diminish the effectiveness of the features.

CHANGE TEXT STYLE

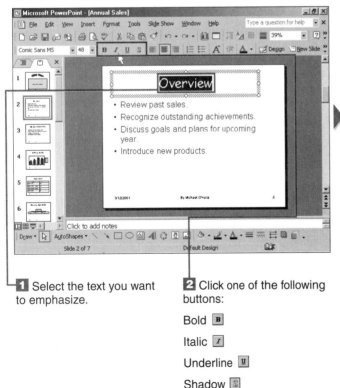

1 Select the text you want to emphasize.

2 Click one of the following buttons:

Bold B

Italic I

Underline U

Shadow S

■ The selected text appears in the new style.

■ The toolbar button is boxed.

■ To deselect text, click outside the selected area.

Note: To remove a style, repeat steps 1 and 2.

CHANGE TEXT ALIGNMENT

You can use the alignment buttons on the Formatting toolbar to change the alignment of text on a slide. Changing the alignment of text can make the text on your slides easier to read and help your audience distinguish between different types of information in the presentation.

PowerPoint uses text boxes to display text on a slide. When you

change the alignment of text, you change the position of the text in the text box. You can also move the text box as covered in Chapter 20.

You can use the left align option to line up text along the left edge of a text box. You may want to left align the main points on a slide.

The center option lets you center text between the left and right

edges of a text box. This is useful for making headings and titles on a slide stand out.

You can use the right align option to line up text along the right edge of a text box. You may want to right align short lists of information on a slide.

CHANGE TEXT ALIGNMENT

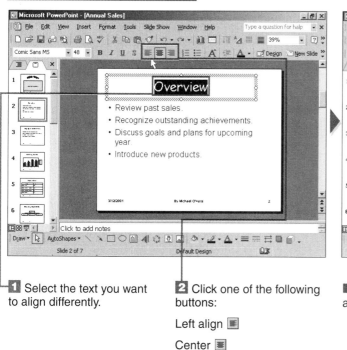

■1 Select the text you want to align differently.

■2 Click one of the following buttons:

Left align 🔲

Center 🔲

Right align 🔲

■ The text displays the new alignment.

■ To deselect text, click outside the selected area.

CHANGE TEXT COLOR

You can change the color of text on a slide. This can help enhance the appearance of a slide or draw attention to important information.

You can choose the text color you want to use from a color palette. The top row of the color palette contains the eight colors used in the color scheme of the current slide. A *color scheme* is a set of coordinated colors for items such as the background, text, shadows, and titles of a slide. For more information on color schemes, see Chapter 22.

Make sure the text color you choose works well with the background color of the slide. For example, your readers may find red text on a blue background difficult to read.

When you change the color of text in the Normal view, the text in the Slide pane displays the new color. The text in the Outline pane does not display the new color. For more on views in PowerPoint, see Chapter 19.

CHANGE TEXT COLOR

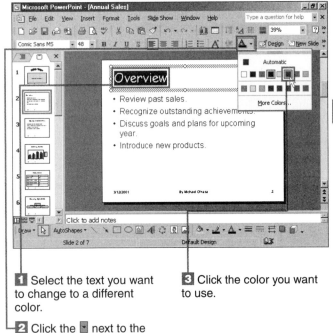

■ Select the text you want to change to a different color.

■ Click the ▼ next to the Font Color button (**A**).

■ Click the color you want to use.

■ The text appears in the color you selected.

■ To deselect text, click outside the text area.

Note: To once again display the text in the default color, repeat steps 1 through 3, except select Automatic in step 3.

COPY FORMATTING

Y ou can make the text on one slide in your presentation appear exactly like the text on another slide.

You may want to copy the formatting of text to make all the titles or important information on your slides look the same. This can help give your presentation a consistent appearance.

The Format Painter tool enables you to copy the formatting of text from one location for applying to text somewhere else in a document. Simply select the text and use the Format Painter button, and PowerPoint copies all formatting applied to that text.

How can I copy the formatting to more than one selection of text?

✔ You can copy formatting to text on several slides in your presentation at once. To do so, perform the steps below, except double-click the Format Painter button ![icon] on the Standard toolbar in step 2. When you finish selecting all the text you want to display the formatting, press Esc to stop copying the formatting.

COPY FORMATTING

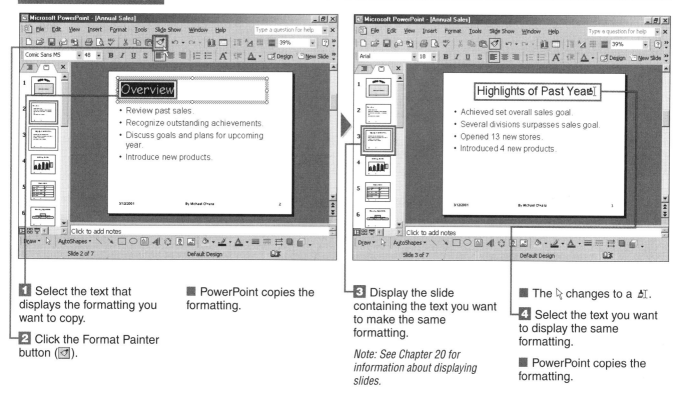

1 Select the text that displays the formatting you want to copy.

2 Click the Format Painter button (![icon]).

■ PowerPoint copies the formatting.

3 Display the slide containing the text you want to make the same formatting.

Note: See Chapter 20 for information about displaying slides.

■ The ▷ changes to a ▵I.

4 Select the text you want to display the same formatting.

■ PowerPoint copies the formatting.

FORMAT BULLETED AND NUMBERED LISTS

Some slide layouts include a placeholder for a bulleted list. If you have added one of these slides and created a bulleted list, you can change the appearance of the bullets on a slide. You can also change the bullets to numbers.

Bullets are useful for items in no particular order, such as a list of expenses. Numbers are useful for items in a specific order, such as the steps required to complete a

project. You can change one, some, or all of the bullets on a slide.

PowerPoint offers several bullet styles for you to choose from, including dots, squares, and check marks.

PowerPoint also provides several number styles you can use, including letters and Roman numerals.

You can change the color of the bullets or numbers you select. The available colors depend on the color scheme of the slide. See Chapter 22 for more information about schemes. If you want to make the bullets or numbers the same color as the default text color on the slide, you can choose the Automatic option.

FORMAT BULLETED AND NUMBERED LISTS

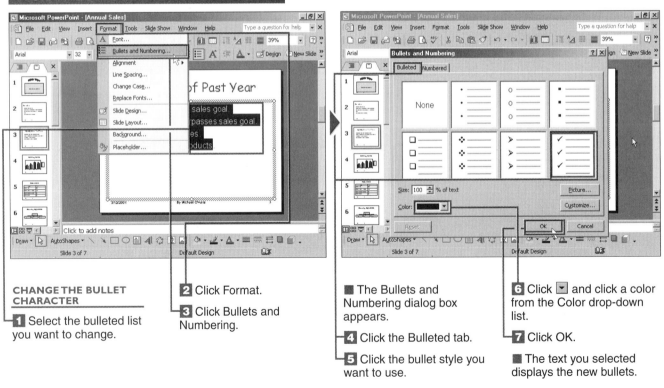

CHANGE THE BULLET CHARACTER

1 Select the bulleted list you want to change.

2 Click Format.

3 Click Bullets and Numbering.

■ The Bullets and Numbering dialog box appears.

4 Click the Bulleted tab.

5 Click the bullet style you want to use.

6 Click ▾ and click a color from the Color drop-down list.

7 Click OK.

■ The text you selected displays the new bullets.

How can I quickly add bullets or numbers to text?

✔ Select the text you want to display bullets or numbers. On the Formatting toolbar, click the Bullets button (▤) to add bullets or click the Numbering button (▤) to add numbers.

How do I remove bullets or numbers?

✔ Select the bulleted list or numbered list and then click the ▤ or the ▤.

How can I add another item to a bulleted list or numbered list?

✔ You can add more items to a bulleted list or numbered list by clicking at the end of the last item in the list and pressing Enter. PowerPoint adds new bulleted point or numbered point. You can type the text for this item.

Are there more bullet styles I can choose from?

✔ Yes. In the Bullets and Numbering dialog box, click the Bulleted tab and then click Customize. In the Symbol dialog box that appears, select the font containing the bullet style you want to use. Click the bullet style you want to use and then click OK.

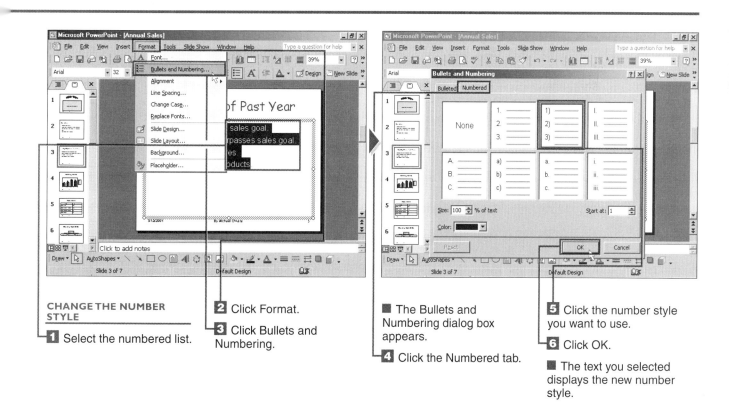

CHANGE THE NUMBER STYLE

1 Select the numbered list.

2 Click Format.

3 Click Bullets and Numbering.

■ The Bullets and Numbering dialog box appears.

4 Click the Numbered tab.

5 Click the number style you want to use.

6 Click OK.

■ The text you selected displays the new number style.

ANIMATE SLIDE OBJECTS

You can add movement to the objects on your slides. You can animate an object such as a title, AutoShape, text effect, table, or picture. Animation helps you emphasize important points and keep your audience's attention.

PowerPoint offers several animation categories that each contain different effects. For example, you can select from Entrance effects, Emphasis effects,

Exit effects, or Motion paths. Each of these categories offers its own set of animations; the available animation effects depend on the object you select.

In addition to the effect, you can select when to start the animation, its properties (for example, the direction), and the speed.

You can preview an effect to see the animation. If you add more than one effect to a slide, PowerPoint

displays the effects in the order you added them to the slide.

When you use the AutoContent Wizard to create a presentation, PowerPoint may automatically include animated objects in the presentation.

To display an animated object during a slide show, you must click the slide that contains the object. For information on viewing a slide show, see Chapter 22.

ANIMATE SLIDE OBJECTS

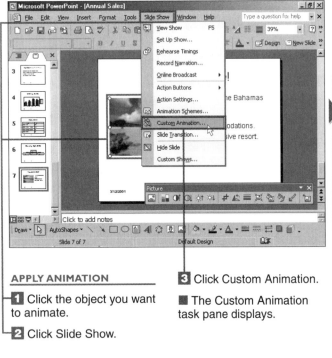

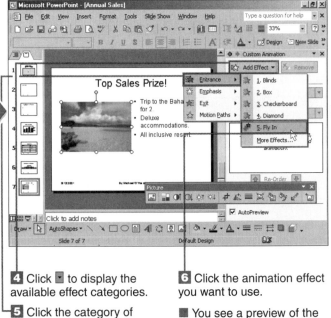

APPLY ANIMATION

■1 Click the object you want to animate.

■2 Click Slide Show.

■3 Click Custom Animation.

■ The Custom Animation task pane displays.

■4 Click ▾ to display the available effect categories.

■5 Click the category of animation effect you want to add.

■ PowerPoint displays a list of the available effects within the selected category.

■6 Click the animation effect you want to use.

■ You see a preview of the animation with the default settings.

How can I have an animated object appear automatically during a slide show instead of waiting for a mouse click?

✔ Click the animated object you want to have automatically appear. Click Slide Show and click Custom Animation. In the Custom Animation task pane, display the Start drop-down list and select when to play the animation.

How do I change the order of animations on a slide?

✔ Click Slide Show, and then click Custom Animation. Click the object you want to move. Click the Up or Down Re-Order buttons to move the object up or down in the animation order.

How do I turn off an animation?

✔ From the Slide Show menu, click Custom Animation. Select the animation to remove and then click Remove.

What are the numbers on the slide?

✔ PowerPoint adds numbers to each animated object so that you can see the order in which they appear. These numbers are not displayed when you play the presentation.

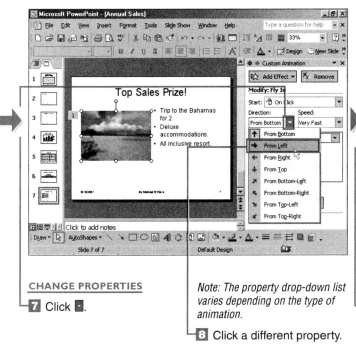

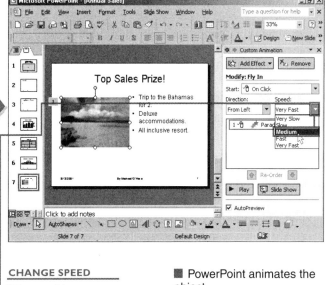

CHANGE PROPERTIES

7 Click ▪.

Note: The property drop-down list varies depending on the type of animation.

8 Click a different property.

CHANGE SPEED

9 Click ▪ and click a speed.

■ PowerPoint animates the object.

10 Click outside the object to deselect it.

USING AN ANIMATION SCHEME

One quick way to animate the items in a presentation is to use an animation *scheme,* a set of animations that PowerPoint applies to selected slides or all slides. An animation scheme animates several items on the slide, including the title and any other objects. Which objects are animated depends on the animation scheme you select.

In the list of animation schemes in the task pane, PowerPoint groups

the animation schemes into Subtle, Moderate, and Exciting. You can select a scheme that best matches the mood and purpose of your presentation. For example, for a business proposal, you may opt for something subtle. On the other hand, in a meeting to introduce a new product or to get your audience's interest, you may prefer a more exciting animation scheme, such as a boomerang or pin wheel scheme.

You can preview an effect to see the animation scheme. By default, PowerPoint checks AutoPreview, and the current slide shows the animation when you select it.

When you use the AutoContent Wizard to create a presentation, PowerPoint may automatically include an animation scheme. For more about the AutoContent Wizard, see Chapter 18.

USING AN ANIMATION SCHEME

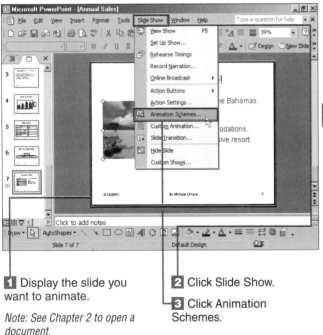

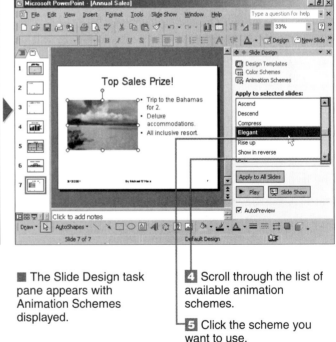

1 Display the slide you want to animate.

Note: See Chapter 2 to open a document.

2 Click Slide Show.

3 Click Animation Schemes.

■ The Slide Design task pane appears with Animation Schemes displayed.

4 Scroll through the list of available animation schemes.

5 Click the scheme you want to use.

How do I remove an animation scheme?

✔ Select the slide(s) from which you want to remove the scheme. Then follow steps 1 through 6, except click No Animation from the Slide Design task pane in step 5.

What happens when I have custom animations and an animation scheme?

✔ PowerPoint retains the custom animation and adds the animation scheme only to objects that currently are not animated.

Can I customize an animation scheme?

✔ Yes. Click Slide Show and then click Custom Animation. The Custom Animation task pane is displayed listing all the animations — custom animations you have added as well as animations added with the animation scheme. You can select any of the animations and modify them.

For additional animation options, click the animation and then click the 🔽 next to it. You see a menu of choices. From this menu, you can change the effect options, set timing, or remove the animation.

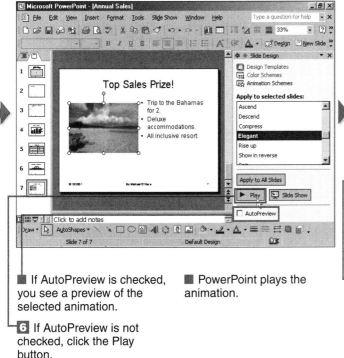

■ If AutoPreview is checked, you see a preview of the selected animation.

■ PowerPoint plays the animation.

6 If AutoPreview is not checked, click the Play button.

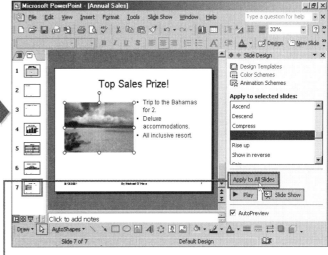

■ By default, PowerPoint adds the animation scheme only to the selected slides. To add the animation scheme to all slides in the presentation, click Apply to All Slides.

■ PowerPoint animates the slide(s) with the selected animation schemes.

CHANGE THE COLOR SCHEME

You can select a new color scheme for an individual slide or all the slides in your presentation. Changing the color scheme for an individual slide is useful when you want to make an important slide stand out from the rest of the slides in your presentation. Changing the color scheme for all the slides is useful

when you want to keep the appearance of the presentation consistent.

The design template you are using for the presentation determines the available color schemes. Each color scheme contains a set of eight coordinated colors, including background, text, shadow, title text, and accent colors. For information

on design templates, see the section "Change the Design Template."

When selecting a color scheme, consider the type of presentation you are giving. If you are using overheads, choose a color scheme with a light background and dark text. If you are using 35mm slides, choose a color scheme with a dark background and light text.

CHANGE THE COLOR SCHEME

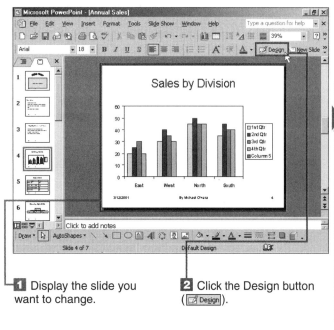

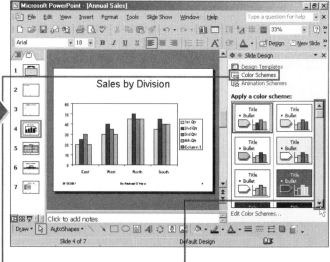

1 Display the slide you want to change.

2 Click the Design button (Design).

■ You see the Slide Design task pane.

3 Click Color Schemes.

■ The Color Scheme task pane appears.

4 Scroll through the list to view the available color schemes.

Note: The available color schemes depend on the current design template.

How can I change a color in a color scheme?

✔ In the Color Scheme task pane, click the scheme you want to modify. Click the Edit Color Schemes link. Click the color you want to change and then click Change Color. Click the color you want to use and then click OK.

Can I change just the background color for a slide?

✔ Yes. Click Format and then click Background. Click the ▼ in the Background fill area and then click the background color you want to use. Click Apply to apply the color to the current slide. To apply to all slides, click Apply to All.

How do I undo a change?

✔ Click the Undo button (⟲). Or if you cannot undo the change — perhaps because you have made other changes after applying the color scheme — go back to the original design template and apply it to the slide. See the section "Change the Design Template" for more information.

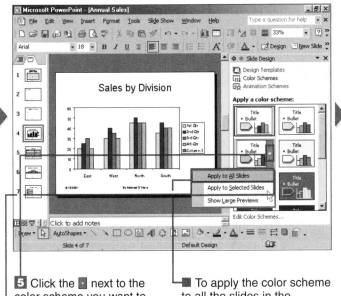

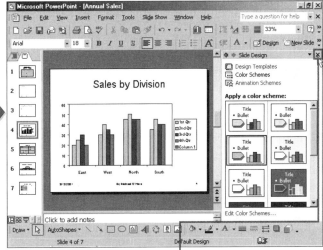

5 Click the ▼ next to the color scheme you want to use.

6 Click Apply to Selected Slides to apply the color scheme to the current slide.

■ To apply the color scheme to all the slides in the presentation, click Apply to All Slides.

■ PowerPoint applies the color scheme to the slide(s).

7 Click ✕ to close the Slide Design task pane.

CHANGE THE DESIGN TEMPLATE

PowerPoint offers many design templates to give the slides in your presentation a new appearance. Changing the design of your slides can help you make your presentation more effective.

When you create a new presentation, you can base it on a design template. If you do not like that template, or if you start with a blank presentation, you can always change to another design template.

Each design template contains fonts, text colors, and a background that work well together. You can choose the design template that best suits your presentation's content and your intended audience. The design template affects only the appearance of the slides, but the slide content does not change.

Changing the design template does not affect any formatting you have

applied directly to a slide. For example, if you change the color of text on a slide and then change the design template, the text color you applied overrides that of the new design.

After you change the design template, review your entire presentation to ensure that your slides appear the way you want.

CHANGE THE DESIGN TEMPLATE

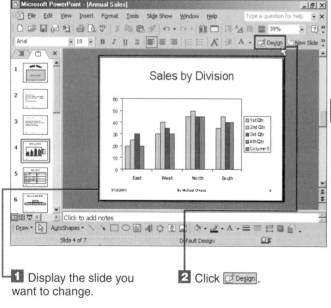

1 Display the slide you want to change.

2 Click ☑ Design.

■ The Slide Design task pane displays.

3 If necessary, click the link for Design Templates.

4 Scroll through the list of templates until you see a template you like.

How can I return to the previous design template?

✔ If you do not like the look of new design template, click the Undo button (🔄) to immediately return to the previous design template.

Can I change the color scheme for my presentation after changing the design template?

✔ Yes. PowerPoint provides several different color schemes for each design template. For more information on changing the color scheme, see the section "Change the Color Scheme."

Can I change the background color of a slide after changing the design template?

✔ Yes. Click Format and then click Background. In the Background fill area, click the ▾ and click a new color. Then click Apply. To change the background color of all the slides in the presentation, click Apply to All.

Can I preview how my slides will look if printed from a black-and-white printer?

✔ You can click the Color/Grayscale button (▣) in the Standard toolbar to preview how your slides will look when printed on a black-and-white printer. Click this button and then click Grayscale or Pure Black and White.

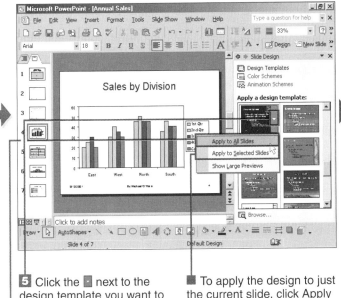

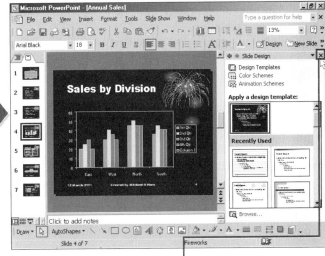

5 Click the ▪ next to the design template you want to use.

6 Click Apply to All Slides to apply the design template to all the slides in the presentation.

■ To apply the design to just the current slide, click Apply to Selected Slides.

■ The presentation updates with the new design template.

7 To close the Slide Design task pane, click ✕.

ADD OR EDIT A HEADER OR FOOTER

You can display additional information at the bottom of every slide in your presentation and the top and/or bottom of notes and handouts. Text that appears at the top of the page, called a *header*, or text that appears at the bottom of the page, called a *footer*, is useful when you want the audience to keep certain information, such as the name of your company, in mind during your presentation.

You can display the date and time, a page or slide number, and text in the footer on every slide in your presentation. You can display the same items and header text on notes and handouts. When you use the AutoContent Wizard to create a presentation, PowerPoint may automatically add this information to your slides for you. For more on the AutoContent Wizard, see Chapter 18.

You can have the date and time update automatically each time you open your presentation. You can also display a fixed date and time, such as the date you created the presentation. If you choose to update the date and time automatically, PowerPoint gives you several options as to how the date and time will appear, such as 4/22/99 3:59 PM.

ADD A HEADER OR FOOTER

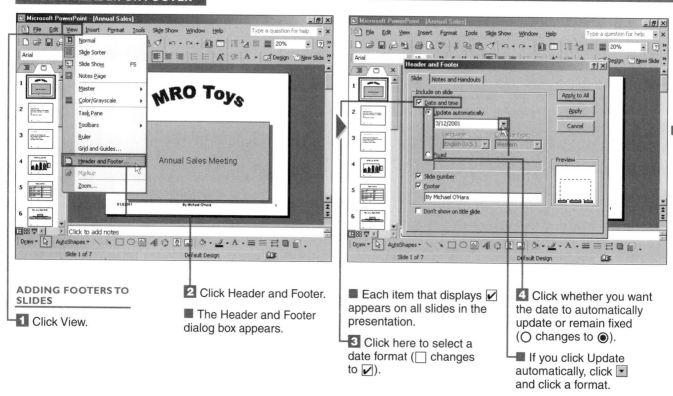

ADDING FOOTERS TO SLIDES

█1 Click View.

█2 Click Header and Footer.

■ The Header and Footer dialog box appears.

■ Each item that displays ☑ appears on all slides in the presentation.

█3 Click here to select a date format (☐ changes to ☑).

█4 Click whether you want the date to automatically update or remain fixed (○ changes to ◉).

■ If you click Update automatically, click ▼ and click a format.

How can I prevent a footer from appearing on the first slide in my presentation?

✔ In the Header and Footer dialog box, check the Don't show on title slide option. This also removes the date and time and the slide number from the first slide.

Can I start numbering the slides in my presentation at a number other than 1?

✔ Yes. Click File and then click Page Setup. Double-click the Number slides from box and then type the number you want to display on the first slide of the presentation. Click OK.

Can I change the appearance and position of text in a header or footer?

✔ You can change the appearance and position of text in a header or footer on your slides, speaker notes, and handouts. Click View, click Master, and then click the appropriate Master. For more information on the Slide Master, see the section "Using the Slide Master."

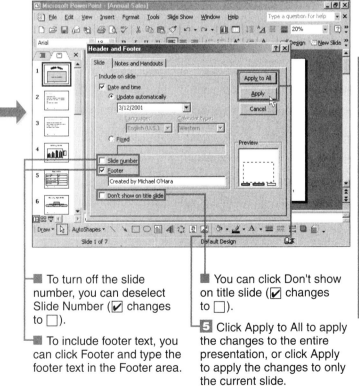

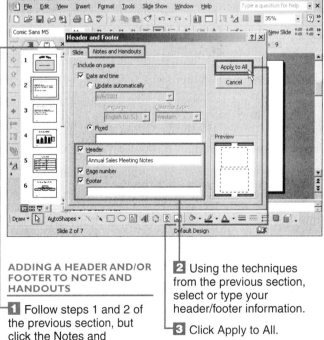

■ To turn off the slide number, you can deselect Slide Number (☑ changes to ☐).

■ To include footer text, you can click Footer and type the footer text in the Footer area.

■ You can click Don't show on title slide (☑ changes to ☐).

5 Click Apply to All to apply the changes to the entire presentation, or click Apply to apply the changes to only the current slide.

ADDING A HEADER AND/OR FOOTER TO NOTES AND HANDOUTS

1 Follow steps 1 and 2 of the previous section, but click the Notes and Handouts tab.

2 Using the techniques from the previous section, select or type your header/footer information.

3 Click Apply to All.

USING THE SLIDE MASTER

You can use the Slide Master to simultaneously change the appearance of all your presentation's slides. Using the Slide Master helps you apply a consistent style to your presentation.

The Slide Master contains a placeholder for the title, points, date, footer text, and slide number on each slide in your presentation.

You can format the sample text in a placeholder to format text on all your slides. Formatting text on the Slide Master does not affect text you previously formatted on individual slides.

You can add an object to the Slide Master, such as a clip art image, picture, or chart, that you want to appear on all your slides. You can move, resize, or delete items on the

Slide Master as you would any object in your presentation. For example, you can change the placement of the text boxes or other slide objects. For more information on moving, resizing, and deleting objects, see Chapter 20.

After changing the Slide Master, review your entire presentation to make sure text and objects do not look out of place.

USING THE SLIDE MASTER

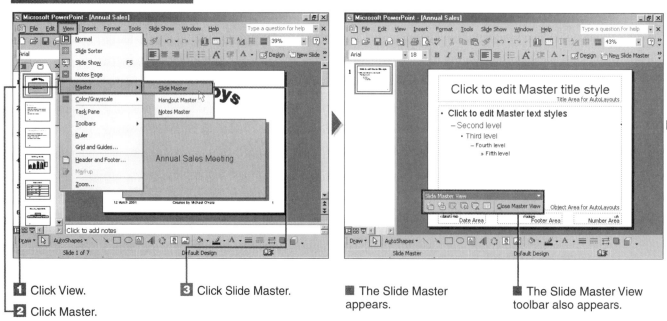

■ Click View.

■ Click Master.

■ Click Slide Master.

■ The Slide Master appears.

■ The Slide Master View toolbar also appears.

Are there other masters available?

✔ Yes. The Handout Master allows you to change the appearance of handouts. The Notes Master allows you to change the appearance of speaker notes. To use one of these masters, click View, click Master, and then select the master you want to use.

Can I apply transitions to the Slide Master?

✔ Yes. Right-click the miniature slide master in the left pane and then select Slide Transition. The Slide Transition task pane appears. Select the transition to use. See Chapter 22 for more information on slide transitions.

Can I restore a placeholder I accidentally deleted from the Slide Master?

✔ Yes. Click Format and then click Master Layout. Click the placeholder you want to restore and then click OK.

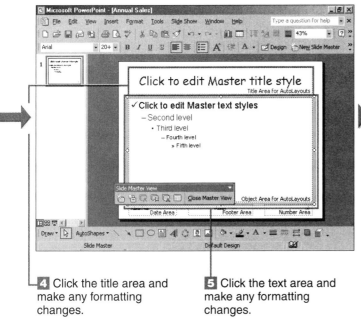

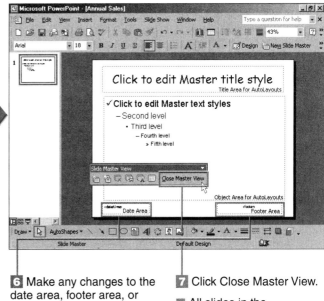

4 Click the title area and make any formatting changes.

5 Click the text area and make any formatting changes.

6 Make any changes to the date area, footer area, or number area.

■ You can add any objects to the Slide Master that you want to appear on every slide.

7 Click Close Master View.

■ All slides in the presentation update to reflect the changes you made to the Slide Master.

REARRANGE SLIDES

Y ou can change the order of the slides in your presentation. This is useful when you have finished creating your presentation and realize you want to present the slides in a different order.

The Slide Sorter view displays a miniature version of each slide so that you can see a general overview

of your presentation. This view allows you to easily reorder your slides. For more information on opening a presentation in different views, see Chapter 19.

A slide number appears below each slide in your presentation. When you move a slide, PowerPoint automatically renumbers the slides for you. These slide numbers do

not appear in the presentation; they simply help you keep track of the number and order of slides.

You can move one slide or several slides at once. To move several slides at once, you must first select the slides you want to move. PowerPoint displays a line to indicate the new location of the slides in the presentation.

REARRANGE SLIDES

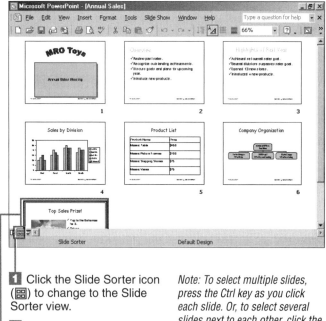

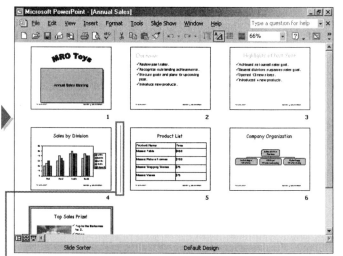

1 Click the Slide Sorter icon (⊞) to change to the Slide Sorter view.

2 To select the slide you want to move, click the slide.

Note: To select multiple slides, press the Ctrl key as you click each slide. Or, to select several slides next to each other, click the first slide and then press the Shift key while clicking the last slide.

3 Drag the slide to a new location.

■ A line shows where the slide will appear.

■ The slide appears in the new location.

DELETE A SLIDE

You can remove a slide you no longer need in your presentation. This is useful when you are reviewing your presentation and realize a slide contains incorrect or outdated information.

The Slide Sorter view displays a miniature version of each slide in your presentation. This view allows

you to easily see the slide you want to delete. For more information on the views, see Chapter 19.

You can delete one slide or several slides at once. To delete several slides at once, you must first select the slides you want to delete.

When you delete a slide, PowerPoint automatically

renumbers the remaining slides in your presentation for you.

PowerPoint remembers the last changes you made to your presentation. If you change your mind after deleting a slide, you can use the Undo feature to immediately cancel the deletion.

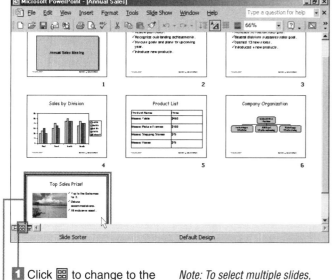

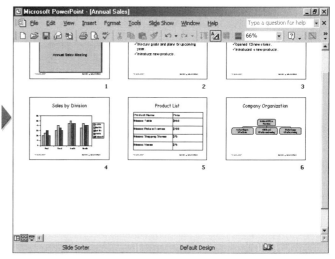

1 Click ⊞ to change to the Slide Sorter view.

2 Click the slide you want to delete.

Note: To select multiple slides, press the Ctrl key as you click each slide. Or, to select several slides next to each other, click the first slide and then press the Shift key while clicking the last slide.

3 Press Delete.

■ PowerPoint deletes the slide.

HIDE A SLIDE

Y ou can hide a slide in your presentation so that the slide does not display when you deliver the presentation.

Hiding a slide is useful when a slide in your presentation contains supporting information you do not want to include unless the audience requires clarification. For example, you may not want to show your audience a slide containing

sensitive financial information unless they ask to see the information.

Hiding a slide can also help you prepare for questions from the audience. You can create slides that answer common questions and then display the slides only when necessary.

When you hide a slide in your presentation, a symbol appears through the number for the slide in the Slide Sorter view.

If you want to present the information on a hidden slide during a slide show, you can easily display the hidden slide. For information on viewing a slide show, See the section "Preview a Slide Show."

HIDE A SLIDE

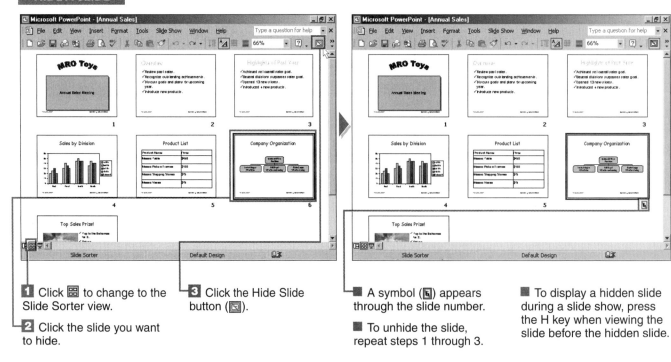

■ **1** Click ▦ to change to the Slide Sorter view.

■ **2** Click the slide you want to hide.

■ **3** Click the Hide Slide button (▧).

■ A symbol (▧) appears through the slide number.

■ To unhide the slide, repeat steps 1 through 3.

■ To display a hidden slide during a slide show, press the H key when viewing the slide before the hidden slide.

CREATE A SUMMARY SLIDE

You can create a summary slide containing the titles of the slides in your presentation. A summary slide is useful for giving your audience an overview of your presentation before you begin.

Before creating a summary slide, you need to decide which slides' titles you want to include on the summary slide. PowerPoint gives you the option of either including all of your slides or selecting certain ones. Depending on the length of your presentation, PowerPoint may make the summary slide more than one slide.

PowerPoint places the summary slide at the beginning of your presentation. If you want to use the summary slide to conclude your presentation, you can move the slide to the end of the presentation. For information on moving slides, see the section "Rearrange Slides."

After creating a summary slide, you can edit the summary slide as you would edit any slide in your presentation. For example, you can remove a slide title you do not want to appear on the summary slide. For information on editing text on a slide, see Chapter 19.

CREATE A SUMMARY SLIDE

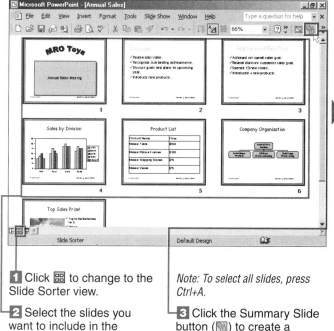

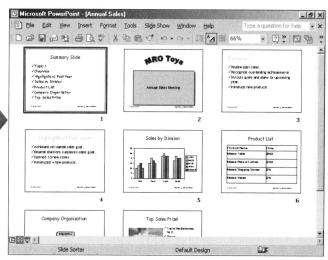

1 Click 🔲 to change to the Slide Sorter view.

2 Select the slides you want to include in the summary by pressing the Ctrl key and clicking each slide.

Note: To select all slides, press Ctrl+A.

3 Click the Summary Slide button (🔲) to create a summary slide.

■ A summary slide appears at the beginning of the presentation, listing the title of each slide.

Note: To move the summary slide to the end of the presentation, see the section "Rearrange Slides."

ADD SLIDE TRANSITIONS

You can use effects called transitions to help you move from one slide to the next. A transition determines how PowerPoint removes one slide and presents the next slide on the screen.

Using transitions can help you introduce each slide during an on-screen slide show, add interesting visual effects to your presentation, and signal to the audience that new information is appearing. When you use the AutoContent Wizard to create a presentation, PowerPoint may automatically add slide transitions to the presentation for you.

PowerPoint offers many slide transitions from which you can choose, including Blinds Vertical, in which the slides appear on the screen like vertical blinds on a window; Checkerboard Across, in which the slide appears in a checkerboard pattern; and Dissolve, in which the slide fades away on the screen. You can preview a slide transition to determine whether it is appropriate for your presentation.

You can set the speed of a slide transition to slow, medium, or fast. You can also add a transition to one slide or to your entire presentation. PowerPoint displays the transition when you rehearse or present your slide show.

ADD SLIDE TRANSITIONS

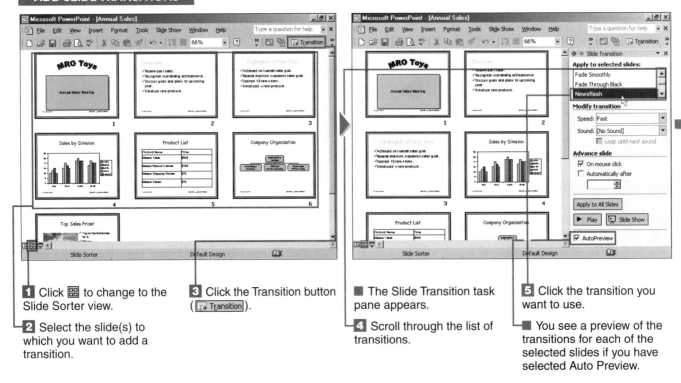

1 Click 🖿 to change to the Slide Sorter view.

2 Select the slide(s) to which you want to add a transition.

3 Click the Transition button (📭 Transition).

■ The Slide Transition task pane appears.

4 Scroll through the list of transitions.

5 Click the transition you want to use.

■ You see a preview of the transitions for each of the selected slides if you have selected Auto Preview.

How do I select when to advance to the next slide?

✔ The default advances to the next slide when you click the mouse. But you can display the next slide after a certain interval. Click Automatically after in the Advance slide area of the Slide Transition task pane (☐ changes to ☑). Then type the number of seconds or minutes to wait.

How do I remove a transition?

✔ Click the slide from which you want to remove a transition. Perform steps 3 through 5 below, except select No Transition in step 5.

How do I add a sound to a transition?

✔ In the Slide Transition task pane, click ⯆ next to the Sound box and then select the sound you want to use.

Can I have a transition sound continue playing?

✔ You can have a transition sound continue playing until PowerPoint displays a slide with a new sound. In the Slide Transition task pane, click the Loop until next sound option (☐ changes to ☑).

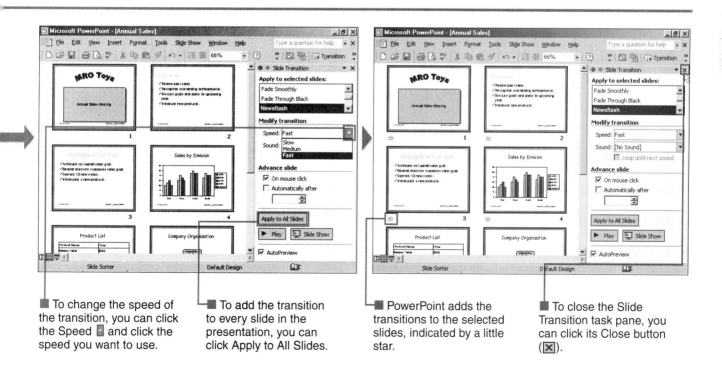

■ To change the speed of the transition, you can click the Speed ⯆ and click the speed you want to use.

■ To add the transition to every slide in the presentation, you can click Apply to All Slides.

■ PowerPoint adds the transitions to the selected slides, indicated by a little star.

■ To close the Slide Transition task pane, you can click its Close button (☒).

REHEARSE A SLIDE SHOW

You can rehearse your slide show and have PowerPoint record the amount of time you spend on each slide. Timing your slide show can help you decide if you need to add or remove information.

While you rehearse your slide show, PowerPoint displays the time you spend on the current slide and

the total time for the slide show. If you make a mistake while rehearsing and want to begin a slide again, you do not have to restart the entire rehearsal. You can restart the timer for the current slide as many times as necessary.

When you finish rehearsing your slide show, PowerPoint displays the total time for the slide show. You

can choose to record the time you spent on each slide.

If you record the timings for each slide, the timings appear below each slide in the Slide Sorter view. PowerPoint uses the timings to advance your slides automatically during a slide show.

REHEARSE A SLIDE SHOW

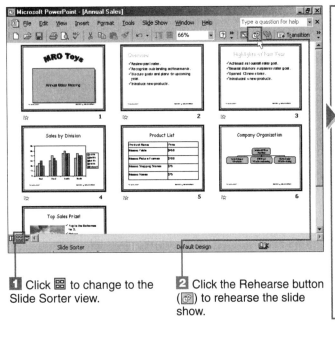

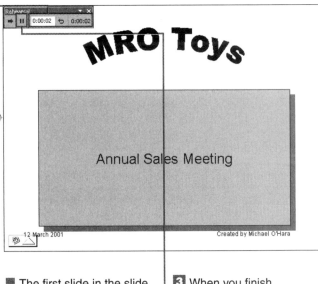

1 Click ▦ to change to the Slide Sorter view.

2 Click the Rehearse button (🖼) to rehearse the slide show.

■ The first slide in the slide show appears.

■ The Rehearsal dialog box displays the time spent on the current slide and the total time spent on the slide show.

3 When you finish rehearsing the current slide, click the mouse button to display the next slide.

■ If you make a mistake and want to reset the timer for the current slide, click the Pause button (❙❙).

Can I change the timing for a slide after rehearsing my slide show?

✔ If you do not like the timing you recorded for a slide, you can change the timing for the slide. Click the slide and then click 🔠. In the Automatically after area, drag the ⌖ over the current timing and type the new timing.

I do not want to use my timings to advance my slides automatically during a slide show. How can I advance my slides manually?

✔ From the Slide Show menu, click Set Up Show. In the Advance slides area, click the Manually option (○ changes to ◉) and then click OK.

Can I preview my presentation as a Web page?

✔ Yes. PowerPoint displays the presentation in frames in your browser window. The left pane contains a list of all the slides in the presentation. The right pane displays the current slide. The bottom pane contains any speaker notes. You can use the navigation bar at the bottom of the browser window to browse from slide to slide. To close the browser window, click its ☒.

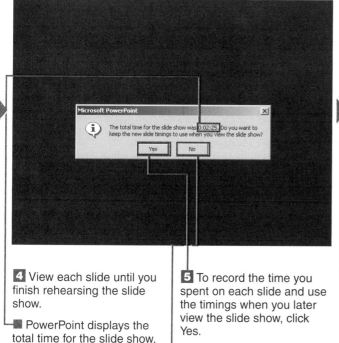

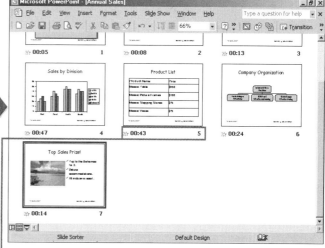

4 View each slide until you finish rehearsing the slide show.

■ PowerPoint displays the total time for the slide show.

5 To record the time you spent on each slide and use the timings when you later view the slide show, click Yes.

■ You can click No if you do not want to update times.

■ The time you spent on each slide appears below the slides.

SET UP A SLIDE SHOW

You can specify how you want to present a slide show on a computer.

You can deliver a slide show in one of three ways. A slide show can be presented by a speaker, browsed by an individual, or set up to run at a kiosk. Kiosks are often found at shopping malls and trade shows.

You can have your slide show run continuously until you press Esc.

This is useful if your slide show runs at a kiosk. If your presentation contains voice narration or animation, you can choose not to include these effects in your slide show.

You can set up your slide show to display all the slides in your presentation or only a specific range of slides.

During a slide show, the slides can be advanced manually or automatically. If you choose to advance slides manually, you must perform an action, such as clicking the mouse, to move to the next slide. If you choose to advance slides automatically, you must set timings for your slides. To set timings for your slides, See the section "Rehearse a Slide Show."

SET UP A SLIDE SHOW

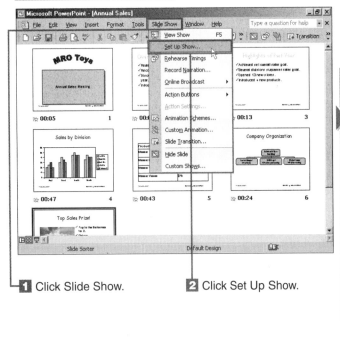

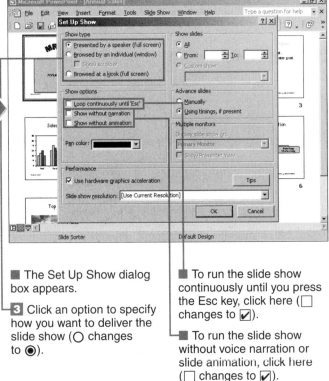

1 Click Slide Show.

2 Click Set Up Show.

■ The Set Up Show dialog box appears.

3 Click an option to specify how you want to deliver the slide show (○ changes to ⦿).

■ To run the slide show continuously until you press the Esc key, click here (☐ changes to ☑).

■ To run the slide show without voice narration or slide animation, click here (☐ changes to ☑).

Can I add tools to help an individual viewing the slide show?

✔ Yes. If you select the Browsed by an individual option, you can display a scroll bar during the slide show that lets an individual easily move through the slide show.

Can I use multiple monitors to present my slide show?

✔ Yes. If you use Windows 98 or Windows ME with multiple monitors, the audience can view the slide show on one monitor while you view the outline, speaker notes, and slides on another. In the Set Up Show dialog box, click ▣ in Display slide show box, and then click monitor.

What does the Pen color option do?

✔ To select the color of pen used to draw on the slides, display this drop-down list and select the color you want to use. See the section "Preview a Slide Show" for more information about drawing on slides.

What are the performance options?

✔ You can use available hardware graphics acceleration by clicking this option (☐ changes to ☑). You can also select a resolution for the slide show by displaying the Slide show resolution drop-down list and selecting a resolution.

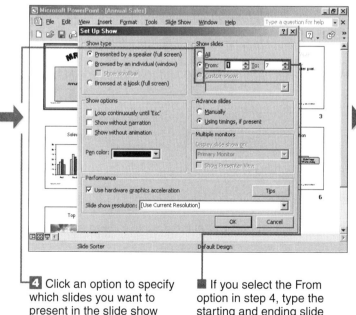

4 Click an option to specify which slides you want to present in the slide show (○ changes to ◉).

■ If you select the From option in step 4, type the starting and ending slide numbers.

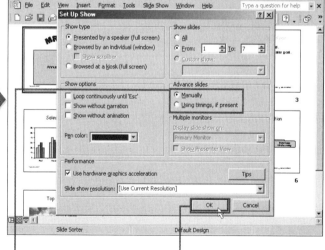

5 Click an option to specify whether you want to advance the slides manually or automatically using timings you have set (○ changes to ◉).

6 Click OK.

■ The slide show is set up with these selections.

PREVIEW A SLIDE SHOW

You can view a slide show of your presentation on a computer screen. A slide show displays one slide at a time using the entire screen.

If you create your presentation for on-screen viewing, a slide show allows you to preview how your slides look and rehearse the pace of your presentation.

Any objects or enhancements you added to your slides, including clip art, animations, or transitions, appear during the slide show.

You can display the next slide or return to the previous slide while viewing a slide show. You can also end the slide show at any time.

PowerPoint allows you to draw on the slides during a slide show. This

is useful if you want to add a check mark beside an important point or circle a key word on a slide. If a slide becomes cluttered with drawings, you can erase all the drawings. The drawings you add during a slide show are temporary and do not appear on the slides when the slide show is over.

PREVIEW A SLIDE SHOW

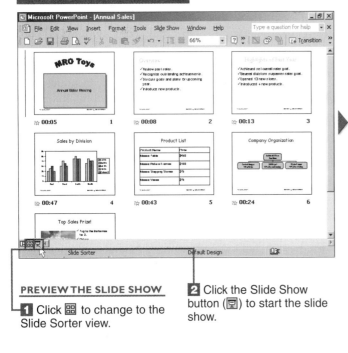

PREVIEW THE SLIDE SHOW

1 Click ⊞ to change to the Slide Sorter view.

2 Click the Slide Show button (🖵) to start the slide show.

■ The first slide fills the screen.

3 Click the current slide or press the Spacebar to view the next slide.

■ To return to the previous slide, press Backspace.

■ Clicking either of these buttons displays a menu with commands for ending the show, adding notes, and so on.

Can I take meeting minutes during a slide show?

✔ Yes. Right-click a slide and then select Meeting Minder. Type the meeting minutes and then click OK. To view the meeting minutes after the slide show, click Tools and then Meeting Minder. You can remind yourself of follow-up topics by noting them on the Action Items tab of the Meeting Minder.

Can I create speaker notes during a slide show?

✔ Yes. Right-click the slide for which you want notes and then select Speaker Notes. Type the notes for the slide and click Close. For more information on speaker notes, see the section "Create Speaker Notes."

How can I pause or end a slide show?

✔ Press the B key to pause the slide show. Press the B key again to resume the slide show. To end a slide show, either press Esc or right-click any slide and click End Show.

What other methods do I have for presenting a slide show?

✔ If you have a microphone and camera, you can record a presentation for broadcasting later. To set up a presentation broadcast, click Slide Show and then click Online Broadcast.

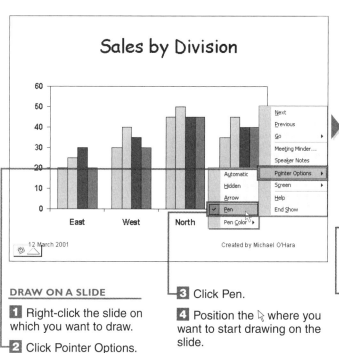

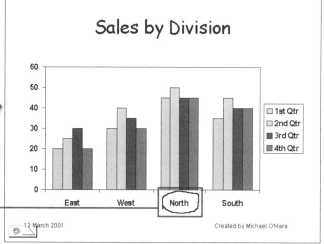

DRAW ON A SLIDE

1 Right-click the slide on which you want to draw.

2 Click Pointer Options.

3 Click Pen.

4 Position the ⬚ where you want to start drawing on the slide.

5 Drag the ⬚ to draw on the slide.

■ To erase all the drawings on the slide, press the E key.

Note: When drawing on a slide, you cannot use the ⬚ to display the next slide. To once again use the ⬚ to move through slides, repeat steps 1 through 3, except click Automatic in step 3.

CHAPTER 22

CREATE SPEAKER NOTES

Y ou can create speaker notes that contain copies of your slides with all the ideas you want to discuss. You can use these notes as a guide when delivering your presentation.

Although you can create speaker notes in all four views, Normal and Notes Page view provide the easiest environment for you to do so. The Normal view provides a notes pane

where you can type speaker notes while creating your slides. This lets you record your ideas while working on your presentation.

The Notes Page view is useful for editing and formatting your speaker notes. Each notes page includes a small version of a slide and a text area. You can magnify the text area to make it easier to see the text. You can edit and

format text in the text area as you would any text in the presentation.

When you finish creating your speaker notes, you can print the notes pages so you have a paper copy of your notes to refer to while delivering your presentation. For information on printing a presentation, See the section "Print a Presentation."

CREATE SPEAKER NOTES

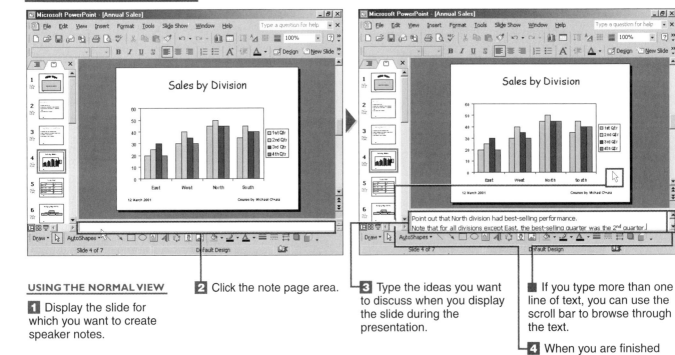

USING THE NORMAL VIEW

1 Display the slide for which you want to create speaker notes.

2 Click the note page area.

3 Type the ideas you want to discuss when you display the slide during the presentation.

■ If you type more than one line of text, you can use the scroll bar to browse through the text.

4 When you are finished adding notes, click back in the slide to exit the note page area.

Can I increase the height of the notes pane in the Normal view?

✔ Yes. Position the ⟲ over the horizontal bar above the notes pane and then drag the bar to a new location.

Can I type speaker notes in other views?

✔ You can type speaker notes in the Outline and Slide Sorter views. Like the Normal view, the Outline view provides a pane where you can type speaker notes. To type speaker notes in the Slide Sorter view, click a slide and then click the Notes button. For more information on the views, see Chapter 19.

I am having trouble formatting my speaker notes in the Normal view. What is wrong?

✔ To view the formatting for speaker notes in the Normal view, click the Show Formatting button (⊞) on the Standard toolbar.

How can I display speaker notes on my screen during a slide show?

✔ Right-click the slide you want to display speaker notes for and then select Speaker Notes.

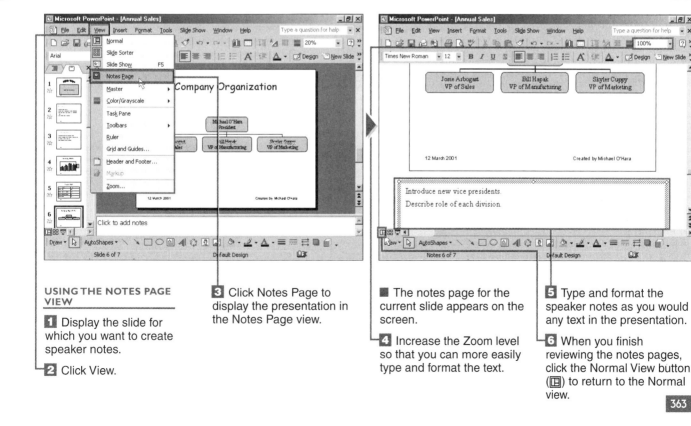

USING THE NOTES PAGE VIEW

■1 Display the slide for which you want to create speaker notes.

■2 Click View.

■3 Click Notes Page to display the presentation in the Notes Page view.

■ The notes page for the current slide appears on the screen.

■4 Increase the Zoom level so that you can more easily type and format the text.

■5 Type and format the speaker notes as you would any text in the presentation.

■6 When you finish reviewing the notes pages, click the Normal View button (⊞) to return to the Normal view.

CHECK SPELLING

Before printing or presenting your presentation, you should verify that it does not contain spelling errors. A misspelled word can mar an otherwise perfect presentation, creating an impression of carelessness. PowerPoint's spell check feature can help you check for spelling errors.

The spell check feature compares every word in your presentation to

words in its dictionary. If PowerPoint does not find the word in the dictionary, it flags the word. A flagged word, however, does not always indicate a misspelled word; the word is just not in Office's dictionary. For each flagged word, PowerPoint usually offers suggestions for correcting the errors in your document. You can accept one of these suggestions, edit the word, ignore the misspelling, or add the word to the dictionary.

Even after using the spell check feature, you should still proofread your presentation. PowerPoint only recognizes spelling errors, not whether you use the word correctly. For example, to, two, and too all have different meanings and uses. If they are spelled correctly, PowerPoint does not flag them, even if you use them incorrectly as in, "I went too the grocery store."

CHECK SPELLING

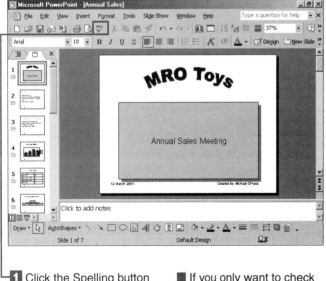

■1 Click the Spelling button (🔤) to start the spell check.

■ If you only want to check a word or a sentence, select the word or sentence first.

■ The Spelling dialog box appears and the spell check commences.

■ This area displays the first misspelled word.

■ This area displays suggestions for correcting the text.

■2 Click to select one of the suggestions or type your own replacement word in the Change to box.

■ To add the flagged word to the PowerPoint dictionary, you can click Add.

What are AutoCorrect options?

✔ AutoCorrect options are changes that PowerPoint makes automatically. For example, if you type two initial capitals, PowerPoint fixes this error. You can review the changes that PowerPoint makes by clicking Tools and then clicking AutoCorrect.

You can turn off any option by unchecking its check box(☑ changes to ☐). Also note that Word automatically replaces some misspelled words with the correct spelling and some characters such as (c) with a symbol ©. You can scroll through the list of AutoCorrect entries to see which changes PowerPoint makes.

How can I stop PowerPoint from flagging words, such as my company name, that are spelled correctly?

✔ PowerPoint considers any words that do not exist in its dictionary to be misspelled. You can add a word to the dictionary so that PowerPoint recognizes the word during future spell checks. When PowerPoint flags the word, click the Add button.

If you want to have Word automatically correct the word, click AutoCorrect in the Spelling dialog box to create an AutoCorrect entry.

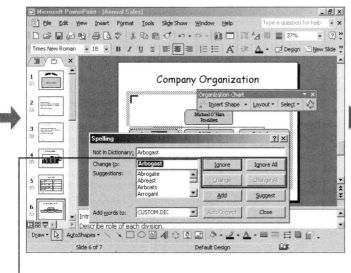

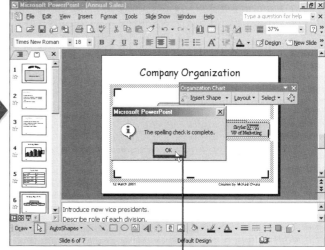

3 Click the appropriate correction button.

■ You can click Change to correct just this error or Change All to correct this flagged word throughout the document.

■ If the word is spelled correctly, you can click Ignore to skip this occurrence or Ignore All to ignore all occurrences.

4 Continue making changes until the spell check is complete.

5 Click OK.

■ The presentation's spelling has been checked.

SET UP A PRESENTATION FOR PRINTING

Before printing your presentation, you can change the setup of the presentation.

PowerPoint allows you to specify how you want to output your presentation, such as on paper, 35mm slides, or overheads.

You can choose the orientation you want to use when printing your presentation. *Orientation* refers to

the way PowerPoint prints information on a page. The orientation you select for the slides affects every slide in your presentation. Portrait orientation prints information across the short side of a page. Landscape orientation prints information across the long side of a page and is the standard orientation for slides.

You can also choose the orientation you want to use for speaker notes, handouts, and the outline of your presentation. Portrait is the standard orientation for speaker notes, handouts, and the outline.

After you set up your presentation for printing, PowerPoint adjusts the presentation to reflect the new settings.

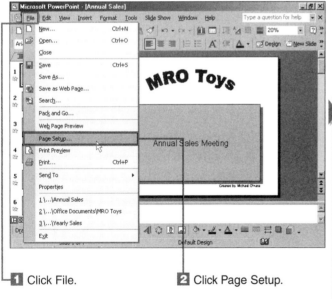

1 Click File.

2 Click Page Setup.

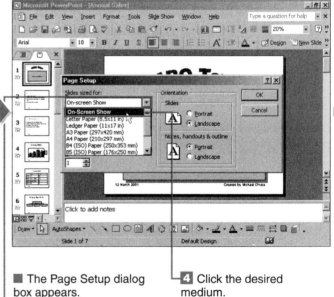

■ The Page Setup dialog box appears.

3 Click here to display the available output media for the slide.

4 Click the desired medium.

Should I review my presentation after setting it up for printing?

✔ You should review your presentation after changing the output or orientation of slides to ensure that the information on your slides still appears the way you want.

The layout of information on my slides does not suit the new orientation. What can I do?

✔ You can move and resize text placeholders and objects on the Slide Master to better suit the new orientation of the slides. Click View, click Master, and then click Slide Master. For information on using the Slide Master, see Chapter 21.

Can I start numbering the slides in my presentation at a number other than 1?

✔ Yes. Changing the numbering of slides is useful if your presentation is part of a larger presentation. In the Page Setup dialog box, double-click the Number slides from area and then type the number you want to use for the first slide of the presentation.

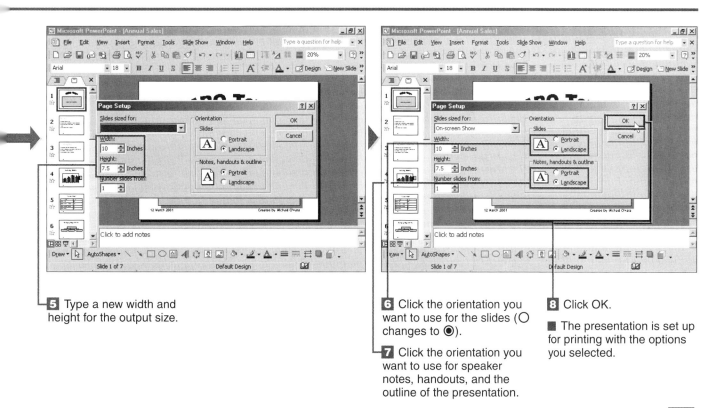

5 Type a new width and height for the output size.

6 Click the orientation you want to use for the slides (○ changes to ●).

7 Click the orientation you want to use for speaker notes, handouts, and the outline of the presentation.

8 Click OK.

■ The presentation is set up for printing with the options you selected.

PRINT A PRESENTATION

You can produce a paper copy of your presentation. PowerPoint lets you specify the part of the presentation you want to print, such as slides or handouts. When printing handouts, you can choose the number of slides you want to appear on each printed page.

You can print every slide in your presentation, the current slide, or a series of slides.

PowerPoint offers several options for changing the appearance of your printed presentation. The Grayscale option improves the appearance of color slides printed on a black-and-white printer. The Pure black and white option eliminates shades of gray and prints in black and white.

The Include animations option prints slides as they appear when animated. For information on animating slides, see Chapter 21.

The Scale to fit paper option adjusts the size of slides to fill a printed page. The Frame slides option adds a border around your slides, handouts, and notes pages. The Print hidden slides option prints slides you have hidden. For information on hiding slides, See the section "Hide a Slide." Note that this option is available only if your presentation includes hidden slides.

PRINT A PRESENTATION

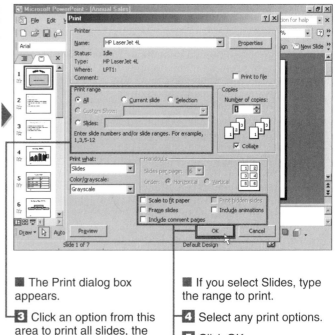

PRINT SLIDES

1 Click File.

2 Click Print.

■ The Print dialog box appears.

3 Click an option from this area to print all slides, the current slide, the selected slides, or a range of slides.

■ If you select Slides, type the range to print.

4 Select any print options.

5 Click OK.

■ PowerPoint prints the presentation.

How do I print notes or an outline?

✔ Click the Print what 🔽 and select Notes Pages to print notes. Select Outline View to print an outline.

Why did only part of my outline print?

✔ Your outline prints as it appears in the Outline pane. If you have hidden text, click the Expand All button (🔳) on the Standard toolbar to display all the text. For information on hiding slide text, see the section "Hide a Slide."

How do I produce 35mm slides?

✔ You can send your presentation to a service bureau to create 35mm slides.

Can I preview how my slides will look when printed on a black-and-white printer?

✔ Yes. Click the Color/Grayscale button (🔳) on the Standard toolbar. Then select Grayscale or Pure Black and White. To return to color, click the button again and select Color.

Can I print more than one copy?

✔ Yes. In the Print dialog box, double-click the Number of copies text box and type the number of copies to print.

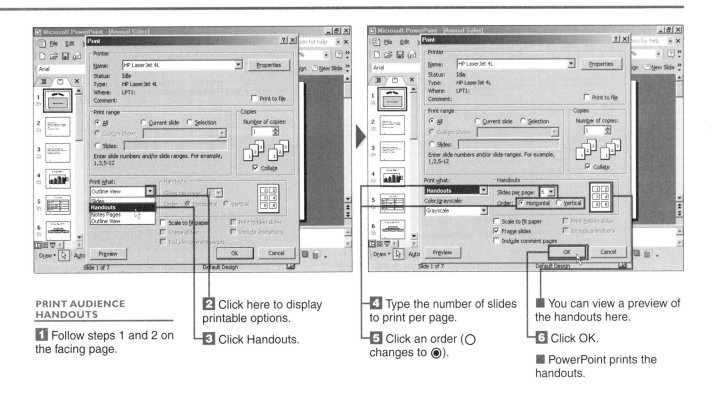

PRINT AUDIENCE HANDOUTS

1 Follow steps 1 and 2 on the facing page.

2 Click here to display printable options.

3 Click Handouts.

4 Type the number of slides to print per page.

5 Click an order (○ changes to ◉).

■ You can view a preview of the handouts here.

6 Click OK.

■ PowerPoint prints the handouts.

SECTION V

23) GETTING STARTED

An Introduction to Access 372

Parts of a Database 373

Plan a Database 374

Start Access 375

Create a Blank Database 376

Create a Database Using a Wizard 378

Parts of the Database Window 384

Rename or Delete an Object 385

Open and Save a Database 386

24) CREATE TABLES

Create a Table in Datasheet View 388

Enter Data in Datasheet View 390

Create a Table Using the Wizard 392

Open a Table 396

Understanding Data Types 397

Add or Delete Records 398

Move through Records 400

Select Data 402

Edit Data 404

Zoom into a Cell 406

Change Column Width 407

Hide a Field 408

Freeze a Field 409

25) CHANGE TABLE DESIGN

Change the Table View 410

Rearrange Fields 411

Display Field Properties 412

Add a Field Description 413

USING ACCESS

Change the Data Type 414
Rename a Field 415
Change the Field Size 416
Select a Data Format 418
Change the Number of Decimal Places 419
Add or Delete a Field 420
Add a Caption 422
Add a Default Value 423
Require an Entry 424
Add a Validation Rule 426
Create a Yes/No Field 428
Create a Lookup Column 430
Use a Lookup Column to Enter Data 432
Create an Index 433
Set the Primary Key 434
Display a Subdatasheet 435
Define Relationships between Tables 436

26) CREATE FORMS

Create a Form Using a Wizard 440
Open a Form 444
Move through Records with a Form 446
Edit Data Using a Form 447
Add or Delete a Record 448
Add a Field to a Form 450
AutoFormat a Form 451
Change a Form Control 452
Change the Appearance of Form Controls 454
Change Form Control Colors and Borders 456

27) FIND AND QUERY DATA

Find Data 458
Sort Records 460
Filter Data 462
Filter Data by Form 464

Create a Query Using the Simple Query
   Wizard 466
Create a Query in Design View 470
Open a Query 474
Change the Query View 475
Set Criteria 476
Examples of Criteria 478
Sort Query Results 479
Perform Calculations 480
Summarize Data 482

28) CREATE REPORTS

Create a Report Using the Report Wizard 484
Open a Report 490
Change the Report View 491
Preview a Report 492
Print Data from a Database 494
Create Mailing Labels 496

AN INTRODUCTION TO ACCESS

Microsoft Access is a database program that enables you to store and manage large collections of information. Access provides you with all the tools you need to create an efficient and effective database. Databases are useful for finding specific data in a large collection of information, and you can perform calculations on the information contained in a database.

For more information on Access, you can visit the following Microsoft Web site at www.microsoft.com/access.

Database Uses

Many people use *databases* to store and organize personal information, such as addresses, music and video collections, recipes, or a wine list — which is much more efficient than using sheets of paper or index cards.

Companies use databases to store information such as mailing lists, billing information, client orders, expenses, inventory, and payroll. A database can help a company effectively manage information that it must constantly review, update, and analyze.

Types of Databases

Flat file databases store information in one large table, and often contain duplicate information. Although easy to set up, a flat file database is not flexible or efficient for storing large amounts of information.

Relational databases store information in separate tables, and enable you to use relationships to bring together information from different tables. This type of database is powerful and flexible, and it effectively stores large amounts of information. A relational database is faster and easier to maintain than a flat file database. Access uses the relationship model for its databases. Therefore, you can link a customer database to an order database, and link the order database to a product database. Each database is separate, but by linking information, you can keep track of orders, inventory, and client billing.

Database Benefits

Databases store and manage collections of information related to a particular subject or purpose. You can efficiently add, update, view, and organize the information stored in a database.

As another benefit, you can instantly locate information of interest in a database. For example, you can find all clients with the last name Smith. You can also perform more advanced searches, such as finding all clients who live in California and who purchased more than $100 worth of supplies last year.

Additional benefits include performing calculations on the information in a database to help you make quick, accurate, and informed decisions. You can also present the information in neat, professionally designed reports.

PARTS OF A DATABASE

ccess databases consist of objects such as tables, forms, queries, reports, pages, macros, and modules.

Tables

A *table* is a collection of related information about a specific topic. You can have one or more tables in a database. A table consists of fields and records. A *field* is a specific category of information in a table, such as the first names of all your clients. A *record* is a collection of information about one person, place, or thing, such as the name and address of one client.

Forms

Forms provide a quick way to view, enter, and modify information in a database by presenting information in an easy-to-use format. A form displays boxes that clearly show you where to enter or modify information. Forms usually display one record at a time so that you can concentrate on that particular record rather than the entire set of records.

Queries

Queries enable you to find information of interest in a database. When you create a query, you ask Access to find information that meets the criteria, or conditions, that you specify. For example, you can create a query to find all items that cost less than $100.

Reports

Reports are professional-looking documents that summarize data from your database. You can perform calculations, such as averages or totals, in a report to summarize information. For example, you could create a report that displays the total sales for each product.

Pages

Pages enable you to access a database on the Internet or an intranet using a Web browser. When you add pages to a database, other users can view and enter information in the database even if they do not have Access installed on their computers.

Macros

A *macro* saves you time by combining a series of actions into a single action. Macros are ideal for tasks you perform frequently. You can, for example, create a macro that calculates and prints daily sales figures. Instead of having to perform each action individually, you can have a macro automatically perform all the actions for you.

Modules

Modules are programs created in a programming language called Visual Basic for Applications (VBA). Modules enable you to efficiently control a database. Access also includes Class modules that enable you to define custom methods and options, called properties, for forms and reports.

PLAN A DATABASE

Take time to properly design a database. Good database design ensures that you can perform tasks efficiently and accurately. As you add information and objects to a database, the database becomes larger and more complex. A properly designed database is easier to modify and work with as it grows. Good planning can also make it easier for other users to work with a database you create.

Determine the Purpose of the Database

Decide what you want the database to do and how you plan to use the information. Consider consulting others concerning their expectations, if you intend to use the database with a group of people. This can help you determine what information you need to include to make the database complete.

Determine the Tables You Need

Gather all the information you want to store in the database and then divide the information into separate tables. A table should contain related information about one subject only. The same information should not appear in more than one table in a database. You can work more efficiently and reduce errors if you need to update information in only one location. And you can link tables together to combine information or show relationships among data in different tables.

Determine the Fields You Need

In each table, you should consider which fields you plan to include. Each field should relate directly to the subject of the table.

When adding fields, make sure to break down information into its smallest parts. For example, break down names into two fields called First Name and Last Name. Doing so provides more flexibility in sorting and using the information. Do not include fields that you can get from other tables or calculations. If you have a total field and a sales tax percentage field, for instance, you can calculate the sales tax by multiplying the total by the sales tax percentage. Tables with many fields increase the time the database takes to process information.

Determine the Relationships Between Tables

A relationship tells Access how to bring together related information stored in separate tables. You can use the primary key to form a relationship between tables. Access defines a *primary key* as one or more fields that uniquely identifies each record in a table. For example, the primary key for a table of employees could be the Social Security number for each employee. You learn more about primary keys in Chapters 24 and 25.

START ACCESS

You can start Access to create a new database or work with an existing database.

Each time you start Access, the New File task pane appears. This task pane enables you to create a blank database or use a template or Database Wizard to create a database. A Database Wizard guides you step-by-step through creating a new database.

You can also use the New File task pane to open an existing database. The dialog box displays a list of the most recently used databases, thus enabling you to quickly open a database that you use often.

For more information on working with task panes, see Chapter 2.

What other ways can I start Access?

✔ You can also start Access from a shortcut icon placed on the desktop. To create this icon, open the program folder that contains Access and then with the *right* mouse button, drag the program icon to the desktop. From the shortcut menu that appears, click Create Shortcut(s) Here.

START ACCESS

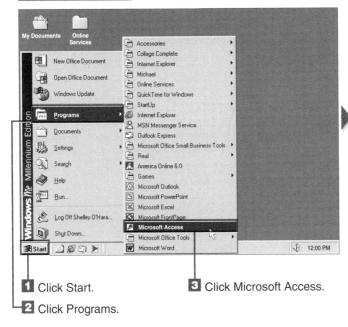

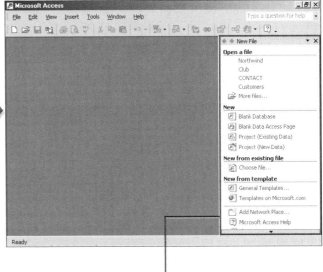

1 Click Start.

2 Click Programs.

3 Click Microsoft Access.

■ The Microsoft Access window appears.

■ The New File task pane appears each time you start Access, enabling you to create a new database or open an existing database.

CREATE A BLANK DATABASE

I f you want to design your own database, you can create a blank database.

Each time you start Access, a New File task pane appears, enabling you to create a blank database or use a template to create a simple database. You can use a blank database when you have experience using Access and know exactly which fields you want to include,

or when you want to create a complex database.

To store the database as a file on your computer, you must give the database a name. Access assigns a default name, such as db1, to each database you create. You should give the database a more descriptive name to help you recognize it later.

Access automatically stores the database in the My Documents folder, but you can specify another location.

Access displays the blank database on your screen. The database does not yet contain any objects, such as forms, reports, or tables.

CREATE A BLANK DATABASE

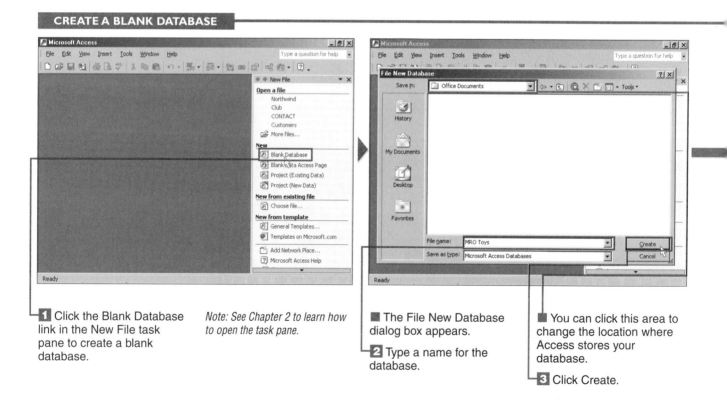

–1 Click the Blank Database link in the New File task pane to create a blank database.

Note: See Chapter 2 to learn how to open the task pane.

■ The File New Database dialog box appears.

–2 Type a name for the database.

■ You can click this area to change the location where Access stores your database.

–3 Click Create.

What folders can I access using the Places Bar?

✔ The History folder lets you access recently used folders. The My Documents folder provides a convenient place to store your database. The Desktop folder lets you store your database on the Windows desktop. The Favorites folder provides a place to store a database you frequently access. You can click any of these folders to change to that folder. For more information on saving documents, see Chapter 2.

Can I create a blank database while working in Access?

✔ Yes. Click the New button (🗋) to display the New File task pane. Then follow the steps in this task.

How do I create a new folder to store my database?

✔ In the File New Database dialog box, click the Create New Folder button (🗀). Type a name for the folder and then press Enter.

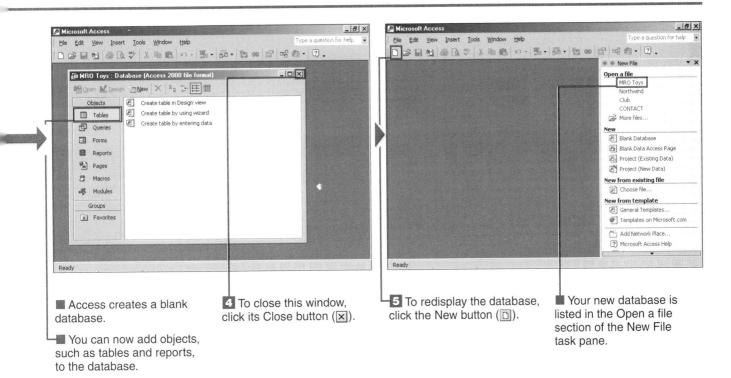

■ Access creates a blank database.

■ You can now add objects, such as tables and reports, to the database.

4 To close this window, click its Close button (✕).

5 To redisplay the database, click the New button (🗋).

■ Your new database is listed in the Open a file section of the New File task pane.

CREATE A DATABASE USING A WIZARD

A Database Wizard lets you create a database quickly and efficiently. The wizard saves you time by providing ready-to-use database templates. To display available template wizards, you can use the General Templates link in the New File task pane to view the database wizard choices in the Databases tab of the Templates dialog box. From this dialog box,

you can then select the type of database you want to create.

Access offers ten database templates, such as the Contact Management, Expenses, Inventory Control and Order Entry databases. You can choose the database that best suits the type of information you want to store. For additional templates, you can visit

http://officeupdate.microsoft.com/downloadCatalog/dldAccess.htm.

The Database Wizard asks you a series of questions to determine how to set up the database to suit your needs. When you start the wizard, the wizard describes the type of information the database stores.

CREATE A DATABASE USING A WIZARD

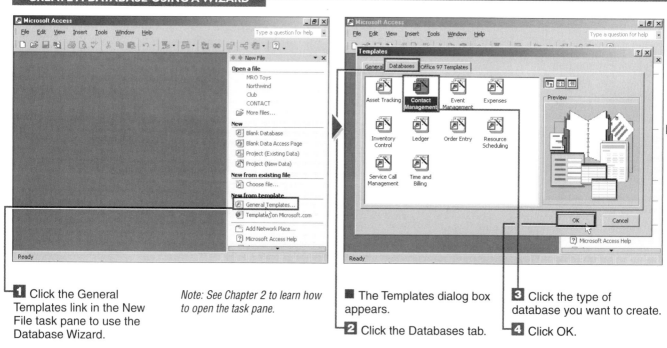

1 Click the General Templates link in the New File task pane to use the Database Wizard.

Note: See Chapter 2 to learn how to open the task pane.

■ The Templates dialog box appears.

2 Click the Databases tab.

3 Click the type of database you want to create.

4 Click OK.

How can I start the Database Wizard while working in Access?

✔ Click the New button (🗋) to display the New File task pane. Then, follow the steps in this task. Access closes the database displayed on your screen when you create a new database.

Can I change the way databases appear in the Template dialog box?

✔ Yes. Click any of the View buttons (🔳, 🔳, or 🔳) to display the databases in Large Icons view, List view, or Details view, respectively. To preview a particular template, click the icon for the template.

What are the options on the General tab of the Templates dialog box?

✔ You can create a blank database, pages, or projects from the General tab. Pages are Web pages you can create to access a database on an intranet or the Internet using a Web browser. Projects enable you to create an Access database for use with more sophisticated programs, such as network database programs.

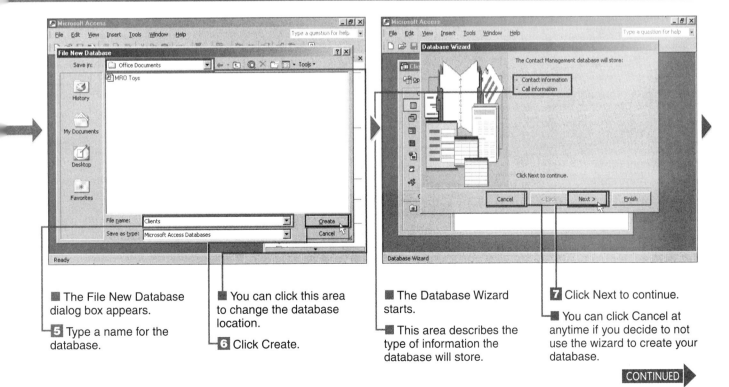

■ The File New Database dialog box appears.

5 Type a name for the database.

■ You can click this area to change the database location.

6 Click Create.

■ The Database Wizard starts.

■ This area describes the type of information the database will store.

7 Click Next to continue.

■ You can click Cancel at anytime if you decide to not use the wizard to create your database.

CONTINUED ▶

CREATE A DATABASE USING A WIZARD
(CONTINUED)

When using a Database Wizard to create a database, the wizard displays all the tables that Access can create. The wizard also displays the fields that will be included in each table.

The wizard automatically includes required fields in each table. You can choose to include optional fields. For example, in the Order

Entry database, the Customer information table includes required fields, such as Company Name, Billing Address, and Phone Number. You can include optional fields in the table, such as E-mail Address and Notes.

The Database Wizard asks you to select the style you want to use for screen displays. A screen display style gives the database a

consistent look. You can choose from several screen display styles, including Blends, International, and Stone.

The wizard also asks you to select a style for printed reports. Using a report style helps you create professional-looking reports. The wizard offers several report styles for you to choose from, including Bold, Corporate, and Formal.

CREATE A DATABASE USING A WIZARD (CONTINUED)

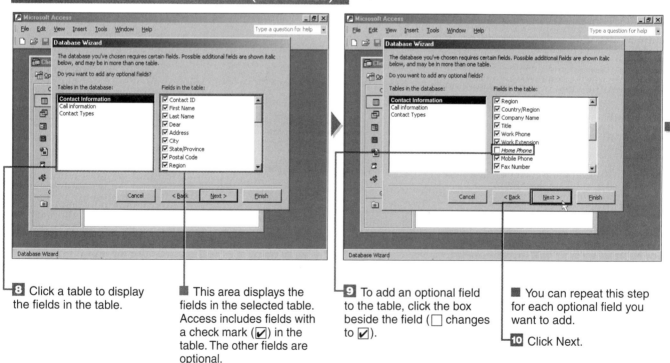

■8 Click a table to display the fields in the table.

■ This area displays the fields in the selected table. Access includes fields with a check mark (☑) in the table. The other fields are optional.

■9 To add an optional field to the table, click the box beside the field (☐ changes to ☑).

■ You can repeat this step for each optional field you want to add.

■10 Click Next.

Can I remove a required field from the Database Wizard?

✔ You can only remove a required field after you finish creating the database. When you try to remove a required field from the Database Wizard, a dialog box appears, stating that the field is required and must be selected. To remove a field from an existing database, see Chapter 25.

Can I change the style of my screen displays later on?

✔ You can easily change the style of your screen displays after you create a database. For more information, see Chapter 26.

Do I have to answer all the questions in the Database Wizard?

✔ No. You can click the Finish button at any time to create a database based on your completed answers so far. If you are using the Database Wizard for the first time, the wizard applies default settings for the questions you do not answer. If you have used the Database Wizard before, the wizard applies the last answers you provided.

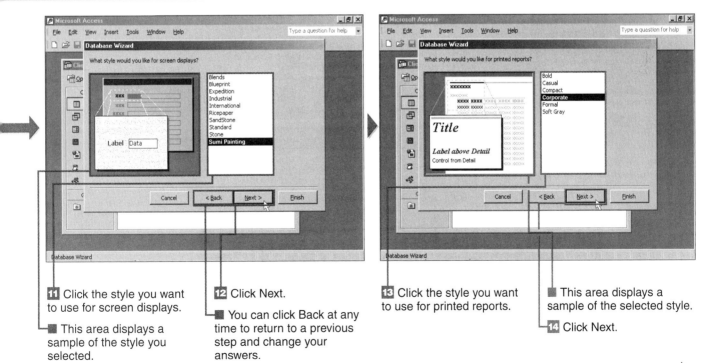

11 Click the style you want to use for screen displays.

■ This area displays a sample of the style you selected.

12 Click Next.

■ You can click Back at any time to return to a previous step and change your answers.

13 Click the style you want to use for printed reports.

■ This area displays a sample of the selected style.

14 Click Next.

CONTINUED ▶

CREATE A DATABASE USING A WIZARD
(CONTINUED)

The Database Wizard asks you to specify a title for the database. Do not confuse the title of the database with the *name* of the database. The title of the database appears on the *switchboard,* which is similar to a main menu for the database. The name of the database is the filename under which you store the database on your computer.

After the wizard finishes creating the database, it opens the database. You can specify whether you want to start using the database immediately after you create it.

The Database Wizard automatically creates objects, such as tables, forms, queries, and reports, for the database.

When the wizard is complete, the switchboard appears on your screen. You can utilize the switchboard to perform common tasks, such as adding records to the database table and exiting the database.

CREATE A DATABASE USING A WIZARD (CONTINUED)

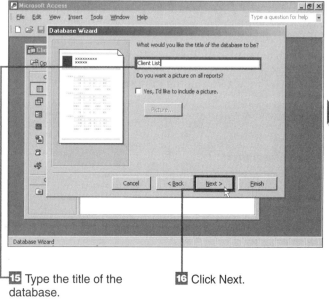

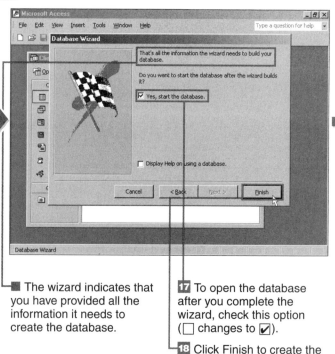

15 Type the title of the database.

16 Click Next.

■ The wizard indicates that you have provided all the information it needs to create the database.

17 To open the database after you complete the wizard, check this option (☐ changes to ☑).

18 Click Finish to create the database.

Can I get help with my new database?

✔ Access can display help information when it starts your newly created database. In the last dialog box of the Database Wizard, click the Display help on using a database option (☐ changes to ✔).

Why does Access ask for information when the database starts?

✔ Access may ask you to type information, such as your company name and address, to finish setting up the database. It uses this information in reports, forms, and other objects to identify your company.

Can I include a picture on all my reports?

✔ You can include a picture, such as a company logo, next to the title on your reports. After you specify a title for the database in the Database Wizard, select the Yes, I'd like to include a picture option (☐ changes to ✔). Then, click Picture and locate the picture you want to use. The picture you select appears in the Database window.

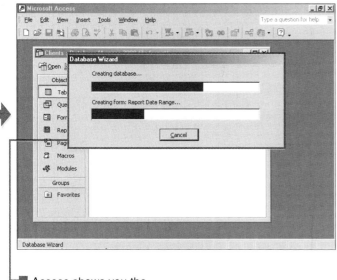

■ Access shows you the progress of creating the objects for the database.

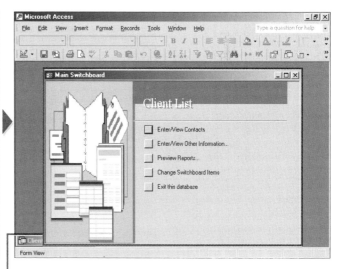

■ When Access finishes creating all the database objects, the Main Switchboard window appears to help you perform common tasks.

PARTS OF THE DATABASE WINDOW

You can use the Database window to view and work with all the objects in a database. Each type of object in the Database window displays a different icon. When the Database window is hidden, you can press the F11 key to bring the Database window in front of all other open windows in Access.

The Database window enables you to quickly open an object in the database to perform a task, such as adding a record to a table or changing a form.

How do I access the Database window when I have other windows open in Access.

✔ When you have the Database window hidden, you can press the F11 key to bring the Database window in front of all other open windows in Access.

Large Icons

Clicking this button displays the objects as large icons.

Small Icons

Clicking this button displays the objects as small icons, enabling you to view more objects at once.

Objects Bar

This area displays the types of objects in the database, including tables (▦), queries (▣), forms (▣), reports (▣), pages (▣), macros (▣), and modules (▣). If you click an object that does not contain any items yet, you do not see any listed. Instead, you see the options available for creating these items. See Chapters 26 and 28 for information on creating these types of objects.

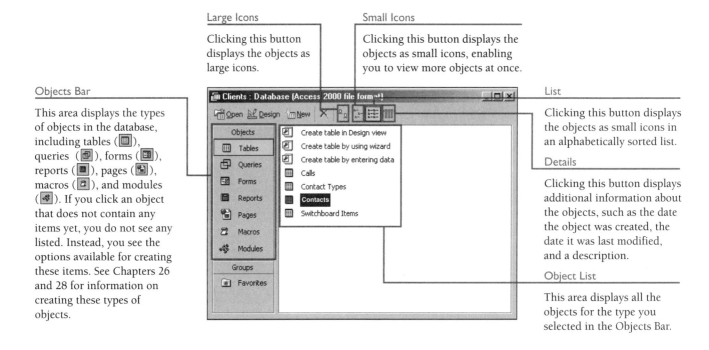

List

Clicking this button displays the objects as small icons in an alphabetically sorted list.

Details

Clicking this button displays additional information about the objects, such as the date the object was created, the date it was last modified, and a description.

Object List

This area displays all the objects for the type you selected in the Objects Bar.

RENAME OR DELETE AN OBJECT

To meet the needs of your constantly changing database, you can change the names of the objects in your database to better identify them. Likewise you can delete objects that you no longer need. Before you can delete a table with a relationship to another table, you must first delete the relationship. You see an error message in this case. For more information on relationships, see Chapter 25.

Can I organize the objects in the Database window?

✔ Yes. You can create groups to keep related objects in one place. To create a group, click the Groups bar in the Database window. Right-click the area below the Groups bar and then select New Group. Type a name for the group and then click OK. To add an object to the group, drag the object from the right pane of the Database window to the name of the group below the Groups bar. To display the objects in a group, click the group.

RENAME OR DELETE AN OBJECT

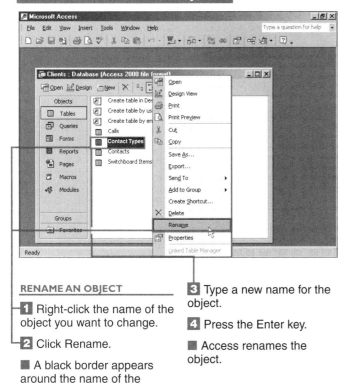

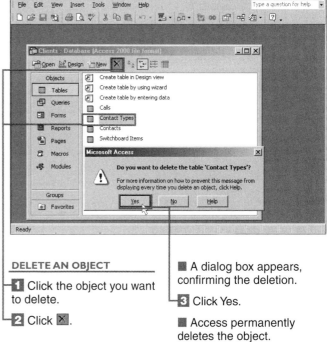

RENAME AN OBJECT

■1 Right-click the name of the object you want to change.

■2 Click Rename.

■ A black border appears around the name of the object.

■3 Type a new name for the object.

■4 Press the Enter key.

■ Access renames the object.

DELETE AN OBJECT

■1 Click the object you want to delete.

■2 Click ☒.

■ A dialog box appears, confirming the deletion.

■3 Click Yes.

■ Access permanently deletes the object.

OPEN AND SAVE A DATABASE

Y ou can open an existing database and display it on your screen. Once you open a database, you can review and make changes to it.

Each time you start Access, the New File task pane appears, displaying a list of recently opened databases. The names of sample databases, such as Contacts Sample

Database, may also appear in the list. You can quickly open one of these databases. If the database you want to open is not in the list, you can use the Open dialog box to open the database.

You can have only one database open at a time. Access closes a database displayed on your screen when you open another database.

When you create a database, you assign it a name and then save it. After that, you do not need to resave the database. Access saves data in tables each time you add a record. You do need to save other objects, such as forms, reports, and queries. Saving these objects is covered in the chapters on each object.

OPEN AND SAVE A DATABASE

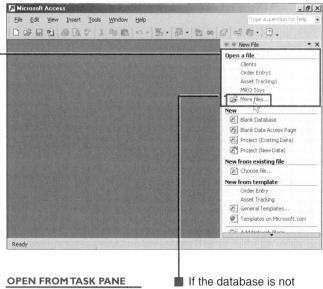

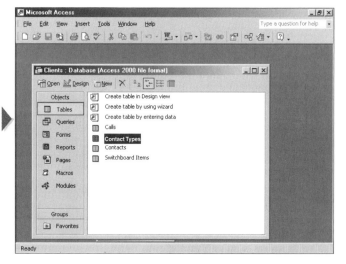

OPEN FROM TASK PANE

1 If the database is listed under "Open a file" in the task pane, click its name.

■ If the database is not listed, you can click the "More files" link.

Note: See Chapter 2 to learn how to open the task pane.

■ Access opens the database.

■ If you used a wizard to create the database, you see the Main Switchboard. You can click any of the options to complete that action.

■ If you used another method to create the database, you see the Database window.

Can I prevent other people on a network from opening a database?

✔ Yes. If you save the database on a network, other people can open it even while you are using it. To prevent others from opening the database while you are working on it, click Open. Then in the Open dialog box, click ⊡ beside the Open button and then click Open Exclusive. Now you have exclusive rights of the file. No one else can open or modify it.

Why do some sample databases require that I insert the Office CD before the database will load?

✔ You may not have installed the database along with Access. You can tell that this is the case if you attempt to open one of the sample databases and a message box appears, prompting you to install the database. Click Yes to install the sample database. A dialog box appears, asking you to insert the Office CD-ROM. Insert the CD-ROM and click OK.

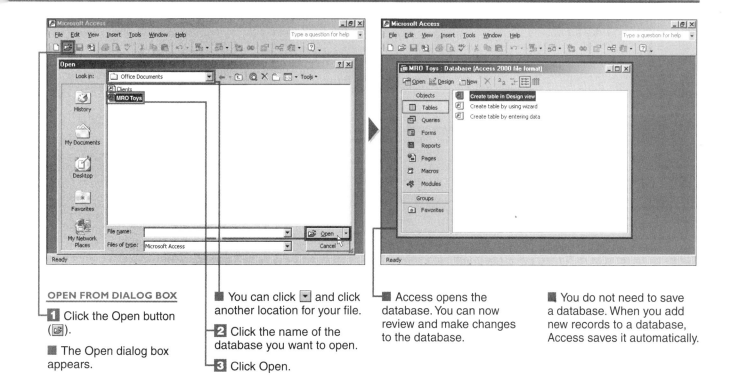

OPEN FROM DIALOG BOX

■1 Click the Open button (📂).

■ The Open dialog box appears.

■ You can click ⊡ and click another location for your file.

■2 Click the name of the database you want to open.

■3 Click Open.

■ Access opens the database. You can now review and make changes to the database.

■ You do not need to save a database. When you add new records to a database, Access saves it automatically.

CREATE A TABLE IN DATASHEET VIEW

A *table* in a database stores a collection of information about a specific topic, such as a list of client addresses. You can create a table in the Datasheet view to store new information in rows and columns.

A table consists of fields and field names. A *field* is a specific category of information in a table. A *field*

name identifies the information in a field. You can use up to 64 characters to name a field.

A *record* is a collection of information — a set of completed fields — about one person, place, or thing in a table.

When you save a table, you give the table a name. You can use up to 64 characters to name a table. Use a

descriptive name so that you can easily identify the table and its purpose or contents.

You can have Access set a primary key in your table for you. A *primary key* is one or more fields that uniquely identify each record in a table, such as an ID number. Each table you create should have a primary key.

CREATE A TABLE IN DATASHEET VIEW

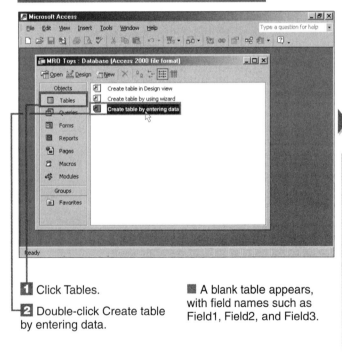

1 Click Tables.

2 Double-click Create table by entering data.

■ A blank table appears, with field names such as Field1, Field2, and Field3.

3 To change a field name, double-click the field name, type the new name, and press Enter.

4 Type a field name for each field you want to include in the table.

5 When you have finished creating the fields, click the Save button (■) to save the table.

Is there another way to create a table?

✔ You can create a table in the Design view. In the Database window, click Tables and then double-click the Create table in Design view option. The Design view gives you more control over the structure of the table and the type of information each field will contain. For information on working in the Design view, see Chapter 25.

Can I use a table I created in another database?

✔ You can import a table from another database. This saves you from having to create a new table. From the File menu, select Get External Data and then click Import. Click the name of the database that contains the table you want to import and then click the Import button. Click the name of the table you want to import and then click OK.

I did not choose to have Access create a primary key for me. Can I set a primary key later?

✔ Yes. You can set the primary key at any time. See Chapter 25 for details on setting a primary key.

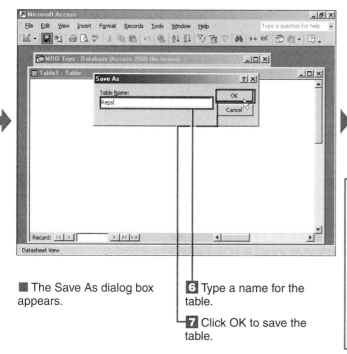

■ The Save As dialog box appears.

6 Type a name for the table.

7 Click OK to save the table.

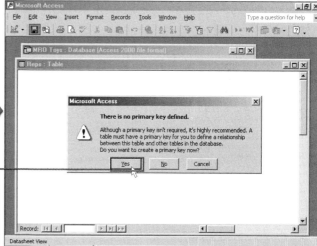

■ After you save a new table, a dialog box appears stating that the table does not have a primary key.

8 To have Access set the primary key, click Yes.

■ The table is created and displayed so that you can enter records.

ENTER DATA IN DATASHEET VIEW

Y ou can enter data into a table in Access as you enter data into a worksheet in Excel. That is, you enter data into a cell, the intersection of a column and row.

After you create and save a table using Datasheet view, Access removes the rows and columns that do not contain data. This reduces

cluttering the table and makes it easier to enter your data.

The field names that you type when you create the table become the column headings and help to identify what contents to enter into each cell. See the section "Create a Table in Datasheet View" for more on creating a table.

Access adds a new row to the table each time you enter another record, so you can enter as many records as you need. Access also automatically saves each record you enter.

When you finish entering the records for a table, you can close the table. The name of the table appears in the Database window.

ENTER DATA IN DATASHEET VIEW

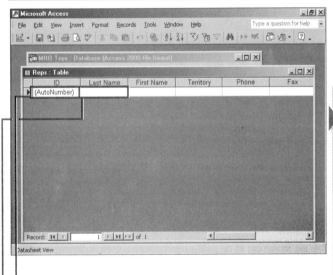

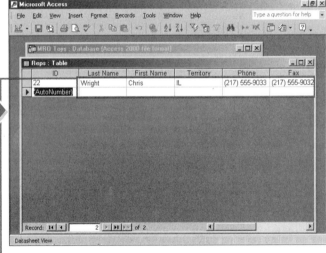

■ If Access creates a primary key field, the ID field is automatically added to the table.

1 Click the first empty cell in the row.

2 Type the data for each field.

3 Press the Tab or Enter key to move from field to field.

4 At the end of each record, press Enter to add a new record.

■ The record is added.

5 Repeats steps 1 through 4 until you have added all the records you need.

Note: Access automatically saves your table after you add a record.

What are the symbols that appear to the left of a record?

✓ The arrow indicates the current record. The pencil indicates the record you are editing. The asterisk indicates where you can enter data for a new record.

How do I insert a new column?

✓ You can insert a column to add a new field to your table. Select the column next to where you want to place the new column by clicking the column header. Click Insert and then click Column. The new column is inserted to the left of the current column. Double-click the field name and type a new field name.

How do I delete a table?

✓ Before you delete a table, make sure other objects in your database, such as a form or report, do not use the table. In the Database window, click Tables. Click the name of the table you want to delete and then press the Delete key.

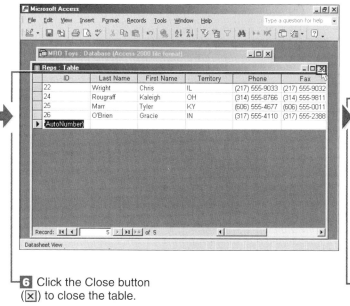

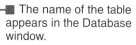

6 Click the Close button (⊠) to close the table.

■ The name of the table appears in the Database window.

CREATE A TABLE USING THE WIZARD

The Table Wizard helps you quickly create a table that suits your needs. The wizard asks you a series of questions and then sets up a table based on your answers.

The Table Wizard can help you create a table for business or personal use. The wizard provides

sample business tables, such as Customers, Products, Orders, and Deliveries. For your personal needs, the wizard offers sample tables, such as Recipes, Plants, Wine List, and Investments. You can select a sample table that is similar to the table you want to create.

The Table Wizard displays the available fields for the sample table you select. You can include all or only some of the available fields in your table. You should make sure that each field you include is directly related to the subject of the table. If you accidentally include a field in your table you do not need, you can remove the field.

CREATE A TABLE USING THE WIZARD

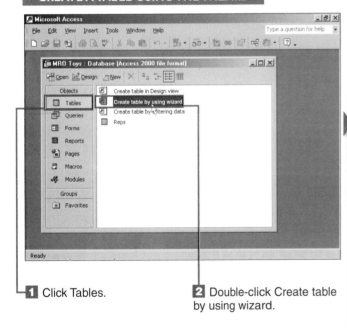

1 Click Tables.

2 Double-click Create table by using wizard.

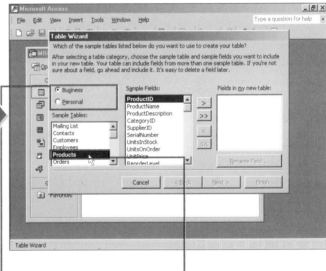

■ The Table Wizard appears.

3 Click an option specifying whether the table is for business or personal use (○ changes to ◉).

4 Click the sample table that best describes the table you want to create.

Note: The available sample tables depend on the option you selected in step 3.

How can I quickly include all the available fields in my table?

✔ In the Table Wizard, click >> to quickly include all the available fields from the sample table in your table.

Can I rename a field in the Table Wizard?

✔ Yes. In the Fields in my new table area, click the field you want to rename and then click Rename Field. Type a new name for the field and then click OK.

How can I quickly remove all the fields I included in my table?

✔ In the Table Wizard, click < to quickly remove all the fields you included.

Do I have to complete all the steps in the Table Wizard?

✔ After you select the fields you want to include, you can click Finish at any time to create your table based on the information you have provided.

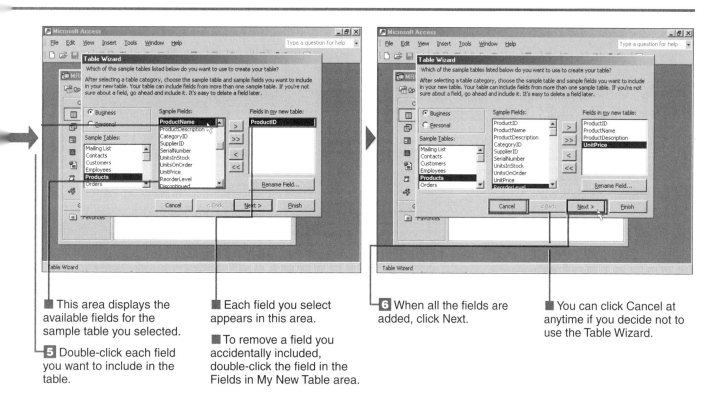

■ This area displays the available fields for the sample table you selected.

5 Double-click each field you want to include in the table.

■ Each field you select appears in this area.

■ To remove a field you accidentally included, double-click the field in the Fields in My New Table area.

6 When all the fields are added, click Next.

■ You can click Cancel at anytime if you decide not to use the Table Wizard.

CONTINUED

CREATE A TABLE USING THE WIZARD
(CONTINUED)

The Table Wizard asks you to name your table. You can use up to 64 characters to name a table. The name you specify appears in the Tables area of the Database window.

You can set a primary key for your table. A primary key is a field that uniquely identifies each record in a table. Each table in a database should have a primary key. If you do not know which field to set as the primary key, you should allow the wizard to set the primary key for you. You can later change the primary key the wizard sets. See Chapter 25.

If other tables already exist in the database, the Table Wizard shows you how your new table relates to the other tables.

Access allows you to choose what you want to do when the wizard finishes creating your table. You can modify the table design, start entering data directly into the table, or enter data using a form the wizard creates.

CREATE A TABLE USING THE WIZARD (CONTINUED)

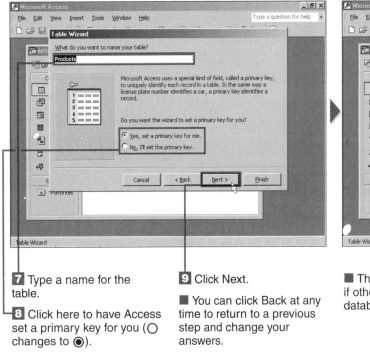

7 Type a name for the table.

8 Click here to have Access set a primary key for you (○ changes to ◉).

9 Click Next.

■ You can click Back at any time to return to a previous step and change your answers.

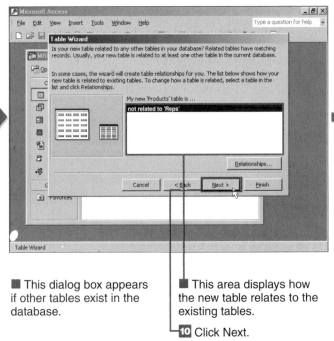

■ This dialog box appears if other tables exist in the database.

■ This area displays how the new table relates to the existing tables.

10 Click Next.

Which field should I use as the primary key?

✔ You should use a field that holds a unique value for each record. For example, in a table that stores data related to inventory, you could use the Part Number field as the primary key because each product has its own unique serial number.

Can I change how my table relates to another table in the database?

✔ Yes. In the Table Wizard, select the table for which you want to change the relationship and then click Relationships. Select the type of relationship you want to create. For more information on relationships, see Chapter 25.

How do I delete a table?

✔ Before you delete a table, make sure the table does not contain information you may need in the future and is not used by any other objects in your database, such as a form or report. Click Tables in the Database window, select the table you want to delete, and then press the Delete key.

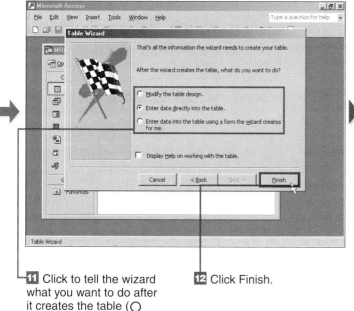

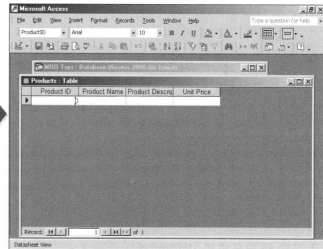

🔟🔢 Click to tell the wizard what you want to do after it creates the table (○ changes to ⦿).

🔢🔢 Click Finish.

■ The new table appears, ready for you to enter data.

Note: To enter data into the table, see the section "Add or Delete Records."

OPEN A TABLE

You can open a table and display its contents on your screen, which lets you review and make changes to the table.

You can open a table in the Datasheet or Design view. The Datasheet view displays all the records in a table so that you can enter, edit, and review records. If

you add records to a table, you do not need to save the table; Access saves the table each time you add or edit a record.

The Design view displays the structure of a table. You can change settings in the Design view to specify the kind of data you want to enter in each field of a table. For

more information on the Design view, see Chapter 25.

When you finish working in Design view, you need to save the changes you made; unlike the Datasheet view, Access does not automatically save changes in Design view.

OPEN A TABLE

1 Click Tables.

■ If the Database window is not visible, you can display it by pressing the F11 key.

2 Double-click the table you want to open.

■ The table appears.

3 Make any editing changes or add any records.

Note: For information about editing table data, see the section "Edit Data." To learn how to add records, see the section "Add or Delete Records."

4 When you finish reviewing the table, click ☒.

■ The table is saved and closed.

UNDERSTANDING DATA TYPES

Each database field accepts a specific type of data. If you use a wizard to create a table, that table's data types are set depending on the contents of the field. If you set up a table by entering data, the data types are all set to match the type of entry you make in that field.

When adding records, you should type the appropriate data type into the field. Chapter 25 explains how you can change the data type.

Text

Accepts entries up to 255 characters long that include any combination of text and numbers, such as an address. Use this data type for numbers that you do not want to use in calculations, such as phone numbers or ZIP Codes.

Memo

Accepts entries up to 64,000 characters long that include any combination of text and numbers. This data type works for notes or lengthy descriptions.

Number

Accepts only numbers. You can type numbers for use in calculations in a field by using the Number data type.

Date/Time

Accepts only dates and times. You can type dates as 6/18/01 or Jun-18-01. You can type times as 6:25AM, 6:25:55, or 18:25.

Currency

Accepts only monetary values. This data type accepts up to 15 numbers to the left of the decimal point and 4 numbers to the right of it. The Currency data type automatically displays data as currency. For example, if you type 3428, the data appears as $3,428.00.

AutoNumber

This data type automatically numbers each record for you. The AutoNumber data type automatically assigns a unique number in a sequential or random order to each record in a table.

Yes/No

Accepts only one of two values — Yes/No, True/False, or On/Off.

OLE Object

Accepts OLE objects. An *OLE object* is an item you create in another program, such as a document in Word or a chart in Excel. OLE objects can also include sounds and pictures.

Hyperlink

Accepts hyperlinks. You can select a hyperlink to jump to another document on an intranet or a Web page on the World Wide Web. You can type a Web site address, such as www.maran.com, in a field using the Hyperlink data type and quickly access the Web site from the table.

ADD OR DELETE RECORDS

You can add a new record to insert additional information into your table. Access automatically saves each new record you add to a table.

You can use the blank row at the bottom of a table to add a record. You cannot add a record to the middle of a table. If you want to change the order of the records, you can sort the records. See Chapter 27 for more on sorting records.

If your table has an AutoNumber field, Access automatically enters a number for each record you add.

In addition to adding records, you can also delete records you no longer need. For example, you can delete a record containing information on a company with which you no longer deal.

When you delete a record, you may also want to delete any related

records in other tables. For example, if you delete a company from your supplier table, you may also want to delete records containing information about the products the company supplies from your product table.

ADD A RECORD

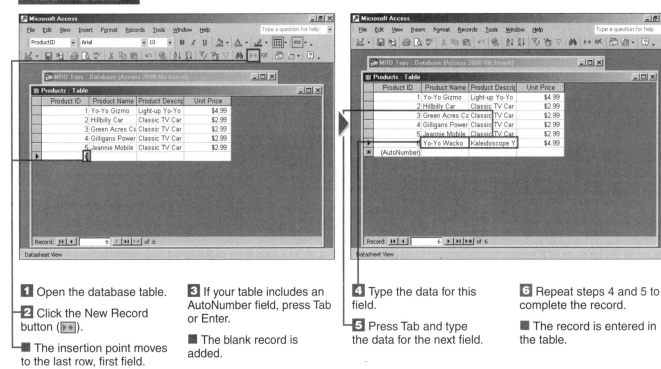

1 Open the database table.

2 Click the New Record button (▶✱).

■ The insertion point moves to the last row, first field.

3 If your table includes an AutoNumber field, press Tab or Enter.

■ The blank record is added.

4 Type the data for this field.

5 Press Tab and type the data for the next field.

6 Repeat steps 4 and 5 to complete the record.

■ The record is entered in the table.

Is there a faster way to enter data into cells in a new record?

✔ Yes, you can copy the data from the cell above the current cell. To do so, press Ctrl + apostrophe key ('). To insert the current date, press Ctrl + semicolon key (;).

Can I use a form to add a record?

✔ Yes, you can use a form to add a record to a table. See Chapter 26 for information on creating and using data forms.

How do I delete several records at once?

✔ Select the records you want to delete by dragging through the row selector for the records you want to delete, and then click the Delete button (⊠). Confirm the deletion by clicking Yes. Note that you cannot delete noncontiguous records.

Can I undo a record deletion?

✔ No, so be sure that you do indeed want to delete a record. If you delete a record by accident, you cannot undo it. You have to re-create the record. To remind you of the consequences, Access displays a dialog box asking you to confirm the deletion.

DELETE A RECORD

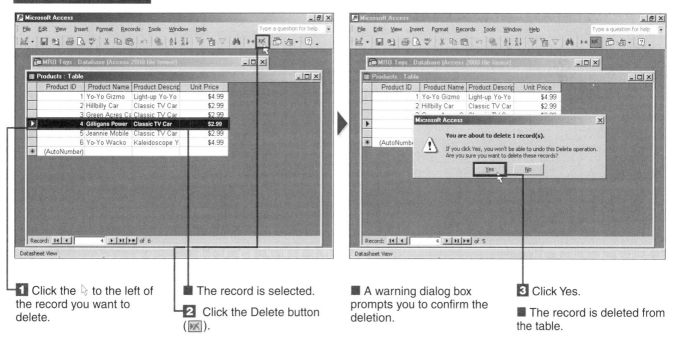

■1 Click the ▷ to the left of the record you want to delete.

■ The record is selected.

■2 Click the Delete button (⊠).

■ A warning dialog box prompts you to confirm the deletion.

■3 Click Yes.

■ The record is deleted from the table.

MOVE THROUGH RECORDS

You can easily move through the records in your table when reviewing or editing information.

You can change the location of the insertion point in your table. The insertion point must be located in the cell you want to edit. You can move from field to field within a record.

Access also provides buttons that allow you to instantly move the insertion point to the first, last, previous, or next record.

If your table contains a large amount of information, your computer screen may not display all the fields and records at once. You can use the scroll bars to view the fields and records that are not

displayed. You can scroll one field or record at a time. You can also quickly scroll to any field or record in your table. The scroll bars do not appear if all the fields and records display on your screen.

Scrolling allows you to see the rest of the table, but does not move the insertion point.

MOVE THROUGH RECORDS

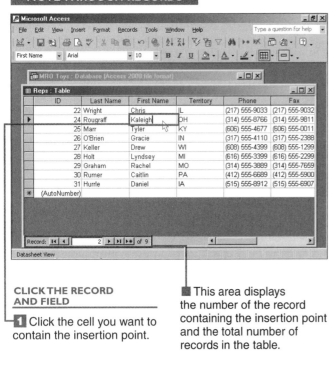

CLICK THE RECORD AND FIELD

■1 Click the cell you want to contain the insertion point.

■ This area displays the number of the record containing the insertion point and the total number of records in the table.

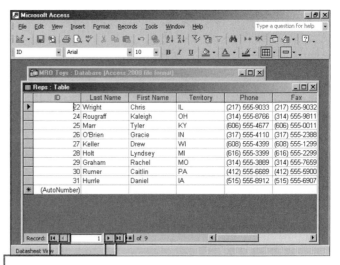

USE THE RECORD BUTTONS

■1 To quickly move to another record, click one of the following buttons:
- |◄ First Record
- ◄ Previous Record
- ► Next Record
- ►| Last Record

■ That record is displayed.

How do I use my keyboard to move through fields and records?

✔ Press the Tab key to move to the next field in the current record. Press the up or down arrow key to move up or down one record. Press the Page Up or Page Down key to move up or down one screen of records.

Can I quickly display a specific record?

✔ Yes. You can either go to a specific record number by double-clicking the current number, typing the record number you want to display, and then pressing Enter. Or you can search for a particular record. For example, you can search for a client that lives in Ohio. See Chapter 27 for help on searching for data.

How can I quickly display a specific field?

✔ You can use the Formatting toolbar to quickly display a specific field. To display the Formatting toolbar, click the View menu, click Toolbars, and then click Formatting (Datasheet). In the Formatting toolbar, click the down arrow next to the Go To Field area and then select the name of the field you want to display.

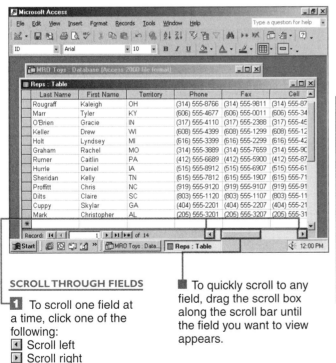

SCROLL THROUGH FIELDS

1 To scroll one field at a time, click one of the following:
◄ Scroll left
► Scroll right

■ To quickly scroll to any field, drag the scroll box along the scroll bar until the field you want to view appears.

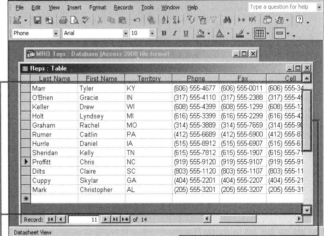

SCROLL THROUGH RECORDS

1 To scroll one record at a time, click one of the following:
▲ Scroll up
▼ Scroll down

■ To quickly scroll to any record, drag the scroll box along the scroll bar until the yellow box displays the number of the record you want to view.

SELECT DATA

B efore performing many tasks in a table, you must select the data you want to work with. For example, you must select data you want to move or copy.

Selected data appears highlighted on your screen, which makes selected data stand out from the rest of the data in your table.

You can select the part of the table you want to work with — either a field, record, cell, or data in a cell. Selecting a field or record is useful when you need to delete a field or record from your table. Selecting one cell or data in a cell is useful when you are editing data in your table.

You can select multiple fields, records, or cells to perform the same task on all the fields, records, or cells at once. This saves you from having to perform the same task again and again.

SELECT DATA

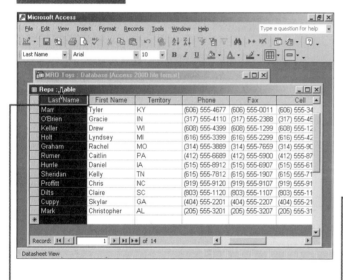

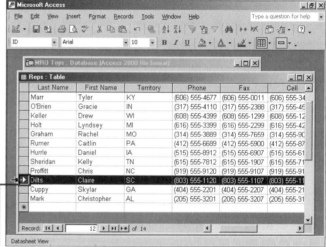

SELECT A FIELD

1 Position the ⃕ over the name of the field you want to select.

2 Click the field name.

■ The column and all its contents are selected.

■ To select multiple fields, position the ⃕ over the name of the first field. Then, drag the ⃕ until you highlight all the fields you want to select.

SELECT A RECORD

1 Click the area to the left of the record you want to select.

■ That record is selected.

■ To select multiple records, position the ⃕ over the area to the left of the first record. Then drag the ⃕ until you highlight all the records you want to select.

How do I deselect data?

✔ To deselect data, click anywhere in the table.

How do I select all the records in a table?

✔ To select all the records in a table, click the blank area to the left of the field names. You can also press the Ctrl+A keys to select all the records in a table.

Is there a fast way to select a word in a cell?

✔ To quickly select a word, double-click the word.

How can I quickly select a large group of cells?

✔ To quickly select a large group of cells, click the first cell in the group you want to select and then scroll to the end of the group. Press the Shift key as you click the last cell in the group. Access highlights all the cells between the first and last cell you select.

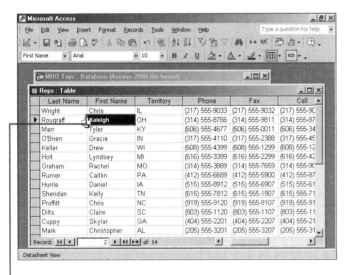

SELECT A CELL

1 Position the ⬚ over the left edge of the cell you want to select.

2 Click that edge to select the cell.

■ That cell is selected.

■ To select multiple cells, position the ⬚ over the left edge of the first cell. Then drag the ⬚ until you highlight all the cells you want to select.

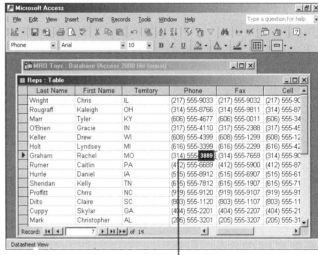

SELECT DATA IN A CELL

1 Position the ⬚ over the data.

2 Drag the ⬚ until you highlight all the data you want to select.

■ The data is selected.

EDIT DATA

After you enter data into your table, you can change the data to correct a mistake or update the data.

The flashing insertion point in a cell indicates where Access will remove or add data. When you remove data using the Backspace key, Access removes the character to the left of the insertion point. When you insert data, Access adds the characters you type at the location of the insertion point.

You can quickly replace all the data in a cell with new data.

As you edit data, Access displays symbols to the left of the records. The arrow indicates the current record. The pencil indicates the record you are editing. The asterisk indicates where you can enter data for a new record.

If you make a mistake while editing data, you can use the Undo feature to immediately undo your most recent change.

You do not have to save the changes you make. When you move from the record you are editing to another record, Access automatically saves your changes.

EDIT DATA

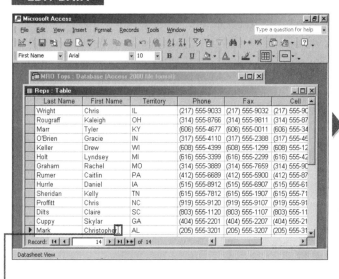

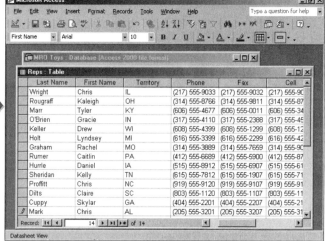

EDIT DATA

1 Click the location in the cell where you want to change the data.

■ A flashing insertion point appears in the cell.

Note: You can press the left or right arrow key to move the insertion point to where you want to remove or add characters.

2 Type or edit your data.

■ To remove the character to the left of the insertion point, press the Backspace key.

■ To insert data where the insertion point flashes on your screen, type the data.

3 Press the Enter key.

■ The record is updated.

How can I quickly find data I want to edit?

✔ Click a cell in the field containing the data you want to find. Click the Find button (📷). Type the data you want to find and then click Find Next.

Can I check my table for spelling errors?

✔ You can find and correct all the spelling errors in a table. Click the Spelling button (📷) to start the spell check. To spell check a single field or record, select the field or record before you begin.

Can I copy data in a table?

✔ Yes. Copying data is useful when you want several records in a table to display the same information. After you edit the data in one record, you can copy the data to other records. Select the data you want to copy and then click the Copy button (📷). Click the location where you want to place the data and then click the Paste button (📷).

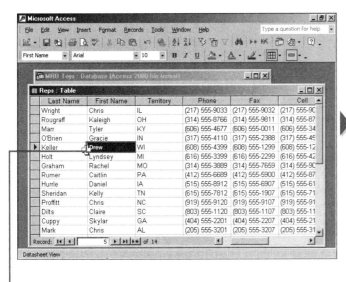

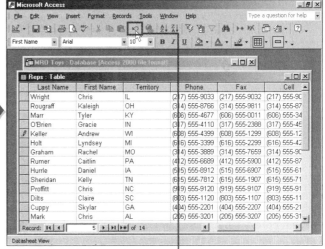

REPLACE ALL DATA IN A CELL

1 Position the ⇧ over the left edge of the cell you want to replace with new data.

2 Click the mouse button.

■ The cell becomes highlighted and is ready to accept new data.

3 Type the new data.

4 Press the Enter key.

■ The new data replaces the original data.

■ To Undo the change, click the Undo button (📷).

ZOOM INTO A CELL

You can zoom into any cell in a table, which can make the contents of the cell easier to review and edit.

Zooming into a cell is useful when the columns in your table are not wide enough to display the entire contents of a cell. For example, a cell may contain a long address or a long description that Access cannot completely display.

When you zoom into a cell, Access displays the contents of the cell in the Zoom dialog box. You can edit the contents of the cell directly in the Zoom dialog box.

If you plan to enter a large amount of data into a cell, you can also zoom into an empty cell, which lets you easily view all the data you are typing into the cell at once.

ZOOM INTO A CELL

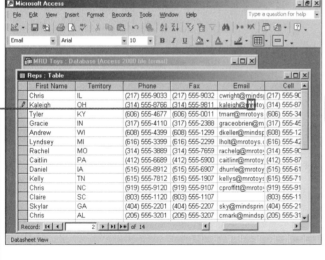

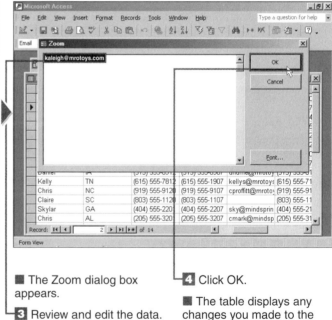

1 Click the cell containing the data you want to review and edit.

2 Press the Shift key as you press the F2 key.

■ The Zoom dialog box appears.

3 Review and edit the data.

Note: See the section "Edit Data" for more about editing table contents.

4 Click OK.

■ The table displays any changes you made to the data.

CHANGE COLUMN WIDTH

You can change the width of a column in your table, which lets you view data that is too long to display in the column. Reducing the width of a column allows you to display more fields on your screen at once.

You can have Access automatically adjust the width of a column to fit the longest item in the column.

After you change the width of a column, you must save the table to have Access save the new column width.

How do I change the height of the rows?

✔ To change the height of rows in your table, position the ⍨ over the bottom edge of the gray area to the left of the row you want to change. You can then drag the row edge to a new location. When you change the height of a row, all the rows in the table automatically change to the new height. You cannot change the height of a single row.

CHANGE COLUMN WIDTH

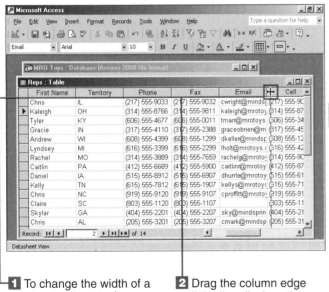

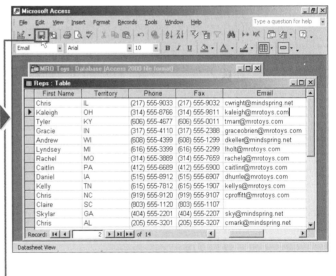

1 To change the width of a column, position the ⍨ over the right edge of the column heading.

■ The ⍨ changes to +.

2 Drag the column edge until the line displays the column width you want.

■ The column displays the new width.

3 Click 🖫.

■ To change a column width to fit the longest item in the column, double-click the right edge of the column heading.

HIDE A FIELD

Y ou can temporarily hide a field in your table to reduce the amount of data displayed on your screen. This can help you work with specific data and can make your table easier to read.

Hiding a field enables you to review only fields of interest. For example, if you want to

browse through the names and telephone numbers of all your clients, you can hide the fields that display all other information.

When you hide a field, Access does not delete the field. The data in the hidden field remains intact.

How do I redisplay a hidden field?

✔ You can redisplay a hidden field to once again view the data in the field. From the Format menu, select Unhide Columns. A dialog box appears, displaying a list of the fields in your table. A check mark beside a field indicates the field is displayed on your screen. Click the box beside the field you want to redisplay and then click Close.

HIDE A FIELD

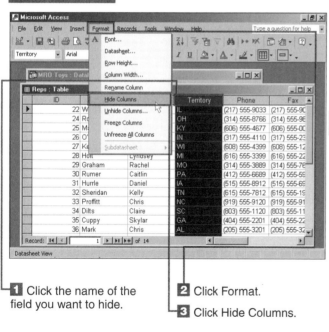

1 Click the name of the field you want to hide.

2 Click Format.

3 Click Hide Columns.

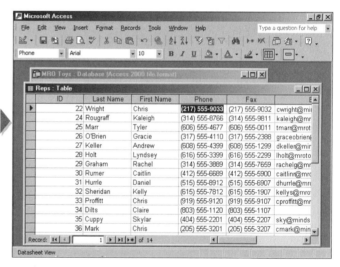

■ The field disappears from the table, and remaining columns shift to the left.

FREEZE A FIELD

You can freeze a field to make it remain on your screen at all times. Freezing a field enables you to keep important data displayed on your screen as you move through a large table. For example, you can freeze a field

containing the names of your clients so that the names remain on your screen while you scroll through the rest of the data for the clients.

You can unfreeze a field at any time. From the Format menu, select Unfreeze All Columns. You can also

hide or freeze more than one field at a time. To hide or freeze multiple fields, you must first select the fields you want to hide or freeze. You can then hide or freeze the fields as you would hide or freeze a single field.

FREEZE A FIELD

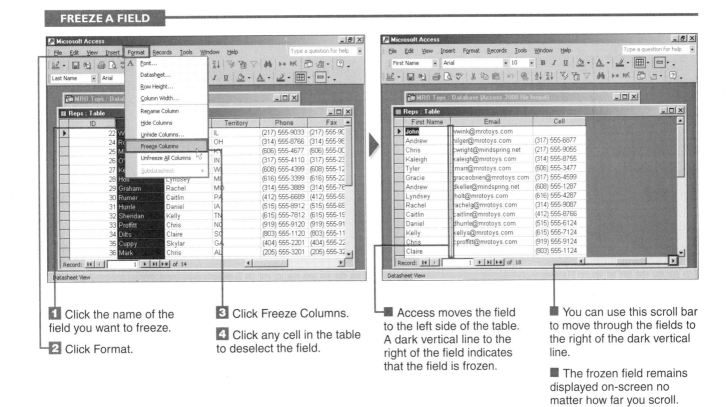

1 Click the name of the field you want to freeze.

2 Click Format.

3 Click Freeze Columns.

4 Click any cell in the table to deselect the field.

■ Access moves the field to the left side of the table. A dark vertical line to the right of the field indicates that the field is frozen.

■ You can use this scroll bar to move through the fields to the right of the dark vertical line.

■ The frozen field remains displayed on-screen no matter how far you scroll.

CHANGE THE TABLE VIEW

Y ou can view a table two ways; each view allows you to perform different tasks.

The Datasheet view displays all the records in a table. You can enter, edit, and review records in this view. Working in this view is covered in Chapter 24.

The Design view displays the structure of a table. Use this view when you want to make changes to the structure, layout, and design of the table.

You can change the data type and field property settings in the Design view. The data type determines the type of information you can enter in a field, such as text, numbers, or dates. Specifying a data type helps ensure that you enter the correct information in a field. For more on date types see Chapter 24 and the section "Change the Data Type."

The field properties are a set of characteristics that provide additional control over the information you can enter in a field. For example, you can specify the maximum number of characters a field accepts. You learn more about fields in this chapter.

Access allows you to quickly switch between the Datasheet and Design views.

CHANGE THE TABLE VIEW

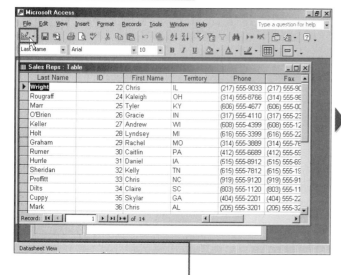

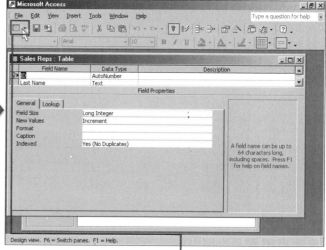

■ In this example, the table appears in the Datasheet view.

1 Click the Design button (⧉).

■ The table appears in the Design view.

■ The View button changes to the Datasheet button (⧉).

2 Click the View button to quickly switch between the Design and Datasheet views.

REARRANGE FIELDS

Y ou can change the order of fields to better organize the information in your table. For example, in a table that stores employee names and phone numbers, you may want to move the field containing work phone numbers in front of the field containing home phone numbers.

Rearranging the fields in a table does not affect how the fields

display in other objects in the database, such as a form. Rearranging fields in the Datasheet view also does not affect the arrangement of fields in the Design view.

A thick line indicates the new location of the field you are moving. If you move a field to an area of your table that is not displayed on the screen, Access

scrolls through the table to show you the new location of the field.

After you change the order of fields in your table, you must save the table to keep the new arrangement of fields.

REARRANGE FIELDS

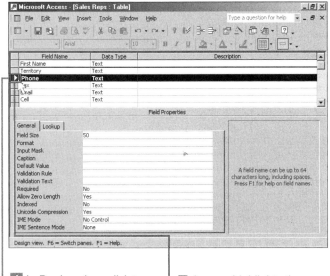

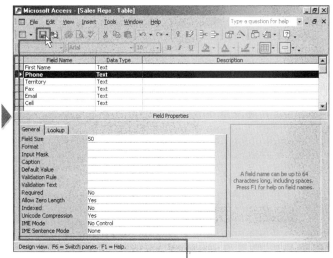

■1 In Design view, click to the left of the name of the field you want to move.

Note: See the section "Change the Table View" to switch to Design view.

■ Access highlights the field.

■2 Position the ⬛ over the triangular field selector and then drag the selector to the new location.

■ A thick line shows the field's new location.

■3 Release the mouse.

■ The field appears in the new location.

■4 Click the Save button (⬛) to save your change.

■ Access saves the table design.

DISPLAY FIELD PROPERTIES

ach field in a table has properties that you can display. The field properties are a set of characteristics that provide additional control over the kind of information you can type in a field. For example, the Field Size property tells Access the maximum number of characters a field can contain. You can display these

properties to see the settings that affect data entry and the table display.

The properties available for a field depend on the type of data the field contains. For example, the Field Size property is available for a field containing text but not for a field containing currency. The Decimal Places property is available for a

field containing currency but not for a field containing text.

You can display the available properties for any field in your table.

If you use a field in other objects in the database, such as a form or report, the other objects also use the properties for the field.

DISPLAY FIELD PROPERTIES

1 Change to Design view.

Note: See the section "Change the Table View" to switch to Design view.

■ This area displays the field name and data type for each field in the table.

■ A triangle appears beside the current field.

■ This area displays the properties for the current field.

2 To display the properties for another field, click the field name.

■ This area displays the properties for the new field you selected.

ADD A FIELD DESCRIPTION

You can add a description to a field to identify the type of information the field contains. You can use up to 255 characters, including spaces, to describe a field.

Adding a description to a field can help you determine what kind of information you should type in the field. For example, if a field has an abbreviated field name such as CNum, you can add a description such as "This field contains customer numbers" to help you enter information in the field.

After you add a description to a field, you must save the table to have Access save the description.

When you display your table in the Datasheet view, you can click anywhere in the field to display the description you added. The description appears on the status bar at the bottom of your screen.

If you use the field in another object in the database, such as a form, the other object displays the description when you are working with the field.

ADD A FIELD DESCRIPTION

1 In Design view, click the description area for the field to which you want to add a description.

Note: See the section "Change the Table View" to switch to Design view.

2 Type the description.

3 Click 🖫.

4 Click 🖩 to display the table in the Datasheet view.

5 Click anywhere in the field to which you added the description.

■ The description for the field appears in this area.

■ To return to the Design view, click 🖳.

CHANGE THE DATA TYPE

You can change the type of data you can type in a field. For more information on available data types, see Chapter 24.

Consider what type of data you want to enter in the field. Access does not accept entries that do not match the data type you specify. This helps prevent errors when entering data. For example, you

cannot type text in a field with the Number data type.

Determine if you want to perform calculations using the data in the field. Access can calculate numbers in a Number or Currency field but cannot calculate numbers in a Text field.

The ability to sort records is also a consideration. Access cannot sort

some data types, such as Memo, Hyperlink, and OLE Object.

If you change the data type for a field, Access may delete data in the field. Access displays a warning message before deleting any data. You can click OK to confirm the change or keep the original data type.

CHANGE THE DATA TYPE

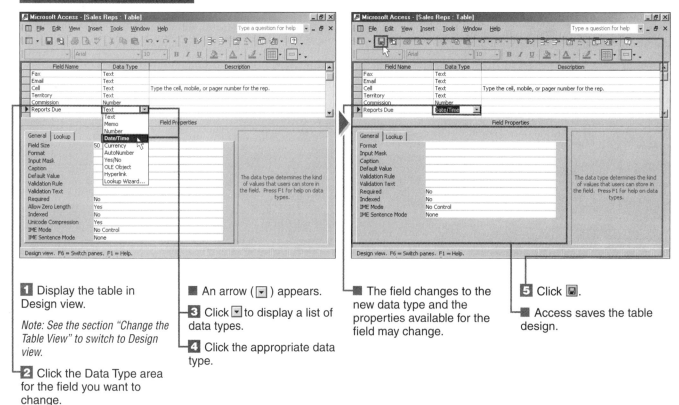

■ **1** Display the table in Design view.

Note: See the section "Change the Table View" to switch to Design view.

■ **2** Click the Data Type area for the field you want to change.

■ An arrow (▼) appears.

■ **3** Click ▼ to display a list of data types.

■ **4** Click the appropriate data type.

■ The field changes to the new data type and the properties available for the field may change.

■ **5** Click 🖫.

■ Access saves the table design.

414

RENAME A FIELD

You can give a field a different name to more accurately describe the contents of the field, which can help prevent confusion between two similar fields in a table.

If you rename a field that is used in other objects in the database, such as a form or report, Access automatically changes the references in the database to ensure the objects can access the information in the renamed field.

You can use up to 64 characters to name a field. You cannot use periods (.), exclamation points (!), or brackets ([or]) in the name of a field. Avoid including spaces when you rename a field if you plan to enter the field name in an expression for a calculation. A field name that contains spaces is more likely to be entered incorrectly than one without spaces. For more information on using expressions in calculations, see Chapter 28.

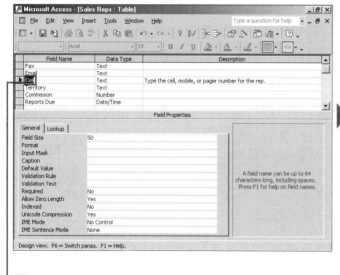

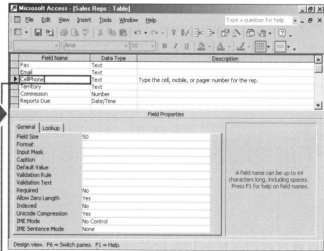

1 Double-click the field name you want to change.

■ Access highlights the field name.

2 Type a new field name.

3 Press Enter.

■ The field displays the new name.

CHANGE THE FIELD SIZE

You can change the field size of a text or number field to specify the maximum size of data you can enter into the field.

You can change the maximum number of characters that a text field accepts. You can specify a field size of up to 255 characters for all fields except Memo, which you can make much larger.

You can change the number field to specify the size and type of numbers that you can type into the field. Most field size options allow you to enter whole numbers only. If you want to enter decimal numbers, such as 1.234, select the Single or Double field size option.

Access processes smaller field sizes more quickly than larger ones. Using smaller field sizes can help speed up tasks, such as searching for data in a field. Using small field sizes can also reduce the amount of space required to store a table on your computer. If a table contains thousands of records, reducing the size of a text field by one or two characters may save a considerable amount of disk space.

CHANGE THE FIELD SIZE

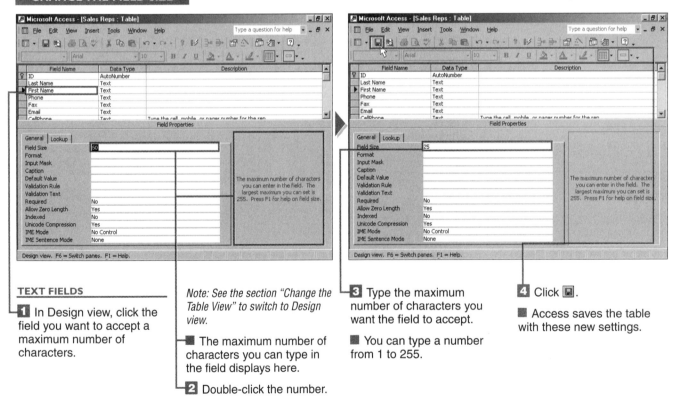

TEXT FIELDS

1 In Design view, click the field you want to accept a maximum number of characters.

Note: See the section "Change the Table View" to switch to Design view.

■ The maximum number of characters you can type in the field displays here.

2 Double-click the number.

3 Type the maximum number of characters you want the field to accept.

■ You can type a number from 1 to 255.

4 Click 💾.

■ Access saves the table with these new settings.

What are the maximum and minimum size settings for number fields?

Setting	Number Size
Byte	Between 0 and 255
Integer	Between -32,768 and 32,767
Long Integer	Between -2,147,483,648 and 2,147,483,647

Can I change the field size that Access automatically uses for new text or number fields?

✔ Yes. Click Tools, Options, and then the Tables/Queries tabs. To change the size of text fields, double-click the Text area and type the new size. To change the size of number fields, click the Number area and choose a new size setting. Then click OK.

Can I change the size of a field that already contains data?

✔ Yes. If you reduce the size of a text field containing data, Access shortens any data longer than the new field size. If you reduce the size of a number field containing data, Access may change or delete data larger than the new field size. Access displays a warning message before changing any data.

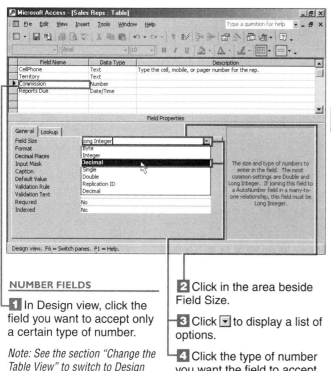

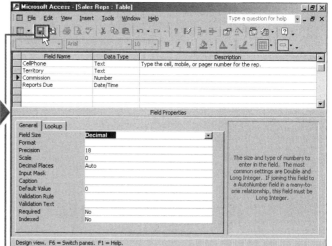

NUMBER FIELDS

■1 In Design view, click the field you want to accept only a certain type of number.

Note: See the section "Change the Table View" to switch to Design view.

■2 Click in the area beside Field Size.

■3 Click ▾ to display a list of options.

■4 Click the type of number you want the field to accept.

■ Access sets the new field size.

■5 Click 🖫.

■ Access saves the table with the new settings.

SELECT A DATA FORMAT

You can select a format to customize the way information appears in a field. When you select a format, you only change the way Access displays information on the screen. The values in the field do not change.

You can select a format for Number, Date/Time, Currency, AutoNumber, and Yes/No fields. Access does not provide formats for Text, Memo, OLE Object, or Hyperlink fields.

In a Number field, you can choose to display numbers in a format such as 1234.00 or $1,234.00. If you want a number to display decimal places, you may also need to change the field size. For information on changing the field size, see the section "Change the Field Size."

In a Date/Time field, you can choose to display a date as Tuesday, July 20, 1999 or 7/20/99. A Yes/No field can display values as True/False, Yes/No, or On/Off.

After you select a format, Access automatically changes any data you enter in the field to the new format. For example, if you type 3456, Access automatically displays the data as $3,456.00.

SELECT A DATA FORMAT

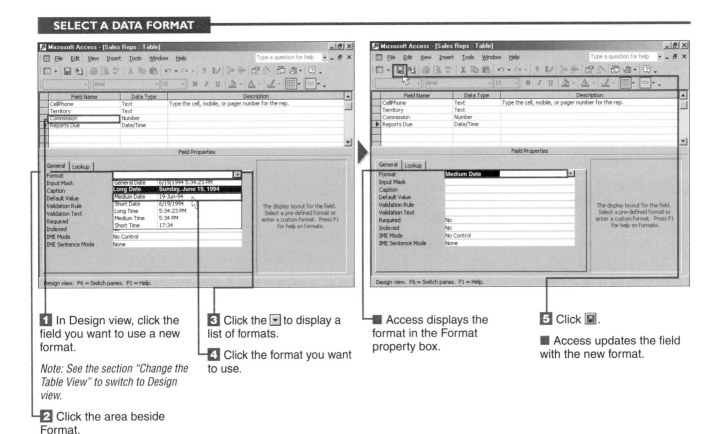

1 In Design view, click the field you want to use a new format.

Note: See the section "Change the Table View" to switch to Design view.

2 Click the area beside Format.

3 Click the ▼ to display a list of formats.

4 Click the format you want to use.

■ Access displays the format in the Format property box.

5 Click 💾.

■ Access updates the field with the new format.

CHANGE THE NUMBER OF DECIMAL PLACES

You can specify how many decimal places Access uses to display numbers in a field. Some numbers, such as prices, require only two decimal places. Numbers you use in scientific calculations may require more decimal places.

You can choose to display between 0 and 15 decimal places after the decimal point.

Changing the number of decimal places only affects how a number displays on the screen, not how Access stores or uses a number in calculations. For example, if you change the number of decimal places to 1, Access displaysthe number 2.3456 is displayed as 2.3. However, Access stores and performs calculations using the number 2.3456.

If the Format property of a field is blank or set to General Number, changing the number of decimal places does not affect the field. For information on selecting a format, see "Select a Data Format."

You may also need to change the field size before the field displays numbers with decimal places. For information on changing the field size, see "Change the Field Size."

CHANGE THE NUMBER OF DECIMAL PLACES

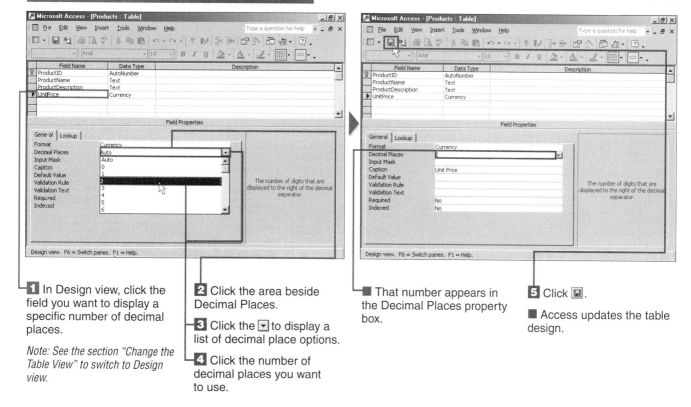

1 In Design view, click the field you want to display a specific number of decimal places.

Note: See the section "Change the Table View" to switch to Design view.

2 Click the area beside Decimal Places.

3 Click the ▼ to display a list of decimal place options.

4 Click the number of decimal places you want to use.

■ That number appears in the Decimal Places property box.

5 Click 🖫.

■ Access updates the table design.

ADD OR DELETE A FIELD

You can add a field to a table when you want the table to include an additional category of information. For example, you may want to add a field for e-mail addresses to a table that contains client information.

If you no longer need a field, you can delete the field from your table.

Deleting a field permanently deletes all the data in the field. Deleting unneeded fields makes your database smaller and may speed up the searches you perform.

Before you delete a field, make sure the field is not used in any other objects in the database, such as a form, query, or report. If you delete

a field used in another object, Access cannot find all the data for the object.

When you add or delete a field, Access automatically saves the changes for you.

ADD A FIELD

1 In Design view, click in the last row of the table in the Field Name column.

Note: See the section "Change the Table View" to switch to Design view.

2 Type the field name and press Tab.

3 Type a Data Type and press Tab.

■ You can type a description.

4 Make any changes to the field properties.

Note: See the other sections in this chapter to change field properties.

5 Click 🔚.

■ Access adds the new blank field to the table.

Do I have to insert my field at the end of the table as the last field?

✔ No. You can insert a new row into the Design view table and then add the field in that location. You can also move fields in Design view. See "Rearrange Fields."

Can I add a field in Datasheet view?

✔ Yes. Select the column where you want the new field to be inserted. Then click Insert and New Column. The field is assigned a generic name, such as Field3. Double-click the field name and type a more descriptive name. Then press Enter.

After I delete a field from a table, can I undo the change?

✔ You cannot use the Undo feature to reverse the results of deleting a field. If you regret deleting a field from your table, you must add the field and all the deleted data again.

Why does Access prevent me from deleting a field?

✔ The field may be part of a relationship. You must delete the relationship before you can delete the field. To delete a relationship, see "Define Relationships Between Tables."

DELETE A FIELD

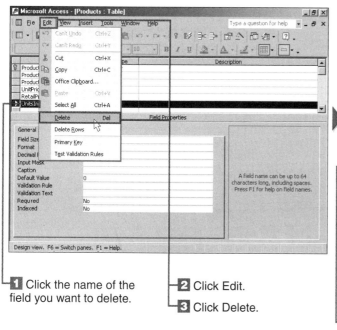

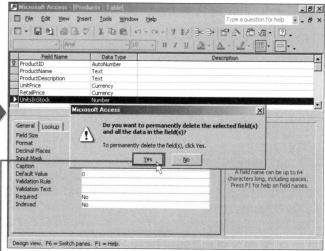

■1 Click the name of the field you want to delete.

■2 Click Edit.

■3 Click Delete.

■ A dialog box appears, confirming the deletion.

■4 Click Yes to permanently delete the field.

■ The field disappears from the table.

ADD A CAPTION

You can create a caption for a field when you want the heading for a field to be longer and more descriptive than the field name allows. Adding a caption can help you recognize the field more easily when you are entering or reviewing data in your table. For example, the caption

Home Phone Number is much easier to understand than the field name HPhone.

The caption appears as the heading for the field instead of the field name. A caption can be up to 2,048 characters in length, including letters, numbers, and spaces.

After adding a caption to a field, any forms, reports, or queries you create that use the field display the caption instead of the field name. Any forms or reports you created before adding the caption continue to display the field name.

ADD A CAPTION

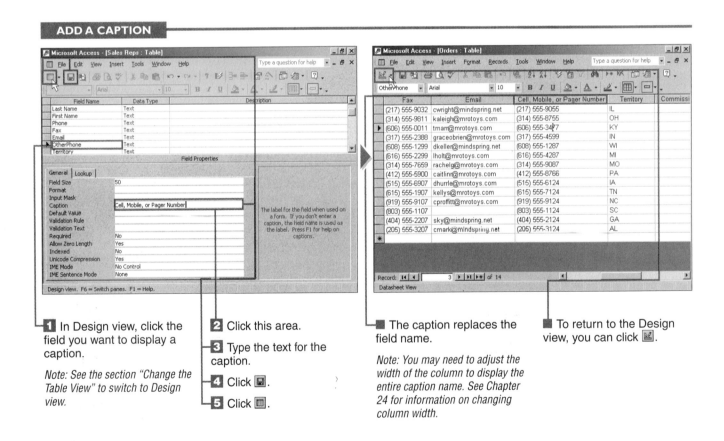

■1 In Design view, click the field you want to display a caption.

Note: See the section "Change the Table View" to switch to Design view.

■2 Click this area.

■3 Type the text for the caption.

■4 Click 🖫.

■5 Click 🖩.

■ The caption replaces the field name.

Note: You may need to adjust the width of the column to display the entire caption name. See Chapter 24 for information on changing column width.

■ To return to the Design view, you can click 🗠.

ADD A DEFAULT VALUE

You can specify a value that you want to appear automatically in a field each time you add a new record, which saves you from having to type the same data repeatedly.

For example, a table containing the addresses of your clients may contain a field for the country in which each client lives. If the

majority of your clients live in the United States, you can set United States as the default value for the field. This can save you a considerable amount of time if the table contains a large number of records.

You do not have to accept the default value for each new record

you add to your table. You can enter another value in the field.

Setting a default value does not affect the existing data in a field. To change existing data to the default value, click a cell containing data you want to change and then press Ctrl + Alt + Spacebar.

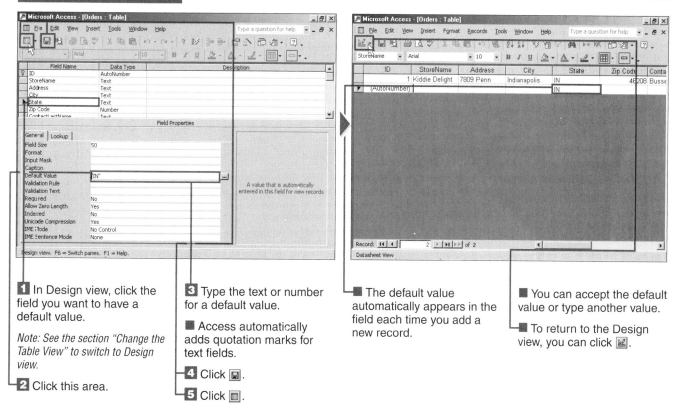

1 In Design view, click the field you want to have a default value.

Note: See the section "Change the Table View" to switch to Design view.

2 Click this area.

3 Type the text or number for a default value.

■ Access automatically adds quotation marks for text fields.

4 Click ▣.

5 Click ▥.

■ The default value automatically appears in the field each time you add a new record.

■ You can accept the default value or type another value.

■ To return to the Design view, you can click ⬚.

REQUIRE AN ENTRY

You can specify that a field must contain data for each record, which prevents you from leaving out important information. For example, in a table that stores invoice information, you can specify that a user must type data in the Invoice Number field.

After you specify that a field must contain data, Access can verify if

the field contains data for all the existing records in the table. When you add a new record in the table, an error message appears if you do not type data in the field.

You can also specify that a field requiring data may accept *zero-length strings*. A zero-length string indicates that no data exists for the field. For example, if you set the Fax Number field to require data, but

one of your clients does not have a fax machine, you need to enter a zero-length string in the field.

To enter a zero-length string in a cell, type "" in the cell. When you enter a zero-length string, the cell in the table appears empty.

REQUIRE AN ENTRY

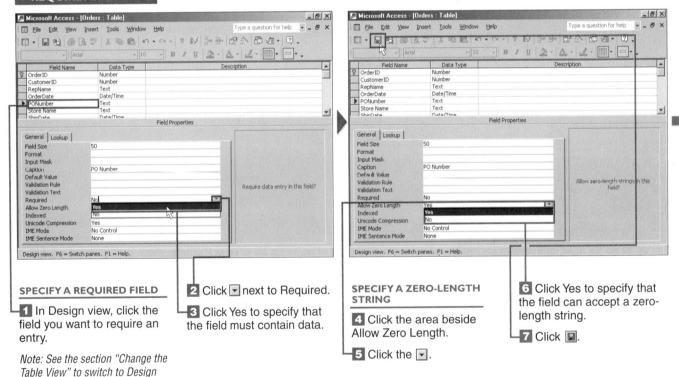

SPECIFY A REQUIRED FIELD

1 In Design view, click the field you want to require an entry.

Note: See the section "Change the Table View" to switch to Design view.

2 Click ▾ next to Required.

3 Click Yes to specify that the field must contain data.

SPECIFY A ZERO-LENGTH STRING

4 Click the area beside Allow Zero Length.

5 Click the ▾.

6 Click Yes to specify that the field can accept a zero-length string.

7 Click 🖫.

What is the difference between a null value and a zero-length string?

✔ A null value indicates that you do not know the information for the field. If the field is not set to require data, you can enter a null value by pressing Enter, which leaves the cell blank and allows you to move to the next field. A zero-length string indicates that no data exists for the field.

I set a field in my table to require data and accept zero-length strings. Are these properties also used in my forms?

✔ Yes. Properties you specify for a table also apply to forms that use data from the table. Make sure you set the properties for a table before using the table to create a form.

Why do I not see the entry for Allow Zero Length in the Design property boxes?

✔ You can set the zero length for only text fields, memo, and hyperlink fields, not numeric or date/time fields. You can require entries for these fields, but they cannot accept zero-length entries.

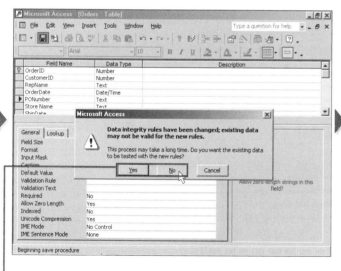

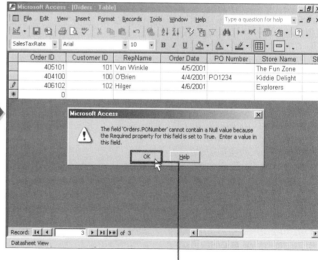

■ A dialog box appears, asking if you want to check if the field contains data for all existing records.

8 Click Yes to check the field or No to avoid checking the fields.

■ If you click Yes, Access checks the current data. If the contents do not meet the requirements, you see an error message allowing you to fix the field content.

■ The field now requires an entry. If you try to skip making an entry, a dialog box appears.

9 Click OK to clear the error message. Then type an entry or enter a zero value ("").

ADD A VALIDATION RULE

You can add a validation rule to a field to help reduce errors when entering data. A field that uses a validation rule can accept only data that meets certain requirements.

Access automatically sets rules based on the data type of the field. For example, you cannot type text in a field that has a Number data type. You can use a validation rule to set more specific rules. For example, you can type <50 so that users do not type a value more than 50 in the field.

Access displays an error message if the data you type does not meet the requirements of the field. You can specify the error message you want Access to display. The error message can contain up to 255 characters. If you do not specify an error message, Access displays a standard error message.

When you add a validation rule, you can check to see if the existing data in the field meets the requirements of the new rule. Access notifies you if any existing data violates the new rule.

ADD A VALIDATION RULE

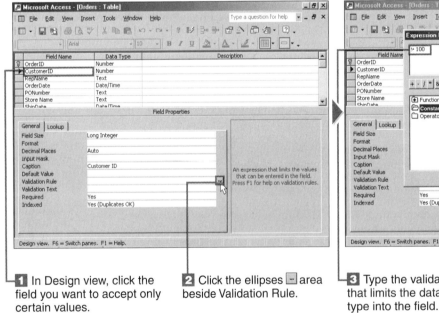

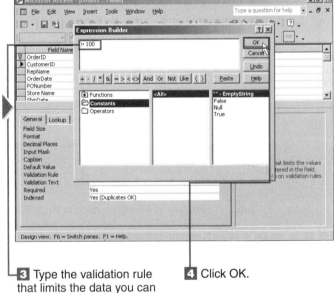

1 In Design view, click the field you want to accept only certain values.

Note: See the section "Change the Table View" to switch to Design view.

2 Click the ellipses ⸱⸱⸱ area beside Validation Rule.

3 Type the validation rule that limits the data you can type into the field.

4 Click OK.

What types of validation rules can I use?

✔ Examples of validation rules include the following:

<1000	Entry must be less than 1000
>M	Entry must begin with M or a letter after M
<>0	Entry cannot be zero
Between 100 and 200	Entry must be between 100 and 200
USA or Canada	Entry must be USA or Canada
Like "????"	Entry must have 4 characters
Like "##"	Entry must have 2 numbers

How do I build the expression?

✔ You build the expression by clicking the appropriate operators to make the comparison and by typing any text or values against which to compare the entry.

What type of error message should I create?

✔ You should create an error message that explains exactly why the data violates the validation rule. For example, the error message "You must enter a number between 0 and 9" is more informative than the message "Data Rejected."

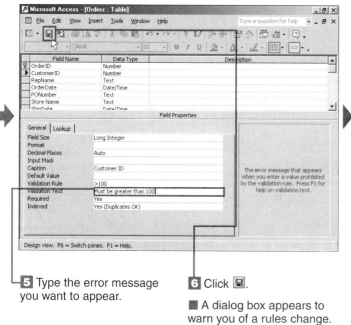

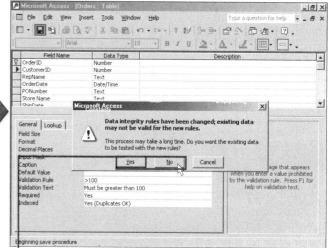

5 Type the error message you want to appear.

6 Click 🔲.

■ A dialog box appears to warn you of a rules change.

7 Click Yes to check the existing data and No if you do not want to check the existing data.

■ If you click Yes, Access tells you whether the current data violates the new rule.

■ When you type data that does not meet the field requirements, the step 5 error message appears.

■ To clear an error message, click OK and then type an entry that is within the specified validation rule(s).

CREATE A YES/NO FIELD

You can create a field that accepts only one of two values, such as Yes or No. Creating a Yes/No field is useful when a field in your table requires a simple answer. For example, a table that stores product information could contain a Yes/No field that indicates whether you have discontinued a product.

You can choose one of three available formats for a Yes/No field: Yes/No, True/False, or On/Off.

Access offers three ways to display data in a Yes/No field. The Check Box option displays a check box to indicate a value, such as Yes or No. The Text Box option displays a text value, such as "Yes" or "No." The

Combo Box option displays a text value, such as "Yes" or "No," and allows you to select the value you want from a drop-down list.

When you display your table in the Datasheet view, the Yes/No field displays the options you selected.

CREATE A YES/NO FIELD

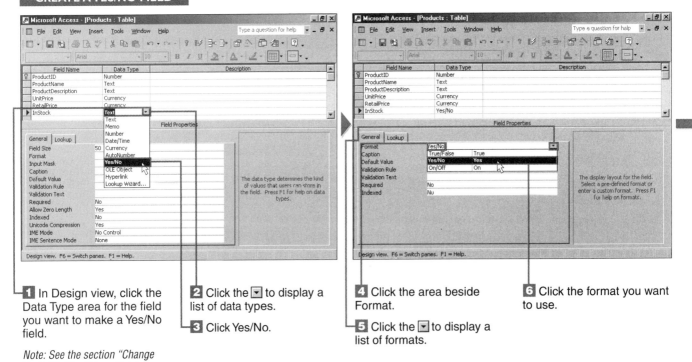

1 In Design view, click the Data Type area for the field you want to make a Yes/No field.

Note: See the section "Change the Table View" to switch to Design view.

2 Click the ▾ to display a list of data types.

3 Click Yes/No.

4 Click the area beside Format.

5 Click the ▾ to display a list of formats.

6 Click the format you want to use.

When would I use the True/False format?

✔ You often use the True/False format to determine if an action is required. For example, you can use a True/False format to indicate whether you should send mailings, such as newsletters, to a client.

How can I speed up the entry of data in a Yes/No field?

✔ By default, Access displays the No value in Yes/No fields. If most of your records require a Yes value, you can change the default value to Yes. See the section "Add a Default Value" for more information.

In the Datasheet view, why does the Combo Box drop-down list not display any values?

✔ You must specify the values you want the drop-down list to display. In the Design view, click the Lookup tab and then click the area beside Row Source Type. Click the arrow that appears and then select Value List. Click the area beside Row Source and then type the values you want to display in the drop-down list, separated by a semicolon. For example, type **Yes;No**.

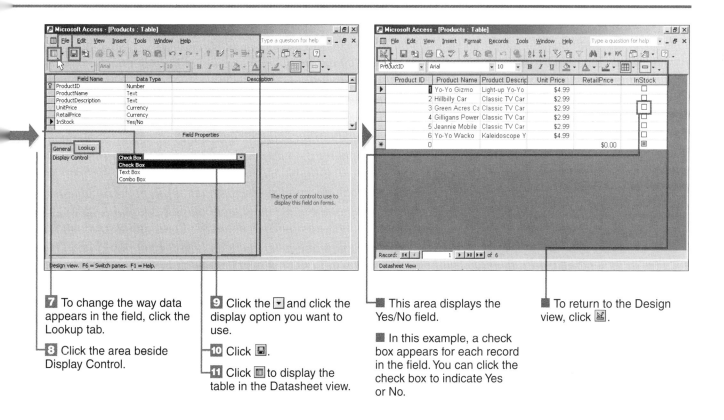

7 To change the way data appears in the field, click the Lookup tab.

8 Click the area beside Display Control.

9 Click the 🔽 and click the display option you want to use.

10 Click 🔲.

11 Click 🖳 to display the table in the Datasheet view.

■ This area displays the Yes/No field.

■ In this example, a check box appears for each record in the field. You can click the check box to indicate Yes or No.

■ To return to the Design view, click 🔲.

CREATE A LOOKUP COLUMN

Y ou can create a list of values, called a lookup column, that gives you a choice when entering information in a field. This can save you time because you do not have to type the values for each record.

Creating a lookup column is very useful if you repeatedly enter the same values in a field. For example, if you always use one of three methods to ship your orders, you can create a lookup column that displays the three shipping methods, such as US Mail, UPS Ground, or Express.

You can enter the values you want to appear in the lookup column using the Lookup Wizard or you can specify a table to use for the values.

The Lookup Wizard displays the name of the field that offers the lookup column. If you want the field to display a different field name, you can enter a new name.

CREATE A LOOKUP COLUMN

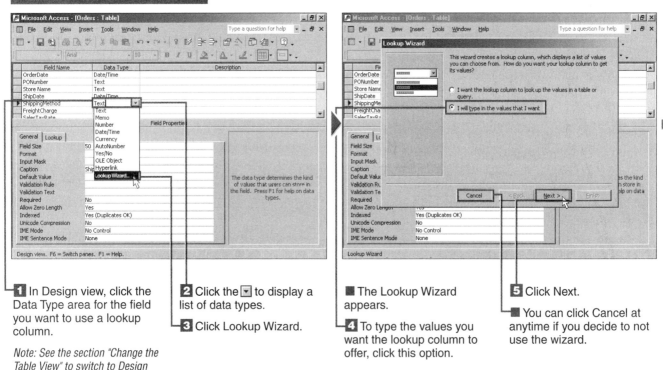

1 In Design view, click the Data Type area for the field you want to use a lookup column.

Note: See the section "Change the Table View" to switch to Design View.

2 Click the ▼ to display a list of data types.

3 Click Lookup Wizard.

■ The Lookup Wizard appears.

4 To type the values you want the lookup column to offer, click this option.

5 Click Next.

■ You can click Cancel at anytime if you decide to not use the wizard.

How can I ensure that users enter a value only from the lookup column?

✔ You can have Access display an error message when a user enters a value that is not displayed in the lookup column. In the Design view, click the field that offers the lookup column, click the Lookup tab, and then click the area beside Limit To List. Click the arrow that appears and then select Yes.

Can I change the values in an existing lookup column?

✔ Yes. In the Design view, click the field that offers the lookup column and then click the Lookup tab. The area beside Row Source displays the values that currently appear in the lookup column. You can delete, edit, or add values in this area. You must use a semicolon (;) to separate the values.

Can I create a lookup column that uses values from a table or query in my database?

✔ Yes. In the Lookup Wizard, choose the I want the lookup column to look up the values in a table or query option (O changes to ●).

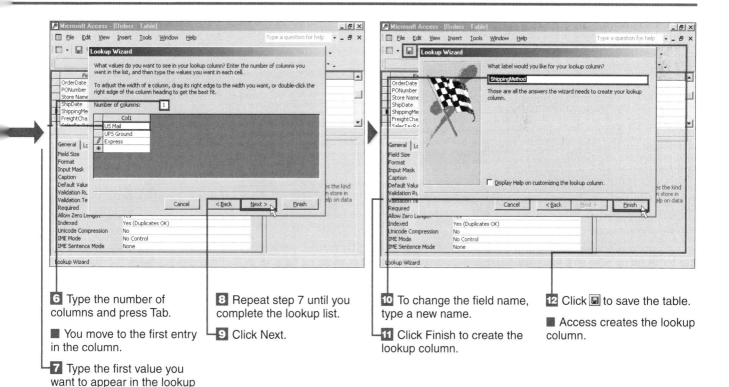

6 Type the number of columns and press Tab.

■ You move to the first entry in the column.

7 Type the first value you want to appear in the lookup column and press Tab.

8 Repeat step 7 until you complete the lookup list.

9 Click Next.

10 To change the field name, type a new name.

11 Click Finish to create the lookup column.

12 Click 🖫 to save the table.

■ Access creates the lookup column.

USE A LOOKUP COLUMN TO ENTER DATA

When users display your table in the Datasheet view, they can display the lookup column and select the value they want to enter in the field. Entering information by selecting a value from a lookup column can help prevent errors, such as spelling mistakes. Using a lookup column can also ensure that users enter the correct type of information in a field.

You can tell which fields have a lookup column because a drop-down arrow appears next to the field when you move to that field to enter data. You can display and then select the data for the field from the list.

If a lookup column does not display the value you want to use, you can type a different value in the field. To hide a lookup column

you displayed without selecting a value, you can click outside the lookup column. Then you can type in any entry you want.

For information on creating a lookup column, see the section "Create a Lookup Column."

USE A LOOKUP COLUMN TO ENTER DATA

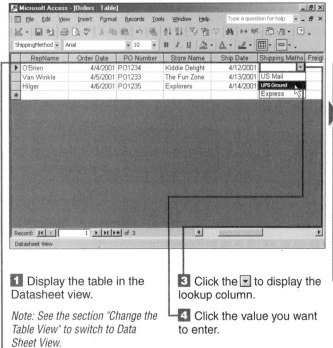

1 Display the table in the Datasheet view.

Note: See the section "Change the Table View" to switch to Data Sheet View.

2 Click a cell in the field that offers the lookup column.

3 Click the ▾ to display the lookup column.

4 Click the value you want to enter.

■ Access enters the value you selected from the lookup column.

CREATE AN INDEX

You can create an index for a field to speed up searching and sorting information in the field. Access uses the index to find the location of information.

Index the fields you frequently search. For example, in a table containing client information, index the Last Name field because you are likely to search for a client using the last name.

You can specify if the field you want to index can contain duplicates. The Yes (Duplicates OK) option allows you to enter the same data in more than one cell in a field. The Yes (No Duplicates) option does not allow you to enter the same data in more than one cell in a field. Use the first option if you enter unique values in this field, such as social security

numbers. Use the second option if the field may contain duplicates, such as last name that you may leave duplicated within the database table.

The primary key, which uniquely identifies each record in a table, is automatically indexed. The index for the primary key is automatically set to Yes (No Duplicates).

CREATE AN INDEX

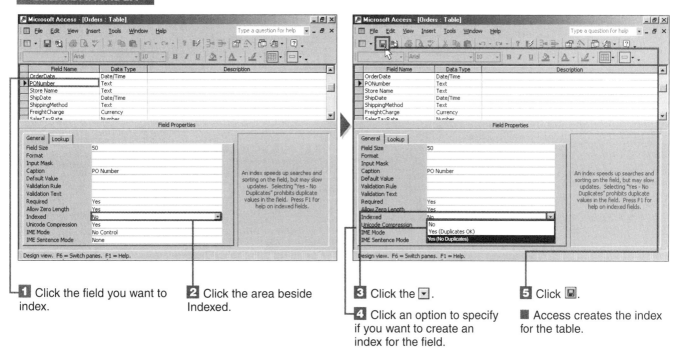

1 Click the field you want to index.

2 Click the area beside Indexed.

3 Click the ⏷.

4 Click an option to specify if you want to create an index for the field.

5 Click 🔲.

■ Access creates the index for the table.

SET THE PRIMARY KEY

A primary key is one or more fields that uniquely identify each record in a table. Each table in a database should have a primary key. You should not change the primary key in a table that has a relationship with another table in the database.

There are three types of primary keys you can create — AutoNumber, single-field, and multiple-field.

The AutoNumber primary key field automatically assigns a unique number to each record you add. When you create a table, Access can create an AutoNumber primary key field for you.

A single-field primary key is a field that contains a unique value for each record, such as a Social Security number.

A multiple-field primary key is two or more fields that together make up a unique value for each record.

Access does not allow you to enter the same value in the primary key field more than once. If you create a primary key for a field that already contains data, Access displays a warning message if the field contains duplicate values or an empty cell.

SET THE PRIMARY KEY

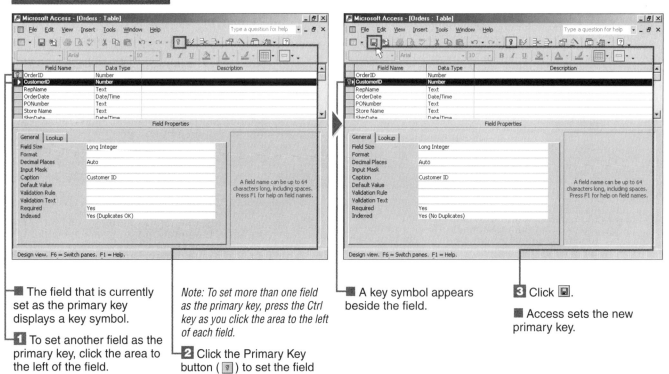

■ The field that is currently set as the primary key displays a key symbol.

1 To set another field as the primary key, click the area to the left of the field.

Note: To set more than one field as the primary key, press the Ctrl key as you click the area to the left of each field.

2 Click the Primary Key button (💡) to set the field as the primary key.

■ A key symbol appears beside the field.

3 Click 🖫.

■ Access sets the new primary key.

DISPLAY A SUBDATASHEET

When viewing the records in a table, you can display a subdatasheet to view and edit related data from another table.

Access displays subdatasheets only for tables that have a relationship. If you used the Database Wizard to create your database, the wizard automatically defined relationships between tables for you. You can

also set relationships yourself. See the section "Define Relationships Between Tables" for more information.

A plus sign appears beside each record that has related data. You can click a plus sign to display the related data in a subdatasheet. For example, a table containing customer information may be related to a table containing

product orders. When viewing the customer table, you can click the plus sign beside the record for a customer. A subdatasheet appears, displaying information about the products the customer has ordered.

When you finish viewing and editing the data in a subdatasheet, you can hide the subdatasheet to remove it from your screen.

DISPLAY A SUBDATASHEET

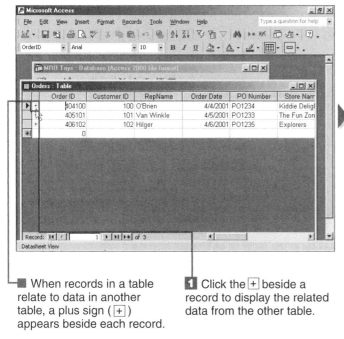

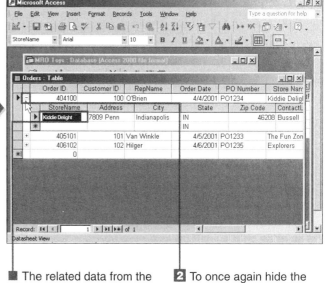

■ When records in a table relate to data in another table, a plus sign (+) appears beside each record.

1 Click the + beside a record to display the related data from the other table.

■ The related data from the other table appears. You can review and edit the data.

2 To once again hide the related data, click the − beside the record.

■ Access hides the related data.

DEFINE RELATIONSHIPS BETWEEN TABLES

You can create relationships between tables to bring together related information. Relationships between tables are essential for creating a form, report, or query that uses information from more than one table in a database.

For example, one table in the database can contain the names and addresses of your clients, while the other table can contain the orders placed by these clients. After you define a relationship between the two tables, you can create a query to have Access display client names and their current orders.

The Relationships window shows the relationships that exist between the tables in your database. You can add tables to this window.

You establish a relationship by identifying matching fields in two tables. The fields do not need to have the same name, but they must use the same data type and contain the same kind of information. You usually relate the primary key in one table to a matching field in the other table. For more information on primary keys, see the section "Set the Primary Key."

DEFINE RELATIONSHIPS BETWEEN TABLES

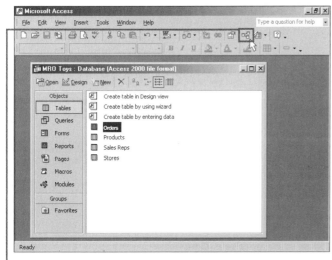

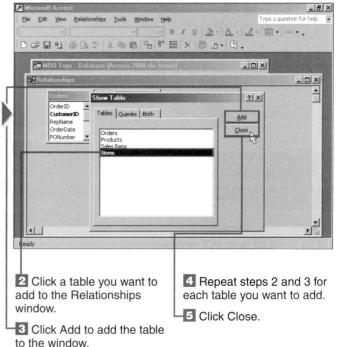

1 In the Database window, click the Relationship button (⊞) to display the Relationships window.

■ If you do not see this button, make sure the Database window is open and no other windows are open on the screen.

■ If the tables contain no relationships, the Show Table dialog box appears.

2 Click a table you want to add to the Relationships window.

3 Click Add to add the table to the window.

4 Repeat steps 2 and 3 for each table you want to add.

5 Click Close.

Why do I see the Relationships window instead of the Show Table dialog box?

✔ If any relationships exist between the tables in the database, a box for each table appears in the window. If you use the Database Wizard to create your database, the wizard automatically creates relationships between tables.

How do I remove a table from the Relationships window?

✔ Click the box for the table you want to remove and then press Delete. This table and any relationships defined for the table are removed from the Relationships window, but not from the database.

How can I view the relationships for just one table?

✔ Click the Clear Layout button (☒) to remove all the tables from the Relationships window. Click Yes in the dialog box that appears and then perform steps 2 through 4 in this section to add a table to the Relationships window. Close the Show Table dialog box and then click the Show Direct Relationships button (☷) to view the relationships for the table.

How can I quickly display all the relationships in the database?

✔ To view all the relationships in the database, click the Show All Relationships button (☷).

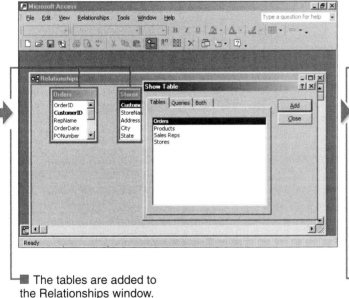

■ The tables are added to the Relationships window.

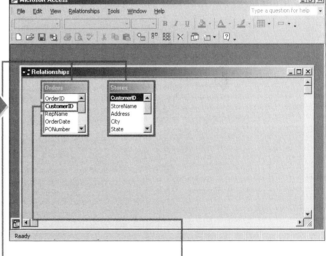

■ The Relationships window displays a box for each table. Each box displays the fields for one table.

■ The primary key in each table appears in bold.

CONTINUED ▶

DEFINE RELATIONSHIPS BETWEEN TABLES (CONTINUED)

The type of relationship Access creates between two tables depends on the fields you use to create the relationship.

If only one field in the relationship is a primary key, Access creates a one-to-many relationship. In this type of relationship, each record in a table relates to one or more records in the other table. For example, if one table stores the names of clients and the other table stores orders, the one-to-many relationship allows each client to have more than one order. This is the most common type of relationship.

If both fields in the relationship are primary keys, Access creates a one-to-one relationship. In this type of relationship, each record in a table relates to just one record in the other table. For example, if one table stores available rental cars and the other table stores the dates the cars are reserved, the one-to-one relationship allows each car to have only one reserve date.

DEFINE RELATIONSHIPS BETWEEN TABLES (CONTINUED)

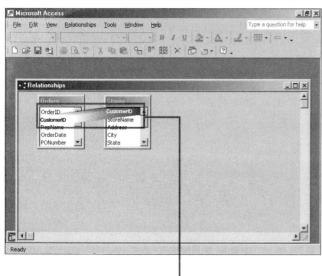

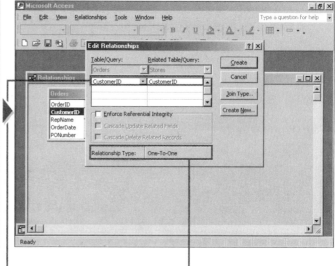

6 Position the ⊳ over the field you want to use to form a relationship with another table.

7 Drag the field over the second table until a small box appears over the matching field.

■ The Edit Relationships dialog box appears.

■ This area displays the names of the tables you are creating a relationship between and the names of the matching fields.

■ This area displays the relationship type.

What is referential integrity?

✔ Referential integrity is a set of rules that prevent you from changing or deleting a record if matching records exist in a related table. Access provides two options that let you override the rules of referential integrity but still protect data from accidental changes or deletions. The Cascade Update Related Fields option allows Access to update matching data in all related records when you change the data in the primary key. The Cascade Delete Related Records option allows Access to delete matching records in related tables when you delete a record.

Can I change the referential integrity options later?

✔ Yes. To redisplay the Edit Relationships dialog box so you can change these options, double-click the line representing the relationship you want to change.

How do I delete a relationship?

✔ In the Relationships window, click the line representing the relationship you want to delete and then press Delete.

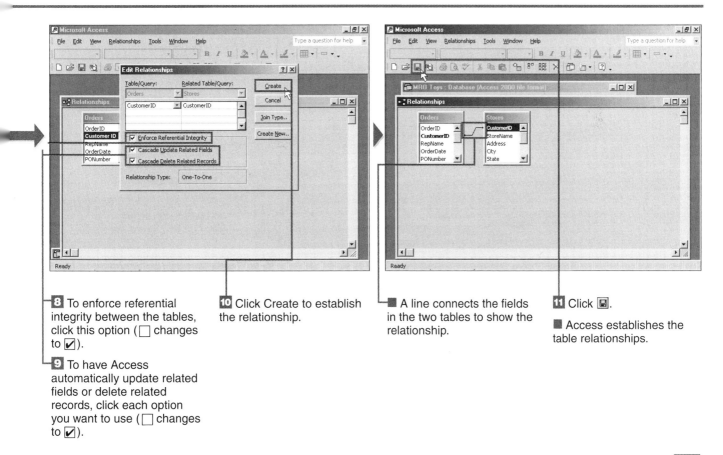

8 To enforce referential integrity between the tables, click this option (☐ changes to ☑).

9 To have Access automatically update related fields or delete related records, click each option you want to use (☐ changes to ☑).

10 Click Create to establish the relationship.

■ A line connects the fields in the two tables to show the relationship.

11 Click 🖫.

■ Access establishes the table relationships.

CREATE A FORM USING A WIZARD

A form presents information from a database table in an attractive format. You can use a form to add, edit, and delete information in a table. You may find that a form is easier to work with than a table. You can also create a form for queries.

The Form Wizard helps you create a form that suits your needs. The wizard asks you a series of questions and then sets up a form based on your answers.

To start, the Form Wizard allows you to select the table containing

the fields you want to include in the form.

After you create a table, you can select the fields you want to include from a list in the table. A form can include all or only some of the fields in a table.

CREATE A FORM USING A WIZARD

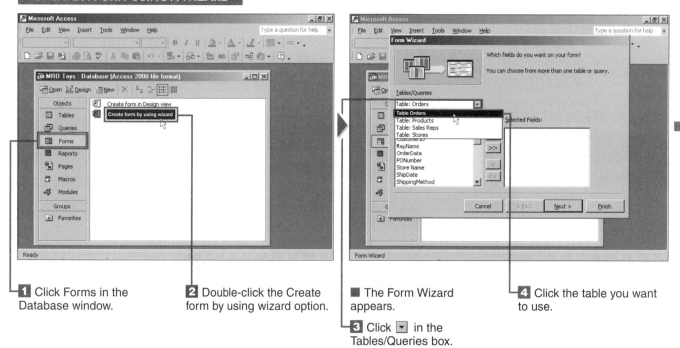

1 Click Forms in the Database window.

2 Double-click the Create form by using wizard option.

■ The Form Wizard appears.

3 Click ▼ in the Tables/Queries box.

4 Click the table you want to use.

Can I create a form that uses fields from more than one table?

✔ Yes. Perform steps 1 through 7 in this section to select the fields you want to include from one table. Then repeat steps 5 through 7 until you have all the tables and fields you want to include. To use more than one table, relationships must exist between the tables. For information on defining relationships between tables, see Chapter 25.

How do I remove a field that I accidentally added?

✔ To remove a field, double-click the field in the Selected Fields list. To remove all the fields at once, click ⟨⟨.

In what order do the fields I select appear in the form?

✔ The fields appear in the form in the order you select them. You can rearrange the fields after you create the form. See the section "Rearrange the Form" for more information.

Is there another way to start the Form Wizard?

✔ Yes. In the Database window, click Forms and then click the New button (⊞). Click Form Wizard and click OK.

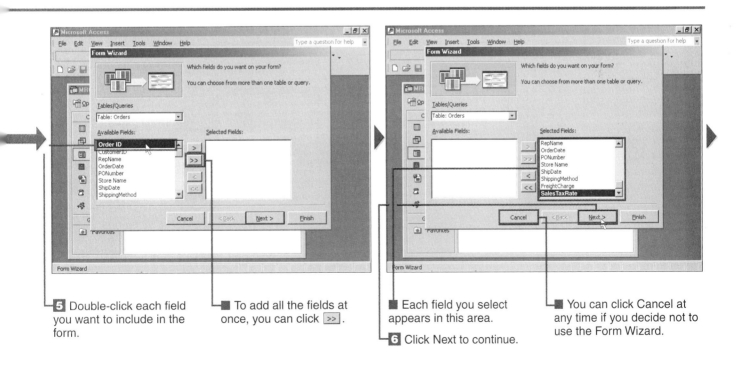

5 Double-click each field you want to include in the form.

■ To add all the fields at once, you can click ⟩⟩.

■ Each field you select appears in this area.

6 Click Next to continue.

■ You can click Cancel at any time if you decide not to use the Form Wizard.

CONTINUED

CREATE A FORM USING A WIZARD
(CONTINUED)

After you select all the fields for your table, you can select which layout you prefer for the form. The layout of a form determines the arrangement of information on the form.

The Columnar layout displays one record at a time and lines up information in a column. The Tabular layout displays multiple records and presents information in rows and columns. The Datasheet layout displays multiple records and is similar to the Datasheet view for tables. The Justified layout displays one record at a time and aligns information along both the left and right sides of a form.

You can apply a style to the form, such as Blends, International, or Stone. Most styles use colors and patterns to enhance the form's appearance.

After you select a layout for your form, Access requires that you name the form. The name, which appears at the top of the form and in the Forms area of the Database window, can contain up to 64 characters.

CREATE A FORM USING A WIZARD (CONTINUED)

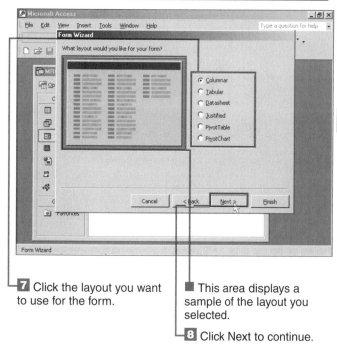

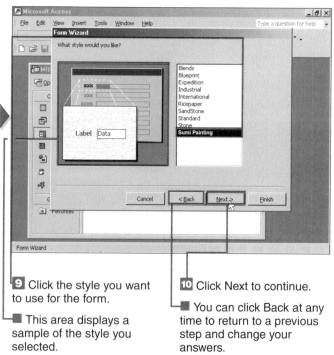

7 Click the layout you want to use for the form.

■ This area displays a sample of the layout you selected.

8 Click Next to continue.

9 Click the style you want to use for the form.

■ This area displays a sample of the style you selected.

10 Click Next to continue.

■ You can click Back at any time to return to a previous step and change your answers.

Is there a faster way to create a form?

✔ Yes. You can use an AutoForm to quickly create a form based on one table in your database. In the Database window, click Forms and then click ⬛. Click the AutoForm you want: Columnar, Tabular, Datasheet, PivotTable, or PivotChart. Click ⬛ in the tables box and then select the table that you want to supply the information for the form. Then click OK.

How do I rename an existing form?

✔ In the Database window, click Forms and then right-click the form you want to rename. From the menu that appears, select Rename. Type a new name for the form and then press Enter.

Can I change the style of an existing form?

✔ You can use the AutoFormat feature to change the style at a later date. To do so, display the form you want to change in the Design view and then click the AutoFormat button (⬛). In the AutoFormat dialog box, select the style you want to use and then click OK. For more information on the AutoFormat feature, see the section "AutoFormat a Form."

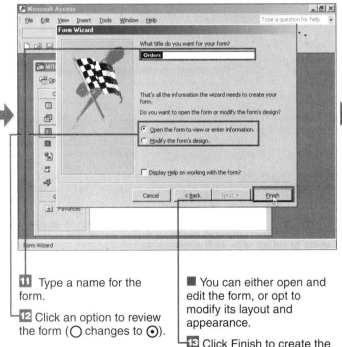

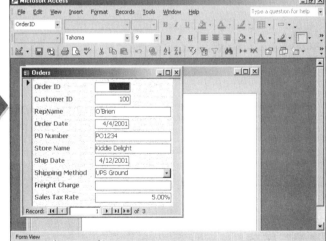

■ Type a name for the form.

■ Click an option to review the form (○ changes to ⊙).

■ You can either open and edit the form, or opt to modify its layout and appearance.

■ Click Finish to create the form.

■ The form appears, displaying the field names you selected and the first record.

OPEN A FORM

You can open a form and display its contents on your screen to review and make changes to the form.

When you double-click a form, you can open the Form view. The Form view usually displays one record at a time in an organized and attractive format. This view is useful for entering, editing, and reviewing records. You can also

delete records that you no longer need from this view.

You can also open a form in Design View. The Design view displays the structure of a form and lets you customize the appearance of a form to make the form easier to use. You can also use this view to change the contents of a form — that is, which fields from the underlying database table are included.

You can find information on changing the form design in several of the sections in this chapter including "Add a Field to a Form," "AutoFormat a Form," and "Change a Form Control."

When you finish working with a form, you can close the form to remove it from your screen.

OPEN A FORM

OPEN A FORM IN FORM VIEW

1 Click Forms in the Database window to display a list of the forms in the database.

2 Double-click the form you want to open.

■ The form opens in Form view.

■ You can make any changes to the records.

Note: To add, delete, or edit a record, see the section "Add or Delete a Record."

3 When you finish using the form, click the Close button (🗵) to close the form.

When do I need to save the form?

✔ Unlike changes made to records, design changes are not automatically saved. If you open a form in Design view and make changes, you can click the Save button (🖫)to save the form. If you close the form in Design view without saving, you are prompted to save it.

What other views can I use for forms?

✔ The Datasheet view displays all the records in rows and columns. Each row displays the information for one record. The field names appear directly above the first record. You can enter, edit, and review records in this view.

Can I change from one view to another after I open a form?

✔ Yes. You can change from Form View to Design View using the view button. In Form View, you see the Design view button. Clicking it changes to Design view. The reverse is also true: In Design View, you see the Form View button. You can click it to change to Form View.

To select a different view, click the 🔽 next to the view button and then select the view you want.

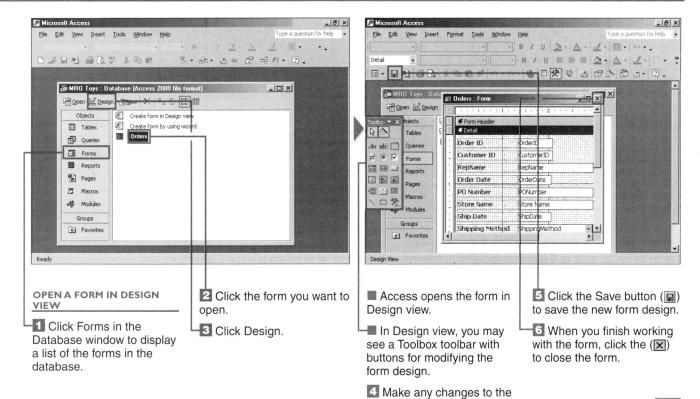

OPEN A FORM IN DESIGN VIEW

1 Click Forms in the Database window to display a list of the forms in the database.

2 Click the form you want to open.

3 Click Design.

■ Access opens the form in Design view.

■ In Design view, you may see a Toolbox toolbar with buttons for modifying the form design.

4 Make any changes to the form design.

5 Click the Save button (🖫) to save the new form design.

6 When you finish working with the form, click the (☒) to close the form.

MOVE THROUGH RECORDS WITH A FORM

You can easily move through the records in a form to review or edit information. Any changes you make to the information in a form also appear in the table(s) you use to create the form.

Access displays the number of the current record and the total number of records in the form. Access also displays buttons that you can use to move through the records. You can quickly move to the first, last, previous, or next record. If you know the number of the record you want to view, you can quickly move to that record.

Can I use the keyboard to quickly move through records?

✔ Yes. Press the Page Up key to move to the previous record. Press the Page Down key to move to the next record. Press Ctrl and the Up Arrow key to move to the first record, or Press Ctrl and the Down Arrow key to move to the last record.

MOVE THROUGH RECORDS WITH A FORM

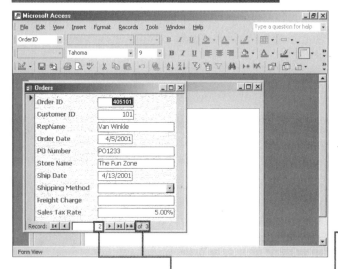

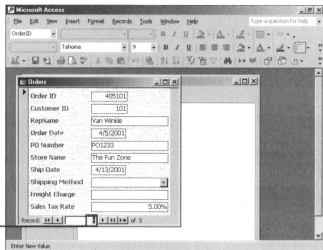

USING FORM BUTTONS

1 Click either First Record (⏮), Previous Record (◀), Next Record (▶), or Last Record (⏭).

■ Access moves to the appropriate record.

■ You can view the number of the current record and the total number of records here.

GO TO A SPECIFIC RECORD

1 Click and drag over the current record number.

2 Type the number of the record to which you want to go.

3 Press Enter.

■ Access displays the record.

EDIT DATA USING A FORM

A ccess enables you to edit the data in a form, which lets you correct a mistake or update the data in a record.

You can insert new data in a cell. The flashing insertion point in a cell indicates where Access inserts new data. You can also delete all or part of the data you no longer need from a cell.

Access remembers the changes you make to a record. If you make a

mistake while editing data in a cell, you can use the Undo feature to immediately reverse the changes in the current cell.

You do not have to save the changes you make. When you move from the record you are editing to another record, Access automatically saves your changes.

I changed a record by mistake. How do I change it back?

✔ If you move the insertion point to another cell and then click the Undo button (⟲), Access reverts your record to its original state.

EDIT DATA USING A FORM

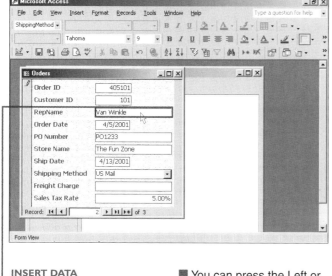

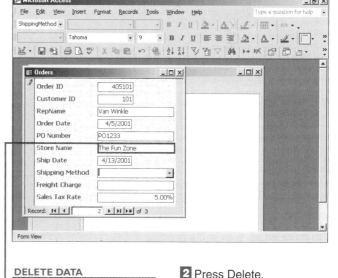

INSERT DATA

1 Click the location in the cell where you want to insert data.

■ A flashing insertion point appears in the cell.

■ You can press the Left or Right arrow key to move the insertion point.

2 Type the data you want to insert.

■ Access adds the data.

DELETE DATA

1 Click and drag ⟍ over the data you want to delete.

2 Press Delete.

■ Access deletes the data.

ADD OR DELETE A RECORD

You can use a form to add a record to the table. Access adds the new record to the table you used to create the form. For example, you may want to add information about a new client.

Access checks to make sure the data you enter in each field is valid for the specified data type and field properties. If an entry is invalid, Access notifies you before you

move to the next field or record. For example, Access tells you if you try to enter text in a Number field.

You can delete a record to remove information you no longer need. Deleting records saves storage space on your computer and keeps the database from becoming cluttered with unnecessary information.

When you delete a record using a form, you may also want to delete any related data in other tables in the database. For example, if you use a form to delete a company from your supplier table, you may also want to delete information about the products the company supplies from your product table.

ADD OR DELETE A RECORD

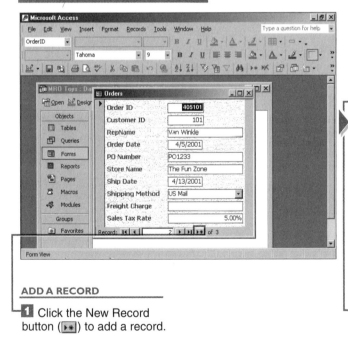

ADD A RECORD

1 Click the New Record button (▶*) to add a record.

■ A blank form appears.

2 Type the data for the first field.

3 Press Tab.

4 Repeat steps 2 and 3 until you finish typing all the data for the record.

Note: Access automatically saves each new record.

■ Access adds the record.

Can I restore a record I accidentally deleted?

✔ When you delete a record from the database, you cannot undo the deletion. If you have a backup copy of the database, you can use the backup to restore a deleted record.

Can I ensure that Access removes related data in the database when I delete a record?

✔ Yes. You can specify that if you delete a record from one table, Access removes related records from another table. To do this, you must establish a relationship between two tables. See Chapter 25 for more information on table relationships.

When I add a record using a form, do I also have to add the record to the table?

✔ No. When you use a form to enter data, Access automatically adds the data to the appropriate table — that is, the table you selected when you created the form. When you edit data in a form, you are actually editing the data in the table. The form is a template that simply organizes the data in a record in a more visually appealing way.

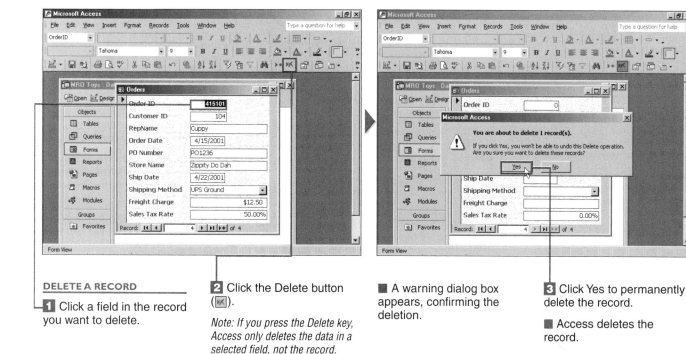

DELETE A RECORD

1 Click a field in the record you want to delete.

2 Click the Delete button (✕).

Note: If you press the Delete key, Access only deletes the data in a selected field, not the record.

■ A warning dialog box appears, confirming the deletion.

3 Click Yes to permanently delete the record.

■ Access deletes the record.

ADD A FIELD TO A FORM

If you neglected to add a field from the table when you created a form, you can add the field. For example, you may want to add a telephone number field to a form that displays client addresses.

Before you can add a field to a form, you must display the form in the Design view. Access enables you to add a field from the table you used to create the form.

Access uses labels and text boxes to display information on a form. When you add a field, Access adds a label and its corresponding text box for you.

Access automatically uses the correct data type and field properties for a field you add to a form. For example, if you add a field that has the Yes/No data type with the Check Box option, Access adds a check box to the form instead of a text box.

You may need to resize a form to make room for a field you add. For information on resizing a form, see the section "Change a Form Control."

ADD A FIELD TO A FORM

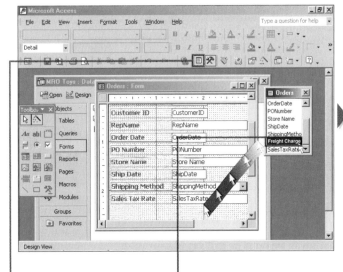

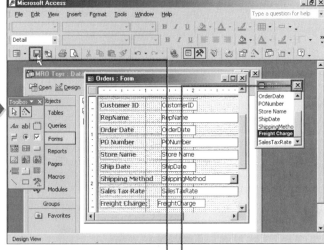

■1 Open the form you want to change in the Design view.

Note: See the section "Open a Form" for help on opening a form in Design view.

■2 Click the Field List button (▦).

■ A list of fields from the table you used to create the form displays.

■3 Click ⬚ over the field you want to add.

■4 Drag the field to where you want it on the form.

■ Access adds the label and corresponding text box for the field to the form.

Note: You may need to move or resize the label or text box. See the section "Change a Form Control" for more information.

■5 Click ✕ to hide the box displaying the list of fields.

■6 Click (▦) to save the form.

AUTOFORMAT A FORM

You can choose to AutoFormat your form to instantly change the overall look of a form. AutoFormatting changes the background and text colors of a form.

Before you can AutoFormat your form, you must display the form in the Design view. You must also select the form to ensure that

Access applies the AutoFormatting to the entire form. You might consider using the same AutoFormatting for all the forms in your database to give the database a more consistent appearance.

You can choose from several AutoFormats including Blends, Industrial, International, and Stone. As mentioned, each one changes

the background color and color of the form controls. Each AutoFormat also uses different font choices for the form controls. Access allows you to preview a sample of the AutoFormat you select before you apply it to a form, which can help you determine if the AutoFormat suits your needs.

AUTOFORMAT A FORM

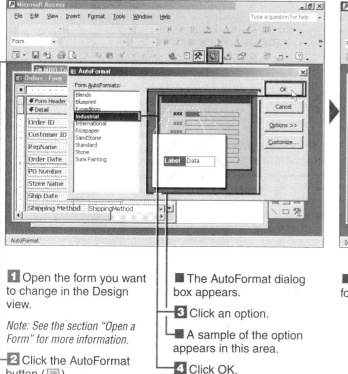

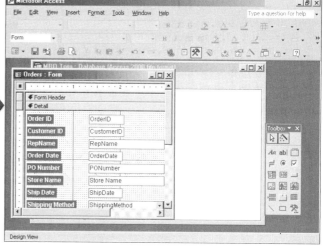

1 Open the form you want to change in the Design view.

Note: See the section "Open a Form" for more information.

2 Click the AutoFormat button (📷).

■ The AutoFormat dialog box appears.

3 Click an option.

■ A sample of the option appears in this area.

4 Click OK.

■ The form displays the new format.

CHANGE A FORM CONTROL

A *control* is an item on a form, such as a label that displays a field name or a text box that displays data from a field. You can move, resize, or delete a control to make the form easier to use.

You can change the location of a control on a form. You can move a label and its corresponding text box together or individually.

You can change the size of a control. Larger controls allow you to display longer entries. You may want to resize a text box that displays long Web page addresses.

When you move or resize a control, Access automatically aligns the control with the dots on the form, which enables you to neatly arrange controls on the form.

You can delete a control you no longer want on a form. Access allows you to delete just a label or a label and its corresponding text box.

Before you close a form, make sure you save the changes you made to the form. If you forget, Access reminds you to save.

CHANGE A FORM CONTROL

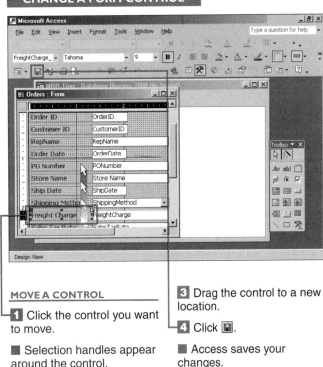

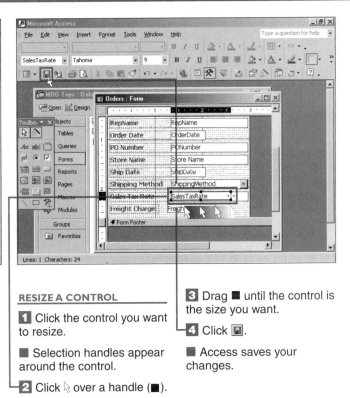

MOVE A CONTROL

■1 Click the control you want to move.

■ Selection handles appear around the control.

■2 Click ⌖ over the border of the control.

■3 Drag the control to a new location.

■4 Click 🖫.

■ Access saves your changes.

RESIZE A CONTROL

■1 Click the control you want to resize.

■ Selection handles appear around the control.

■2 Click ⌖ over a handle (■).

■3 Drag ■ until the control is the size you want.

■4 Click 🖫.

■ Access saves your changes.

Can I resize an entire form?

✔ Yes. Resizing a form is useful when you want to increase the space available for moving and resizing controls. Click and drag the ⬚ over an edge of the form until the form is the size you want.

If I delete a field from a form, is it deleted from the table? Is the data deleted?

✔ No. The field is not deleted from the table, only from the form. Also, the data is unaffected in the table.

How do I move, resize, or delete several controls at once?

✔ To select multiple controls, press the Shift key as you click each control.

Can I undo a change?

✔ Yes. You can undo it by clicking ⬚.

Can I move a label or text box individually?

✔ Yes. Click ⬚ over the large handle (■) at the top-left corner of the label or text box in step 3.

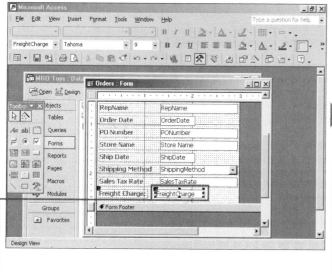

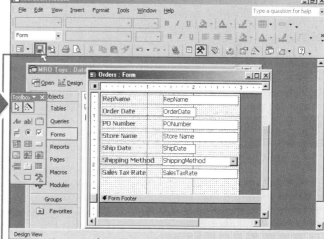

DELETE A CONTROL

1 Click the control you want to delete.

■ Selection handles appear around the control.

■ You can click a label to delete only the label or click a text box to delete the label and the corresponding text box.

2 Press Delete.

■ Access deletes the control.

3 Click ⬚.

■ Access saves your changes.

CHANGE THE APPEARANCE OF FORM CONTROLS

Y ou can change the font, size, style, and alignment of text in a control to customize the appearance of a form. You must display the form in the Design view before you can format the text in a control.

Access provides a list of fonts from which you can choose. The fonts appear in the list as they will appear in the control, which

enables you to preview a font before you select it.

You can increase or decrease the size of text in a control, which Access measures in points. There are 72 points in an inch.

You can use the Bold, Italic, and Underline features to change the style of text in a control. This can help you emphasize important information on a form.

Access automatically aligns text to the left and numbers to the right in a control. You can choose to align data to the left, to the right, or in the center of a control.

After you make changes to the form design, you must save the form to apply all of your changes.

CHANGE THE APPEARANCE OF FORM CONTROLS

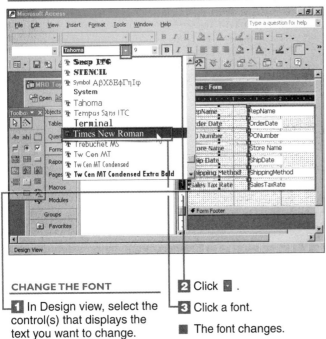

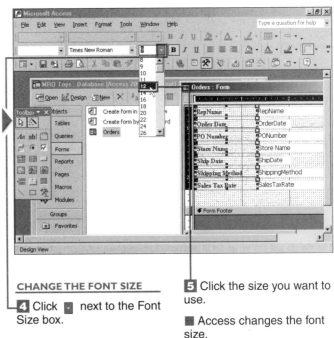

CHANGE THE FONT

1 In Design view, select the control(s) that displays the text you want to change.

Note: To open your form in Design view, see the section "Open a Form."

2 Click ▼.

3 Click a font.

■ The font changes.

CHANGE THE FONT SIZE

4 Click ▼ next to the Font Size box.

5 Click the size you want to use.

■ Access changes the font size.

My formatted text no longer fully displays in the control. Why not?

✔ Changing the font or size of the text may make the text too large to fully display in the control. To display all the text, you can resize the control. Click the control you want to resize. From the Format menu, select Size and then click To Fit.

How can I preview the form?

✔ To check the appearance of the form as you make changes, click the Form view button (Design) to see how the form will look. To change back to Design view, click the Design view button.

Can I format several controls at once?

✔ Yes. To select multiple controls, press the Shift key as you click each control. Most often, you want to maintain a consistent appearance for the controls, so save time by selecting all the controls you want to change and then make the change.

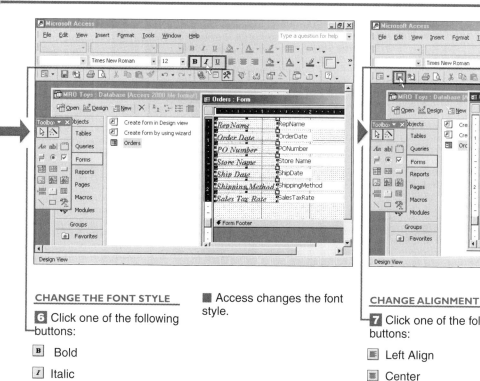

CHANGE THE FONT STYLE

6 Click one of the following buttons:

B Bold

I Italic

U Underline

■ Access changes the font style.

CHANGE ALIGNMENT

7 Click one of the following buttons:

▤ Left Align

▤ Center

▤ Right Align

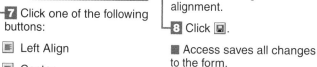

■ Access changes the alignment.

8 Click 🖫.

■ Access saves all changes to the form.

CHANGE FORM CONTROL COLORS AND BORDERS

You can change the background, text, and border colors of a control on a form. You can also change the width of a control's border. Changing the background and text colors of a control can help draw attention to important information on a form. Access provides several background and text colors from which to choose. You can change the color and width of a control's border to make the control stand out.

Before formatting a control, you must display the form in the Design view. When you change the colors and borders, make sure that your text remains legible and that the colors do not clash. Also remember that if you are printing a form using a black-and-white printer, any colors you add to the text, background, or border of a control appear as shades of gray.

Before you close a form, you must save your changes you made to the controls or Access does not apply them.

CHANGE FORM CONTROL COLORS AND BORDERS

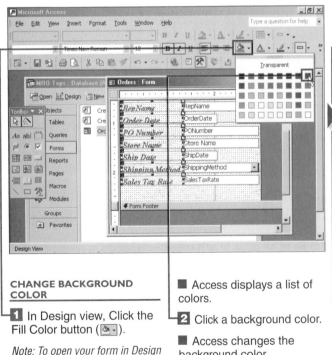

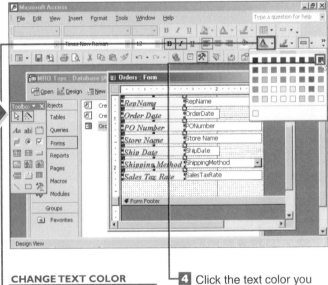

CHANGE BACKGROUND COLOR

■1 In Design view, Click the Fill Color button (⬛▾).

Note: To open your form in Design view, see the section "Open a Form."

■ Access displays a list of colors.

■2 Click a background color.

■ Access changes the background color.

CHANGE TEXT COLOR

■3 Click the Font/Fore Color button (A▾).

■ Access displays a list of colors.

■4 Click the text color you want to use.

■ Access changes the text color.

Is there another way to enhance the appearance of a control?

✔ Yes. You can make a control appear raised, sunken, or shadowed. Click the control you want to enhance. Click beside the Special Effect button (⬜) on the Formatting toolbar and then click the effect you want to use.

How can I quickly change the text color in a control?

✔ The Font/Fore Color button (🅰) on the Formatting toolbar displays the last text color you selected. To quickly add this color to text in a control, click the control you want to change and then click 🅰.

How do I apply the same formatting options to another control on the form?

✔ To save time, you can copy the formatting — not just the borders and colors, but also the font changes and alignment. Select the control with the formatting you want to copy, click the Format Painter button (🖌), and then click the control to which to copy the formatting.

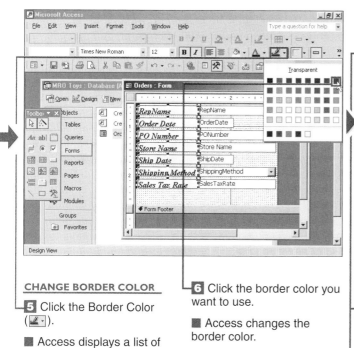

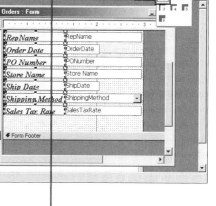

CHANGE BORDER COLOR

5 Click the Border Color (🖊).

■ Access displays a list of colors.

6 Click the border color you want to use.

■ Access changes the border color.

CHANGE BORDER WIDTH

7 Click the Border Width button (🔲).

■ A list of border widths displays.

8 Click the border width you want to use.

■ Access applies the new border to the control.

9 Click 🖫.

■ Access saves all changes to the form.

FIND DATA

You can search for records that contain specific data. You can search for data in tables, queries, and forms.

By default, Access performs a search of the current field. To perform a more advanced search, you can create a query. For more information, see the later sections in this chapter on creating queries.

You can specify how you want Access to search for data in a field. The Any Part of Field option allows you to find data anywhere in a field. For example, a search for smith finds Smithson and Macsmith. The Whole Field option allows you to find data that is exactly the same as the data you specify. For example, a search for smith finds Smith but not

Smithson. You can also choose the Start of Field option to find data only at the beginning of a field. For example, a search for smith finds Smithson but not Macsmith.

After you start the search, Access finds and highlights the first instance of the data. You can continue the search to find the next instance of the data.

FIND DATA

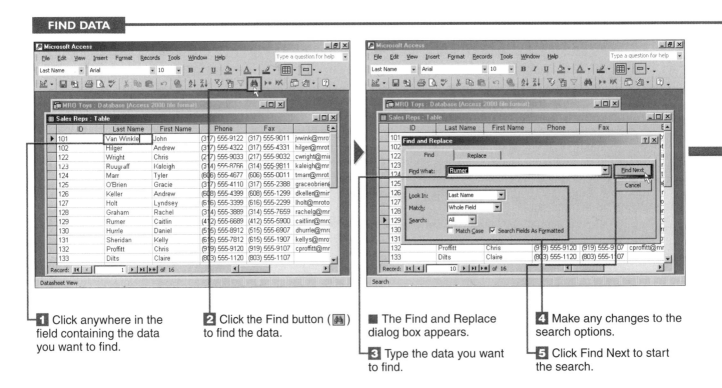

1 Click anywhere in the field containing the data you want to find.

2 Click the Find button (🔍) to find the data.

■ The Find and Replace dialog box appears.

3 Type the data you want to find.

4 Make any changes to the search options.

5 Click Find Next to start the search.

How do I specify a search direction?

✔ In the Find and Replace dialog box, click the Search 🔽 and click either Up or Down to search above or below the current record.

How can I have Access replace the data I find with new data?

✔ Perform steps 1 through 3 in this section and then click the Replace tab. In the Replace With text box, type the new data. Click Find Next. To replace the data Access finds with the new data, click Replace. To ignore the data and continue with the search, click Find Next.

Can I find data that matches the case of the data I specify?

✔ Yes. You can have Access find only data with exactly matching uppercase and lowercase letters. In the Find and Replace dialog box, click the Match Case option (☐ changes to ☑).

What if I selected the wrong field?

✔ The Look In box displays the current field. If this is not the field you want to search, click the 🔽 next to this list box and then click the appropriate field.

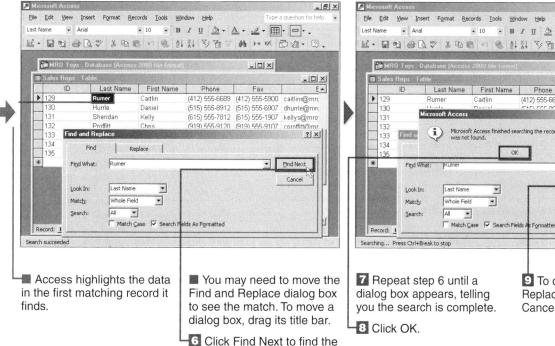

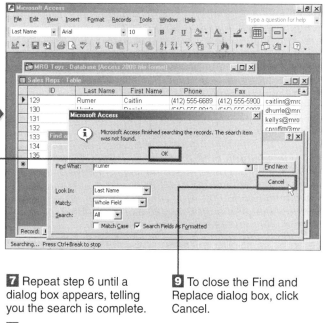

■ Access highlights the data in the first matching record it finds.

■ You may need to move the Find and Replace dialog box to see the match. To move a dialog box, drag its title bar.

6 Click Find Next to find the next matching record.

7 Repeat step 6 until a dialog box appears, telling you the search is complete.

8 Click OK.

9 To close the Find and Replace dialog box, click Cancel.

SORT RECORDS

You can change the order of records in a table, query, or form to help you find, organize, and analyze data.

You can sort by one or more fields. Sorting by more than one field can help you refine the sort. For example, if several of your clients have the same last name, you can sort by the last name field and the first name field. When you sort by multiple fields, you must place the fields side-by-side and in the order you want to perform the sort. Access sorts the records in the far left field first.

You can sort records in ascending or descending order. Sorting in ascending order displays text in alphabetical order from A to Z and displays numbers from smallest to largest. The opposite occurs when you sort text or numbers in descending order.

When you save the table, query, or form, Access saves the sort order you specified.

SORT RECORDS

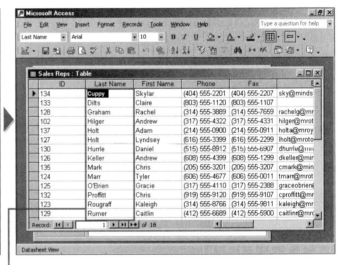

SORT BY ONE FIELD

1 Click anywhere in the field you want to use to sort the records.

2 Click one of the following buttons:
- Sort A to Z, 1 to 9
- Sort Z to A, 9 to 1

■ The records appear in the new order. In this example, the records are sorted by last name.

How do I rearrange the fields in a table?

✔ You may need to rearrange the fields when sorting records by two fields. Click the name of the field you want to move. Position the ▷ over the field name and then drag the field to a new location. A thick black line shows where the field appears.

Can I also use a menu command to perform a sort?

✔ Yes. Click Records and then click Sort. Click either Sort Ascending or Sort Descending.

Why are the Sort buttons unavailable?

✔ Excel does not make the Sort buttons available when you select a field that has a Hyperlink, Memo, or OLE Object data type. Access does not allow you to sort a field that has one of these data types.

How do I remove a sort from my records?

✔ If you no longer want to display your records in the sort order you specified, you can return your records to the primary key order at any time. Click Records, and then Remove Filter/Sort.

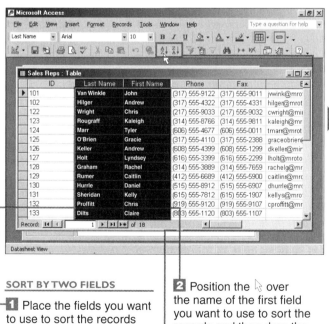

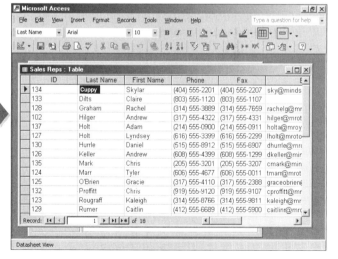

SORT BY TWO FIELDS

1 Place the fields you want to use to sort the records side-by-side and in the order you want to perform the sort.

2 Position the ▷ over the name of the first field you want to use to sort the records and then drag the mouse until you highlight the second field.

3 Click 🔼 or 🔽.

■ The records appear in the new order.

■ In this example, the records are sorted by last name and then first name.

FILTER DATA

You can filter records in a table, form, or query to display only specific records. Filtering data can help you review and analyze information in your database by temporarily hiding information not currently of interest. For example, in a table that stores client addresses, you can filter out clients who do not live in Indiana.

When you filter by selection, you select data and have Access display only the records that contain the same data.

When you filter by input, you enter data or criteria and have Access display only the records that contain matching data or data that meets the entered criteria. Filtering by input is useful when you want

to specify exact data or find records within a specific range.

Filtering data does not change how Access stores the records in the database.

You can add, delete, or edit records when you are viewing filtered records. Access updates changes you make to filtered data in the table.

FILTER DATA

FILTER BY SELECTION

1 Click a field that contains the data you want to use to filter the records.

2 Click the Filter By Selection button ( ) to filter the records.

■ Access displays the records that contain the matching data. All other records are hidden.

■ The word **(Filtered)** appears in this area to indicate that you are looking at filtered records.

3 Click the Remove Filter button ( ) to once again display all the records.

■ Access removes the filter and displays all records.

Is there another way to filter by selection?

✔ Yes. You can select specific characters you want to use to filter the records. For example, select "Smi" in Smith to display records containing data starting with "Smi." If you do not select the first character, Access displays all the records containing the characters. For example, select "mi" in Smith to display records containing Jamison and Farmington.

Can I use a filter to hide records that contain specific data?

✔ Yes. Click the data you do not want to display. Click Records, Filter, and then Filter Excluding Selection.

How can I use criteria to filter data?

✔ When filtering by input, you can use criteria to define which records Access displays. For example, type <1/1/01 to display records with dates before January 1, 2001. See the section "Examples of Criteria" for more information.

Can I filter records that have already been filtered?

✔ Yes. You can continue to narrow the records by filtering them again and again, until you see the records you want to view. When you perform multiple filters, you cannot back up one filter. When you remove the filter, Access displays all of the records.

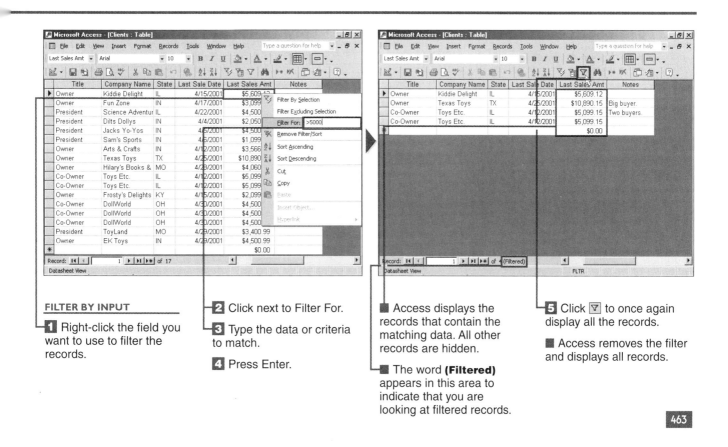

FILTER BY INPUT

1 Right-click the field you want to use to filter the records.

2 Click next to Filter For.

3 Type the data or criteria to match.

4 Press Enter.

■ Access displays the records that contain the matching data. All other records are hidden.

■ The word **(Filtered)** appears in this area to indicate that you are looking at filtered records.

5 Click 🔽 to once again display all the records.

■ Access removes the filter and displays all records.

FILTER DATA BY FORM

You can use the Filter by Form feature to perform powerful searches of a table, form, or query in a database. Filtering records allows you to quickly find and display records of interest.

When you filter by form, you can specify the criteria that records

must meet to be displayed. For example, you can have Access find clients who made purchases of more than $3,000.

You can specify multiple criteria to filter records. Access displays only records that meet all the criteria you specify. For example, you can have Access find clients in Indiana

who made purchases of more than $3,000. For more information on search criteria, see the section "Examples of Criteria."

When you save a table, form, or query, the last filter you performed is also saved. You can quickly apply the same filter again later.

FILTER DATA BY FORM

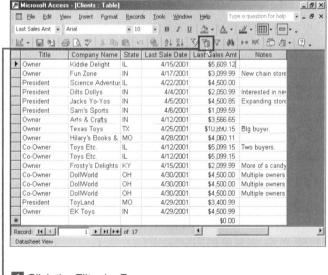

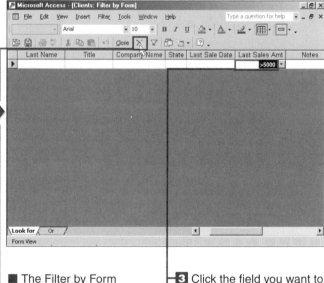

1 Click the Filter by Form button () to filter by form.

■ The Filter by Form window appears.

2 To clear any information used for the last filter, click the Clear button (⊠).

3 Click the field you want to use to filter the records.

4 Type the data or criteria to specify which records you want to find.

How can I quickly enter the data I want to use to filter records?

✔ Click the field you want to use to filter records. To display a list of the values in the field, click the arrow that appears. Then click the value you want to use to filter the records.

What types of criteria can I use?

✔ You can use the typical comparison operators, such as = (equal to), < (less than), > (greater than), and others. For more information on search criteria, see the section "Examples of Criteria."

Can I display records that meet one of several criteria I specify?

✔ You can use the Or tab when filtering by form to display records that meet at least one of the criteria. For example, you can find clients with the first name Bill or William. Perform steps 1 through 3 in this section to enter the first criteria you want the records to meet. Click the Or tab in the bottom left corner of the Filter by Form window and then enter the second criteria.

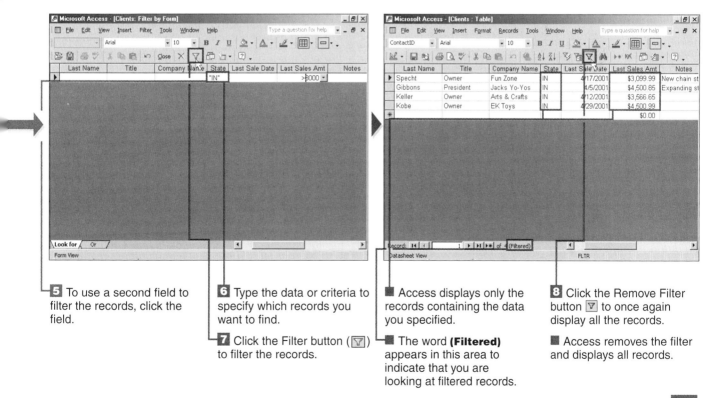

5 To use a second field to filter the records, click the field.

6 Type the data or criteria to specify which records you want to find.

7 Click the Filter button (▽) to filter the records.

■ Access displays only the records containing the data you specified.

■ The word **(Filtered)** appears in this area to indicate that you are looking at filtered records.

8 Click the Remove Filter button ▽ to once again display all the records.

■ Access removes the filter and displays all records.

CREATE A QUERY USING THE SIMPLE QUERY WIZARD

query is similar to asking a question of the database and getting a response. The response you get is a set of records, much like a filter. With a query, you have a great deal more control. You can perform calculations on the data, use more than one table, and save queries.

You can use the Simple Query Wizard to gather information from

one or more tables in a database. The wizard asks you a series of questions and then sets up a query based on your answers. The Simple Query Wizard is useful when you want to perform simple calculations in a query, such as finding the sum.

The Simple Query Wizard allows you to choose the table containing the fields you want to include in

the query. After you choose a table, you can select the fields you want to include. A query can include all or only some of the fields in a table.

You can select fields from multiple tables if they are related. For information on relationships between tables, see Chapter 25.

CREATE A QUERY USING THE SIMPLE QUERY WIZARD

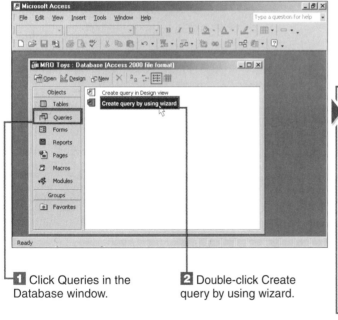

1 Click Queries in the Database window.

2 Double-click Create query by using wizard.

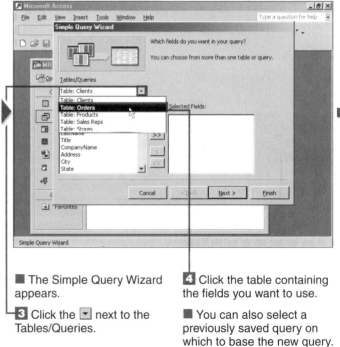

■ The Simple Query Wizard appears.

3 Click the ▼ next to the Tables/Queries.

4 Click the table containing the fields you want to use.

■ You can also select a previously saved query on which to base the new query.

Can I use other wizards to create a query?

✔ Yes. In the Database window, click Queries and then click New. The Crosstab Query Wizard allows you to create a query that groups related information together and displays summarized information. The Find Duplicates Query Wizard allows you to find records that contain the same values to avoid duplication. The Find Unmatched Query Wizard allows you to compare two tables to find records in one table that do not have related records in the other table.

Why should I use a wizard instead of creating my own query?

✔ Using a wizard is a fast way to create a basic query. If you want to plan and set up your own query, you can create a query in the Design view. For more information, see the section "Create a Query in Design View."

Can I remove fields I have added to the query by mistake?

✔ Yes. You can remove the field in question by double-clicking the field in the Selected Fields list in the Simple Query Wizard dialog box.

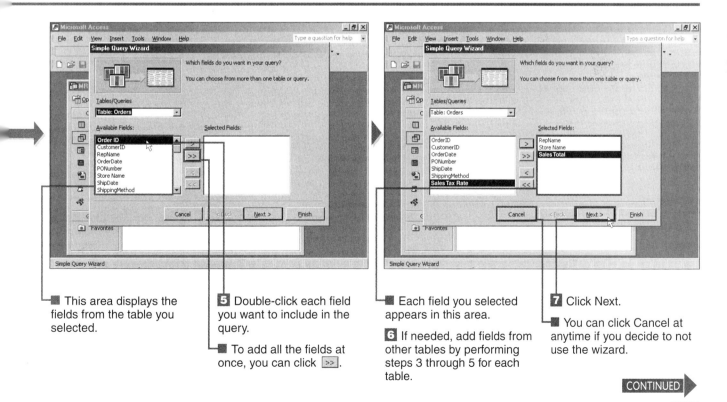

■ This area displays the fields from the table you selected.

5 Double-click each field you want to include in the query.

■ To add all the fields at once, you can click >> .

■ Each field you selected appears in this area.

6 If needed, add fields from other tables by performing steps 3 through 5 for each table.

7 Click Next.

■ You can click Cancel at anytime if you decide to not use the wizard.

CONTINUED ▶

CREATE A QUERY USING THE SIMPLE QUERY WIZARD (CONTINUED)

If the fields you selected for a query contain information that can be calculated, you can choose to display all the records or a summary of the records in the results of the query.

You can calculate values in a query to summarize information. The Sum option adds values. The Avg option calculates the average value. The Min and Max options find the smallest or largest value.

When you calculate values in a query, Access groups related records together. For example, in a query that contains an Employee Name field and a Products Sold field, Access groups together the records for each employee to find the total number of products each employee sold.

You can have Access count the number of records used in each

group to perform a calculation. The count appears as a field in the query results.

To finish creating a query, you must name the query. Choose a descriptive name that can help you recognize the query in the future.

CREATE A QUERY USING THE SIMPLE QUERY WIZARD (CONTINUED)

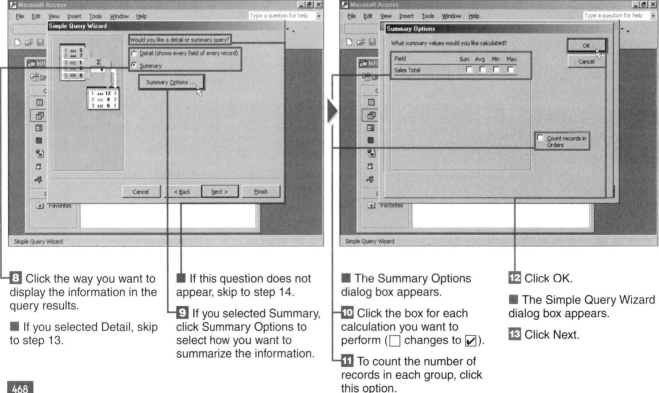

8 Click the way you want to display the information in the query results.

■ If you selected Detail, skip to step 13.

■ If this question does not appear, skip to step 14.

9 If you selected Summary, click Summary Options to select how you want to summarize the information.

■ The Summary Options dialog box appears.

10 Click the box for each calculation you want to perform (□ changes to ☑).

11 To count the number of records in each group, click this option.

12 Click OK.

■ The Simple Query Wizard dialog box appears.

13 Click Next.

How can I make changes to a query I created using the Simple Query Wizard?

✔ You can use the Design view to make changes to any query you create. You can sort records, add and remove fields, and more. See the section "Change the Query View."

Why does another dialog box appear, asking me how I would like to group dates in my query?

✔ It may appear if one of the fields in your query stores dates. You can choose to group the dates in your query by the individual date, day, month, quarter, or year.

Why did Access not summarize my information properly in the query?

✔ Make sure you include only the fields you need to create the query. Also, make sure you select the field you want to group the records by first. Access groups records starting with the first field and then considers the data in each of the following fields.

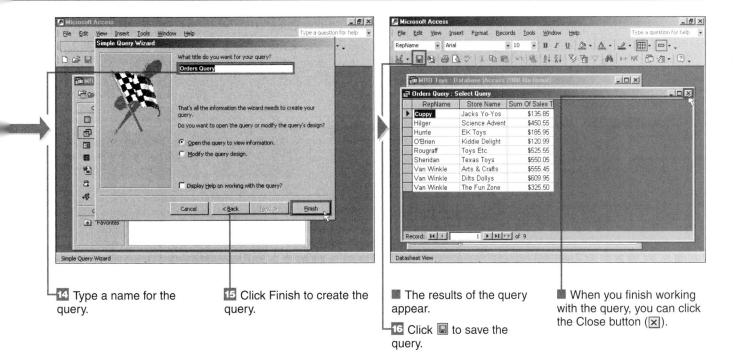

-14 Type a name for the query.

-15 Click Finish to create the query.

■ The results of the query appear.

-16 Click 🖫 to save the query.

■ When you finish working with the query, you can click the Close button (☒).

CREATE A QUERY IN DESIGN VIEW

The Design view allows you to plan and set up your own query. If you cannot find a wizard that matches your query needs, you can build one from scratch. You might also build a query using Design view if you need to create a complex query that finds results based on multiple criteria.

To start, select each table that contains information you want to use in a query. To perform a query on more than one table, the tables you select must be related.

The tables you use in the query appear in the top half of the Select Query window.

The bottom half of the window displays a grid, called the design grid, where you can specify the information you want the query to display. You can use this grid to select the field, sort order, and criteria. You can type the criteria to match. See "Set Criteria" later in this section for information on entering criteria.

CREATE A QUERY IN DESIGN VIEW

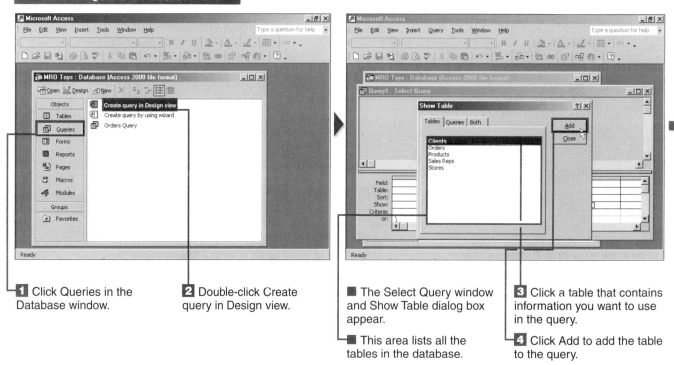

1 Click Queries in the Database window.

2 Double-click Create query in Design view.

■ The Select Query window and Show Table dialog box appear.

■ This area lists all the tables in the database.

3 Click a table that contains information you want to use in the query.

4 Click Add to add the table to the query.

How do I add another table to a query?

✔ Click the Show Table button ( ) on the toolbar to redisplay the Show Table dialog box. Double-click the table you want to add to the query and then click Close.

How do I remove a table from a query?

✔ In the Select Query window, click the box displaying the fields for the table you want to remove and then press Delete. Access removes the table from the query but not from the database.

Can I use an existing query to create a new query?

✔ Yes. This is useful if you want to refine an existing query to produce fewer records. In the Show Table dialog box, click the Queries tab and then double-click the name of the query you want to use. Click Close and then perform steps 7 through 9 to create the new query.

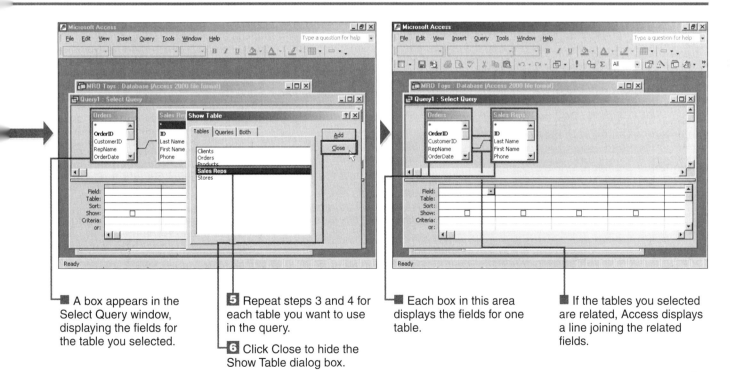

■ A box appears in the Select Query window, displaying the fields for the table you selected.

5 Repeat steps 3 and 4 for each table you want to use in the query.

6 Click Close to hide the Show Table dialog box.

■ Each box in this area displays the fields for one table.

■ If the tables you selected are related, Access displays a line joining the related fields.

CONTINUED ▶

CREATE A QUERY IN DESIGN VIEW
(CONTINUED)

After you select the fields you want to include, you can choose to hide a field. Hiding a field is useful when you need to use a field to find information in the database but do not want the field to appear in the results of the query.

When you run a query, Access displays the results of the query in the Datasheet view. If you change the information when the query is displayed in the Datasheet view, the table that supplies the information for the query also changes.

If you want to run a query later, you must save the query. When you save a query, you save only the conditions you specified. You do not save the information gathered by the query. This allows you to view the most current information each time you run the query.

You can give the query a name. Make sure you use a descriptive name that allows you to distinguish the query from the other queries in the database.

CREATE A QUERY IN DESIGN VIEW (CONTINUED)

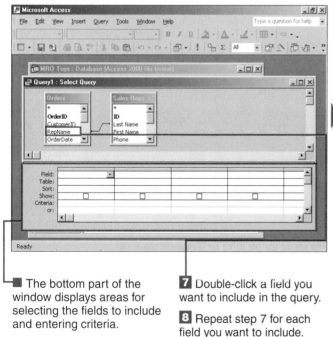

■ The bottom part of the window displays areas for selecting the fields to include and entering criteria.

7 Double-click a field you want to include in the query.

8 Repeat step 7 for each field you want to include.

■ Each field displaying a check mark (☑) appears in the results of the query.

■ If you do not want a field to appear in the results of the query, uncheck the Show box for the field (☑ changes to ☐).

■ The query is complete. You can now run the query to see the results.

9 Click the Run button (🗓) to run the query.

How do I quickly include all the fields from a table in a query?

✓ In the Select Query window, double-click the title bar of the box displaying the fields for the table. Position the ⇨ over the selected fields and then drag the fields to the first empty column in the design grid.

Can I clear a query and start over?

✓ If you make mistakes while selecting fields for a query, you can start over by clearing the design grid. Click Edit, and then Clear Grid.

Can I change the order of fields in a query?

✓ Yes. Rearranging fields in a query affects the order the fields appear in the results. In the design grid, position the ⇨ over the top of the field you want to move and click to select the field. Then position the ⇨ directly above the selected field and drag the field to a new location.

How do I remove a field I included in a query?

✓ Click anywhere in the field. Click Edit, and then Delete Columns.

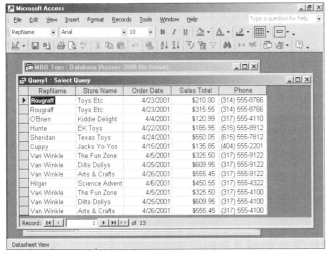

■ The results of the query appear.

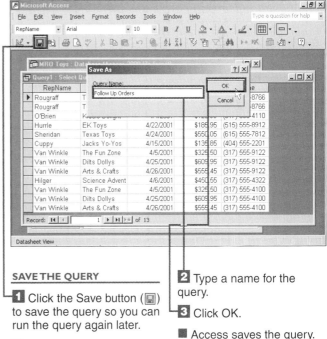

SAVE THE QUERY

1 Click the Save button (🖫) to save the query so you can run the query again later.

■ The Save As dialog box appears.

2 Type a name for the query.

3 Click OK.

■ Access saves the query.

OPEN A QUERY

You can open a query to display the results of the query or change the design of the query. You can open a query in the Datasheet or Design view.

When you open a query in the Datasheet view, Access runs the query and displays the results. This

view is similar to the Datasheet view for tables but displays only the information that meets the criteria or conditions of the query.

In the Design view, you can make changes to the structure of a query. You can use this view to tell Access what data you want to find, where

to find the data, and how you want to display the results.

When you have finished working with a query, you can close the query to remove it from your screen. A dialog box appears if you have not saved changes you made to the query.

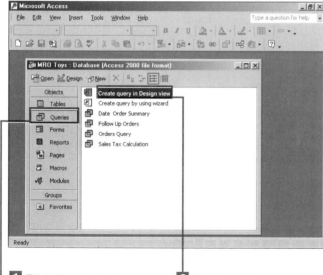

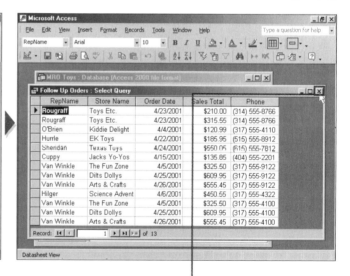

1 Click Queries in the Database window to display a list of the queries in the database.

2 Double-click the query you want to open.

■ Access opens the query.

3 When you finish viewing the query, click ⊠ to close the query.

CHANGE THE QUERY VIEW

There are several ways you can view a query. Each view allows you to perform different tasks.

The Design view allows you to plan your query. You can use this view to tell Access what data you want to find, where Access can find the data, and how you want to display the results.

The Datasheet view allows you to review the results of a query. The field names appear across the top of the window. Each row shows the information for a record that meets the criteria or conditions you specify.

The SQL view displays the SQL statement for the current query. *Structured Query Language (SQL)* is

a computer language. When you create a query, Access creates the SQL statement that describes your query. You do not need to use this view to effectively use Access.

You can also use the new PivotTable and PivotChart views to view and change this type of query.

CHANGE THE QUERY VIEW

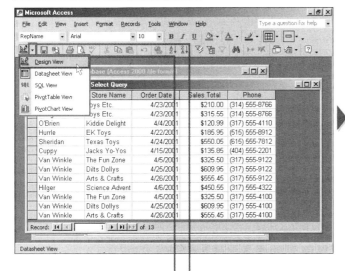

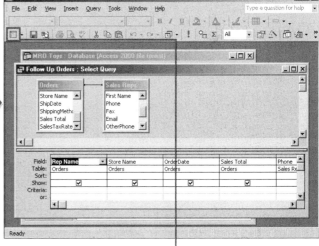

■ In this example, the query appears in the Datasheet view.

1 Click ⦁ next to the View button (📊) to display the query in another view.

2 Click the view you want to use.

■ The query appears in the view you selected.

■ This example shows the Design view.

■ The View button changes to Datasheet view (🏷).

■ You can click the View button to quickly switch between the Design and Datasheet views.

SET CRITERIA

You can use criteria to find specific records in a database. *Criteria* are conditions that identify which records you want to find. To set criteria, display the query in Design view. You can enter a single criteria — for example, type IN in the State field to find all clients in Indiana.

You also can use multiple criteria. Using the OR condition allows you to find records that meet at least one of the criteria you specify. For example, you can find clients in Indiana or Texas. You can use the OR condition with one or more fields.

You can combine criteria. For example, you can enter criteria for more than one field. Access displays only records that match all the criteria you enter.

Using the AND condition allows you to find records that meet all the criteria you specify. You can use the AND condition with one or more fields. For example, you can find clients in Indiana or Texas who bought more than $150 worth of products. This example includes both OR and AND conditions.

SET CRITERIA

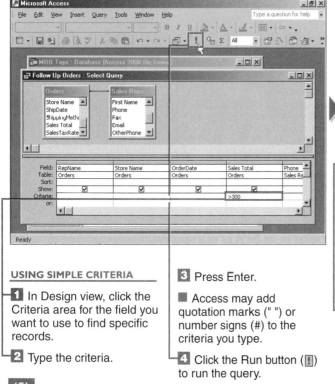

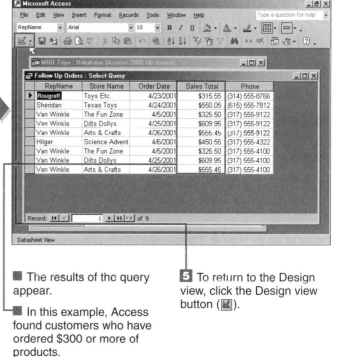

USING SIMPLE CRITERIA

1 In Design view, click the Criteria area for the field you want to use to find specific records.

2 Type the criteria.

3 Press Enter.

■ Access may add quotation marks (" ") or number signs (#) to the criteria you type.

4 Click the Run button (!) to run the query.

■ The results of the query appear.

■ In this example, Access found customers who have ordered $300 or more of products.

5 To return to the Design view, click the Design view button (⊠).

Can I have Access display only a portion of the records in the results?

✔ Yes. When you know there will be many records in the results of a query, you can have Access display only the top or bottom values in the results. Click the Sort area for the field you want to show the top or bottom values. Click the arrow that appears. Select Ascending to display the bottom values or Descending to display the top values. In the Top Values box on the toolbar, click and then select the values you want to display.

How do I use the AND condition in one field?

✔ In the Criteria area for the field, enter both criteria separated by the word "And." For example, to find records that contain invoice numbers between 100 and 150, type **>100 And <150** in the Criteria area of the Invoice Number field.

Should I save the query?

✔ Yes, save the query if you want to use it again. Click the Save button (■).

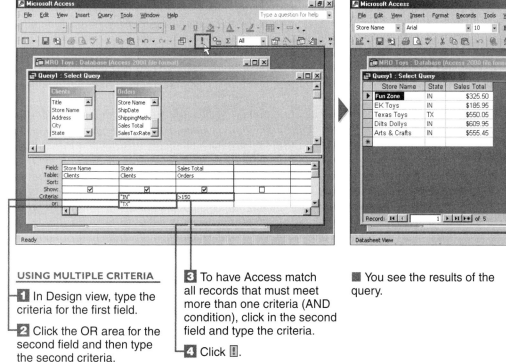

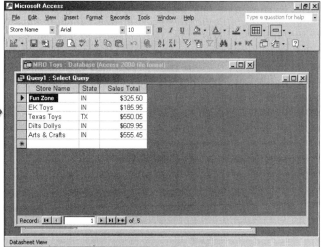

USING MULTIPLE CRITERIA

1 In Design view, type the criteria for the first field.

2 Click the OR area for the second field and then type the second criteria.

3 To have Access match all records that must meet more than one criteria (AND condition), click in the second field and type the criteria.

4 Click ■.

■ You see the results of the query.

■ In this example, Access displays stores in Indiana or Texas who have placed orders greater than $150.

EXAMPLES OF CRITERIA

Exact Matches

=100 . . . . . . .Finds the number 100
=California . . .Finds California
=1/5/01 . . . . . .Finds the date 5-Jan-01

Less Than

<100 . . . . . . .Finds numbers less than 100
<N . . . . .Finds text starting with the
letters A to M
<1/5/01 . . . . . .Finds dates before 5-Jan-01

Less than or equal to

<=100 . . . . . . .Finds numbers less than or
equal to 100
<=N . . . . . . .Finds text starting with the
letters A to N
<=1/5/01 . . . . .Finds dates on or before
5-Jan-01

Greater than

>100 . . . . . . .Finds numbers greater than 100
>N . . . . .Finds text starting with the
letters O to Z
>1/5/01 . . . . . .Finds dates after 5-Jan-01

Greater than or equal to

>=100 . . . . . . .Finds numbers greater than or
equal to 100
>=N . . . . . . .Finds text starting with the
letters N to Z
>=1/5/01 . . . . .Finds dates on or after 5-Jan-01

Not equal to

<>100 . . . . . .Finds numbers not equal to 100
<> . . . . .Finds text not equal to California
<>1/5/01 . . . . .Finds dates not on 5-Jan-01

Empty Fields

Is Null . . . . . .Finds records that do not
contain data in the field
Is Not Null . . .Finds records that do contain
data in the field

Find list of items

In (100,101) . . . . . . .Finds the numbers 100
and 101
In (California, CA) . . . .Finds California and CA
In (#1/5/01#,#1/6/01#) . .Finds the dates 5-Jan-01
and 6-Jan-01

Between..And...

Between 100 And 200 . .Finds numbers from
100 to 200
Between A and D . . . . . .Finds text starting with
the letters A through D
Between 1/5/01 . . . . . .Finds dates on and
and 1/15/01   between 5-Jan-01 and
15-Jan-01

Wildcards

The asterisk (*) wildcard represents one or
more characters. The question mark (?)
wildcard represents a single wildcard.
Like Br* . . . .Finds text starting with Br, such
as Brenda or Brown
Like *ar* . . .Finds text containing ar such as
Arnold or Mark
Like Terr? . . .Find 5 letters starting with Terr
such as Terri or Terry

SORT QUERY RESULTS

You can sort the results of a query to better organize the results. This can help you find information of interest more quickly.

The results of a query can be sorted in ascending or descending order. Sorting in ascending order sorts text in alphabetical order from A to Z and sorts numbers from smallest

to largest. When you sort in descending order, the opposite occurs.

You can choose not to sort the results of a query. If you do not sort the results, Access displays the results in the order they are found.

You can sort by one or more fields. When you sort by more than one

field, you must place the fields in the order you want to perform the sort. Access sorts the records in the far left field first.

You cannot sort a field that has a Hyperlink, Memo, or OLE Object data type.

SORT QUERY RESULTS

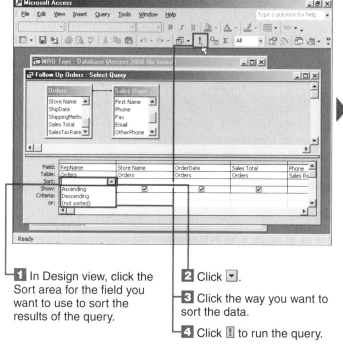

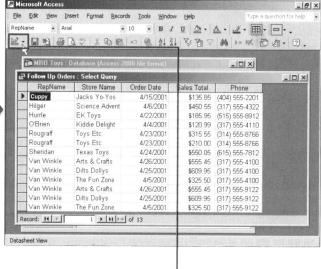

1 In Design view, click the Sort area for the field you want to use to sort the results of the query.

2 Click ▾.

3 Click the way you want to sort the data.

4 Click ▯ to run the query.

■ The records appear in the new order.

■ In this example, the records are sorted alphabetically by rep name.

5 To return to the Design view, click ▨.

PERFORM CALCULATIONS

You can perform calculations on records in a database. You can then review and analyze the results.

In a blank field, you can type a name for the field that displays the results of the calculation, followed by an expression. An *expression* tells Access which items to use in the calculation. An expression also contains operators that tell Access to multiply (*), add (+), subtract (-),

divide (/), or raise values to a power (^).

To enter a field name in an expression, type the field name in square brackets. For example, type **[Quantity]*[Cost]** to multiply the Quantity field by the Cost field. Make sure you type the field names exactly.

If the same field name is found in more than one table, type the table

name in square brackets followed by a period (.) and the field name in square brackets. For example, type **[Products].[Quantity]** to ensure Access uses the Quantity field in the Products table.

The results of a calculation are not stored in the database. If you run the query again, Access uses the most current data in the database to perform the calculation.

PERFORM CALCULATIONS

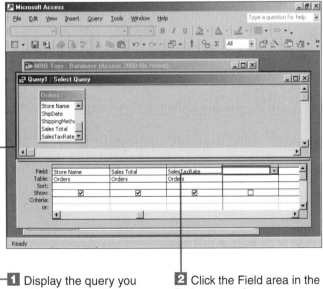

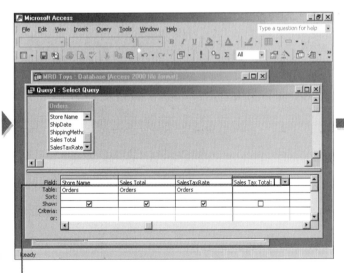

1 Display the query you want to change in the Design view.

2 Click the Field area in the first empty column.

3 Type a name for the field that will display the results of the calculation, followed by a colon (:).

4 Press the Spacebar to leave a blank space.

Can I change the format of calculated information?

✔ Yes. In the Design view, click anywhere in the calculated field. Click the Properties button and then click the Format area. Click the down arrow that appears and then select the format you want to use. You can also specify the number of decimal places to display for numeric fields.

How can I display an entire expression?

✔ An expression you type may be too long to fit in the Field area. To display the entire expression, click the cell containing the expression and then press Shift + F2. The Zoom dialog box appears, displaying the entire expression.

What types of expressions can I use?

✔ Here are some examples of expressions you can use.

Inventory Value: [Price]*[Quantity]

Total Price: [Cost]+[Profit]

New Price: [Price]-[Discount]

Item Cost: [Price of Case]/[Items]

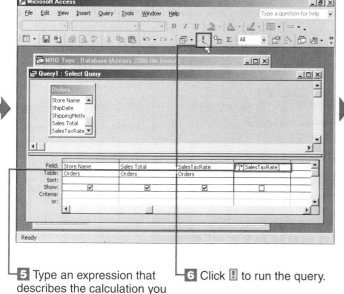

5 Type an expression that describes the calculation you want to perform.

6 Click 🔳 to run the query.

■ The result of the calculation for each record appears.

7 To return to the Design view, click 🔳.

SUMMARIZE DATA

Y ou can summarize the information in a database to help you analyze the information.

You can divide records into groups and summarize the information for each group. For example, you can summarize information grouped by date to determine the number of orders for each day.

To group records, you must display the Total row. The words "Group

By" automatically appear in each field in the Total row. You can leave the words "Group By" in the field you want Access to use to group the records. In the other field, you can specify the calculation you want to perform on the group to summarize the information.

Access provides several calculations you can perform. The Sum option adds the values. The Avg option calculates the average value. You

can use the Min or Max option to find the smallest or largest value. The Count option calculates the number of values, excluding empty records. You can use the StDev (standard deviation) or Var (variance) option to perform statistical functions. You can use the First or Last option to find the value of the first or last record.

SUMMARIZE DATA

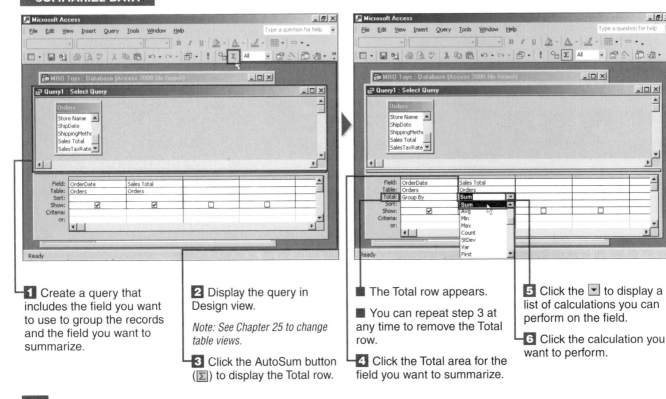

1 Create a query that includes the field you want to use to group the records and the field you want to summarize.

2 Display the query in Design view.

Note: See Chapter 25 to change table views.

3 Click the AutoSum button (Σ) to display the Total row.

■ The Total row appears.

■ You can repeat step 3 at any time to remove the Total row.

4 Click the Total area for the field you want to summarize.

5 Click the ▼ to display a list of calculations you can perform on the field.

6 Click the calculation you want to perform.

Can I use more than one field to group records?

✔ Yes. You can group records using more than one field. For example, you can use the Company and Product fields to group the records and the Quantity Ordered field to summarize the data. This lets you display the total amount of each product purchased by each company. Access groups records using fields from left to right. In the Design view, place each field in the order you want to group the records.

Do I have to use more than one table in a query?

✔ No. You can create a query based on one table, as in this example.

Can I limit the records that appear in the results?

✔ Yes. You can summarize all the records in a query but show only some of the records in the results. For example, you may want to display only the companies who had orders totaling more than $100. In the Criteria area of the field you are summarizing, type the criteria you want to limit the records that show in the results. For more information on search criteria, see the section "Examples of Criteria."

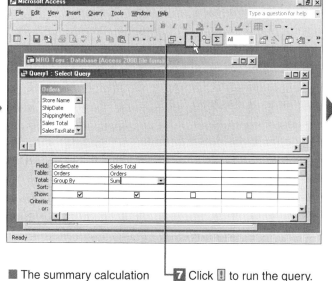

■ The summary calculation is set up.

7 Click to run the query.

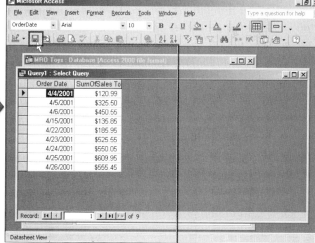

■ The results of the calculations appear.

■ In this example, Access calculates the sum of products purchased for each order date.

8 To save the query, click and type a query name.

9 Click OK.

■ Access saves the summary query.

CREATE A REPORT USING THE REPORT WIZARD

Y ou can use the Report Wizard to help you create a professionally designed report that summarizes the data from a table or a query. The Report Wizard asks you a series of questions and then creates a report based on your answers.

You can choose the table that contains the fields you want to

include in the report. After you choose a table, you can select the fields you want to include. For example, in a report that displays monthly sales, you may want to select the Date, Customer, Sales Rep, and Order Total fields. A report can include all or only some of the fields in a table.

The Report Wizard can help you organize the data in the report by grouping related data together. If you choose to group related data together, Access automatically places the data in the appropriate sections in the report. For example, you can group data by the Date field to have Access place all the sales for the same month together.

CREATE A REPORT USING THE REPORT WIZARD

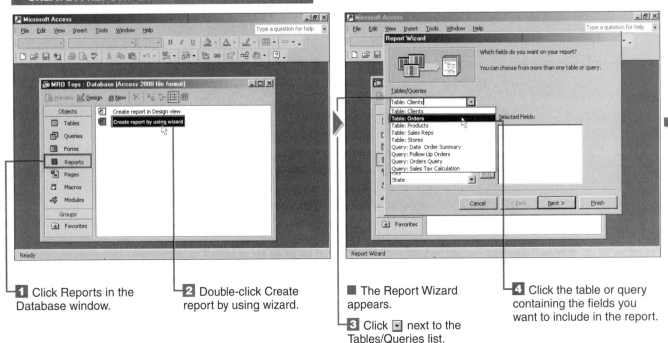

■1 Click Reports in the Database window.

■2 Double-click Create report by using wizard.

■ The Report Wizard appears.

■3 Click ▾ next to the Tables/Queries list.

■4 Click the table or query containing the fields you want to include in the report.

Can I specify how I want Access to group data in my report?

✔ Yes. After you select the field you want to use to group data, click Grouping Options. In the Grouping intervals area, click the ▪ and click how to group the data. The available options depend on the type of field you selected.

How do I remove fields I added by accident?

✔ To remove fields, double-click the field in the Selected Fields list. To remove all fields, click ◄ .

Can I create a report based on more than one table?

✔ Yes. Relationships must exist between the tables you use. For information on relationships, see Chapter 25. To create the report, perform steps 1 through 5 below and then repeat steps 3 through 5 until you have chosen all the tables and fields you want to include. Click Next. If prompted to select how to view data, click the fields below the question until the preview area displays the view you want. Finally, perform steps 6 through 25 to finish the report.

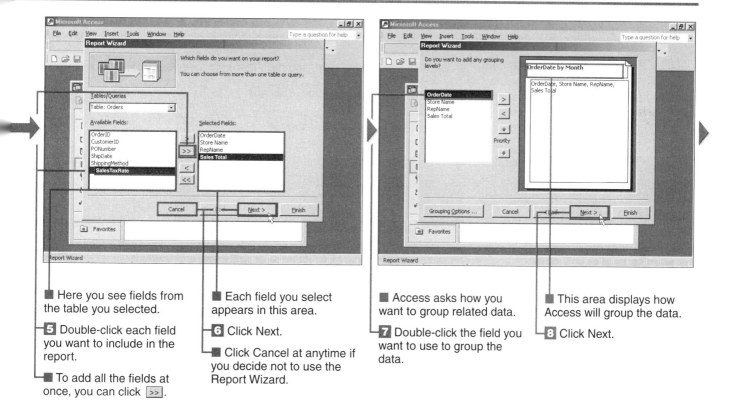

■ Here you see fields from the table you selected.

5 Double-click each field you want to include in the report.

■ To add all the fields at once, you can click ⟩⟩ .

■ Each field you select appears in this area.

6 Click Next.

■ Click Cancel at anytime if you decide not to use the Report Wizard.

■ Access asks how you want to group related data.

7 Double-click the field you want to use to group the data.

■ This area displays how Access will group the data.

8 Click Next.

CONTINUED ▶

CREATE A REPORT USING THE REPORT WIZARD (CONTINUED)

You can sort the records in a report to better organize the records. The Report Wizard lets you select the fields you want to use to sort the records. For example, you can alphabetically sort records by the Last Name field. If the same data appears more than once in the field, you can sort by a second field, such as First Name.

You can sort records in ascending or descending order. When you sort in ascending order, Access sorts the text from A to Z and the numbers from 1 to 9. When you sort in descending order, the opposite occurs.

You can perform calculations to summarize the data in a report. When you perform calculations, you can have Access display all the records and the calculated summary for each group of records or just the calculated summaries in the report.

You can also choose to display the percentage of the total that each group represents. For example, in a database that stores sales information, you can calculate the percent of total sales for each region.

CREATE A REPORT USING THE REPORT WIZARD (CONTINUED)

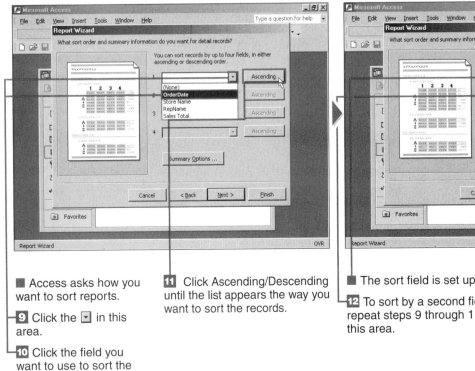

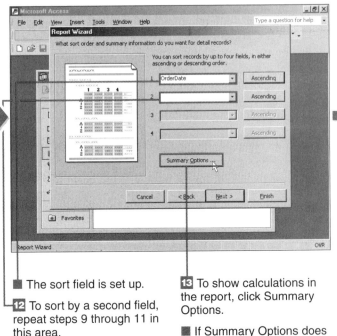

■ Access asks how you want to sort reports.

9 Click the ▼ in this area.

10 Click the field you want to use to sort the records.

11 Click Ascending/Descending until the list appears the way you want to sort the records.

■ The sort field is set up.

12 To sort by a second field, repeat steps 9 through 11 in this area.

13 To show calculations in the report, click Summary Options.

■ If Summary Options does not display, skip to step 18.

Why does summary options not display?

✔ Summary Options does not display if you do not include any fields that store numbers in the report or if you do not choose to group related data together in your report. For information on grouping related data, see the preceding pages of this section.

What calculations can I perform on the data in my report?

✔ Access offers several calculations you can perform. The Sum option adds values. The Avg option calculates the average value. The Min and Max options find the smallest or largest value.

Is there a faster way to create a report?

✔ You can use an AutoReport to quickly create a report based on one table in your database. In the Database window, click Reports and then click New. Choose the Columnar or Tabular AutoReport style. Click the ▾ and click the table that you want to supply the information for the report. Then click OK.

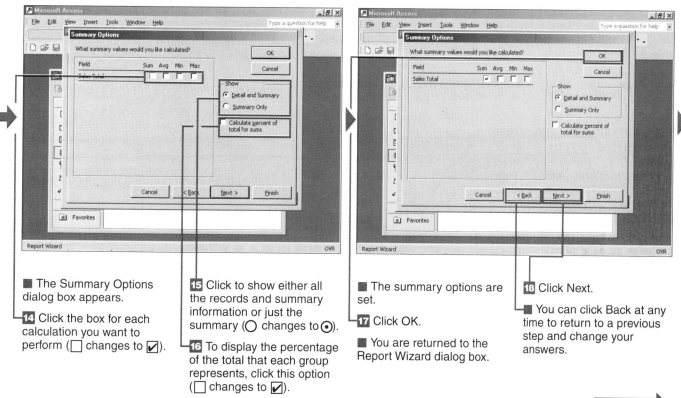

■ The Summary Options dialog box appears.

14 Click the box for each calculation you want to perform (☐ changes to ☑).

15 Click to show either all the records and summary information or just the summary (○ changes to ⊙).

16 To display the percentage of the total that each group represents, click this option (☐ changes to ☑).

■ The summary options are set.

17 Click OK.

■ You are returned to the Report Wizard dialog box.

18 Click Next.

■ You can click Back at any time to return to a previous step and change your answers.

CONTINUED ▶

CREATE A REPORT USING THE REPORT WIZARD (CONTINUED)

You can choose among several layouts for a report. The layout you choose determines the arrangement of data in the report.

The available layouts depend on the options you previously selected for the report. If you chose to group related data, Access makes the Stepped, Block, Outline, and Align Left layouts available. If you chose not to group related data, Access

makes the Columnar, Tabular, and Justified layouts available.

You can specify the page orientation of the printed report. The portrait orientation prints data across the short side of a page. The landscape orientation prints data across the long side of a page.

You can choose a style for the report, such as Casual, Corporate, or Formal. Most styles use colors

and patterns to enhance the appearance of a report.

The Report Wizard asks you to name your report. The name you select appears in the Reports area of the Database window.

The report appears in a window on your screen. If the report consists of more than one page, you can move through the pages in the report to view them.

CREATE A REPORT USING THE REPORT WIZARD (CONTINUED)

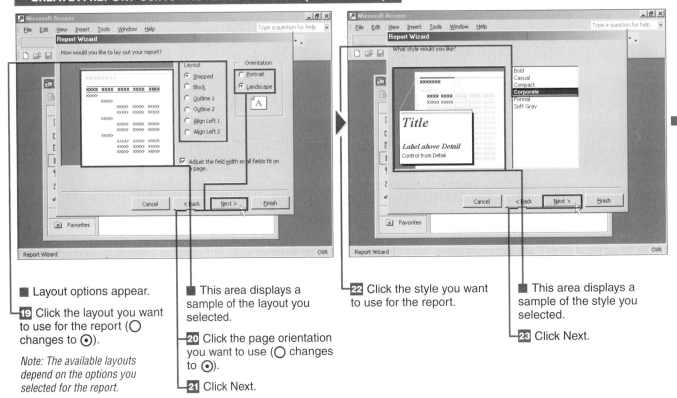

■ Layout options appear.

19 Click the layout you want to use for the report (○ changes to ⦿).

Note: The available layouts depend on the options you selected for the report.

■ This area displays a sample of the layout you selected.

20 Click the page orientation you want to use (○ changes to ⦿).

21 Click Next.

22 Click the style you want to use for the report.

■ This area displays a sample of the style you selected.

23 Click Next.

How do I print a report?
✔ When the report displays on your screen, click the Print button (🖨) to print the report.

When viewing my report, how can I display an entire page on my screen or display other pages?
✔ You can click the ▾ next to the Zoom box (100% ▾) to display the entire page on your screen. You can also use the scroll buttons at the bottom to display other pages. For more information on changing the magnification of a page, see the section "Preview a Report."

Can I later change the style of a report?
✔ Yes. In the Database window, click Reports. Select the name of the report you want to change and then click the Design button. Click the AutoFormat button (▨) and select the style you want to use. Then click OK.

I changed data in a table I used to create a report. How do I update the report?
✔ When you open the report, Access automatically gathers the most current data from the table. Access also updates the date it displays in the report.

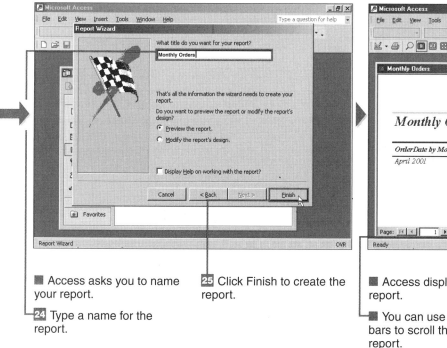

■ Access asks you to name your report.

24 Type a name for the report.

25 Click Finish to create the report.

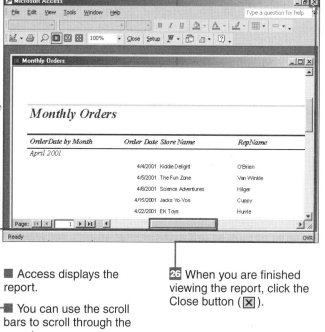

■ Access displays the report.

■ You can use the scroll bars to scroll through the report.

26 When you are finished viewing the report, click the Close button (☒).

OPEN A REPORT

Y ou can open a report to display its contents and to review its information.

You can open a report in the Print Preview or Design view. The Print Preview view allows you to see how a report looks when you print it. The Design view allows you to change the design of a report, make formatting changes, or rearrange the report items.

When you open a report, Access gathers the most current data from the table or query used to create the report. If the table or query contains a large amount of data, it may take a few moments for the report to appear on your screen.

When you finish working with a report, you can close the report to remove it from your screen. A dialog box appears if you have not saved changes you made to the design of the report, such as changing the font or size of text. You can select to save the report or cancel the changes.

OPEN A REPORT

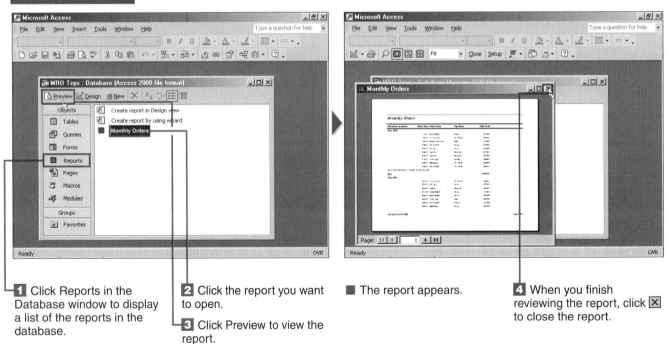

1 Click Reports in the Database window to display a list of the reports in the database.

2 Click the report you want to open.

3 Click Preview to view the report.

■ The report appears.

4 When you finish reviewing the report, click ☒ to close the report.

CHANGE THE REPORT VIEW

You can view a report in three ways. Each view allows you to perform a different task.

The Design view allows you to change the layout and design of a report. The Design view displays a grid of small, evenly spaced dots to help you line up the items in a report. This view displays information in several sections,

such as the report header and page footer sections.

The Print Preview view allows you to display all the pages in the report and examine how each page will print.

The Layout Preview view allows you to quickly view the layout and style of a report. The Layout

Preview view is available only when you display a report in the Design view. The Layout Preview view is similar to the Print Preview view, but allows you to see only a few pages of a report. The data from the table or query you use to create the report may not update properly in the Layout Preview view.

CHANGE THE REPORT VIEW

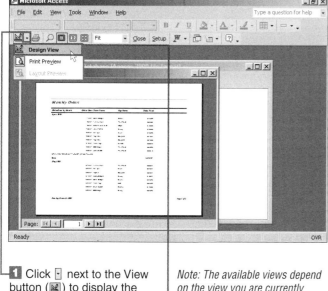

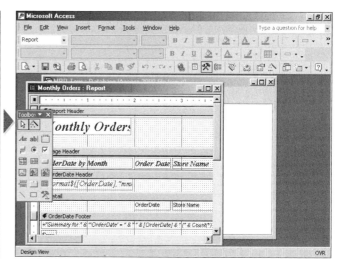

1 Click ⊡ next to the View button (■) to display the report in another view.

Note: The available views depend on the view you are currently using.

2 Click the view you want to use.

■ The report appears in the view you selected.

PREVIEW A REPORT

You can use the Print Preview feature to see how your tables, queries, forms, and reports look when you print them. Using the Print Preview feature can help you confirm that the printed pages appear the way you want.

The Print Preview window indicates which page you are

currently viewing. If an object contains more than one page, you can easily view the other pages.

You can magnify an area of a page. This allows you to view the area in more detail. When you magnify a page, Access displays scroll bars that you can use to move through the information on the page.

You can have Access display several pages in the Print Preview window at once. This gives you an overall view of the pages in an object.

When you finish using the Print Preview feature, you can close the Print Preview window to return to the Database window.

PREVIEW A REPORT

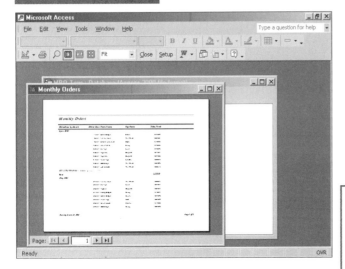

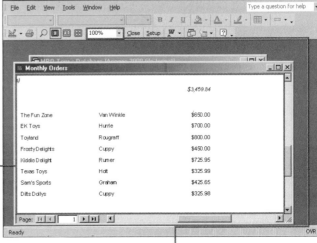

■1 Open the report by double-clicking its name in the Database window.

■ The Print Preview window appears.

■2 Click one of these buttons to view the other pages:

◼◀ First Page

◀ Previous Page

▶ Next Page

▶◼ Last Page

MAGNIFY A PAGE

■1 Position the ⊕ over the area of the page you want to magnify.

■2 Click the area to magnify it.

■ The page is magnified. You can see the magnification percent in the Zoom box.

■3 To once again display the entire page, click anywhere on the page.

Can I preview an object at different magnification levels?

✔ Yes. In the Print Preview window, you can select a new zoom setting to change the level of magnification. Click the ▾ next to 100% ▾ and then click the zoom setting you want to use. By default, Access displays an object in the Fit zoom setting, which allows Access to use the magnification level that displays all of the currently displayed page(s).

Can I print directly from the Print Preview window?

✔ Yes. To print an object directly from the Print Preview window, click the Print button (🖨).

How can I quickly display two pages of an object in the Print Preview window?

✔ To quickly display two pages, click the Two Pages button (▣).

How do I preview only one page of an object after displaying multiple pages?

✔ To preview one page of an object, click the One Page button (▣) in the Print Preview window.

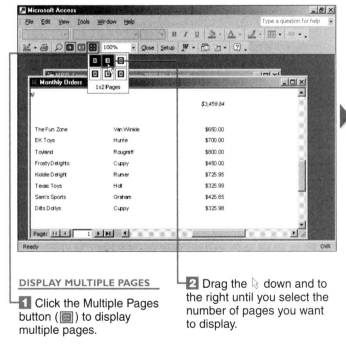

DISPLAY MULTIPLE PAGES

1 Click the Multiple Pages button (▦) to display multiple pages.

2 Drag the ⬚ down and to the right until you select the number of pages you want to display.

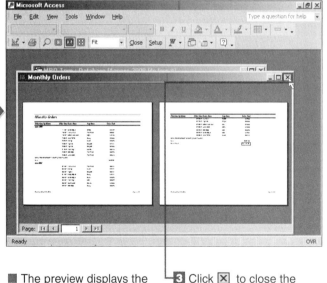

■ The preview displays the selected number of pages.

3 Click ✕ to close the Print Preview window.

PRINT DATA FROM A DATABASE

You can produce a paper copy of a table, query, form, or report. A paper copy is often referred to as a hard copy.

Before printing, make sure your printer is on and contains an adequate supply of paper.

You can choose the information you want to print. You can print all the records, specific pages, or specific records. Printing only specific records saves you from printing information you do not want to review. To print only specific records, you must select the records before you begin.

If the current printer settings suit your needs, you can use the Print button to quickly print all the records without displaying the Print dialog box.

When you print a table or query, Access prints the title, date, and page number on each page. This information can help you organize the printed data.

PRINT DATA FROM A DATABASE

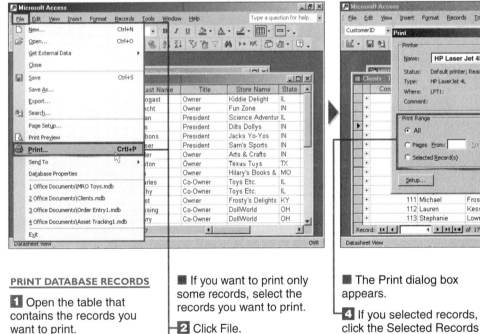

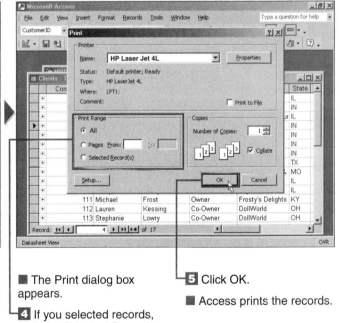

PRINT DATABASE RECORDS

1 Open the table that contains the records you want to print.

■ If you want to print only some records, select the records you want to print.

2 Click File.

3 Click Print.

■ The Print dialog box appears.

4 If you selected records, click the Selected Records option. To print all records, click All.

5 Click OK.

■ Access prints the records.

Can I specify the printer I want to use to print information?

✔ If you have more than one printer installed, you can select the printer you want to use. For example, you may want to use your color printer to print forms and a black-and-white printer to print tables. In the Print dialog box, click the Name area and then select the printer you want to use.

Can I print multiple copies?

✔ Yes. In the Print dialog box, double-click the Number of Copies area and then type the number of copies to print.

How do I change the page margins?

✔ Click File and then Page Setup, or click Page Setup in the Print dialog box. In the Page Setup dialog box, click the Margins tab and then type the margins you want to use for the top, bottom, left, and right. The default margin setting is 1 inch. Click OK to confirm your new margins.

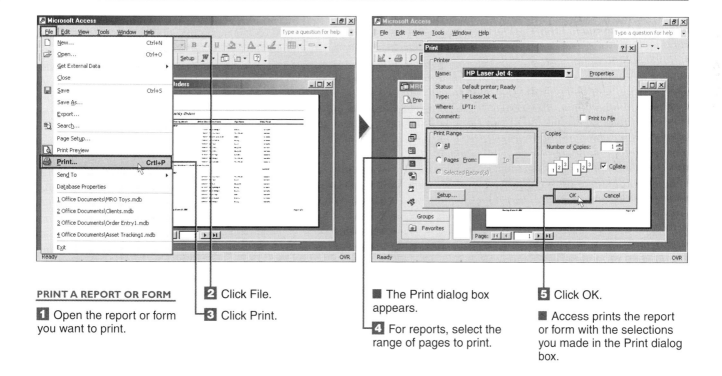

PRINT A REPORT OR FORM

1 Open the report or form you want to print.

2 Click File.

3 Click Print.

■ The Print dialog box appears.

4 For reports, select the range of pages to print.

5 Click OK.

■ Access prints the report or form with the selections you made in the Print dialog box.

CREATE MAILING LABELS

You can create a mailing label for every person in a database table. You can use labels for addressing envelopes and packages, labeling file folders, and creating name tags.

The fastest way to create mailing labels is to use Access's Label Wizard. The Label Wizard asks you a series of questions and then creates labels based on your answers.

You can choose the table that contains the names and addresses you want to appear on the labels.

You can use two types of labels — sheet feed and continuous. Sheet feed labels are individual sheets of labels. Continuous labels are connected sheets of labels, with holes punched along each side.

You can select the label size you want to use. Check your label

packaging to determine which label size to select.

The wizard allows you to change the appearance of the text on the labels. You can choose between various fonts, sizes, weights, and colors. The text appearance you choose affects all the text on every label.

CREATE MAILING LABELS

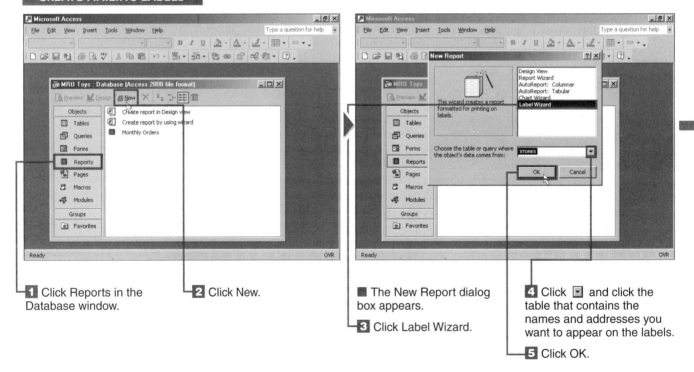

1 Click Reports in the Database window.

2 Click New.

■ The New Report dialog box appears.

3 Click Label Wizard.

4 Click ▾ and click the table that contains the names and addresses you want to appear on the labels.

5 Click OK.

I cannot find the label size I want in the Label Wizard. What is wrong?

✔ By default, the Label Wizard displays standard Avery labels. You can display a list of label sizes for a different manufacturer. Click the Filter by manufacturer ▪ and then click the manufacturer of the labels you are using.

How do I specify a custom label size in the Label Wizard?

✔ Click Customize and then click New. A dialog box appears, displaying sample labels and areas where you can enter measurements for your labels. Type in the measurements you want to use and then click OK.

How do I change the Text appearance options in the Label Wizard?

✔ You can click ▪ in the Font name, Font size, or Font weight areas to display a list of options. You can then select the option you want to use. Click ▪ beside the Text color area to display a list of colors and then click the color you want to use. To italicize or underline text, click the appropriate option (☐ changes to ☑).

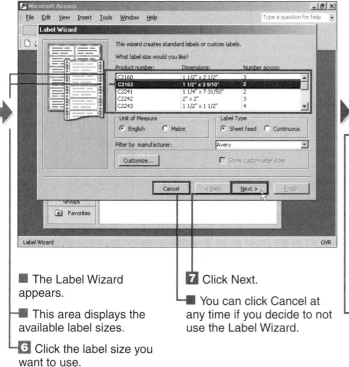

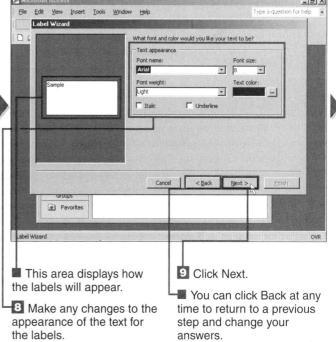

■ The Label Wizard appears.

■ This area displays the available label sizes.

6 Click the label size you want to use.

7 Click Next.

■ You can click Cancel at any time if you decide to not use the Label Wizard.

■ This area displays how the labels will appear.

8 Make any changes to the appearance of the text for the labels.

9 Click Next.

■ You can click Back at any time to return to a previous step and change your answers.

CONTINUED ▶

CREATE MAILING LABELS (CONTINUED)

Y ou can select the fields you want to appear on the labels. You do not have to select all the fields from the table.

The fields you select should appear in the Label Wizard in the order and location that you want them to print on the labels. Make sure you add spaces or commas where needed, such as a space between

the first and last name, or a comma between the city and state.

You can specify how you want to sort the labels. Sorting the labels determines the order that Access arranges the labels on a printed sheet. For example, you may want to sort mailing labels by city to place all labels for the same city together.

You can type a name for the labels. Access stores the labels as a report that you can open as you would open any report. To open a report, see the section "Open a Report."

The labels appear on your screen as they look when printed. This allows you to preview the labels before you print them.

CREATE MAILING LABELS (CONTINUED)

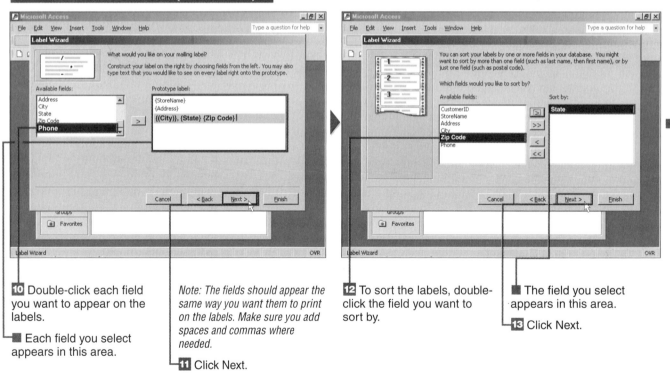

10 Double-click each field you want to appear on the labels.

■ Each field you select appears in this area.

Note: The fields should appear the same way you want them to print on the labels. Make sure you add spaces and commas where needed.

11 Click Next.

12 To sort the labels, double-click the field you want to sort by.

■ The field you select appears in this area.

13 Click Next.

Can I sort the labels by more than one field?

✔ Yes. If the first field you are using to sort the labels contains matching data, you can sort by a second field. In the Label Wizard, double-click the first field you want to sort by and then double-click the second field you want to sort by.

How do I edit labels I created?

✔ You must change the data in the table you used to create the labels. Changes you make in the table automatically appear in the labels.

What if I see a mistake when I am previewing the labels?

✔ You can start over and create new mailing labels, being sure to make the appropriate changes to the label format. Or you can edit the label report design, inserting spaces and punctuation as needed. To edit a report design, open the report and then click the Design View button (🖹). Make any changes to the layout and then click the Save button (💾).

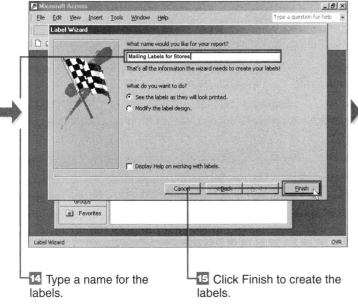

14 Type a name for the labels.

15 Click Finish to create the labels.

■ A new window opens, displaying a personalized label for each person or company in the table.

16 To print the labels, insert the labels into your printer and then click the Print button (🖨).

29) SEND AND RECEIVE E-MAIL

An Introduction to Outlook 502
Start Outlook 503
Using Outlook Today 504
Change the Outlook Window 505
Read Messages 506
Create a New Message 508
Select a Name from the Address Book 510
Attach a File to a Message 512
Open and Save Attachments 514
Reply to or Forward a Message 516

30) ORGANIZE MESSAGES

Open E-mail Folders 518
Print a Message 520
Delete a Message 521
Create a New Mail Folder 522
Move a Message 523
Archive Messages 524
Format a Message 525
Sort and Find Messages 526

31) MANAGE INFORMATION

Keep Notes 528
Create a Task List 530
Manage a Task List 532
Schedule Appointments with Calendar 534
Display the Calendar 536
Manage Contacts 538

SECTION VI

AN INTRODUCTION TO OUTLOOK

Outlook is an e-mail and personal information manager. The program includes tools for sending, receiving, and handling e-mail messages and also other program components for keeping track of people, appointments, and to-do tasks.

For more information on Outlook, you can visit the following Web site: www.microsoft.com/outlook.

Electronic Mail

The main purpose of Outlook is to handle your electronic mail or e-mail. If you have an Internet or other communication connection such as America Online (AOL) or a network e-mail system, you can send e-mail to others. To use your connection, you must set up Outlook to dial in or make the network connection to your e-mail account. For this procedure, you enter specific information about your system, including information about the mail server, your username, and your password. Outlook includes a wizard

for setting up an account, which prompts you for this information. Because everyone may have a unique system, the steps for setup are not provided in this chapter. Check with your network administrator or your e-mail provider for the exact information and steps to follow to set up your e-mail account.

After Outlook is set up to handle e-mail, you can send and receive e-mail. You can delete, print, forward, and respond to messages. You can even attach files and open files attached to a message. E-mail has many benefits: It is inexpensive, convenient, and quick. Your message is sent instantaneously, and you can send messages at any time you choose. See Chapters 29 and 30 for more on sending and handling e-mail.

Appointments, Contacts, and To-Do Lists

In addition to handling e-mail, you can also use Outlook and its various components to schedule appointments and other events on the Calendar; to keep track of friends, employees, business clients, and other contacts using Contact; to keep a to-do list of tasks; and to record notes or other journal entries. See Chapter 31 for more on these features of Outlook.

START OUTLOOK

Y ou can start Outlook to access a wide range of e-mail features. When you start the program, you see the Microsoft Outlook window, which is divided into two areas. The area on the left side of the window contains the Outlook Bar. The Outlook Bar displays icons for the different features of Outlook. The area on the right side of the window displays the current feature.

You can use Outlook's features to manage many different types of information. The Inbox lets you send and receive e-mail messages. The Calendar helps you keep track of your appointments. You can use Contacts to store information about people with whom you correspond. Tasks allows you to create a list of duties you want to accomplish. Notes lets you create brief reminder notes. Deleted Items stores items you have deleted.

Note: The first time you start Outlook, a wizard appears that allows you to set up Outlook on your computer. Follow the instructions on your screen to set up Outlook.

START OUTLOOK

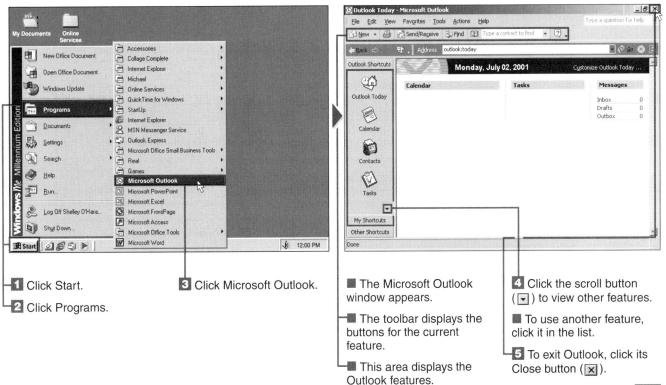

1 Click Start.

2 Click Programs.

3 Click Microsoft Outlook.

■ The Microsoft Outlook window appears.

■ The toolbar displays the buttons for the current feature.

■ This area displays the Outlook features.

4 Click the scroll button (▾) to view other features.

■ To use another feature, click it in the list.

5 To exit Outlook, click its Close button (✕).

USING OUTLOOK TODAY

You can use Outlook Today to display a summary of your day, which includes your upcoming appointments, a list of your tasks, and a summary of your e-mail messages.

By default, Outlook Today is selected as the default feature when you start Outlook.

The first list contains any appointments or events you have

scheduled with the Calendar. You can view the details of and make changes to any scheduled event. For example, you can mark an event as complete. For information on using Calendar, see Chapter 31.

The second list contains any tasks you add to your task list. Again, you can view details of a task or mark it complete. For information on adding tasks, see Chapter 31.

The third list contains the Inbox, Draft, and Outbox folders. The Inbox contains a short list of messages you have received from other people. You can view and edit messages that you are currently composing but have not yet sent in your Drafts folder. You can see completed and unsent messages in your Outbox. For more on e-mail, see the later sections in this chapter.

USING OUTLOOK TODAY

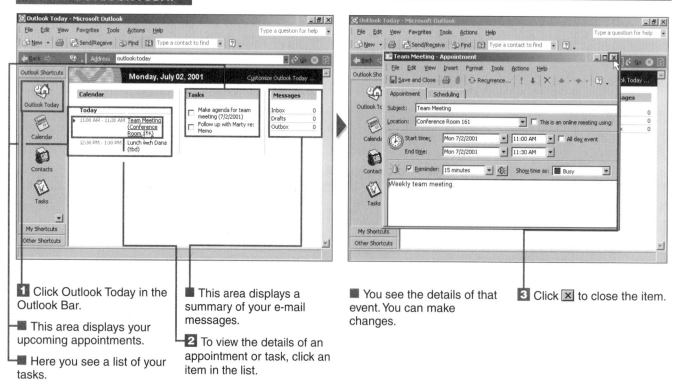

■ 1 Click Outlook Today in the Outlook Bar.

■ This area displays your upcoming appointments.

■ Here you see a list of your tasks.

■ This area displays a summary of your e-mail messages.

■ 2 To view the details of an appointment or task, click an item in the list.

■ You see the details of that event. You can make changes.

■ 3 Click ⊠ to close the item.

CHANGE THE OUTLOOK WINDOW

You can change what appears in the Outlook window so that the most important elements, the features you use most often, are readily available.

For example, if you do not like scrolling through the list of icons in the Outlook bar, you can replace it with a folder list. Or you can display both a folder list and the Outlook bar. As another example, you can hide the Outlook Bar and

the folder list to increase the viewing area of the current feature.

Outlook lists the available items you can display and turn off on the view menu. Check boxes allow you to display or remove an item from view.

Can I change the way Outlook Today displays information?

✔ Yes. Click Outlook Today to display the feature, and then click Customize Outlook Today. Choose the options for the items you want to display differently. You can select what Outlook Today displays at startup, which message folders it displays, how many days you see in the calendar, as well as other options. Make your changes and then click Save Changes.

CHANGE THE OUTLOOK WINDOW

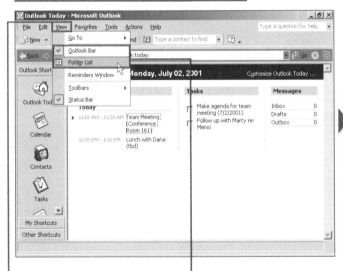

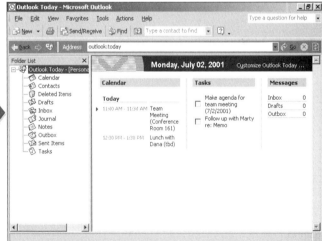

1 Click View.

■ Active items have a check mark (✔) or an indented symbol next to their names.

2 Click the menu item you wish to turn on or off.

■ To turn an item on or off, click View and then click the command again.

■ Outlook makes the changes. In this example, the Outlook bar is hidden, and the Folder list is displayed.

READ MESSAGES

Outlook allows you to exchange electronic mail, or e-mail, with friends, family members, colleagues, and clients. When you receive new e-mail messages, Outlook stores the messages you receive in the Inbox. You can use the Inbox to open the messages and read their contents.

Outlook displays the number of new messages in bold next to the

Inbox under Message in Outlook Today. If you opt to display the Folder List, the Inbox appears bold and indicates the number of new messages in parentheses when you have new mail. Also, if you have Outlook open and you receive new mail, an envelope icon appears in the taskbar of Windows.

Each unread message displays a closed envelope and appears in

bold type. After you read a message, Outlook displays an open envelope that appears in regular type. For each e-mail you receive, Outlook displays the author, subject, and date.

READ MESSAGES

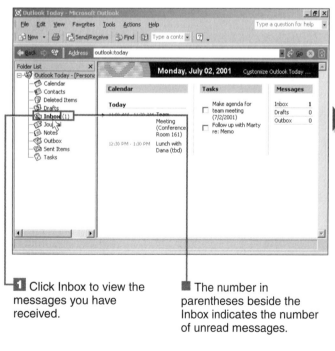

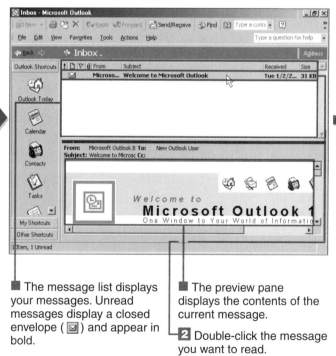

■1 Click Inbox to view the messages you have received.

■ The number in parentheses beside the Inbox indicates the number of unread messages.

■ The message list displays your messages. Unread messages display a closed envelope (✉) and appear in bold.

■ The preview pane displays the contents of the current message.

■2 Double-click the message you want to read.

How do I check for new messages?

✔ To check for new messages immediately, click the Send/Receive button (📧). You need to connect to your e-mail provider, and that server (computer) downloads your message to your computer.

How can I go directly to my Inbox?

✔ If you prefer to go directly to your Inbox, rather than Outlook Today, you can do so. Click the Customize Outlook Today link in the Outlook Today window. In the Startup area, uncheck the When starting, go directly to Outlook Today option (☑ changes to ☐).

Does Outlook ever automatically check for new messages?

✔ If you are connected to your e-mail server, Outlook checks for new messages at regular intervals. To change how often Outlook checks for messages, click Tools, Options, and then click the Mail Setup tab. Be sure that Include this group in send/receive is checked for When Outlook is Online. In the minutes area beside the Schedule an automatic send/receive every [xx] minutes option in this same area, double-click the number and then type the number of minutes you want to use. Click Close, and then click OK.

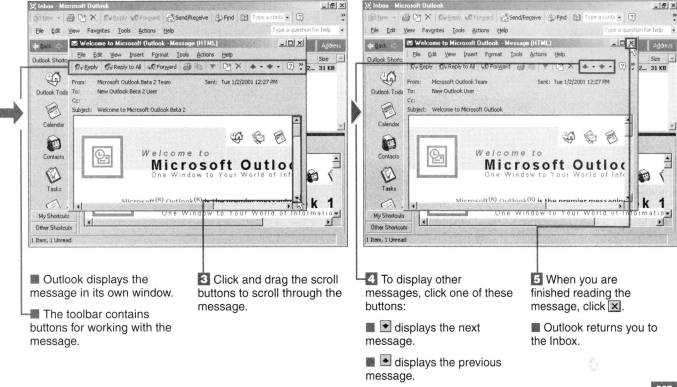

■ Outlook displays the message in its own window.

■ The toolbar contains buttons for working with the message.

3 Click and drag the scroll buttons to scroll through the message.

4 To display other messages, click one of these buttons:

■ 🔽 displays the next message.

■ 🔼 displays the previous message.

5 When you are finished reading the message, click ✖.

■ Outlook returns you to the Inbox.

CREATE A NEW MESSAGE

Y ou can create and send an
e-mail message to exchange
ideas or request information.

Outlook allows you to send a
message to more than one person.
To send a message, you must know
the e-mail address of each person
you want to receive the message.
You can type the address of each
recipient in the To area. You can
type the address or select it from
an address list. See the section

"Select a Name from the Address
Book" for more information on the
address list.

You can also type an address in the
Cc, or *carbon copy*, to send a copy
of the message to a person who is
not directly involved in the subject
of the e-mail, but who may find the
message of interest.

When you create a message, be
sure to type a subject that helps the

reader quickly identify the contents
of your message.

Outlook stores messages you have
sent or are planning to send in
three mail folders. The Drafts
folder stores incomplete messages.
The Outbox folder stores messages
that you have not yet sent. The
Sent Items folder stores sent
messages.

CREATE A NEW MESSAGE

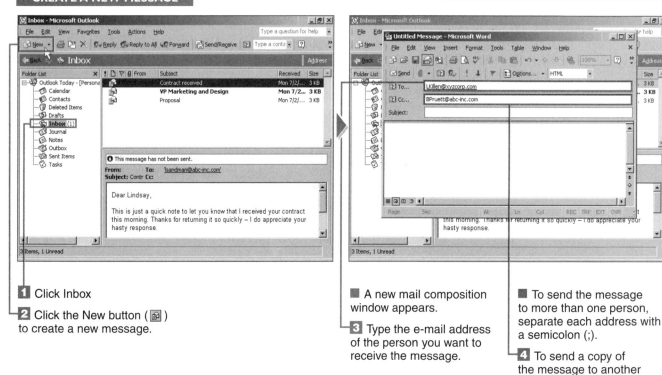

1 Click Inbox

2 Click the New button (🖹)
to create a new message.

■ A new mail composition
window appears.

3 Type the e-mail address
of the person you want to
receive the message.

■ To send the message
to more than one person,
separate each address with
a semicolon (;).

4 To send a copy of
the message to another
person, click here and type
the e-mail address.

Can I correct spelling errors in my message?

✔ Yes. To find and correct spelling errors in a message, click Tools and then click Spelling to start the spell check.

How can I prevent Outlook from saving my messages in the Sent Items folder?

✔ In the Microsoft Outlook window, click Tools, click Options, and then click the Preferences tab. Click E-mail and deselect the Save copies of messages in Sent Items folder option (☑ changes to ☐). Then click OK.

Can I add a priority to my message?

✔ Yes. You can change the priority of the message, flagging it as high or low priority. The default is regular priority. Click the Importance: High button (❗) to assign a high importance, or click the Importance: Low button (⬇) to assign a low priority.

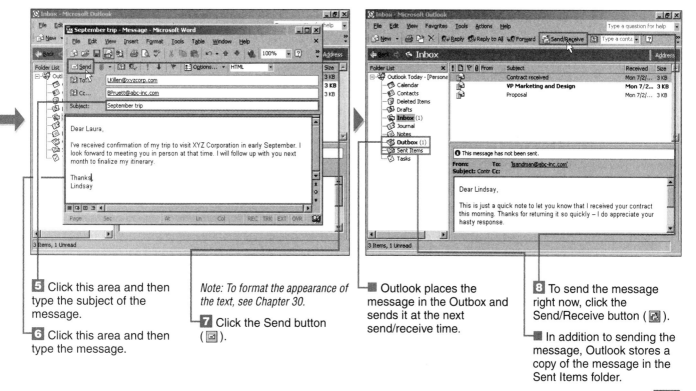

5 Click this area and then type the subject of the message.

6 Click this area and then type the message.

Note: To format the appearance of the text, see Chapter 30.

7 Click the Send button (▣).

■ Outlook places the message in the Outbox and sends it at the next send/receive time.

8 To send the message right now, click the Send/Receive button (▣).

■ In addition to sending the message, Outlook stores a copy of the message in the Sent Items folder.

SELECT A NAME FROM THE ADDRESS BOOK

When creating a message, you can select from an address book the name of the person you want to receive the message. Using an address book makes it easy to send a message without remembering the exact spelling of the recipient's address and reduces the possibility that your e-mail service cannot deliver your e-mail due to a typing mistake in the address.

You can use an address book to send a message to more than one person. You can specify whether the recipients receive the original message or a carbon copy, Cc, of the message. You use the Cc option if your recipient is not directly involved in the e-mail, but may find the message of interest. Outlook also lets you send a blind carbon copy, Bcc, which lets you send a copy of the message to a person

without anyone else knowing that the person received the message.

You must list the address of your recipients in the address book before you can select their names. See Chapter 31 for information on adding names to an address book.

SELECT A NAME FROM THE ADDRESS BOOK

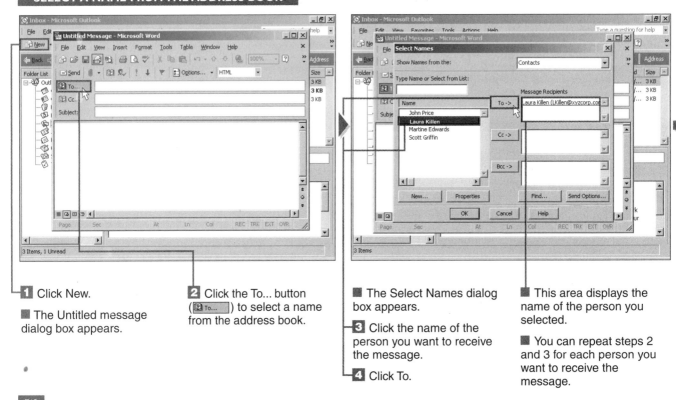

■1 Click New.

■ The Untitled message dialog box appears.

■2 Click the To... button (To...) to select a name from the address book.

■ The Select Names dialog box appears.

■3 Click the name of the person you want to receive the message.

■4 Click To.

■ This area displays the name of the person you selected.

■ You can repeat steps 2 and 3 for each person you want to receive the message.

How can I quickly select a group of people from my address book?

✔ You can create a distribution list. In the Select Name dialog box, click New, Distribution List, and OK. Type a name for the list and then click the Select Members button. Double-click the name of each person you want to add to the list and then click OK. Click Save and Close to add the list to the address book. When you send a message with the distribution list name as the recipient, Outlook sends the message to each person on the list.

What is the format for an e-mail address?

✔ The format for an e-mail address is *username@servername.ext*. The *username* is the person's assigned username, and the *servername* is the name of that person's server or domain. The extension indicates the type of server. For example, lgodiva.@aol.com is an example of an e-mail address, where the server name is America Online.

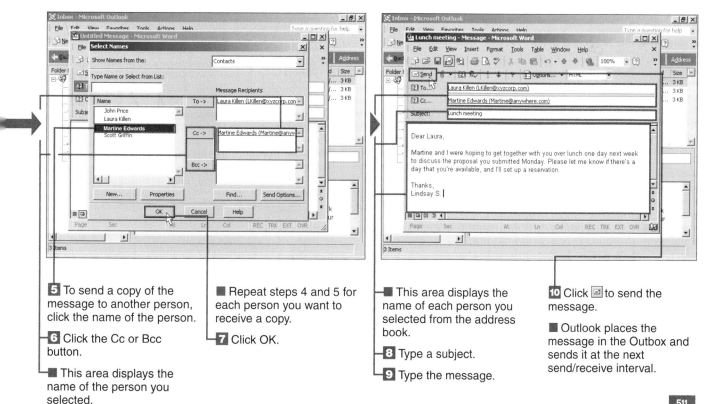

5 To send a copy of the message to another person, click the name of the person.

6 Click the Cc or Bcc button.

■ This area displays the name of the person you selected.

■ Repeat steps 4 and 5 for each person you want to receive a copy.

7 Click OK.

■ This area displays the name of each person you selected from the address book.

8 Type a subject.

9 Type the message.

10 Click ☑ to send the message.

■ Outlook places the message in the Outbox and sends it at the next send/receive interval.

ATTACH A FILE TO A MESSAGE

You can attach a file to a message you are sending. Attaching a file is useful when you want to include additional information with a message. To learn how to send a message, see the section "Create a New Message."

Outlook allows you to attach many different types of files to a message, including images, documents, videos, sound recordings, and program files.

To attach a file, you must select the drive and folder where the file is placed. Outlook lists the attached file in the message header. While Outlook does not restrict the number of attachments you can send with a message, the size of your file may prevent you from sending it. Many e-mail servers on the Internet do not transfer large messages properly, if at all. Also, some mail recipients may block file attachments over a certain size.

When sending e-mail messages over the Internet, you should keep the total size of attachments to less than 150 kilobytes.

The recipient of your message must have the necessary hardware and software installed on their computer to display or play the file you attach.

ATTACH A FILE TO A MESSAGE

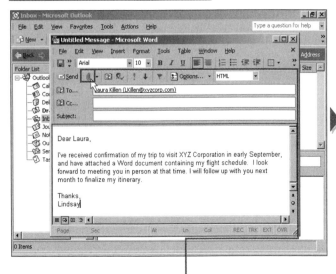

1 Create a new message.

Note: To create a new message, see the section "Create a New Message."

2 Click the Insert File button ( ).

■ The Insert File dialog box appears.

■ By default, Outlook displays the My Documents folder if this is the first time you attach a file. If you attached a file previously in this session, you see the last folder you selected.

3 Change to the drive and folder that contains the file you want to attach.

■ Click any of these areas to change to another drive or directory.

How do I remove a file I attached to a message?

✔ Right-click the icon or name of the file and then click Remove.

How can I send large files?

✔ If you do need to send large files, you can compress them before sending. You can do so using a compressed folder, which is a Windows feature. Or you can use a compression program such as WinZIP. You can also find other available zip or compression programs.

Why is it taking so long to send the message?

✔ Outlook sends a simple text message quickly, but depending on the file size, a message with an attachment may take more time to send. You can display the status of the send/receive operation by clicking the status bar message that says Send/Receive Status and then clicking Details. To close the Outlook Send/Receive Progress dialog box, click its ☒.

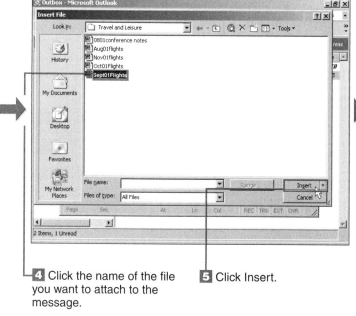

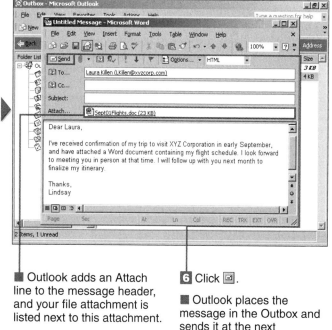

4 Click the name of the file you want to attach to the message.

5 Click Insert.

■ Outlook adds an Attach line to the message header, and your file attachment is listed next to this attachment.

6 Click 🖃.

■ Outlook places the message in the Outbox and sends it at the next send/receive time.

OPEN AND SAVE ATTACHMENTS

When you receive a message with an attached file, you can open or save the file. Messages with an attached file display a paper clip icon in the message list.

When you select an attached file you want to view, Outlook asks if you want to open the file or save the file on your computer.

What happens when you open the file depends on the file type. If the file is a graphic file or document, that file or document displays. If the file attachment is a program, Office executes the program.

Some files, such as program files, can contain viruses. If you open and run a file that contains a virus, the virus could damage information on your computer. You should only open files sent by people you trust and even then, scan the attachment with a virus scan program before opening it.

If you receive an attachment that you want to save, you can save it to your hard drive or floppy disk.

OPEN AND SAVE ATTACHMENTS

OPEN AN ATTACHED FILE

1 Open a message with an attached file.

■ The attachment(s) is listed here.

2 Double-click the file you want to open.

■ Outlook asks if you want to open or save the file.

3 Click Open it (○ changes to ◉).

4 Click OK.

How can I check an attached file for viruses before opening the file?

✔ When Outlook asks if you want to open or save the attached file, save the file to a folder on your computer. You can then use an anti-virus program to check the file for viruses before opening it.

If I do not save the attachment, can I open it again?

✔ Yes. Outlook stores the attachment with the mail message, and you can open it again by displaying the message. If you delete the message permanently, you cannot open the attachment again. For information on deleting messages, see Chapter 30.

I see an error message when I open a file. What is wrong?

✔ Each type of file is associated with one or more programs, which can be used to open or run that file. If you do not have the appropriate programs and attempt to open the file, Outlook prompts you to select the program to use to display the file. Click the appropriate program and click OK. If you do not have the appropriate program, you cannot open the file.

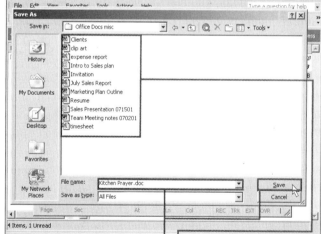

■ The appropriate program opens and displays the file on-screen. Here a Word document is displayed.

5 Click ✕ to close the file attachment.

SAVE AN ATTACHED FILE

1 Follow steps 1 through 3 from the facing page, but in step 3 click Save it to disk (○ changes to ◉).

■ The Save As dialog box appears.

2 Click a drive and folder to store the file.

3 You can change the file name.

4 Click Save.

■ Outlook saves the file to the location you specified.

REPLY TO OR FORWARD A MESSAGE

You can reply to a message to answer a question, express an opinion, or supply additional information.

You can send a reply to just the person who sent the message or to the sender and everyone else who received the original message.

When you reply to a message, a new window appears, displaying the name of the recipient(s) and the subject of the message to which you are replying. The reply includes a copy of the original message, which Outlook calls *quoting*. Including a copy of the original message helps the reader identify to which message you are replying. To save the reader time, you can delete all parts of the original message that do not directly relate to your reply.

You can also forward a message to another person. When you forward a message, you can add your own comments to the original message.

Outlook stores a copy of each message you send in the Sent Items folder. For information on the mail folders, see Chapter 30.

REPLY TO OR FORWARD A MESSAGE

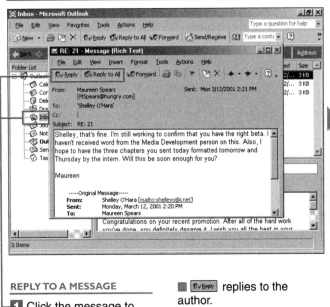

REPLY TO A MESSAGE

1 Click the message to which you want to reply in the Inbox.

■ The message displays.

2 Click a reply button.

■ **Reply** replies to the author.

■ **Reply to All** replies to the author and everyone who received the original message.

■ A window appears, displaying a copy of the original message.

■ Outlook fills in the e-mail address(es) and subject for you.

3 Type your reply.

4 Click to send the reply.

■ Outlook places the message in the Outbox and then sends it at the next send/receive time.

Can I respond only to that person?
✔ No. When you reply, the recipient's name is used as the address, but you can also select other recipients for the To or CC fields. Either type the address(es) or use the address book to add them to the message.

How do I forward multiple messages?
✔ Hold down the Ctrl key as you click each message you want to forward. Then perform steps 2 to 5 on this page. If you forward more than one message at a time, Outlook sends the messages as attachments.

Can I prevent Outlook from including a copy of the original message in my replies?
✔ Yes. Choose the Tools menu and then click Options. Click the Preferences tab and then click the E-mail Options button. In the E-mail Options dialog box, display the When replying to a message drop-down list and select Do not include original message. Then click OK.

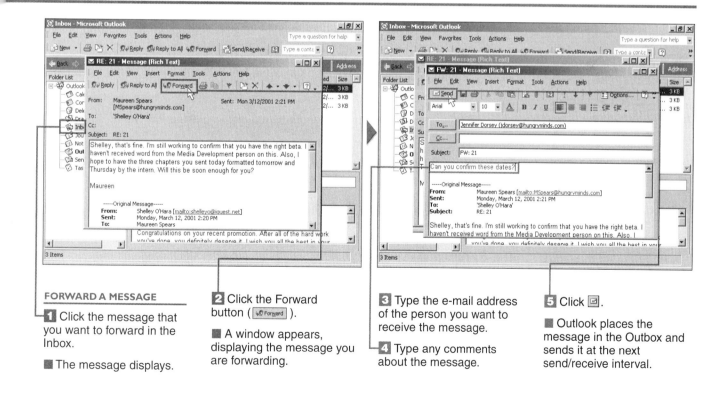

FORWARD A MESSAGE

1 Click the message that you want to forward in the Inbox.

■ The message displays.

2 Click the Forward button (Forward).

■ A window appears, displaying the message you are forwarding.

3 Type the e-mail address of the person you want to receive the message.

4 Type any comments about the message.

5 Click .

■ Outlook places the message in the Outbox and sends it at the next send/receive interval.

OPEN E-MAIL FOLDERS

Outlook includes several e-mail folders so that you can use to keep your messages organized. You can view any of these folders to review and work with any of the messages stored in that folder.

The Inbox contains messages that you have received. This includes messages you have read and have not read. Messages you have not read appear in bold.

The Outbox stores messages that you have created but not yet sent. You can click Send/Receive to send these messages. Otherwise, Outlook sends them during the next send/receive interval.

The Drafts folder contains messages you have created, but not yet sent. By default, Outlook saves messages every three minutes as you create them.

When you delete a message, Outlook does not actually delete the message, but simply moves the message to the Deleted Items folder. You must delete the message from the Deleted Items folder or empty the entire folder to permanently remove the message.

The Sent Items folder contains a copy of all messages you have sent.

OPEN E-MAIL FOLDERS

1 If the Folder List is visible, skip to step 3; otherwise, click View.

2 Click Folder List.

■ The Folder List appears.

3 Click the desired folder in the Folder List.

■ Outlook highlights the selected folder and displays its contents.

■ To view deleted items, click the Deleted Items folder.

■ You see all of the messages you have deleted.

How can I prevent Outlook from saving my messages in the Sent Items folder?

✓ In the Microsoft Outlook window, click Tools, Options and then click the Preferences tab. Click E-mail Options and uncheck the Save copies of messages in Sent Items folder option (☑ changes to ☐). Then click OK.

How do I empty the Deleted Items folder?

✓ Click Tools and then click Empty "Deleted Items" Folder. Click Yes to confirm that you want to permanently delete all items.

What are the Back and Forward buttons used for?

✓ You can click the Back ⬛ and Forward ⬛ buttons to move back to the previous folder or forward to the last folder (if you have gone back a folder). Click the appropriate button.

Can I change the width of the columns?

✓ Yes. You can change the width of the folder list column or the panes for the message list and preview pane. To do so, put the mouse pointer on the border of the pane and drag to resize.

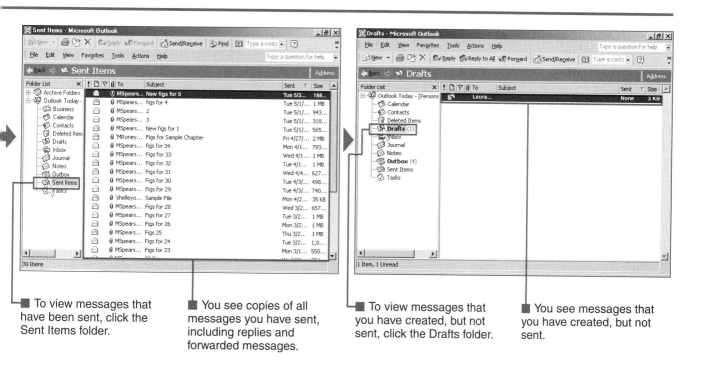

■ To view messages that have been sent, click the Sent Items folder.

■ You see copies of all messages you have sent, including replies and forwarded messages.

■ To view messages that you have created, but not sent, click the Drafts folder.

■ You see messages that you have created, but not sent.

PRINT A MESSAGE

Y ou can produce a paper copy of a message. A printed message is useful when you need a reference copy of the message. For example, you might print directions to a meeting to take with you. Or a message might include phone numbers or other information for which you need a paper copy.

Outlook prints information such as the date and time the message was sent on the first page of the message. The page number appears at the bottom of each page of the printed message. If the message includes replies and responses, all of the messages are printed.

You can select which printer is used, the print style, whether

attachments are printed, and the number of copies to print if you use the Print dialog box.

If you do not need to set printing options, you can print using the Print button. You can print messages using this button from the Inbox or from an open message.

PRINT A MESSAGE

1 Open the message you want to print.

2 Click File.

3 Click Print.

■ The Print dialog box appears.

4 Make any changes to the print options.

5 Click OK.

■ Outlook prints the message.

DELETE A MESSAGE

You can delete a message you no longer need. Deleting messages prevents your mail folders from becoming cluttered with unneeded messages.

You can delete a message from an open message window or from the Inbox.

When you delete a message, Outlook places the deleted message in the Deleted Items folder. You can view the contents of the Deleted

Items folder by selecting the folder in the Folder List. See the section "Open E-mail Folders" for more information.

To undelete a message, you can move it from the Deleted Items folder to another folder. See the section "Move a Message" for more information.

Can I permanently delete selected messages?

✔ Yes. Open the Deleted Items folder and then select the message(s) you want to permanently delete. Click the Delete button (☒). When a dialog box appears questioning whether you really want to delete the item, confirm the deletion by clicking Yes.

DELETE A MESSAGE

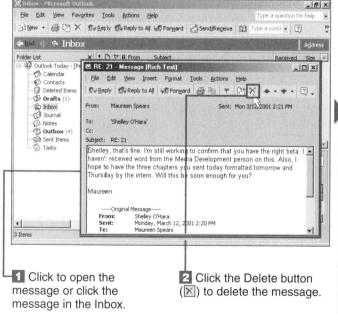

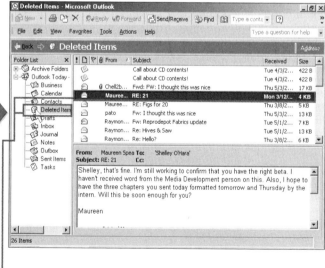

1 Click to open the message or click the message in the Inbox.

2 Click the Delete button (☒) to delete the message.

3 In the Folder List, click the Deleted Items folder.

■ Outlook places the deleted message in the Deleted Items folder.

■ You can permanently delete the message from the Deleted Items folder.

CREATE A NEW MAIL FOLDER

As you use e-mail more and more, you may find that your folders get cluttered with messages. To keep your e-mail correspondence organized, you can create mail folders.

For example, you may want to set up one folder for personal correspondence and another for business correspondence. If you

receive a lot of jokes, you may want to set up a folder for jokes that you want to save. If you subscribe to mailing lists, you may want to store these e-mail messages in their own separate folder.

You can also nest folders, creating folders inside folders. For example, under business correspondence, you can set up folders for specific

clients or for correspondence regarding specific projects.

You can set up as many folders as needed. You can then move messages from one folder to another to keep them organized. See the section "Move a Message" for help on moving a message from one folder to another.

CREATE A NEW MAIL FOLDER

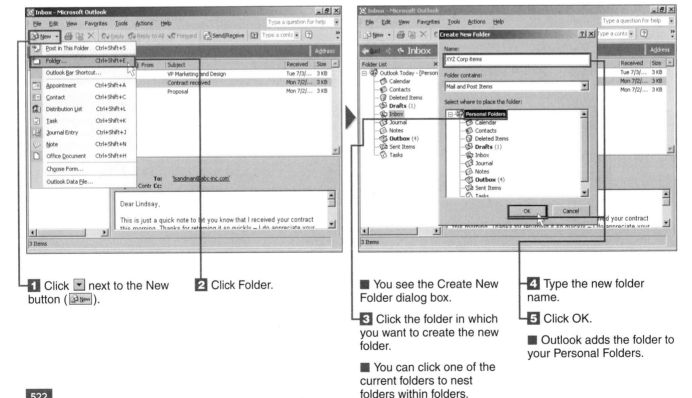

1 Click ▾ next to the New button (📇 New).

2 Click Folder.

■ You see the Create New Folder dialog box.

3 Click the folder in which you want to create the new folder.

■ You can click one of the current folders to nest folders within folders.

4 Type the new folder name.

5 Click OK.

■ Outlook adds the folder to your Personal Folders.

MOVE A MESSAGE

To keep your e-mail correspondence organized, you can create mail folders and then move messages to the appropriate folder.

For example, you can set up folders named Personal and Business and move messages from your Inbox to the appropriate folder. This way you have a copy, but your Inbox is not cluttered with read messages.

As another example, you may want to move messages from one of Outlook's default folders. For example, if you delete a message by mistake, you can move it from the Deleted Items folder to another folder.

For information on creating mail folders, see the section "Create a New Mail Folder."

Is there another way to move messages?

✓ Yes. You can display the message in the message list and then drag it to the appropriate folder in the Folder List. You can also use a shortcut menu for working with messages. To display the shortcut menu, right-click the message and then select the command you want. For example, right-click a message and then click the Move to Folder.

MOVE A MESSAGE

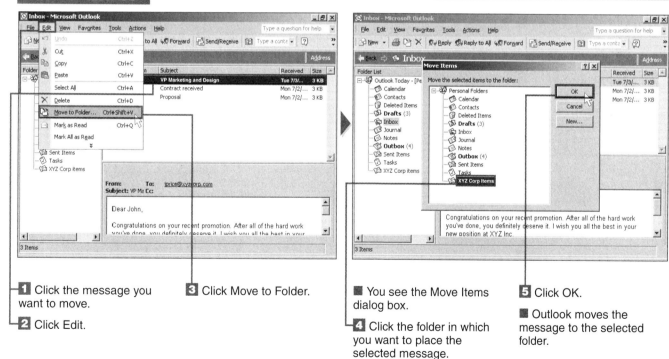

■ Click the message you want to move.

② Click Edit.

③ Click Move to Folder.

■ You see the Move Items dialog box.

④ Click the folder in which you want to place the selected message.

⑤ Click OK.

■ Outlook moves the message to the selected folder.

ARCHIVE MESSAGES

To periodically make a back up copy of the messages in your folder, you can archive them. Archiving messages copies them to a special mail archive file and removes the archived items from the original folders.

Archiving offers several advantages over manually moving or copying messages. You can set up a schedule so that you are reminded to archive. And you can also archive several folders at once.

When you use AutoArchive, you select which folder(s) to archive and Outlook archives the selected folder and any folders within that folder (subfolders).

You can also select a date. Outlook archives any items older than the specified date. Finally, you can select the name and folder for the archive file.

How do I view archived messages?

✔ When you archive the messages, Outlook creates a file with the extension .pst. You can open this file if you need to access archived messages. To open an archive file, click File, Open, and then Outlook Data File. Change to the folder that contains your file, select it, and then click OK.

ARCHIVE MESSAGES

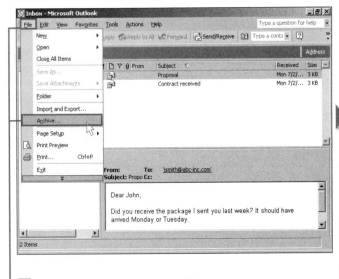

1 Click File.

2 Click Archive.

■ You see the Archive dialog box.

3 Click the top-level folder of the material you want to archive.

4 Click ▼ and click a date to use as the archive date.

■ Outlook archives any items older than the selected date.

■ You can change the name and location for the archive file.

5 Click OK.

■ Outlook archives the messages.

FORMAT A MESSAGE

When you create a mail message, you can select the format for the message. You can select HTML (the same format as Web pages), Rich Text (text that allows formatting), and Plain Text (no formatting).

If you select HTML or Rich Text, the formatting tools become available, and you can use these tools to make formatting changes to the text.

The formatting options you can make to message text are similar to other formatting changes you can make in other Office programs. You can change the font, font size, font style, and font color. You can also add bullets, indent text, or change the text alignment.

Keep in mind a few cautions. First, do not overdo the formatting. Too many changes not only distract from your message, but also make

the message file size larger, which takes the message longer for your recipient to download. Second, some mail programs can handle only certain mail formats. If you send a message to someone and they have trouble reading or opening the message, try a plain text message without any formatting.

FORMAT A MESSAGE

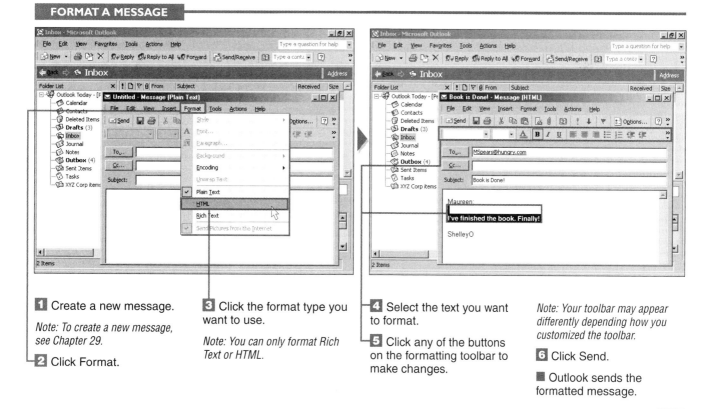

1 Create a new message.

Note: To create a new message, see Chapter 29.

2 Click Format.

3 Click the format type you want to use.

Note: You can only format Rich Text or HTML.

4 Select the text you want to format.

5 Click any of the buttons on the formatting toolbar to make changes.

Note: Your toolbar may appear differently depending how you customized the toolbar.

6 Click Send.

■ Outlook sends the formatted message.

SORT AND FIND MESSAGES

Messages are usually sorted by the date they were received in descending order, but you can select a different sort order so that you can more easily find messages.

You can sort by the name of the people who sent the messages, the subjects of the messages, or the dates the messages were received.

You can sort messages in ascending or descending order.

You can sort not only the messages in the Inbox, but messages in any folder.

If you cannot find a message by sorting, you can use Outlook's Find command to search for a message. You can search any folders in

Outlook. By default, Outlook searches all text in each message in that folder for the text you enter.

When the search is complete, Outlook displays the matching messages. You can then open, move, or delete these message(s) as needed.

SORT AND FIND MESSAGES

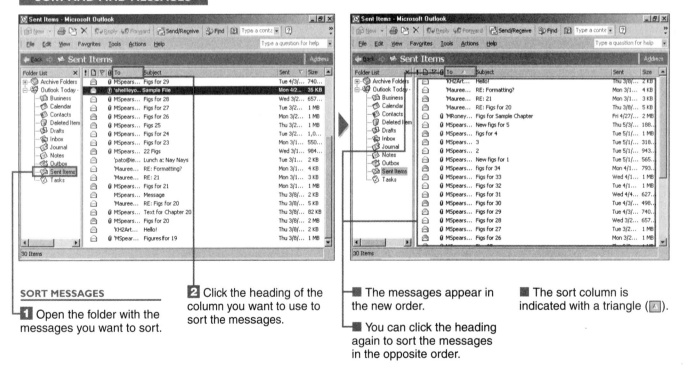

SORT MESSAGES

1 Open the folder with the messages you want to sort.

2 Click the heading of the column you want to use to sort the messages.

■ The messages appear in the new order.

■ You can click the heading again to sort the messages in the opposite order.

■ The sort column is indicated with a triangle (▣).

The wrong folder is selected. How can I select another folder?

✔ By default, Outlook selects the current folder to search in and displays this folder name next to Search In. If the wrong folder is selected, click the down arrow next to Search In and select the folder you do want to search.

Outlook found too many matches. How can I better refine the search?

✔ If you use a common word or phrase, you may get too many matches. Try searching for a unique word or phrase, or try using the advanced options.

What other options can I use for searching?

✔ Click Tools and then click Advanced Find. With the options in the Advanced Find dialog box, you can select what to search, such as the subject field or subject and message. You can also select the sender using the From text button or the recipient using the Sent To button.

In the Advanced Find dialog box, click the More Choices tab to search for messages by read/unread, with or without attachments, file size, or by importance.

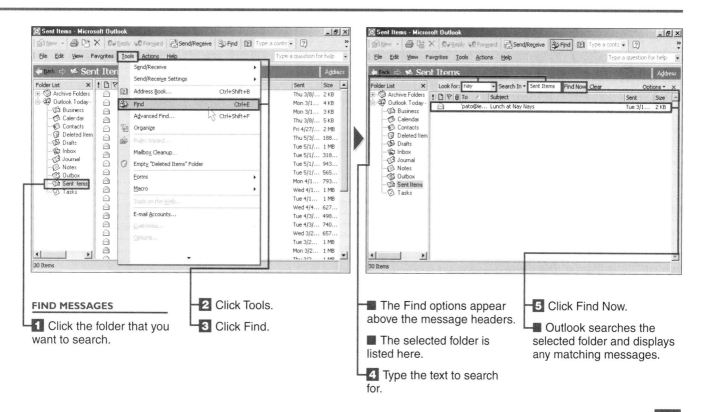

FIND MESSAGES

1 Click the folder that you want to search.

2 Click Tools.

3 Click Find.

■ The Find options appear above the message headers.

■ The selected folder is listed here.

4 Type the text to search for.

5 Click Find Now.

■ Outlook searches the selected folder and displays any matching messages.

KEEP NOTES

Using Outlook, you can create electronic notes that are similar to the paper sticky notes often used in offices.

Notes are useful for storing small pieces of information such as reminders, questions, ideas, and anything else you would record on note paper. Notes are often used to store information on a temporary basis.

When you create a note, Outlook records and saves the current date and time at the bottom of the note. This information helps you keep track of your notes and identify notes that are outdated.

You can open a note to read or edit the contents of the note. When you make changes to the contents of a note, the changes are automatically saved.

You can delete a note you no longer need. Deleting old notes reduces the number of notes on your screen and makes it easier to see new or important notes.

KEEP NOTES

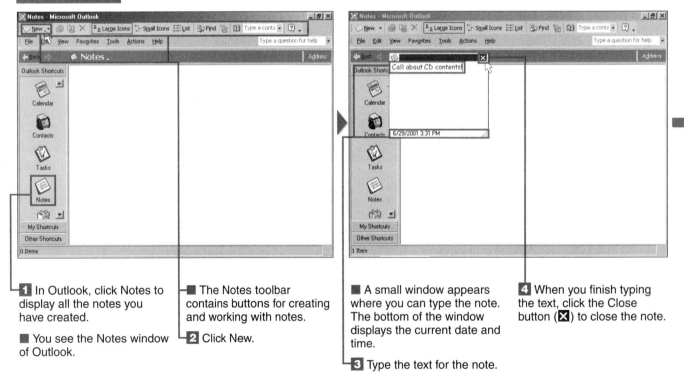

■1 In Outlook, click Notes to display all the notes you have created.

■ You see the Notes window of Outlook.

■ The Notes toolbar contains buttons for creating and working with notes.

■2 Click New.

■ A small window appears where you can type the note. The bottom of the window displays the current date and time.

■3 Type the text for the note.

■4 When you finish typing the text, click the Close button (✖) to close the note.

Can I change the size of a note?

✔ Yes. Display the contents of the note. Position the mouse pointer over the bottom right corner of the note window and then drag the corner until the note displays the size you want.

Can I change the color of a note?

✔ Yes. Display the contents of the note and then click the note icon (⬜) in the top left corner of the note window. From the menu that appears, click Color and then select the color you want to use.

Can I locate a specific word or phrase in my notes?

✔ Yes. Click the Find button on the toolbar. The Find tools appear at the top of the Notes screen. In the Look for area, type the word or phrase you want to locate and then click Find Now. Outlook lists the notes that contain the word or phrase you specified. You can double-click a note to display its contents.

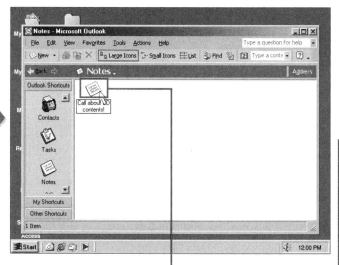

■ The note appears on the screen.

5 To open the note to display its contents, double-click the note.

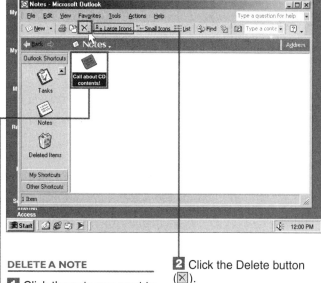

DELETE A NOTE

1 Click the note you want to delete.

2 Click the Delete button (✕).

■ Outlook deletes the note.

CREATE A TASK LIST

The Tasks feature of Outlook allows you to create an electronic to-do list of personal and work-related tasks that you want to accomplish. A task is a duty or errand you want to keep track of until it is complete.

When you create a new task, enter a descriptive subject that will help you recognize the task later, such as "submit marketing report" or "book airline reservations." The subject appears in your task list.

You can also specify a due date for a task. The due date appears in your task list and helps remind you of upcoming deadlines.

Outlook allows you to specify the status and priority of a task. Setting the status of a task can help you monitor your progress. Assigning a priority can help you organize your tasks and budget your time. You can also add comments to a task to record details about the task.

CREATE A TASK LIST

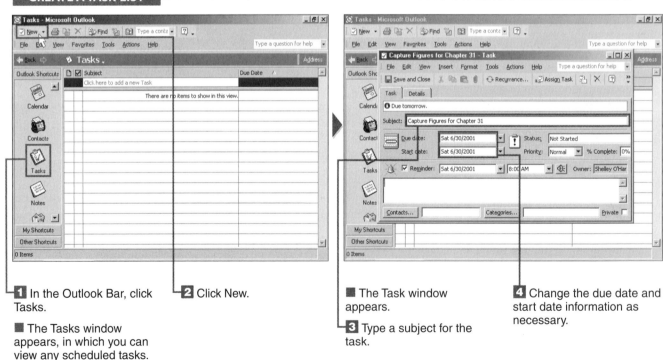

1 In the Outlook Bar, click Tasks.

■ The Tasks window appears, in which you can view any scheduled tasks.

2 Click New.

■ The Task window appears.

3 Type a subject for the task.

4 Change the due date and start date information as necessary.

How do I edit a task?

✔ To change the information for a task, double-click beside the task to redisplay the Task window. Make any changes and click OK.

Can I create a recurring task?

✔ Yes. Click the Recurrence button in the Task window. In the Task Recurrence dialog box, click the Daily, Weekly, Monthly, or Yearly option to specify the frequency of the task. The available options vary depending on your selection. Select the options you want to use to specify when the task occurs. Then click OK.

Is there another way to create a new task?

✔ In the task list, click the area that says "Click here to add a new Task" and then type a subject for the task. To specify a due date, press Tab and then type the due date. Then press Enter.

Can I have Outlook remind me of a task?

✔ Yes. In the Task window, check the Reminder check box. Then set the date and time for the reminder in the appropriate areas. Outlook displays a Reminder dialog box on your screen at the time you specify.

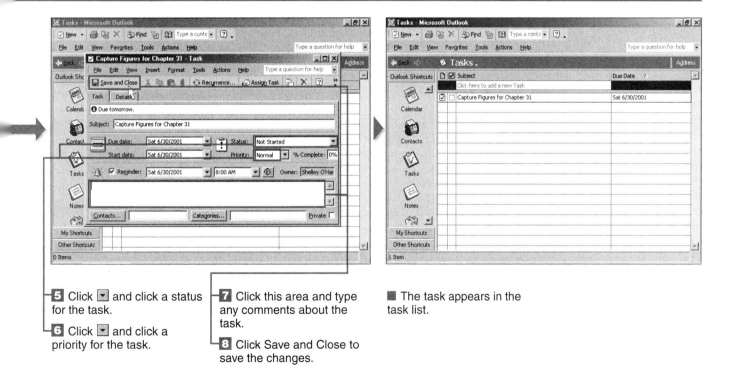

-5 Click ▼ and click a status for the task.

-6 Click ▼ and click a priority for the task.

-7 Click this area and type any comments about the task.

-8 Click Save and Close to save the changes.

■ The task appears in the task list.

MANAGE A TASK LIST

You can sort the tasks in your task list by subject or due date to help you find tasks of interest. You can sort tasks in ascending or descending order.

After you have accomplished a task, you can mark the task as complete. Outlook draws a line through each completed task. This allows you to see at a glance which tasks are outstanding and which tasks are complete.

You can delete a task you no longer want to display in your task list. Deleting tasks reduces clutter in your task list.

By default, Outlook displays your task list in the Simple List view. You can change the view of your tasks at any time. Outlook offers several views for you to choose from. For example, the Detailed List view displays details about each task, including the priority of the tasks. The Active Tasks view displays only tasks that are incomplete. The Next Seven Days view displays tasks that are due in the next week.

MANAGE A TASK LIST

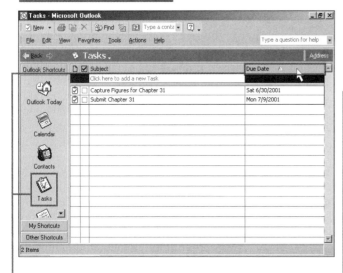

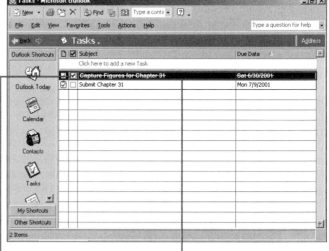

SORT TASKS

1 Click Tasks in the Outlook Bar.

2 Click the heading of the column you want to use to sort the tasks.

■ A small arrow appears in the heading of the column indicating the order in which the items are sorted. You can click the heading again to sort the tasks in the opposite order.

MARK A TASK COMPLETE

1 In the task list, click the box next to the completed task (☐ changes to ☑).

■ Outlook marks the task as complete and draws a line through the task.

Can I restore a task I have deleted?

✔ When you delete a task, Outlook places the task in the Deleted Items folder. To restore a task, click the Deleted Items icon in the Outlook Bar and then drag the task you want to restore to the Tasks icon.

How do I display comments in my task list?

✔ If you entered comments about a task, you can display the first few lines of the comments in your task list. Click View, AutoPreview. Repeat this procedure to once again hide the comments.

Can I change the color of tasks?

✔ You can change the color of overdue and completed tasks. Click Tools, Options, and then click the Task Options button. In the Task Options dialog box, click the Overdue task color drop-down arrow and select the color to use. Click the Completed task color drop-down arrow and select a new color for completed tasks. Then click OK twice.

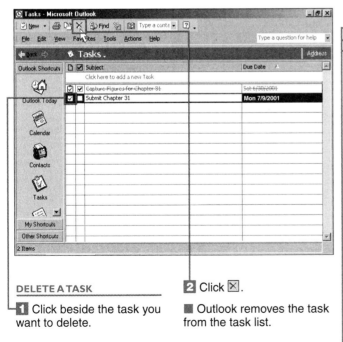

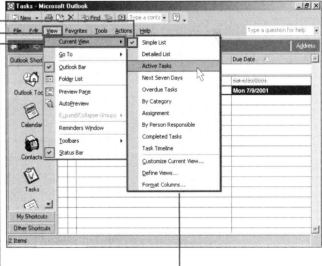

DELETE A TASK

–1 Click beside the task you want to delete.

2 Click ☒.

■ Outlook removes the task from the task list.

CHANGE VIEW OF TASKS

–1 Click View.

–2 Click Current View.

■ A check mark appears beside the current view.

3 Click the way you want to view the tasks.

■ Outlook displays the tasks in the selected view.

SCHEDULE APPOINTMENTS WITH CALENDAR

You can use the Calendar to keep track of your appointments. An appointment can be an activity such as going to the dentist, attending a meeting, or having lunch with a prospective client.

Calendar allows you to enter information about each appointment you want to schedule. You can enter a subject for an appointment. The subject is the description of an appointment that appears in the Calendar. You can also enter the location for an appointment and add comments about the appointment.

When you enter a start date, end date, or time for an appointment, you can type text such as "next Tuesday," "tomorrow," or "noon" instead of typing a date or time.

Outlook plays a brief sound and displays a dialog box 15 minutes before a scheduled appointment.

If an appointment will last an entire day, you can make the appointment an all-day event. Outlook displays an all-day event just below the date in the Calendar. You can still schedule other appointments after scheduling an all day event.

SCHEDULE APPOINTMENTS WITH CALENDAR

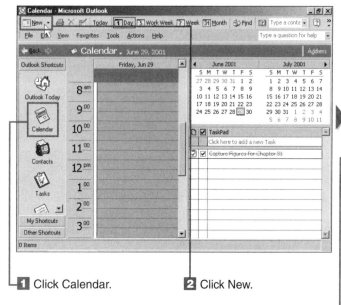

1 Click Calendar.

2 Click New.

■ The Appointment window appears.

3 Type a subject for the appointment.

4 Click this area and type the room or location for the appointment.

5 Click this area and type any comments about the appointment.

Can I schedule a recurring appointment?

✔ Yes. In the Appointment window, click the Recurrence button. In the Appointment Recurrence dialog box, specify the information about the recurring appointment including the start and end time, duration, and reoccurrence pattern. Select when to start and end the recurring appointment.

How do I delete an appointment?

✔ You can delete an appointment that has been canceled or that you no longer want to keep. Click the left side of the appointment and then click the Delete button (✕).

How can I quickly schedule an appointment?

✔ In the Day view, drag the mouse pointer over the yellow area to select the time for the appointment. Type a subject for the appointment and then press Enter.

How do I print the information in the Calendar?

✔ Click the Print button (🖨) to display the Print dialog box. Click the print style you want to use. Click the first and the last date you want to print. Then click OK.

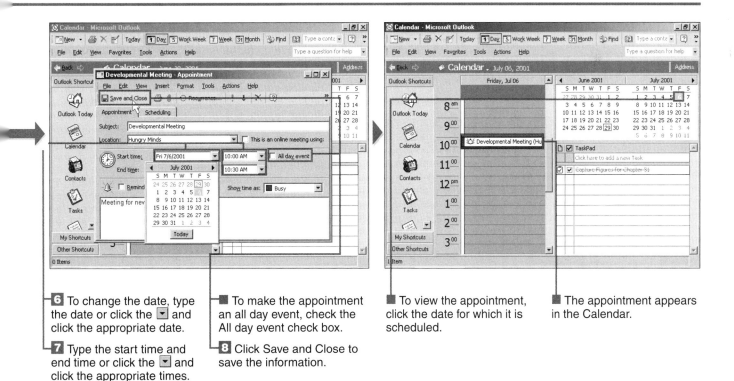

6 To change the date, type the date or click the ▼ and click the appropriate date.

7 Type the start time and end time or click the ▼ and click the appropriate times.

■ To make the appointment an all day event, check the All day event check box.

8 Click Save and Close to save the information.

■ To view the appointment, click the date for which it is scheduled.

■ The appointment appears in the Calendar.

DISPLAY THE CALENDAR

The Outlook Calendar window gives you a handy way to quickly view all of your appointments. By default, the Calendar displays the appointments you have scheduled for the current day. But you can easily display the appointments for another day.

The Calendar window also displays all the days in the current month and the next month. Today's date displays a red outline and days with appointments appear in bold. Clicking on any day brings up the appointments for that day.

You can flip through all the months in the Calendar to view past or future appointments. Viewing past appointments is useful when you have to report the amount of time you spent working on a particular project.

The Calendar also displays a list of tasks you created using the Tasks feature. For information on the Tasks feature, see "Create a Task List."

By default, the Calendar displays your appointments in Day view. You can change the view to display your appointments in the Work Week, Week, or Month view.

DISPLAY THE CALENDAR

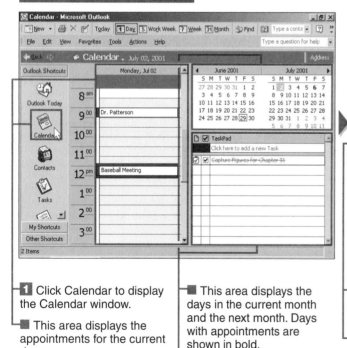

1 Click Calendar to display the Calendar window.

■ This area displays the appointments for the current day.

■ This area displays the days in the current month and the next month. Days with appointments are shown in bold.

■ This area displays the task list.

2 To display the appointments for another day, click the day.

■ Outlook highlights the day you select on the calendar, and you see the scheduled activities for that day in the appointment list.

■ The current day displays a red outline.

3 To display the days in the previous or next month, click the back or forward buttons.

Why is the Calendar displaying the wrong date for today?

✔ Outlook uses the date and time set in your computer to determine today's date. Your computer's clock may be set incorrectly. Use the Date/Time Control Panel in Windows to change the date.

Are there other views available in the Calendar?

✔ The Calendar also offers the Active Appointments, Events, Annual Events, Recurring Appointments, and By Category views. To change to one of these views, choose the View menu and select Current View. Then select the view you want to use.

How do I quickly display today's appointments?

✔ You can click the Today button at any time to display today's appointments.

How do I add holidays to the Calendar?

✔ Click the Tools menu and select Options. Click the Calendar Options button. Click the Add Holidays button and then select the country for the holidays you want to add. Click OK. Outlook adds the holidays to the calendar. Click OK three more times to close the message box and the two dialog boxes.

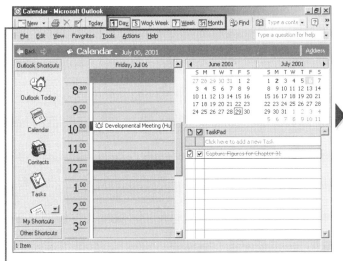

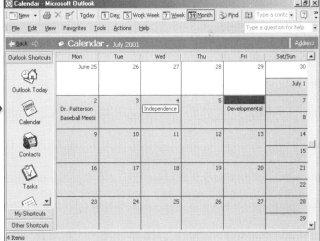

CHANGE VIEW OF CALENDAR

1 Click the button representing how you want to view the Calendar:

Day
Work Week
Week
Month

■ That view is displayed. Here you see a Month view.

MANAGE CONTACTS

Outlook supplies a contacts list where you can keep detailed information about your friends, family members, colleagues, and clients.

When you add a contact to the list, Outlook provides spaces for you to enter information about the contact. You can enter the contact's full name, job title, company name, and address. You can also enter the contact's business phone, home phone, business fax, and mobile phone numbers.

You can also include the contact's e-mail address. This information is necessary if you intend to use the Address Book/Contact List when creating e-mail messages. See Chapter 29 for more information.

You also can enter comments about the contact and the contact's Web page address, although you do not need to enter information in all the spaces Outlook provides.

You can update or add additional information to a contact in your list at any time. Over time, friends and colleagues may move and you will need to record their new addresses. Also, as you learn more about your contacts, you can add information such as directions to their house or the names of their children.

MANAGE CONTACTS

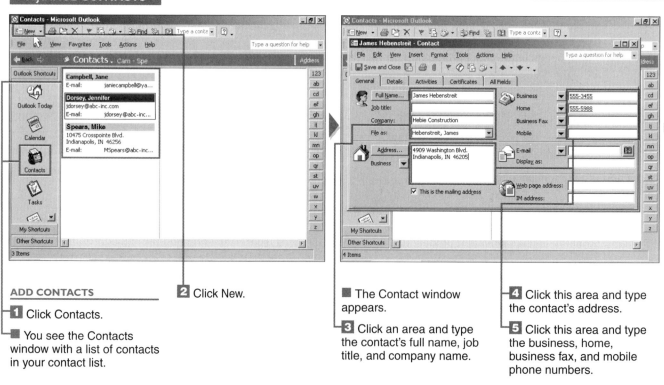

ADD CONTACTS

1 Click Contacts.

■ You see the Contacts window with a list of contacts in your contact list.

2 Click New.

■ The Contact window appears.

3 Click an area and type the contact's full name, job title, and company name.

4 Click this area and type the contact's address.

5 Click this area and type the business, home, business fax, and mobile phone numbers.

Why did the Check Address dialog box appear after I entered an address?

✔ If the address you entered is incomplete, the Check Address dialog box appears to help you complete the address.

Where can I enter more information about a contact?

✔ In the Contact window, click the Details tab. You can enter personal information about the contact, such as the contact's birthday, the assistant's name, and the name of the contact's spouse.

Can I view a list of e-mail messages I have exchanged with a contact?

✔ Yes. In the Contact window, click the Activities tab. This tab displays a summary of Outlook items, such as e-mail messages and tasks, that relate to the contact.

Can I display a map showing a contact's address?

✔ If a contact's address is in the United States, you can view a map for the address. In the Contact window, click the Display Map of Address button (🗺). Your Web browser opens and displays the map.

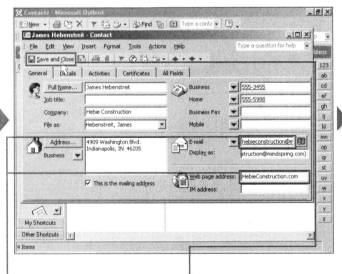

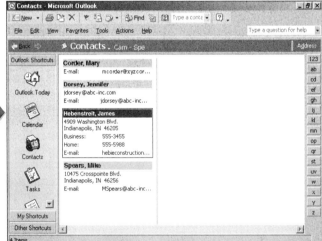

-6 Click this area and type the contact's e-mail address.

-7 Click this area and type the contact's Web page address.

8 Click Save and Close to save the information for the contact.

■ The contact appears in the contact list.

■ To change the information for a contact, double-click the contact to redisplay the Contact window.

CONTINUED ▶

MANAGE CONTACTS (CONTINUED)

Like a paper address book, the contact list displays tabs you can use to browse through your contacts alphabetically. When you select a tab, Outlook selects the first contact that begins with the letters on the tab. You can then scroll to see the other contacts in that range.

You can delete a contact you no longer need. This helps make the contact list smaller and easier to manage.

Outlook offers several ways you can display the contact list. You can choose the view that best suits your needs. The Address Cards view displays the mailing address, phone numbers, and e-mail address for each contact. The Detailed Address Cards view is useful when you want to display all the information for each contact. The Phone List view lists the business phone, business fax, home phone, and mobile phone numbers for each contact. You can also choose a view that groups related contacts together, such as the By Category view, By Company view, or By Location view.

MANAGE CONTACTS (CONTINUED)

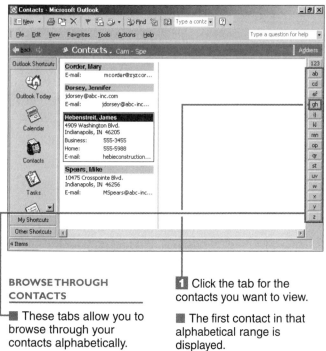

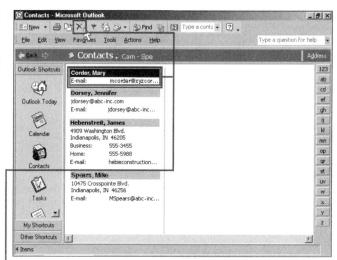

BROWSE THROUGH CONTACTS

■ These tabs allow you to browse through your contacts alphabetically.

1 Click the tab for the contacts you want to view.

■ The first contact in that alphabetical range is displayed.

DELETE A CONTACT

1 Click the contact you want to delete.

2 Click ✕ to delete the contact.

■ The contact is sent to the Deleted Items folder. To permanently delete the contact, delete it from the Deleted Items folder.

Can I restore a deleted contact?

✔ When you delete a contact, Outlook places the contact in the Deleted Items folder. To restore a contact, click the Deleted Items icon in the Outlook Bar and then drag the contact you want to restore to the Contacts icon.

How do I print the information for a contact?

✔ In the contact list, click the contact whose information you want to print and then click the Print button (🖨). In the Print range area, click the Only selected items option. Select a print style and then click OK.

Can I quickly send an e-mail message to a contact?

✔ You can quickly send an e-mail message to a contact if you entered an e-mail address for the contact. In the contact list, click the contact you want to send a message to and then click the New Message to Contact button (📧). Outlook automatically displays the contact's e-mail address in the To area of the message. Complete and send the message. Sending messages is covered in Chapter 29.

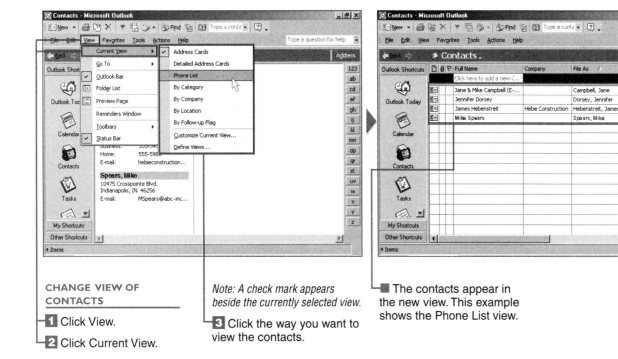

CHANGE VIEW OF CONTACTS

1 Click View.

2 Click Current View.

Note: A check mark appears beside the currently selected view.

3 Click the way you want to view the contacts.

■ The contacts appear in the new view. This example shows the Phone List view.

32) CREATE A WEB SITE

Introduction to FrontPage 544
Start FrontPage 545
Create a New Web Site 546
Create a New Page 548
Save a Page 550
Open a Web Page 552
Add or Edit Text on a Page 553
Change Font and Size of Text 554
Using Bold, Italic, or Underline 556
Change Color of Text 557
Change Alignment of Text 558
Indent Text 559
Add Numbers or Bullets 560
Create a Heading 561
Add a Picture 562
Insert a Table 564
Create a Hyperlink 566
Preview and Print a Page 568

33) ENHANCE A WEB SITE

Check Spelling 570
Apply a Theme 572
Add a Hit Counter 574
Work with Web Files and Folders 576
View Web Reports 578
View Hyperlinks 580
Check Site Navigation 582
Publish a Web Site 584

SECTION VII

INTRODUCTION TO FRONTPAGE

FrontPage is a program that you can use to create and edit Web pages. A Web page is a document on the World Wide Web. FrontPage also allows you to create and maintain Web sites. A Web site is a collection of Web pages.

The *World Wide Web* is part of the Internet and consists of a huge collection of sites stored on hundreds of thousands of computers around the world. A computer that stores Web pages is called a *Web server.*

For more information on FrontPage, you can visit the following Web site: www. microsoft.com/frontpage.

Web Pages

A Web page can contain text, pictures, sound, and video. A Web page can also contain special text and images, called *hyperlinks.* When you click a hyperlink, the connected page appears on the screen. That page may be another page in the current Web, another Web page at the current site, or another page at a totally different site. Hyperlinks allow you to easily navigate through a vast amount of information by jumping from one Web page to another. Hyperlinks can also start downloading a file or open an e-mail window.

You can find Web pages on every subject imaginable. Each page has a unique address, called a *Uniform Resource Locator (URL).* You can quickly display any page if you know its URL. A URL usually has this type of format:

www.hungryminds.com

The first part describes the type of site; *www* stands for World Wide Web. The remainder is the domain or server name and has two parts. The first part is the name, and the second part is the extension and indicates the type of

server. Common server types include com (commercial), edu (educational), org (non-profit organization), net (Internet server), gov (government organization), and so on.

Create and Publish Web Pages

After you have created a Web site, you can work with pages in the Web site. You can edit and format the pages or add items such as pictures, links, and tables.

After you have created all the pages for your Web site, you can publish the Web site on the World Wide Web. To publish your site, you transfer your Web site to a Web server. You can also place pages you create on a corporate intranet. An *intranet* is a small version of the Internet within a company or organization.

Reasons for Publishing

Publishing pages on the Web allows you to share information with millions of people around the world. Companies often place pages on the Web to keep the public informed about new products, interesting news, and job openings within the company. Companies can also allow readers to use their Web pages to place orders for products and services.

Many individuals use the Web to share information about a topic that interests them. For example, you can create pages to discuss a favorite celebrity or hobby, show your favorite pictures, promote a club, or present a resumé to potential employers.

START FRONTPAGE

You can use FrontPage to create and maintain Web sites. A Web site is a collection of Web pages.

When you start FrontPage for the first time, only the Views bar is displayed. But after you create a Web site, the FrontPage screen is similar to the screens in other Office programs. For example, like the screens in Word and Excel, the FrontPage screen displays toolbars that allow you to quickly select common commands.

The FrontPage screen also contains icons you can use to change the view of a Web site. For more information on working in the different views, see Chapter 33.

After you start FrontPage, you can create a Web site using a template or wizard. For information on creating a Web site, see "Create a New Web Site."

START FRONTPAGE

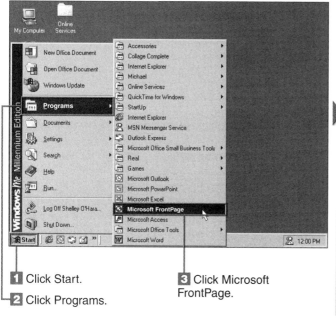

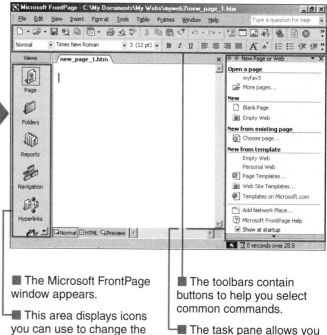

■1 Click Start.

■2 Click Programs.

■3 Click Microsoft FrontPage.

■ The Microsoft FrontPage window appears.

■ This area displays icons you can use to change the way you view a Web site.

■ The toolbars contain buttons to help you select common commands.

■ The task pane allows you to create new pages or Webs, insert pictures, and more.

CREATE A NEW WEB SITE

FrontPage provides several templates and wizards you can use to create a new Web site.

Some templates and wizards provide sample text for the Web site. You can select the sample text on a page and type your own information to replace the text.

When you use a wizard to create a Web site, the wizard asks you a series of questions and then sets up a Web site based on your answers. FrontPage offers the Corporate Presence Wizard, Discussion Web Wizard, Database Interface Wizard, and Import Web Wizard.

The One Page Web template creates a Web site containing a single blank page. The Empty Web template creates a Web site with nothing in it. These templates are useful when you want to design your own Web site one page at a time.

The Customer Support Web, Personal Web, and Project Web templates create Web sites with multiple pages. These templates provide the layout and formatting for your site so that you can concentrate on the content of your pages.

CREATE A NEW WEB SITE

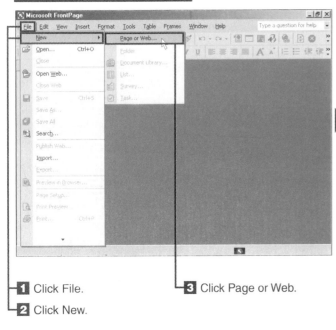

1 Click File.

2 Click New.

3 Click Page or Web.

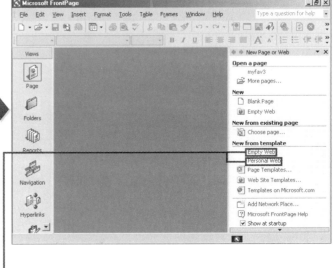

■ The New Page or Web task pane appears.

4 Click Personal Web.

■ To create an empty Web and add your own pages, click Empty Web.

Note: To learn how to add new pages, see "Create New Pages."

■ When you select Personal Web, you see the Web Site Templates dialog box.

How do I select an appropriate wizard?

✔ When you click the wizard, FrontPage displays a short description in the dialog box. For example, if you select Database Interface Wizard, the description tells you this wizard "enables you to connect to a database, and then view, update, delete, or add records."

Where can I find other templates?

✔ You can visit the Web to find other templates. Click the Web Site Templates or Templates on Microsoft .com links under New from template. You are and taken to the appropriate site with these templates.

Can I use more than one template or wizard to create a Web site?

✔ You can add a new Web site to an existing Web site to combine features from two templates or wizards. Open the Web site to which you want to add another Web site. Perform the steps below, except click the Add to current Web check box in step 5. If the Web sites contain duplicate features, FrontPage asks if you want to replace the current feature with the new one. Make your selection and click OK.

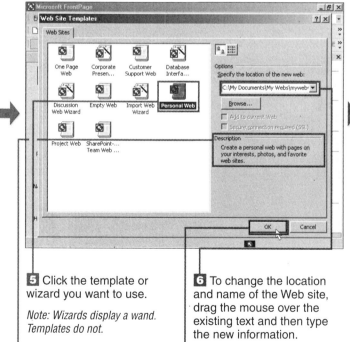

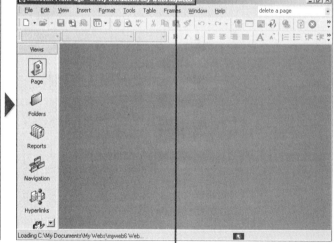

5 Click the template or wizard you want to use.

Note: Wizards display a wand. Templates do not.

■ Here you see a description of the template or wizard you selected.

6 To change the location and name of the Web site, drag the mouse over the existing text and then type the new information.

7 Click OK.

■ If you selected a template in step 5, FrontPage creates the Web site. You see a blank screen; you can then open pages in the Web or add new pages.

Note: If you selected a wizard in step 5, FrontPage asks you a series of questions before creating the Web site.

■ The location and name of the Web site appear in the title bar.

CREATE A NEW PAGE

You can create new pages to fill out a Web created with a blank Web site template or just to add additional pages. For example, you may need pages for product details, company information, or your resume.

You can choose to either create a blank page or use a page template. When you create a blank page,

FrontPage displays the page on your screen. You can immediately start typing the text you want to appear on the new page.

FrontPage provides page templates to help you create a new, professional-looking page. You can select templates from one of three category tabs: General, Frames Pages, and Style Sheets. When you

use a template, FrontPage provides a design and sample text for the page. You can replace the sample text with your own information.

FrontPage gives each new page a temporary name, such as new_page_2.htm. You can change the temporary name when you save the page. For information on saving a page, see "Save a Page."

CREATE A NEW PAGE

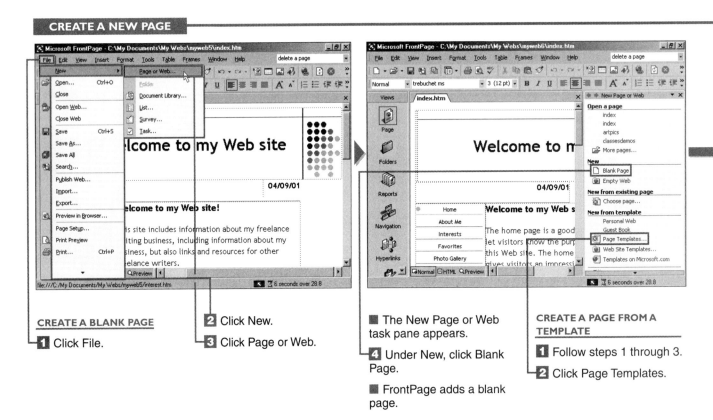

CREATE A BLANK PAGE

■1 Click File.

■2 Click New.

■3 Click Page or Web.

■ The New Page or Web task pane appears.

■4 Under New, click Blank Page.

■ FrontPage adds a blank page.

CREATE A PAGE FROM A TEMPLATE

■1 Follow steps 1 through 3.

■2 Click Page Templates.

What kinds of general templates are available?

✔ You can select from page templates such as bibliography, confirmation form, guest book, one-column, table of contents, search page, and others.

How do I delete a page I have added by mistake?

✔ If you have not saved the page, you can click the Close button to remove the page from the Web. If you have saved it, you need to change to folders view and delete the page from that list. See Chapter 33.

What kinds of frames templates are available?

✔ Frames enable you to display different contents in each part of the page. You can select a banner and contents page, a vertical split, a horizontal split, and others.

What are typical style sheet templates?

✔ Style sheet templates include formatting such as font style, hyperlink colors, and backgrounds. Click a style sheet to see a preview and short description.

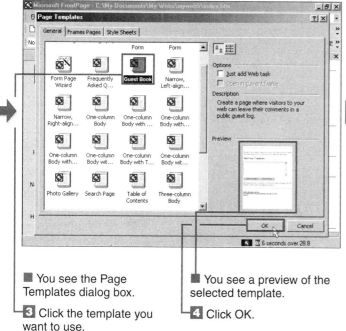

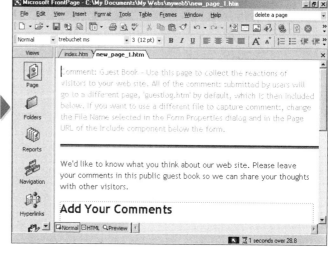

■ You see the Page Templates dialog box.

■ 3 Click the template you want to use.

■ You see a preview of the selected template.

■ 4 Click OK.

■ FrontPage adds the page. Notice that the page includes filler text and placeholders for other items such as graphic files. You can replace the filler text with your own text.

SAVE A PAGE

Y ou can save a page to store it for future use. This allows you to later review and make changes to the page.

To avoid losing your work, regularly save changes.

The first time you save a page, the Save As dialog box appears, allowing you to name the page.

FrontPage suggests a name for the page based on the first line of text on the page. You can give the page a more descriptive name that will help you identify the page later.

By default, FrontPage saves the page in the current Web site in the My Webs folder.

When you create a page, FrontPage gives the page a temporary title,

such as New Page 1. You can change this title to reflect the content of your page when you save the page.

The next time you save the page, the Save As dialog box does not appear because you have already named the page. This is also true for pages that are included in a Web template. You can simply click the Save button to save these pages.

SAVE A PAGE

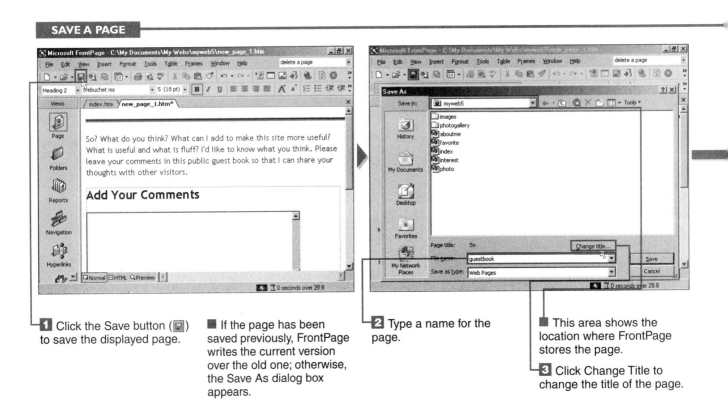

■1 Click the Save button (image) to save the displayed page.

■ If the page has been saved previously, FrontPage writes the current version over the old one; otherwise, the Save As dialog box appears.

■2 Type a name for the page.

■ This area shows the location where FrontPage stores the page.

■3 Click Change Title to change the title of the page.

Are the page title and the page name the same?
✔ No. The page title is the text that appears in the title bar at the top of the Web browser window when a reader views your page. The file name is the name you use to store the page as a file on your computer.

How can I change the title after I have saved the page?
✔ To change the page title, click File and then click Properties. In the Page Properties dialog box, type a new title for the page. Then click OK.

What should I use as the page title?
✔ When changing the page title, use a brief, descriptive title that interests people in reading your page. For example, the title "Advanced Golf Techniques" is more interesting and informative than "Chapter Two" or "My Home Page." Using a descriptive page title can also help people find your page on the Web, since many search tools use page titles in their searches.

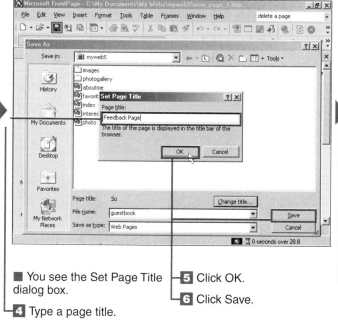

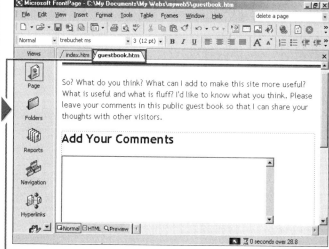

■ You see the Set Page Title dialog box.

4 Type a page title.

5 Click OK.

6 Click Save.

■ FrontPage saves the page, and the page title appears in the title bar and on the page tab.

OPEN A WEB PAGE

You can open and edit the pages in a Web site. For example, you can add your own content to predesigned pages from a template or a wizard or change content in previously saved pages.

FrontPage considers any open Web site to be the default. When you select the Open command, FrontPage displays the pages, folders, and images stored with the open Web site. If you want to open another Web site, you can use the Open Web command and the Look in field to find the desired site.

When you open a Web site, FrontPage displays the Web site elements on your screen. If you make changes to a page, you should save the page. For information on saving a page, see "Save a Page."

What do the symbols next to the Web site elements mean?

✔ FrontPage uses icons to indicate the different items that appear in Webs. Folders use the traditional folder icon (▢). Web pages use a special Web file icon (▣). Graphic files use a file icon indicating the specific graphic file type.

OPEN A WEB PAGE

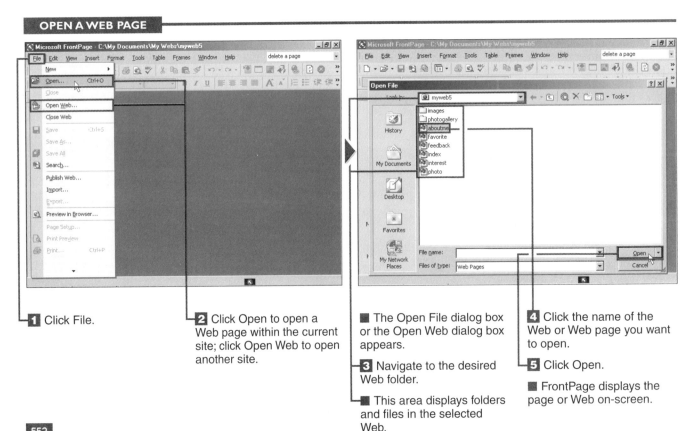

1 Click File.

2 Click Open to open a Web page within the current site; click Open Web to open another site.

■ The Open File dialog box or the Open Web dialog box appears.

3 Navigate to the desired Web folder.

■ This area displays folders and files in the selected Web.

4 Click the name of the Web or Web page you want to open.

5 Click Open.

■ FrontPage displays the page or Web on-screen.

ADD OR EDIT TEXT ON A PAGE

You can add text to a page or edit existing text, such as filler text that you want to replace with your own material.

To add text, click where you want to insert the new text and type. You can add text to any of the text areas on the page. When editing text, you can select a single word or any amount of text on the page. After the filler text is selected, you can type the replacement text.

To avoid losing your work, regularly save changes you make to a page. Pages that are included in a template already have a name and page title assigned, so you simply have to save the page without going to the Save As dialog box.

When I tried to select text, why could I not drag across the text?

✔ Some text looks like text but is actually a graphic element. For example, page banners are often graphical text. You can edit this type of text by double-clicking the item and then typing your replacement text in the text area of the dialog box that appears.

ADD OR EDIT TEXT ON A PAGE

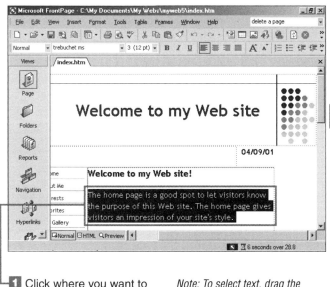

1 Click where you want to place the new text or select the text you want to replace.

Note: To select text, drag the mouse pointer across the text you want to replace. You can also double-click any word you want to select or triple-click a word to select an entire paragraph.

2 Type the text.

■ FrontPage adds your text. If you first selected text, the new text replaces the selected text.

3 Click ⊟ to save the pages with the changes you made.

CHANGE FONT AND SIZE OF TEXT

You can enhance the appearance of your page by changing the font and size of text.

FrontPage automatically uses the default font setting and sets the font size to Normal. Using these settings allows a reader's Web browser to determine the font and size of text displayed on a page.

FrontPage provides a list of fonts you can use to give your text a different look. The fonts appear in the list as they will appear on your page. To avoid problems when people view your page, use common fonts such as Arial, Times New Roman, and Courier.

You can increase or decrease the size of text on your page. Larger text is easier to read, but smaller text allows you to fit more information on a screen. FrontPage offers seven font sizes. Size 1 is the smallest and size 7 is the largest.

Web browsers can be set to override the formatting you define so readers can display pages with the formatting they prefer. Therefore, the formatting you choose for your page may not appear the way you expect on some computers.

CHANGE FONT AND SIZE OF TEXT

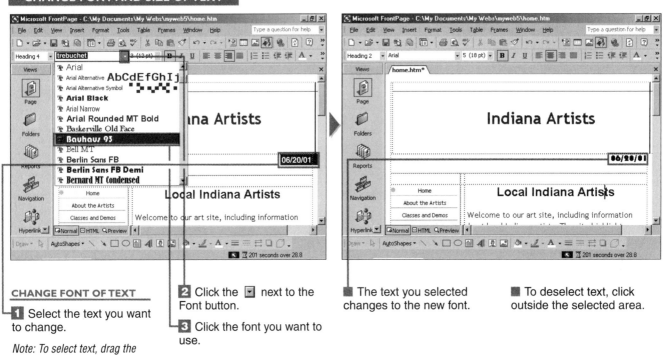

CHANGE FONT OF TEXT

1 Select the text you want to change.

Note: To select text, drag the mouse pointer across the text. You can also double-click individual words or triple-click to select entire paragraphs.

2 Click the ▼ next to the Font button.

3 Click the font you want to use.

■ The text you selected changes to the new font.

■ To deselect text, click outside the selected area.

Can I quickly remove all the formatting I added to text?

✔ Yes. Select the text from which you want to remove formatting. Click Format and then click Remove Formatting.

Is there another way to change the font and size of text?

✔ Yes. Select the text you want to change. Click Format and then click Font. The Font dialog box appears, allowing you to select a font and size as well as many other options. FrontPage displays a preview of how the text will look once the formatting is applied.

I changed the font on my text, but I do not like the result. Can I cancel the change?

✔ You can immediately click the Undo button (🔄) to cancel the last change you made to your page.

Can I copy formatting?

✔ Yes. To copy formatting, select the text that is formatted with the selections you want. Click the Format Painter button (🖌) and then drag across the text to which you want to copy the formatting.

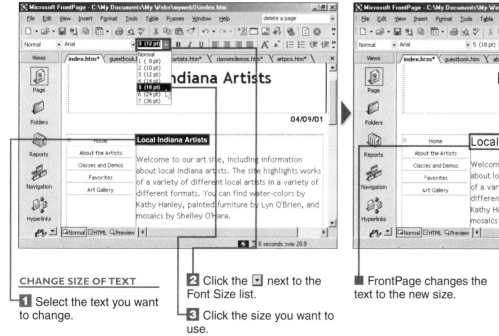

CHANGE SIZE OF TEXT

1 Select the text you want to change.

2 Click the 🔽 next to the Font Size list.

3 Click the size you want to use.

■ FrontPage changes the text to the new size.

■ To deselect text, click outside the selected area.

USING BOLD, ITALIC, OR UNDERLINE

To enhance the appearance of the text on your page, you can make formatting changes. A common change is to boldface, italicize, and/or underline key information to add emphasis.

You can use one feature at a time or any combination of the three formatting features to change the style of text.

The Bold feature makes text appear darker and thicker than other text. You can bold headings and titles to make them stand out from the rest of the text on the page.

The Italic feature tilts text to the right. You may want to italicize quotations and definitions on the page.

The Underline feature adds a line underneath text. You should use underlines only when necessary, because people viewing your page may confuse underlined text with hyperlinks.

Only emphasize important information. If you emphasize too many words and phrases on a page, the important information does not stand out.

USING BOLD, ITALIC, OR UNDERLINE

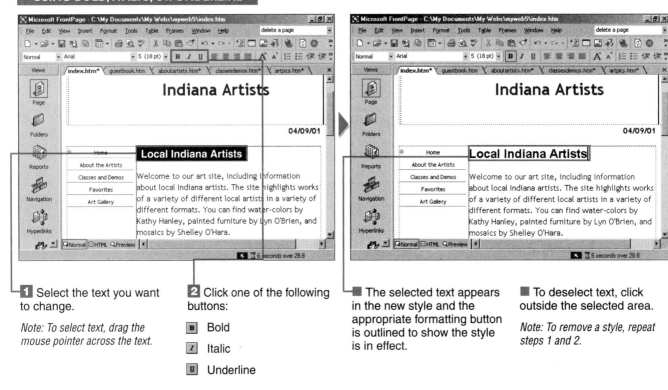

■1 Select the text you want to change.

Note: To select text, drag the mouse pointer across the text.

■2 Click one of the following buttons:

B Bold

I Italic

U Underline

■ The selected text appears in the new style and the appropriate formatting button is outlined to show the style is in effect.

■ To deselect text, click outside the selected area.

Note: To remove a style, repeat steps 1 and 2.

CHANGE COLOR OF TEXT

You can change the color of text on a page to draw attention to headings or important information. Changing the color of text also allows you to enhance the appearance of your page.

FrontPage provides a variety of colors for you to choose from.

Make sure the text color you choose works well with the background color of the page. For example, red text on a blue background may be difficult to read.

When selecting the text color you want to use, consider that the colors you choose for your page

may not appear the way you expect on some computers. Web browsers can be set to override the colors used on a page. This allows people to display your page in the colors they prefer.

If the color you select does not suit your needs, you can return to the default color at any time.

CHANGE COLOR OF TEXT

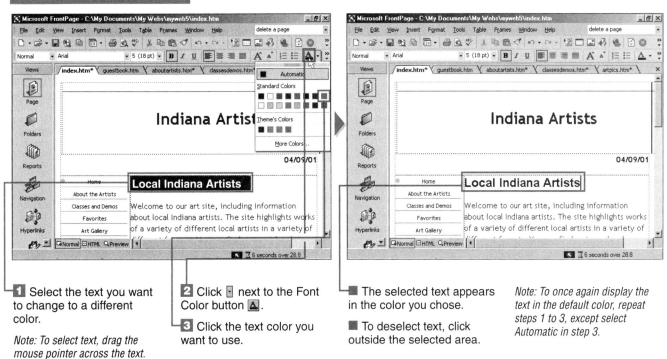

1 Select the text you want to change to a different color.

Note: To select text, drag the mouse pointer across the text.

2 Click next to the Font Color button.

3 Click the text color you want to use.

■ The selected text appears in the color you chose.

■ To deselect text, click outside the selected area.

Note: To once again display the text in the default color, repeat steps 1 to 3, except select Automatic in step 3.

CHANGE ALIGNMENT OF TEXT

You can use the alignment buttons on the Formatting toolbar to change the alignment of text on your page. Changing the alignment of text can help organize your page and make the page easier to read.

By default, FrontPage aligns text along the left side of a page.

FrontPage allows you to center text between the left and right sides of

your page. This is useful for making headings and titles on your page stand out. Center only short sections of text, because long paragraphs can be difficult to read when centered.

You can align text along the right side of your page. You may want to right align a column of text, such as a description of a product, to make the text stand out from the rest of the text on your page.

Justified text makes the right and left margins flush. Justified text is often used for paragraphs in columns.

Note that some pages are divided into frames or tables. Therefore, when you make an alignment change, the text is aligned within that frame or table cell, not within the entire page.

CHANGE ALIGNMENT OF TEXT

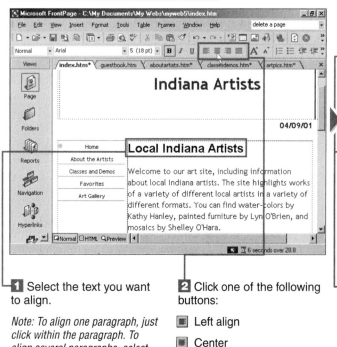

1 Select the text you want to align.

Note: To align one paragraph, just click within the paragraph. To align several paragraphs, select the ones you want to change.

2 Click one of the following buttons:

▣ Left align

▣ Center

▣ Right align

▣ Justified

■ The text displays the new alignment and the appropriate formatting button is outlined to show the style is in effect.

■ To deselect text, click outside the selected area.

INDENT TEXT

You can use the Indent feature to make important text on your page stand out.

FrontPage allows you to quickly move text away from or closer to the left and right edges of your page. Indenting lets you position text. Increasing the indent moves text away from the edges of your page. Decreasing the indent moves text closer to the edges of your page.

Note that if the page is divided into frames, the text is indented with that particular frame. Also, some templates use a table to organize text on the page. If you indent text in a table, the text is indented within that cell, not the entire page.

When you indent a paragraph, all the lines of text in the paragraph are indented together. Indenting text is useful when you want to set

quotations or references apart from the rest of the text on your page.

Indenting text can also help you emphasize a content change. For example, you may want to indent your e-mail address or copyright information.

INDENT TEXT

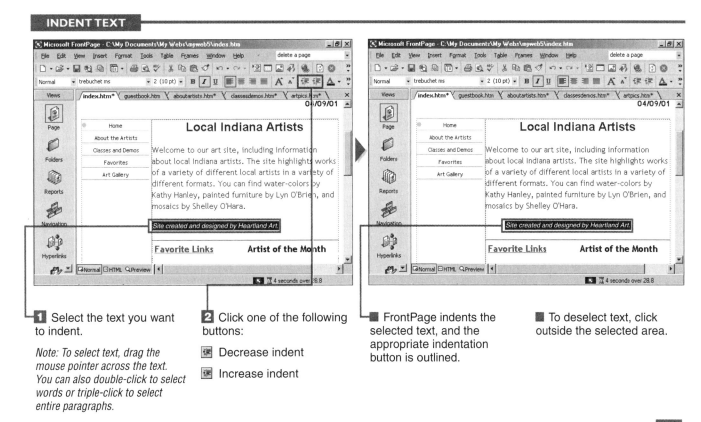

1 Select the text you want to indent.

Note: To select text, drag the mouse pointer across the text. You can also double-click to select words or triple-click to select entire paragraphs.

2 Click one of the following buttons:

Decrease indent

Increase indent

■ FrontPage indents the selected text, and the appropriate indentation button is outlined.

■ To deselect text, click outside the selected area.

ADD NUMBERS OR BULLETS

Y ou can separate items in a list by beginning each item with a number or a bullet. This can help make the list easier to read.

Numbers are useful for items in a specific order, such as a set of instructions or a table of contents. Bullets are useful for items in no

particular order, such as a list of products or a series of hyperlinks. By default, FrontPage uses the bullets from the template. If a template was not used, FrontPage uses round bullets.

When you add numbers or bullets to a list, FrontPage indents the list slightly. This enhances the

appearance of the list and separates the list from the other text on the page. When you add a new item to a list displaying numbers or bullets, FrontPage automatically adds a number or bullet to the new item. If you add an item within a numbered list, FrontPage automatically renumbers all the items in the list for you.

ADD NUMBERS OR BULLETS

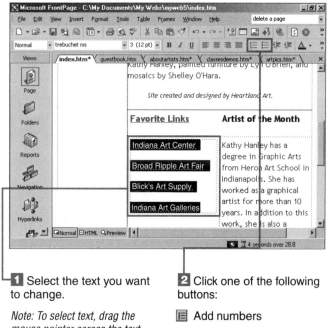

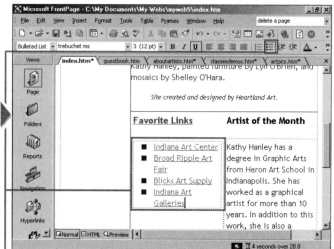

1 Select the text you want to change.

Note: To select text, drag the mouse pointer across the text.

2 Click one of the following buttons:

▤ Add numbers

▤ Add bullets

■ FrontPage adds the numbers or bullets to the selected paragraphs and the appropriate toolbar button is outlined.

■ To deselect text, click outside the selected area.

Note: To remove numbers or bullets, repeat steps 1 and 2.

CREATE A HEADING

You can use headings to indicate the importance of text, such as section titles, on your page.

You can create headings to separate the text on a page into smaller sections. There are six heading levels, ranging in size from very large to very small. Levels 1, 2, and 3 are large and are often used for page and section titles. Level 4 is

the same size as the main text on a page. Levels 5 and 6 are smaller and are often used for copyright information. Most pages use a maximum of three heading levels.

Make sure you use the same heading level for all the text of equal importance. This helps your readers determine the importance of the text on the page.

You can also create headings to provide an outline of the page for your readers. By scanning the headings, a reader should get a general overview of the information covered on the page and be able to quickly locate topics of interest.

If you use a template to create the Web, headings may already be assigned.

CREATE A HEADING

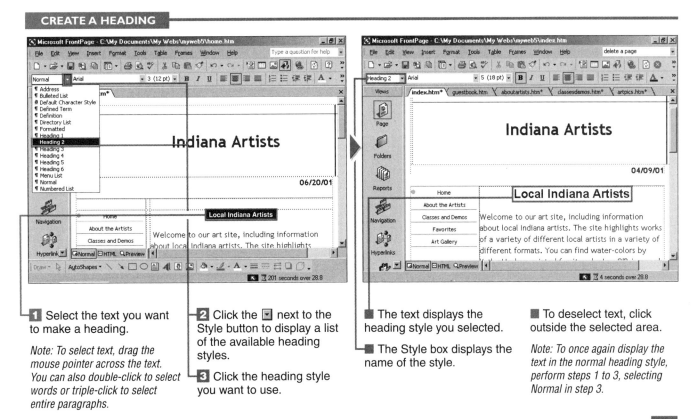

1 Select the text you want to make a heading.

Note: To select text, drag the mouse pointer across the text. You can also double-click to select words or triple-click to select entire paragraphs.

2 Click the ▼ next to the Style button to display a list of the available heading styles.

3 Click the heading style you want to use.

■ The text displays the heading style you selected.

■ The Style box displays the name of the style.

■ To deselect text, click outside the selected area.

Note: To once again display the text in the normal heading style, perform steps 1 to 3, selecting Normal in step 3.

ADD A PICTURE

You can add pictures to your page to make it more interesting and attractive, or to help clarify a concept. For example, you can add a diagram to explain a product.

You can find pictures to add to your page from many sources. Many pages on the Web offer pictures you can use for free. You can also scan pictures or use a drawing program to create your

own pictures. Make sure you have permission to use any pictures you did not create yourself.

Adding pictures increases the time it takes for a page to appear on a screen. The bottom right corner of the Microsoft FrontPage window indicates how long it takes to display your page using a 28.8 Kbps modem. Whenever possible, use pictures with a small file size.

Use pictures in the GIF or JPG format. These picture formats are supported in all Web browsers.

When you save the page, if the picture is not within the current Web site folder, you are prompted to save the embedded file. Doing so saves the picture within the Web site folder so that it is available for viewing.

ADD A PICTURE

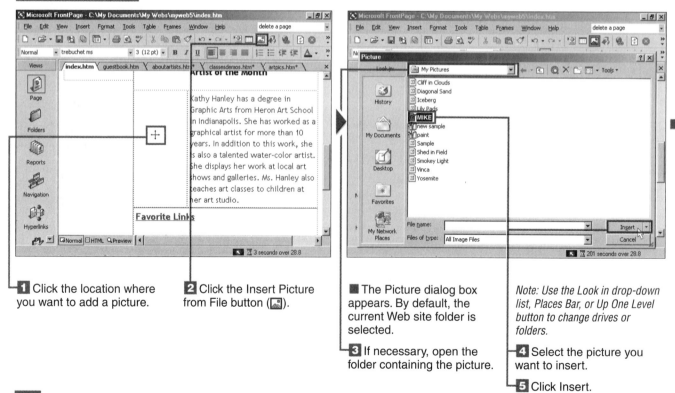

■1 Click the location where you want to add a picture.

■2 Click the Insert Picture from File button ().

■ The Picture dialog box appears. By default, the current Web site folder is selected.

■3 If necessary, open the folder containing the picture.

Note: Use the Look in drop-down list, Places Bar, or Up One Level button to change drives or folders.

■4 Select the picture you want to insert.

■5 Click Insert.

Can I add a clip art image to my page?
✔ Yes. Office includes many ready-made clip art images that you can add. Click Insert, Picture, and then Clip Art to display the Insert Clip Art task pane. Search for the clip art image of interest. Then, in the search results, click the down arrow next to image you want to insert and click Insert.

How do I delete a picture?
✔ Click the picture to select it and then press Delete.

How do I move a picture on my page?
✔ Position the mouse pointer over the picture, click to select the picture, and then drag the picture to a new location on your page.

How can I resize a picture?
✔ Click the picture to display selection handles around the picture. Position the mouse pointer over one of the handles and then drag the handle until the picture is the size you want.

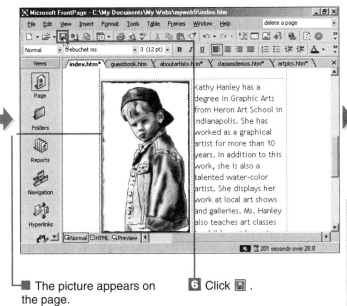

■ The picture appears on the page.

Note: You may need to resize the figure to fit the page.

6 Click 🖫 .

■ You are prompted to save the embedded file.

7 Click OK to save the picture file within the current Web site folder.

■ FrontPage saves the page and picture.

INSERT A TABLE

Y ou can insert a table to neatly display information on a page. You can also use a table to control the placement of text and pictures on a page. If you use a template, you may find that many of the pages are set up as a table, with different elements within each cell.

A table is made up of rows, columns, and cells. A *row* is a horizontal line of cells. A *column* is a vertical line of cells. A *cell* is the area where a row and column intersect.

You can enter any amount of text in a cell. When the text you enter reaches the end of a line, FrontPage automatically wraps the text to the next line in the cell and increases the size of the cell to accommodate the text.

You can edit and format text in a table the same way you edit and format any text on your page.

When you create a table, all the cells are the same size. You can adjust the column width to make columns wider or narrower.

INSERT A TABLE

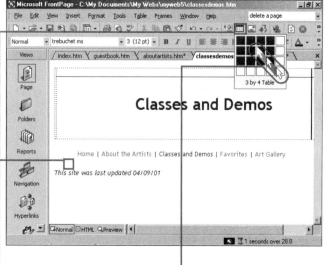

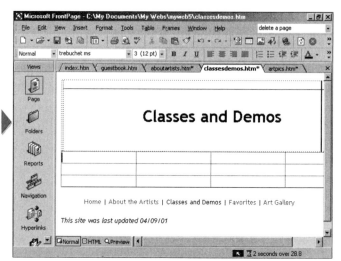

CREATE A TABLE

■1 Click the location where you want the table to appear.

■2 Click the Insert Table button (▦).

■3 In the mini-table that appears, drag the mouse pointer until you highlight the number of rows and columns you want the table to contain.

■ The table appears on the page.

Can I change the background color of my table?

✔ Yes. Click anywhere in the table. Click Table, Properties, and then Table. Click the ▼ next to the Color drop-down list and click the color you want to use. Then click OK.

What other graphical elements can I add to my page?

✔ You can place a horizontal line across your page. Click the location where you want to add a horizontal line. Click Insert, Horizontal Line. A horizontal line appears on the page. To remove the line, click it and then press Delete.

How do I insert a new row or column?

✔ Click the location in the table where you want to insert rows or columns. Click Table, Insert, and then Rows or Columns. In the Insert Rows or Columns dialog box, select to insert a row or column and then select its placement. Click OK.

How do I delete a row or column?

✔ Drag the mouse over all the cells in the row or column to select it. After the row or column is selected, click Table, Delete Cells.

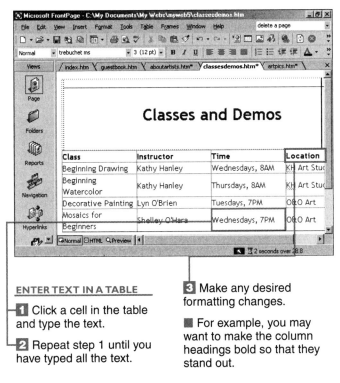

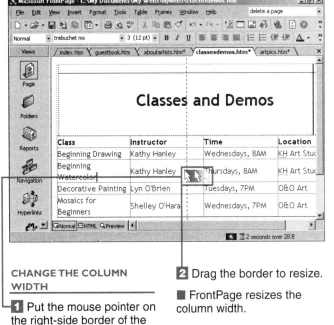

ENTER TEXT IN A TABLE

1 Click a cell in the table and type the text.

2 Repeat step 1 until you have typed all the text.

3 Make any desired formatting changes.

■ For example, you may want to make the column headings bold so that they stand out.

CHANGE THE COLUMN WIDTH

1 Put the mouse pointer on the right-side border of the column you want to resize.

2 Drag the border to resize.

■ FrontPage resizes the column width.

CREATE A HYPERLINK

You can create a hyperlink to connect a word, phrase, or picture on your page to another page in your Web site or to related information on the Web. When a reader clicks the word, phrase, or picture in a Web browser, the other page appears on the screen. Adding a hyperlink to your page gives readers quick access to information that relates to the page.

You can use any text or picture on your page as a hyperlink. Make sure the text or picture you choose clearly indicates where the hyperlink takes the reader.

You can also create a hyperlink by typing a Web page address or

e-mail address on your page. FrontPage automatically converts the address to a hyperlink for you.

By default, text hyperlinks appear underlined and blue in color. When you position the mouse pointer over a hyperlink in FrontPage, the bottom of your screen displays where the hyperlink takes you.

CREATE A HYPERLINK

LINK TO ANOTHER PAGE

1 Select the text or click the picture you want to make a hyperlink.

2 Click the Insert Hyperlink button (🖳).

■ The Create Hyperlink dialog box appears.

3 Click the page you want to link to.

Note: When the reader clicks this link, the page you selected is displayed.

4 Click OK.

■ FrontPage creates the hyperlink.

How do I remove a hyperlink without removing the text or picture from my page?

✔ Select the hyperlink on your page and then click 🔲. Click the Remove Link button.

Can I verify all the hyperlinks in my Web site at once?

✔ Yes. Click View, Reports, Problems, Broken Hyperlinks. FrontPage changes to Reports view and displays a list of hyperlinks in your Web site. To fix a Hyperlink with a Broken status, double-click it. In the Replace hyperlink with area, type the correct address or click Browse to locate the correct file. Then click Replace.

Can I preview the link?

✔ Yes. To preview links to other sites, you must be connected to the Internet. Then you can use the Preview tab to test your hyperlinks. This process lets you make sure the correct page appears when you click a hyperlink.

Can I create a hyperlink that sends e-mail?

✔ Yes. Select the text you want to make a hyperlink and then click the Insert Hyperlink button (🔲). In the Link to area, click E-mail Address and then type the E-mail address for the link. Click OK.

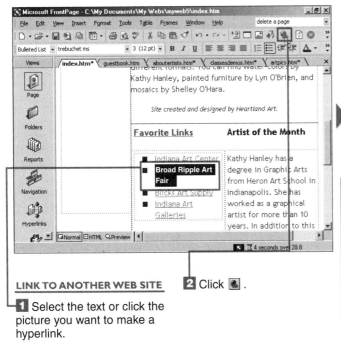

LINK TO ANOTHER WEB SITE

1 Select the text or click the picture you want to make a hyperlink.

2 Click 🔲 .

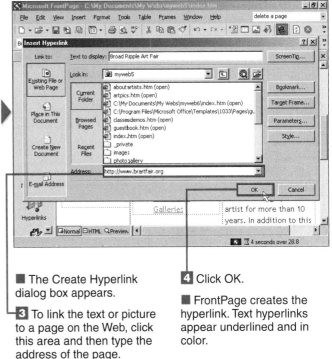

■ The Create Hyperlink dialog box appears.

3 To link the text or picture to a page on the Web, click this area and then type the address of the page.

4 Click OK.

■ FrontPage creates the hyperlink. Text hyperlinks appear underlined and in color.

PREVIEW AND PRINT A PAGE

You can preview your page to see how the page appears when readers view the page on the Web. This lets you make sure your page appears the way you want.

FrontPage offers two ways you can preview your page — in a Web browser and in FrontPage. When you preview a page in your Web browser, the Web browser opens and displays the page. When you preview a page in FrontPage, FrontPage displays the page on the Preview tab as it appears on the Web.

You can produce a paper copy of the page displayed on your screen. Printing your page lets you exchange information with people who do not have access to the Web. You can also work on design changes by marking up the hard copy.

You can print your entire page or only part of the page. Long pages may consist of several printed pages, but you can specify the range of printed pages you want to produce.

PREVIEW AND PRINT A PAGE

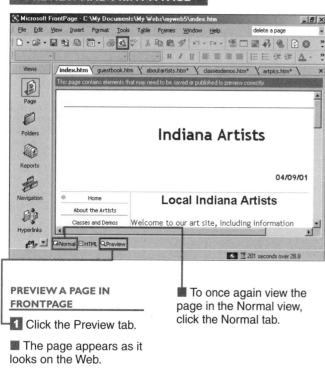

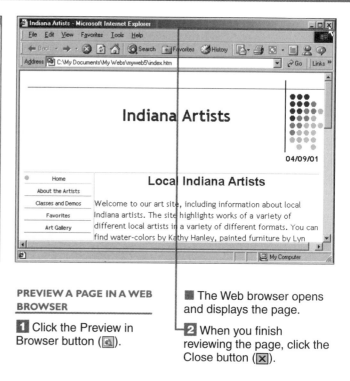

PREVIEW A PAGE IN FRONTPAGE

1 Click the Preview tab.

■ The page appears as it looks on the Web.

■ To once again view the page in the Normal view, click the Normal tab.

PREVIEW A PAGE IN A WEB BROWSER

1 Click the Preview in Browser button ([image]).

■ The Web browser opens and displays the page.

2 When you finish reviewing the page, click the Close button ([X]).

Can I print when I am previewing the page in FrontPage?

✓ No. You must use the File, Print command. You can, though, print when you are previewing in the Web browser. To do so, click the Print button.

Why does my printed page look different than the preview?

✓ Your printed page may look different than the page displayed on your screen. For example, FrontPage may adjust the layout of text and graphics on the printed page due to the size difference between the paper and your computer screen.

The preview in my Web browser looks different than the preview in FrontPage. What is wrong?

✓ Different Web browsers may display items such as text and tables differently. If your Web browser is different than Internet Explorer, the Web browser FrontPage uses, the previews may not look the same. Make sure you are satisfied with the way your page appears in both your Web browser and FrontPage before you publish your Web site.

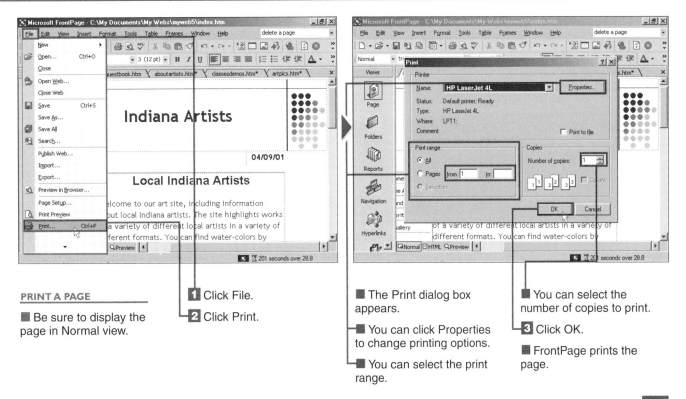

PRINT A PAGE

■ Be sure to display the page in Normal view.

1 Click File.

2 Click Print.

■ The Print dialog box appears.

■ You can click Properties to change printing options.

■ You can select the print range.

■ You can select the number of copies to print.

3 Click OK.

■ FrontPage prints the page.

CHECK SPELLING

You can find and correct spelling errors on your page. Correcting spelling errors makes your page appear more professional.

FrontPage checks spelling by comparing words on your page to words in its dictionary. If a word on your page does not exist in the dictionary, FrontPage considers the word misspelled.

Although FrontPage automatically checks your page for spelling errors as you type and underlines potentially misspelled words in red, you can locate and correct all the spelling errors at once by using the spell check feature when you finish creating your page.

When FrontPage finds a misspelled word, it provides a list of suggestions to correct the word.

You can either replace the word with a suggested word or ignore the misspelled word and continue checking your page.

If FrontPage repeatedly finds a misspelled word that you know is correct, such as a name, you can make FrontPage ignore all occurrences of the word on your page.

CHECK SPELLING

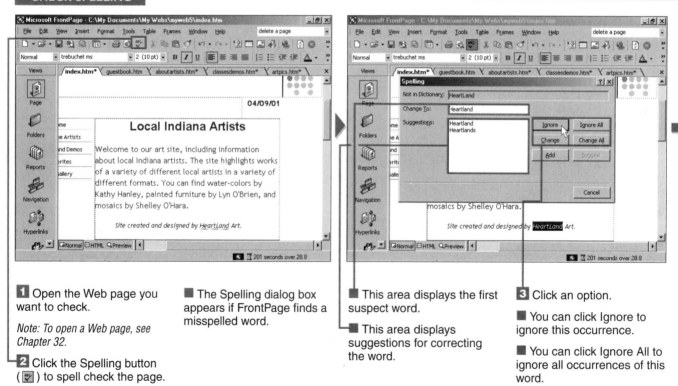

■ Open the Web page you want to check.

Note: To open a Web page, see Chapter 32.

■ Click the Spelling button (✔) to spell check the page.

■ The Spelling dialog box appears if FrontPage finds a misspelled word.

■ This area displays the first suspect word.

■ This area displays suggestions for correcting the word.

■ Click an option.

■ You can click Ignore to ignore this occurrence.

■ You can click Ignore All to ignore all occurrences of this word.

MASTER IT

Why did FrontPage underline a correctly spelled word?

✔ FrontPage flags all words that do not exist in its dictionary as misspelled. You can add a word to the dictionary so that FrontPage recognizes it during future spelling checks. To do so, right-click the word you want to add to the dictionary and then click Add.

How can I spell-check all the pages in my Web site at once?

✔ Click Views, click Folders and then click the Spelling button ([ABC]). From the dialog box that appears, click the Entire web option and then Start. To correct the errors, double-click the first page from the list FrontPage displays. After finishing the first page, FrontPage asks if you want to continue, which you can do by clicking Next Page. When you finish correcting all the pages, you see the Spelling dialog box, which lists all the checked pages. Click the Close button [X] to close the Spelling dialog box.

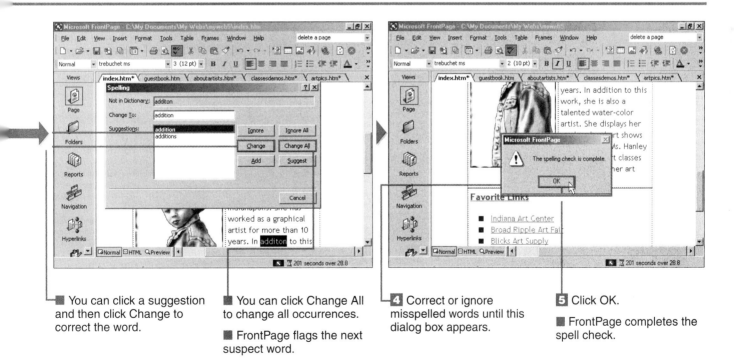

■ You can click a suggestion and then click Change to correct the word.

■ You can click Change All to change all occurrences.

■ FrontPage flags the next suspect word.

■4 Correct or ignore misspelled words until this dialog box appears.

■5 Click OK.

■ FrontPage completes the spell check.

APPLY A THEME

FrontPage offers many themes that you can apply to give the pages in your Web site a new appearance. A *theme* consists of a coordinated set of design elements that includes fonts, background images, navigation buttons, bullets, banners, and a color scheme.

Applying a theme to all pages in your Web site enables you to keep the appearance of your Web site consistent. After you apply a theme to the Web site, FrontPage automatically applies the theme to any new pages you create.

You can also apply a theme to only the current page, which is useful when you want to make an important page stand out from the rest of the pages in your Web site.

To apply a theme to only one page, you must first display the page you want to change.

Some of the available themes include Blueprint, Expedition, and Romanesque. You can view a sample of a theme to help you choose the theme that best suits the content of your pages and your intended audience.

APPLY A THEME

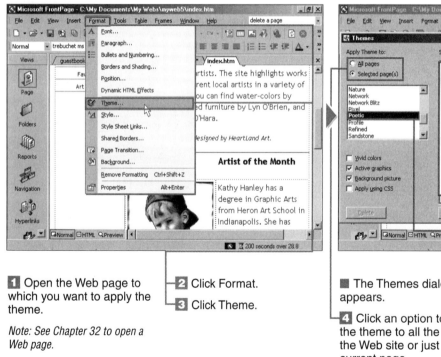

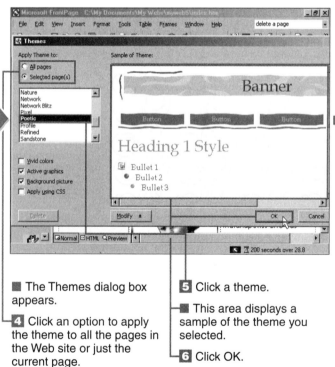

1 Open the Web page to which you want to apply the theme.

Note: See Chapter 32 to open a Web page.

2 Click Format.

3 Click Theme.

■ The Themes dialog box appears.

4 Click an option to apply the theme to all the pages in the Web site or just the current page.

5 Click a theme.

■ This area displays a sample of the theme you selected.

6 Click OK.

Can I personalize a theme to suit my pages?

✔ Yes. FrontPage provides additional options for the themes in the Themes dialog box. The options include Vivid colors, Active graphics, Background picture, and Apply using CSS. Each option that that FrontPage includes in the current theme displays a check mark (☑). You can click an option to add or remove it (☐ changes to ☑ or ☑ changes to ☐). The Apply using CSS option applies the current theme with an external style sheet rather than changing the HTML code for the page(s). Some Web browsers and Web servers cannot properly display pages that use this option.

Does FrontPage offer any other themes?

✔ Yes. When choosing the theme you want to use in the Themes dialog box, you can click Install Additional Themes to have FrontPage display more themes. Click Yes to install the themes. Follow the on-screen prompts, inserting the CD-ROM disc you used to install Office and then clicking OK.

You can also find various themes available for use or purchase on the Internet. To start, visit www.office.microsoft.com/Downloads/default Insert.

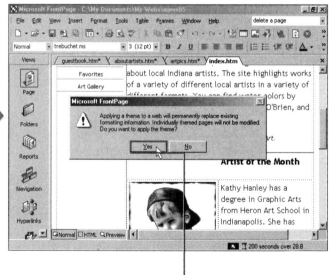

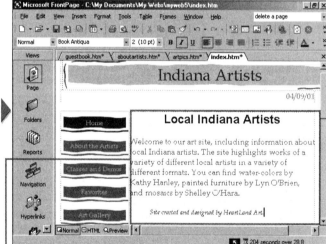

■ A dialog box may appear, indicating that applying the theme will change the way fonts, colors, bullets and lines appear on the page(s) in the Web site.

7 Click Yes.

■ The page(s) in the Web site display the new theme.

■ To remove a theme from page(s) in the Web site, perform steps 1 through 5, except select [No Theme] in step 5.

ADD A HIT COUNTER

You can use a hit counter to keep track of the number visitors to your Web site, and thus, determine the popularity of the site.

FrontPage provides five counter styles from which you can choose. You should choose a counter style that works well with the design of your page. Although you can start

your hit counter at any number, by default, FrontPage starts the hit counter at 0.

You can limit the number of digits your hit counter can display. For example, if you limit the number of digits to five, the hit counter resets to 00000 after 99999.

You must publish your page before you can view a hit counter you add

to the page. For information on publishing Web sites, see the section "Publish a Web Site."

To display a hit counter, your Web server must use FrontPage Server Extensions. You can consult your Web presence provider (WPP) to determine if your Web server uses FrontPage Server Extensions.

ADD A HIT COUNTER

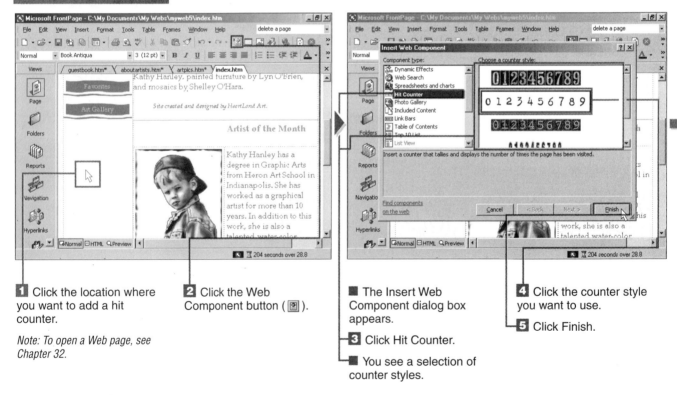

1 Click the location where you want to add a hit counter.

Note: To open a Web page, see Chapter 32.

2 Click the Web Component button (🖼).

■ The Insert Web Component dialog box appears.

3 Click Hit Counter.

■ You see a selection of counter styles.

4 Click the counter style you want to use.

5 Click Finish.

To which page in my Web site should I add a hit counter?

✔ A hit counter keeps track of the number of people who visit the page where the counter is located. Because people visit your home page first, consider adding the hit counter to your home page.

Can adding a hit counter slow the display of my page?

✔ Yes. A hit counter is a small program that must run each time your page displays in a Web browser. As a result, the page may take slightly longer to display.

Can changing the theme of a page change the appearance of my hit counter?

✔ No. If you change the theme of a page containing a hit counter, you must change the counter style to one that works well with the new theme. Double-click [Hit Counter] on your page to open the Hit Counter Properties dialog box. Click a new counter style and then click OK.

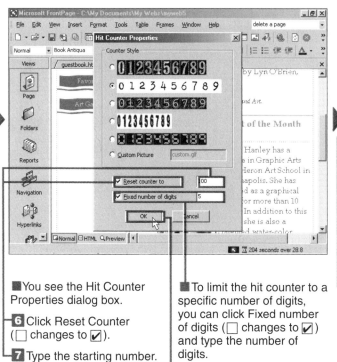

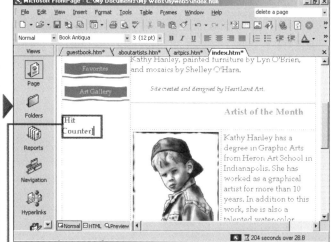

■ You see the Hit Counter Properties dialog box.

▌6 Click Reset Counter (☐ changes to ☑).

▌7 Type the starting number.

■ To limit the hit counter to a specific number of digits, you can click Fixed number of digits (☐ changes to ☑) and type the number of digits.

▌8 Click OK.

■ The text [Hit Counter] appears on the page. The actual counter appears after you publish your Web site.

Note: See the section, "Publish a Web Site" for more information.

■ To remove a hit counter, click [Hit Counter] and then press the Delete key.

WORK WITH WEB FILES AND FOLDERS

When you create a Web site using a template or wizard, FrontPage automatically creates a folder structure for the Web site. You can use the Folders view to see this folder structure. The Folders view displays the folder structure for the Web site on the left side of the window and the contents of the current folder on the right side of the window.

The folder structure includes a main folder for the Web site, a private folder, and an images folder. The main folder stores all the folders and pages in your Web site. The private folder stores information you do not want to appear on your pages, such as the results of forms. The images folder stores pictures and other images.

When you display the contents of a folder, you can view information

about the contents, such as the name, title, and size of each item. You can also sort the contents of a folder to help you find an item of interest. Finally, you can use the Folders view to delete pages in the Web site.

WORK WITH WEB FILES AND FOLDERS

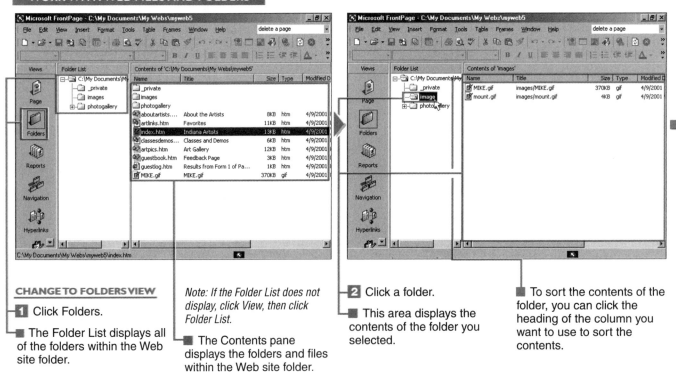

CHANGE TO FOLDERS VIEW

■1 Click Folders.

■ The Folder List displays all of the folders within the Web site folder.

Note: If the Folder List does not display, click View, then click Folder List.

■ The Contents pane displays the folders and files within the Web site folder.

■2 Click a folder.

■ This area displays the contents of the folder you selected.

■ To sort the contents of the folder, you can click the heading of the column you want to use to sort the contents.

How do I return to Page view from Folders view?

✔ The default view for working in FrontPage is Page view. In this view, you can edit, format, and create new pages. You can change back to this view by clicking Page in the Views bar.

How do I display the Views bar?

✔ If FrontPage does not display the Views bar, click View and then click Views Bar. You can also change views using the View menu. Click View and then click the view you want to use.

How do I rename my Web?

✔ Although FrontPage assigns a generic numbered name for the Webs, such as myweb1, myweb2, and so on, you can rename your Web with a more descriptive name. To do so, open the folder to which FrontPage saved the Web. Right-click the Web folder, click Rename, type a new name, and press Enter.

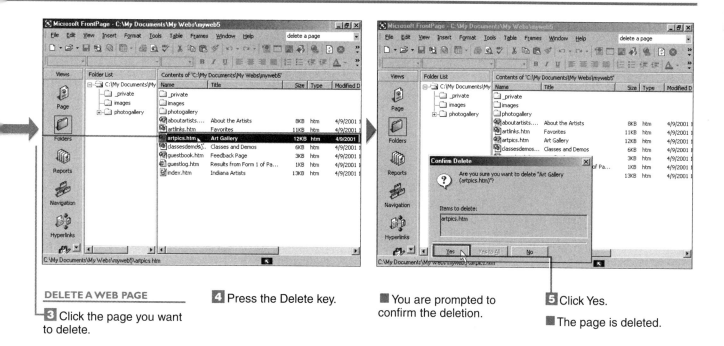

DELETE A WEB PAGE

3 Click the page you want to delete.

4 Press the Delete key.

■ You are prompted to confirm the deletion.

5 Click Yes.

■ The page is deleted.

VIEW WEB REPORTS

Y ou can use the Reports view to see information about your Web site. FrontPage offers many reports that you can display in the Reports view, each displaying different information about the Web site.

The Site Summary report displays an overview of your Web site, including information such as the number of pictures and hyperlinks in the Web site.

The Files menu lets you view reports on All Files, Recently Added Files, Recently Changed Files, and Older Files. These reports display details about the files in your Web site. For example, you can view the title, size, and type of each file.

The Problems menu lets you display the Broken Hyperlinks report. This report shows the status of the hyperlinks in your Web site

so that you can quickly determine which hyperlinks are working. You can also display slow pages and component errors.

The Usage menu lets you view many reports on monthly, weekly, and daily usage. You can also view monthly, weekly, and daily hits reports.

VIEW WEB REPORTS

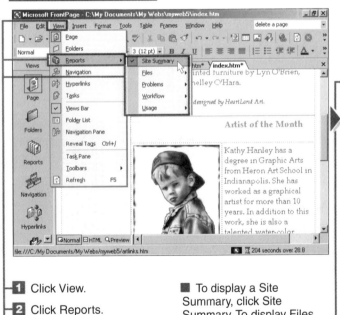

-1 Click View.

-2 Click Reports.

-3 Click the report you want to view.

■ To display a Site Summary, click Site Summary. To display Files, Problems, Workflow, or Usage reports, click that command and then click the desired report on the submenu that appears.

■ The report you selected appears.

■ The Site Summary report shows you a good overview of the site.

-4 Click any underlined link in the Name column to view an additional report.

I clicked Reports in the Views bar, but I do not see all of the reports listed. What happened?

✔ If you click Reports, FrontPage displays the last report with which you worked. This feature helps you if you frequently use the same report. To display a different report, you must use the View menu.

What are Workflow reports?

✔ Workflow reports include Review Status, Assigned To, Categories, and Publish Status. These reports enable you to chart the progress of publishing and maintaining the Web site, a very useful monitoring tool when several people are working on the same Web site.

How do I fix a broken link?

✔ To fix a broken link, double-click the link name in the Hyperlink column of the Broken Hyperlinks report. In the Edit Hyperlink dialog box that appears, either type the correct address or click Browse and click the file. Then click Replace. To edit the page, and delete or change the link, click Edit Page and make any changes to the page.

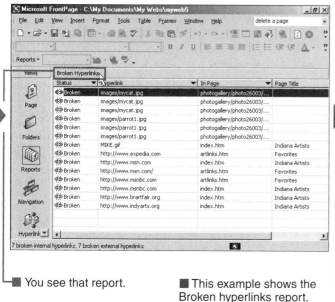

■ You see that report.

■ This example shows the Broken hyperlinks report.

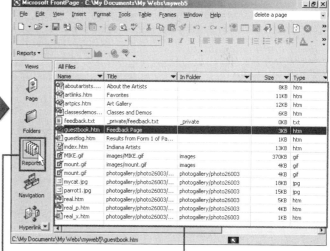

■ To quickly display the last report with which you worked, click Reports.

■ Here you see the All Files report.

VIEW HYPERLINKS

A *hyperlink* connects information on a page to another page in the Web site or to related information on the Web. When a reader clicks a hyperlink in a Web browser, the other page appears on the screen. You can display your Web site in the Hyperlinks view to see the hyperlinks that connect a page to other information.

If you use a template or wizard to create your Web site, FrontPage may have automatically added hyperlinks to the pages for you. You can also add your own hyperlinks to pages. For information on creating a hyperlink, see Chapter 32.

The Hyperlinks view displays a list of the folders and pages in your Web site on the left side of the window and a map of the hyperlinks to and from the current page on the right side of the window. You can hide or display the list of folders and pages. Hiding the list gives you more room to see the hyperlinks for a page. Displaying the list lets you quickly display the hyperlinks for another page.

VIEW HYPERLINKS

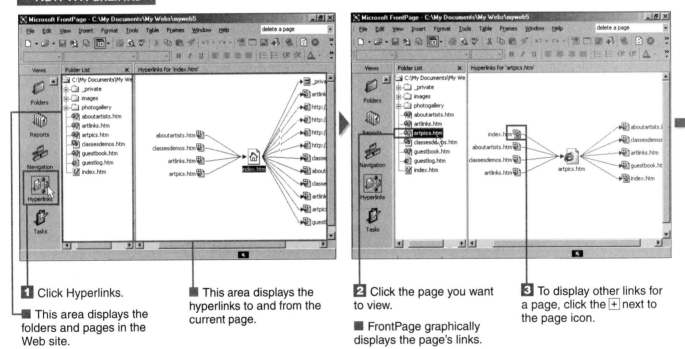

■1 Click Hyperlinks.

■ This area displays the folders and pages in the Web site.

■ This area displays the hyperlinks to and from the current page.

■2 Click the page you want to view.

■ FrontPage graphically displays the page's links.

■3 To display other links for a page, click the ➕ next to the page icon.

How do I delete a hyperlink?

✔ Open the page that contains the link. Click the link and then click the Insert Hyperlink button 🔖 to display the Edit Hyperlink dialog box. Click Remove Link. The text remains on the page, but FrontPage removes the link. To delete the text, select it and press the Delete key.

How can I distinguish between types of link?

✔ If the link is to another Web site or page, you see a page icon with the browser icon. For example, you see **e** for Internet Explorer. If the link is to the home page, you see an icon of a house.

How can I check that links are accurate?

✔ You can view the broken links report to verify all of the links in a web. See the section "View Web Reports" for more information.

Can I print a diagram of the links?

✔ FrontPage dims both the Print button and command in Hyperlinks view, indicating that you cannot print the diagram of links. You can, however, print the Navigation page. See the section "Check Site Navigation" for more information.

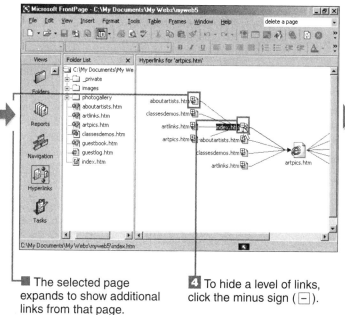

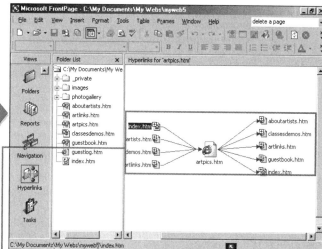

■ The selected page expands to show additional links from that page.

■ If you cannot see all of the links, scroll through the contents pane.

4 To hide a level of links, click the minus sign (−).

■ The links for the selected page are hidden.

CHECK SITE NAVIGATION

Y ou can use the Navigation view to see how the various pages in your Web site relate to each other. Although some templates and wizards automatically set up a navigational structure for you, you can change this structure.

The navigational structure of your Web site determines the layout of your page's navigation bars, which

is a set of hyperlinks at the top, bottom, right, or left edge of each page that readers can use to move through your Web site. When you change the navigational structure of your Web site, FrontPage automatically updates the navigation bars for you.

The Navigation view displays the folders and pages in your Web site on the left side of the window and

the navigational structure on the right side of the window. Boxes represent pages in the navigational structure. A line between boxes indicates how the pages interrelate.

In the Navigation view, you can connect new or existing pages to the navigational structure. You can also move pages to change the way the pages relate to each other.

CHECK SITE NAVIGATION

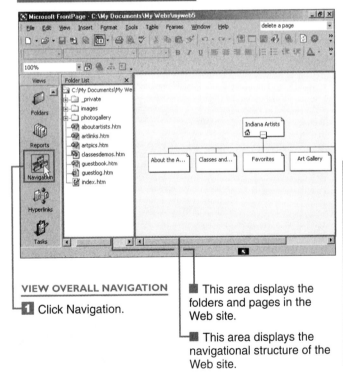

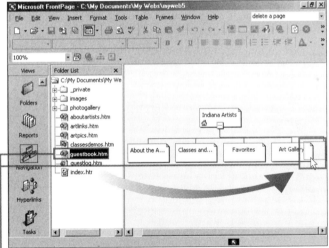

VIEW OVERALL NAVIGATION

■1 Click Navigation.

■ This area displays the folders and pages in the Web site.

■ This area displays the navigational structure of the Web site.

ADD A PAGE TO THE NAVIGATION FLOW

■1 Click the page you want to add to the navigational structure of the Web site.

■2 Drag the ▹ to where you want the page to appear.

■ An outline shows where the page will appear.

■ The page appears in the navigational structure.

How can I add navigation bars to my pages?

✔ If your pages do not display navigation bars, you can have FrontPage automatically add navigation bars to the pages. Click Format, click Shared Borders, and then click All Pages. Click an option to specify where you want the navigation bars to appear, and then click Include navigation buttons. Click OK.

How can I view the entire navigational structure?

✔ If you cannot view your entire structure on-screen, you can click the minus sign (⊟) on a page in the structure to hide the pages below the page. To once again display the pages, click the plus sign (⊞).

How do I remove a page from the navigational structure?

✔ Click the page in the navigational structure and then press the Delete key. Click the Remove this page from all navigation bars option and then click OK. Doing this deletes only the navigational structure, and does not delete the page from the Web site.

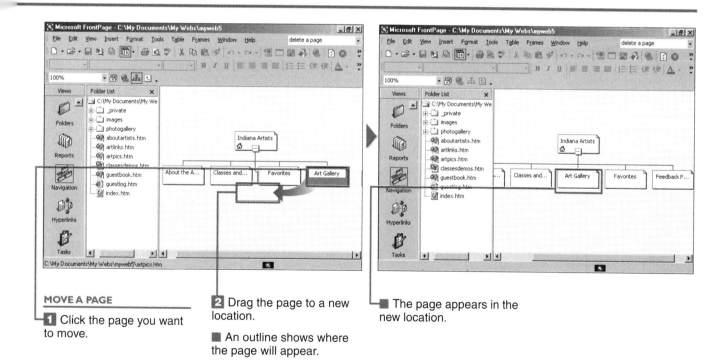

MOVE A PAGE

1 Click the page you want to move.

2 Drag the page to a new location.

■ An outline shows where the page will appear.

■ The page appears in the new location.

PUBLISH A WEB SITE

When you finish creating your Web site, you can transfer the pages to a computer called a *Web server*. When stored on the Web server, pages become available for other people to view. You can publish your Web site to a Web server on the Internet or on your company's intranet.

The company that gives you access to the Internet usually offers space on its Web server where you can publish your Web site. The Internet also has sites that allow you to publish your Web site for free, such as GeoCities (www.geocities.com).

Before publishing your Web site, you should preview the pages to ensure they look the way you want. For information on previewing pages, see Chapter 32.

To publish your Web site, you must enter the Internet address of the Web server where you want to publish your Web site. You must also enter your user name and password. If you do not know this information, you can contact your Internet Service Provider (ISP) or system administrator.

PUBLISH A WEB SITE

1 Click File.

2 Click Publish Web.

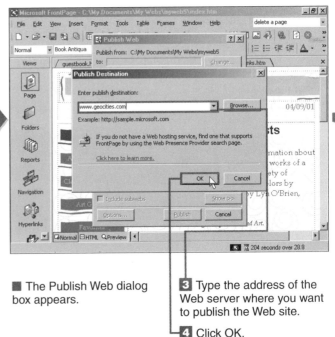

■ The Publish Web dialog box appears.

3 Type the address of the Web server where you want to publish the Web site.

4 Click OK.

How do I publish changes to my Web site?

✔ You can click the Publish Web button 🔳. Although FrontPage does not redisplay the Publish Web dialog box, you can change your options, by clicking File and then clicking Publish Web.

How do I determine if my Web server uses FrontPage Server Extensions?

✔ You need to contact your Internet service provider or system administrator. If your Web server does not use FrontPage Server Extensions, advanced features may not function. For example, a hit counter may not work properly. For information on hit counters, see the section "Add a Hit Counter."

Do I have to publish all the pages in my Web site?

✔ No. You may not want to publish a page still under construction. Click View, click Reports, and then Workflow. Click Publish Status. You see a list of all the pages and related files in the Web site. Right-click the name of the page you do not want to publish and click Don't Publish from the menu that appears.

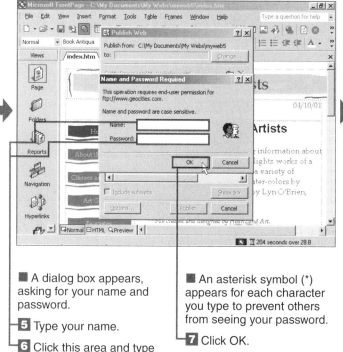

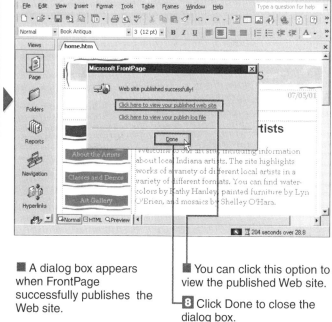

■ A dialog box appears, asking for your name and password.

5 Type your name.

6 Click this area and type your password.

■ An asterisk symbol (*) appears for each character you type to prevent others from seeing your password.

7 Click OK.

■ A dialog box appears when FrontPage successfully publishes the Web site.

■ You can click this option to view the published Web site.

8 Click Done to close the dialog box.

34) SHARE DATA

Move or Copy Information between
    Documents 588
Work with the Clipboard 590
Embed Information 592
Edit Embedded Information 594
Link Information 596
Edit Linked Information 598
Create a File Hyperlink 600
Insert a Web Hyperlink 602

35) CUSTOMIZE OFFICE

Set Toolbar and Menu Options 604
Add or Remove Office XP Features 606
Using Handwriting or Speech Recognition 608
An Introduction to Additional Office XP
    Programs and Features 610

SECTION VIII

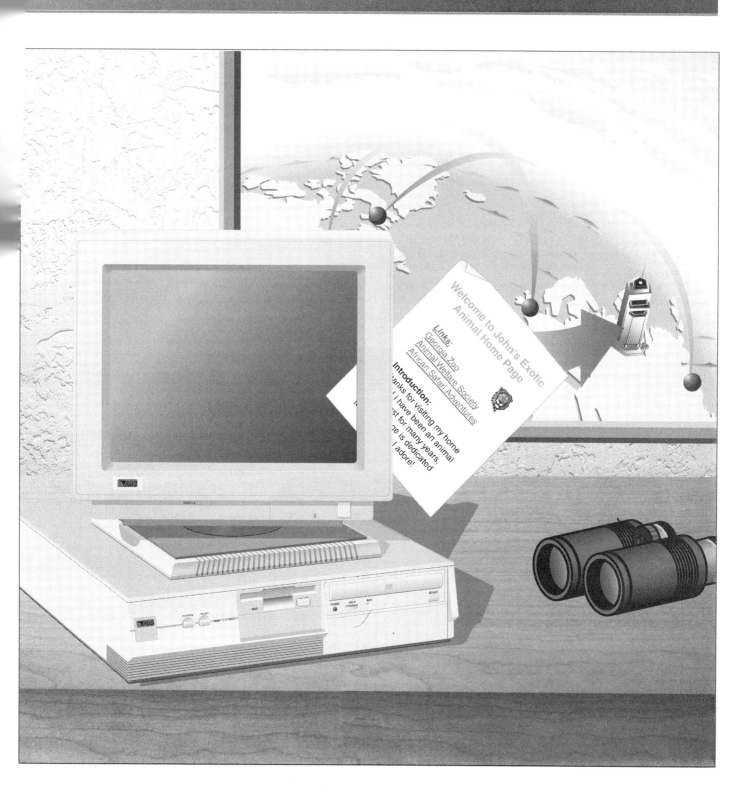

MOVE OR COPY INFORMATION BETWEEN DOCUMENTS

You can move or copy information from one document to another. This saves you time when you want to use the same information in more than one document.

Moving or copying information allows you to use text and objects from one document in another document without having to retype or re-create the information. You can also move or copy information between Office programs, such as Word, Excel, PowerPoint, and Access. For example, you can move an Excel chart to a Word document.

Office places the information you move or copy in a temporary storage area, called the Office Clipboard. When you move information, Office takes it from the original document and places it in the Office Clipboard. When you copy information, the information remains in the original document and Office places a copy of the information in the Office Clipboard.

When you paste information into a document, the information from the Office Clipboard appears in the document.

MOVE OR COPY INFORMATION BETWEEN DOCUMENTS

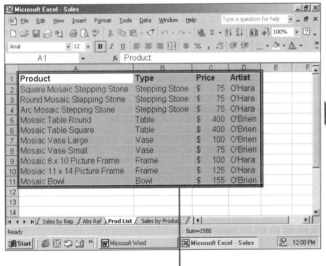

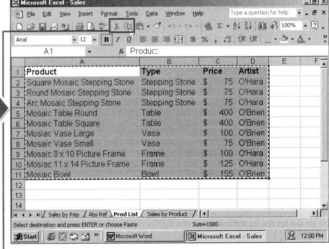

1 Open the document containing the information you want to appear in another document.

2 Select the information you want to move or copy.

3 Click the Cut button (✄) to cut or the Copy button (▤) to copy the information.

■ Office places the information in the Office Clipboard.

How do I select the information I want to move or copy?

✔ To select text in most Office programs, drag the mouse over the text. Selected text appears highlighted on your screen. To select an object, click the object. Selection handles appear around the selected object.

Can I drag and drop information from one document to anther?

✔ Yes. Display both documents side-by-side or top to bottom. Select the information you want to move or copy. To move the information, drag the information to the other document. To copy the information, hold down Ctrl as you drag the information.

Why does the Clipboard button appear when I paste data?

✔ The Clipboard Smart Tag is displayed so that you can select specific options for pasting the item you just inserted. For more information on using the Clipboard, see "Work with the Clipboard."

Can I use keyboard shortcuts to cut and paste?

✔ You can use the following keyboard shortcuts for cutting, copying, and pasting from one program or document to another:

Cut	Ctrl+X
Copy	Ctrl+C
Paste	Ctrl+V

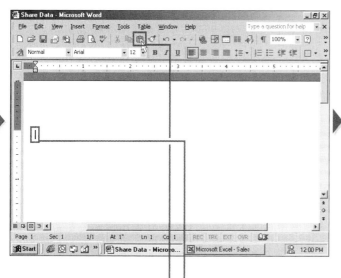

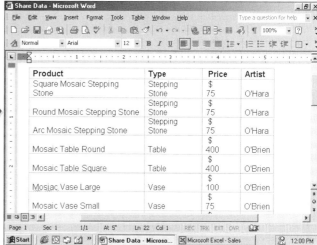

4 Open the document you want to display the information.

Note: See Chapter 2 to learn how to open a document.

5 Click where you want to place the information.

6 Click the Paste button (📋).

■ The information appears in the document.

WORK WITH THE CLIPBOARD

With newer versions of Office, including Office XP, you can cut or copy several items, and then using the Clipboard, decide which items to paste into another document or Microsoft Office program. The Clipboard task pane lets you view up to 24 different cut or copied items, which allows you to select and paste individual or multiple items. Depending on the compatibility, you can even paste items from non-Microsoft programs.

Office represents each item in the Clipboard with an icon to help you determine the item's program. Please note that when you fill the Clipboard, Office begins deleting older items. For this reason, you may want to clear all or some of the items in the Clipboard before you start a large pasting project.

Also new with Office XP, the Clipboard Smart Tag appears when you paste an item. You can use this Smart Tag to view a list of item-specific commands for pasting. For example, when you paste an Excel range, Office lists commands for keeping the source formatting and column widths, matching the destination formatting, and so on.

WORK WITH THE CLIPBOARD

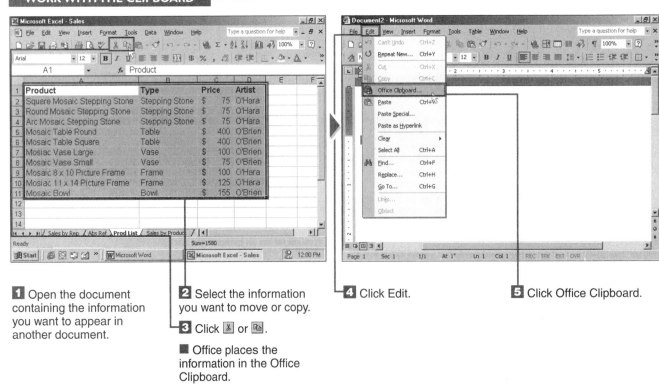

1 Open the document containing the information you want to appear in another document.

2 Select the information you want to move or copy.

3 Click ✂ or 📋.

■ Office places the information in the Office Clipboard.

4 Click Edit.

5 Click Office Clipboard.

What other benefits does the Clipboard task pane provide?

✔ Rather than cutting and pasting individual selections, you can use the Clipboard task pane to paste several cut or copied items. Cut or copy the items to the Clipboard and then display the Clipboard task pane. Select where you want to paste all of the Clipboard items and click the Paste All button.

How do I delete a particular item in the Clipboard?

✔ Click the down arrow next to the item you want to remove from the Clipboard. Then click Delete.

What does the Options button do in the Clipboard task pane?

✔ Click the Options button to display a menu of choices for when and how the Office displays the Clipboard. You can select to show the Office Clipboard automatically or not at all. You can select to show the Office Clipboard icon on the taskbar and show the status of the copying near the taskbar. Click an item that is not checked to turn it on, or click an item that is checked to turn it off.

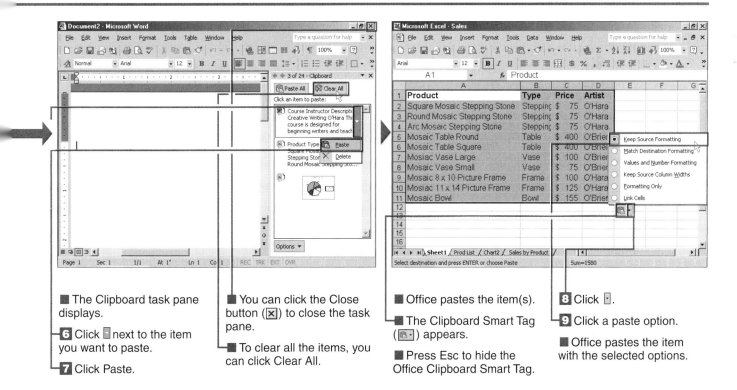

■ The Clipboard task pane displays.

6 Click ▪ next to the item you want to paste.

7 Click Paste.

■ You can click the Close button (✕) to close the task pane.

■ To clear all the items, you can click Clear All.

■ Office pastes the item(s).

■ The Clipboard Smart Tag (🗐▾) appears.

■ Press Esc to hide the Office Clipboard Smart Tag.

8 Click ▪.

9 Click a paste option.

■ Office pastes the item with the selected options.

EMBED INFORMATION

Y ou can use Object Linking and Embedding (OLE) to create a document that contains text, charts, images, sounds, and video clips from other applications. Each piece of information you embed in a document is an object. To use OLE, you create an object in another program and then embed that object in an Office document. For example, you can

use Excel to create a chart and then embed the chart in a Word document.

The document you use to create the object is called the *source file*. The document in which you embed the object is the *destination file*. When you embed an object, the object becomes part of the destination file and is no longer connected to the source file.

A document with an embedded object is often large because it stores information about the object and the program that you used to create the object.

Use an embedded object to share data when you do not need to keep the source file separate. Use another data sharing method if you used the source files in other documents and want to keep it separate.

EMBED INFORMATION

■1 Select the data you want to place in another document.

■2 Click 📋.

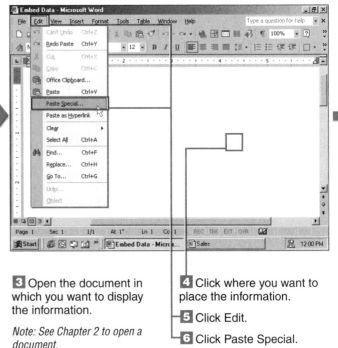

■3 Open the document in which you want to display the information.

Note: See Chapter 2 to open a document.

■4 Click where you want to place the information.

■5 Click Edit.

■6 Click Paste Special.

How can I tell if a program supports OLE?

✔ Display the Edit menu in the program. If the Paste Special command appears in the menu, the program supports OLE.

Can I drag and drop an object to embed it?

✔ Yes. Display the source and destination files side-by-side on your screen. Select the object in the source file. To move the object, drag the object to the destination file. To copy the object, hold down the Ctrl key as you drag the object to the destination file.

Can I embed and create a new object at the same time?

✔ Open the document you want to display the new object. Click Insert, Object. Click the Create New tab and then click the type of object you want to create. Create the object and then click back in the destination document.

Can I embed an entire file in a document?

✔ Yes. Click Insert, Object. Click the Create from File tab and then click Browse. Click the file and click Insert. Click OK to insert the file.

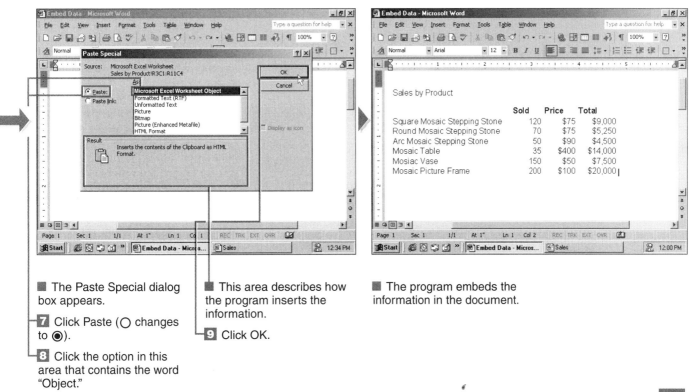

■ The Paste Special dialog box appears.

7 Click Paste (○ changes to ◉).

8 Click the option in this area that contains the word "Object."

■ This area describes how the program inserts the information.

9 Click OK.

■ The program embeds the information in the document.

EDIT EMBEDDED INFORMATION

You can change an object you have embedded in a document. When you need to modify an object, you can edit the object using the same tools you used to create the object. To learn more about embedding objects, see the section "Embed Information." You might need to change the object to alter its content or change its appearance.

When you embed, you insert an item, or *object*, from its original

file, or *source file*, into another file, called the *destination file* so that the object becomes part of that file. Therefore, changing an embedded object, does not affect the source.

When you double-click an embedded object, the menus and toolbars from the source file appear on your screen allowing you to edit the embedded object. When you finish editing the embedded object, Office replaces the menus and toolbars from the source program

with the menus and toolbars from the destination program.

A document containing an embedded object is often large because it stores information about the object and the program that you used to create the object. If large documents are a problem, consider another data-sharing method, as covered in this section.

EDIT EMBEDDED INFORMATION

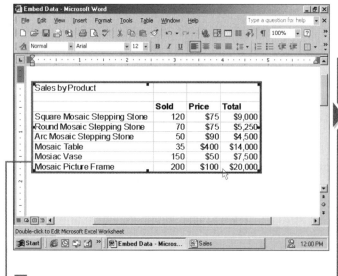

1 Double-click the embedded information you want to change.

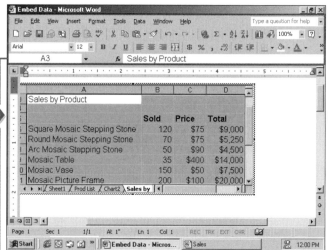

■ The menus and toolbars from the program you used to create the information appear. You can access all the commands you need to make the necessary changes.

When I double-click an embedded object, it appears in a separate window. What should I do?

✔ You can edit the object in the window. After you make your changes, save the document and then select the File menu and then click Exit to return to the destination file.

Can I change the size of an embedded object?

✔ Yes. Click the object. Selection handles appear around the object. Click the ⬚ over one of the handles and then drag the handle to a new location.

How do I edit an embedded sound or video clip?

✔ Some embedded objects, such as sound and video clips, play automatically when you double-click them. To edit an embedded sound or video clip, right-click the object. Click the object type and then click Edit.

Can I edit an embedded object that someone else created?

✔ You can edit the object only if you have the program used to create the source file installed on your computer.

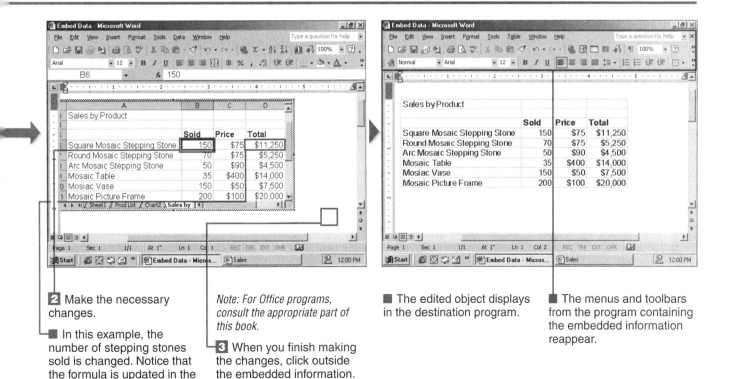

■2 Make the necessary changes.

■ In this example, the number of stepping stones sold is changed. Notice that the formula is updated in the Excel object.

Note: For Office programs, consult the appropriate part of this book.

■3 When you finish making the changes, click outside the embedded information.

■ The edited object displays in the destination program.

■ The menus and toolbars from the program containing the embedded information reappear.

LINK INFORMATION

You can use Object Linking and Embedding (OLE) to link the information in one document, called a source file, to another document, called a destination file. A destination file can contain linked information from several source files.

Each piece of information you link between documents is called an

object, which you can make a picture, chart, worksheet, or text. You can link an object between documents in the same or different programs. For example, you can link a chart in a worksheet to another worksheet in Excel or to a report in Word.

When you link an object, the destination file displays the object

but does not contain the object itself. The object remains in the source file, and a connection, or *link*, exists between the source file and the destination file. Because the linked object remains a part of the source file, you cannot delete, move, or rename the source file.

LINK INFORMATION

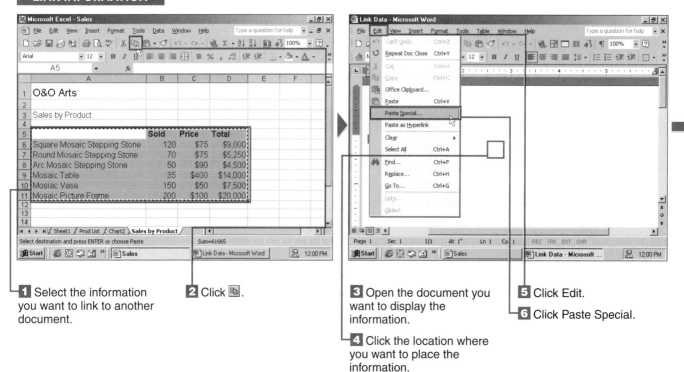

1 Select the information you want to link to another document.

2 Click 📋.

3 Open the document you want to display the information.

4 Click the location where you want to place the information.

5 Click Edit.

6 Click Paste Special.

How should I insert information I want to link?

✔ The available options for inserting information depend on the information you select. Inserting information as an object is ideal if you later want to edit the linked information. Some of the other available options include formatted text, unformatted text, picture, bitmap, and HTML format.

Can I use drag and drop to link objects?

✔ No. When you drag and drop an object, the object is embedded in the destination file, not linked.

What is the difference between linking and embedding?

✔ When you link an object, the object remains a part of the source file. Changes you make to the object in the source file appear in the destination file. When you embed an object, the object becomes part of the destination file and is no longer connected to the source file. Changes you make to the object in the source file do not appear in the destination file.

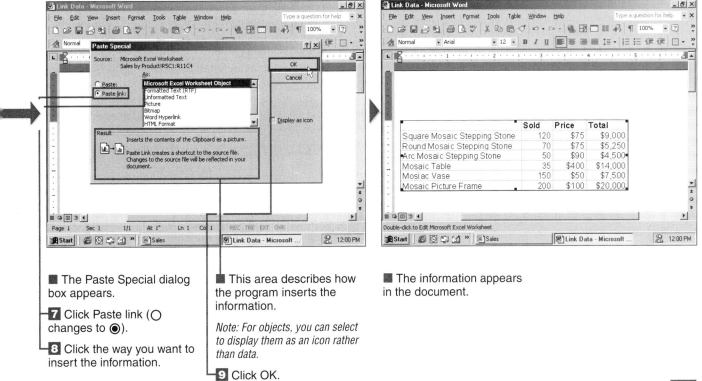

■ The Paste Special dialog box appears.

7 Click Paste link (○ changes to ◉).

8 Click the way you want to insert the information.

■ This area describes how the program inserts the information.

Note: For objects, you can select to display them as an icon rather than data.

9 Click OK.

■ The information appears in the document.

EDIT LINKED INFORMATION

You can make changes to a linked object so that both the source and destination files reflect the changes. This is useful when you want several documents to display the same up-to-date information. The file to which you linked the object is the destination file and displays the linked object but does not contain the object itself. The file in which you created

the object is the source file. If you linked the same object to several documents, all the documents display the changes.

To edit the linked object, you must have both the source file and the program you used to create the file installed on your computer or network.

To edit a linked object, you can select it in the destination file and then display the object in the source file. You can also go directly to the source program to open the source file and display the object.

EDIT LINKED INFORMATION

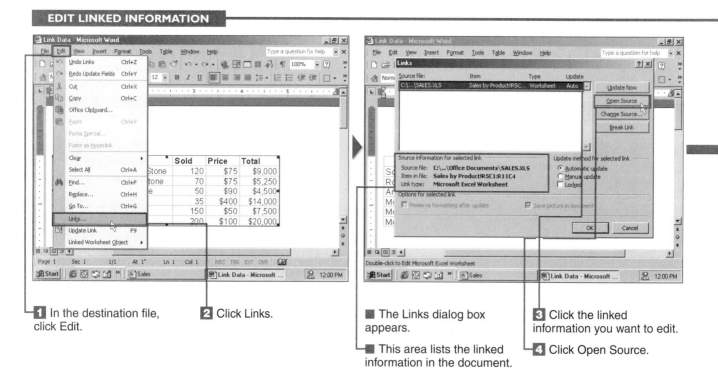

1 In the destination file, click Edit.

2 Click Links.

■ The Links dialog box appears.

■ This area lists the linked information in the document.

3 Click the linked information you want to edit.

4 Click Open Source.

Can I manually update linked information?

✔ By default, when you change linked information in the source file, the information automatically updates in the destination file. However, you can have linked information update only when you choose to update it. Click Edit, Links. Click the linked information you want to update manually and click Manual update. When you want to update the linked information, display the Links dialog box, click the linked information, and then click Update Now. Or as a shortcut, you can select the manually linked object and press F9.

Is there another way to edit linked information in the destination file?

✔ If you inserted the linked information as an object, you can double-click the information to quickly open the source file and edit the information.

Can I break a link?

✔ Yes. Click Edit and then Links. Click the linked information and then click the Break Link button. The object becomes part of the destination file and you can no longer update it when you change the object in the source file.

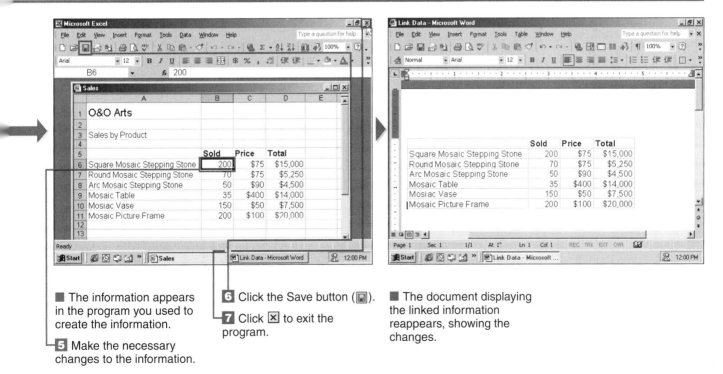

■ The information appears in the program you used to create the information.

5 Make the necessary changes to the information.

6 Click the Save button (🖫).

7 Click ⊠ to exit the program.

■ The document displaying the linked information reappears, showing the changes.

CREATE A FILE HYPERLINK

You can create a hyperlink to connect a word, phrase, or graphic in your document to another document on your computer, network, corporate intranet, or the Internet. You can create a hyperlink in Word, Excel, PowerPoint, or Access. You can also create Web pages and Web sites, including hyperlinks, in FrontPage. See Chapters 32 and 33 for information on FrontPage.

You can use any text or graphic in your document as a hyperlink. Make sure the text or graphic you choose clearly indicates where the hyperlink takes you.

You can also create a hyperlink by typing a Web page address or e-mail address in your document. The program automatically converts the address to a hyperlink for you. You can easily identify hyperlinks in a document.

By default, hyperlinks appear underlined and in color. When you position the mouse pointer over a hyperlink, a yellow box appears, displaying where the hyperlink takes you. When you select a hyperlink, the connected document appears on your screen.

CREATE A FILE HYPERLINK

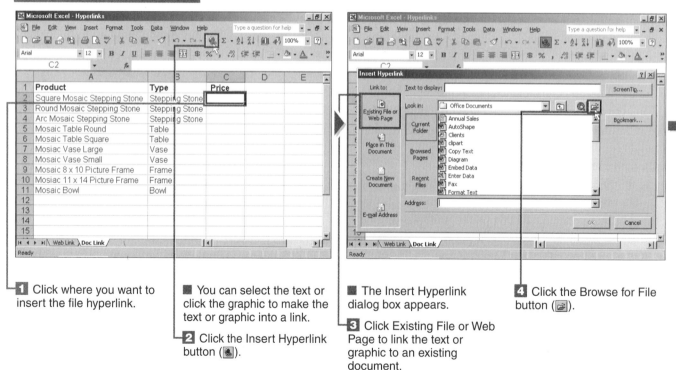

1 Click where you want to insert the file hyperlink.

■ You can select the text or click the graphic to make the text or graphic into a link.

2 Click the Insert Hyperlink button (⬛).

■ The Insert Hyperlink dialog box appears.

3 Click Existing File or Web Page to link the text or graphic to an existing document.

4 Click the Browse for File button (📂).

Can I create a hyperlink that allows people to send me e-mail?

✔ Yes. Select the text or graphic you want to make a hyperlink and then click the Insert Hyperlink button (🖱). Click E-mail Address and type the e-mail address you want to use in the E-mail address text box. Then click OK.

How do I remove a hyperlink?

✔ Right-click the hyperlink in your document. A menu appears. Click Hyperlink and then click Remove Hyperlink.

How do I make a hyperlink appear as regular text?

✔ You can make a hyperlink appear as regular text by right-clicking the link and then selecting Hyperlink, Remove Hyperlink. You might do this for readers that do not have e-mail or Internet access. Or if you have to submit a document without formatting, you can turn off the automatic hyperlink. When the hyperlink is removed, the text appears as regular text. Clicking it does not open that Web page.

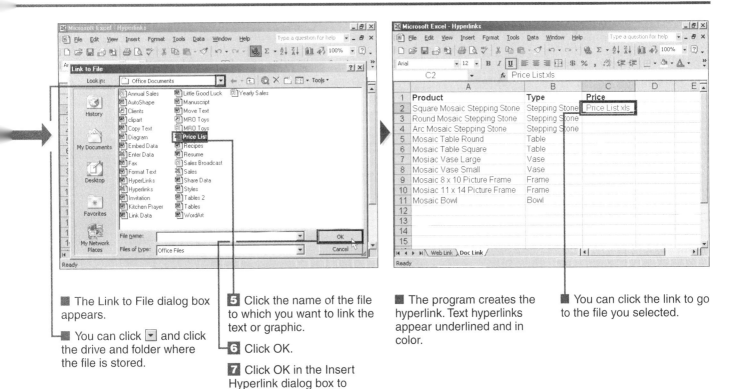

■ The Link to File dialog box appears.

■ You can click ▾ and click the drive and folder where the file is stored.

5 Click the name of the file to which you want to link the text or graphic.

6 Click OK.

7 Click OK in the Insert Hyperlink dialog box to create the hyperlink.

■ The program creates the hyperlink. Text hyperlinks appear underlined and in color.

■ You can click the link to go to the file you selected.

INSERT A WEB HYPERLINK

You can insert a hyperlink in your document, enabling you to go from the current document to another file, a Web page, another place in the current document, or an e-mail address. Because hyperlinks require you to click to them, they are most useful in documents that you send via e-mail or display on-screen. Office displays them in a unique color to distinguish them from regular text. For more information on Web sites, see Part VII of this book.

You have several options for creating the Web link. You can type the address. You can click the Browsed Pages button and select the address from a list of recently visited files or Web pages. You can also use the Browse the Web button to start your Web browser and go to the page.

By default, Office displays the Web page address as a ScreenTip, which appears when a user positions the mouse pointer over it. You can change this text to anything you want.

INSERT A WEB HYPERLINK

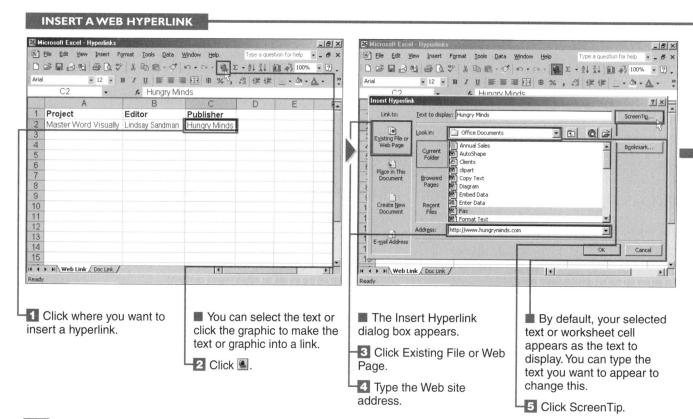

■ Click where you want to insert a hyperlink.

■ You can select the text or click the graphic to make the text or graphic into a link.

■ Click ⬛.

■ The Insert Hyperlink dialog box appears.

■ Click Existing File or Web Page.

■ Type the Web site address.

■ By default, your selected text or worksheet cell appears as the text to display. You can type the text you want to appear to change this.

■ Click ScreenTip.

How do I insert a link to a new document?

✔ Click Create New Document and then type the name of the new document text to display. Select to Edit the document now. Click OK. The new document opens, using the name you entered. Create, save, and then close this document.

How do I edit a link I have inserted?

✔ Start by selecting that link. Then click Insert and click Hyperlink. You see the Edit Hyperlink dialog box listing the text and link information. Make any changes and click OK.

How do I insert a link to a place within the current document?

✔ Create bookmarks (Word) or cell names (Excel) to the places you want to link to. Then when creating the link, select Place in This Document. In the Select a place in this document list, click the bookmark or cell name to which you want to go and then click OK.

How do I browse to find a link?

✔ Click the Browse the Web button (🔍) and then click to display the page to which you want to link.

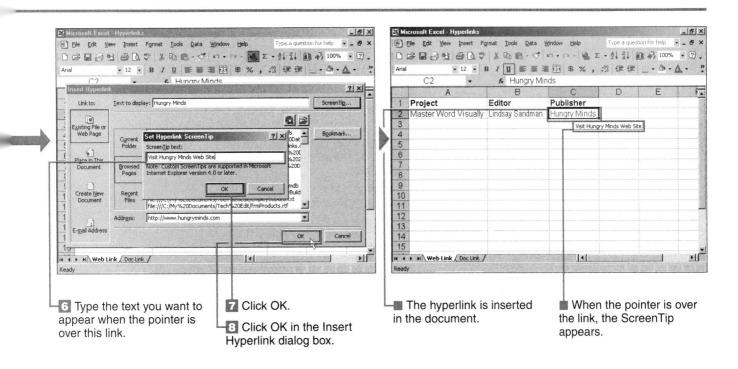

6 Type the text you want to appear when the pointer is over this link.

7 Click OK.

8 Click OK in the Insert Hyperlink dialog box.

■ The hyperlink is inserted in the document.

■ When the pointer is over the link, the ScreenTip appears.

SET TOOLBAR AND MENU OPTIONS

You can customize the toolbars in an Office program to help you work more efficiently. You can also customize the menus and other on-screen tools. For example, the two default toolbars, Standard and Formatting, can share a row or display as two separate rows depending on your preference.

For menus, you can always display a complete list of menu commands.

Or, you can have the program show the most recently used commands. With the most recently used commands option, you can still access the other commands by using the down arrow at the bottom of the menu.

You have several other options for customizing on-screen elements. You can select to use large icons for the toolbar buttons, to list font names in the actual font, and to

show or hide ScreenTips. As a final option, you can select from several menu animations.

Office programs keep track of what commands and buttons you most frequently use. You can reset the data usage option so that Office clears any previous choices and starts from scratch building your list of frequently used commands.

SET TOOLBAR AND MENU OPTIONS

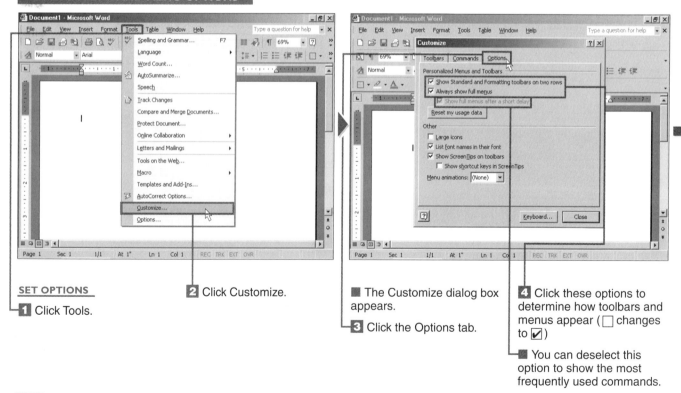

SET OPTIONS

1 Click Tools.

2 Click Customize.

■ The Customize dialog box appears.

3 Click the Options tab.

4 Click these options to determine how toolbars and menus appear (☐ changes to ☑)

■ You can deselect this option to show the most frequently used commands.

Can I create my own toolbar?

✔ Yes. Click the Toolbars tab in the Customize dialog box and then click New. Type a name for your toolbar and then click OK. The toolbar displays very small because it does not contain any buttons. Click the Commands tab and then drag the commands you want to add to the new toolbar.

How do I return a toolbar to its original settings?

✔ Click Tools, Customize, and then click the Toolbars tab. Click the toolbar and then click Reset. Click OK in the dialog box that appears and then click Close.

Can I move the buttons on the toolbars?

✔ Yes. You can customize the toolbars by removing infrequently used buttons, moving buttons to a different location, or adding new buttons. To make these changes, click the Commands tab of the Customize dialog box. You can then drag buttons off of the toolbar, drag buttons to another location, or drag commands from the Commands list to the toolbar.

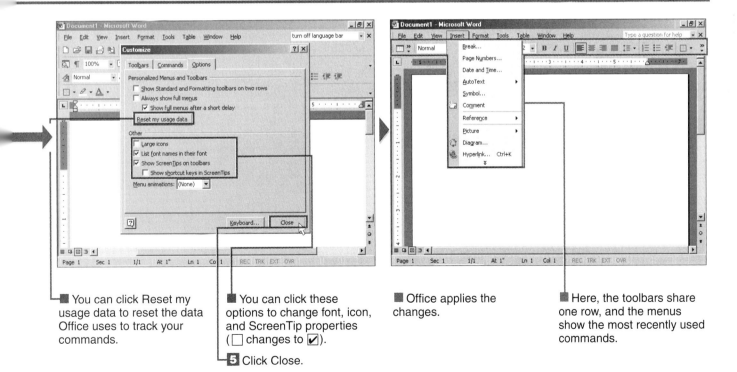

■ You can click Reset my usage data to reset the data Office uses to track your commands.

■ You can click these options to change font, icon, and ScreenTip properties (☐ changes to ☑).

5 Click Close.

■ Office applies the changes.

■ Here, the toolbars share one row, and the menus show the most recently used commands.

ADD OR REMOVE OFFICE XP FEATURES

Depending on your initial installation selections, you can install additional Office XP features on your computer to add additional capabilities and enhancements. You can also remove Office XP features to free up storage space on your computer.

Office organizes the available features by program, which you can display or hide. You can add or

remove all features and subfeatures within a program.

Each feature displays an icon that indicates the feature's current installation status. You can select a different icon for a feature to change the way the feature installs. The Run from My Computer icon (🖳) indicates a previously installed feature. The Installed on First Use icon (🖳) indicates that Office

installs this feature only when you first install it. When you select the Run All from My Computer icon (🖳), you change the way Office installs a feature and all its subfeatures. For example, you might choose to install templates on first use. That way, you do not use the disk space to store these files, but they are available when and if you need them.

ADD OR REMOVE OFFICE XP FEATURES

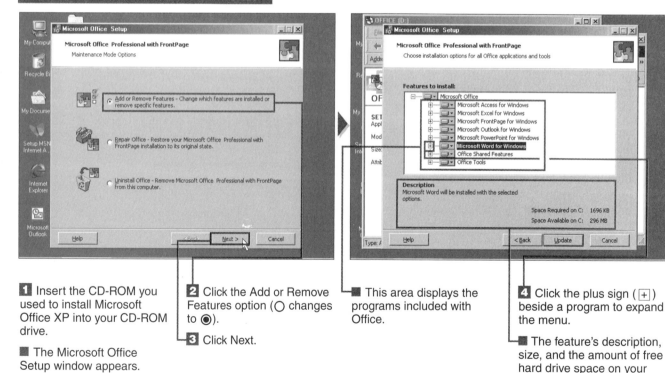

1 Insert the CD-ROM you used to install Microsoft Office XP into your CD-ROM drive.

■ The Microsoft Office Setup window appears.

2 Click the Add or Remove Features option (○ changes to ◉).

3 Click Next.

■ This area displays the programs included with Office.

4 Click the plus sign (⊞) beside a program to expand the menu.

■ The feature's description, size, and the amount of free hard drive space on your computer appears.

Can I close the window without adding or removing any Office features?

✔ Yes. Click Cancel to exit without making any changes. Click Yes in the confirmation dialog box that appears.

Why are the icons for some features gray?

✔ When Office displays a gray icon, the feature has subfeatures which you cannot collectively install the same way. For example, Office may allow you to install some subfeatures on your computer, and others the first time you use the feature. To display the subfeatures for a feature, click the plus sign (⊞) beside the feature.

The Microsoft Office Setup window did not appear. What is wrong?

✔ You may need to set up your computer to automatically run a CD-ROM. To display the Microsoft Office Setup window, double-click My Computer on your desktop and then double-click the icon for your CD-ROM drive. If necessary, double-click the Setup icon.

When would I select the other two Maintenance Mode Options?

✔ You can select Repair Office to restore Office to its original state. You can select Uninstall Office to remove the Office programs from your computer. See Appendix A for more on these options.

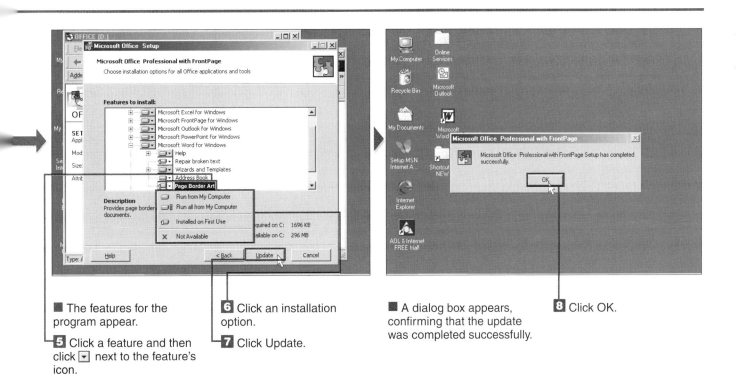

■ The features for the program appear.

5 Click a feature and then click ▾ next to the feature's icon.

6 Click an installation option.

7 Click Update.

■ A dialog box appears, confirming that the update was completed successfully.

8 Click OK.

USING HANDWRITING OR SPEECH RECOGNITION

You can use Microsoft's handwriting and speech recognition features to input text without typing on a keyboard. You can enter either text or handwriting by using a handwriting device such as a digital pen and tablet, a PDA with handwriting features, or using the mouse to draw text in the Writing Pad within a program. You can use the speech recognition feature in any Office XP program, Internet Explorer, and

Outlook Express so long as you have a microphone and sound card or a USB port.

When you add handwriting and speech components, Office automatically displays the Language bar in the various Office programs. See the section "Add or Remove Office XP Features" for help on adding or removing components. Office places these features in the Office Shared

Features folder within the Alternative User Input subfolder.

Because handwriting and voice recognition features can introduce unwanted mistakes into your text, remember to proofread your work. Also, you may consider deactivating these features if you do not use them because they slow down the performance of the program.

USING HANDWRITING RECOGNITION

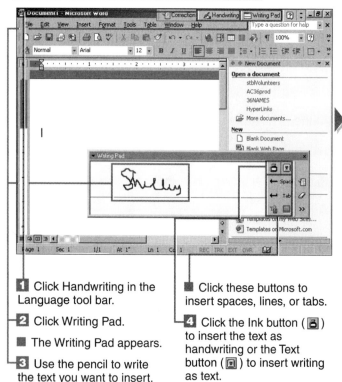

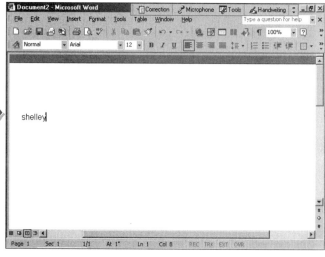

■1 Click Handwriting in the Language tool bar.

■2 Click Writing Pad.

■ The Writing Pad appears.

■3 Use the pencil to write the text you want to insert.

■ Click these buttons to insert spaces, lines, or tabs.

■4 Click the Ink button (🖊) to insert the text as handwriting or the Text button (🔲) to insert writing as text.

■ Office inserts the text into the document.

What do I do if I do not see the Language bar after adding the language components?

✔ You may need to active the Language bar. In the status bar, you should see EN, if you are working in English and have the components installed properly. Right-click EN and click Show the Language bar.

How do I close the Language Bar?

✔ Right-click the Language Bar and click Close Language Bar.

What are the Write Anywhere and Drawing Pad options on the Language bar?

✔ You use Write Anywhere to write anywhere on-screen and Drawing Pad to draw and insert pictures.

How do I set up my microphone for the Speech feature?

✔ To set up your microphone, click Tools and then Speech to start the Microphone Wizard. Follow the Wizard's step-by-step instructions to install the Microphone.

How do I train the speech recognition engine to recognize my voice?

✔ To train speech recognition, click the Speech Tools button on the Language bar. Speak slowly and clearly without emphasizing each syllable. If possible, eliminate any background noise by turning off your TV or radio. Microsoft recommends a headset microphone connected via a USB port.

USING SPEECH RECOGNITION

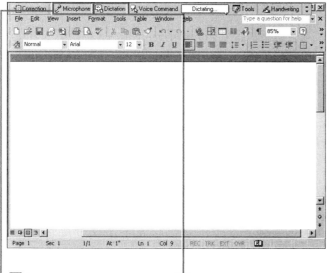

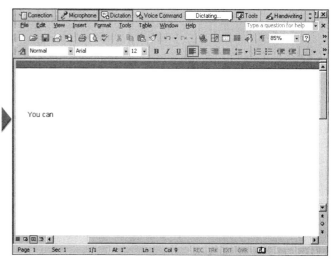

1 Set up the microphone and train the speech tool.

Note: See the appropriate product documentation to set up these features.

2 Click Microphone.

3 Click Dictation.

4 Talk into the microphone.

■ The words appear on-screen.

■ If you want to spell a word, especially terminology or someone's name, you can say "Spelling mode" and then spell the name.

AN INTRODUCTION TO ADDITIONAL OFFICE XP PROGRAMS AND FEATURES

Each Office program is packed full of features; this book highlights the most important and commonly used. The features that may benefit you most are covered in the particular program sections of this book.

In addition to each program, Office XP has some shared features that work throughout all programs. Because some of these features remain in the background, you never notice them, or know they exist. Others are worth

investigating for special situations. For example, if you need to type in Japanese or another language, you can investigate the language resources.

Program Maintenance

Office XP programs are self-repairing applications. When you start an Office XP program, the program determines whether any essential files are missing and then re-installs the files if necessary in the background. The program may also check your registry files and make any necessary repairs.

You can also use the Detect and Repair feature to find and correct problems with a program's files. Available on the Help menu of most Office programs, Detect and Repair compares the program files on your computer to the files that were installed when you installed Office XP. The feature then automatically replaces any corrupt or missing files. When it is repairing a program, Office may ask you to insert the Microsoft Office XP installation disc into your CD-ROM drive.

Scanner and Camera Add-In

The Scanner and Camera Add-In allows you to scan an image or download an image from a digital camera while working in an Office program and then insert the image directly into the current document. This saves you from having to leave the Office program to scan or download an image.

In an Office program, you can access the From Scanner or Camera option by clicking Insert, and then Picture. The first time you use the From Scanner or Camera option, Office may ask you to install the feature from the Microsoft Office XP installation CD-ROM disc.

Text Converters

Text converters allow Office programs to work with a wide variety of file formats. For example, you can create a document in Word and then save the document in a format that you or another person can use with another program, such as WordPerfect or an earlier version of Word. Text converters make it easy to exchange data with friends and colleagues who do not use Office XP.

The first time you use a text converter, Office may ask you to install the text converter from the Microsoft Office XP installation CD-ROM disc. Office automatically installs some text converters when you install Office XP.

Microsoft Office Language Settings

Microsoft Office Language Settings allow you to change the language Office displays in programs, including the menus, dialog boxes, the Help feature as well as the dictionary so you can use the spell checker for a given language.

You access the Microsoft Office Language Settings feature by clicking Start, then Programs and then Microsoft Office Tools. Upon first use, Office may ask you to install the feature and the MultiLanguage Pack from the Microsoft Office XP installation CD-ROM disc.

Microsoft Photo Editor

Microsoft Photo Editor allows you to scan an image and change the appearance of an image on your computer. With various tools, you can smudge colors, make an area transparent, or change the contrast. You can also emboss or apply a watercolor or stained glass effect to an image.

You save the image like any other computer file. Photo Editor supports many popular image file formats, including Graphics

Interchange Format (.gif), JPEG (.jpeg), Tag Image File Format (.tif) and Windows Bitmap (.bmp). This enables you to print, or e-mail an image to a colleague.

To access the Photo Editor, click Start menu, click Programs and then click Microsoft Office Tools. Upon first use, Office may ask you to install the program from the Microsoft Office XP installation CD-ROM disc.

Collaboration and Document Management Features

Office XP includes several new collaboration features that you can use to track, review, and merge changes to Word documents, spreadsheets, and presentations. You can schedule online meetings and track changes to documents sent via e-mail. You can use Track Changes to track revisions, and Compare and Merge Documents to merge several versions of a document. You find all these commands in the Tools menu.

Another component, Microsoft Binder, enables you to bring together related documents from different Office programs to create a single document, called a binder. For example, a binder may include a Word document that provides background information about your company, an Excel worksheet that displays your company's sales figures, and a PowerPoint presentation about your company's objectives.

Like other components, you may need to install Binder from the Microsoft Office XP installation CD-ROM disc.

INSTALL OFFICE XP

You can install Office XP from the Microsoft Office CD-ROM. When you insert the CD-ROM into your CD-ROM drive, Microsoft's Setup program checks your system and then starts the installation process.

Before you can install Office XP, Microsoft may need to update your

system files. If you do not have Office 2000 SR1 or Windows 2000 or greater system files, Setup prompts to update the system files. You must complete the installation of these system components before you can install Office XP.

During the process of updating, you must restart your computer.

When the program is finished updating system files, it begins Office XP Setup. If your system files are up to date, Setup begins immediately after you insert the CD-ROM. The steps in this section focus on installing Office XP without updating the system files.

INSTALL OFFICE XP

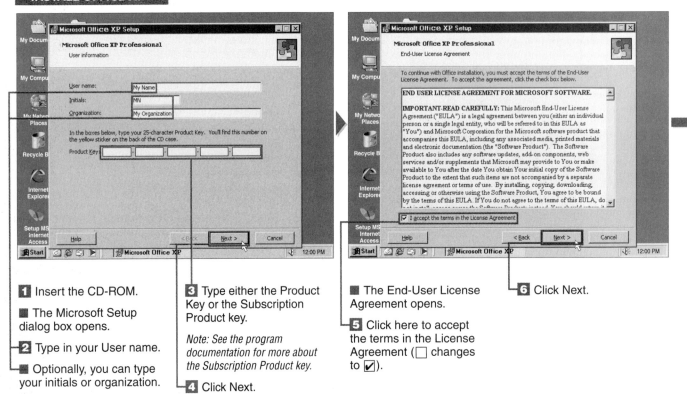

■1 Insert the CD-ROM.

■ The Microsoft Setup dialog box opens.

■2 Type in your User name.

■ Optionally, you can type your initials or organization.

■3 Type either the Product Key or the Subscription Product key.

Note: See the program documentation for more about the Subscription Product key.

■4 Click Next.

■ The End-User License Agreement opens.

■5 Click here to accept the terms in the License Agreement (☐ changes to ☑).

■6 Click Next.

Is there anything I need to do before I start installing Office XP?

✔ Make sure that no other programs, including virus protection, are running on your computer. If you are installing to Windows NT or Windows 2000, you must be logged on with administrative privileges.

What are the system requirements for installing Office XP?

✔ System requirements include Windows 98, NT 4 with at least Service Pack 6A, Windows 2000, or Windows Millennium Edition.

Are there other requirements I need to know for installing Office XP?

✔ Microsoft lists minimum requirements for using Office XP, but there are also optimum requirements you may want to meet. Optimum requirements mean that Office XP runs more efficiently on your computer. Additional requirements are a PC with a Pentium 133 or comparable processor, 32MB RAM, 360MB free hard-disk space, 4MB free space in the registry for Windows NT only, and a CD-ROM drive. For optimum performance, add 64MB or even 128MB RAM to your computer.

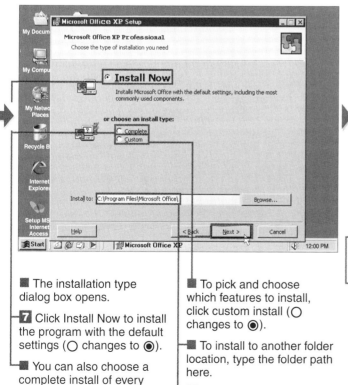

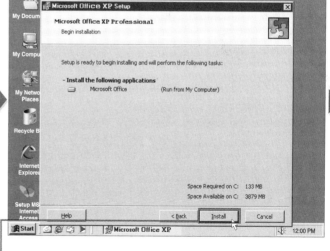

■ The installation type dialog box opens.

7 Click Install Now to install the program with the default settings (○ changes to ◉).

■ You can also choose a complete install of every feature (○ changes to ◉).

■ To pick and choose which features to install, click custom install (○ changes to ◉).

■ To install to another folder location, type the folder path here.

8 Click Next.

9 Click Install.

■ If you chose a complete or custom installation, you are presented with another dialog box of options from which to choose.

CONTINUED ▶

INSTALL OFFICE XP (CONTINUED)

Depending on the installation type you select, Office XP may take several minutes to install the files to your computer. During the course of installing, you can view your installation progress using the bar in the middle of the Setup dialog box. Files are copied to your computer based on the installation options you chose.

When Setup is finished, it notifies you, and you can then start working in Office XP. To learn more about starting an Office XP program, see Chapter 2.

You can return to the Setup program at any time by reinserting the CD-ROM. Setup offers several maintenance modes, including adding or removing features, repairing damaged files, and uninstalling the program.

For example, you may decide to add other fonts included on the CD-ROM or remove a feature you do not use, such as some of the Microsoft Office tools. When you choose a maintenance option, Setup walks you through the process of adding, removing, repairing, or uninstalling. For more on adding or removing Office XP features, see Chapter 35.

INSTALL OFFICE XP (CONTINUED)

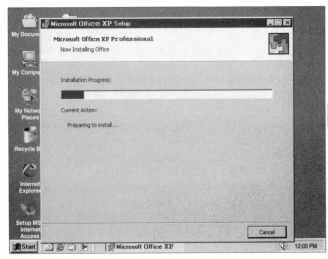

■ Setup begins installing the files.

■ When the installation is complete, this prompt box appears

10 Click OK.

■ Office is installed on your computer and the Office applications appear on your Program menu.

Note: See Chapter 2 to learn how to start an Office program.

MASTER IT

Setup starts automatically when I insert the CD-ROM. Why is that?

✔ If you have your CD-ROM drive's Auto Play feature activated, your computer automatically starts the Setup program for you. You do not have to click Start and use the Run command to begin the Setup program.

How do I stop the installation?

✔ Click the Cancel button in the Setup dialog box at any time to stop the installation. A prompt box appears, asking if you really want to stop the process. Click Yes, and another prompt tells you that Setup was cancelled. Click OK.

What exactly does the repair option repair in maintenance mode?

✔ If for some reason Office XP files are damaged or missing, you can run the repair maintenance mode to reinstall missing files or registry settings associated with Office XP. This option does not repair files you have created yourself, only program files installed by Setup.

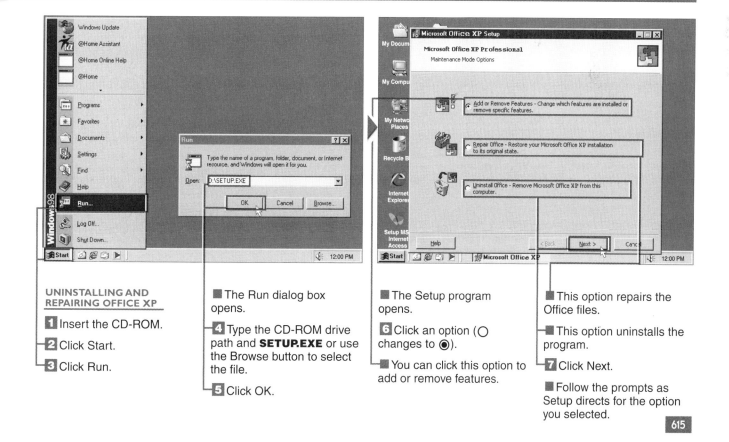

UNINSTALLING AND REPAIRING OFFICE XP

1 Insert the CD-ROM.

2 Click Start.

3 Click Run.

■ The Run dialog box opens.

4 Type the CD-ROM drive path and **SETUP.EXE** or use the Browse button to select the file.

5 Click OK.

■ The Setup program opens.

6 Click an option (○ changes to ●).

■ You can click this option to add or remove features.

■ This option repairs the Office files.

■ This option uninstalls the program.

7 Click Next.

■ Follow the prompts as Setup directs for the option you selected.

TROUBLESHOOT INSTALLATION

You can troubleshoot problems you have with Office XP before calling in technical help. You might have trouble with the installation, the connection to your network, or other problems with which this appendix can help you.

Installation Problems

If Office XP fails to install properly, it may be for any of several reasons. First, make sure all programs are closed except for the Setup program. You should also turn off anti-virus software while you install Office XP. Next, open the CD-ROM and run Setup again. Often, the second time you run Setup, the installation process continues from where it left off.

Another installation problem sometimes happens if you are using an older version of Internet Explorer. If the Setup program stops or hangs and you receive no message, you may need to install a later version of Internet Explorer. See the Microsoft Web site for more information about downloading upgrades for Internet Explorer.

Setup Log Files

Office Setup creates two log files during the installation process you can check to see details about the installation. This information may help if you are experiencing a problem. One log file is for the Setup.exe and named SetupLog(####). The other log file is for the Windows Installer. Setup creates these files in your C:\Windows\Temp folder. Both files are text files so you can open them in a text editor, such as Notepad, for viewing. In addition, these files list the number of times you ran Setup; for example SetupLog(0005) defines the fifth time you ran setup. The log file with the highest number is the file for the last time you ran Setup.

The SetupLog file is relatively short and it displays information about checking the system for the appropriate files, such as the correct operating system and service pack, the version of the Msi.dll file, the version of Internet Explorer, and so on. Setup.exe also installs the Windows Installer. After installation, Setup.exe passes control to the Windows Installer if all of the criteria were met.

If Setup.exe cannot install the Windows Installer, you may see a message. If the message says you do not have an MSI.dll file on your computer, or if you see an error-1157 in the SetupLog file, you can ignore the error. In the next step of Setup, the Setup.exe runs the Instmsi.exe file which installs Msi.dll. If you see a problem with the Instmsi.exe file listed in your SetupLog file, you may have trouble with a software conflict. You can call Microsoft technical support for help resolving this problem.

Windows Installer Log File

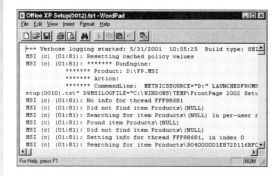

If you cannot find resolution to the installation problem in the SetupLog file, you can check the Installer log file. The Installer log file may be named something similar to Office Setup(####)_Task(####). The Installer log file is usually too large to open in Notepad. When you double-click the file in the Windows Explorer, Windows suggests you want to open the file in WordPad instead of Notepad. The Installer log file uses verbose logging to create a detailed log file of the installation process.

To use the Installer log file, you can search for the error number contained in the error message you received during setup. For example, if you received an "Internal Error 2343" during Setup, search for "2343" in the log. Read the text around the found text to see if the log suggests a solution, such as "Contact product support for assistance." You might also find help on the Microsoft technical sight (http://support.microsoft.com) through some of Microsoft's Knowledge Base articles.

Network Connectivity Problems in FrontPage

When working with FrontPage, you can test your network connection if you have problems accessing or opening Webs on the server. Testing the network connection displays your host name, local host, IP address, and other information about the network. For more on FrontPage, see Part VII.

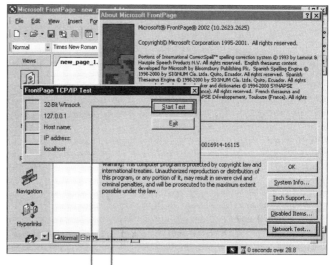

1 In FrontPage, click Help in the main menu, then click About Microsoft FrontPage from the drop-down menu.

2 In the About Microsoft FrontPage dialog box, click Network Test.

■ The FrontPage TCP/IP Test dialog box opens.

3 Click Start Test.

■ The test checks for a working network connection, and displays the results. For example, the test shows a host is present and lists the host's name. The test shows your IP address is valid and then shows your IP address.

WHAT'S ON THE CD-ROM

The CD-ROM disc included in this book contains many useful files and programs that can be used when working with Windows Me Millennium Edition. You will find a Web page providing one-click access to all the Internet links mentioned in the book, as well as several popular programs you can install and use on your computer. Before installing any of the programs on the disc, make sure a newer version of the program is not already installed on your computer. For information on installing different versions of the same program, contact the program's manufacturer.

SYSTEM REQUIREMENTS

While most programs on the CD-ROM disc have minimal system requirements, your computer should be equipped with the following hardware and software to use all the contents of the CD-ROM disc:

- A Pentium or faster processor.
- Microsoft Windows 95 or later.
- At least 32MB of RAM.
- At least 200 MB of hard drive space.
- A double-speed (2x) or faster CD-ROM drive.
- A monitor capable of displaying at least 256 colors or grayscale.
- A modem with a speed of at least 14,400 bps.
- A sound card.

DOCUMENT FILES

This CD contains several of the document example files used throughout the book. When you want to practice a particular task, you can use these documents to do so. You can check the title bar in the figures to see which document was used in the steps.

WEB LINKS

This CD contains a Web page that provides one-click access to all the Web pages and Internet references in the book. To use these links you must have an Internet connection and a Web browser, such as Internet Explorer, installed.

ACROBAT VERSION

The CD-ROM contains an e-version of this book that you can view and search using Adobe Acrobat Reader. You can also use the hyperlinks provided in the text to access all Web pages and Internet references in the book. You cannot print the pages or copy text from the Acrobat files. An evaluation version of Adobe Acrobat Reader is also included on the disc.

INSTALLING AND USING THE SOFTWARE

This CD-ROM disc contains several useful programs.

Before installing a program from this CD, you should exit all other programs. In order to use most of the programs, you must accept the license agreement provided with the program. Make sure you read any Readme files provided with each program.

Program Versions

Shareware programs are fully functional, free trial versions of copyrighted programs. If you like a particular program, you can register with its author for a nominal fee and receive licenses, enhanced versions, and technical support.

Freeware programs are free, copyrighted games, applications and utilities. You can copy them to as many computers as you like, but they have no technical support.

GNU software is governed by its own license, which is included inside the folder of the GNU software. There are no restrictions on distribution of this software. See the GNU license for more details.

Trial, demo, and evaluation versions are usually limited either by time or functionality. For example, you may not be able to save projects using these versions.

For your convenience, the software titles on the CD are listed alphabetically.

Acrobat Reader

For Microsoft Windows 95/98/NT/2000. Freeware.

This disc contains an evaluation version of Acrobat Reader from Adobe Systems, Inc. You will need this program to access the e-version of the book also included on this disc.

WinZip

For Windows 95/98/NT/2000. Shareware version.

WinZip compresses files to make it easier and faster to transfer information from one computer to another. WinZip is commonly used to reduce the amount of disk space consumed by files and to reduce the size of files sent by e-mail. WinZip is a shareware version from Nico Mak Computing, Inc. You can use the program for free for 21 days. If you wish to continue using the program, you must pay a registration fee. For more information about WinZip, visit www.winzip.com.

TROUBLESHOOTING

We have tried our best to compile programs that work on most computers with the minimum system requirements. Your computer, however, may differ, and some programs may not work properly for some reason.

The two most likely problems are that you do not have enough memory (RAM) for the programs you want to use or you have other programs running that are affecting the installation or running of a program. If you get error messages while trying to install or use the programs on the CD-ROM disc, try one or more of the following methods and then try installing or running the software again:

- Close all running programs.
- Restart your computer.
- Turn off any anti-virus software.
- Close the CD-ROM interface and run demos or installations directly from Windows Explorer.
- Add more RAM to your computer.

If you still have trouble installing the programs from the CD-ROM, please call the Hungry Minds Customer Service phone number: 800-762-2974. Outside the United States, call 1(317) 572-3994. You can also contact Hungry Minds Customer Service by e-mail at techsupdum@hungryminds. com. Hungry Minds will provide technical support only for installation and other general quality control items; for technical support on the applications themselves, consult the program's vendor or author.

MASTER VISUALLY OFFICE XP ON THE CD-ROM

You can view *Master VISUALLY Office XP* on your screen using the CD-ROM included at the back of this book. The CD-ROM allows you to search the contents of the book for a specific word or phrase. The CD-ROM also provides a convenient way of keeping the book handy while traveling.

You must install Acrobat Reader on your computer before you can view the book on the CD-ROM. This program is provided on the disc. Acrobat Reader allows you to view Portable Document Format, or PDF, files. These files can display books and magazines on your screen exactly as they appear in printed form.

To view the contents of the book using Acrobat Reader, display the contents of the disc. Open the PDF folder. Then double-click the chapter you want to view.

MASTER VISUALLY OFFICE XP ON THE CD-ROM

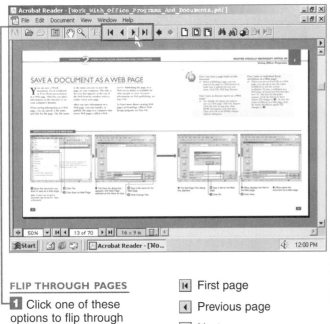

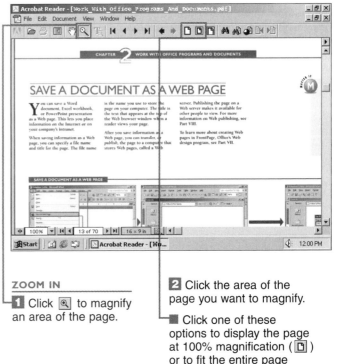

FLIP THROUGH PAGES

1 Click one of these options to flip through the pages of a section.

|◄| First page

|◄| Previous page

|►| Next page

|►| Last page

ZOOM IN

1 Click 🔍 to magnify an area of the page.

2 Click the area of the page you want to magnify.

■ Click one of these options to display the page at 100% magnification (🗎) or to fit the entire page inside the window (🗎).

How do I install Acrobat Reader?

✔ Open the `Software\Reader` folder on the CD-ROM disc. Double-click the `AR405eng.exe` file and then follow the instructions on your screen. Or, you can use the visual interface to install Acrobat Reader. (Begin by clicking the idg.exe icon.)

How do I search all the sections of the book at once?

✔ You must first locate the index. While viewing the contents of the book, click 🔍 in the Acrobat Reader window. Click Indexes and then click Add. Locate and click the index.pdx file, click Open and then click OK. You need to locate the index only once. After locating the index, you can click ⬛ to search all the sections.

How can I make searching the book more convenient?

✔ Copy the Acrobat Files folder from the CD-ROM disc to your hard drive. This enables you to easily access the contents of the book at any time.

Can I use Acrobat Reader for anything else?

✔ Acrobat Reader is a popular and useful program. There are many files available on the Web that are designed to be viewed using Acrobat Reader. Look for files with the `.pdf` extension.

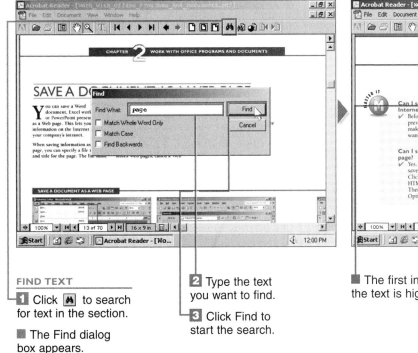

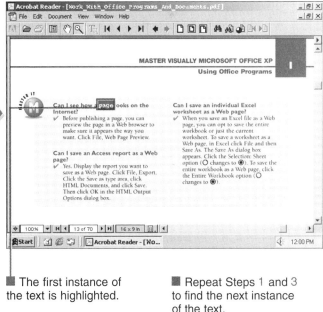

FIND TEXT

1 Click 🔍 to search for text in the section.

■ The Find dialog box appears.

2 Type the text you want to find.

3 Click Find to start the search.

■ The first instance of the text is highlighted.

■ Repeat Steps 1 and 3 to find the next instance of the text.

TECHNIQUES DESCRIBED IN THIS BOOK. HMI DOES NOT WARRANT THAT THE FUNCTIONS CONTAINED IN THE SOFTWARE WILL MEET YOUR REQUIREMENTS OR THAT THE OPERATION OF THE SOFTWARE WILL BE ERROR FREE.

(c) This limited warranty gives you specific legal rights, and you may have other rights that vary from jurisdiction to jurisdiction.

6. Remedies.

(a) HMI's entire liability and your exclusive remedy for defects in materials and workmanship shall be limited to replacement of the Software Media, which may be returned to HMI with a copy of your receipt at the following address: Software Media Fulfillment Department, Attn.: *Master VISUALLY Office XP*, Hungry Minds, Inc., 10475 Crosspoint Blvd., Indianapolis, IN 46256, or call 1-800-762-2974. Please allow four to six weeks for delivery. This Limited Warranty is void if failure of the Software Media has resulted from accident, abuse, or misapplication. Any replacement Software Media will be warranted for the remainder of the original warranty period or thirty (30) days, whichever is longer.

(b) In no event shall HMI or the author be liable for any damages whatsoever (including without limitation damages for loss of business profits, business interruption, loss of business information, or any other pecuniary loss) arising from the use of or inability to use the Book or the Software, even if HMI has been advised of the possibility of such damages.

(c) Because some jurisdictions do not allow the exclusion or limitation of liability for consequential or incidental damages, the above limitation or exclusion may not apply to you.

7. U.S. Government Restricted Rights. Use, duplication, or disclosure of the Software for or on behalf of the United States of America, its agencies and/or instrumentalities (the "U.S. Government") is subject to restrictions as stated in paragraph (c)(1)(ii) of the Rights in Technical Data and Computer Software clause of DFARS 252.227-7013, or subparagraphs (c) (1) and (2) of the Commercial Computer Software - Restricted Rights clause at FAR 52.227-19, and in similar clauses in the NASA FAR supplement, as applicable.

8. General. This Agreement constitutes the entire understanding of the parties and revokes and supersedes all prior agreements, oral or written, between them and may not be modified or amended except in a writing signed by both parties hereto that specifically refers to this Agreement. This Agreement shall take precedence over any other documents that may be in conflict herewith. If any one or more provisions contained in this Agreement are held by any court or tribunal to be invalid, illegal, or otherwise unenforceable, each and every other provision shall remain in full force and effect.

INDEX

Symbols and Numbers

; (semicolon) between addresses in Outlook, 31, 508

' (apostrophe) before an Excel numeric entry, 179

signs in Excel, 179, 209

$ (dollar sign) in an absolute reference, 214

% (percent) operator in Excel, 208

* (asterisk) wildcard in Access, 478

* (multiple) operator in Access expressions, 480

* (multiplication) operator in Excel, 208

* wildcard in Word, 55

+ (add) operator in Access expressions, 480

+ (addition) operator in Excel, 208

+ (plus sign) beside Access records with related data, 435

, (commas), separating Excel arguments, 216

- (subtract) operator in Access expressions, 480

- (subtraction) operator in Excel, 208

/ (divide) operator in Access, 480

/ (division) operator in Excel, 208

: (colon), separating Excel arguments, 216

< (less than) operator
    in Access criteria, 478
    in Excel, 208

<= (less than or equal to) operator
    in Access criteria, 478
    in Excel, 208

<> (not equal to) operator in Excel, 208

= (equal to) operator in Excel, 208, 212

> (greater than) operator
    in Access criteria, 478
    in Excel, 208

>= (greater than or equal to) operator
    in Access criteria, 478
    in Excel, 208

? (question mark) wildcard in Access, 478

? wildcard in Word, 55

^ (exponent) operator in Excel, 208

^ (power) operator in Access expressions, 480

3-D effect
    adding to a PowerPoint AutoShape, 325
    adding to Excel AutoShapes, 269

3-D Effects AutoFormats, 236

3-D effects table designs in Word, 136

35mm slides
    color schemes for, 342
    creating, 369

1157 error, 616

A

absolute reference, 214, 215

Access, 5
    introduction to, 372–373
    starting, 375

Access reports, saving as a Web page, 25

Accounting AutoFormats, 236

accounting underline styles, 229

Acrobat Reader on CD-ROM in this book, 619, 621

active cell in Excel, 177, 178

active chart in PowerPoint, 316

Activities tab in Contact window, 539

add (+) operator in Access expressions, 480

Add bullets button in FrontPage, 560

Add Holidays button in Outlook, 537

Add numbers button in FrontPage, 560

addition (+) operator in Excel, 208

address block
    formatting, 168
    inserting for a letter, 160
    linking to, 166, 167

address book, 510–511

Address Book button, 30

Address Cards view for Outlook contacts, 540

Address Information dialog box in Mail Merge, 167

Address list, 167

addresses, printing on envelopes in Word, 170–171

Advance slide area in PowerPoint, 355

Advanced Find dialog box in Outlook, 527

Advanced link in Search task pane, 35

Align button in Tables and Borders toolbar in Word, 135

Align Left button in Word, 78

Align Left report layout in Access, 488

Align Right button in Word, 78

alignment
    applying to Word text, 78–79
    changing for controls in Access forms, 455
    changing for FrontPage text, 558
    changing for Word tables, 131
    on a page in Word, 108
    removing in Word, 79

Alignment box in Page Number dialog box in Word, 111

alignment buttons
    on Formatting toolbar in PowerPoint, 333
    on Formatting toolbar in Word, 78

Alignment drop-down list in Word, 79

All caps option in Word, 75

all-day events, 534

All Files report in FrontPage, 579

Alt+Tab, cycling through open programs, 32

AND condition with Access criteria, 476, 477

animation categories, 338

animation schemes, 340–341

Answer Wizard, 16

Any Part of Field option for Access searching, 458

apostrophe (') before an Excel numeric entry, 179

applications. See programs

Apply to All Slides option, 295

Apply to Selected Slides option, 297, 309

Apply using CSS option in FrontPage, 573

Appointment Recurrence dialog box, 535

Appointment window, 534

appointments
    deleting, 535
    displaying, 504
    scheduling, 534–535
    viewing past or future, 536

archiving messages in Outlook, 524

area charts, 254, 260

arguments in Excel functions, 208, 216

Arial font as default for Excel, 224

arithmetic operators in Excel formulas, 208

Arrow button on Word Drawing toolbar, 139

arrow buttons in scroll bars, 9

arrow keys in Access, 401

art, adding to page borders in Word, 91

ascending order
    sorting query results in, 479
    sorting records in, 460, 486

ascending sort for Excel data lists, 278

asterisk (*) wildcard in Access, 478

At least spacing option in Word, 85

Attach line, adding to Outlook message header, 513

attachments
    opening and saving, 514–515
    sending documents as, 31

audience handouts, 369
auditing tools, 211, 213
AutoArchive in Outlook, 524
AutoCalculate feature, 210, 211
AutoComplete, 183
AutoContent Wizard, 286, 290–293, 300
AutoCorrect dialog box, 59
    Automatic bulleted lists option in
      Word, 87
    Automatic numbered lists option in
      Word, 89
AutoCorrect feature
    in Excel, 183, 191
    in PowerPoint, 365
    in Word, 42, 58–59
AutoFilter feature in Excel, 280–281
AutoFit command, 137
AutoForm, creating Access forms, 443
AutoFormat As You Type tab in Word, 101
AutoFormat feature in Access, 443, 451, 489
AutoFormat tab in Word, 101
AutoFormats, applying in Excel, 236–237
Automatic bulleted lists option, 87
automatic formatting, turning off in Excel, 237
Automatic number lists option, 89
Automatically update option, 93, 95
AutoNumber data type in Access, 397
AutoNumber field in Access, 398
AutoNumber primary key, 434
AutoPreview of animations in PowerPoint, 341
AutoReport, 487
AutoShapes
    adding in PowerPoint, 324–325
    adding in Word, 138–139
    adding to Excel worksheets, 268–269
    changing appearance of PowerPoint,
      325
    in Excel, 175
AutoSum button
    in Access, 482
    in Excel, 210, 211
AutoSum function, 174
AutoText feature, 38, 42, 43, 66–67
Average calculation in Excel AutoCalculate, 211
Avg option in Access, 468, 482, 487
award certificates, creating, 152
axes in Excel charts, 255

B

B key, pausing slide shows, 361
background color
    changing for a slide, 343, 345
    changing for form controls in Access,
      456
    changing for FrontPage tables, 565
Backspace key
    deleting characters, 49
    removing data in Access, 404
    removing data in Excel, 186
bar charts, 254, 260
Bar Tab in Word, 82
Basic Shapes category
    of AutoShapes in Excel, 268
    of AutoShapes in PowerPoint, 324
    of AutoShapes in Word, 138
between..and... Access criteria, 478
binder, 611
Black and white print option in Excel, 245
black-and-white printer, previewing slides on,
    345
blank database, creating, 376–377
blank lines
    adding to Word documents, 48
    adding within cells of Word tables,
     124
blank pages, creating Web pages in, 548
blank presentation, creating in PowerPoint, 288
blind carbon copy (Bcc), 510, 511
Blinds Vertical slide transition, 354
Block Arrows category
    of AutoShapes in PowerPoint, 324
    of AutoShapes in Word, 138
Block report layout in Access, 488
blue lines, showing Excel page breaks, 247
Blueprint theme in FrontPage, 572
Bold feature
    in Access, 454, 455
    in Excel, 220
    in FrontPage, 556
    in PowerPoint, 332
    in Word, 72
Border button in Word, 90
Border Color button
    in Access, 457
    in Word, 133
Border Width button in Access, 457

borders
    adding in Excel, 232–233
    adding in Word, 90, 91
    changing for text boxes in Excel, 271
    changing for Word tables, 132–133
    removing from Excel worksheets,
     233
    removing from Word tables, 133
bottom alignment of text, 108
bottom result values for Access queries, 477
Break dialog box, 34–35, 53
Break Link button, 599
brightness of pictures in PowerPoint, 323
broken hyperlinks, fixing in FrontPage, 567
Broken Hyperlinks report, 578, 579
Browse for File button in Insert Hyperlink
    dialog box, 600
Browse the Web button, 602, 603
Browsed Pages button, 602
browsing PowerPoint presentations, 306–307
bullet character, changing in PowerPoint, 336
bullet point
    adding to a PowerPoint slide, 301
    selecting in PowerPoint, 298
bulleted list slide in PowerPoint, 296
bullets
    adding in FrontPage lists, 560
    adding in Word, 86–87
Bullets and Numbering dialog box
    adding bullets in Word, 86, 87
    creating numbered lists in Word, 89
    in PowerPoint, 336, 337
business tables sample in Access, 392
buttons
    activating in toolbars, 10
    identifying in toolbars, 10
    moving on toolbars, 605
By Column button, changing chart plots in
    PowerPoint, 317
Byte number field, size settings for, 417

C

calculations in Access, 480–481, 482, 486, 487
Calendar, 5, 503, 534–535, 536–537
calendar order, sorting in Excel, 279
Callouts category
    of AutoShapes in PowerPoint, 324
    of AutoShapes in Word, 138

INDEX

cameras, inserting pictures from, 145
Canvas in Word, 138
Caps Lock key, 43
captions, adding for Access fields, 422
Carnegie Coach category of PowerPoint
  presentations, 290
Cascade Delete Related Records option, 439
Cascade Update Related Fields option, 439
case
  changing for text in Word, 49
  changing in Word, 43
case sensitive sort in Excel, 279
categories of PowerPoint presentations, 290
category names in an Excel chart, 255
Cc (carbon copy) area, 30, 31, 508
CD-ROM in this book, 618–621
cell references in Excel, 208, 212, 214
cells
  adding shading or color to Word,
    134
  adding to Word tables, 129
  applying a number style to Excel,
    221
  assigning names to Excel, 200, 201
  attaching hidden notes to, 271
  changing borders for Word, 132
  changing text position in Word, 135
  checking spelling in Excel, 190
  deleting a group of Excel, 197
  in Excel, 176, 177
  in FrontPage tables, 564
  inserting a group of Excel, 195
  inserting data into Access, 447
  moving from one to another in Word
    tables, 124
  in PowerPoint tables, 310
  printing selected in Excel, 240, 241
  protecting in Excel, 202–203
  searching for Excel, 192, 193
  selecting a range of Excel, 184–185
  selecting for Excel charts, 256
  selecting in Access, 403
  unlocking in Excel, 203
  zooming into Access, 406
Center align button in Excel, 230
center-align option in Word, 78
center alignment of text in Word, 108
Center button
  in Access, 455
  in FrontPage, 558

in PowerPoint, 333
in Word, 78
Center on page options in Excel, 243
center option
  in Excel, 230
  in PowerPoint, 333
Center Tab in Word, 82
changes, undoing in Word, 49, 52
character styles in Word, 92
chart elements, formatting in Excel, 262–263
Chart menu
  Chart command in PowerPoint, 317
  Chart Type command in Excel, 260
  Location command in Excel, 264
chart plots in PowerPoint, 317
chart sheets, 258, 259, 265
chart titles, 255, 256, 257, 262
Chart toolbar, 258, 259, 262, 263
Chart Type dialog box, 260–261
chart types
  changing in Excel, 260–261
  changing in PowerPoint, 316–317
  in Microsoft Graph program, 316
Chart Wizard in Excel, 256–259
charts
  adding data to Excel, 266
  adding in PowerPoint, 314–315
  creating based on Excel list subtotals,
    283
  creating with Chart Wizard in Excel,
    256–259
  deleting in Excel, 265
  displaying in Excel Print Preview
    window, 239
  editing and formatting in PowerPoint,
    316–317
  in Excel, 175
  introduction to Excel, 254–255
  moving in Excel, 264
  printing in Excel, 267
  resizing in Excel, 264
Check Address dialog box in Outlook, 539
Check Box option for Yes/No fields in Access,
    428, 429
Check grammar as you type check option, 63
Check grammar with spelling option, 63
Checkerboard Across slide transition, 354
circles, drawing in Word, 139
circular reference in an Excel formula, 209
class modules in Access, 373

Classic table designs in Word, 136
clearing, formatting in Excel, 235
Click and Type feature, 43, 78, 79
clip art images. See also images; pictures
  adding in PowerPoint, 320–321
  adding to Excel worksheets,
    272–273
  adding to Web pages, 563
  adding to Word documents,
    140–141
  browsing through Excel, 273
  changing from inline to floating in
    Word, 149
  editing in Word, 141
  searching for by keyword in Word,
    140–141
  searching for Excel, 272–273
Clip Organizer, 273
Clipboard, 588, 589, 590–591
Clipboard Smart Tag, 589, 590, 591
Clipboard toolbar, 51, 189
Clips Online button, 141
Close button, 7, 9
Closing category for AutoText entries, 66
collaboration features in Office XP, 611
colon (:), separating Excel arguments, 216
color code, applying to Excel worksheets, 205
Color/Grayscale button in PowerPoint, 345, 369
color palette in PowerPoint, 334
color schemes, 334, 342–343
Colorful AutoFormats, 236
Colorful table designs in Word, 136
colors
  adding to Word table cells, 134
  applying to text in Word, 76
  changing for AutoShapes in Excel,
    269
  changing for FrontPage text, 557
  changing in a PowerPoint
    AutoShape, 325
  combining with patterns for shading
    in Word, 91
column break inserting in Word, 117
column charts, 254, 260
column headings
  freezing in Excel, 187
  as names in Excel, 201
  repeating in Excel, 249
column width
  in Access, 407
  in Excel, 218, 219

in FrontPage, 565
in PowerPoint tables, 312
in Word tables, 126
Columnar AutoForm in Access, 443
Columnar layout for an Access form, 442
Columnar report layout in Access, 488
columns
adding in PowerPoint tables, 313
adding in Word tables, 128, 129
centering data across Excel, 231
changing width of Excel, 218, 219
changing width of Word, 117
creating in Word, 116–117
deleting from FrontPage tables, 565
deleting from PowerPoint tables, 313
deleting in Excel, 196, 197
deleting in Word tables, 128, 129
in Excel, 177
in FrontPage tables, 564
hiding in Excel, 198, 199
inserting in Access, 391
inserting in Excel, 194, 195
inserting in FrontPage tables, 565
in PowerPoint tables, 310
selecting in Excel, 185
sorting data lists by, Excel, 278, 279
unhiding in Excel, 198, 199
in Word, 122
Columns button on Standard toolbar in Word, 117
Columns with Depth custom chart type in Excel, 261
Combo Box option for Yes/No fields in Access, 428, 429
Comic Sans MS font in PowerPoint, 330
Comma button in Excel, 221
Comma format in Excel, 221, 222
commands, displaying the most currently used, 604
commas (,), separating Excel arguments, 216
comments
displaying in a task list, 533
displaying in Excel, 270
Compare and Merge Documents feature, 611
Compare to another selection, 99
comparison operators in Excel, 208
compression programs, 513
contacts, 5, 503
adding, 538–539
browsing through, 540

deleting, 540
managing, 538–541
Contacts Sample Database, 386
Contemporary Memo template in Word, 120
Contents tab of Help dialog box, 17
continuous labels, 496
contrast of pictures, changing in PowerPoint, 323
controls, 452
deleting, 453
enhancing appearance of, 456–457
copies, printing multiple, 28, 29, 241, 495
Copy button, 588
in Access, 405
in Excel, 189, 214, 266
in Word, 51
copying data in Excel, 188, 189
Corporate category of PowerPoint presentations, 290
Corporate Presence Wizard in FrontPage, 546
Count calculation in Excel AutoCalculate, 211
Count Nums calculation in Excel AutoCalculate, 211
Count option in Access, 482
counter styles in FrontPage, 574
Create a copy option in Excel, 207
Create AutoText dialog box, 66
Create form by using wizard option in Access, 440
Create Hyperlink dialog box, 566, 567
Create link in Mail Merge task pane, 156
Create New Folder button, 23, 377
Create New Folder dialog box in Outlook, 522
Create query by using wizard option in Access, 466
Create table by entering data option in Access, 388
Create table by using wizard option in Access, 392
Create table in Design view option in Access, 389
criteria
examples of Access, 478
filtering data in Access, 463
filtering Excel list data, 280, 281
filtering records in Access, 465
setting in Access, 476–477
Crop button on Picture toolbar in PowerPoint, 323
Crosstab Query Wizard in Access, 467
Ctrl + 1 in Word, 85
Ctrl + 2 in Word, 85

Ctrl + 5 in Word, 85
Ctrl + A
selecting all cells in an Excel worksheet, 185
selecting all records in an Access table, 403
selecting all text in a PowerPoint presentation, 299
in Word, 47
Ctrl + Alt + Spacebar in Access, 423
Ctrl + apostrophe key (') in Access, 399
Ctrl + C (copy), 589
Ctrl + Down Arrow in Access, 446
Ctrl + End in Word, 45
Ctrl + Home in Word, 45
Ctrl + semicolon (;) in Excel, 182
Ctrl + Up Arrow in Access, 446
Ctrl + V (paste), 589
Ctrl + X (cut), 589
Currency button in Excel, 221
Currency data type in Access, 397
Currency format in Excel, 221, 222
current date, inserting in Word, 68
Custom Animation task pane, 338, 339, 341
Custom AutoFilter dialog box in Excel, 281
Custom border option in Word, 90, 91
custom footers in Excel, 252–253
custom headers in Excel, 252–253
Custom Types tab in Chart Type dialog box, 261
Customer Support Web template in FrontPage, 546
Customize Address List dialog box in Mail Merge, 157
Customize dialog box, Options tab, 604–605
Customize Outlook Today option, 505
Cut button, 588
in Excel, 188
in Word, 50

D

daily activities, displaying a summary of, 504
Dale Carnegie Training, presentations provided by, 290
dashed borders for text boxes in Excel, 271
data
adding to Excel charts, 266
aligning in Excel, 230–231
changing size of Excel, 224
(continued)

data *(continued)*
>> copying from previous Access cell, 399
>> copying in Excel, 188, 189
>> deleting in Excel, 186, 187
>> deselecting in Access, 403
>> editing in Access, 404–405
>> editing in Excel, 186, 187
>> editing with forms in Access, 447
>> entering in Datasheet view, 390–391
>> entering in lookup columns in Access, 432
>> entering into Excel lists, 276
>> filtering by form in Access, 464–465
>> filtering in Excel lists, 280–281
>> finding in Access, 458–459
>> finding in Excel, 192–193
>> grouping in Access reports, 485
>> hiding in Excel, 198–199
>> managing in an Excel list, 175
>> moving in Excel, 188, 189
>> moving or copying between documents, 588–589
>> replacing in an Access cell, 405
>> rotating in Excel cells, 231
>> selecting in Access, 402–403
>> selecting to move or copy, 589
>> summarizing in Access, 482–483
data format, selecting in Access, 418
data forms in Excel, 276, 277
data lists, 276
>> adding subtotals, 282–283
>> creating, 276
>> filtering, 280–281
>> sorting, 278–279
data markers in Excel charts, 255
Data menu
>> Filter command, 280
>> Form command, 277
>> Sort command, 278
>> Subtotals command, 282
data series, 258, 260
>> adding to a chart, 266
>> in a chart, 255
>> formatting, 262
data source, 156
>> creating, 156–157
>> creating and saving, 152–153
>> saving, 158–159
>> selecting a different, 155

Data Table button in PowerPoint, 317
data types, 397
>> changing, 410, 414
>> sorting not allowed for certain, 461
Database Interface Wizard in FrontPage, 546
database templates, 378
Database window, 384, 385
Database Wizard, 375, 378–383
databases, 5, 372
>> creating blank, 376–377
>> creating with Database Wizard, 378–383
>> designing, 376–377
>> installing sample, 387
>> naming, 376
>> opening and saving, 386–387
>> opening existing, 375
>> parts of, 373
>> planning, 374
>> printing data from, 494–495
>> types of, 372
datasheet
>> displaying in PowerPoint, 317
>> for a PowerPoint chart, 314–315
Datasheet AutoForm in Access, 443
Datasheet button in Access, 410
Datasheet layout for an Access form, 442
Datasheet view, 396
>> adding fields in, 421
>> creating tables in, 388–389
>> entering data in, 390–391
>> opening a query in, 474
>> rearranging fields in, 411
>> viewing query results, 475
>> viewing tables, 410
Date number format in Excel, 222
Date/Time data type in Access, 397, 418
dates
>> displaying current in Outlook, 536
>> displaying in a slide header or footer, 346
>> entering into Excel, 182
>> grouping in Access queries, 469
>> including on PowerPoint slides, 292
>> inserting current in Mail Merge, 155
>> inserting current in Word, 43, 68
>> inserting into a header or footer in Word, 112, 113
Day view for displaying Calendar appointments, 536, 537

days of the week, completing a series for in Excel, 181
decimal places
>> changing number displayed in Access, 419
>> increasing or decreasing in Excel, 221
Decimal Places property box in Access, 419
Decimal Places property in Access, 412
Decimal Tab in Word, 82
Decrease Decimal button in Excel, 221
Decrease Font Size button in PowerPoint, 331
Decrease Indent button
>> in Excel, 230
>> in FrontPage, 559
>> in Word, 80
default folder locations, 21
default font settings, 75, 229
default margins
>> in Excel, 242
>> in Word, 106
default table style in Word, 122
default tables in Word, 123
default template, 18
default values for fields in Access, 423
Delete button
>> in Access, 399, 449
>> in Outlook messages, 521
Delete key
>> deleting characters, 49
>> removing data in Excel, 186, 187
Deleted Items folder in Outlook, 503, 518, 519, 521
delivery addresses for Word envelopes, 170
dependents in Excel formulas, 213
descending order
>> sorting query results in, 479
>> sorting records in, 460, 486
descending sort for Excel data lists, 278
descriptions, adding to Access fields, 413
deselecting
>> data in Access, 403
>> text in Word, 47
Design button
>> in Access, 410
>> in PowerPoint, 295, 342
Design Gallery Live Web site, 321
design grid in Select Query window, 470
design templates in PowerPoint, 291, 294–295, 344–345

Design view, 396
  adding fields in, 421, 450
  changing layout and design of a report, 491
  creating queries in, 470–473
  creating tables in, 389
  opening a form, 444, 445
  opening a query in, 474
  opening reports in, 490
  planning queries in, 475
  rearranging fields in, 411
  viewing tables in Access, 410
desktop, adding shortcut icons to, 7
Desktop folder, 22, 377
destination cells, replacing contents of, 189
destination file, 594
  embedding OLE objects, 592
  for linked information, 598
  linking a source file to, 596
Detailed Address Cards view, 540
Details button in Access, 384
Details tab in Contact window, 539
Details view in Access, 379
Detect and Repair feature, 610
diagrams
  adding to Word documents, 146–147
  editing text in, 147
  in PowerPoint, 318, 319
Dictation option in Language toolbar, 609
dictionary
  adding words to, 61
  adding words to Excel's, 191
digital photographs. See pictures
Discussion Web Wizard, 546
Display Map of Address button, 539
Dissolve slide transition, 354
Distance from text area, 151
distribution lists, 511
#DIV/0! error message in Excel, 209
divide (/) operator in Access expressions, 480
division (/) operator in Excel, 208
Do not include original message option in Outlook, 517
docking toolbars, 13
document area on Word screen, 41
document files on CD-ROM in this book, 618
document windows, 9. See also windows
documents
  changing orientation for part of, 109
  closing, 20, 21

correcting spelling errors in, 60–61
creating, 18–19
e-mailing, 30–31
finding, 34–35
formatting in Word, 38–39
merging in Mail Merge, 153, 162–163
merging versions of, 611
moving or copying information between, 588–589
moving through, 44–45
naming, 20
numbering the pages of, 110–111
opening, 19, 26–27
previewing, 29, 104–105
printing, 28–29, 39
renaming, 21
saving, 20–21, 22–23, 24–25
scrolling through Word, 45
sending as attachments to e-mail, 31
sharing with non-Office XP users, 21
sorting any text in, 125
switching among, 33
taskbar buttons for, 33
viewing in Word, 39
Documents folder in Access, 377
dollar sign ($) in an absolute reference, 214
double line spacing, 84, 85
doughnut charts, compared to pie charts, 261
Down Arrow, 45
Draft quality print option in Excel, 245
Drafts folder in Outlook, 504, 508, 518, 519
Drag-and-drop text editing option, 51
Draw Table button, 133
Drawing button
  in Excel, 268
  in Word, 138
Drawing Pad option on Language toolbar, 609
Drawing toolbar, 12
  in Excel, 268
  in PowerPoint, 289
  in Word, 138, 139, 142, 149
drawings, adding as slides, 360, 361
duplicate entries, allowing in indexed Access fields, 433

E

Edit Hyperlink dialog box, 579, 581, 603
Edit menu
  Clear command in Excel, 235
  Delete command in Access, 421

Delete command in Excel, 196, 197
Find command in Excel, 192
Find command in Word, 54
Links command, 598, 599
Move or Copy Sheet command in Excel, 207
Move to Folder command in Outlook, 523
Office Clipboard command, 590
Paste Special command, 592, 593, 596
Replace command in Word, 56
Undo command in Excel, 187
Edit recipient list link in Mail Merge task pane, 167
Edit Relationships dialog box in Access, 438–439
Edit WordArt Text dialog box
  in PowerPoint, 327
  in Word, 143
editing data in Access, 404--405
electronic mail in Outlook, 502
electronic notes. See notes
em dash, inserting, 69
e-mail, creating hyperlinks for sending, 567
e-mail account, setting up, 502
e-mail addresses
  adding for contacts, 539
  format for, 511
E-mail button, 30
e-mail folders, 518–519
e-mail messages. See messages
e-mail server, 507
embedded information, 592–593
embedded objects
  for data sharing, 592
  double-clicking, 594, 595
  editing, 594–595
embedding, compared to linking, 597
Emboss option in Word, 75
Emphasis category in PowerPoint, 338
empty fields in Access criteria, 478
Empty Web template in FrontPage, 546
End key in Word, 45
End-User License Agreement, 612
endnotes, 65, 114–115
Engrave option in Word, 75
Enhanced Metafile (.emf), 322
Enter, pressing in Word, 42, 48
Entrance effects category in PowerPoint, 338

entries
  adding to AutoCorrect, 58–59
  requiring in Access fields, 424–425
envelope icon in Outlook, 506
Envelope size area in Word, 171
envelopes, printing in Word, 170–171
Envelopes and Labels dialog box, 170–171
E-postage, 171
Equal column width option in Word, 117
equal to (=) operator in Excel, 208, 212
Eraser button in Word, 127
Error button in Excel, 209
error messages
  for Access validation rules, 426, 427
  for Excel formulas, 209
e-version of this book, 618, 620–621
exact matches in Access criteria, 478
Exactly spacing option in Word, 85
Excel, 4, 174
  AutoComplete feature, 183
  copying charts, 315
  introduction to, 174–175
  printing in, 175
  saving files as Web pages, 25
  screen, 177
  starting, 176
  typing numbers into, 179
  typing text into, 178
Exciting animation schemes, 340
Exclude Recipient link in Mail Merge, 163
exclusive rights in Access, 387
Exit effects category in PowerPoint, 338
Exit option in File menu, 7
Expand All button in PowerPoint, 305
Expedition theme in FrontPage, 572
exponent (^) operator in Excel, 208
expressions, 427, 481

F

F4 key, creating an absolute reference in
  Excel, 215
F11 key
  bringing Database window in front
    in Access, 384
  creating charts in Excel, 257
faint borders. *See* gridlines
Favorites folder, 22, 377
fax templates in Word, 120

features
  adding or removing in Office XP,
    606–607
  shared in Office XP, 610
field descriptions, adding in Access, 413
Field List button in Access, 450
field names
  in Access, 415
  in database tables, 388
  entering in expressions, 480
  for form letters in Mail Merge, 156
field properties in Access, 410, 412
field size, changing in Access, 416
fields
  adding captions for Access, 422
  adding descriptions for Access, 413
  adding in Access, 420, 421
  adding to forms in Access, 450
  changing order of, in an Access
    query, 473
  consequences of deleting Access,
    421
  creating indexes for Access, 433
  customizing in Mail Merge, 157
  in a data source in Mail Merge, 156
  in database tables, 388
  in databases, 373
  deleting from forms, 453
  deleting in Access, 420, 421
  displaying properties for Access, 412
  displaying specific, 401
  freezing in Access, 409
  hiding from query results, 472
  hiding in Access, 408
  including all in an Access query, 473
  in a Mail Merge data source, 152
  planning for database tables, 374
  rearranging in Access, 411
  removing from forms, 441
  removing from queries, 467
  renaming in Access, 415
  renaming in Table Wizard, 393
  scrolling through, 401
  searching for data in Access, 458
  selecting for Access forms, 441
  selecting for Access reports, 485
  selecting for mailing labels in
    Access, 498
  selecting in Access, 402

setting default values for, in Access,
  423
sizing in Access, 416–417
sorting by one or more in Access,
  460–461
file extension, 20
file hyperlinks, 600–601
File menu
  Archive command in Outlook, 524
  Exit option, 7
  Open command, 26
  Page Setup command in Excel, 242,
    244, 245, 248, 249, 250, 252
  Page Setup command in PowerPoint,
    366
  Page Setup command in Word, 106,
    108, 109
  Print command, 28
  Print command in Access, 494
  Print command in Excel, 240, 267
  Print command in FrontPage, 569
  Print command in Outlook, 520
  Print command in PowerPoint, 368
  Print Preview command, 29
  Print Preview command in Excel,
    238
  Print Preview command in Word,
    104
  Publish Web command, 584
  Save As command, 22
  Save as Web page command, 24
  viewing reports in FrontPage, 578
  Web Page Preview command, 25
file names, 20, 24
File New Database dialog box, 376, 379
files
  attaching to Outlook messages,
    512–513
  sending large in Outlook, 513
fill a series in Excel, 180–181
fill color, changing in Excel, 226, 227
Fill Color button
  in Access, 456
  in Excel, 227
Fill Weekdays option in Excel, 181
Filter by Form feature in Access, 464–465
filter by input in Access, 462, 463
filter by selection in Access, 462, 463
filtering data in Excel lists, 280–281

Find a recipient link in Mail Merge, 163
Find and Replace dialog box
- in Access, 458–459
- in Excel, 192–193
- in Word, 54–55, 56–57
Find button in Access, 405, 458
Find Duplicates Query Wizard in Access, 467
Find entire cells only option in Excel, 193
Find Entry dialog box in Mail Merge, 163
Find feature
- in Excel, 192–193
- in Word, 54–55
find list of items in Access criteria, 478
Find Next button in Find and Replace dialog box, 54, 55, 56
Find options in Outlook, 527
Find tools in Notes screen in Outlook, 529
Find Unmatched Query Wizard, 467
Find whole word option in Word Find and Replace dialog box, 55
first-line indents, setting in Word, 80, 81
First Record button in Access, 400, 446
flashing insertion point
- in Access, 404
- in Excel, 186
flat file databases, 372
floating palette, 13
floating toolbar, 13
flow charts
- adding to Word documents, 146
- in PowerPoint, 319
folder icon in FrontPage, 552
Folder list in Outlook, 505, 518
folder locations, changing default, 21
folder structure
- creating for a Web site, 576
- navigating through, 23
folders. See also mail folders
- creating, 22, 23, 377
- nesting, 522
Folders view in FrontPage, 576–577
Font button in PowerPoint, 330
Font Color button
- in Excel, 226, 227
- in Word, 76
Font dialog box
- in FrontPage, 555
- special effects options in, 75
Font drop-down list in Word, 73
Font/Fore Color button in Access, 456, 457

Font Size button in PowerPoint, 331
font sizes
- changing, 74
- changing for controls in Access forms, 454
- changing in Excel, 224, 225
- for FrontPage text, 554
font style
- changing in Access forms, 455
- changing in Word, 73
Font tab in Excel, 228–229
fonts
- availability in Excel, 229
- changing for controls in Access forms, 454
- changing for PowerPoint text, 330
- changing in Excel, 224, 225
- changing in Web pages, 554, 555
- changing size of Word, 74
- changing style of Word, 73
- listing available in Word, 73
- in Word, 70
footers, 112, 346
- adding in Excel, 250–251
- adding in Word, 112–113
- adding to PowerPoint slides, 346–347
- creating custom in Excel, 252–253
- deleting in Word, 113
- displaying on PowerPoint slides, 292
- removing from Excel, 251
- viewing in Word, 111
footnotes, 65, 114–115
form buttons in Access, 446
form letter, creating in Mail Merge, 154–163
Form view, opening in Access, 444
Form view button in Access, 455
Form Wizard, 440–443
Format button in Page Numbers dialog box in Word, 111
Format Cells dialog box in Excel, 202, 220, 228–229, 232–233
Format dialog box for active PowerPoint charts, 317
Format menu
- AutoFormat command in Excel, 236
- Borders and Shading command in Word, 90, 91
- Bullets and Numbering command in PowerPoint, 336, 337
- Bullets and Numbering command in Word, 86, 88

Cells command in Excel, 202, 222, 227, 228, 232
Column command in Excel, 198, 199, 219
Font command in Word, 75, 76
Freeze Columns command in Access, 409
Hide Columns command in Access, 408
Hide command in Excel, 199
Paragraph command in Word, 80
Picture command in Word, 149
Replace Fonts command in PowerPoint, 331
Reveal Formatting command in Word, 99
selecting graphics commands in Word, 150
Styles and Formatting command in Word, 92, 95, 96
Theme command in FrontPage, 572
Unfreeze All Columns command in Access, 409
Unhide Columns command in Access, 408
Unhide command in Excel, 199
Format Painter button
- in Access, 457
- copying formatting in Word, 98
- in Excel, 234
- formatting Excel rows, 194
- in FrontPage, 555
- in PowerPoint, 335
Format Painter Smart Tag in new Excel rows or columns, 195
Format Picture dialog box in Word, 150–151
Format property box in Access, 418
formats
- for date and time in Word, 68
- for Excel dates and times, 182
- opening files in different, 26
- for saving documents, 21
formatting
- changing a style in Word, 97
- changing default in Word, 101
- changing with Replace feature, 57
- clearing in Excel, 235
- comparing in Word, 99
- copying for form controls, 457
- copying in Excel, 234

(continued)

formatting *(continued)*

    copying in FrontPage, 555

    copying in PowerPoint, 335

    copying in Word, 98

    dates and times in Excel, 182

    messages in Outlook, 525

    new rows or columns, 195

    options for Word tables, 136

    options in Word, 38

    removing from FrontPage, 555

    revealing in Word, 99

    worksheets in Excel, 174

formatting marks, displaying and hiding in Word, 100

Formatting toolbar, 12

    in Access, 401

    displaying, 10, 11, 12

    in Excel, 177

    in PowerPoint, 289

    in Word, 41

forms, 440, 449

    in Access, 5

    adding fields to, 450

    adding or deleting records, 448–449

    changing appearance of controls in, 454–455

    changing controls on, 452–453

    creating with fields from more than one table, 441

    creating with Form Wizard, 440–443

    in databases, 373

    editing data using, 447

    formatting controls in, 456–457

    moving through records with, 446

    naming, 442, 443

    opening, 444–445

    printing, 495

    renaming existing, 443

    resizing entire, 453

    saving, 445

    selecting layouts for, 442

Forms button in Objects bar in Access, 384

formula bar in Excel, 177, 178, 187, 212

formulas, 174, 208

    copying, 214–215

    editing, 212, 213

    entering, 212, 213

    error messages resulting from, 209

    examples of, 209

    names in, 200, 201

    referencing a cell in another workbook, 213

    referencing a cell in another worksheet, 213

    tracing, 211

Forward button in Outlook, 517

Frame slides option for printed presentations, 368

frames, indenting in, 559

frames templates in FrontPage, 549

Freeform tool for drawing custom shapes in Word, 139

freezing row or column headings in Excel, 187

From File command in Word, 144

From Scanner or Camera command, 144

From Scanner or Camera option, 610

FrontPage, 5

    introduction to, 544

    network connectivity problems, 617

    previewing Web pages in, 568, 569

    screen, 545

    starting, 545

FrontPage Server Extensions, 574, 585

FrontPage TCP/IP Test dialog box, 617

frozen fields in Access, 409

functions, 4, 174, 208

    entering, 216–217

    examples of, 209

    searching for particular, 217

G

General category of PowerPoint presentations, 290

General tab of Templates dialog box in Access, 379

general templates in FrontPage, 549

General Templates link in Access, 378

GeoCities, 584

Go To command in Word, 45

grammar, checking in Word, 62–63

grammatical mistakes, underlining in Word, 42

grand total, displaying in Excel, 282, 283

graphical text, editing in FrontPage, 553

graphics

    deleting in Excel, 274, 275

    deleting in Word, 149

    in Excel, 175

    inserting in Word, 39

    moving in Excel, 274

    moving in Word, 148, 149

    resizing in Excel, 274

    resizing in Word, 148, 149

    rotating in Excel, 275

    wrapping text around in Word, 150–151

graphics file formats, available in PowerPoint, 322

Graphics Interchange Format (.gif), 322

gray icons, 607

Grayscale option for printed presentations, 368

greater than (>) operator

    in Access criteria, 478

    in Excel, 208

greater than or equal to (>=) operator

    in Access criteria, 478

    in Excel, 208

green underlining in Word, 42, 63

Greeting Line dialog box in Mail Merge, 161

gridlines, 133

    adding to Excel charts, 258

    hiding or displaying in PowerPoint charts, 317

    printing in Excel, 233, 239

Gridlines print option in Excel, 245

Group By in Total row in Access, 482

Grouping Options button in Access, 485

Groups bar in Access, 385

H

H key, displaying hidden slides in PowerPoint, 352

handles. *See* selection handles

Handout Master in PowerPoint, 349

handouts in PowerPoint, 287, 369

Handwriting in Language tool bar, 608

handwriting recognition, 608, 609

hanging indents in Word, 81, 82

hard breaks in Word, 42

hard copy, 494

headers, 112, 346

    adding in Excel, 250–251

    adding in Word, 112–113

    adding to PowerPoint slides, 346–347

    creating custom in Excel, 252–253

    deleting in Word, 113

    removing from Excel, 251

    viewing in Word, 111

headings, creating in FrontPage, 561

Help button, 17

help information for databases, 383

help options in Office XP, 16
hidden columns in Excel, 198, 199
hidden fields, redisplaying in Access, 408
hidden notes, adding to cells, 271
hidden slides, displaying, 352
hidden text, displaying in Word documents, 100
Hide Gridlines command in Word, 133
Hide Slide button in PowerPoint, 352
Hide spelling errors in this document option, 61
hiding page numbers in Word, 110
high importance for Outlook messages, 509
Highlight button in Word, 77
highlighted text in Word, 77
History folder, 22, 377
hit counter, 574–575
holidays, adding to Calendar, 537
Home key in Word, 45
horizontal axis, 255
horizontal lines, inserting in FrontPage, 565
horizontal page breaks in Excel, 246, 247
HTML, formatting for messages in Outlook, 525
HTML Documents, saving Access reports as, 25
Hyperlink data type in Access, 397
hyperlinks, 544, 580, 600
    allowing receipt of e-mail, 601
    creating, 566–567
    deleting, 581
    editing, 603
    fixing broken, 567
    inserting in documents, 602–603
    making to appear as regular text, 601
    printing a diagram of, 581
    removing, 567, 601
    types of, 581
    verifying all in a Web site, 567
    viewing, 580–581
hyphenation, controlling, 69

I

I-beam cursor, 40, 44
icons, displaying gray, 607
ID field as a primary key in Access, 390
images. *See also* clip art images; pictures
    aligning in a document, 149
    scanning or downloading, 610
images folder for a Web site, 576
Import Web Wizard in FrontPage, 546

importing external data into Access, 389
In line with text option for Word graphics, 150
Inbox in Outlook, 503, 504, 507, 518
Include animations option for printed presentations, 368
Increase Decimal button in Excel, 221
Increase Font Size button in PowerPoint, 331
Increase Indent button
    in Excel, 230
    in FrontPage, 559
    in Word, 80
Indent feature
    in FrontPage, 559
    in Word, 80
Indents and Spacing tab in Word, 81, 84–85
Index tab in Help window, 17
indexes, creating in Access, 433
index.pdx file, 621
information. *See* data
Ink button in Writing Pad, 608
inline images in Word, 149
Insert Address Block dialog box, 160, 168
Insert AutoText in Word, 113
Insert Chart button in PowerPoint, 315
Insert Clip Art button
    in Excel, 272
    in PowerPoint, 321
Insert Clip Art task pane
    in Excel, 272, 273
    in FrontPage, 563
    in Word, 140–141
Insert File dialog box in Outlook, 512
Insert Function dialog box, 217
Insert Hyperlink button, 566, 600
Insert Hyperlink dialog box, 600, 602–603
Insert menu
    AutoText command in Word, 66, 67
    Break command in Word, 53, 117
    Cells command in Excel, 195
    Column command in Access, 391
    Columns command in Excel, 195
    Comment command in Excel, 271
    Diagram command in Word, 146
    Function command in Excel, 217
    Name command in Excel, 201
    Page Break command in Excel, 246
    Page Numbers command in Word, 110
    Picture command in PowerPoint, 322
    Picture command in Word, 140, 144

Reference command in Word, 114
Rows command in Excel, 194
Symbol command in Word, 69, 70
Worksheet command in Excel, 204
Insert Merge Field dialog box, 161
Insert Picture dialog box
    in PowerPoint, 322
    in Word, 144–145
Insert Picture from File button in FrontPage, 562
Insert Table button
    in FrontPage, 564
    on Standard toolbar in PowerPoint, 311
    on Standard toolbar in Word, 123
    in Tables and Borders toolbar in Word, 129
Insert Table dialog box in PowerPoint, 310
Insert Web Component dialog box in FrontPage, 574
Insert WordArt button
    in Excel, 271
    in PowerPoint, 326
insertion point
    in Access tables, 400
    in Word, 40, 44
installation problems with Office XP, 616
Installed on First Use icon, 606
Installer log file, 617
Instmsi.exe file, 616
Integer number field, 417
intranet, 544
IP address, 617
Italic feature
    in Access, 454, 455
    in Excel, 220
    in FrontPage, 556
    in PowerPoint, 332
    in Word, 72
items, clearing from Clipboard, 590

J

jobs, stopping, 29
JPEG (.jpg), 322
justified alignment of text, 108
Justified button in FrontPage, 558
Justified form layout in Access, 442
Justified report layout in Access, 488
Justify button in Word, 78

K

keyboard
browsing through presentations, 307
changing line spacing in Word, 85
moving through Access fields and records, 401
moving through Access records, 446
moving through Word documents, 45
keyboard shortcuts
assigning to styles in Word, 93
creating charts in Excel, 257
for cutting and pasting, 589
inserting symbols in Word, 71
for selecting text in Word, 47
kiosks, running slide shows as, 358

L

label document, saving in Mail Merge, 168
Label Options dialog box in Mail Merge, 165
Label Wizard in Access, 496–497
labels. *See also* mailing labels
in Access forms, 452, 453
landscape orientation, 109
in Excel, 244
for PowerPoint slides, 366
for printed reports, 488
Language command in Word, 64
Language tool bar
activating, 609
Handwriting option, 608
Large Icons button in Access, 384
Large Icons view in Access, 379
Last Record button in Access, 400, 446
Layout Preview view, viewing layout and style of reports, 491
Layout tab
of Format Picture dialog box in Word, 151
in Page Setup dialog box in Word, 108
Layout view, inserting a page break, 53
layouts
for reports in Report Wizard, 488
selecting for Access forms, 442
leader characters, setting before tabs, 83
Left align button
in Access, 455
in Excel, 230

in FrontPage, 558
in PowerPoint, 333
left alignment in Word, 78
left alignment of text in Excel, 178
Left Arrow in Word, 45
left indents, setting in Word, 80
Left Tab in Word, 82
Legend tab in Chart Wizard in Excel, 258
legends, 258
in Excel charts, 255, 258
hiding for Excel charts, 259
hiding in PowerPoint charts, 317
Less Brightness button in PowerPoint, 323
Less Contrast button in PowerPoint, 323
less than (<) operator
in Access criteria, 478
in Excel, 208
less than or equal to (<=) operator
in Access criteria, 478
in Excel, 208
letter templates in Word, 120
letters
creating with Mail Merge, 154–163
previewing merged, 162
levels for FrontPage headings, 561
Limit To List option in Access, 431
Line button in Word, 139
line charts, 254, 260
line color, changing in PowerPoint, 325
line spacing in Word, 84, 85
Line Style button in Word, 132
line styles in Word, 123, 132
Line Weight button in Word, 132
lines
adding blank to Word documents, 48
adding to Word tables, 123
erasing in Word tables, 127
Lines category
for AutoShapes in Excel, 268
for AutoShapes in Word, 138
Link to File dialog box, 601
linked information, 596–599
linked objects, 596, 598
linking, compared to embedding, 597
links, 599. *See also* hyperlinks
Links dialog box, 598, 599
List button in Access, 384
List view in Access, 379
lists. *See* data lists
log files, 616–617

logo, including in Access, 383
Long Integer number field, 417
long lines of text in Excel, 231
Look in drop-down list, 26, 27
lookup columns in Access, 430–431, 432
Lookup Wizard, 430
Loop until next sound option, 355
low priority for Outlook messages, 509
lowercase in Word, 49

M

macros, 373
Macros button in Access, 384
magnification levels in Access, 493
magnifying pages in Word, 105
mail folders, 522
Mail Merge feature
creating letters, 154–163
introduction to, 152–153
printing mailing labels, 164–169
in Word, 39
Mailing Instructions category for AutoText entries, 66
mailing labels
creating in Access, 496–499
editing in Access, 499
editing in Mail Merge, 169
naming, 498, 499
printing in Mail Merge, 164–169
sizing in Access, 496, 497
sorting in Access, 498, 499
types of, 496
updating in MailMerge, 169
main document, 154
completing in Mail Merge, 153, 160–161
creating in Mail Merge, 152, 154–155
main folder for a Web site, 576
Main Switchboard window in Access, 383
Maintenance Mode Options, 607
map, displaying for a contact's address, 539
margins, 106, 242
changing for printing in Access, 495
changing in Excel, 239, 242–243, 253
changing in Word, 106–107
viewing changes in, 107
visually adjusting in Print Preview in Word, 104, 105
Margins button in Excel, 239

Margins tab in Page Setup dialog box, 106–107, 109

Master VISUALLY Office XP on CD-ROM in this book, 620–621

masters in PowerPoint, 349

Match Case option

    in Excel, 193

    in Find and Replace dialog box in Access, 459

    in Word Find and Replace dialog box, 55

matching fields, identifying in two Access tables, 436

Max calculation in Excel AutoCalculate, 211

Max option in Access, 468, 482, 487

Maximize button, 9

maximized windows, 8

Measurement units area in Word, 107

Media Gallery Online, 141

Meeting Minder, 361

Memo data type in Access, 397

menu bar

    in Excel, 177

    in PowerPoint, 289

    on Word screen, 41

menus, customizing in an Office program, 604

Merge and Center button in Excel, 231

merge fields, 160, 161

Merge to Printer dialog box, 163, 169

message list in Outlook, 506

messages

    archiving, 524

    attaching files to, 512–513

    checking for new, 507

    creating, 508–509

    deleting, 521

    dragging to folders, 523

    finding, 526, 527

    formatting, 525

    forwarding, 516, 517

    moving, 523

    printing, 520

    reading, 506–507

    replying to, 516, 517

    sending copies to other persons, 511

    sending to contacts, 541

    sorting, 526, 527

    total size of, 512

Microphone option in Language toolbar, 609

Microphone Wizard, 609

Microsoft Access. *See* Access

Microsoft Access window, 375

Microsoft Binder, 611

Microsoft Clip Organizer, 320

Microsoft Excel. *See* Excel

Microsoft Excel window, 176

Microsoft FrontPage window, 545

Microsoft Graph program, 314, 315, 316

Microsoft Help dialog box, 17

Microsoft IntelliMouse. *See* wheeled mouse

Microsoft Office CD-ROM, installing Office XP, 612–615

Microsoft Office Language Settings, 611

Microsoft Office Setup window, 606–607

Microsoft Office XP. *See* Office XP

Microsoft Outlook. *See* Outlook

Microsoft Outlook window. *See* Outlook window

Microsoft Photo Editor, 611

Microsoft PowerPoint. *See* PowerPoint

Microsoft PowerPoint window, 288, 289

Microsoft Setup dialog box, 612–614

Microsoft Word. *See* Word

Microsoft Word window, 40

Min calculation in Excel AutoCalculate, 211

Min option

    in Access, 482, 487

    for query results, 468

Minimize button, 9

misspelled words

    correcting with AutoCorrect, 58, 59

    underlining of, 42

Moderate animation schemes, 340

Modify Style dialog box in Word, 96, 97

modules, 373

Modules button in Access, 384

monitors, presenting slide shows on, 359

Month view for Calendar appointments, 536, 537

More Brightness button in PowerPoint, 323

More button in Find and Replace dialog box, 54, 56

More Contrast button in PowerPoint, 323

Motion paths category in PowerPoint, 338

mouse, 45, 46. *See also* wheeled mouse

Move Items dialog box in Outlook, 523

Move or Copy dialog box in Excel, 207

move table handle in Word, 130

moving text. *See* Cut button; Paste button

Msi.dll, installing, 616

MultiLanguage Pack, installing, 611

multiple (*) operator in Access expressions, 480

multiple-field primary key, 434

Multiple Pages button

    in Access, 493

    in Word, 105

Multiple spacing option in Word, 85

multiplication (*) operator in Excel, 208

multitasking, 32

My Documents folder, 20, 22

My Pictures file, 144

My Pictures folder, 119

N

#N/A error message in Excel, 209

name badges, creating, 152

name box in Excel, 177

#NAME? error message in Excel, 209

named cells, going to Excel, 200

names. *See also* file names

    for Access fields, 415

    assigning to cells in Excel, 200, 201

    of databases, 382

    deleting defined in Excel, 201

    selecting from Outlook address book, 510–511

    for tables, 388

    typing in Excel formulas, 200, 201

naming

    Access forms, 442, 443

    databases, 376

    mailing labels in Access, 498, 499

    queries, 468, 472

    reports, 488, 489

    worksheets in Excel, 206

navigation bars, adding to Web pages, 583

Navigation view in FrontPage, 582–583

navigational structure of a Web site, 582, 583

negative numbers

    automatically changing to red, 227

    entering into Excel, 179

nesting folders, 522

network connection, testing in FrontPage, 617

network connectivity problems in FrontPage, 617

New Address List dialog box, 156–157

New button, 18

    in Access, 377

    in Outlook, 508

    in Word, 154

New Document task pane, 14, 120

New File task pane in Access, 375, 376, 377, 386

new mail composition window, 508

New Message to Contact button, 541

New Page or Web task pane, 546, 548

New Presentation task pane, 290, 294

New Record button, 398, 448

New Report dialog box, 496

New section in task pane, 18

New Slide button, 296, 301

New Style dialog box, 93

Next Record button in Access, 400, 446

Next Record code in Mail Merge, 169

No watermark option, 119

nonbreaking hyphen, 69

Normal category for AutoText entries, 66

Normal Slides view, 307

Normal tab in FrontPage, 568

Normal view

    displaying Word columns, 116

    inserting a page break, 53

    notes pane in, 362, 363

    in PowerPoint, 286, 292, 304, 305

    selecting text in, 299

    in Word, 39, 102

Norton Utilities, 619

not equal to (<>) operator

    in Access criteria, 478

    in Excel, 208

notes, 5, 503, 528–529

Notes and Handouts tab in PowerPoint, 347

Notes Master in PowerPoint, 349

Notes Page view in PowerPoint, 305, 362, 363

Notes pane in PowerPoint, 289

#NULL! error message in Excel, 209

null value, compared to a zero-length string, 425

Num Lock key, 179

Number data type in Access, 397

number fields, 417, 418

number formats in Excel, 222–223

number series in Excel, 180, 181

number signs (###) in Excel cells, 222

number styles

    applying to Excel cells, 221

    in PowerPoint, 336, 337

    in Word, 88

Number tab in Excel, 222–223

numbered lists

    creating in Word, 88–89

    in PowerPoint, 336

Numbering button

    in PowerPoint, 337

    in Word, 88

numbers

    adding in FrontPage lists, 560

    formatting in Excel, 222–223

    summing in Excel, 210–211

    typing into Excel, 179

numeric keypad, entering numbers into Excel, 179

O

object layouts in PowerPoint, 297

Object Linking and Embedding. *See* OLE

Object List area in Access, 384

objects

    in Access, 373

    in Access database window, 384

    adding to PowerPoint slides, 286–287

    animating in PowerPoint slides, 338–339

    dragging and dropping for embedding, 593

    embedding OLE objects, 594

    linking, 596

    moving, resizing, or deleting in PowerPoint slides, 328–329

    renaming or deleting in Access, 385

Objects bar in Access, 384

Office Assistant, 16, 17

Office Clipboard. *See* Clipboard

Office Language Settings, 611

Office programs. *See* programs

Office Setup, log files created by, 616

Office Shared Features folder, 608

Office XP, 4

    adding or removing features, 606–607

    documents, 18–31, 33–35

    exiting programs, 6, 7

    help options, 16–17

    installation problems, 616

    installing, 612–615

    optimum requirements for, 613

    programs in, 4–5

    repairing, 615

    restoring deleted, 607

    shared features, 610–611

    starting programs, 6–7

    system requirements for installing, 613

    task panes, 14–15

    toolbars, 10–13

    troubleshooting, 616–617

    uninstalling, 615

    windows, 8–9

OLE, 592–593, 596

OLE Object data type in Access, 397

On/Off format. *See* Yes/No fields

One Page Web template in FrontPage, 546

one-to-many relationship in Access, 438

one-to-one relationship in Access, 438

Online Broadcast command for slide shows in PowerPoint, 361

Open button in Access, 387

Open command in FrontPage, 552

Open dialog box, 26–27

    in Access, 386

    opening databases from, 387

    searching documents from, 35

Open File dialog box in FrontPage, 552

Open Source button in Links dialog box, 598

Open Web command in FrontPage, 552

optimal fields, adding to Database Wizard tables, 380

Options button in Clipboard task pane, 591

Options tab in Customize dialog box, 604–605

OR condition with Access criteria, 476, 477

Or tab for filtering by form, 465

order for performing calculations in Excel, 208

organization charts

    adding in PowerPoint, 318–319

    adding to Word documents, 146

orientation

    for presentations in PowerPoint, 366, 367

    for printed reports, 488

    in Word, 109

Outbox folder in Outlook, 504, 508, 518

Outline option in Font dialog box in Word, 75

Outline report layout in Access, 488

Outline tab in PowerPoint, 293, 304
Outline tab/slides tab in PowerPoint, 289
Outline view
  browsing through outlined slides, 306, 307
  editing in PowerPoint text, 301
  in PowerPoint, 286, 298
  selecting text in, 299
  typing speaker notes, 363
  in Word, 39, 102
outlined buttons in a toolbar, 11
outlines
  creating in Word, 89
  printing in PowerPoint, 369
Outlook, 5, 502, 503
Outlook Bar, 503, 505
Outlook Calendar window. *See* Calendar
Outlook Today, 504, 505
Outlook window, 503, 505
output for presentations in PowerPoint, 366
Oval button on Drawing toolbar in Word, 139
overheads, color schemes for, 342
Overtype feature in Word, 49

P

page borders, adding in Word, 91
page breaks, 246
  inserting in Excel, 246, 247
  inserting in Word, 53, 115
  removing from Excel, 247
  removing in Word, 53
  viewing in Excel, 246, 247
Page Down key
  in Access, 401
  moving to next Access record, 446
Page Number button in Excel, 253
page numbers
  adding in Word, 110–111
  displaying in a slide header or footer, 346
  hiding in Word, 110
  inserting in Excel headers or footers, 253
  removing from Word documents, 111
  viewing in Word, 111
page orientation, changing in Excel, 244
page ranges, printing selected in Excel, 240, 241

Page Setup dialog box
  Header/Footer tab in Excel, 250–251, 252, 253
  Margins tab in Access, 495
  Margins tab in Excel, 242, 243
  Margins tab in Word, 109
  Page tab in Excel, 244, 248
  in PowerPoint, 366–367
  Sheet tab in Excel, 245, 249
  in Word, 106–107, 108
Page tab of Page Setup dialog box in Excel, 248
page templates, creating Web pages in, 548
Page Templates dialog box in FrontPage, 549
page titles in FrontPage, 551
Page Up key in Access, 401, 446
Page view in FrontPage, 577
Page Width zoom setting in Word, 103
pages. *See also* Web pages
  adding to databases, 373
  changing orientation of Word, 109
  displaying in Word, 45
  displaying multiple in Word, 105
  magnifying in Print Preview window, 492
  magnifying in Word, 105
  moving to specific in Word, 45
  numbering in Word documents, 110–111
Pages button in Access, 384
panes. *See* task panes
paper clip icon in Outlook message list, 514
Paragraph dialog box, 80, 81
  changing line spacing in Word, 85
  changing paragraph spacing in Word, 84
  Indents and Spacing tab in Word, 79
paragraph formatting options in Word, 38
paragraph marks, displaying and hiding in Word, 100
paragraph spacing, changing in Word, 84, 85
paragraph styles in Word, 92, 93
paragraphs
  indenting in Word, 80
  justifying last line of, 79
  selecting in Word, 47
parentheses ( ) in Excel formulas, 208
Paste button, 589
  in Access, 405
  in Excel, 188, 214, 266
  in Word, 50

Paste Special dialog box, 593, 597
patterns
  adding to background of Excel cells, 227
  combining with colors for shading in Word, 91
.pdf extension, 621
Pen color option in PowerPoint, 359
percent (%) operator in Excel, 208
Percent format in Excel, 221, 222
personal tables sample in Access, 392
Personal Web template in FrontPage, 546
personalized letters. *See* letters
Phone List view for Outlook contacts, 540, 541
Photo Editor, 611
photographs. *See* pictures
phrases, locating in Outlook notes, 529
Picture dialog box in FrontPage, 562
Picture toolbar
  displaying in Word, 141, 148
  in PowerPoint, 320, 321, 322, 323
picture watermark, 118–119
pictures. *See also* clip art images; images
  adding in FrontPage, 562–563
  adding in PowerPoint, 322–323
  deleting in FrontPage, 563
  including in Access, 383
  inserting into Word, 144–145
  moving in FrontPage, 563
  resizing in FrontPage, 563
pie charts, 254, 260
  compared to doughnut charts, 261
  moving slices, 264
PivotChart AutoForm, 443
PivotChart view, 475
PivotTable AutoForm, 443
PivotTable view, 475
placeholders
  on PowerPoint slides, 300
  in slide layouts in PowerPoint, 308, 309
Places Bar
  accessing folders from Access, 377
  in Open dialog box, 26
  in PowerPoint, 322
  in Save As dialog box, 22, 23
Plain Text (no formatting) in Outlook, 525
plot area in an Excel chart, 255
plus sign (+) beside Access records with related data, 435

INDEX

points, 74
Portable Network Graphics (.png), 322
portrait orientation, 109
    in Excel, 244
    for PowerPoint slides, 366
    for printed reports, 488
power (^) operator in Access expressions, 480
PowerPoint, 5, 286–287
precedence, 208
precedents, tracing in Excel formulas, 213
presentations
    browsing through, 306–307
    changing order of slides in, 350
    creating, 286, 287, 288, 290–293, 295
    enhancing, 287
    fine-tuning, 287
    magnifying, 305
    previewing as Web pages, 357
    printing, 368–369
    recording for broadcast, 361
    replacing fonts throughout, 331
    setting up for printing, 366–367
preset borders in Excel, 232
Preview command for images in Word, 145
Preview in Browser button in FrontPage, 568
Preview tab in FrontPage, 567, 568
previewing
    merged letters, 162
    reports in Access, 490
Previous Record button in Access, 400, 446
primary key, 374, 388
    index for, 433
    setting, 389, 394, 395, 434
print areas, setting in Excel, 241
Print button, 29
    in Access, 489
    in Excel, 240, 267
    in Outlook, 520
Print dialog box, 28–29
    in Access, 494, 495
    in Excel, 240
    in FrontPage, 569
    in Mail Merge, 163, 169
    in Outlook, 520
    in PowerPoint, 368

Print Layout view
    displaying documents in, 79
    displaying footnotes or endnotes, 114
    displaying Word columns, 116
    moving or resizing Word tables, 130
    in Word, 39, 102
Print link in Mail Merge task pane, 169
print options, 29, 245
Print Preview button
    in Excel, 238
    in Page Setup dialog box, 242
    in Word, 105
Print Preview command in File menu, 29
Print Preview view
    changing margins in, 243
    for displaying report pages, 491
    opening reports in, 490
Print Preview window
    in Access, 492
    in Excel, 238–239
    in Word, 104, 105, 107
print queue, displaying, 29
printed data, changing size of Excel, 248
printed presentations, changing appearance of, 368
printed reports in Access, 380, 381
Printed Watermark dialog box, 118
printer font, 224
printer symbol, indicating a printer font in Excel, 224
printers
    accessing and changing settings for, in Excel, 243
    margin settings for, 106
    selecting, 28
    selecting in Excel, 240
    specifying for Mail Merge, 165
    specifying in Access, 495
printing in Excel, 175
priorities
    assigning for tasks, 530, 531
    for Outlook messages, 509
private folder for a Web site, 576
Product Key, 612
program maintenance features, 610
program window, 6
programs
    on CD-ROM in this book, 618–619
    closing from taskbar button, 32

    exiting, 6, 7
    in Office XP, 4–5
    starting, 6–7
    switching among Office, 32
    taskbar buttons for, 32
Project Web template in FrontPage, 546
Projects category of PowerPoint presentations, 290
properties
    displaying for fields, 412
    selecting for PowerPoint animations, 339
Protect Sheet dialog box in Excel, 203
Protection tab in Excel, 202
.pst files in Outlook, 524
Publish Web dialog box in FrontPage, 584
publishing Web pages, 24, 544
Pure black and white option for printed presentations, 368

Q

queries, 5, 466
    building from scratch in Design view, 470–473
    changing view for, 475
    creating, 373, 466–469, 470–473
    naming, 468, 472
    opening, 474
    saving, 472, 473
    sorting results of, 479
    summarizing result information, 468
Queries button in Objects bar in Access, 384
question mark (?) wildcard in Access, 478
questions, typing in Help text box, 16
queue, 29
quotation marks in Access text fields, 423
quotations, indenting in Word, 80
quoting in Outlook, 516

R

range names for Excel cells, 200, 201
range of cells in Excel, 184–185
recipients
    searching for individual, 163
    selecting, 159
    selecting for mailing labels, 167

record buttons in Access, 400

records

adding in Access, 398, 399, 448, 449

adding in Mail Merge, 157, 159

consequences of deleting in Access, 399, 449

in a data source in Mail Merge, 156

in database tables, 388

in databases, 373

deleting in Access, 398, 399, 448, 449

displaying in Datasheet view in Access, 396

displaying specific, in Access, 401

displaying the top 10 in an Excel list, 281

editing in Mail Merge, 159

entering for Access tables, 390

in Excel data lists, 276, 277

filtering in Access, 462–463

grouping in Access, 482, 483

limiting in Access query results, 483

moving through in Access, 400–401, 446

printing databases, 494

scrolling through, 401

searching for particular in Mail Merge, 167

selecting all in an Access table, 403

selecting in Access, 402

sorting in Access, 460–461

sorting in Access reports, 486

Records menu, Sort command in Access, 461

Recount button in word count toolbar, 65

Rectangle button on Drawing toolbar in Word, 139

Recurrence button in Task window, 531

recurring appointments, scheduling in Outlook, 535

recurring tasks, 531

red underlining

in PowerPoint presentations, 301

in Word, 42, 60

Redo button in Word, 52

#REF! error message in Excel, 197, 209

Reference box in Excel, 200, 201

references. See cell references in Excel

referential integrity, 439

regular priority for Outlook messages, 509

Rehearsal dialog box in PowerPoint, 356

Rehearse button in PowerPoint, 356

relational databases, 372

relationships

defining between tables, 436–439

deleting in Access, 439

determining between database tables, 374

Relationships button in Table Wizard in Access, 395

relative reference in an Excel formula, 214

Reminder check box in Task window in Outlook, 531

Remove Filter button in Access, 462, 463, 465

Remove Link button in FrontPage, 567

renaming objects in Access, 385

repair maintenance mode, 615

Repair Office option, 607

repeating row or column labels in Excel, 249

Replace feature in Word, 56

Replace Fonts command in PowerPoint, 331

Replace tab of Excel Find and Replace dialog box, 193

Replace with box in Word Find and Replace dialog box, 56

Replace With text box in Access, 459

reply buttons in Outlook, 516

report design, editing for mailing labels, 499

Report Wizard, 484–489

reports, 5

basing on more than one table, 485

changing view for, 491

creating from databases, 373

creating with Report Wizard, 484–489

naming, 488, 489

opening, 490

previewing, 492–493

printing, 489, 495

viewing on screen, 489

Reports button in Objects bar in Access, 384

Reports view in FrontPage, 578

required fields

including in Database Wizard tables, 380

removing from Database Wizard tables, 381

specifying in Access, 424

Reset my usage data option, 605

resizing handles for graphics in Word, 148, 149

Restore button, 9

results of queries, sorting, 479

return addresses, specifying for envelopes in Word, 170, 171

Reveal Formatting task pane, displaying in Word, 99

reverse video for selected text, 46

Rich Text, formatting for messages in Outlook, 525

Right align button

in Access, 455

in Excel, 230

in FrontPage, 558

in PowerPoint, 333

right-align option in Word, 78

right alignment of numbers in Excel, 179

Right Arrow in Word, 45

Right Tab in Word, 82

Rolodex cards, creating, 152

Romanesque theme in FrontPage, 572

Rotate handle in Excel, 275

rotating data in Excel cells, 231

Row and column headings print option in Excel, 245

row headings, freezing in Excel, 187

row height

in Access, 407

in Excel, 218, 219

for PowerPoint tables, 312

in Word tables, 126

row labels

as names in Excel, 201

repeating in Excel, 249

rows

adding to Access tables, 390

adding to PowerPoint tables, 313

adding to Word tables, 124, 128, 129

changing height of Excel, 218, 219

deleting from Excel, 196, 197

deleting from FrontPage, 565

deleting from PowerPoint, 313

deleting in Word tables, 128, 129

in Excel, 177

in FrontPage tables, 564

hiding in worksheets, 199

inserting in Excel, 194, 195

inserting in FrontPage tables, 565

in PowerPoint tables, 310

selecting in Excel, 185

in Word, 122

INDEX

Ruler

    changing margins in Print Preview in Word, 105

    setting indents in Word, 81

    on Word screen, 41

Run button, running Access queries, 472, 476

Run from My Computer icon, 606

S

Sales/Marketing category of PowerPoint presentations, 290

Salutation category for AutoText entries, 66

sample databases, installing, 387

sample tables in Table Wizard, 392

Save Address List dialog box in Mail Merge, 158

Save As dialog box, 20, 22–23

    in Access, 389

    saving queries in Access, 473

    saving Web pages in FrontPage, 550

Save As Web page command in File menu, 24

Save button, 20

    in Design view in Access, 445

    in FrontPage, 550

Save in drop-down list, 22

Scale to fit paper option, 368

scanned images. *See* pictures

Scanner and Camera Add-In, 610

Scientific number format in Excel, 222

screen display styles in Access, 380, 381

ScreenTip button, 602–603

ScreenTip feature

    displaying name of a toolbar button, 10

    turning on, 11

scroll bars

    in Excel, 177

    in windows, 9

    in Word documents, 44, 45

    on Word screen, 41

scroll boxes in Access, 401

Search button in Search task pane, 35

search criteria for documents, 34

Search dialog box, accessing from Open dialog box, 35

search direction, specifying, 459

Search task pane, displaying, 34–35

searches, refining in Outlook, 527

Section break types options in Break dialog box, 53

section formatting in Word, 99

sections, breaking documents into, 53

Select Data Source dialog box, 157, 166

Select Names dialog box, 510

Select Picture dialog box

    in PowerPoint, 320, 321

    in Word, 119

Select Query window in Access, 470–472

Selected Fields list in Simple Query Wizard dialog box, 467

selecting data in Access, 402–403

selection bar, 46, 47

selection handles

    for AutoShapes in Excel, 269

    for charts in Excel, 264

    for graphics in Excel, 274

    for graphics in Word, 148, 149

    for PowerPoint objects, 328

self-repairing capabilities of Office XP programs, 610

semicolon (;) between addresses in Outlook, 31, 508

Send a Copy button, 31

Send button in Outlook, 509

Send/Receive button in Outlook, 507, 509

send/receive operation, 513

Sent Items folder in Outlook, 508, 509, 518, 519

Sentence case in Word, 49

sentences, selecting in Word, 47

serial number, storing Excel data as, 182

series, 180, 181

servername in an e-mail address, 511

Set Page Title dialog box, 25, 551

Set Print Area option in Excel, 241

Set Up Show dialog box in PowerPoint, 358–359

Setup program in Office XP, 615

SetupLog file, 616

shading

    adding in Word, 90, 91

    adding to Word table cells, 134

shadow

    adding to a PowerPoint AutoShape, 325

    adding to AutoShapes in Excel, 269

Shadow feature in PowerPoint, 332

Shadow option in Font dialog box in Word, 75

shapes, 138, 139. *See also* AutoShapes

sheet feed labels, 496

Sheet tab of Excel Page Setup dialog box, 245, 249

Shift + F2

    in Access, 406

    displaying an entire expression, 481

shortcut icons

    creating, 7, 375

    deleting, 7

    starting programs from, 7

shortcut keys. *See* keyboard shortcuts

Show All Relationships button, 437

Show Direct Relationships button, 437

Show Gridlines command in Word, 133

Show Large Previews option, 295

Show ScreenTips on toolbars option, 11

Show Table dialog box in Access, 470–471

Show Toolbar box in Word Count dialog box, 65

Shrink to Fit button in Word, 105

Shrink to fit option in Excel, 225

Simple Query Wizard, 466–469

Simple table designs in Word, 136

single-field primary key, 434

single line spacing, 84, 85

Site Summary report in FrontPage, 578

slices, moving in a pie chart in Excel, 264

Slide Design task pane, 294–295, 340, 342, 343, 344–345

Slide Layout task pane, 296–297, 308–309

Slide Master, 346, 348–349

    adding clip art images to, 321

    displaying, 348–349

slide numbers, 292, 346, 350

slide pane, 289

Slide Show button, 305, 360

Slide Show menu

    Animation Schemes command, 340

    Custom Animation command, 338

    Set Up Show command, 358

Slide Show view, 286

slide shows

    methods of delivery, 358

    pausing or ending, 361

    presenting on multiple monitors, 359

    previewing, 360–361

    rehearsing, 356–357

    setting up, 358–359

Slide Sorter view, 286, 304, 305, 350, 351, 363
Slide Transition task pane, 349, 354–355
slide transitions, 354–355
slides
adding, 296–297
adding AutoShapes to, 324–325
adding charts to, 314–315
adding clip art images to, 320–321
adding headers or footers to, 346–347
adding objects to, 286–287
adding pictures to, 322–323
adding tables to, 310–311
adding text effects to, 326–327
adding transitions to, 354–355
advancing manually in slide shows, 357
advancing manually or automatically, 358–359
animating objects on, 338–339
changing alignment of text in, 333
changing color schemes for, 342–343
changing layout for, 308–309
changing numbering of, 367
changing order of objects on, 323
changing text color on, 334
creating, 286, 353
deleting, 351
displaying previous or next, 307
drawing on, during slide shows, 360, 361
hiding in, 352
inserting duplicate, 297
moving, resizing, or deleting objects on, 328–329
previewing for black-and-white printing, 369
rearranging, 350
Slides tab in PowerPoint Normal view, 304
Slides view in PowerPoint, 298, 306, 307
Small caps option in Font dialog box in Word, 75
Small Icons button in Access, 384
Smart Tag. See Clipboard Smart Tag
software suite, 4
Sort Ascending button
in Excel, 279
in Word, 125
Sort Descending button
in Excel, 279
in Word, 125

Sort dialog box in Excel, 278
sort order for Outlook messages, 526
sorting
records in Access, 460–461
tasks in Outlook, 532
sounds
adding to slide transitions in PowerPoint, 355
editing embedded, 595
source file, 594
creating an OLE object, 592
for linked information, 598
linking to a destination file, 596
spaces, compared to tabs, 82
speaker notes
browsing in presentations, 307
creating, 287, 361, 362–363
special appearance effects, applying in Excel, 228–229
special characters, 69
Special Effect button on Formatting toolbar in Access, 457
special text effects, applying, 75
speech recognition, 608, 609
Speech Tools button on Language toolbar, 609
speed
selecting for PowerPoint animations, 339
setting for slide transitions, 354, 355
spell check in PowerPoint, 364–365
spelling
checking in Excel, 190–191
checking in FrontPage, 570–571
checking in Word, 60–61
Spelling and Grammar button in Word, 60
Spelling and Grammar dialog box in Word, 61, 62–63
Spelling button
in Access, 405
in Excel, 190
in FrontPage, 570, 571
in PowerPoint, 364
spelling errors
correcting in Outlook messages, 509
correcting with AutoCorrect, 59
hiding underlining of, 61
spreadsheet program. See Excel
SQL, 475
SQL view, 475

square brackets [ ] around field names in Access expressions, 480
squares, drawing in Word, 139
Standard toolbar, 12
displaying, 10, 11, 12
in Excel, 177
in PowerPoint, 289
on Word screen, 41
Stars and Banners category
for AutoShapes in Excel, 268
for AutoShapes in PowerPoint, 324
for AutoShapes in Word, 138
Start menu, starting programs, 6, 7
Start of Field option for searching in Access, 458
status bar
in Access, 413
in Excel, 177
OVR in, 49
in PowerPoint, 289
on Word screen, 41
StDev (standard deviation), 482
Stepped report layout in Access, 488
Strikethrough effect in Excel, 228
Strikethrough option in Word, 75
Structured Query Language. See SQL
style sheet templates in FrontPage, 549
styles
applying in Word, 94–95
applying to Access forms, 442, 443
creating in Word, 92–93
deleting in Word, 97
modifying in Word, 96–97
selecting for reports, 488, 489
for Word tables, 122
subdatasheets, displaying in Access, 435
subjects, creating for e-mail, 30, 31
Subscript effect in Excel, 228
Subscript option in Font dialog box in Word, 75
Subscription Product key, 612
subsets of fonts in Word, 71
Subtle animation schemes, 340
Subtotal dialog box in Excel, 282
subtotals, 282–283
subtract (-) operator in Access expressions, 480
subtraction (-) operator in Excel, 208
SUM function, automatically inserting, 210

Sum option
  in Access, 482, 487
  adding query result values, 468
Summary Options button in Report Wizard, 486, 487
summary reports, creating for Excel data lists, 282
summary slides in PowerPoint, 353
Superscript effect in Excel, 228
Superscript option in Word, 75
Switch Between Header and Footer button in Word, 112
switchboard for a database, 382
symbols, inserting in Word, 70–71
synonyms, finding in Word, 64
system files, updating, 612

T

Tab key, moving to next Access field, 401
tab scroll buttons in Excel, 177
Table AutoFormat dialog box in Word, 136–137
table designs in Word, 136, 137
Table menu
  AutoFit command in Word, 137
  Delete command in Word, 129
  Hide Gridlines command in Word, 133
  Insert command in Word, 128
  Show Gridlines command in Word, 133
  Table AutoFormat command in Word, 136
table resize handle in Word, 130, 131
table structure, displaying in Design View in Access, 396
Table Wizard, creating tables, 392–395
tables
  in Access, 5
  adding rows or columns in Word, 128–129
  adding shading or color to cells in Word, 134
  adding to Design view queries, 471
  adding to slides in PowerPoint, 310–311
  changing alignment of Word, 131
  changing borders of Word, 132–133
  changing column width in Word, 126
  creating in Datasheet view, 388–389
  creating in FrontPage, 564

creating in Word, 122–123
creating with Table Wizard, 392–395
in databases, 373, 388
defining relationships between, 436–439
deleting entire in Word, 129
deleting in Access, 391
deleting in Table Wizard, 395
deleting rows or columns in Word, 128–129
determining relationships between database, 374
drawing in Word, 122
enforcing referential integrity between Access, 439
erasing lines in Word, 127
formatting in PowerPoint, 312–313
importing from other databases, 389
inserting in FrontPage, 564–565
inserting in Word, 39
moving in Word, 130, 131
naming, 388, 394
opening in Access, 396
planning for databases, 374
removing from Design view queries, 471
removing from Relationships window, 437
resizing in Word, 130, 131
sorting text in Word, 125
typing text in Word, 124
viewing in Access, 410
Tables and Borders toolbar
  in PowerPoint, 311, 313
  in Word, 122–123
Tables button in Access, 384
tabs, 82–83
Tabular AutoForm in Access, 443
Tabular layout for an Access form, 442
Tabular report layout in Access, 488
task list
  creating in Outlook, 530–531
  displaying comments in, 533
  managing in Outlook, 532–533
Task Pane command in View menu, 15
task panes, 14
  closing, 15
  creating new documents, 18
  in different Office XP programs, 15
  options in, 14
  in PowerPoint, 289

resizing, 15
  on Word screen, 41
Task Recurrence dialog box, 531
taskbar, switching among documents within, 33
taskbar buttons, 6
  for programs, 32
  redisplaying windows, 9
  in Word, 40
tasks, 5, 503, 530
  creating recurring, 531
  deleting, 533
  displaying, 504
  marking as complete, 532
  restoring deleted, 533
  sorting, 532
telephone numbers, entering in Access, 397
templates, 18. See also design templates in PowerPoint
  categories of FrontPage, 548
  creating, 19, 121
  creating new documents, 19
  in FrontPage, 546, 547
  storing Word styles in, 92
  using in Word, 120–121
Templates dialog box, 19
  Databases tab in Access, 378
  in Word, 120–121
text
  adding bullets or numbers to in PowerPoint, 337
  adding in PowerPoint, 300
  adding or editing on Web pages, 553
  adding to a PowerPoint AutoShape, 325
  adding to AutoShapes in Excel, 269
  adding to AutoShapes in Word, 139
  aligning in FrontPage, 558
  aligning in Word, 78–79
  aligning on a page in Word, 108
  applying different alignments in a single line, 79
  applying special effects, 75
  bolding in Word, 72
  changing alignment of PowerPoint, 333
  changing case of, 49
  changing cell position of, in Word tables, 135
  changing color of FrontPage, 557
  changing color of PowerPoint, 334
  changing color of Word, 76

changing font and size of PowerPoint, 330–331

changing margin settings for selected in Word, 107

copying formatting of, in PowerPoint, 335

copying in Word, 50, 51

deleting in PowerPoint, 301

deleting in Word, 48, 49

deleting in Word tables, 129

deselecting in Word, 47

displaying hidden in Word documents, 100

displaying in columns in Word, 116–117

displaying long lines in Excel cells, 231

dragging and dropping in Word, 51

editing graphical in FrontPage, 553

editing in diagrams in Word, 147

editing in PowerPoint, 300–301

editing in Word, 38

editing WordArt in PowerPoint, 327

entering automatically in Word, 43

entering in a FrontPage table, 565

entering in PowerPoint tables, 310, 311

entering in Word, 38

finding in Word, 54–55

formatting in Excel headers or footers, 253

formatting in Word, 38

highlighting in Word, 77

indenting in FrontPage, 559

inputting without typing, 608–609

inserting in Word, 48, 49

italicizing in Word, 72

moving and copying in PowerPoint, 302

moving in Word, 50, 51

recovering deleted in Word, 49

reorganizing in PowerPoint presentation, 302

replacing existing in PowerPoint, 301

replacing in PowerPoint, 301

replacing in Word, 56–57

selecting all formatted with a specified style in Word, 97

selecting all in a Word document, 47

selecting in PowerPoint, 298–299, 302

selecting in Word, 46–47

sizing on Web pages, 554, 555

sorting in Word tables, 125

typing in Word tables, 124

typing into Excel, 178

typing into Word documents, 42–43

underlining in Word, 72

wrapping around graphics in Word, 150–151

text and object layouts in PowerPoint, 297

Text appearance options in Label Wizard, 497

Text Box button
in Excel, 270
in PowerPoint, 303

Text Box option for Yes/No fields in Access, 428, 429

text boxes
in Access forms, 452, 453
in Excel, 270–271
in PowerPoint, 299, 303, 333

Text button in Writing Pad, 608

text color in Access, 456

text converters, 610–611

Text data type in Access, 397

text effects
adding to PowerPoint slides, 326–327
adding to Word documents, 142–143

text fields in Access, 416, 417

text hyperlinks
appearance of, 601
in FrontPage, 566

text layouts in PowerPoint, 297

text phrase, searching for, 34

text placeholders
on PowerPoint slides, 293, 300
in Word diagrams, 147

text series in Excel, 180

text style in PowerPoint, 332

text watermark in Word, 118, 119

Text Width zoom setting in Word, 103

texture, adding to a PowerPoint AutoShape, 325

themes, applying to Web sites or pages, 572–573

thesaurus in Word, 64

time
displaying in a slide header or footer, 346
entering into Excel, 182
inserting into a header or footer in Word, 112, 113
inserting the current in Mail Merge, 155
inserting the current in Word, 43, 68

Time data type. *See* Date/Time data type in Access

Time number format in Excel, 222

Times New Roman font
as default Word font, 74
in PowerPoint, 330, 331

timing slide shows in PowerPoint, 356, 357

title bar
in Excel, 177
in PowerPoint, 289
on Word screen, 41

Title Case in Word, 49

titles
adding to PowerPoint charts, 317
specifying for databases, 382
specifying for presentations in PowerPoint, 292
for Web pages, 24, 25, 550–551

Titles tab in Excel, 257

To area in Outlook, 508

To... button in Outlook, 510

to-do list. *See* task list

tOGGLE cASE in Word, 49

toggles, toolbar buttons as, 11

toolbar buttons in Help window, 17

toolbars, 10–13
additional options for buttons in, 11
buttons in, 10–11
creating, 605
customizing in an Office program, 604, 605
displaying, 10, 11, 12
hiding, 12
listing, 12
moving, 13
moving buttons on, 605
in Outlook, 503
placing, 13
for PowerPoint diagrams, 319
resetting, 605
resizing, 13

Tools menu
AutoCorrect Options command, 101
Customize command, 604
Find command in Outlook, 527
Formula Auditing command in Excel, 211, 213

(continued)

INDEX

Tools menu *(continued)*

Language command in Word, 64

Letters and Mailings command in Word, 154, 164, 170

Protection command in Excel, 203

Spelling and Grammar command in Word, 60

Spelling command in Outlook, 509

Word Count command in Word, 65

Top 10 AutoFilter dialog box, 281

top result values for Access queries, 477

Total Number of Pages button in Word, 113

Total Pages button in Excel, 253

tracer lines in Excel, 213

tracing formulas and errors, 211

Track Changes feature, 611

Transition button in PowerPoint, 354

transitions, applying to Slide Master in PowerPoint, 349

troubleshooting Office XP, 616–617

True/False format. *See* Yes/No fields

TrueType font, 224

truncated entries in Excel cells, 178

TT symbol, indicating a TrueType font in Excel, 224

TWAIN driver, 145

Two Pages zoom setting in Word, 103

Type a question button in menu bar, 16, 17

typographical characters, inserting special, 69

U

Underline feature

in an Access control, 454, 455

in Excel, 220

in FrontPage, 556

in PowerPoint, 332

in Word, 72

underline styles, applying in Excel, 228, 229

Undo button

in Excel, 187

undoing a sort, 125

in Word, 49, 52

Unhide command for columns in Excel, 199

Uniform Resource Locators. *See* URLs

Uninstall Office option, 607

unlocking cells in Excel, 203

Unprotect Sheet option in Excel, 203

Up Arrow in Word, 45

Update to Match Selection option, 96, 97

UPPERCASE in Word, 49

URLs, 544

Usage menu in FrontPage, 578

Use wildcards option, 55

username in an e-mail address, 511

V

validation rules in Access, 426–427

#VALUE! error message in Excel, 209

Var (variance) option in Access, 482

vertical alignment of Excel cell data, 231

vertical alignment options in Word, 108

vertical axis, 255

vertical line, placing between Word columns, 116, 117

vertical page breaks in Excel, 246, 247

video clips, editing embedded, 595

View buttons

in Access, 379, 410, 491

in PowerPoint, 289

on Word screen, 41

View Datasheet button in PowerPoint, 316

View menu

Current View command in Outlook, 533, 541

Header and Footer command in Word, 112, 113

Master command in PowerPoint, 346, 348

Normal command in Excel, 247

Notes Page command in PowerPoint, 363

in Outlook, 505

Page Break Preview command in Excel, 247

Reports command in FrontPage, 578

Task Pane command, 15

views

changing for Outlook Calendar, 537

changing for queries, 475

changing for reports, 491

changing in forms, 445

changing in PowerPoint, 304–305

changing in Word, 102

switching between Datasheet and Design in Access, 410

in Word, 39

Views bar in FrontPage, 577

viruses in attachments to messages, 514, 515

visitors to Web sites, tracking number of, 574

W

watermark, 118–119. *See also* picture watermark; text watermark in Word

Web browser, previewing Web pages in, 25, 568, 569

Web Component button in FrontPage, 574

Web file icon in FrontPage, 552

Web hyperlinks, inserting, 602–603

Web Layout view in Word, 102

Web links on CD-ROM in this book, 618

Web Page Preview command in File menu, 25

Web pages, 544

adding or editing text on, 553

changing fonts in, 554, 555

creating, 5, 544, 548–549

deleting, 577

moving in navigation structure, 583

opening, 552

previewing, 25

previewing and printing, 568–569

previewing presentations as, 357

publishing, 544

removing from navigation structure, 583

saving, 550–551

saving documents as, 24–25

Web server, 24, 544, 584

Web sites, 5, 544

creating, 546–547

hyperlinking to other, 567

navigating, 582–583

opening, 552

publishing, 584–585

renaming, 577

viewing information about, 578–579

Week view for displaying Calendar appointments, 536, 537

wheeled mouse, 307

white space, 106

Whole Field option for searching in Access, 458

Whole Page zoom setting in Word, 103

Width/Height option in Excel, 237

width of columns
    changing in Access, 407
    changing in Word tables, 126
wildcard characters in Word searches, 55
wildcards in Access criteria, 478
Window menu
    commands in, 33
    Freeze Panes command in Excel, 187
    Unfreeze Panes command in Excel, 187
windows, 8–9. *See also* document windows
Windows Bitmap (.bmp), 322
Windows Installer log file. *See* Installer log file
Windows menu, searching documents from, 35
Windows Metafile (.wmf), 322
WinFax Pro on CD-ROM in this book, 619
Wingdings font in Word, 70
WinZip on CD-ROM in this book, 619
Wizard templates in Word, 121
wizards. *See also* Chart Wizard in Excel
    creating documents, 19
    creating queries, 467
    selecting in FrontPage, 547
Word, 4
    introduction to, 38–39
    screen, 41
    starting, 40
Word Count in Word, 65
word wrap feature in Word, 42
WordArt feature
    in PowerPoint, 326–327
    in Word, 142–143
WordArt text, inserting in Excel text boxes, 271
words
    adding to Excel's dictionary, 191
    correcting automatically, 61
    counting in Word, 65

finding whole in Word, 55
locating in Outlook notes, 529
selecting in Access cells, 403
selecting in PowerPoint, 298
selecting in Word, 47
Work Week view, 536, 537
workbooks, 174
    protecting entire, 203
    reorganizing, 207
    saving, 178
Workflow reports in FrontPage, 579
Worksheet Tabs in Excel, 177
worksheets, 174, 176
    adding, 204
    adding AutoShapes to, 268–269
    adding borders to, 233
    applying color-coding to, 205
    automatically adjusting column widths, 219
    changing order of, 205
    checking spelling in several, 191
    consequences of deleting, 205
    copying, 207
    correcting spelling errors, 190–191
    deleting, 204, 205
    fitting to pages, 248
    formatting, 174
    hiding entire, 199
    hiding rows and columns, 198–199
    moving, 207
    moving data to different, 189
    previewing, 238
    printing, 239, 240–241
    protecting cells in, 202–203
    renaming, 206
    reorganizing, 188–189
    selecting all cells in, 185

World Wide Web (WWW), 544
Wrap text option in Excel, 231
wrapping styles in Word, 151
Write Anywhere option on Language toolbar, 609
Writing Pad, 608
writing style, changing, 62, 63

X

x-axis, 255
X-axis title in Excel, 256

Y

y-axis, 255
Y-axis title in Excel, 256
Yes (Duplicates OK) setting in Access, 433
Yes/No data type in Access, 397
Yes (No Duplicates) setting in Access, 433
Yes/No fields
    creating in Access, 428–429
    selecting a display format for, 418

Z

z-axis, 255
zero-length string ("") in Access, 424–425
ZIP codes, entering in Access, 397
Zoom box in Word, 103
Zoom button in Excel, 239
Zoom dialog box in Access, 406
Zoom feature in Excel, 225